Uniform Commercial Code

Editorial Advisory Board

Little, Brown and Company
Law Book Division

Uniform Commercial Code
Terms and Transactions in Commercial Law

An adaptation for law students of
Fundamentals of Commercial Activity:
A Lawyer's Guide

John F. Dolan
Professor of Law
Wayne State University

Little, Brown and Company
Boston Toronto London

Library of Congress Catalog No. 90-64115

ISBN 0-316-18905-7

Second Printing

EB

Published simultaneously in Canada
by Little, Brown & Company (Canada) Limited

Printed in the United States of America

For Jim, Ben, and Sarah

Summary of Contents

Table of Contents

PART II

SECURED LENDING 179

PART IV

TRANSPORT AND STORAGE 451

Preface

The purpose of this book is to provide sufficient introduction to commercial activity to enable students taking law school courses in commercial law or contracts to study the Uniform Commercial Code efficiently, that is, with a maximum of learning and a minimum of pain. Study of the Uniform Commercial Code is more difficult than it needs to be. By introducing the reader to the commercial practices that the statute governs, this book makes that study simpler.

We know that law is culture. When the first-year law teacher announces that he or she will teach students to "think like lawyers," a process of acculturation is beginning. Without experiencing that process, people cannot behave in their new culture without looking a bit like buffoons. The Uniform Commercial Code, which embodies a good bit of statutory commercial law, is a subculture of the law, and students of the Code need to absorb that subculture.

This book is an introduction to the transactions that the Code governs and as such is a first step in that process. It consists of four Parts that correspond to four traditional areas of law school study: Sales (Contracts), Payments Systems, Secured Lending, and Transport and Storage (Bailments), and it describes the commercial activity that commercial law serves. Given the traditional nature of law school texts, most textbook authors are unable to spend sufficient time explaining the underlying transaction, and most teachers cannot spend enough classroom time on the subject. Students, especially those who do not come to law school with a business major, find themselves having to deal with reported decisions that involve activity foreign to the students' experience.

A case involving the manufacture of a specially designed printing press for the wine label industry makes a little more sense if the student knows what a specialty manufacturer is and how it differs from General Motors or IBM. Cases growing out of the construction of a manufacturing facility make more sense when the student understands something about the construction industry and its multitude of players. A lawsuit arising out of the collection of a wire transfer payment under a contract for the international shipment of goods will make more sense to the student who understands the way banks collect international payments, what international buyers and sellers do, and why an international carrier operates the way it does than to the student who is struggling without that understanding.

Law study, moreover, is normative. Students and faculty constantly ask whether the rules established by the courts are "fair," "efficient," or "good." Yet, students, or any lawyer for that matter, cannot fully appreciate the success or failure of the rule established by the case or by the statute without understanding the activity the rule governs and the reasonable expectations of the participants in the activity. In many cases, the student must decide whether rules of law should be prescriptive or descriptive. Should the law tell people how to behave in a given context, or should the conduct of the parties in that context dictate the rules of law? As you will soon learn, the practicing lawyer and the business person complain most often about rules of law on the grounds that they are not realistic — that they do not rest on an understanding of the practices in question.

Nothing in this book challenges basic law school methods. Rather, the information here is supplemental. It is an introduction to the kind of inquiry that any lawyer soon realizes is necessary to a proper understanding of the legal system.

Finally, it is necessary to emphasize that this book is only an introduction. As you begin your practice, you will quickly become expert in certain areas. For the most part, you will learn what you need to know about client activity in those areas from those greatest law teachers of all — your clients. In the commercial area, this book is a beginning. It should be helpful in your study of the law and in your understanding of the cases. It is fashioned with a view to making the Code more understandable. If it succeeds, this little primer will assist you in the important task of beginning to make the public policy judgments about commercial law that we, as members of the bar, must make as our law grows to meet the needs of a dynamic commercial society.

Using the Book

In each Part the first chapter serves to introduce the subject matter, following chapters deal with specific practices, and the last chapter is a glossary. Most chapters have figures and illustrative documents; their function is to elucidate. Documents are for you to skim or examine closely, as you see fit. They should help you understand what the parties are doing. Bear in mind, however, that this is not a form book, and I have made no attempt to provide the latest forms available. These are forms, however, that parties are using.

The chapters are generally short, and the text of the chapters and of the Parts tends to move from the less complex to the more complex. It will benefit many students to start with the first two or three chapters of a Part and then to look at the Table of Contents again to determine what additional chapters merit reading. The Tables of Documents are also helpful.

I have made a special effort to create a comprehensive index. One of the secrets to good teaching is to remember what parts of an area trouble the student. We all approach subject matter from different perspectives, but students tend to stumble at the same places. The index rests on 15 years' experience in teaching commercial subjects.

The last chapter in each Part is a glossary. If commercial law is a subculture, it must have a language, and, indeed, commercial law and commercial activity do have their own lexicon. Placement of this chapter at the end of the Part reflects deference to custom rather than the judgment that the glossaries are mere reference chapters. On the contrary, the glossary chapters are worth reading as chapters. In fact, some readers may find it helpful to read the glossary right after the introductory chapter. There are terms and explanations in the glossaries that do not appear in the substantive chapters. Once read, the glossary resumes its role as a handy reference defining terms that recur in the substantive chapters.

The glossaries are somewhat long, but they are written in essay fashion. Textual explanations follow many of the dictionary definitions. In preparing the glossaries, I have been guided less by the rules of lexicography and more by a desire to make commercial activity clear. The definitions in Part I, for example, may not be helpful to the reader of Part II. Thus, each glossary is fashioned for the Part in which it appears.

Acknowledgments

I could not have written this book without the generous assistance of friends and colleagues. I have acknowledged the help of corporations and banks in captions to the documents reproduced here that their people so kindly supplied.

A number of people spent significant amounts of time in my behalf. They deserve special mention. Perry Flanagan read chapters and made lengthy and helpful comments. Thanks to her efforts, all of the lame jokes about bank loan officers fell by the wayside before I submitted the manuscript to Little, Brown. Frederick C. Winke provided patient explanation of the marketing and transportation of gas and other petroleum derivatives in the United States. Kim Hall explained agricultural marketing and finance. Carl Hammerl provided review, helpful comments, and gentle criticism of the secured lending chapters. Egon David took time to explain international banking practices. David Barnett provided cheerful responses to urgent requests for help, as he and his colleague, Johan Wendt, have done on other occasions. Finally, a word of thanks is in order to Barton R. Nelson, who, with his father, Russell, has taught this lawyer about law and about business over a long period and in the grand manner.

These professionals recognize the value to an academic of working with people who know an industry, and they are generous enough and confident enough to teach. In this case, they taught the professor; and he is grateful for it. Some of them and others reviewed early drafts of these chapters, but any errors here are my responsibility, not theirs.

Law libraries are indispensable to any work such as this. Wayne State University is fortunate to have a fine law library and, more importantly, an excellent staff. Georgia Clark, Director of the Law Library, and her staff of librarians afforded assistance in the preparation of this book that was invariably professional and cheerful. Similar thanks are due Professor Dan F. Henke, Librarian at the University of California, Hastings College of the Law, where I spent the spring semester in 1988 and prepared drafts of several chapters. He and his staff were always patient and generous with their visitor.

In my view the most significant contribution to this work was the idea for it. The idea was not mine; it was that of Richard Heuser, Vice President and Publisher of Law Books at Little, Brown and Company. When he approached me with the suggestion, it occurred to me that on many occasions the lawyer's edition of this work would have been helpful to me during the years that I practiced law. I am confident, furthermore, that a student edition will be invaluable to my students and to me, as I teach Contracts and the Uniform Commercial Code courses. Thus, I accepted his invitation to participate in what I view as an important pedagogical exercise. I hope I have done his suggestion justice.

Finally, I owe a debt of gratitude to my dean, John W. Reed, for support he provided and to the Detroit law firm of Clark, Klein & Beaumont for grants they generously made to the law school so that I could work on this book. Thanks are also due my former student John F. Mahoney for research help and June Frierson for secretarial assistance.

John F. Dolan

January 1991

Uniform Commercial Code

PART I

SALES

1

Scope

§1.1 SUBJECT MATTER

This Part covers those commercial activities that generally fall under the typical law school courses that we denominate contracts and sales. There is bound to be some overlap in any arbitrary classification of commercial activity, which has the tendency not to follow law school course headings. Most lawyers are comfortable with the classifications or at least familiar with them, and they serve as a good starting point.

Chapters in this Part generally emphasize the *commercial* aspects of sales and contracts law. Unfortunately, law study at times emphasizes *consumer* aspects. While there is nothing wrong with attention to consumer transactions, the fact is that the law surrounding consumer sales and consumer contracts tends to be fashioned with considerations peculiar to the consumer, and to limit the inquiry to the consumer setting distorts that study. The commercial aspects of sales and contracts are far richer in diversity than consumer transactions and tend to be less familiar to the reader to whom this book is addressed. In short, the commercial aspects of sales and contracts law are the primary concern of this Part, though there is some attention from time to time to the consumer transaction. The focus is narrowed further by the effort to include here contract activity that involves or is related to the sale of goods or services.

§1.2 EXCLUSIONS

Some features of contract and sales law are either too broad or too specialized to fit here. Real estate contracts and collective bargaining agreements are sufficiently broad to merit books of their own. They appear here in the first case rarely and in the second not at all. Contracts peculiar to the activity of corporations, partnerships, and joint ventures fall into a similar class, as do government contracts. Contracts for a celebrity's services, agreements for the transfer of a liquor license, prenuptial contracts, and agreements between federal and local agencies are rather specific for a work whose focus is general. Other contracts, such as those peculiar to bailments (Part IV), secured lending (Part II), or international sales (Part IV) appear in other parts where they seem more appropriate and where study of them is easier by virtue of their place in an industry or legal classification.

2 Consumer Sale

§2.1 CASH

In the simplest and probably oldest sales transaction, the buyer either barters one **chattel** for another or pays "cash on the barrelhead" for the goods. In these transactions, there is no **contract** for the sale of the goods, there is simply a *sale*, which consists of the passing of **title** to the goods from the seller to the buyer for a price. There are a number of reasons to distinguish these **cash sales** from **credit sales,** and the Uniform Commercial Code warns that an **agreement** between the parties for delay in payment by even one day turns the transaction into one for credit. In many **consumer** sales at the counter of a retail store the buyer will pay for the goods against immediate delivery in a cash-sale transaction. Credit sales, however, now comprise a significant part of sales activity. Most **merchant-to-merchant** sales are on credit, and the number of consumer sales on credit has grown at a dizzying pace.

§2.2 SALES CONTRACT

We know that the consumer sale for cash will not involve any explicit contract of **purchase,** but we can say in theory that the cash-on-the-barrelhead sale involves an implicit contract, and the law reads into that contract a number of terms. For example, if a buyer approaches a sales counter and gives the sales clerk a **check,** the law will impose on the buyer a contractual duty to pay the seller if the check bounces. That duty exists in addition to obligations the buyer has under the law of negotiable instruments as the drawer of an instrument that is dishonored. By the same token, the law reads into the cash-sale transaction seller **warranties** of merchantability and good title.

In some consumer large-dollar, cash-sale transactions, the parties will enter into a written contract. If, for example, a consumer agrees to purchase a new automobile, the seller, an automobile **dealer,** will usually prepare a contract of purchase such as Document 2-1.

§2.3 CREDIT

With the advent of reliable consumer credit reporting agencies and the recognition by merchandisers that the consumer will buy more if he can obtain credit, retailers began actively campaigning to promote consumer credit sales. In these transactions, the seller can grant credit to the buyer directly, or the seller can arrange to have a third party grant the credit. In both transactions, the seller takes a contract of sale usually calling for a down payment and deferred payments, the total of which equals the "cash price" plus interest charges variously referred to as the *time price differential* or the *finance charge*. In most instances, state law regulates the consumer credit contract under a Retail **Installment** Sales Act that protects the consumer by requiring, among other things, that the seller disclose credit terms clearly. Document 2-2 is an example of a consumer retail installment sales contract.

The retail installment sale often stretches the dealer's capital to its limits or beyond. An automobile dealer that sells half of the cars on its lot under retail installment contracts will be concerned that it cannot pay with the retail contracts salespeople or taxing bodies or its manufacturer supplier that is providing new inventory. Salespeople, local governments, the IRS, and General Motors want cash or bank credit from the dealer.

Dealers are always anxious to make sales. That is their primary business. They are aware, furthermore, that easy credit for their customers will increase sales, so they often make credit available even when they do not have the capital to finance the buyer's purchase. They also try to get their customers to arrange their own credit. The dealer might encourage the buyer to obtain his own financing through a third-party financial institution, such as the buyer's credit union or a local finance company. Frequently, it is in the buyer's best interest to arrange a loan, say, from a financial institution with which he regularly does business, since "direct" loans from these institutions to the consumer are often less expensive than an "indirect" loan, under a retail installment sales agreement, the retailer's charge plan, or a credit-card sale.

Figure 2-1. Direct Consumer Loan

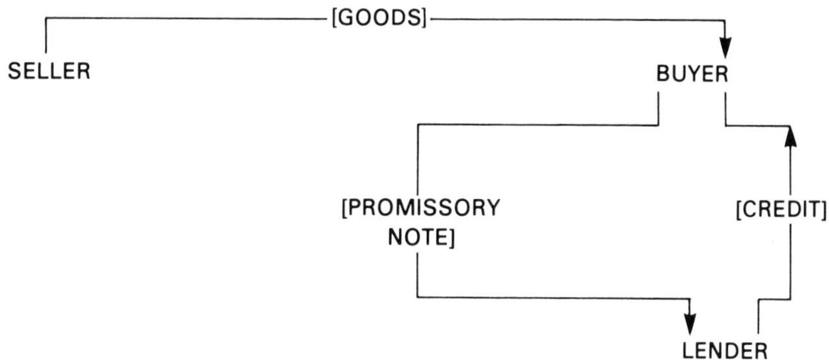

In the indirect loan, the seller might take an installment sales contract from the consumer and assign it to a financing institution, such as a bank. Figures 2-1 and 2-2 illustrate the direct and indirect credit arrangements.

In the retailer charge-plan transaction, the retailer ostensibly grants credit to the consumer under the retailer's own charge account plan. Thus, a buyer may purchase luggage and simply tell the sales clerk to charge it, that is, to charge the amount of the purchase to the buyer's revolving charge account with the seller. In fact, most retailers that maintain their own charge accounts do not have the resources to carry those accounts and finance those accounts at a bank or other commercial lender. Chapter 15 explains the retailers' account financing. Document 2-3 is a typical charge-account agreement.

The buyer in this luggage example may prefer to use a bank credit card to finance the purchase. Bank credit card arrangements have grown dramatically in the last 20 years. The two national credit card systems have worked remarkably well despite the fact that there is little regulatory law on the subject and that there are several parties involved.

In a typical bank card system, commercial banks or other financial institutions enter into an agreement with the system itself for the purpose of being able to issue cards and to access the national bank card collection network. Each bank member, in turn, enters into cardholder agreements with its customers. In a second role, banks in the credit card network enter into contracts with merchants in their market under which (1) the merchants agree to accept charges by cardholders and (2) the banks agree to take the charges from the merchants.

When the cardholder purchases luggage from a merchant member, the merchant notes a description of the goods on the familiar sales slip, which records the transaction. The merchant uses the slip, which banks call an *item* — the term banks use for checks and other instruments that pass through the check-collection system — to obtain credit (less a **discount**) from its bank. The bank uses the slip to charge the cardholder's account at the card issuer bank, which gives credit for the sales slip through the

Figure 2-2. Indirect Consumer Loan

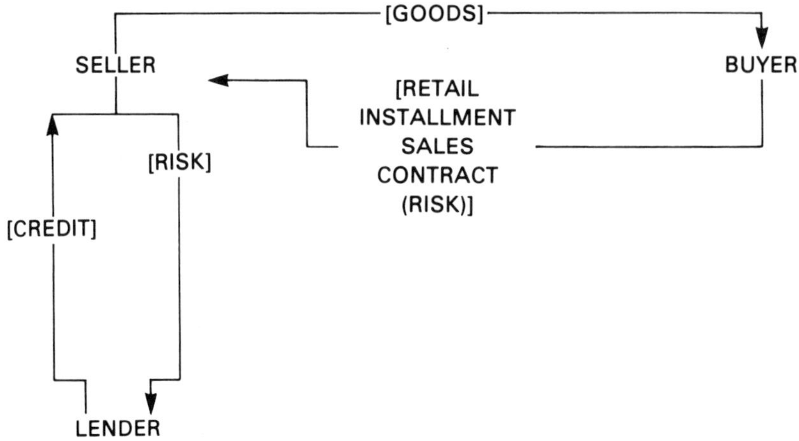

system. Periodically, the bank card issuer bills its customer. Note that under bank card arrangements, the card holder does not have to pay off the entire monthly **statement** but has the option of paying only a portion of the outstanding balance each month plus interest on the balance remaining unpaid. Figure 2-3 illustrates the bank credit card relationships.

There is a second species of credit card that differs from the bank credit card. For a long time, some national or large regional retailers have used credit cards in connection with their marketing. These credit cards are in the nature of open-account arrangements whereby, for example, a customer may purchase gasoline from the oil company's dealer with the understanding that the customer will pay his bill periodically. Under these credit card agreements, installment credit is not available to the customer, as it is under bank card agreements, and the merchandiser does not use the bank collection system to obtain payment for charges but bills the consumer directly.

Other nonbank credit card issuers, such as Diners Club and American Express, issue similar cards, called *travel and entertainment cards,* that permit cardholders to charge purchases at merchant establishments that agree to take such cards.

Recently, national retailers have blended the aspects of bank cards and merchant cards to permit cardholders to pay card balances in installments and to permit retailers to use the bank collection system to collect on the sales slips they generate through the sales of their goods and services.

§2.4 HOMEMADE CONTRACTS

There is an abundance of case law, most of it the subject of study in the contracts course, that deals with the homemade contract that is the prod-

Figure 2-3. Bank Credit Card Sales Relationships

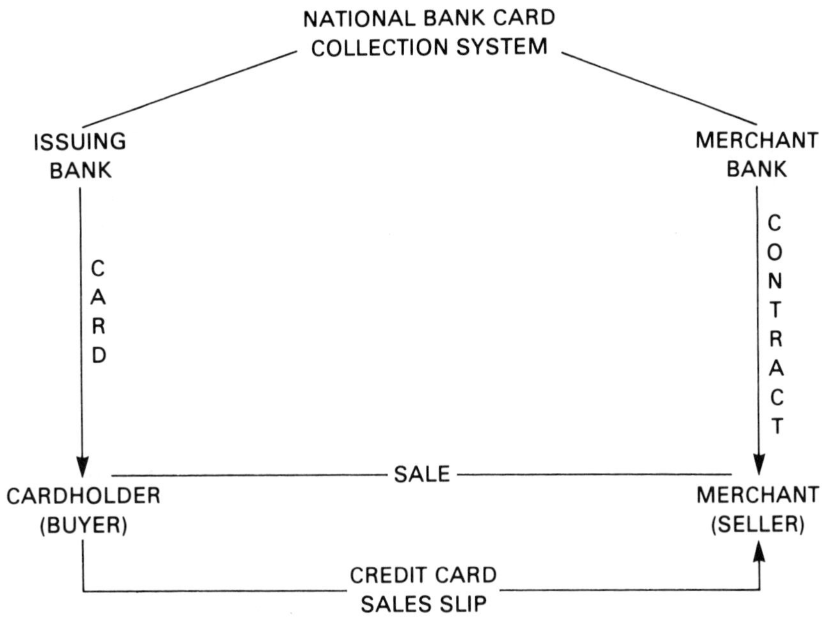

uct of pencil scratching on a pad of paper or the back of an envelope done at the kitchen table. These horrors are not significant to the national economy, but they frequently are significant to the parties that enter into them, and the courts have sometimes stuffed square pegs into round holes and otherwise punched the law of contract out of shape to effect a modicum of justice in these settings. No one can quarrel with these efforts, but the student and the lawyer must recognize them for what they are — ad hoc jurisprudence that should not extend to the regular and sophisticated transactions that are described in the first three sections of this chapter and surely should not apply to commercial contracts and transactions.

12829

CHRYSLER-PLYMOUTH 001200

PLEASE ENTER MY ORDER FOR:

STOCK # | VIN | SALESMAN | ORDER #

YR | MAKE | MODEL | BODY | SERIES | STAT | DATE | TIME

ODOMETER | LICENSE NUMBER | CYL | FUEL | COLOR | TRIM | KEY - 1 | KEY - 2

VEHICLE DISCLOSURE - VEHICLE PRESENTED TO BE
☐ NEW ☐ DEMO ☐ USED ☐ LEASE

	PRICE OF UNIT	
ALL USED VEHICLES SOLD AS IS		
ALL NEW VEHICLES SOLD AS EQUIPPED		
DEALER INSTALLED ACCESSORIES		
RUSTPROOFING	249	50
PAINT PROOFING	199	50
FABRIC PROOFING	179	50
TOTAL SELLING PRICE		
SALES TAX		
TAG, TITLE & FEES		
DOCUMENT SERVICE FEE	97	50
TOTAL PRICE		
EXTENDED SERVICE CONTRACT		
TOTAL CASH DELIVERY PRICE		
PARTIAL PAYMENT (NON-REFUNDABLE)		
FACTORY REBATE (IF APPLICABLE)		
DEALER REBATE (IF APPLICABLE)		
TRADE EQUITY		
CASH DUE ON DELIVERY:		
TOTAL DOWN PAYMENT		
BALANCE TO FINANCE		
TOTAL		

BUYER'S NAME

ADDRESS - 1

ADDRESS - 2

CITY | ST | ZIP

HOME PHONE | BUSINESS PHONE | EXT

CO-BUYER

DOB - 1 | DL - 1

DESCRIPTION OF TRADE-IN

YEAR | MAKE | MODEL

LICENSE NUMBER | BODY TYPE

VEHICLE ID NUMBER | ODOMETER

TRADE-IN ALLOWANCE | DATE | AMOUNT

BALANCE OWED TO | AMOUNT

TRADE EQUITY | AMOUNT

TRADE-IN VERIFICATION

NET TO ADDRESS: ______

ACCOUNT NUMBER: ______

AMOUNT: $

GOOD UNTIL:

HOW TITLED:

ANY 2ND LIEN:

TO WHOM: SPOKE TO:

VERIFIED BY: VERIFIED ON:

Buyer acknowledges and agrees that he has not relied upon any statements or representations of seller or any salespersons, employee or agent of seller and that no statements or representations shall be binding on seller unless contained in a writing executed by seller.

I acknowledge receipt of a true copy of this instrument. I completely understand all the terms and conditions of this purchase.

THIS IS NOT AN ORDER UNTIL ACCEPTED BY AN OFFICIAL OF THE COMPANY AND APPROVED BY A RESPONSIBLE FINANCE COMPANY TO ANY DEFERRED BALANCE.

SPECIMEN

BUYER'S SIGNATURE

DATE

ACCEPTED – Pointe Chrysler-Plymouth – By

Printed with the permission of Chrysler Motors Corp.

CONDITIONS

It is further understood and agreed:

The order on the reverse side hereof is subject to the following terms and conditions which have been mutually agreed upon:

1. The manufacturer has reserved the right to change the list price of new motor vehicles without notice and in the event that the list price of the new vehicle ordered hereunder is so changed, the cash delivered price, which is based on list price effective on the day of delivery, will govern in this transaction. But if such cash delivered price is increased the buyer may, if dissatisfied with such increased price, cancel this order, in which event if a used vehicle has been traded in as a part of the consideration herein, such used vehicle shall be returned to the buyer upon the payment of a reasonable charge for storage and repairs (if any) or, if the used vehicle has been previously sold by the dealer, the amount received therefor, less a selling commission of 15% and any expense incurred in storing, insuring, conditioning or advertising said vehicle for sale, shall be returned to the buyer.

2. If the used vehicle is not to be delivered to the dealer until the delivery of the new vehicle, the used vehicle shall be reappraised at that time and such reappraisal value shall determine the allowance made for such used vehicle. The buyer agrees to deliver the original bill of sale and the title to any used vehicle traded herein along with the delivery of such vehicle, and the buyer warrants such used vehicle to be his property free and clear of all liens and encumbrances except as otherwise noted herein.

3. Upon the failure or refusal of the buyer to complete said purchase for any reason other than cancellation on account of increase in price, the cash deposit may be retained as liquidated damages, or in the event a used vehicle has been taken in trade, the buyer hereby authorizes dealer to sell said used vehicle, and the dealer shall be entitled to reimburse himself out of the proceeds of such sale, for the expenses specified in paragraph 1 above and also for his expenses and losses incurred or suffered as the result of buyer's failure to complete said purchase.

4. The manufacturer has the right to make any changes in the model or design of any accessories and part of any new motor vehicle at any time without creating any obligation on the part of either the Dealer or the Manufacturer, to make corresponding changes in the vehicle covered by this order either before or subsequent to the delivery of such vehicle to the buyer.

5. Dealer shall not be liable for delays caused by the manufacturer, accidents, sureties, fires, or other causes beyond the control of the dealer.

6. The price of the vehicle quoted herein does not include any taxes imposed by any governmental authority prior to or at the time of delivery of such vehicle unless expressly so stated, but the buyer assumes and agrees to pay, unless prohibited by law, any taxes, except income taxes, imposed on or incidental to the transaction herein, regardless of the person having the primary tax liability.

7. NO WARRANTIES ARE MADE OR WILL BE DEEMED TO HAVE BEEN MADE BY EITHER THE DEALER OR THE MANUFACTURER OF THE NEW MOTOR VEHICLE OF MOTOR VEHICLE CHASSIS FURNISHED HEREUNDER, EXCEPTING ONLY FORD MOTOR CORPORATION'S CURRENT PRINTED WARRANTY APPLICABLE TO SUCH VEHICLE OR VEHICLE CHASSIS, WHICH WARRANTY IS INCORPORATED HEREIN AND MADE A PART HEREOF AND A COPY OF WHICH WILL BE DELIVERED TO BUYER AT THE TIME OF DELIVERY OF THE NEW MOTOR VEHICLE OR MOTOR VEHICLE CHASSIS. SUCH WARRANTY SHALL BE EXPRESSLY IN LIEU OF ANY OTHER WARRANTY, EXPRESSED OR IMPLIED, INCLUDING, BUT NOT LIMITED TO, ANY IMPLIED WARRANTY OF MERCHANTABILITY OR FITNESS FOR A PARTICULAR PURPOSE, AND THE REMEDIES SET FORTH IN SUCH WARRANTY WILL BE THE ONLY REMEDIES AVAILABLE TO ANY PERSON WITH RESPECT TO SUCH NEW MOTOR VEHICLE OR MOTOR VEHICLE CHASSIS.

   NO WARRANTIES, EXPRESSED OR IMPLIED, ARE MADE BY THE DEALER WITH RESPECT TO USED MOTOR VEHICLES OR MOTOR VEHICLE CHASSIS FURNISHED HEREUNDER EXCEPT AS MAY BE EXPRESSED IN WRITING BY THE DEALER FOR SUCH USED MOTOR VEHICLE OR MOTOR VEHICLE CHASSIS, WHICH WARRANTY, IF SO EXPRESSED IN WRITING, IS INCORPORATED HEREIN AND MADE A PART HEREOF.

8. In case the vehicle covered by this order is a used vehicle, no warranty or representation is made as to the extent such vehicle has been used, regardless of the mileage shown on the speedometer of said used vehicle.

9. In the event that the transaction referred to in this order is not a cash transaction, the buyer herein, before or at the time of delivery of the vehicle ordered, and in accordance with the terms and conditions of payments indicated on the front of this order, will execute either a chattel mortgage, conditional sales contract, or such other form of security agreement as may be required to complete this transaction upon a time credit price basis.

10. This order is subject to acceptance by the dealer, which acceptance shall be signified by the signaure of Dealer, Dealer's Manager or other authorized signature on the reverse side hereof.

I understand the Terms and Conditions of this instrument. X ______________________________

Document 2-2. Retail Installment Sales Contract

SEARS, ROEBUCK and CO.
HOME IMPROVEMENT PLAN
RETAIL INSTALLMENT CONTRACT and SECURITY AGREEMENT

ACCOUNT NUMBER	

BUYER: Name ______________________________

Address ______________________________
Street Number City State Zip

Installation Address–If Different ______________________________

SELLER: Sears, Roebuck and Co. (Sears) ______________________________
Store Number Address

DESCRIPTION OF MERCHANDISE:

STOCK NUMBER	DESCRIPTION OF MERCHANDISE	CASH PRICE

ITEMIZATION OF AMOUNT FINANCED:

TOTAL FOR MERCHANDISE	
TAX	
TOTAL CASH PRICE	
LESS CASH DOWN PAYMENT	
AMOUNT FINANCED	

TRUTH IN LENDING DISCLOSURES:

ANNUAL PERCENTAGE RATE The cost of your credit as a yearly rate.	*FINANCE CHARGE* The dollar amount the credit will cost you.	*Amount Financed* The amount of credit provided to you.	*Total of Payments* The amount you will have paid after you have made all payments as scheduled.	*Total Sale Price* The total cost of your purchase on credit, including your down-payment of $______
______%	$______	$______	$______	$______

Your payment schedule will be:

Number of Payments	Amount of Payments	When Payments Are Due
		______, 19___ and same date of each following month.

Security: You are giving a security interest in the goods purchased.

Prepayment: If you pay off early you may be entitled to a refund of part of the FINANCE CHARGE.

You should refer to the remainder of your contract for information about non-payment default, any required repayment in full before the scheduled date, prepayment refunds and penalties.

SEE OTHER SIDE FOR IMPORTANT TERMS OF THIS CONTRACT

Document 2-2. (*continued*)

I agree to purchase and Sears agrees to sell the merchandise described on the reverse side for the total credit sales price consisting of the cash price plus the **FINANCE CHARGE** according to the terms on the reverse side and the following terms and conditions.

1. **SECURITY INTEREST IN GOODS.** I give Sears a security interest under the Uniform Commercial Code in all merchandise purchased under this contract identified on the reverse side until paid in full. If I do not make payments as agreed, the security interest allows Sears to repossess the merchandise. I am responsible for any loss or damage to the merchandise until the purchase price is fully paid.

2. **FAILURE TO MAKE MINIMUM PAYMENT.** Subject to applicable state law limitations, if I do not make at least the minimum required monthly payment when due, Sears may declare my entire balance immediately due and payable.

3. **PREPAYMENT.** If I pay in full in advance, any unearned **FINANCE CHARGE** will be rebated under the Actuarial Method. This is a mathematical formula which allows Sears to retain a proportionately higher percentage of the **FINANCE CHARGE** if the account balance is paid off in the early part of the term.

4. **SUBSEQUENT PURCHASES—CONSOLIDATED BILLING STATEMENT.** If I make any other purchases from Sears under a Home Improvement Credit Plan similar to this contract Sears may add together all minimum required monthly payments and send me one consolidated billing statement each month. A consolidated billing statement will not change any of the terms of this contract.

5. **CREDIT INVESTIGATION.** Sears has the right to investigate my credit, employment and income records and to verify my credit references.

6. **CREDIT REPORTING.** Sears has the right to report my performance of this contract to credit bureaus and other interested parties. If my monthly payments required under this contract are consolidated with my monthly payments required under any other Sears Home Improvement Credit Plan contracts on a single monthly statement, the total unpaid balance of all such contracts will be treated as a single amount owing to Sears for credit reporting purposes.

7. **CONTRACT SUBJECT TO APPROVAL OF SEARS CREDIT SALES DEPARTMENT.** This contract is subject to the approval of Sears Credit Sales Department.

8. **LATE PAYMENT CHARGES.** If I fail to make an installment payment within 10 days of the due date in any month, Sears may charge me and I agree to pay a late payment charge equal to the lesser of 5% of the installment or $5.

9. **ATTORNEYS' FEES.** Subject to applicable state law limitations, upon my default, Sears may charge me and I agree to pay reasonable attorneys' fees and collection costs.

10. **ASSIGNMENT OF CONTRACT—PROTECTION OF BUYER'S RIGHTS.** Sears may sell, assign or transfer this contract to another creditor without further notice to me. If so, the notice below, which is required by Federal law, is intended to protect any claim or defense I have against Sears.

NOTICE: ANY HOLDER OF THIS CONSUMER CREDIT CONTRACT IS SUBJECT TO ALL CLAIMS AND DEFENSES WHICH THE DEBTOR COULD ASSERT AGAINST THE SELLER OF THE GOODS OR SERVICES OBTAINED PURSUANT HERETO OR WITH THE PROCEEDS THEREOF. RECOVERY HEREUNDER BY THE DEBTOR SHALL NOT EXCEED AMOUNTS PAID BY THE DEBTOR HEREUNDER.

NOTICE TO OWNER

DO NOT SIGN THIS CONTRACT IN BLANK.

YOU ARE ENTITLED TO A COPY OF THE CONTRACT AT THE TIME YOU SIGN.

KEEP IT TO PROTECT YOUR LEGAL RIGHTS.

DO NOT SIGN ANY COMPLETION CERTIFICATE OR AGREEMENT STATING THAT YOU ARE SATISFIED WITH THE ENTIRE PROJECT BEFORE THIS PROJECT IS COMPLETE. HOME REPAIR CONTRACTORS ARE PROHIBITED BY LAW FROM REQUESTING OR ACCEPTING A CERTIFICATE OF COMPLETION SIGNED BY THE OWNER PRIOR TO THE ACTUAL COMPLETION OF THE WORK TO BE PERFORMED UNDER THE HOME REPAIR CONTRACT.

11. **DELIVERY OF CONTRACT.** I ACKNOWLEDGE RECEIPT OF A COPY OF THIS CONTRACT.

RETAIL INSTALLMENT CONTRACT and SECURITY AGREEMENT

SEARS, ROEBUCK AND CO.

Customer's Signature SPECIMEN ____________

Date ____________

The Terms of This Contract Are Contained on Both Sides Of This Page.

11084-224 Rev. 4/88 New Jersey
Sears Forms Management

Document 2-3. Charge Account Agreement

AR-19 9/89 HLN 30-Day or Option

JACOBSON'S APPLICATION FOR CREDIT

ACCOUNT NUMBER

Extended Payment

	Approved by	☐☐☐—☐☐☐—☐☐☐☐		Approved by

IMPORTANT: READ THESE DIRECTIONS BEFORE COMPLETING THIS APPLICATION AND CHECK APPROPRIATE BOX BELOW.

(1) ☐ If you are applying for an individual account in your own name and relying on your own income or assets and not the income or assets of another person as the basis for repayment of the credit requested, complete only Section A and sign reverse side of application.

(2) ☐ If you are applying for a joint account or an account that you and another person will use, complete all sections, providing information in Section B about the joint applicant or user and both sign the reverse side of application.

(3) ☐ If you are applying for an individual account, but relying on income from alimony, child support, or separate maintenance, or on the income or assets of another person as the basis for repayment of the credit requested, complete all sections to the extent possible, providing information in Section B about the person on whose alimony, support, or maintenance payments or income or assets you are relying. The individual upon whose income you are relying must sign below the authorization to allow Jacobson's to investigate his or her credit record.

SECTION A — INFORMATION REGARDING APPLICANT

Courtesy title optional	First Name of Applicant	Middle Intial	Last Name

Street No.	Street	Apt./RFD # (Specify)	City or Town	State	Zip Code	Additional persons authorized to use account excluding spouse.

Previous Address if at Above Less than 3 Yrs.	Nearest Relative Name and Address	Phone No.

Social Security No.	Driver License No.	Phone No.	Bank Reference

Employer	Years	Firm Address	Phone No.	Position

SECTION B — INFORMATION ON APPLICANT'S SPOUSE, FORMER SPOUSE OR JOINT APPLICANT

Name	Social Security No.	Address (if different than applicant)	Phone No.

Employer	Years	Firm Address	Phone	Position

Jacobson's is authorized to investigate my credit record and to verify my credit, employment and income references.

Signature of individual you are depending on for alimony, child support or separate maintenance as described in #3 above. X____________________ Date__________

SPECIMEN

STORE USE ONLY

VISA/MC/AMX #____________________ EXP__________ Employee No.__________ Dept. No.__________

Printed with the permission of Jacobson Stores, Inc.

Document 2-3. *(continued)*

JACOBSON'S CHARGE ACCOUNT AGREEMENT

I apply for credit with Jacobson's and warrant that the information provided by me is true. I understand that I may apply for either a 30 Day or an Option charge account. I may also apply for an Extended Payment account, but, Jacobson's may limit the types of goods and services which I may purchase under the Extended Payment Account.

(1) CREDIT INVESTIGATION REPORTING

I authorize Jacobson's to investigate my credit record including my references and statements and report my performance of this agreement to any consumer reporting agency or other credit grantor.

(2) PAYMENT TERMS

I agree to pay all purchases made by me and others allowed to use my account. The monthly statement from Jacobson's will show my account balance (the amount I owe) at the bill closing date and the date by which payment must be made. The statement will also show a minimum payment due (the amount which must be paid by the next billing date) and finance charge, if any and the average daily balance on which the finance charge was calculated. The time between closing dates is referred to as a billing period. Whenever I have an account balance, I agree payments will made in accordance with the terms of the account type(s) selected by me below.

☐ 30 DAY I expect to pay the full amount of my new balance. If I do not pay the full amount of my account balance on or before my next bill closing date, I agree that Jacobson's may upon notice to me, convert my 30 Day account to an Option account.

☐ OPTION Whenever I have a balance, I agree to pay Jacobson's whichever of the following is greater (1) 20% of my account balance or (2) $10.

☐ EXTENDED PAYMENT Whenever I have an account balance, I agree to pay Jacobson's whichever of the following is the greatest (1) 5% of my highest account balance since the last time I had a zero balance (2) $50 (3) monthly amount agreed to in writing by Jacobson's and me.

(3) FINANCE CHARGE CALCULATION

There is no finance charge in a billing period if there is no beginning balance or if the new balance is paid in full by the bill closing date. When a finance charge is imposed on an Option or Extended Payment Account, it is applied to the average daily balance at the rate of 1½% per month. The average daily balance is figured by adding the outstanding balance (including new charges and deducting payments and credits) for each day in the billing period and then dividing by the number of days in the billing period. I may pay the full balance of my Option or Extended Payment account at any time to avoid additional finance charge.

(4) DEFAULT

If I fail to make payment when due, all sums owed by me to Jacobson's immediately become due. Payments are not considered made until received by Jacobson's. If I fail to pay the amount owed in full and you give my account to an attorney (who is not one of your salaried employees) for collection, I will pay you a reasonable amount to cover the attorney fee and court cost.

(5) SECURITY INTEREST

Jacobson's will retain security interest in all merchandise charged to an account, to secure the payment of the purchase price of the merchandise. Jacobson's will apply payments on my account first to unpaid finance charges, and then to unpaid purchases and other charges in the order in which they were posted to my account. If more than one charge was posted on the same day, the lowest priced charges shall be considered paid for first. The security interest on each item of merchandise will terminate when such item has been paid for in full. Jacobson's is authorized to file a financing statement in connection with any security interest related by Jacobson's under this agreement, and to sign the financing statement on my behalf.

(6) LOSS OR THEFT OF CHARGE ID CARD

I will notify Jacobson's immediately of loss or theft of my charge card. I will not be responsible for use which occurs after I notify Jacobson's orally or by writing to the address shown on the back of my bill. In any case, my liability will not exceed $50.

(7) REVISION OF TERMS

Jacobson's may revise the terms of this agreement after notifying me, but the changes may not increase the payment required for previous purchases. Revisions in the calculation of finance charges or annual percentage rate may not exceed the legal limits.

(8) AGREEMENT ASSIGNMENT

From time to time, Jacobson's may assign this agreement or its rights hereunder. Notice to me is not required.

ANNUAL PERCENTAGE RATE FOR PURCHASES	VARIABLE RATE INFORMATION	GRACE PERIOD FOR REPAYMENT OF THE BALANCE FOR PURCHASES	METHOD OF COMPUTING THE BALANCE FOR PURCHASES	ANNUAL FEES	MINIMUM FINANCE CHARGE	TRANSACTION FEE FOR PURCHASES
18%	NONE	NOT LESS THAN 28 DAYS SINCE LAST BILLING PERIOD	AVERAGE DAILY BALANCE INCLUDING CURRENT CHARGES	NONE	NONE	NONE

NOTICE: ANY HOLDER OF THIS CONSUMER CREDIT CONTRACT IS SUBJECT TO ALL CLAIMS AND DEFENSES WHICH THE DEBTOR COULD ASSERT AGAINST THE SELLER OF GOODS OR SERVICES OBTAINED PURSUANT HERETO OR WITH THE PROCEEDS HEREOF. RECOVERY HEREUNDER BY THE DEBTOR SHALL NOT EXCEED AMOUNTS PAID BY THE DEBTOR HEREUNDER.

NOTICE TO THE BUYER: DO NOT SIGN THIS AGREEMENT BEFORE YOU READ IT, OR IF IT CONTAINS BLANK SPACES. A COPY OF THIS AGREEMENT WILL BE ENCLOSED WITH YOUR ID CARDS OR IS AVAILABLE AT ANY JACOBSON'S CREDIT OFFICE. RETENTION OR USE OF THE JACOBSON'S CHARGE ID CARDS ACKNOWLEDGES RECEIPT OF THIS AGREEMENT AND ACCEPTANCE OF ALL TERMS AND CONDITIONS THEREOF. IT FURTHER ACKNOWLEDGES RECEIPT OF A COPY OF THE NOTICE OF RIGHTS TO DISPUTE BILLING ERRORS.

Applicant Signature ______ SPECIMEN ______ Joint Applicant or Co-Signature ______ Date ______

Address ______ Address ______

3

Open Account Sales

§3.1 THE TRANSACTION

As all students who have taken the contracts course know, contracts fall into two categories. The first category includes the recurring transaction, e.g., insurance arrangements, retail installment sales agreements, loan agreements, collective bargaining agreements, and real estate sales contracts. The second category includes everything else. Many of the standard agreements in commercial law appear at one place or another in this book.

For the purposes of introducing readers to commercial activity the hard part is the "everything else" category. The fact is that no teacher can cover that category, for while one teaches, the merchants and consumers that comprise the players on the commercial field are inventing new commercial devices and new contracts. Nowhere is that fact more evident than in the sales context. For while there are a number of recurring patterns in sales, many sales are unique.

This book generally attempts to deal with recurring commercial transactions. In sales those include, among others, retail installment contracts (*see* Section 2.3); consumer purchases on open credit (*see* Section 2.3); documentary draft transactions (*see* Chapter 4); imports and exports (*see* Chapter 5); consignments (*see* Chapter 6); and sales disguised as leases (*see* Chapter 9).

In domestic merchant-to-merchant sales there has also emerged an efficient and standard practice known as the *open account sale*. With the exception of those transactions described elsewhere in this chapter, the open account sale dominates domestic sales transactions between merchants when one of the merchants sells out of inventory to another.

The significant exception to that domination arises in the agricultural sector, where farm producers often sell their inventory to **brokers** or large corporate purchasers. The farmer selling his crop might do so not on open account but under a **futures contract**. Document 3-1 is an illustration of such a contract. Many agricultural sales follow the open account paradigm, however, such as those covering milk, eggs, poultry, some vegetables, and livestock, all of which are often subject to sale on open account.

This is probably as good a place as any to make the point that farmers are really merchants, most of them quite sophisticated. Even the small farmer who does not use computer terminals to gain access to markets, modern drip irrigation techniques, or scientific advances for soil testing will know as much about the agricultural enterprise as any small business entrepreneur knows about bank credit, markets, supply **costs,** taxes, and all the other areas of commerce and learning from which any business enterprise will benefit. The nation has long enjoyed something of a romance with the farm producer. There is allure in that romance, which a drive through the countryside on a fine summer evening inevitably nurtures. That romance must not mask the facts of agricultural commerce, however. It is best to think of the farmer as a merchant; the farmer has earned that respect.

Farmers and other merchants who sell to nonconsumer buyers have devised the open account sale as an efficient sales mechanism.

The open account sale involves massive amounts of goods and trillions of dollars of sales yearly in the domestic economy. In the overwhelmingly large percentage of merchant-to-merchant sales transactions, the parties will resort to the cheap, efficient device of the open account sale. A bit of history is helpful to understand open account sales.

There was a time when merchants were not often able to sell on open account. Credit reporting was slow and often unreliable. A New York manufacturer in the nineteenth century was not willing to ship on credit to a buyer way off in Tennessee unless the manufacturer had hard facts supporting the buyer's credit standing. The manufacturer certainly would not extend credit (i.e., ship on open account) on the basis of an order on the buyer's letterhead. Some manufacturers, however, were large enough to support a network of sales personnel ("drummers" who "drummed" up business) who would visit the buyer's establishment, talk to local merchants about the buyer, and report back to the manufacturer with a recommendation on credit. That system was expensive, and the volatile nature of many industries and many local economies rendered it imprecise and rendered the information generated by it of doubtful validity after short periods of time.

The day of the drummer is over. We encounter him in Meredith Wilson's catchy lyrics from the Music Man or in tired jokes modernized into stories about "travelling salesmen." Time has transmuted that commercial personage into a "marketing analyst" or the like. With the advent of accurate, reliable credit reporting agencies, sellers were in a better position to know the current state of a potential buyer's economic strength and, especially, to know when danger (usually foretold by late payments on current accounts) lurked. Specialized *credit agencies* accumulate data on customers in an industry and reported that information for a fee that is far less than the cost of maintaining a cadre of drummers. Document 3-2 is an illustration of a modern commercial credit report.

In the past, sellers had to acquire periodic, written credit reports from the credit-reporting agencies. That process was slow enough that the information could lose its value as circumstances changed and the report's data became dated. The advent of computerized communications, however, has generally guarded against data obsolescence and has rendered the credit-reporting process more immediate and therefore more reliable. Today, any high-volume, open account seller will have access to the credit-reporting agency's database. When a seller needs information about an account, a clerk in the seller's credit department will access the base by telephone wire and see on a computer terminal up-to-date credit information on the account in question.

The development of such credit reporting, faster communications methods, and the general standardization of many industries permitted sellers to do away with their costly in-house system of monitoring accounts and permitted them to sell to a vastly greater number of potential buyers. By the same token, the open account sale gives buyers tremendous advantages to the extent that it encourages sellers to sell on industry credit terms to new accounts and to new ventures that have in some way established a good credit rating.

It is important to understand that the open account sale is a credit sale. At the very least, the seller is giving the buyer credit during the time it takes for the seller's **invoice** to arrive at buyer's office and for buyer's purchasing people to forward payment to seller. In most industries, the credit terms are longer. Sellers in these industries ship on the understanding that payment is not due until the end of the month or 30 or even 60 days after the invoice date or after the end of the month. Many sellers, moreover, quote their prices in terms of discounts to those buyers that pay early.

§3.2 THE PARTIES

The efficiency of the typical open account sale is reflected in its simplicity. There are only two parties, the buyer and the seller, and the documentation is often minimal. Figure 3-1 illustrates the simplicity of the open account sale.

§3.3 DOCUMENTATION

In the open account sale, there may be little documentation. For example, a buyer in Tennessee may order merchandise from a New York seller by telephone. The seller's salesperson will book the order for internal purposes but probably will not send any acknowledgment, other than the sales invoice, to the buyer. Upon approval of the order by the seller's credit department, the shipping instructions, usually contained in a carbon copy of the invoice or the document that will become the invoice, go to the shipping department, which in the course of a few days or less will ship the merchandise to the buyer.

At the same time that the shipping information goes to shipping, billing information goes to the credit department, which will invoice the buyer without delay. Document 3-3 is a typical invoice, sometimes referred to as a *commercial invoice*.

Note that the invoice includes significant information, enough to satisfy the Statute of Frauds certainly, and note the economy of the document. By using computers, sellers with any significant volume of open account sales can generate all of the information they need concerning the

Figure 3-1. Open Account Sale

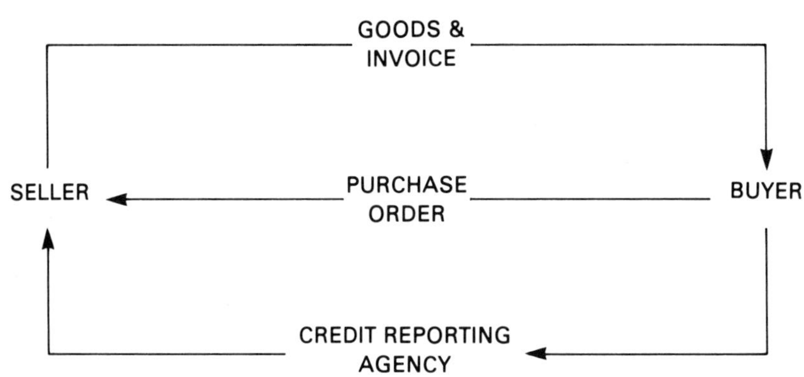

sale from the invoice itself, copies of which will serve as shipping tickets, sales records, and account records.

Briefly, then, the open account sale involves four simple steps. First, the sales department must determine that the sale is in the house, that is, that the buyer and the seller have agreed to a contract for the sale of the goods. Lawyers should be wary of importing into this determination their own legal culture. Business people may not always know whether the correspondence or telephone communications between the parties rise to the level of an enforceable contract. They do know, usually much better than the lawyers, what activity in the trade is sufficient for the seller to act upon. It is true that many times a court will subsequently decide that there was no contract. That **risk** is usually minimal in the minds of open account sellers, however. They act on the basis of commercial considerations that may not influence the court, and they are usually right.

The second step involves the credit evaluation. The credit department may make periodic preauthorizations, so that the sales people can skip this step in the process unless the order takes the account over the preauthorized limit. If there is no preauthorization, the credit department must look in the reporting-agency's database and determine whether the account merits credit under the seller's standards. If the credit department decides that the customer is worthy of customary industry credit terms, the department gives its approval to the order and initiates the invoicing process.

The third step is for the shipping department to arrange to ship the goods. The final step is to send the invoice.

§3.4 FURTHER DOCUMENTATION

In many cases, parties are not willing to rely on the telephone method of initiating an open account sale that is described in the foregoing paragraphs. Some buyers invariably follow the practice of issuing **purchase orders** in all of their purchase transactions or in those above a certain dollar amount or those from certain suppliers. Document 3-4 is a purchase order.

Many sellers also resort to documentation in the form of **order acknowledgments**. As all law students know, more often than not, the terms of the purchase order and the order acknowledgment differ in some respects. Those differences give rise to the famous "battle of the forms" that contracts law teachers have so much fun with in the basic contracts course. In real life, those battles are less significant than they are in the classroom. Most merchants do not rely on the boilerplate provisions that they incorporate into their forms. (At least they do not rely on them until the matter reaches litigation.) The disputes arise not because of the variances in the forms but because one or the other of the parties to the contract of sale no longer values it. In most cases, the buyer and the seller whose forms conflict go merrily on their way, often with no knowledge of the conflict; and if there are problems, say over the time period within which a buyer must examine goods and report defects, they work them out in a manner that is satisfactory to both. Only their lawyers worry about it. Document 3-5 is a typical order acknowledgment.

§3.5 AN IMPORTANT VARIATION

In some industries, a growing number it would appear, and in all industries to some extent, sellers will refuse to sell on open account without some assurance that the buyer will pay. There are two reasons for the seller's reluctance. First, if money is tight and interest rates are correspondingly high, some sellers find it difficult to finance their accounts. The open account sale leaves sellers with significantly high levels of accounts receivable. The seller can borrow on those accounts. (See Chapter 15 for a description of account financing.) The cost of that borrowing may be significant, however, and the seller can reduce its borrowing costs and be able to borrow more, if the accounts are secured by a financially strong guarantor of some kind. Second, in some cases, a buyer's credit rating will not qualify it for open account credit. In that case, the buyer may resort to some kind of **guaranty** arrangement in order to qualify for industry credit terms.

The invoice **letter of credit** provides an efficient device for satisfying both the seller's needs and the buyer's lack of creditworthiness. In this three-party variation of the open account sale, the buyer's bank or other financial institution issues a standby letter of credit in favor of the seller. Figure 3-2 illustrates the transaction.

After the buyer causes the letter of credit to be established, the open account sale proceeds as usual. The buyer submits orders, and the seller ships on open account with customary terms. The seller resorts to the letter of credit only in the event that the buyer fails to pay the invoice when it is due.

The standby, carefully drawn, incorporates as an exhibit the certificate that the seller must execute in order to draw on the letter of credit. Also the letter of credit contains a definite expiry, as all letters of credit should. The expiry, however, is often subject to what merchants and bankers call an *evergreen clause* that renders the credit automatically renewed in the event that the issuer of it does not give the seller 60 days' notice that it will not be renewed. When the seller receives notice of nonrenewal, it will stop selling on open account unless the buyer obtains a new credit from another issuer.

Figure 3-2. Invoice Standby Letter of Credit Transaction

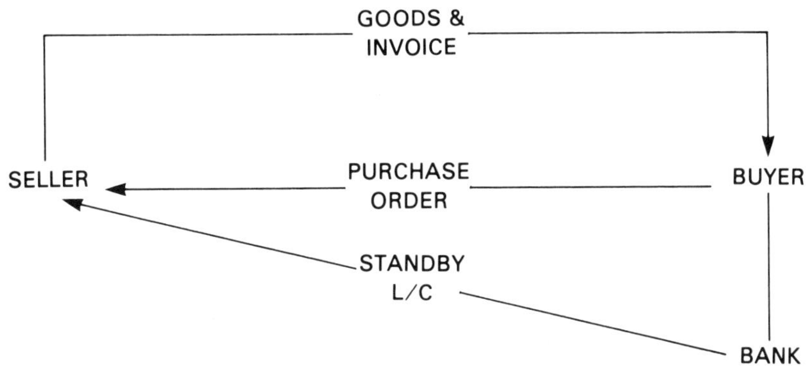

Invoice letters of credit are common in the automobile industry where the sellers, automobile manufacturers, are typically strong and the buyers, automobile dealers, are relatively weak. Automobile manufacturers have used their market strength to require dealers to obtain invoice standby credits, though they do not call them such. Document 3-6 is a typical automobile manufacturer's required invoice standby. Such letters of credit are appearing with increasing frequency in other industries.

§3.6 ELECTRONIC DATA INTERCHANGE

Recently, buyers and sellers have been experimenting with computer technology in an effort to reduce the amount of costly paper work. **Electronic data interchange** (EDI) is one innovation that effects that reduction, and although it is still in its infancy, some buyers and sellers have adapted it to the open account sale and have been able to reduce the use of purchase orders and invoices.

EDI is the transmission by modern communications methods of business forms in a standardized format. In order to utilize EDI, therefore, parties in an industry must establish a trade organization that will undertake to standardize forms. Because of the advanced technology involved, progress in the area is slow. Parties must have computer capabilities and sophisticated computer personnel. The equipment and education costs are considerable, and because only a small segment of any industry is ready for EDI, those with the capability must retain their paper-based procedures to service non-EDI customers or suppliers.

To date, EDI has achieved some success in the sales transaction by standardizing invoices and purchase orders. Under the trade group's standardization procedures, a party preparing a purchase order, for example, provides a minimum amount of information to the computer in language defined in a data dictionary. A buyer would need to enter a description of the merchandise, the price and **delivery terms**, and the identity of the parties. Much of the input is in codes, which the computer translates into a purchase order that appears on the prospective seller's computer terminal.

If the parties engage in frequent buy-sell transactions, the arrangement has obvious advantages. First, it is speedy. By using telephone lines, for example, the parties can transmit the purchase orders or invoices instantly. The parties, moreover, have eliminated paper, so that there is no need to store or transport documents. Finally, because the information is in the parties' computers, they can gain access to it quickly, manipulate it (e.g., change quantity or **price terms** or call for monthly summaries), and retrieve it instantly, even at locations distant from the office that initially received it.

Document 3-1. Grain Contract

GRAIN AND BEAN SALE AND PURCHASE AGREEMENT

This Agreement is entered into between ______________________________ of ______________________________, hereinafter referred to as the "Seller," and ______________________________ of ______________________________, hereinafter referred to as the "Purchaser."

In consideration of the mutual promises of the parties hereto and other good and valuable considerations, Seller agrees to sell and deliver to the Purchaser __________ (bu.) (cwt.) on or before ______________ at the price of $ __________ (per bu.) (per cwt.) net weight of ______________ (grade) ______________ (commodity) in marketable condition. Premiums and discounts at the time of delivery shall apply. Seller agrees to make delivery at the ______________________ elevator at ______________, Michigan. Seller further agrees that, at the discretion of the Purchaser, he will make delivery at an alternate elevator designated by the Purchaser at the time of delivery, in which case the standard transportation cost differential shall be applied to the price provided for above.

Seller hereby warrants that he has good and merchantable title and right to sell the commodity hereinabove described and that said commodity is free and clean of all liens, mortgages, and encumbrances of any kind or nature whatsoever.

Purchaser agrees to pay for said commodity at the above stipulated price and subject to the stated conditions above, and will accept delivery accordingly.

It is further agreed that title to the said commodity shall pass to the Purchaser at the time delivery is made and the commodity received at the point of delivery stated in this Agreement, or at the alternate point of delivery designated by the Purchaser.

In the event delivery is not completed by the delivery date specified herein due to the Seller's inability to harvest the commodity, the Seller shall make such circumstances known to the Purchaser and upon request by the Seller, an extension of not to exceed 60 days to complete delivery may be granted by the Purchaser. If the Seller then fails to complete delivery by the date on which the extension expires, the Seller agrees to immediately contact the Purchaser and pay to the Purchaser, as liquidated damages for breach of this Agreement, a sum equal to the difference between the above stipulated price and the board price of the commodity on the day after the date on which the extension expired, times the undelivered quantity, plus a penalty of 5 cents per (bu.) (cwt.).

If the Seller fails for any reason to complete delivery by the delivery date specified herein and has failed to request an extension of such delivery date, he shall be granted an extension of 60 days to deliver. However, if delivery is not completed at the expiration of the 60 days extension period, the Seller agrees to pay to the Purchaser, as liquidated damages for breach of this Agreement, a sum equal to the difference between the above stipulated price and the board price of the commodity on either the day after the last delivery date provided hereinabove or on the day after the date on which the extension expires, whichever difference is greater, times the undelivered quantity, plus a penalty of 5 cents per (bu.) (cwt.).

This Agreement shall be binding upon, and inure to the benefit of, the parties hereto, their heirs, personal representatives, successors, and assigns.

Signed this ______________ day of ______________, 19 ____.

____
(Corporation or Partnership)

Witness: ______________________ By: ______________________
Seller

Delivery date extended to ______________________

____
Address

Per: ______________________

____
Purchaser

____
Date

By: ______________________

Document 3-2. Commercial Credit Report

The Business Information Report

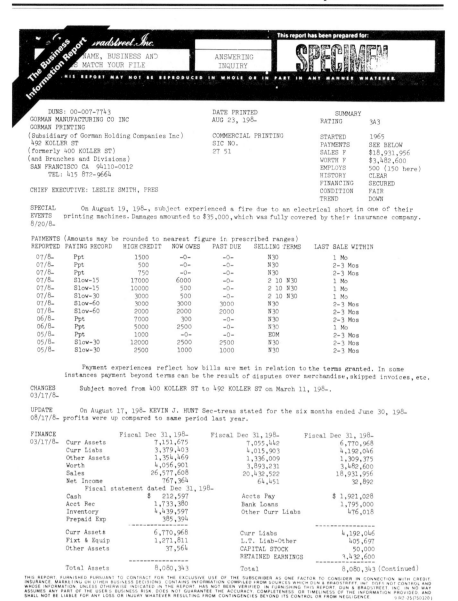

...radstreet, Inc.

...NAME, BUSINESS AND ...S MATCH YOUR FILE

ANSWERING INQUIRY

This report has been prepared for:

SPECIMEN

...HIS REPORT MAY NOT BE REPRODUCED IN WHOLE OR IN PART IN ANY MANNER WHATEVER.

DUNS: 00-007-7743
GORMAN MANUFACTURING CO INC
GORMAN PRINTING
(Subsidiary of Gorman Holding Companies Inc)
492 KOLLER ST
(formerly 400 KOLLER ST)
(and Branches and Divisions)
SAN FRANCISCO CA 94110-0012
TEL: 415 872-9664

DATE PRINTED
AUG 23, 198–

COMMERCIAL PRINTING
SIC NO.
27 51

SUMMARY	
RATING	3A3
STARTED	1965
PAYMENTS	SEE BELOW
SALES F	$18,931,956
WORTH F	$3,482,600
EMPLOYS	500 (150 here)
HISTORY	CLEAR
FINANCING	SECURED
CONDITION	FAIR
TREND	DOWN

CHIEF EXECUTIVE: LESLIE SMITH, PRES

SPECIAL EVENTS 8/20/8– On August 19, 198–, subject experienced a fire due to an electrical short in one of their printing machines. Damages amounted to $35,000, which was fully covered by their insurance company.

PAYMENTS (Amounts may be rounded to nearest figure in prescribed ranges)

REPORTED	PAYING RECORD	HIGH CREDIT	NOW OWES	PAST DUE	SELLING TERMS	LAST SALE WITHIN
07/8–	Ppt	1500	-0-	-0-	N30	1 Mo
07/8–	Ppt	500	-0-	-0-	N30	2-3 Mos
07/8–	Ppt	750	-0-	-0-	N30	2-3 Mos
07/8–	Slow-15	17000	6000	-0-	2 10 N30	1 Mo
07/8–	Slow-15	10000	500	-0-	2 10 N30	1 Mo
07/8–	Slow-30	3000	500	-0-	2 10 N30	1 Mo
07/8–	Slow-60	3000	3000	3000	N30	2-3 Mos
07/8–	Slow-60	2000	2000	2000	N30	2-3 Mos
06/8–	Ppt	7000	300	-0-	N30	2-3 Mos
06/8–	Ppt	5000	2500	-0-	N30	1 Mo
05/8–	Ppt	1000	-0-	-0-	EOM	2-3 Mos
05/8–	Slow-30	12000	2500	2500	N30	2-3 Mos
05/8–	Slow-30	2500	1000	1000	N30	2-3 Mos

Payment experiences reflect how bills are met in relation to the terms granted. In some instances payment beyond terms can be the result of disputes over merchandise, skipped invoices, etc.

CHANGES 03/17/8– Subject moved from 400 KOLLER ST to 492 KOLLER ST on March 11, 198–.

UPDATE 08/17/8– On August 17, 198– KEVIN J. HUNT Sec-treas stated for the six months ended June 30, 198– profits were up compared to same period last year.

FINANCE 03/17/8–

	Fiscal Dec 31, 198–	Fiscal Dec 31, 198–	Fiscal Dec 31, 198–
Curr Assets	7,151,675	7,055,442	6,770,968
Curr Liabs	3,379,403	4,015,903	4,192,046
Other Assets	1,354,469	1,336,009	1,309,375
Worth	4,056,901	3,893,231	3,482,600
Sales	26,577,608	20,432,522	18,931,956
Net Income	767,364	64,451	32,892

Fiscal statement dated Dec 31, 198–

Cash	$ 212,597	Accts Pay	$ 1,921,028
Acct Rec	1,733,380	Bank Loans	1,795,000
Inventory	4,439,597	Other Curr Liabs	476,018
Prepaid Exp	385,394		
Curr Assets	6,770,968	Curr Liabs	4,192,046
Fixt & Equip	1,271,811	L.T. Liab-Other	405,697
Other Assets	37,564	CAPITAL STOCK	50,000
		RETAINED EARNINGS	3,432,600
Total Assets	8,080,343	Total	8,080,343

(Continued)

Printed with the permission of Dun & Bradstreet Business Credit Services, Murray Hill, NJ.

Dun & Bradstreet, Inc.

This report has been prepared for:

GORMAN MANUFACTURING CO INC
SAN FRANCISCO CA

AUG 23 198-

PAGE 2
CONSOLIDATED REPORT

THIS REPORT MAY NOT BE REPRODUCED IN WHOLE OR IN PART IN ANY MANNER WHATEVER.

FINANCE (Cont'd) Annual sales $18,931,956; cost of goods sold $16,777,064. Gross profit $2,154,892; net income $32,892; dividends $29,640; monthly rent $2,500. Lease expires 1999. Fire insurance on mdse & fixt $6,000,000.

Submitted by Kevin J. Hunt, Sec-Treas. Prepared from statement(s) by Accountant: Fred Mitchel, San Francisco, CA. Prepared from books without audit.

Other assets are tangible, composed of miscellaneous deposits and deferred items. Other current liabilities and long term liabilities are notes due on equipment.

On Mar 15, 198- Kevin J. Hunt, Sec-Treas, referred to the above figures as still representative.

He stated that sales for the 12 months ended Dec 31, 198- were down compared to the same period last year. Profit for the period was down but is expected to increase. Kevin J. Hunt stated that the net worth decreased at 12/31/8-, attributed to the purchase and retirement to treasury of a portion of the capital stock.

Current debt is in excess of net worth. Inventory is large in relation to sales and working capital is light compared to volume transacted.

PUBLIC FILINGS 03/17/8- On Mar 25, 198-, a suit in the amount of $500 was filed against Gorman Manufacturing Co Inc. by Z Henric Assoc.(Docket #27511) in San Francisco, CA. Cause of action was Goods sold and delivered.

Financing statement #741170 filed 01-28-8_ with the Secretary, State of CA. Debtor: Gorman Manufacturing Co., Inc., San Francisco, CA. Secured party: Swinger Corp., Malibu, CA. Collateral: Equipment.

On March 17, 198- Kevin J. Hunt reported action filed by Z Henric Associates was due to damages caused by faulty printer and has been settled. Count records reveal suit was withdrawn.

BANKING 03/8- Balances average moderate six figures. Account open over three years. Loans extended to low seven figures, now owes low seven figures, secured by accounts receivable and inventory, and relation satisfactory.

HISTORY 03/17/8- LESLIE SMITH, PRES KEVIN J. HUNT, SEC-TREAS
DIRECTOR(s): THE OFFICER(s)

Incorporated California May 21, 1965. Authorized capital consists of 200 shares common stock, no par value.

Business started 1965 by principals. 100% of capital stock is owned by parent.

LESLIE SMITH born 1926 married. Graduated from the University of California, Los Angeles, June 1947. 1947-1965 was the general manager for Raymor Printing Co.San Francisco, CA. 1965 formed subject with Kevin J. Hunt.

KEVIN J. HUNT born 1925 married. Graduated from Northwestern University, Evanston, IL, in June 1946. 1946-1965 was the production manager for Raymor Printing Co., San Francisco, CA. 1965 formed subject with Leslie Smith.

Related Companies: Through the financial interest of Gorman Holding Companies Inc., the Gorman Manufacturing Co Inc. is related to two other sister companies (Smith Lettershop Inc, San Diego, CA and Gorman Suppliers Inc., Los Angeles, CA). These sister companies are also engaged in commercial printing. There are no intercompany relations.

OPERATION 03/17/8- Subsidiary of Gorman Holding Companies Inc.,Los Angeles, CA, which operates as a holding company for its underlying subsidiaries. Parent company has two other subsidiaries. There are no intercompany relations between parent and subject. A consolidated financial statement on the parent company, dated Dec 31, 198- showed a net worth of $7,842,226, with a fair financial condition indicated.

Commercial printing, engaged in letterpress and screen printing. Sells for cash 30% balance net 30 days. Has 1,000 accounts. Sells to commercial concerns. Territory: Nationwide. Nonseasonal.

EMPLOYEES: 500 including officers. 150 employed here.

FACILITIES: Rents 40,000 sq. ft. in 1 story concrete block building in good condition. Premises neat.

LOCATION: Industrial section on side street.

BRANCHES: Subject maintains a branch at 1073 Boyden Road, Los Angeles, CA.

07-23)9D9 /5)0039/02 00000 052

INVOICE
4874-A

CHRYSLER MOTORS

PLANT	ZONE	DEALER	VEHICLE IDENTIFICATION NO.	INVOICE NO.	INVOICE DATE
TOLEDO I	43	23507	1J4FJ57L2LL120593	L-XJJ-GN343001	08/16/89

SHIP TO: THOMAS GARAGE INC
252 EAST MAIN STREET
ST. CLAIRSVILLE OH 43950

IGN KEY 9014
TRK KEY 0431
ACC KEY

SOLD TO: THOMAS GARAGE INC
252 EAST MAIN STREET
ST. CLAIRSVILLE OH 43950

2459-01-8L12

M.S.O.WT. 3050
SAE HP 36.1

PAID FOR BY: BELMONT COUNTY NATIONAL BANK 000-560701-00

☐ CREDIT SALE ☒ CASH SALE SEE DEFINITION BELOW

BODY & EQUIP.	DESCRIPTION	FACTORY WHOLESALE PRICE
XJJL72	JEEP CHEROKEE 4WD 2DR	13025.60
PB3	SPINNAKER BLUE METALLIC	148.75
Q7SA	RECLINER WING BACK BUCKETS-FABRIC	NO CHARGE
ADH	H.D ALTERNATOR/BATTERY GROUP	62.05
AHT	TRAILER TOW PACKAGE B	207.40
ALR	**************************	
ARC	PKG PREMIUM RADIO SPEAKER SYSTEM	149.60
ARN	PKG LAREDO DECOR GROUP INCLUDES:	2968.20
AWE	OFF ROAD SUSPENSION PACKAGE	497.25
AWH	PKG POWER WINDOW AND LOCK GROUP-2	374.85
BGK	FOUR WHEEL ANTI LOCK BRAKE SYSTEM	848.30
DGB	AUTOMATIC TRANSMISSION	696.15
DHP	"SELECT TRAC" FULL/PART-TIME 4WD	338.30
DSA	REAR TRAC LOCK DIFFERENTIAL	243.95
ERB	4.0 LITRE "POWER-TECH SIX" ENGINE	PACKAGE
GTJ	DUAL MIRRORS-ELECTRIC	85.85
GWB	SUN ROOF-MANUAL	306.85
HAA	PKG AIR CONDITIONING	718.25
JPT	POWER SEATS-DRIVER & PASSENGER	357.00
LNJ	PKG FOG LAMPS	94.35
NHM	PKG CRUISE CONTROL	194.65
RAF	PKG AM/FM CASSETTE RADIO	172.55
SUA	PKG TILT STEERING WHEEL	113.05
TRN	TIRES P225/75R15 OWL WRANGLER(4)	PACKAGE
WJN	ALUMINUM WHEELS-5 SPOKE	NO CHARGE
YDH	OWNER COMMUNICATION PROGRAM	15.00
YEP	MANUFACTURERS STATEMENT OF ORIGIN	1.00
YGG	GASOLINE 9 GALLONS	11.25
5KR	***OPTION GROUP DISCOUNT - ALR**	935.00-
420	JEDAA - PITTSBURG EAST	195.00
441	DESTINATION CHARGE	450.00
	HB70458	
	** TENTATIVE BILLING - SUBJECT TO LATER ADJUSTMENT **	

SPECIMEN

MSRP RETAIL TOTAL 23,936.00 **TOTAL** 21340.20

ORIGINAL INVOICE **1**

IMPORTANT - CHECK VEHICLE IDENTIFICATION NUMBER OF MOTOR VEHICLE RECEIVED WITH VEHICLE IDENTIFICATION NUMBER ON THIS INVOICE. NOTIFY US OF ANY DIFFERENCE.

CREDIT SALE: THIS SALE IS MADE PURSUANT TO THE TERMS AND CONDITIONS OF A CERTAIN WHOLESALE FINANCING AGREEMENT FOR CREDIT SALE SHIPMENTS ENTERED INTO BETWEEN CHRYSLER MOTORS CORPORATION, THE DEALER INDICATED ABOVE AS "SOLD TO:" AND THE DEALERS'S FINANCIAL INSTITUTION INDICATED ABOVE AS "PAID FOR BY:"

CASH SALE: TITLE TO THE ABOVE DESCRIBED MOTOR VEHICLE PASSES ON DELIVERY TO THE DEALER, HIS AGENT OR THE CARRIER. CHRYSLER MOTORS CORPORATION RETAINS A LIEN FOR PAYMENT ON THE MOTOR VEHICLE UNTIL PAID FOR IN FULL. IN CASH. NEGOTIABLE INSTRUMENTS ARE RECEIVED ONLY AS CONDITIONAL PAYMENT.

83-175-0025 (9/86)

Printed with the permission of Chrysler Motors Corp.

PURCHASE ORDER

VENDOR	PURCHASER
PRO FORMA INVOICE NO. — DATE	PURCHASE ORDER NO. — DATE
CONSIGNEE	NOTIFY INTERMEDIATE CONSIGNEE

MFR. ITEM NO., SYMBOL, OR BRAND	QUANTITIES, FULL DESCRIPTION OF MERCHANDISE, AND PACKAGING INSTRUCTIONS	UNIT PURCHASE PRICE CURRENCY	TOTAL PURCHASE PRICE CURRENCY
	SPECIMEN		

SPECIAL PACKAGING REQUIREMENTS		
	OCEAN/AIR FREIGHT	________
	INCLUDED COSTS ________	________
	________	________
	TOTAL	

RELEASE NO.	ITEM AND QUANTITY	DELIVERY DATE	PORT OF ENTRY	CARRIER

DOCUMENT REQUIREMENTS	TERMS OF PAYMENT

Form 16-310 Printed and Sold by UNZ&CO 190 Baldwin Ave., Jersey City, NJ 07306 • (800) 631-3098 • (201) 795-5400

Reprinted with the permission of Unz & Co., 190 Baldwin Ave., Jersey City, NJ 07306 USA.

ORDER CONTRACT

THIS ORDER NOT AUTHORIZED BY K MART UNLESS COUNTER SIGNED AT INT'L. HDQRS.

Kmart Corporation
INTERNATIONAL HEADQUARTERS
3100 WEST BIG BEAVER
TROY, MICHIGAN 48084

Page 1

STORE No. ____________

ORDER No. ____________ DEPT. # ____________

MAIL INVOICE AND BILL OF LADING TO STORE TO WHICH GOODS ARE SHIPPED.

DATE ____________

Vendor ____________
Street ____________
City ____________ Zip Code ____________

Terms ____________

F.O.B. ____________
Merchandise Must Be In Store On ____________

Via ____________
Cancel ____________

NOTE — SEE SECTION TWO OF LIST OF STORES BOOK FOR SHIPPING AND INVOICING INSTRUCTIONS.
Delivery Dates (Are split shipments involved?) ____________

Order Detail:

ASSORTMENT ORDERED							Unit	Item No.	DESCRIPTION (On all wearing apparel show desc. of material, size cut to doz. and colors)	Unit Cost Price	Pkg. Qty.	Ctn. Wgt.
1	2	3	4	5	6	7						

SPECIMEN

If additional space is needed use page 2 (Both pages must be signed)

(Check below only if applicable.)

☐ Check here if any payments are to be held back to cover returns and adjustments. If checked ________% of Seller's total invoices submitted for payment shall be held back until ________ (period of time) has elapsed after Buyer's receipt of all Merchandise oredered under this Order Contract.

☐ Check here if this is a guaranteed sale (sale or return). If checked, Merchandise delivered under this Order Contract which is not resold may be returned in lieu of payment even if Merchandise is conforming.

____________ SALES DEPARTMENT

____________ BUYER

IMPORTANT: SEE REVERSE SIDE FOR ADDITIONAL TERMS AND CONDITIONS

CODE 912-59—Pads 50's—(Rev. 6/87)—CCI—S—Litho in U.S.A.

Document 3-5. (*continued*)

ADDITIONAL TERMS AND CONDITIONS

Seller and K mart Corporation ("Buyer") agree to be bound by all terms and conditions contained or incorporated herein, all of which are a part of this Order Contract and should be carefully read. Any provisions in Seller's invoices, billing statements, acknowledgment forms or similar documents which are inconsistent with the provisions of this Order Contract shall be of no force or effect.

1. **SELLER'S ACCEPTANCE.** Seller's commencement of or promise of shipment of the Merchandise shall constitute Seller's agreement that it will deliver the Merchandise in accordance with the terms and conditions of this Order Contract. Seller agrees to follow the shipping and invoicing instructions issued by Buyer's stores, warehouses, buying offices and Traffic and Accounting Departments, which instructions are incorporated by reference into this Order Contract.
2. **SELLER'S REPRESENTATIONS AND WARRANTIES.** Seller represents and warrants to Buyer, in addition to all warranties implied by law, that each item of merchandise described on the face hereof, together with all related packaging and labeling and other material furnished by Seller ("Merchandise"), shall (a) be free from defects in design, workmanship or materials including, without limitation, such defects as could create a hazard to life or property; (b) conform in all respects with all applicable federal, state and local laws, orders and regulations, including but not limited to those regarding occupational safety and health; (c) not infringe or encroach upon Buyer's or any third party's personal, contractual or proprietary rights, including patents, trademarks, copyrights, rights of privacy or trade secrets; (d) conform to all of Buyer's specifications and to all articles shown to Buyer as Merchandise samples.
3. **SELLER'S INDEMINIFICATION OF BUYER.** Seller agrees to reimburse, indemnify, hold harmless and to defend at its expense (or to pay any attorney's fees incurred by Buyer) K mart Corporation and its subsidiary companies against all damage, loss, expense, claim, liability or penalty, including (but not limited to) claims of infringement of patents, copyrights, trademarks, unfair competition, bodily injury, property or other damage, arising out of any use, possession, consumption or sale of said Merchandise and from any failure of Seller to properly perform this Order Contract. Seller shall obtain adequate insurance to cover its liability under this Order Contract and shall provide copies of the applicable certificate(s) of insurance upon request of Buyer.
4. **DEFECTIVE OR NON-CONFORMING MERCHANDISE.** If any Merchandise is defective, unsuitable, does not conform to all terms of this Order Contract and all warranties implied by law, Buyer may at its option return it to Seller for full credit or refund of the purchase price or repair it at Seller's expense, and may charge Seller such price or expense and the cost of any incurred inbound and outbound freight and a handling, storage and inspection charge of 7½% of the returned Merchandise' invoice price.
5. **BUYER'S RIGHT TO CANCEL.** Buyer may terminate and rescind all or part of the Order Contract in the event Seller breaches or fails to perform any of its obligations in any material respect, or in the event Seller becomes insolvent or proceedings are instituted by or against Seller under any provision of any federal or state bankruptcy or insolvency laws or Seller ceases its operation. Time is of the essence to this Order Contract, and Seller's failure to meet any delivery date shall constitute a material breach of the Order Contract.
6. **SPECIAL FEATURES.** All Merchandise designs, patents and tradenames which are supplied by Buyer to Seller or which are distinctive of Buyer's private label merchandise ("Special Features") shall be the property of Buyer and shall be used by Seller only for Buyer. Buyer may use the Special Features on or with respect to goods manufactured by others and obtain legal protection for the Special Features including, without limitation, patents, patent designs, copyrights and trademarks.
7. **DEDUCTIONS AND SET OFF.** Any sums payable to Seller shall be subject to all claims and defenses of Buyer, whether arising from this or any other transaction or occurrence, and Buyer may set off and deduct against any such sums all present and future indebtedness of Seller to Buyer. Buyer shall provide a copy of the deduction voucher(s) for debits taken by Buyer against Seller's account as a result of any returns or adjustments. Seller shall be deemed to have accepted each such deduction unless Seller, within 90 days following receipt of the deduction voucher, notifies Buyer in writing as to why a deduction should not be made and provides documentation of the reason(s) given. Such written notice shall be directed to: Vendor Audit Department, K mart Corporation, 3100 West Big Beaver Road, Troy, Michigan 48084.
8. **MICHIGAN CONTRACT AND JURISDICTION. This Order Contract shall be construed and enforced in accordance with the laws of the State of Michigan, and it is agreed that Seller shall exercise any right or remedy hereunder in, and hereby consents to the jurisdiction of, the State of Michigan Courts of Oakland County, Michigan or the United States District Court in Detroit, Michigan.**
9. **MISCELLANEOUS.** (a) All rights granted to Buyer hereunder shall be in addition to and not in lieu of Buyer's rights arising by operation of law; (b) any provisions of this Order Contract which are typewritten or handwritten by Buyer shall supersede any contrary or inconsistent printed provisons; (c) no modification of terms of this Order contract shall be valid unless in writing and signed by Buyer; (d) should any of the provisions of this Order Contract be declared by a court of competent jurisdiction to be invalid, such decision shall not affect the validity of any remaining provisions; (e) all of the terms herein shall apply to additional quantities of Merchandise orderded by Buyer except to the extent covered by a new written agreement, (f) the cost price set forth in this Order Contract includes the cost of manufacturing, packaging, labeling and shipping unless otherwise specified herein.

CODE 912-59

CHRYSLER MOTORS

Clean Letter of Credit

TO: Chrysler Motors Corporation, Vehicle Credit Section, P. O. Box 2319, Detroit, Michigan 48288
Telephone 1-800-521-1202, except in Michigan call 313-956-4956. Telefax 313-252-6806

We hereby authorize you or any bank designated by you to draw cash drafts (the "Drafts") on us in payment for motor vehicles sold, delivered or shipped to the undersigned Chrysler Motors Corporation dealer (the "Dealer"), pursuant to the Dealer Agreement or Agreements in effect from time to time between you and the Dealer.

We authorize you to sell, deliver or ship vehicles to the Dealer without our prior approval and we agree to pay you therefor by paying at par upon presentation your Drafts drawn on us in payment for said vehicles. Each Draft will specify, among other things, the invoice number, serial number and amount for each vehicle for which the Draft is drawn. The foregoing applies to all forms of sale, delivery, release or shipment. We understand and agree that this authorization for you to draw Drafts on us and our commitment to pay you therefor (the "Authorization") is unconditional and that it is in no way related to or limited by any payment obligation that the Dealer may have or incur pursuant to any agreement(s) with us.

Until further notice, this Authorization is limited to $____________ for all vehicles sold, delivered or shipped to the Dealer on any one day, and we may return any Drafts drawn in excess of such limit.

This Authorization is not subject to any floor plan limit that we may have established with the Dealer, and we agree not to return Drafts solely because payment thereof would cause such limit to be exceeded.

We may notify you by telephone or in writing to suspend or terminate this Authorization at any time. However, such suspension or termination shall not become effective until the close of business on your first business day following the day you receive such notice. If such notice is given by telephone we will confirm the same in writing. We agree to honor and pay all Drafts in payment for vehicles sold, delivered or shipped to the Dealer prior to the time such suspension or termination becomes effective. We understand that you incur no obligation hereunder to sell, deliver or ship vehicles to the Dealer and that you reserve the right to suspend or discontinue shipments or deliveries to the Dealer at any time at your sole discretion and without notice.

This Authorization is and is intended to be a clean letter of credit, and Drafts issued hereunder are not and are not intended to be documentary drafts or documentary demands for payment. Honor of such Drafts is not and is not intended to be conditioned upon the presentation of any document or documents.

This Authorization is effective immediately and supersedes any previous Authorization, if any, wherein we have agreed to pay for motor vehicles sold, delivered or shipped to the Dealer.

Your right to draw Drafts hereunder is transferable and assignable by you and your assignees to any bank or Federal Reserve Bank. Any rights of Dealer hereunder shall not be transferable or assignable.

Until notified to the contrary, all Manufacturers Certificates of Origin are to be mailed under separate cover to:

☐ The Dealer ☐ The Bank

SPECIMEN

____________________ (BANK NAME) ____________________ (... TO BE PRINTED ON DRAFTS) __________ (TELEPHONE NO.)

By ____________________ (AUTHORIZED OFFICER) ____________________ (BANK STREET ADDRESS)

Title ________________ Date __________ ____________________ (CITY, STATE, ZIP CODE)

Chrysler Motors Corporation Dealer Acknowledgement

We acknowledge the above Authorization and request that Chrysler Motors Corporation draft on the above-named bank in payment for vehicles sold, shipped or delivered to us. We further request that Chrysler Motors Corporation set forth a notation on the invoice for each vehicle sold, shipped or delivered to us that such vehicle is paid for by the above-named bank. We understand that the above Authorization does not affect our obligation to pay for said vehicles.

____________________ (DEALER NAME) ____________________ (DEALER CODE NUMBER) __________ (TELEPHONE NO.)

DBA ____________________ ____________________ (DEALER STREET ADDRESS)

By ____________________ (AUTHORIZED SIGNATURE) ____________________ (CITY, STATE, ZIP CODE)

Title ________________ Date __________

DAP-13C (Rev. 4-89)

Printed with the permission of Chrysler Motors Corp.

4

Sale by Documentary Draft

§4.1 CASH AGAINST DOCUMENTS

While the open account sale of Chapter 3 is the most common setting for sales between merchants, sellers have devised a number of ways to protect themselves against the uncreditworthy buyer. The first and easiest form of protection is for the seller to insist on payment in advance. Sellers who do not have confidence in a buyer can ask for a down payment or for a lump-sum cash payment against which the buyer's purchases will be charged. Down payments are not uncommon when merchants sell on credit to consumers, and some professional providers of services, such as lawyers, will require new accounts to pay a retainer in advance of rendering any services. Some sellers will ship C.O.D., that is, cash on delivery.

All of these methods entail risk on the part of the buyer that it may be unwilling to assume. Any buyer that pays for goods or services before delivery runs the serious risks of seller insolvency or nonperformance. In fact, it is safe to say that in most sale-of-goods transactions few professional buyers will ever pay in advance, and a transaction in which that practice appears may be an instance of fraud or other commercially baleful practice. Sometimes prepayment is an attempt by the buyer to finance his seller, and in that case, the buyer is probably a lender attempting to take a security interest in goods. In these circumstances, the **prepaying buyer** should be considered a secured lender subject to the rules of Article 9.

In order to avoid the risks and baleful commercial effects of prepay-

Figure 4-1. Documentary Draft Transaction

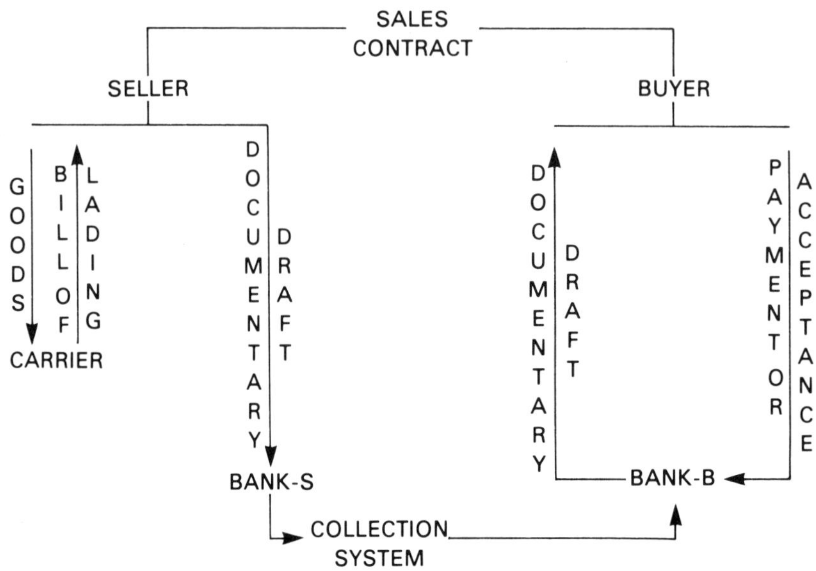

ment, most buyers that confront a seller who is unwilling to ship on open account will suggest a sale for cash against documents or some variation thereof. Under this arrangement, which is illustrated in Figure 4-1, the buyer can assure himself with reasonable certainty before payment that the goods have in fact been shipped and that when they arrive in the buyer's city the carrier will deliver them.

§4.2 THE DOCUMENTS

Formerly, in the domestic sale and, today, in most international sales, two documents are necessary for the **documentary draft** transaction. The first is a negotiable **document of title** called an order **bill of lading**. Document 4-1 is a standard form order bill of lading.

The seller obtains the order bill from a common carrier, fills it out, and tenders it to the carrier along with the goods. The carrier then executes the bill, returns it to the seller (the "shipper" in transport language), and dispatches the goods to the buyer's city. Note that under the order bill, the carrier will deliver the goods only to the holder of the bill. Any delivery to another person is a violation of the carrier's obligation under the bill and under federal and state laws that govern bills of lading. Thus, when the seller's agent asks the buyer to pay against delivery of the bill, the buyer can rely on that obligation and can generally assume that if it has possession of the order bill, it will obtain delivery of the goods when they arrive at the destination specified in the bill. It is fair to say that a negotiable document of title stands for the goods themselves, which are "mere shadows" as long as the bill is outstanding. Chapter 31 discusses negotiable bills and the concept of **negotiability** for documents of title in more detail.

There is one important caveat of which buyers and their lawyers must be aware with regard to order bills of lading. Merchandise is often shipped in cartons or other packaging, and even bulk cargo may be shipped in containers that are loaded at the seller's facility and remain sealed until they arrive at the buyer's facility. The containerization of shipments has done much to reduce pilferage and damage to cargo. It makes no sense to lose the efficiencies that are achieved by shipping in such fashion by insisting that carriers open the packages or containers to inspect the goods. Bills of lading traditionally contain disclaimers by the carrier concerning the contents of the packages. If the bill contains such a disclaimer, and it usually does, buyers generally do not rely and should not rely on the carrier's obligation to deliver goods that conform to the description in the underlying transaction or even in the bill or lading. Buyers that are concerned about the integrity of the seller or otherwise about the conformity of the goods should engage an independent inspector and should not pay against the bill of lading unless the inspector's certificate indicates that the goods conform. Document 4-2 is an example of an inspection certificate.

In most domestic transactions, parties no longer use the negotiable bill of lading. There are distinct advantages to the negotiable bill, the primary one being the fact that the carrier will deliver only to the holder of it; but there are disadvantages too. First, since it stands for the goods, if it becomes lost, the carrier will insist on indemnity (a **bond** of some kind) before it will release the goods. Second, because of the risk of losing the bill, the parties do not send it through the mail but use the bank collection chain. Indemnities and bank collection services cost money and increase the **transaction costs** for buyers and sellers. If the buyer is willing to trust the seller, it will pay the seller upon receipt of a nonnegotiable or "straight" bill of lading. Document 4-3 is a straight bill.

This straight bill does not stand for the goods, and there is a risk that the dishonest seller will stop delivery or redirect a shipment after the buyer pays in reliance on the straight bill as evidence that the goods have been "consigned" to it. The straight bill and the law governing it make it proper for the carrier to deliver the goods according to the seller's instructions after the bill issues and contrary to the original terms of the bill. The suspicious buyer must insist on a negotiable bill.

In addition to the document of title, be it negotiable or nonnegotiable, the documentary draft transaction calls for a **draft**. Document 4-4 is a sight draft. This instrument, which should be negotiable in form, is an order, similar to a check, by the seller (the drawer) to the buyer (the drawee) for payment of the purchase price of the goods. Drafts may be payable at sight, that is, on demand, or may be credit instruments that are payable a specified period of time after a specified date or after sight. Document 4-5 is a time draft, sometimes called a ***usance*** *draft.*

Sight drafts are payable on presentation, and the refusal of the drawee to pay the draft constitutes dishonor. Some time drafts are payable a number of days (30, 60, or 90 are common periods) after sight, that is, after the instrument is presented to the buyer, or a number of days after date. Time drafts are not payable until the time specified, e.g., 30 days after sight, but they are presented to the drawee for "**acceptance**" as soon as possible after they issue. The drawee (here, the buyer) accepts the draft by executing it on its face and dating the acceptance. Document 4-6 is an accepted draft, called a "**trade acceptance.**"

§4.3 MECHANICS OF THE TRANSACTION

In order to provide the buyer and the seller with the full protection of the documentary draft sales transaction, the parties will use the negotiable bill of lading and a negotiable draft, payable either at sight or at a given time, as the underlying contract stipulates. If the underlying contract provides for credit terms, the draft will be a time draft, if it calls for cash against documents, the parties will use a sight draft. Assuming a seller in Detroit and a buyer in Fresno, the parties will then proceed with the following steps.

First, the seller will prepare the goods for shipment and fill out the negotiable bill of lading form supplied by the carrier. Next, the shipper will deliver the goods to the carrier and the carrier's agent will sign the bill and issue it to the seller's order. The seller will then indorse the bill of lading on its back and will draw a negotiable draft on the buyer for the amount of the contract purchase price. At that point the seller has created a documentary draft: the draft with the negotiable bill attached.

Second, the seller will take the draft and the bill to a financial institution in Detroit, probably the bank with whom she does business and will ask the bank to collect the draft. The bank will give the seller provisional credit and often will let the seller draw on the credit. The bank feels safe in doing so (1) because it will require the seller to indorse the draft, so that if the buyer dishonors, the bank is a holder and the seller is liable to it in the seller's capacity as drawer and as indorser; (2) because the bank holds the negotiable bill of lading, which stands for the goods, to which the bank will have resort if the buyer dishonors and the seller defaults on its obligation to reimburse the bank in the event of dishonor; and (3) because often the seller is a valued customer of the bank whose drafts are invariably honored by buyers or invariably made good by the seller in the event the buyers do not honor.

Third, the Detroit bank will forward the documentary draft through the bank collection system to a bank in Fresno. The Fresno bank will notify the buyer that the draft and bill have arrived and will *present* the draft and ask the buyer to honor it. That presentation may be effected by calling the buyer and telling him the draft and bill of lading are at the Fresno bank. Recall that if the draft is a sight draft, the buyer honors it by paying the face amount. If it is a time draft, the buyer honors it by accepting the draft (signing its face), thereby creating a trade acceptance. The buyer later pays the face amount of the acceptance to the holder of it at maturity.

Fourth, upon the buyer's payment of the sight draft or acceptance of the time draft, the Fresno bank will surrender the properly indorsed bill of lading to the buyer, who will then hold a document that stands for the goods and who will be in a position to claim the goods from the carrier when they arrive in Fresno.

Note that the buyer achieves considerable protection under the negotiable bill. He has not paid for the goods in advance, even if the draft is a sight draft, since delivery of the bill to him, which is contemporaneous with his payment of the sight draft or acceptance of the time draft, is the virtual equivalent of delivery of the goods.

There are considerable transaction costs in the documentary draft sale. Many sellers are unwilling to pay those costs and find it more efficient to pay the cost of taking a risk that the buyer will not pay. In domestic sales, the documentary draft transaction has largely fallen into disuse. In international commerce or in those cases where the value of the goods is high, say, the shipment of a super tanker of petrochemicals, the parties will pay the documentary draft transaction's costs and may incur even greater costs under the letter-of-credit variation of the documentary draft sale that is described in the next section.

Note that there are also some efficiencies in the documentary draft sale. Because the Detroit bank will make an advance against the seller's draft when she takes it to the bank for collection, the seller receives funds more quickly than she would under the open account sale. Note also that if insolvency or lack of interest prompts the buyer to dishonor the draft, the seller will still have control of the goods, since the Fresno bank will not surrender the bill of lading to the buyer that dishonors the draft. (Dishonor occurs upon one of three failures of the buyer: (1) to accept a time draft upon presentment for acceptance; (2) to pay a time draft upon maturity; or (3) to pay a sight draft upon presentment.) In the event of dishonor, the Fresno bank will notify the Detroit bank, which in turn will notify the seller to provide instructions for disposal of the goods. The seller can order the sale of the goods in Fresno, can direct their shipment elsewhere, or can ask that the goods be returned to Detroit. None of those choices are happy for the seller, since they inevitably result in increased sales costs; but all of the choices are better than having the buyer with the goods and the seller with no purchase price — the result that will obtain if the seller sells on open account to a buyer that does not pay the invoice. By the same token, the documentary draft sale protects the buyer, since he does not have to advance funds before he gets the bill of lading, which stands for the goods.

The documentary sale also facilitates the financing of the sale. Sometimes the buyer is a middleman that is going to resell the goods promptly. He needs financing during the brief period between the time he receives the goods and the time he receives payment from his subpurchaser. During that brief period, which may be 45 or 60 days, the buyer can avoid having to pay cash to anyone by bargaining with the seller for a documentary sale that involves a time draft. By negotiating for a sales contract that calls for a time draft due 60 days after sight, for example, the buyer can accept the draft (sign it on its face) and not have to come up with the cash to pay it until after his subpurchaser has paid the buyer.

At the same time, the seller achieves significant credit advantages from the documentary sale. Even when the draft calls for payment 60 days after sight, the Detroit bank will usually be willing to advance funds to the seller, less a discount for interest. The bank's willingness is increased by the fact that the draft is going to be accepted by the buyer. That acceptance renders the buyer liable on the instrument to the holder. If the seller is a small automobile parts manufacturer and the buyer is a General Motors Corporation facility in Fresno, the value of the trade acceptance goes up substantially upon the buyer's acceptance of it. In fact, such acceptances are attractive money-market instruments. Institutional investors often buy them for short periods if the interest yields are attractive. By virtue of this feature of trade acceptances, banks themselves find them attractive, since there is a ready market for some of them in the event the bank wants to **liquidate** its investment in the trade acceptance in order to raise cash.

§4.4 LETTER OF CREDIT VARIATION

There is one gaping flaw in the documentary draft transaction. There is no way for the seller to insulate itself against the possibility that the buyer will dishonor the draft by refusing to accept or pay a time draft or refusing to pay a sight draft. In virtually all cases, that dishonor raises serious problems for the seller, and in some cases it has disastrous consequences. If, for example, the seller specially manufactures the goods for the buyer, or if the sale is international, the buyer's dishonor of the draft leaves the seller in a serious fix. If it has specially manufactured for the buyer's unique requirements, the seller may not be able to find any buyer and will have to sell the merchandise for scrap. In international sales, if the buyer dishonors the draft, the seller will have goods in a distant market with which it may be entirely unfamiliar but in which it must dispose of the merchandise, often at distressed prices, the cost of returning them to the seller often being too great.

The commercial letter of credit is the obvious answer to the seller's problems, and by fashioning the transaction carefully, the parties can also achieve added protection for the buyer. Chapter 5 explains the use of the commercial letter of credit.

Document 4-1. Negotiable Bill of Lading

62007

EBW/1

BILL OF LADING

SHIPPER

CONSIGNEE

NOTIFY

CARRIER CODE	CARGO CONTROL NO.	CONTRACT NO.	VOYAGE NO.	B/L NO.	PAGE OF
9050					

NUMBER OF ORIGINAL B/L (ISSUED)	INTENDED OCEAN VESSEL

HS #

CAST An operation of **Cast (1983) Ltd**

Managing Agents North America:
Cast North America (1983) Inc.
4150 Ste-Catherine Street West
Montreal (Quebec) H3Z 2R8
Telex: 05-25441 · 055-60712

Managing Agents Europe:
Cast Europe (1983) Limited
C/O Cast Europe Belgium (1983) N.V.
Noorderlaan 147 Bus 8
2030 Antwerpen Belgium Telex: 71783

REFERENCE

REFERENCE

TERM	PLACE OF RECEIPT	AREA	ZONE	GRID	PORT OF LOADING	RATE SHEET NUMBER
TERM	PLACE OF DELIVERY	AREA	ZONE	GRID	PORT OF DISCHARGE	ESTIMATED ARRIVAL DATE

PARTICULARS FURNISHED BY SHIPPER

CONTAINER NO.	CONTENTS AND DESCRIPTION OF GOODS	WEIGHT
	The Blue Box System	M T

Specimen

FREIGHT PAYABLE AS PER CARRIER'S INVOICE

BY

EXPORT

☐ RECEIVED by the Carrier from the merchant in apparent good order and condition unless otherwise indicated herein, the goods, or the container(s) or package(s) said to contain the cargo herein mentioned, to be carried subject to all the terms and conditions provided for on the face and back of the bill of lading by the vessel named herein or any substitute at the Carrier's option and/or other means of transport, from the place of receipt or the port of loading to the port of discharge, or the place of delivery shown herein and there to be delivered unto order or assigns.

In accepting this bill of lading the merchant agrees to be bound by the specifications, exceptions, terms and conditions, on the face and back hereof, whether written, typed, stamped or printed as followed as if signed by the merchant, in legal custom or privilege to the control not withstanding, and agrees that all claims or freight engagements in or in connection with the carriage of the goods are superseded by this bill of lading.

IN WITNESS whereof the Master or Agent on behalf of the Master of the said vessel has signed the number of Bills of Lading stated above, all of this tenor and date, one of which being accomplished, the others to stand void.

BY AUTHORITY OF MASTER AS AGENT ONLY:

IMPORT

☐ Consignees or agents to pay charges indicated on CUSTOMER'S INVOICE. Any charges for equipment, cartage, transfer to points beyond terminal, penalty storage, delays or any other costs are payable by the cargo at current rates. Consignee should confirm goods and released by Customs and Ocean Carrier before delivery can be arranged, no claim for damages will be entertained by Ship's Owners unless Agent notified to attend survey before goods removed from Terminal. Condition of contents of full containers is Shipper/Consignee's responsibility.

IMPORTANT NOTICE — CONTAINER TRAFFIC

It is the consignee's interest to arrange prompt discharge of containers within the free time allowance otherwise demurrage in accordance with Tariff regulations must be assessed.

LCL Cargo subject to storage charges, after free time at current rates.

INVOICE	PLACE AND DATE OF ISSUE

VALUE	AD VALOREM CARGO Value of goods may be declared provided merchant gives prior notice and agrees to pay greater freight on an ad valorem basis. *See clause 10 on back hereof.

CAST

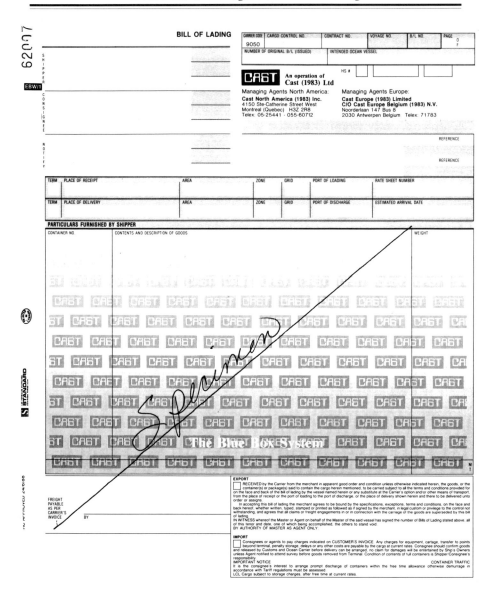

Reprinted with the permission of Cast (Agencies) Ltd.

Document 4-1. (*continued*)

STIPULATIONS, EXCEPTIONS AND CONDITIONS

1. Definitions in this Bill of Lading:

The term "Vessel" means the intended Ocean Vessel on the front hereof and any vessel, craft, lighter or other means of conveyance which is or shall be substituted in whole or in part for such named ocean vessel and also includes any other vessel(s) onto which goods may be loaded for the purpose of being transported thereon in furtherance of the carriage covered by this Bill of Lading or any part thereof.

The term "Carrier" means the Carrier by or on behalf of which this Bill of Lading is signed and issued, as defined in sub paragraph a) of this article.

The term "Merchant" means the shipper, consignor, consignee, the holder of this Bill of Lading and/or the receiver or the owner of the goods. The term "Merchant" also means a forwarder or broker when, even though acting on behalf of a principal, the forwarder or broker's name is entered as shipper or consignee and the principal's name is not divulged.

The term "Container" means container, flat, pallet and any other receptacle for goods (excluding a ship, a rail or road vehicle or aircraft but including a trailer towed or intended to be towed by a road vehicle) supplied or intended to be supplied by or on behalf of the Carrier for the carriage of the goods.

The terms "Place of Receipt", "Intended Port of Loading" or "Port of Loading", "Intended Port of Discharge" or "Port of Discharge" and "Intended Place of Delivery" or "Place of Delivery" mean respectively the place of receipt, port of loading (ocean vessel), port of discharge (ocean vessel) and place of delivery nominated on the front hereof.

The term "Goods" includes anything (other than a container supplied by or on behalf of the Carrier) used or intended to be used to pack or secure goods carried or intended to be carried from one place to another place.

a) Parties to the contract:

The Contract evidenced by this Bill of Lading is between the Merchant and the Owner of the vessel named herein (or substitute) and it is therefore agreed that said Shipowner alone shall be liable for any damage or loss due to any breach or non-performance of any obligation arising out of the contract of carriage whether or not relating to the vessel's seaworthiness. If despite the foregoing it is adjudged that any other is the Carrier and/or bailee of the goods shipped hereunder, all limitations of and exonerations from liability provided for by the law or by this Bill of Lading shall be available to such other.

It is further understood and agreed that as the Company or Agents who has executed this Bill of Lading for and on behalf of the Master is not a principal in the transaction, said Company or Agents shall not be under any liability arising out of the contract of carriage, nor as Carrier, nor as bailee of the goods.

2. Jurisdiction:

This Bill of Lading or any questions arising thereunder shall be governed by the Law of Canada where all proceedings against the Carrier hereon or hereunder are to be taken.

3. Paramount Clause:

The contract evidenced by this Bill of Lading shall have effect subject to the Hague Rules or any legislation making such rules or the Hague/Visby Rules compulsorily applicable to this Bill of Lading (such as the Canadian Water Carriage of Goods Act) and the provisions of the Hague Rules or applicable legislation shall be deemed to be incorporated herein. If more than one national law make such rules compulsorily applicable those most favourable to Carrier shall apply. If and to the extent the said rules are not by legislation compulsorily applicable to this Bill of Lading, the provisions of the Canadian Water Carriage of Goods Act shall apply.

Nothing herein shall be deemed a surrender by the Carrier of any of its rights and immunities or an increase of any of its responsibilities conferred or authorized by any applicable law or statute of any country, and the Carrier at all times whether acting as Carrier, bailee or otherwise howsoever shall be entitled to the benefit of all rights, exemptions and limitations of liability contained therein and of the legislation referred to in the preceding paragraph.

4. Both-To-Blame Collision Clause:

If the ship comes into collision with another ship as a result of the negligence of the other ship and any act, neglect or default of the master, mariner, pilot or servant of the Carrier in the navigation or in the management of the ship, the owners of the goods carried hereunder will indemnify the Carrier against all loss or liability to the other or non-carrying ship or her owners in so far as such loss or liability represents loss of, or damage to, or any claim whatsoever of the owners of said goods, paid or payable by the other non-carrying ship of her owners to be owners of said goods and set off, recouped or recovered by the other or non-carrying ship or her owners as part of their claim against the carrying ship or Carrier.

The foregoing provisions shall also apply where the owners, operators or those in charge of any ship or ships or objects other than, or in addition to, the colliding ships or objects are at fault in respect to a collision or contact.

5. Antwerp Clause:

Cargo carried to Antwerp to be landed and received by the Corporation appointed by the Carrier or its agents. The Merchant paying current charges whether delivery is taken overside or on the quay.

6. General Average and New Jason Clause:

General average shall be adjusted, stated and settled according to York-Antwerp rules 1974, at such port or place as may be selected by the Carrier. In such adjustment, disbursements in foreign currencies may at Carrier's option be converted into United States currency at the rate prevailing on the dates made and allowances for damage to goods claimed in foreign currency may at Carrier's option be converted at the rate prevailing on the last day of discharge at the port of final discharge of such damaged goods from the ship. Average agreement or bond and such additional security as may be required by the Carrier, must be furnished before delivery of the goods.

In addition to the circumstances dealt with in the York-Antwerp rules, it is agreed that if the Carrier has used diligence in the stowage of the container(s) and if the prosecution of the voyage is thereafter imperilled in consequence of the disturbance of stowage, the cost of handling, discharge, reloading, and restowing container(s) shall be allowed in general average even though the handling of said container(s) is not necessary for the purpose of effecting repairs to the vessel.

Where the adjustment is made in accordance with the law and practice of the United States of America, the following clause shall apply: in the case of accident, danger, damage or disaster, before or after commencement of the voyage, resulting from any cause whatsoever whether due to negligence or not, for which, or for the consequence of which the shipowner is not responsible by statute, contract or otherwise, the goods, shippers, consignees or owners of the goods shall contribute with the Carrier in general average to the payment of any sacrifices, losses or expenses of a general average nature that may be made or incurred and shall pay salvage and special charges incurred in respect of goods. If a salving ship is owned or operated by the Carrier, salvage shall be paid for as fully as if the said salving ship or ships belonged to strangers. Such deposit as the Carrier of his agents may deem sufficient to cover the estimated contribution of the goods and any salvage and special changes thereon shall, if required, be made by the goods, shippers, consignees or owners of the goods before delivery.

7. Government directions etc.:

The Carrier, Master and vessel shall have liberty to comply with any orders or directions as to loading, departure, arrival, routes, ports of call, stoppages, discharge, destination, delivery or otherwise howsoever given by the government of any nation or department thereof or any person acting or purporting to act with the authority of such government or of any department thereof, or by any committee or person having, under the terms of war risk insurance on the vessel, the right to give such orders or directions. Delivery or other disposition of the goods in accordance with such orders or directions shall be fulfilment of the contract voyage.

In addition to all other liberties herein, the Carrier shall have the right to withhold delivery of, reship to, deposit or discharge the goods at any place whatsoever, surrender or dispose of the goods or permit inspection or other control in accordance with any direction, condition or agreement imposed upon or extracted from the Carrier by any government or department thereof or any person purporting to act with the authority of either of them. In any of the above circumstances the goods shall be solely at their risk and expense and all expenses and charges so incurred shall be payable by the cargo owner or consignee and shall be a lien on the goods.

8. Merchant's responsibility:

Merchants and their authorized representatives shall assume full responsibility for any loss or damage to containers or contents while in their possession or the possession of their representatives. The Carrier shall not in any event be liable for any loss, delay, damage or injury to the goods, or to other property or to any persons arising out of the use or handling of Carrier's containers by Merchants, consolidators, inland Carriers, or any third parties before delivery to Carrier in accordance with the provisions of Article 9, nor shall the Carrier be responsible for the conditions of the containers or any of their parts or machinery during such times. The Merchant, consolidator, inland Carrier and any other party having custody or control of the container shall indemnify and hold the Carrier harmless from and against any damage or injury done by a container or its contents before delivery to the Carrier at the port of loading or between delivery by the Carrier at port of discharge and redelivery of the containers to the Carrier. If the goods are delivered in a container, the Merchant undertakes to return the container promptly to the Carrier, clean and in the same good order and condition as when filled. The Merchant agrees to be liable for, and shall indemnify the Carrier for any injury, loss or damage, including fines, arising from Shipper's failure to declare correctly herein any of the particulars furnished by him, including marks, quantity and description of goods, weight and cubic measurement of goods, and the exact total gross weight of container (container tare wt. and cargo wt.), also for any kind of damage or expense caused by the contents of said container(s) to other property or to persons, for re-routing of the goods at the Shipper's request, or for any other act, fault or neglect of the Shipper, his agent, or his servants for which the Carrier may become liable. If the container is discharged from the vessel with seals intact, the Carrier shall not be liable for any loss or damage to contents of container unless it be proven that such loss or damage was caused by the Carrier's negligence.

Shippers shall be liable for and shall indemnify the Carrier against any loss or damage to vessel or cargo or to any persons or property, caused by inflammable, explosive, or dangerous goods, shipped without full disclosure of their nature, whether such shipper be principal or agent, and such goods so shipped may be thrown overboard or destroyed at any time without compensation.

9. Carrier's Responsibility:

Except as otherwise provided herein, the Carrier's responsibility for goods shall commence at the time when such goods are received by the Carrier at the port of loading and shall terminate when such goods are delivered by or on behalf of the Carrier at the port of discharge. Notwithstanding the above, where the space(s) entitled "Place of Receipt" and/or "Place of Delivery" on the face hereof are completed, or it is otherwise agreed with Merchant that the contract contained in or evidenced by the Bill of Lading is for through transportation, Carrier undertakes as agent only for the Merchant to procure transportation (by any route whatsoever whether or not the most direct, appropriate or customary) from one or more Carriers apparently authorized to engage in such transportation which shall be effected by such Carriers subject to the terms, conditions, exceptions and limitations of liability in use by each such Carrier and establishing such Carrier's liability in all respects at the minimum level permitted by law, even if less favourable than this Bill of Lading or containing more stringent requirements as to notice of claim, time for suit, exemption from liability or otherwise Carrier not making any declaration of value (other than the minimum where compulsory) unless expressly otherwise instructed by shipper. Carrier guarantees the fulfilment by such Carriers of their obligations as above described.

Where it cannot be proved in whose custody or at what stage of the carriage the goods were when the loss or damage occurred it shall be presumed to have occurred during sea carriage and any liability therefor shall be governed as provided for in clause 3 above.

10. Limitation of liability:

For the purpose of calculating liability (if any) of the Carrier in respect of goods carried in a container under any legislation whereby the carrier is entitled to limit his liability per package, it is agreed that such container constitutes a package except as provided by such legislation where it applies, and except where a lower limit of liability is applicable under clause 9 hereof the liability (if any) of the Carrier shall not exceed dlrs 500 canadian currency per container lost or damaged.

11. Refrigerated Cargo:

The Carrier has no responsibility whatsoever for the functioning of reefer containers or trailers, not owned or leased by the Carrier.

12. Goods of perishable nature:

Carrier not to be responsible for deterioration, however caused, of goods of a perishable nature or as a result of inherent vice of the goods. Merchant to be responsible for damage to other goods and/or the vessel resulting from such causes.

13. Delay:

The Carrier shall in no circumstances whatsoever be responsible for any direct or indirect loss or damage sustained by the Merchant through delay.

14. Options of the Carrier:

a) Subcontracting:

The Carrier shall be entitled to sub-contract on any terms the whole of any part of the handling. Storage or carriage of the goods and any and all duties whatsoever undertaken by the Carrier in relation to the goods.

Subject to clause 9 hereof no Servant of Carrier (including any agent, independent contractor or other person and the servant, agents and independent contractors thereof, from time to time performing services or providing facilities whether in connection with the goods herein described any other goods carried or placed therewith or otherwise howsoever) shall in any circumstances whatsoever be under any liability whatsoever to Merchant for any loss or damage to or in connection with the goods or delay of any kind arising from any act, neglect or default and, without limitation, every exemption, limitation, condition and liberty herein and every right, exemption from liability, defence and immunity of whatsoever nature applicable to Carrier or to which Carrier is entitled shall also be available and shall extend to protect every such Servants and for the purpose of all the foregoing provisions of this clause Carrier is or shall be deemed to be acting as agent and trustee on behalf of and for the benefit of all persons who are or may be his said Servants from time to time and all such persons shall to this extent be or be deemed to be parties to the contract evidenced by this Bill of Lading. Carrier shall be entitled to be paid by Merchant on demand any sum recovered by Merchant from any such Servant for any such loss.

b) Route:

The goods may be carried by any route whatsoever, whether or not the most direct or advertised or customary route, via any ports or places in any order whatsoever and for whatsoever purpose visited, together with other goods of every kind, dangerous or otherwise whether stowed on or under deck. Vessels may sail with or without pilots, undergo repairs, adjust equipment, drydock and tow vessels, or be towed, in all situations.

c) Transhipment:

The goods may be carried by any vessel either belonging to the Carrier or not, or by land or air transport. The Carrier may discharge the goods at any port for transhipment, tranship, land or store the goods either on shore or afloat and reship or forward the same at Carrier's expense.

d) Delivery of goods:

If the goods are not taken by the Merchant within a reasonable time of the Carrier calling upon him to take delivery, the Carrier shall be at liberty to put the goods in safe custody on behalf of the Merchant at the Merchant's risk and expense, but subject to Carrier's lien and Carrier shall be considered as having effected delivery of the goods as per this contract and Carrier's responsibility and liability shall thereupon altogether cease.

e) Ice, canals, strikes, war, etc.:

In any case, actual or apprehended (whether before or after receipt of the goods or commencement of the voyage) and considered by Carrier (whose decision to such effect shall be absolute and binding on all parties) as 1) likely to prohibit, prevent, delay or render unsafe or impracticable entering or leaving any port of loading or discharge of any goods carried or intended to be carried aboard the vessel any such loading or discharge, the voyage itself, continuance of any one or more of them or 2) likely to give rise to danger, injury, loss, delay or disadvantage to the vessel, Carrier, any person, goods or other property whatsoever including without limitation ice, weather, closing or obstruction of any canal, lock or navigable waterway by any cause whatsoever (including without limitation orders or actions of any person having, or purporting to have control thereof) strikes, lock-outs or labour troubles (whether Carrier or its servants are party thereto or not), congestion, shortage, slowdown, or absence of labour or facilities for handling the goods, disease, civil commotion, riot, piracy, insurrection, rebellion, war, hostilities, warlike operations or demonstrations, blockade, interdict, cessation or prohibition or restriction of intercourse commercial or otherwise between nations, or sanctions imposed or measures taken by or against any government (De Jure or De Facto) or international authority in connection with any of the above matters, or any other cause of whatever nature beyond Carrier's reasonable control and/or so long as any control over the use or movements of the vessel may be exercised by any government or other authority and/or space on the vessel is requisitioned or controlled, then Carrier (if any such circumstances make it in its absolute discretion reasonable to do so) in addition to all the liberties set forth in this Bill of Lading, may at its sole option: a) decline to receive, keep or load the goods, or may land the same or put them into lighters there or at the vessel's most convenient port of ports, which shall be selected by Carrier, and goods and Merchant shall bear and pay all charges and expenses incurred in respect of and in consequence of such discharge; or b) may take any other route by water available to the vessel to permit or assist in the delivery of the goods or c) may delay or detain the vessel whether on the voyage or at or off any ports or places, or d) may retain the goods on board the vessel until any return voyage or so long as Carrier deems advisable, Merchant paying to Carrier in cases b), c), or d) or any one or more of them, reasonable additional freight for the services so rendered or e) may effect transhipment of the goods into another vessel or other means of transportation. All actions so taken by Carrier shall be at the expense and risk in every respect of Merchant, who shall be informed if possible, Carrier, master and agents acting solely as agent of Merchant after the goods are discharged from the vessel. The vessel in addition to any liberties expressed or implied herein shall have to comply with any orders, directions or suggestions (including any given under any agreement exacted from or considered advisable to be given by Carrier) as to departure, arrival, routes, ports of call, stoppages, transhipment, discharge or destination, or otherwise howsoever given by the United Nations or other international organization, any sovereign state or political sub-division thereof or any organization or person exercising or purporting to exercise political or military power, or by any committee or person having under the terms of the war risks or other insurance of the vessel the right to give such orders or directions.

f) Stowage in containers:

Goods may be stowed by the Carrier or his agents in containers.

g) On deck stowage:

Containers, whether the goods therein be stowed by the Carrier or by the Merchant, and uncontained unit load machinery, may be carried on or under deck without notice to the shippers, and if they are so carried, the Hague Rules as incorporated herein shall be applicable notwithstanding carriage on or under deck and the goods and/or containers shall contribute in General Average whether carried on or under deck.

15. Cargo stowed in containers by Merchant etc.:

The Carrier shall not be responsible for the safe and proper stowing of cargo in containers, if such containers are loaded with cargo by Merchant, consolidator or inland Carrier, and no responsibility shall attach to the Carrier for any loss or damage caused to contents by shifting, overloading or improper packing of the container. Containers loaded by the shipper, consolidator or inland Carrier shall be properly sealed and the seal identification reference, as well as the container reference, shall be shown herein. The Merchant, consolidator or inland Carrier shall inspect containers before loading them and loading of the containers shall be prima facie evidence that the containers were found suitable for use. The Carrier will not be liable in any event for the particulars furnished by the shipper. The Carrier has counted only the number of containers (if containers received already loaded), or the number of packages or pieces (if the Carrier has loaded the container) and under no circumstances shall the Bill of Lading be prima facie evidence of the marks, quantity, description, weight, measurement and other particulars furnished by the Shipper on reverse hereof, or of gross weight of containers.

16. Freight and charges:

(a) Freight shall be payable on gross intaken weight or measurement or gross discharge weight or measurement or on ad valorem basis, or on a per package or per unit basis all at Carriers' option. Goods may be reweighed or remeasured by the Carrier in his sole option, in order to verify particulars provided by the shipper, but such verification to be at the risk and expense of the goods.
Full freight and charges to final destination shall be considered earned as soon as goods are received, irrespective of whether freight is stated or intended to be prepaid or collect. Freight and charges are due and payable under all circumstances, vessel and/or cargo lost or not lost or the voyage or transit be broken up or abandoned, or packages be delivered damaged or empty. Interest at 10% per annum shall run from the time date when freight and charges are due.

(b) The Merchant shall be liable for expenses of fumigation and of gathering and sorting loose cargo and or weighing on board and expenses incurred in repairing damage to and replacing of packing due to excepted causes and for all expenses caused by extra handling of the cargo for any of the aforementioned reasons.

(c) Any dues, duties, taxes and charges which under any denomination may be levied on any basis such as amount of freight, weight of cargo or tonnage of the vessel shall be paid by the Merchant.

(d) The Merchant shall be liable for all fines and/or losses which the Carrier, vessel or cargo may incur through nonobservance of Custom House and/or import or export regulations.

(e) The Carrier is entitled in case of incorrect declaration of contents, weight, measurements or value of the goods to claim double the amount of freight which would have been due if such declaration had been correctly given. For the purposes of ascertaining the actual facts, the Carrier reserves the right to obtain from the Merchant the original invoice and to have the contents inspected and the weight, measurement of value verified.

(f) Free Time
— on equipment
if precarriage or oncarriage is arranged in containers by the Carrier, unless otherwise specified free time allowed in Europe for stuffing or unstuffing is 2 hours per container, in North America free time is respectfully 4 hours and 2 hours per container and charges assessable on equipment will be charged even in addition to the container demurrage - if the latter should apply.
— on containers
container free time is 48 hours and time counts from the moment container is made available to the Merchant, Sundays and official holidays excluded.
After these 48 hours, for delays at the port of discharge or any other inland terminal due to late instructions for inland re-routing from the Merchant and/or for the return of the empty container to the point designated by the Carrier, container demurrage shall accrue at the rate provided in the applicable tariffs, copies of which may be obtained from the Carrier on request.

17. Devaluation Clause:

If the tariff currency is devalued between the date of the freight agreement and the date when the freight and charges are paid, then all freight and charges shall be automatically and immediately increased equivalent to the extent of the devaluation of the tariff currency. In case the Carrier has consented to payment in another currency than the tariff currency, then all freight and charges shall - subject to the preceding paragraph - be paid at the highest selling rate of exchange for banker's sight draft current on the day when such freight and charges are paid. If the banks are closed on the day when the freight is paid the rate to be used will be the one in force on the last day the banks were open.

18. Lien:

The Carrier shall have a lien on the cargo for any amount due under the contract and for cost of recovering same and shall be entitled to sell the goods privately or by auction without prior notice, advertisement or legal authority to cover any claim.

The Carrier shall have the right to withhold delivery pending payment of outstanding charges, no matter how incurred and irrespective of whether stated to be prepaid or collect.

If on sale of the goods, the proceeds fail to cover the amount due and the cost and expense incurred, the Carrier shall be entitled to recover the difference from the Merchant.

19. Notice of claim and time for suit:

(1) Unless notice of loss or damage and the general nature of such loss or damage be given in writing to the Carrier at the port of discharge or place of delivery before or at the time of delivery of the goods, or if the loss or damage be not apparent, within 3 days after delivery, the goods shall be deemed to have been delivered as described in this Bill of Lading.

(2) In any event the Carrier shall be discharged from all liability in respect of non-delivery, misdelivery, delay, loss or damage unless suit is brought within one year after delivery of the goods, or if the date when the goods should have been delivered.

20. Surrender of Bill of Lading:

If required by the Carrier, this Bill of Lading duly endorsed, must be surrendered to the agent of the Carrier at the port of discharge or at final destination in exchange for delivery order.

21. Interpretation Clause:

Anything done or not done by reason of, or in compliance with the provisions of this Bill of Lading shall be deemed to be done or not done as part for as the case may be fulfilment of the contractual and intended voyage, and all the remedies and rights of Carrier shall have effect accordingly, and nothing so done or not done shall be deemed a deviation.

Any provision hereof prohibited or unenforceable in any applicable jurisdiction shall, as to such jurisdiction only, be ineffective to the extent of such prohibition or unenforceability but shall not affect the validity and enforceability of the remaining provisions hereof. No provision hereof may be changed, waived, discharged or terminated other than as herein provided or in writing by a duly authorized agent or Carrier. The headings herein are for convenience or reference only and shall not define or limit the substance hereof. The shipper agrees that this Bill of Lading be executed in the English language.

ENDORSEMENT

Document 4-2. Inspection Certificate

International Cargo Surveyors, Inc.

MARINE, CARGO,
EQUIPMENT AND
INTERMODAL SURVEYS

DUNDALK MARINE TERMINAL
DUNMAR BLDG. NORTH, SUITE 103
2700 BROENING HIGHWAY
BALTIMORE, MD 21222
(301) 633-3340/41
FAX (301) 633-7848

OFFICES IN: NEW YORK (201) 352-0020, NORFOLK (804) 483-4772

INSPECTION CERTIFICATE

TO WHOM IT MAY CONCERN:

INTRODUCTION

On October 17, 1988, we upon request, attended at the LMD Warehouse, 600 North Union Avenue, Hillside, New Jersey, for the purpose of examining the condition and ascertaining the quantity and type of bagged Titanium Dioxide Pigments.

INSPECTION

Upon our arrival to the above mentioned warehouse, we found the bags of Titanium Dioxide stored on wood shipping pallets. The area in which the commodity was being stored was well lit, clean and dry.

We gathered the following cargo marks from the bags.

SCM CHEMICAL
TITANIUM DIOXIDE PIGMENT
TiONA RCL - 9
50 lbs. Net.

The commodity was stuffed into four-ply paper bags with polyethylene liners, all of which were found to be in good order.

The bags of RCL-9, Titanium Dioxide Pigment were stacked on wood shipping pallets, thirty-eight pallets holding fifty bags (50) per pallet (ten (10) tiers of five (5) each) and one pallet holding twenty (20) bags (four tiers of five) all of the bags were in good condition and were evenly stacked on their pallets. None of the pallet loads were observed to be leaning or distorted in any way.

We then proceeded to count the individual bags of the Titanium Dioxide Pigments. We counted 1,920 bags of the commodity. At 50 lbs. each, the 1,920 bags represent 96,000 lbs. net. of the commodity, RCL-9, Titanium Dioxide Pigment.

This inspection has been performed without prejudice.

Stephen D. Miernicki

Stephen D. Miernicki, President
International Cargo Surveyors, Inc.

SPECIMEN

Document 4-3. Straight Bill of Lading

Form 35-643 Printed and Sold by UNZ&CO 190 Baldwin Ave., Jersey City, NJ 07306 • (800) 631-3098 • (201) 795-5400

STRAIGHT BILL OF LADING—SHORT FORM—ORIGINAL—NOT NEGOTIABLE

RECEIVED, subject to the classifications and tariffs in effect on the date of the issue of this Bill of Lading, the property described above in apparent good order, except as noted (contents and condition of contents of packages unknown), marked, consigned, and destined as indicated above which said carrier (the word carrier being understood throughout this contract as meaning any person or corporation in possession of the property under the contract) agrees to carry to its usual place of delivery at said destination, if on its route, otherwise to deliver to another carrier on the route to said destination. It is mutually agreed as to each carrier of all or any of said property over all or any portion of said route to destination and as to each party at any time interested in all or any said property, that every service to be performed hereunder shall be subject to all the bill of lading terms and conditions in the governing classification on the date of shipment.

Shipper hereby certifies that he is familiar with all the bill of lading terms and conditions in the governing classification and the said terms and conditions are hereby agreed to by the shipper and accepted for himself and his assigns.

From ____________________

DESIGNATE WITH AN (X)

At ____________________ 19 ____ BY TRUCK ☐ FREIGHT ☐ Shipper's No. ____________

Carrier ____________________ Agent's No. ____________

(Mail or street address of consignee—For purposes of notification only.)

Consigned to ____________________

Destination ____________________ State of ____________ County of ____________

Route ____________________

Delivering Carrier ____________________ Vehicle or Car Initial ____________ No. ____________

No. Packages	Kind of Package, Description of Articles, Special Marks, and Exceptions	*Weight (Sub. to Cor.)	Class or Rate	Check Column
	SPECIMEN			
TOTAL PIECES				

†"The fibre containers used for this shipment conform to the specifications set forth in the box maker's certificate thereon, and all other requirements of Rule 41 of the Uniform Freight Classification and Rule 5 of the National Motor Freight Classification." †Shipper's imprint in lieu of stamp, not a part of bill of lading approved by the Interstate Commerce Commission.

____________________ Shipper, Per

____________________ Agent, Per ____________________

Permanent post-office address of shipper

Subject to Section 7 of conditions of applicable bill of lading, if this shipment is to be delivered to the consignee without recourse on the consignor, the consignor shall sign the following statement:

The carrier shall not make delivery of this shipment without payment of freight and all other lawful charges.

Per ____________________
(Signature of Consignor.)

If charges are to be prepaid, write or stamp here, "To be Prepaid."

Received $ ____________
to apply in prepayment of the charges on the property described hereon.

____
Agent or Cashier

Per ____________________
(The signature here acknowledges only the amount prepaid.)

Charges Advanced:

C.O.D. SHIPMENT

Prepaid [ ]
Collect [ ] $ ____________

Collection Fee ____________

Total Charges ____________

*If the shipment moves between two ports by a carrier by water, the law requires that the bill of lading shall state whether it is "Carrier's or Shipper's weight."

†Shipper's imprint in lieu of stamp; not a part of bill of lading approved by the Department of Transportation.

NOTE—Where the rate is dependent on value, shippers are required to state specifically in writing the agreed or declared value of the property.

THIS SHIPMENT IS CORRECTLY DESCRIBED. CORRECT WEIGHT IS

____________ LBS.

Subject to verification by the Respective Weighing and Inspection Bureau According to Agreement.

Per ____________________

If lower charges result, the agreed or declared value of the within described containers is hereby specifically stated to be not exceeding 50 cents per pound per article.

This is to certify that the above-named materials are properly classified, described, packaged, marked and labeled and are in proper condition for transportation according to the applicable regulations of the Department of Transportation.

____________ SIGNATURE

Document 4-4. Sight Draft

Bank of America

BILL OF EXCHANGE

Place of Drawing Los Angeles, CA

Date May 1, 1990

No. 1 of 1

At ------------------------- Sight Of This Bill Of Exchange

Pay To The Order Of Ourselves

XXXXXXXXXXXXXX and XX/100 Dollars

Value Received And Charge To Account Of Buyer Co.

To B of A N.T. & S.A.

At

Seller Co.

Drawer

SPECIMEN

Authorized Signature

FX-200 2-52 Bank of America NT&SA (Reprint 9-88)

Printed with the permission of Bank of America N.T. & S.A.

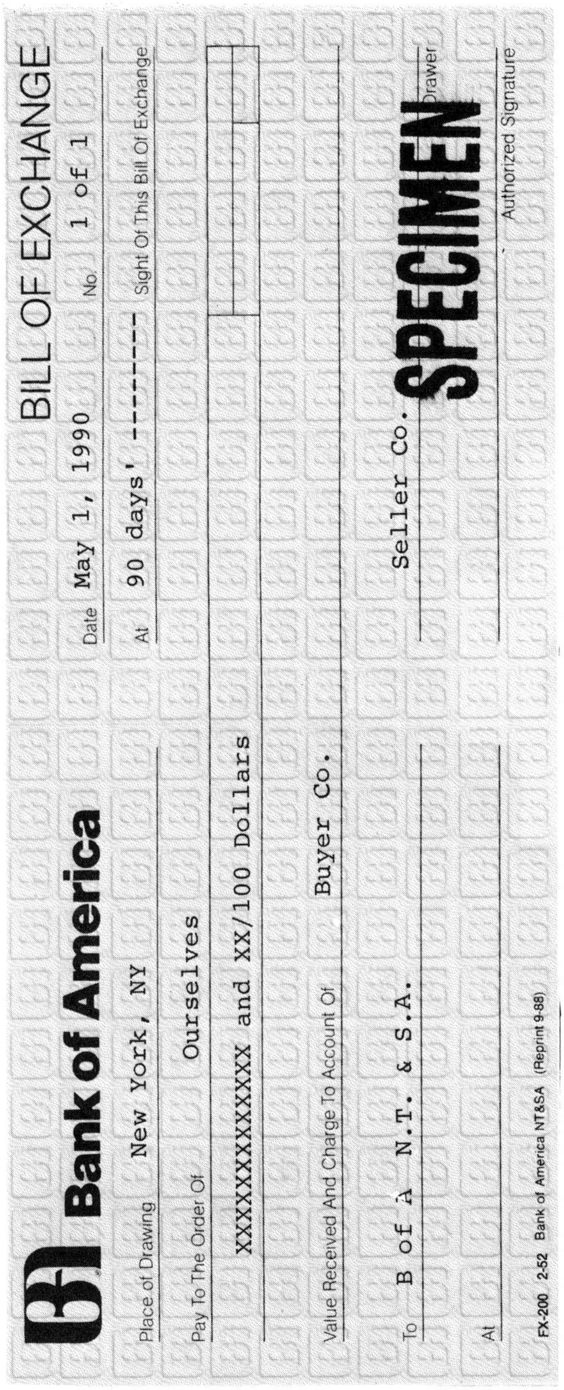

Bank of America — BILL OF EXCHANGE

Place of Drawing New York, NY   Date May 1, 1990   No. 1 of 1

Pay To The Order Of Ourselves   At 90 days' -------- Sight Of This Bill Of Exchange

XXXXXXXXXXXXX and XX/100 Dollars

Value Received And Charge To Account Of Buyer Co.

To B of A N.T. & S.A.   Seller Co.
Drawer

SPECIMEN

At   Authorized Signature

FX-200 2-52 Bank of America NT&SA (Reprint 9-88)

Printed with the permission of Bank of America N.T. & S.A.

Document 4-6. Trade Acceptance

$ XXXXXX.XX　　　　　　　　May 1　19 90

AT 60 days' sight　　　　PAY TO THE ORDER OF

Ourselves

XXXXXX.XX　　　　　　　　DOLLARS

ACCEPTED
May 10, 1990
BUYER CO.
By: Joe Buyer
AGENT

TO

Buyer Co.
123 Main St.
Detroit, MI

Seller Co.
by Joe Seller
(authorized agent)

MULTI - 1179

5

Sale by Commercial Letter of Credit

§5.1 THE SETTING

There are circumstances in which the buyer and the seller are not willing to enter into an open account sale. That arrangement assumes a number of facts, not the least of which is that the seller has access to reliable credit information on the buyer. In addition, the open account seller assumes that the buyer values his credit rating. There is a measure of ad terrorem pressure that the open account seller can bring to bear on his defaulting buyer. Open account buyers are aware that they risk much in defaulting on an open account obligation: They could jeopardize their all-important credit rating. In the event a buyer does default on its current obligations, it runs the risk that other open account sellers, having learned through credit reporting services of the default history, will not extend credit to that buyer. Such an eventuality can cause the demise of the buyer's enterprise, so important is open account credit to the vast majority of commercial buyers in the domestic economy.

In the international setting and in the event the buyer is an infrequent player in open account sales, the open account seller's assumptions may not be valid. First, there may not be reliable credit information on buyers in Portugal, Singapore, or Zimbabwe. The buyer may have a poor credit history, but the seller may not be able to learn of it or may not be able to learn of it without expensive credit inquiry. Second, the buyer may be a fictitious entity — a fact that the seller cannot discern easily or inexpensively without reliable credit reporting agencies. Finally, the buyer may be a new entrant with little creditworthiness, not having established itself as an enterprise that will pay its debts. In short, there are a number of situations in which the seller cannot rely on credit reports, and if the seller cannot rely on the credit report, it is reluctant to sell on open account.

That failure of credit reporting in the international setting and in cases of new entities' entering the trade should not prevent sellers from making sales to many buyers who do in fact have the financial resources to pay for goods, as many new entrants and many buyers in Portugal, Singapore, and Zimbabwe do. The seller who refuses to sell to these accounts will lose sales and profits. The fact is that these buyers are known to their banks, and to the extent the buyer can substitute the known credit of its bank for its own unknown credit, it may be able to satisfy the seller. The commercial letter of credit is the device merchants and bankers have invented to cover these situations.

§5.2 THE PARTIES

In the simplest commercial letter of credit there are only three parties. The buyer, whom merchants and bankers variously call the account party (i.e., the one for whose account the credit is issued), the customer (i.e., the customer of the issuer of the credit), or the applicant (i.e., the party that applies for the letter of credit), asks a strong financial institution, usually its bank, to issue a credit in favor of the seller, the beneficiary of the credit. Figure 5-1 illustrates this simple commercial letter of credit.

In most international letter of credit transactions the issuer opens the credit by **telex**. The telex is a common method of international communication that has replaced the telegram. A telegram relies on the translation of a telegraph operator to render the message readable. A telex message, however, arrives at the receiver's place of business where a telex machine reads the signals emanating from the sender's place of business and automatically prints the message on paper stored in the machine. A telex machine with enough paper can read a night's or weekend's worth of traffic with no difficulty. The telex system is cheap and quick, but it is now being replaced itself by electronic data interchange (EDI). Under EDI, which is even quicker and cheaper than telex, computerized messages are transmitted globally at lightning speed and very little cost. Chapter 27 explains the use of this technology in international payments systems.

In most transactions involving the international sale of goods, the parties use the services of a second financial institution, usually a commer-

Figure 5-1. Commercial Letter-of-Credit Transaction

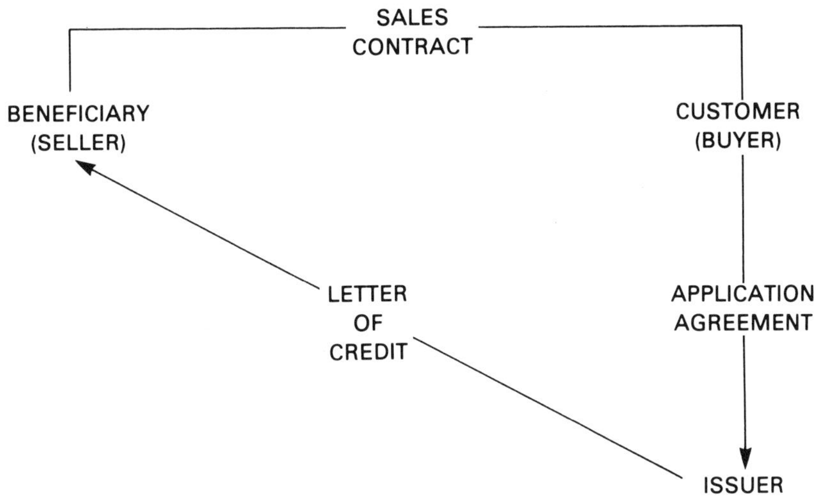

cial bank in the seller's market, to advise or confirm the letter of credit. The appearance of this second bank, the advising bank or the confirming bank, in the transaction facilitates the seller's use of the credit. Commercial letters of credit call for the presentation of certain documents on or before the letter of credit's expiry. It is problematic for a seller in Houston, for example, to present documents at a bank in the buyer's city, say, London. There is a danger that the documents may be lost or mangled in the mail or that one of the documents might contain an error or fail to show a signature or an important date. With a bank in its own market, the seller can submit its documents more easily and can submit them early and correct any defects that appear before the credit expires. Figure 5-2 illustrates the traditional four-party commercial letter of credit.

In addition, the issuer of a credit may designate some bank other than itself to honor the credit. The issuer may choose another bank as the *paying bank,* for example, when the issuer does not have sufficient amounts of the currency in which the credit is available. A Pakistani bank issuing a credit payable in U.S. dollars to a French seller might designate a New York bank as the paying bank, since the New York bank will have a dollar-denominated account in the name of its Pakistani correspondent.

Often, though less frequently than in former times, the buyer's bank, being perhaps a country bank, has little familiarity with letters of credit. In that case, buyer's bank will contact its big-city correspondent, a regional or money center bank with an international letter of credit department, that will issue the credit, not on behalf of the buyer alone, whom the issuer does not know, but on behalf of the buyer and the country correspondent, whom the issuer does know.

Figure 5-2. International Commercial Letter-of-Credit Transaction

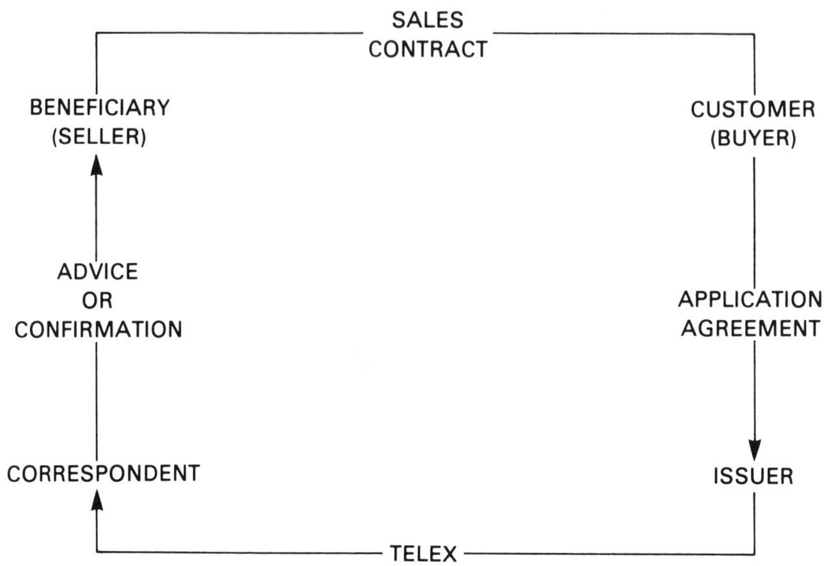

§5.3 PERFORMANCE OF THE COMMERCIAL CREDIT TRANSACTION

The following nine steps describe the complete performance of a typical commercial credit transaction.

Step 1

In the commercial letter of credit transaction, the first and indispensable act is the creation of a sales contract between a seller and a buyer. This contract is the underlying transaction that the letter of credit serves. Often, much of the activity of the parties is simultaneous, that is, while the buyer and the seller are settling the terms of the sales contract, the buyer is contacting its bank to have the credit issue, and the seller is getting the goods ready for shipment. Sometimes the parties get ahead of themselves. The buyer may cause the credit to issue before it has concluded all of the contract terms with the seller, or the seller may actually ship the goods before it sees the terms of the letter of credit. Lawyers cringe when merchants behave in such fashion, but it is naive to expect the busy merchant to be as concerned with details as lawyers are. The cautious lawyer would probably be an unsuccessful merchant. In any event, the transaction does not always proceed as this section describes it, but for optimal protection, the parties should proceed in this manner.

Step 2

After the buyer and the seller hammer out the terms of the underlying sales contract, the buyer should approach its bank and apply for the commercial letter of credit. The terms of the underlying contract dictate the terms of the credit: the description of the goods, the latest date of shipment, the credit's expiry, the requirement for insurance or inspection certificates, the amount of the credit, whether partial shipments are permitted, the mode of transport, the shipment destination, and so forth. Often these terms are not expressed in the underlying contract of sale but are incorporated into it by industry custom and practice or by course of dealing.

Step 3

The next step in the transaction is that of the credit issuer, who will telex the advising bank (or confirming bank, as the case may be) the terms of the credit.

Step 4

After it receives the telex, the advising or confirming bank (the documents in this section assume that the correspondent will only advise the credit) will send the credit advice to the seller. Document 5-1 illustrates an advice.

Step 5

After it receives the advice, the seller-beneficiary should compare the terms of the credit with the terms of the underlying contract. If there are any problems, it must insist at this point that the buyer and the issuer amend the credit, so that the terms of the credit do comply with the terms of the sales agreement. Such an amendment will originate from the issuing bank and be advised by the advising bank to the seller.

Step 6

Once the credit is in order, the seller can begin its performance without risk. Note that the seller must act promptly, since the credit usually has a short expiry and often contains dates relating to the time within which the goods must be shipped or the bill of lading must be issued. The first step in the seller's performance is to generate the documents needed to satisfy the credit. The seller's billing department will prepare the invoice in as many copies as the credit requires. Its shipping department will prepare the goods for shipment and will deliver them to the carrier (or to a freight forwarder) and obtain a bill of lading that complies with the terms of the credit. Other agents of the seller, perhaps a freight forwarder or an in-house employee, will obtain the necessary insurance and inspection certificates and other documents. Finally, the seller will draw the all-important draft. Often, the credit will contain a requirement that the draft bear a legend identifying the credit under which it is drawn. Document 5-2 is a draft that might be used with a letter of credit.

Step 7

After the seller has obtained the necessary documents from third parties and generated those documents that are prepared by its own personnel, the seller is ready to initiate presentation of the documents to the paying bank. The paying bank in this example is the issuer itself, and the seller will commence collection of the draft by taking it and the accompanying documents to a local bank for collection. The seller may take them to the advising bank. In any case, the seller will indorse the draft, and if the seller's credit with the bank is good, the seller may be able to draw against the provisional credit that the collecting bank gives it, though there will be charges. If the draft is a time draft with a specified date for payment, the collecting bank may charge the seller by computing the interest until the date of payment and discounting the draft by that amount. In any event, the seller will normally be liable to the collecting bank if the issuer does not honor the draft.

Step 8

The collecting bank will present the draft and accompanying documents to the issuer through customary bank collection channels. Under most credits, which expire on a given date, that presentation must occur on or before the expiry.

Step 9

Once the draft and the documents arrive at the counters of the paying bank, document examiners begin the process of determining whether the presentation satisfies the documentary conditions of the credit. In that process, the examiners use banking industry practices that are codified in the Uniform Customs and Practice for Documentary Credits, a code that is drafted by the Commission on Banking Technique and Practice of the International Chamber of Commerce and is adopted by the international banking organizations of virtually all countries. If a document appears to be nonconforming, the examiner will take it to a discrepancy clerk. If the clerk agrees that there is a discrepancy, the issuer will usually contact its customer, the buyer, and ask whether the buyer is willing to waive the discrepancy. If the buyer does waive it, as buyers do in a majority of cases, the issuer will honor the beneficiary's draft. If the buyer does not waive the defect, the issuer will promptly notify the presenting bank, which will give that notice to the seller, who will then attempt to cure the defect before the credit expires.

§5.4 DOCUMENTS

Unless the credit is "clean," that is, a credit that calls only for the beneficiary's draft, the credit will contain rather explicit terms relating to the documents that the paying bank must have before it will honor the beneficiary's draft. These documents are similar to the documents that a buyer will request in the documentary draft transaction that is the subject of Chapter 4, but the letter of credit transaction is usually more complicated and entails greater documentation than the documentary sale. Clean credits arise rarely in the commercial credit transaction and only a little more frequently in the standby credit transaction that is discussed in Section 3.5.

Invoice

The seller's invoice, sometimes referred to as a *commercial invoice*, presumably to differentiate it from a proforma invoice, a customs invoice, or other government-regulated document, is a shorthand summary of the underlying sales agreement between the buyer (account party) and the seller (beneficiary). Traditionally, letter-of-credit law puts great store by the description of the goods in the invoice and requires that description to track the description of the goods in the letter of credit. Descriptions of the goods in other documents need not be so precise, so long as they do not vary the description in the credit. An invoice description of goods that refers to them as "imported acrylic yarn" is not sufficient if the credit refers to the goods as "100% acrylic yarn"; nor is an invoice that refers to goods as "woolen knitwears," when the letter of credit described the goods as "ladies sweaters, dresses, pants, and skirts." The careful beneficiary will instruct his billing department that in drafting the invoice description of the goods it is essential to lift the description verbatim from the credit itself. From time to time, in the press of making prompt delivery, sellers will prepare their documents in advance of receiving the credit. They do so at their peril, for it may be too late to recall the invoice when the credit (with a short expiry) arrives containing a description the seller did not anticipate. A copy of a commercial invoice is set out in Chapter 3 as Document 3-3.

Bill of Lading

As Chapter 31 explains in more detail, the bill of lading, if it is negotiable, stands for the goods and plays an important role in the documentary sale and in the commercial letter of credit transaction. Courts and lawyers are apt to give it more credit than it deserves. The bill of lading is not a guaranty by the carrier that the goods described in it have, in fact, been shipped. Generally, the bill of lading contains disclaimer language that the law generally, though not without exception, respects. If the buyer is concerned about the contents of the seller's containers, it should insist on an inspection certificate and should expect to pay for it. The fact that inspection certificates are more common in international sales and less in domestic sales should not surprise anyone. Document 4-1 in Chapter 4 is a negotiable bill of lading of the type that is common in commercial letter of credit transactions.

Some bill of lading forms are "on board" forms. Carriers will not issue these bills unless the goods are loaded on board a ship. Often, bills of lading are in "received for shipment" form. This form merely recites that the carrier has received the goods. Carriers will execute such a bill, which the shipper prepares, upon the shipper's delivery of the goods to the carrier. Later, after the goods pass the ship's rail, the shipper presents the bill to the carrier's agent, who will affix an on board stamp to the bill and date and sign the stamped language. For the on board stamp to be missing would signal danger, since most insurance coverage does not commence until the goods are on board.

In order to be acceptable to banks and buyers, moreover, a bill of lading should be "clean," that is, it should not contain any notation that the goods or containers are damaged. "Dirty" bills are "claused." Such clauses indicate, for example, that some containers are open or water damaged. Claused bills are another danger signal. Under letter of credit law, unless the credit expressly provides otherwise, a paying bank will not honor a draft accompanied by a claused bill or a "received for shipment" bill that fails to carry a properly signed and dated on board stamp.

Inspection Certificate

The buyer that is unwilling to trust the seller must ask for an inspection certificate. In the underlying transaction, the contract of sale between seller and buyer, the buyer will negotiate a term that specifies that payment will be by letter of credit calling for, among other documents, an inspection certificate. That certificate should specify the name of the inspecting agency and should indicate what the certificate should say. If the credit does not lay out the details of the certificate, the paying bank will accept any certificate, even one signed by the seller, or one saying that the inspector has examined one of 4,000 cartons of goods. In many industries, inspection criteria are standardized, and buyers can rely on the assertion of the inspector that the shipment contains 30,000 bushels of #2 yellow corn, without concern that the inspector may not have examined the corn adequately. Document 4-2 in Chapter 4 is an inspection certificate.

Insurance Certificate

Because under sales law the risk of loss often shifts to the buyer when the goods pass over the ship's rail, it is not only important that the bill of lading indicate that the goods are on board, it is also important that the buyer know that the goods are insured at that point. The insurance certificate is generally sufficient proof of that coverage, and most buyers under commercial letters of credit will require an insurance certificate unless they have some kind of broad insurance coverage that covers off-premises goods that are in transit from sellers. Document 5-3 is an insurance certificate.

Certificates of Origin

On occasion, a buyer may be concerned about the origin of goods that it is purchasing. It may, for example, be concerned about the quality of goods and not want the seller to supply it with goods that are manufactured in countries that do not have adequate standards for product quality or safety. In such cases, a certificate of origin is appropriate and may be called for in the credit. In other cases, certificates of origin may be utilized as devices to further politically motivated boycotts of a country's products. United States law generally renders it unlawful to participate in such boycotts against countries friendly to the U.S. Banks and merchants must take care that they do not run afoul of these laws, which carry heavy fines. Document 5-4 is a certificate of origin.

Other Documents

It would be futile to attempt to set out in any book all of the certificates and documents that might arise in a commercial letter of credit transaction. Suffice it to say that the only limit on the documents that may arise is the imagination of the merchants and bankers that use commercial credits. There are a number of documents in addition to those described above that appear in the commercial letter of credit transaction with some frequency. Countries that have enacted foreign exchange laws or import regulations often use letters of credit to monitor the payment of currency out of the country and the importation of goods that may compete with domestic producers. These countries frequently require "customized" or "consularized" invoices or other documents. Those terms refer to the need for a customs or consular official to sign and stamp the document in question. Often, letters of credit will refer to the need for a document to be "countersigned." That language requires the beneficiary of the credit to obtain the signature of some party on a document other than the party that issues the document or other than the party whose signature one would expect to find on the document. For example, if the credit calls for a commercial invoice "countersigned by the purchasing vice president of the buyer," the seller must present the paying bank with a copy of the invoice containing that signature. Note that such a requirement puts the seller-beneficiary at the buyer's mercy. If the vice president refuses to countersign the invoice, the seller cannot comply with the terms of the credit and will not get paid under it. Courts have indicated that they will order a buyer to countersign a document if the refusal is arbitrary and if the buyer does not have the right arbitrarily to refuse to countersign, but the time it takes to obtain such an order probably will run beyond the expiry of the credit. Remember that the credit is not the obligation of the buyer. It is the obligation of the bank issuer, and the courts have generally refused to reform a credit after a bank issues it. The documents are critical, therefore, and the seller beneficiary must be concerned with them. The common practice of submitting documents that do not conform with the credit's terms or of shipping goods before the seller receives the credit and knows its terms are dangerous. True, in most cases, buyers act in good faith and waive documentary discrepancies, but sometimes they do not, and bank document examiners are not in a position to waive discrepancies. They do not know enough about the underlying transaction to make the decision that a discrepancy is immaterial.

Document 5-1. Advice of Credit

Bank of America

Date

Our Ref.

Mail To

Favor

GENTLEMEN:

WE HAVE BEEN REQUESTED BY OUR CORRESPONDENT TO ADVISE THE ENCLOSED LETTER OF CREDIT, WHEN PRESENTING DOCUMENTS FOR NEGOTIATION/PAYMENT PLEASE ALSO PRESENT THE ORIGINAL LETTER OF CREDIT AND AN EXTRA COPY OF THE INVOICE.

THIS IS SOLELY AN ADVICE OF THE LETTER OF CREDIT OPENED BY OUR CORRESPONDENT AND CONVEYS NO ENGAGEMENT FROM BANK OF AMERICA.

PLEASE EXAMINE THIS LC CAREFULLY. IF YOU ARE UNABLE TO COMPLY WITH ANY TERM OR CONDITION YOU SHOULD COMMUNICATE WITH YOUR BUYER FOR AN AMENDMENT. THIS PROCEDURE SHOULD FACILITATE PROMPT HANDLING WHEN DOCUMENTS ARE PRESENTED. THIS LC IS SUBJECT TO THE UNIFORM CUSTOMS & PRACTICES FOR DOCUMENTARY CREDITS (1983 REVISION) INTERNATIONAL CHAMBER OF COMMERCE, PUBLICATION #400.

SPECIMEN

Very Truly Yours

Authorized Signature(s)

SOLE BILL OF EXCHANGE

US $ ________ DATE ________ NO. ________

TENOR ________

PAY TO THE ORDER OF ________ Payee must endorse draft on reverse side prior to payment

________ U.S. Dollars

DRAWN UNDER LETTER OF CREDIT NO. ________ DATED ________

ISSUED BY ________

DRAWN ON ________

SPECIMEN

AUTHORIZED SIGNATURE

Printed with the permission of the First National Bank of Chicago.

ACORD. **CERTIFICATE OF INSURANCE**

ISSUE DATE (MM/DD/YY)

PRODUCER

THIS CERTIFICATE IS ISSUED AS A MATTER OF INFORMATION ONLY AND CONFERS NO RIGHTS UPON THE CERTIFICATE HOLDER. THIS CERTIFICATE DOES NOT AMEND, EXTEND OR ALTER THE COVERAGE AFFORDED BY THE POLICIES BELOW.

COMPANIES AFFORDING COVERAGE

COMPANY LETTER A

CODE SUB-CODE

COMPANY LETTER B

INSURED

COMPANY LETTER C

COMPANY LETTER D

COMPANY LETTER E

COVERAGES

THIS IS TO CERTIFY THAT THE POLICIES OF INSURANCE LISTED BELOW HAVE BEEN ISSUED TO THE INSURED NAMED ABOVE FOR THE POLICY PERIOD INDICATED, NOTWITHSTANDING ANY REQUIREMENT, TERM OR CONDITION OF ANY CONTRACT OR OTHER DOCUMENT WITH RESPECT TO WHICH THIS CERTIFICATE MAY BE ISSUED OR MAY PERTAIN, THE INSURANCE AFFORDED BY THE POLICIES DESCRIBED HEREIN IS SUBJECT TO ALL THE TERMS, EXCLUSIONS AND CONDITIONS OF SUCH POLICIES. LIMITS SHOWN MAY HAVE BEEN REDUCED BY PAID CLAIMS.

CO LTR	TYPE OF INSURANCE	POLICY NUMBER	POLICY EFFECTIVE DATE (MM/DD/YY)	POLICY EXPIRATION DATE (MM/DD/YY)	ALL LIMITS IN THOUSANDS
	GENERAL LIABILITY COMMERCIAL GENERAL LIABILITY CLAIMS MADE OCCUR. OWNER'S & CONTRACTOR'S PROT.				GENERAL AGGREGATE $ PRODUCTS-COMP/OPS AGGREGATE $ PERSONAL & ADVERTISING INJURY $ EACH OCCURRENCE $ FIRE DAMAGE (Any one fire) $ MEDICAL EXPENSE (Any one person) $
	AUTOMOBILE LIABILITY ANY AUTO ALL OWNED AUTOS SCHEDULED AUTOS HIRED AUTOS NON-OWNED AUTOS GARAGE LIABILITY				COMBINED SINGLE LIMIT $ BODILY INJURY (Per Person) $ BODILY INJURY (Per accident) $ PROPERTY DAMAGE $
	EXCESS LIABILITY OTHER THAN UMBRELLA FORM				EACH OCCURRENCE $ AGGREGATE $
	WORKER'S COMPENSATION AND EMPLOYERS' LIABILITY				STATUTORY $ (EACH ACCIDENT) $ (DISEASE—POLICY LIMIT) $ (DISEASE—EACH EMPLOYEE)
	OTHER				

SPECIMEN

DESCRIPTION OF OPERATIONS/LOCATIONS/VEHICLES/RESTRICTIONS/SPECIAL ITEMS

CERTIFICATE HOLDER

CANCELLATION

SHOULD ANY OF THE ABOVE DESCRIBED POLICIES BE CANCELLED BEFORE THE EXPIRATION DATE THEREOF, THE ISSUING COMPANY WILL ENDEAVOR TO MAIL _____ DAYS WRITTEN NOTICE TO THE CERTIFICATE HOLDER NAMED TO THE LEFT, BUT FAILURE TO MAIL SUCH NOTICE SHALL IMPOSE NO OBLIGATION OR LIABILITY OF ANY KIND UPON THE COMPANY, ITS AGENTS OR REPRESENTATIVES.

AUTHORIZED REPRESENTATIVE

ACORD 25-S (3/88)

CERTIFICATE OF ORIGIN

The undersigned ____
(Owner or Agent, or &c)

for ____ declares
(Name and Address of Shipper)

that the following mentioned goods shipped on S/S ______________________________
(Name of Ship)

on the date of ______________ consigned to ______________________________

______________________________ are the product of the United States of America.

MARKS AND NUMBERS	NO. OF PKGS., BOXES OR CASES	WEIGHT IN KILOS GROSS	NET	DESCRIPTION

SPECIMEN

Sworn to before me

Dated at ____________ on the ______ day of ______ 19 ____

this __________ day of __________ 19 ____

______________________________ ______________________________
(Signature of Owner or Agent)

The ______________________________, a recognized Chamber of Commerce under the laws of the State of ______________________________, has examined the manufacturer's invoice or shipper's affidavit concerning the origin of the merchandise and, according to the best of its knowledge and belief, finds that the products named originated in the United States of North America.

Secretary ______________________________

6 Consignments and the Like

§6.1 THE BRIGHT IDEA

We do not know how property concepts evolved, but we suppose that at times "might made right" and that the person with the biggest fist or the biggest band of followers got the buffalo carcass whenever a dispute arose, just as that "rule" of property sometimes obtains today. At other times, kings or other rulers owned all or virtually all of the valuable property in a society. In some societies, no one owned anything, all property being owned in common and being available for those who needed or took it. Those legal systems of allocating resources have generally not survived in today's world, which tends to look on them as more inefficient or tending to cause resentment than the notion of personal property. Eventually, any society works out one system or another for allocating property on its notions of fairness or efficiency. Schoolyard societies reflect the notion that possession connotes ownership. "Finders keepers" enjoys a certain amount of success in resolving ownership disputes over marbles. "Possession is nine points of the law" has attracted more than the schoolyard lawyer. Ultimately, many societies opt for notions of title — a purely metaphysical idea that often yields results contrary to the possessory rules of the schoolyard. Title often gives us comfort against the fear of lawlessness, the fear that some bully will come along and "steal" (an idea that proceeds from the concept of title) our property. Cases that defend the notion of title often quote an old saw to the effect that "no man may be deprived of his property without his consent."

Figure 6-1. Consignment Fiction

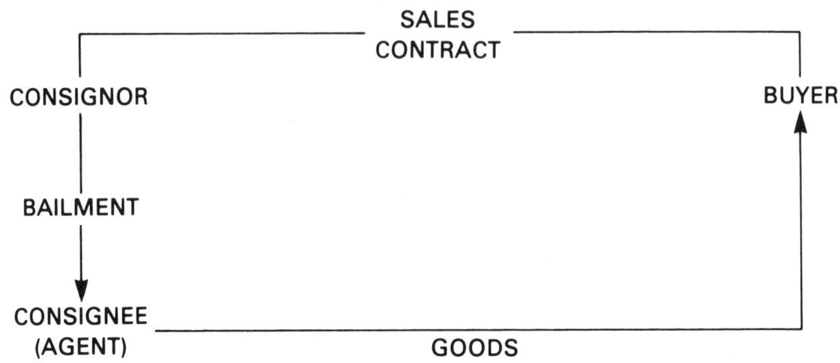

The success of title as a concept for allocating resources has not usurped the role of possession entirely. The possession rule, that is, the notion that possession connotes title and may even defeat title, is still very much alive, especially in commercial law, as the doctrines of voidable title and some buyer-in-ordinary-course rules, for example, suggest.

All of this discussion is necessary to understand what it is that merchants are doing when they enter into **consignments** and similar transactions. On the surface, when an owner (the consignor) consigns her property to another (the consignee), the parties agree quite simply that the owner does not part with title and has merely created a **bailment,** with the consignee holding possession of the goods but having no interest other than a possessory interest. Document 6-1 is a consignment agreement.

While the law does not really care about such an arrangement insofar as it affects the consignor and the consignee, it should care very much about the effects of the agreement on third parties, such as buyers from and creditors of the consignee. If the consignment theory works, Owner (the consignor) will deliver the goods to Agent (the consignee) as agent. Sales transactions that Agent enters into with third parties will bind Owner only under the rules of agency law. If Agent exceeds his actual authority, under primitive agency rules, the third party takes nothing, since Agent has nothing to give unless he acts within the scope of his agency. Figure 6-1 illustrates the agency sale with the consignee acting as an agent, a conduit. The figure illustrates a quite successful fiction in property law.

Agency law, if its crafters want us to take it seriously, cannot persist with a foolish rule such as this one, and it eventually fashioned *estoppel* and *apparent authority* inconsistencies to the logically consistent result that an agent cannot give good title to a buyer if the buyer takes from an agent acting outside the scope of his agency. Under the exceptions, the transaction takes the form of Figure 6-2, rather than that in 6-1.

By the same token, property law fashioned exceptions to its title rules. Owner may argue that she never agreed to let Agent sell to Third Party under the terms of the sales contract Agent entered into with Third Party,

Figure 6-2. Consignment Reality

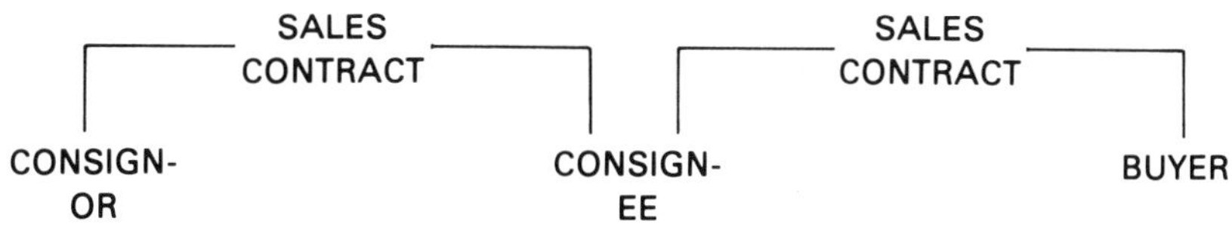

but the law estops Owner. Lord Ellenborough once observed that "[i]f the owner of a horse send it to a repository of sale, can it be implied that he sent it hither for any other purpose than that of sale?"

During a period when a merchant's wealth often consisted of his stock in trade, many were concerned that consignments served to mislead creditors of the consignee. Owner, a woolen company, for example, would "consign" a large shipment of worsteds to Agent, a **distributor.** Agent's creditors would enter her premises and incorrectly assume that Agent was a solvent, going concern, given the large stock of valuable merchandise in her warehouse. If the fiction of the consignment worked, those creditors might suffer unfairly if they extended credit to Agent on the basis of the false impression her possession of the worsteds produced.

It is probably no longer true to say that creditors rely on a merchant's possession of merchandise, though buyers certainly do. In any event, the law is quite chary of the consignment and has developed a number of rules that protect the buyer of goods from the consignee and, importantly, to protect the creditors of the consignee. It is probably fair to say that all good-faith buyers from the consignee will defeat the **claim** of the true owner. Creditors of the consignee are not always so successful, though often they prevail. Secured transactions law is quite suspicious of the consignment, which resembles a loan secured by a security interest in inventory. There remain for consideration in this chapter "true" consignments, that is, consignments that are not disguised secured transactions.

§6.2 THE CONSIGNMENT TRANSACTION

In the last century, **factors** (sometimes referred to as "old" factors to distinguish them from the "new" factor, who is basically an account lender and who is the subject of discussion in Chapter 15) would take merchandise or, sometimes, agricultural produce, and move it to markets where it could be sold. For example, a Kentucky tobacco farmer might deliver his tobacco to such a factor, who would take it by river barge to New Orleans and sell it. Earlier in the century and probably for a long time before, English merchants and American merchants on the east coast would deliver merchandise to ship captains who would take it abroad to trade in various ports. In order to protect these farmers and merchants, the parties used the idea that the delivery to the factor, as the agent came to be called, was a consignment with limits on the transfers of the merchandise that the factor could make. It was long-accepted doctrine, for example, that a factor could sell merchandise entrusted to him but could not pledge it to a lender as security. The world knew that these factors were holding the merchandise of others and had not paid for it, but the world could assume that the factor had the authority to sell the merchandise, such activity being consistent with the common consignment arrangement.

The advent of modern marketing techniques that include instant communication, commodity exchanges, and credit arrangements spelled doom for the old-time factor. Yet, as is so often the case in commercial transactions, where a device that once was an innovation enjoyed something of a heyday and then fell into disuse, but was reinvented or rediscovered, the consignment found new applications. At one time, vagaries in the antitrust laws, for example, permitted manufacturers to fix the resale prices of goods they sold to their customers. For years, General Electric sold its light bulbs to retail and wholesale establishments on consignment with instructions on the prices to be charged to customers of the General Electric buyer. Although the law did not permit a seller to fix resale prices on goods that it "sold," it did permit **resale price maintenance** when the goods were "consigned." Generally, such consignments no longer protect sellers from rules against price fixing, and the use of the consignment for that purpose has not survived as a widespread practice.

Consignments also appear in a few commercially unimportant areas. For example, artists and artisans frequently resort to consignment arrangements under which they entrust their work to a shop or theater for sale. The shopkeeper or theater may post signs indicating that the goods are consigned. The Uniform Commercial Code provides in Article 2 that such "true" consignments must take place in a way that creditors of the consignee will not be misled.

There are a few instances in which consumers or other favorites of the law run afoul of the consignment rules. For example, if a buyer of a mobile home decides she does not want to keep it, she might take it back to the dealer from whom she purchased it and ask the dealer to sell it for her. Although the consumer and the dealer do not think about it and do not say anything to each other about it, both of them assume that the title to the mobile home remains in the consumer and that the dealer is a mere agent for the purposes of arranging the sale for which he will receive some agreed-upon commission. In fact, the arrangement is a consignment, and the consumer may be trapped unfairly when her failure to comply with the rules of Article 2 leave her with a mobile home subject to the claims of the dealer's creditors. The law should probably fashion some exceptions for innocent consumers such as the one in this example, but so far in most jurisdictions no principled exception has emerged.

It is probably fair to say that all consignments are disguised lending arrangements. Even the consumer in the mobile home example and the artist who entrusts his paintings to the summer theater are providing inventory to a business enterprise on credit and retaining title to protect themselves. To the extent that the entruster is a commercial enterprise, the law has no trouble with the characterization: The arrangement is a secured transaction subject to Article 9 of the Uniform Commercial Code. To the extent that the consignor is a nonmerchant, the consequences of permitting him to use the consignment are probably of little commercial significance and should not offend anyone. Such arrangements will probably survive in the consumer and artist situations.

There is one other kind of consignment that has arisen from time to time. In certain industries, some large sellers will consign stock to a **commission merchant** or the like. These merchants travel from market to market much as the old factors did. Generally, they do not use their stock of goods as collateral for loans. In fact, they do not generally borrow from commercial lenders. The commission merchant arrangement, therefore, has generally escaped the attention of the law and its animus against the consignment.

§6.3 LIKE TRANSACTIONS

Sometimes, merchant or consumer sellers will invent other schemes to keep their buyers from obtaining title to the goods that are the subject of their agreement. Most of these inventions have been tried before, and most of them are disguised secured transactions. Some sellers or buyers, for example, have sold merchandise with the understanding that title does not pass to the buyer until the buyer pays. Others use **leases** under which the buyer is designated lessee and the seller lessor. The former reserved title transaction is known as a conditional sale, the latter as a lease-purchase arrangement. Both are disguised secured transactions, and the law is clear that they come within the scope of Article 9 of the Code. That clarity will not prevent some merchant or consumer in the future from fashioning a transaction with such ideas, and sometime, someplace an ill-advised court will accept the argument, and we will have a new device for selling goods without the immediate passage of title.

FROM

MEMORANDUM

TO

NO.__________

__________ 19 ____

The merchandise described herein is delivered to you on MEMORANDUM only, at your risk of loss, or damage from all hazards, whether by theft, robbery, fire or otherwise. Title to said merchandise is and shall remain in ________________ (Your Name) and is held by the undersigned subject to my/our order, the delivery thereof being for the purpose of inspection only, and is to be returned to me/us on demand. It is understood and agreed by the undersigned that nothing contained in this memorandum shall be construed to be, nor has there otherwise been an extension of credit to the undersigned. The undersigned has no right to transfer the said merchandise to any other person, firm or corporation, whether on memorandum or otherwise, without the WRITTEN permission of ________________ (Your Name). Sale of this merchandise can only be effected and title will pass only if, as., and when ________________ (Your Name), the said owner, shall agree to such sale and a bill of sale rendered therefor. All the above is binding on me/us, regardless of prior transactions.

SPECIMEN

4-E3795 GENSUP STATIONERY CO., 1 WEST 47TH ST., NEW YORK, N. Y. 10036

Reprinted with the permission of the New York Diamond Cutting Co.

7 Distribution Arrangements

§7.1 MARKETING THROUGH THIRD PARTIES

Although many sellers to merchant buyers maintain a sales force that solicits accounts and arranges sales through the open account sale described in Chapter 3, many merchant sellers find it necessary to establish a more elaborate sales organization with local distributors, dealers, franchisees, or **wholesalers**. While a giant firm might choose to integrate the distribution function and establish firm-owned distributors and the like, most industries involve independent parties that play important warehousing, warranty service, credit, and delivery functions to the ultimate consumer or to intermediaries as the goods pass from manufacturer to consumer.

§7.2 THE PARTIES

In the simplest distribution arrangement, the manufacturer or other seller of a finished product or commodity will sell directly to the consumer.

Mail-order houses, retailers, and farmstand operators make **direct sales.** Newspaper publishers, automobile manufacturers, and similar sellers need a distribution system. In a way, even a small parts manufacturer for

Figure 7-1. Distribution System (Finished Goods)

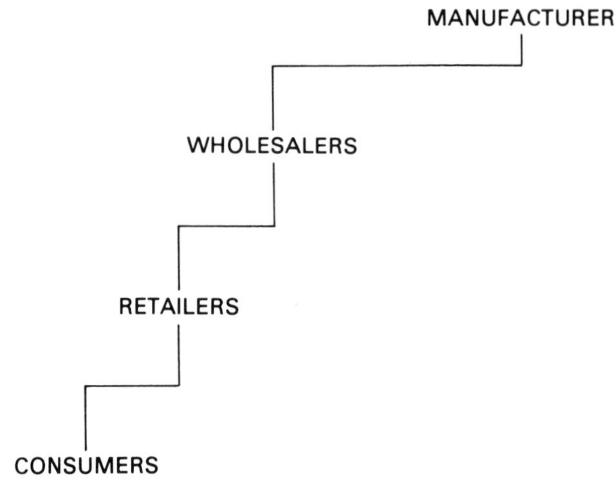

the automobile industry or a small die and mold company will use an **original equipment manufacturer's** distribution system to move the small manufacturer's product from the manufacturer's plant to the ultimate consumer. In the same way, a raw materials supplier uses a manufacturer's distribution system. If we consider only finished goods, Figure 7-1 illustrates a typical distribution system.

In all probability, however, that finished-goods manufacturer buys parts from **vendors** and raw materials from suppliers, so that Figure 7-2 is a more accurate illustration of the movement of goods through the distribution system.

In fact, vendors and even some raw materials suppliers have received goods from their own vendors or suppliers, sometimes through a distribution chain, so that Figure 7-2 is a simplification of the usually more complicated process of moving goods through the **channel of distribution** from mines and farms to consumer.

It is not possible to describe all distribution systems. It is probably not possible even to know all of them, since merchants are continuously devising new methods of relating to their distributors and new modes of distribution. This chapter describes some common distribution arrangements.

§7.3 DISTRIBUTION THROUGH WHOLESALERS

In a classic wholesale distribution arrangement, the wholesaler will perform warehousing and delivery functions for the manufacturer. If a brewery, for example, intends to market its products in a city, it will need warehousing facilities to take delivery from the manufacturer, probably at a rail siding; to store the product until retailers, who traditionally have small storage space, can take delivery; and to deliver the product when retailers order

Figure 7-2. Distribution System

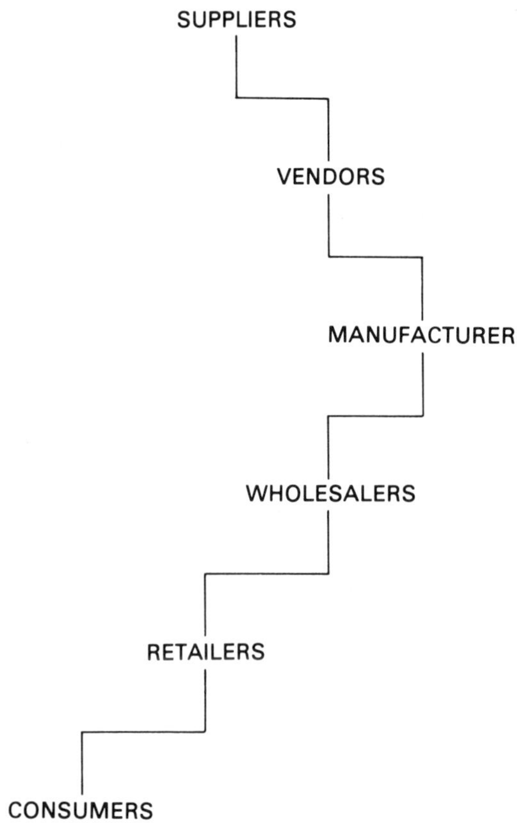

it. The investment in warehouse space, trucks, and personnel is considerable, and brewers may well not have the capital or the management needed to operate their own warehouses all over the country or all over the regions in which they market their products. The wholesaler can serve these functions and can save the brewer the cost of building the system. Note also that the distributor plays a financing role for the brewer. By virtue of the fact that the wholesaler usually pays for product before its customers (the retailers), pay it, the wholesaler cuts the period of time during which the brewer must finance inventory. The wholesaler will pay the brewer and finance its own inventory until the retailer pays it, thereby shortening the time it takes for the brewer to receive cash for its product and reducing the interest charges that the brewer must pay its inventory lender. The wholesaler pays its bank for financing inventory at the wholesaler's warehouse.

§7.4 DISTRIBUTION THROUGH DEALERS

Dealers usually buy from manufacturers or wholesalers and resell to consumers. The dealer performs some of the same functions as the wholesaler. He provides some warehousing, though usually less than a wholesaler, and pays for goods before he receives payment from the consumer. Retailers also expend considerable effort in developing the market through sales promotion, advertising, and the like. Dealers may perform a warranty service function. Customers with warranty complaints can return defective products to dealers who will service the complaint and charge the manufacturer for the work done. In some industries, such as the automobile industry, where manufacturers are strong, dealers play a key role in the financing of the manufacturer's product. In such an industry, the dealer may pay for the goods before they are delivered and may have to cause a bank to guaranty payment under a letter of credit. Manufacturers with the market strength to exact this kind of arrangement from dealers have an enormous benefit — they incur little credit risk and receive payment promptly, thereby achieving significant cash flow advantages not available to manufacturers in most industries.

In this rather sophisticated dealer arrangement, there is a key player in addition to the dealer and his supplier (the manufacturer). That player is the dealer's financer, often a bank or finance company. Chapter 17 explains in more detail the mechanics of the arrangement, but it is worth noting here that the lender, sometimes called a *floorplanner,* is interested not only in lending money to the dealer to buy merchandise from the manufacturer but, often, is more interested in lending to the buyers from the dealer. The volume of credit from those buyers and the all-important interest charges that the lender will earn on its loans is more significant than the volume of credit and interest on the loans to the dealer itself. A dealer with an inventory loan of $2 million may generate enough credit sales to his customer to give the lender $12 million in consumer paper, which yields interest rates in the range of 13 or 14 percent, compared to the modest 8.5 to 9.5 percent interest on the inventory loan.

Often, manufacturers are big enough to incorporate or acquire their own finance companies to play the lender role. In such a case, the manufacturer will ultimately make a profit on the sale of the automobile to the dealer, on the loan the finance company makes to the dealer to buy the vehicle from the manufacturer, and on the loan the finance company makes to the consumer to buy the car from the dealer. Document 7-1 is an agreement between a manufacturer and a dealer.

§7.5 DISTRIBUTION THROUGH FRANCHISEES

Franchising is a very old idea. Whenever a party with a power or a right that he cannot fully exploit himself conveys a part of that power or that right to another, he has, in a sense, created a franchisee. Emperors granted **franchises** to vassals to govern in a given territory; governments sometimes grant franchises to accord privileges or to generate income. Thus the Queen once granted a franchise to import playing cards into England. A state might grant a franchise to build a bridge over the Charles River and collect tolls from travelers. Cities have granted franchises to street railways in the past and to cable television companies in the present. This section deals with commercial franchises, that is, franchises between private parties wherein one, the franchisor, gives something of value to another, the franchisee, usually for a fee based on the franchisee's volume of business or on the condition that the franchisee will buy product from the franchisor.

Despite its long history, franchising is the great commercial innovation of the last 25 years, as entrepreneurs adapted it to a host of new industries and, in some cases, used it to create new industries. For a long time, product franchise arrangements have been common, especially in the retail gasoline, automobile dealership, and wholesale soft-drink bottling trades. Independent, local operators obtain franchises from national corporations.

The number of these "product" franchises has been declining somewhat, but that decline has witnessed the enormous growth of the "service" franchise, common to the fast-food restaurant, car rental, health spa, and similar industries. The number of product franchises is approximately 150,000, while the number of retail service establishments is in the range of 350,000, with the former number shrinking and the latter growing. The volume of sales in product franchises is still strong, being in excess of $400 billion a year, while the sales from retail service franchises are in the range of $170 billion a year.

There are a number of features common to any franchise. First is a trade name or trademark. Under the franchise, the franchisee obtains the right to exploit that proprietary interest of the franchisor. Second is the exclusivity feature. Nearly all franchises contain some exclusivity feature, usually a prohibition against the franchisor's granting of additional franchises in a designated territory. Third is the requirement that the franchisee take steps to protect the quality of the franchisor's name or mark. In product franchises, the franchisee is usually restricted to sales of the franchisor's products. In service franchises, the franchisor must provide the franchisee with instructions and training, so that the franchisee will provide the service in a manner that enhances the service mark. The service franchisee may also be required, under the service franchise agreement, to carry the franchisor's products. Frequently, franchisees must engage in a minimum amount of local advertising and promotion and must use signs, uniforms, and even build facilities that comport with the franchisor's marketing schemes.

The franchise agreement's exclusivity provisions vary but usually are geographic in nature. Thus a franchise might provide that the franchisee has the exclusive right to exploit the franchisor's mark or brand in a given town or county, or the agreement might stipulate that the franchisor will not grant any other franchise to a party located within a certain radius of the franchisor's location. Often, franchisors that have trained one franchisee will grant the franchisee additional franchises in a market in order to minimize development costs for the franchisor and enhance the franchisee's return on investment of time and start-up costs. This type of "horizontal" extension of franchising is quite benign. It does not resemble the vertical proliferation of franchising that is evident in pyramid franchising.

Franchising is subject to considerable regulation under state and federal law. The definitions in these laws are not always consistent, and it is sometimes difficult to distinguish distributors and dealers from franchisees. In fact, of course, sometimes distributors and dealers are franchisees.

The franchise serves a number of purposes. First, it permits an entrepreneur with a good idea and some trade secret, trade name, or trademark to exploit the full potential of those trade advantages. Second, it does so without requiring a great deal of capital, since the franchisee, not the franchisor, must finance the local franchise. Third, it permits small business people to launch a business that they own with the advantages of the goodwill of the franchisor's name, mark, or secret. Fourth, it often permits the franchisor to market goods and make a profit on the goods as well as on the fees for the franchise itself.

In a typical product franchise, such as that involving an oil company and a local service station, there may be little control by the franchisor over the franchisee's method of doing business; while in the typical service franchise, such as a fast-food restaurant, the method of doing business is crucial to the protection of the franchisor's name or mark.

A typical service franchise agreement covers such matters as the hours that the franchisee's establishment is open, hiring practices, sight selection, and facility design.

In the simplest territorial franchising arrangements, the franchisor is a national or regional organization that licenses retail operations at given locations with territorial restrictions. In a successful franchise operation, there may be as many as 10,000 franchisees. Figure 7-3 illustrates the simple territorial allocation.

In other franchising schemes, the franchisor may allocate large territories to a franchisee with the power in the franchisee to grant sublicenses. The original franchisor may obtain fees from its franchisees based in part on the fees the franchisees receive from their subfranchisees. If there are no limits on the number of franchisees and subfranchisees, a franchise scheme approaches the pyramid model with sub-subfranchisees to varying levels, such as that illustrated in Figure 7-4, a model suggesting that subfranchising and subinfeudation have something in common. Franchising laws and regulations generally prohibit such schemes, which are a classic violation of fairness in franchising and, often, of criminal statutes.

Figure 7-3. Franchise System

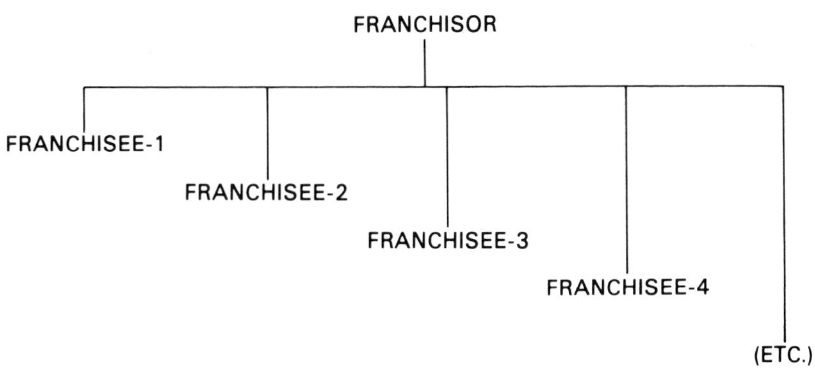

§7.6 DISTRIBUTION THROUGH SALES REPRESENTATIVES

A sales representative customarily takes possession of a manufacturer's or distributor's merchandise and sells it to retailers or consumers. In the simplest arrangement, a salesman, who may represent a number of manufacturers or distributors, either in the same line of products or complementary lines, will put merchandise in the trunk of his car and travel throughout his territory hawking the merchandise. At the other end of the scale is the broker who takes merchandise to the leased premises of a larger retail

Figure 7-4. Franchise Pyramid

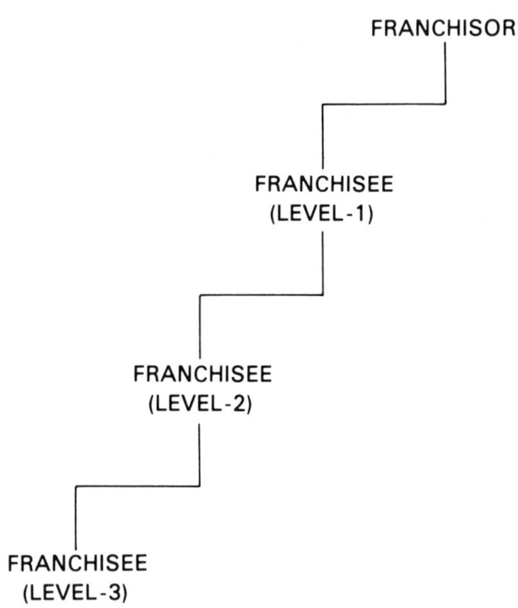

operation, usually a department store, and sells merchandise to walk-in customers. Often, the salesman who markets out of the trunk of his car has a loose relationship with his supplier, and the delivery of the goods to him is probably a consignment, subject to the problems that arise in consignment selling, problems that have not manifested themselves in this relationship in part because the consignments tend to be small and because the creditors of the broker tend not to rely on his stock in trade. Clearly, this merchandise broker is often at the margin of commercially important transactions. There are times, however, when merchandise brokers handle valuable stock, such as precious gems.

In the commercially more important transaction, the merchandise broker will take delivery of significant volumes of merchandise and will have a carefully drawn agreement with her supplier, for whom she acts as broker, and with the store in which she displays and sells the merchandise, the latter agreement being in the nature of a lease.

§7.7 DISTRIBUTION BY LICENSE

To a significant extent, franchise agreements entail licensing provisions that render the franchisee a licensee of a copyright or trademark. There are also licensees who serve as marketers of a licensor's secrets or registered name through licenses that are not franchises.

Patent licenses, for example, grant the licensee the right to make, use, or sell a patented invention. The invention may be a product that comprises a major part of the licensee's business, but more often it is a small part of that business and may be only a component of a small part of the business. Patent licenses, for example, may cover the right of an automobile manufacturer to use a piece of equipment on its assembly line, the right of a food processor to use paper bags in which it markets its products, or an earthmoving equipment manufacturer to incorporate a small roller bearing assembly in a road grader.

Sometimes, an inventor will grant an exclusive patent, thereby granting to another, usually an organization with a distribution system or a manufacturer that is willing to pay high fees to obtain the patent monopoly, the sole right to exploit the patent. At other times, the inventor or owner of the patent will grant nonexclusive patents to a number of licensees, either in a fashion that permits them to exploit the patent in a single territory or market, or as a means of generating license fees, that is, as a means of getting parties to use the patent. Patent licenses can take on many forms. Document 7-2 is an example of a patent license.

Frequently, an inventor will assign his rights as inventor to his employer or to another who desires to exploit the invention, and other inventors sometimes assign or even license their application rights.

Sometimes, a licensee will have the right to sublicense. Thus a bag manufacturer with the right to manufacture a patented paper bag that it sells to the grain industry might sublicense a bag manufacturer who sells bags to the fertilizer industry.

Trademarks and copyrights are also frequently the subject of license. If, because of limited production capacity or limited distribution capacity, for example, a manufacturer is unable to exploit its mark fully in some markets, it might license manufacturers to make and market products under the trademark. Such arrangements are potentially fatal for the trade name owner. Unless it retains the right to control the quality of the licensee's product, that mark might be significantly diluted to the point that the mark loses its value. Franchisees are often licensees of marks, and franchise agreements usually contain the grant of a license in them and invariably contain stiff requirements designed to protect the quality of the mark. Many licensees, of course, are not franchisees.

Trade secrets sometimes do not meet the requirements of patent, copyright, or trademark law and cannot be protected by registration or patent. In that case, parties that develop the trade secret may attempt to exploit it by contract, that is, by licensing the secret. Those attempts are often perilous, since the very disclosure of the trade secret tends to increase the risk that the cat will get out of the bag, leaving the licensor with nothing to license. Disclosure of secrets is also a problem for licensees, who may feel, after they learn the secrets, that they knew them already or would have learned them in the normal course of business in a short time. Disgruntled employees or former employees of licensors and licensees may destroy the secret intentionally or unintentionally.

Since licenses are, by their nature, anticompetitive, they sometimes run afoul of antitrust laws or other regulatory laws or rules. Parties to such agreements sometimes have to prove to a government official or a jury that the secrets are indeed secret and are not fabricated for the purposes of restricting competition. The transfer of technology, which is the outcome under any trade secret license, is often a carefully regulated matter in third world and even western countries, and licensors may find their licenses unenforceable (and their license fees uncollectible) after disclosure, if a foreign tribunal decides that the information was in the public domain.

Sometimes, inventors or people with ideas will ask an enterprise to enter into a nondisclosure agreement in advance of disclosure of a secret or invention. Those agreements are potential problems for the enterprise, since the invention or secret may already be in the public domain or may be known to the enterprise. After disclosure, the inventor will argue that any exploitation was a result of her disclosure, and the evidentiary battle is on. It is often difficult for an enterprise to prove that, in fact, it did have the information prior to the disclosure. Such disclosure arrangements are also a problem for the inventor, since she may have a difficult time proving that, in fact, the enterprise did not have knowledge of her invention or secret. Many parties avoid nondisclosure agreements altogether or water them down to the point that the inventor has no protection.

Copyrights protect tangible expressions in books, articles, films, and other reproductions of intellectual work. To a significant extent, a copyright protects the owner against commercial exploitation of the intellectual property by anyone not licensed and will permit the owner to exploit the product fully. At times, the owner will not be in a position to exploit the product. The author of a short story, for example, might grant a nonexclusive license to a magazine to publish the story and later grant an exclusive license to a publisher who will try to have the story published in anthologies or other collections. Studies of economic and social conditions often yield copyrighted material, which can be the subject of license.

§7.8 DISTRIBUTION THROUGH BROKERS

In some industries, sellers do not market their products to the ultimate consumer but store it or continue to use it until a broker finds a purchaser. Brokers differ from many other middlemen in that they do not take possession of the merchandise or real estate that they are attempting to sell. Frequently, brokers underwrite advertising costs and sometimes maintain their own publications with pictures and descriptions of the seller's property. The broker arrangement best known to consumers is the real estate broker, who lists a seller's property and attempts to find a buyer.

Commodity brokers describe their merchandise by industry standards, e.g., "Number 2 yellow corn," "West Texas Intermediate crude." These brokers often sell goods that are stored with commercial **bailees** who have issued documents of title covering the commodity. The brokers can then sell the commodity by transferring the document in the fashion that is described in Chapter 4 and in Section 31.3. Some brokers buy occasionally for their own account, but most buy only for their clients. Raw materials sellers and agriculture producers frequently rely on brokers and often do so without any written agreement, it being understood in such arrangements that the broker does not have an exclusive and earns his commission only when the seller sells to a buyer.

§7.9 GROUP BUYERS

In industries where some retailers are small, and suppliers diverse, retailers band together for the purpose of saving on transaction costs in their purchases and to obtain quantity discounts. For example, small hardware outlets and grocery stores that compete with much larger operations have sometimes set up cooperatives or merchandise brokers to do their buying. These arrangements permit the small operator to avoid the cost of contacting all of the small manufacturers or even the large distributors that supply such an operation. Under the arrangements, the cooperative or the broker will contact the various sources of supply, negotiate price terms, contact the local operator to determine his needs and delivery requirements, and place the orders. Usually, the cooperative will not serve any wholesale function, that is, it will not take delivery of the goods but will cause them to be **drop shipped** directly to the local enterprise or will simply give the local operator information and let him place the order directly with the supplier.

Chrysler Motors Corporation

CHRYSLER

SALES AND SERVICE AGREEMENT

____
(Dealer Name)

located at ____
(Street) (City) (State)

a(n) ______________________ hereinafter called DEALER, and Chrysler Motors Corporation, a
(Individual, Corporation or Partnership)

Delaware corporation, hereinafter sometimes referred to as "CMC," have entered into this Chrysler Motors Corporation Chrysler Sales and Service Agreement, hereinafter referred to as "Agreement," the terms of which are as follows:

INTRODUCTION

The purpose of the relationship established by this Agreement is to provide a means for the sale and service of specified Chrysler vehicles and the sale of CMC vehicle parts and accessories in a manner that will maximize customer satisfaction and be of benefit to DEALER and CMC.

While the following provisions, each of which is material, set forth the undertakings of this relationship, the success of those undertakings rests on a recognition of the mutuality of interests of DEALER and CMC, and a spirit of understanding and cooperation by both parties in the day to day performance of their respective functions. As a result of such considerations, CMC has entered into this Agreement in reliance upon and has placed its trust in the personal abilities, expertise, knowledge and integrity of DEALER'S principal owners and management personnel, which CMC anticipates will enable DEALER to perform the personal services contemplated by this Agreement.

It is the mutual goal of this relationship to promote the sale and service of specified CMC products by maintaining and advancing their excellence and reputation by earning, holding and furthering the public regard for CMC and all CMC dealers.

1 PRODUCTS COVERED

DEALER has the right to order and purchase from CMC and to sell at retail only those specific models of CMC vehicles, sometimes referred to as "specified CMC vehicles," listed on the Motor Vehicle Addendum, attached hereto and incorporated herein by reference. CMC may change the models of CMC vehicles listed on the Motor Vehicle Addendum by furnishing DEALER a superseding Motor Vehicle Addendum. Such a superseding Motor Vehicle Addendum will not be deemed or construed to be an amendment to this Agreement.

2 DEALER'S MANAGEMENT

CMC has entered into this Agreement relying on the active, substantial and continuing personal participation in the management of DEALER'S organization by:

NAME	POSITION

88C

Reprinted with the permission of Chrysler Motors Corp.

DEALER represents and warrants that at least one of the above named individuals will be physically present at the DEALER'S facility (sometimes referred to as "Dealership Facilities") during most of its operating hours and will manage all of DEALER'S business relating to the sale and service of CMC products. DEALER shall not change the personnel holding the above described position(s) or the nature and extent of his/her/their management participation without the prior written approval of CMC.

3 DEALER'S CAPITAL STOCK OR PARTNERSHIP INTEREST

If DEALER is a corporation or partnership, DEALER represents and agrees that the persons named below own beneficially the capital stock or partnership interest of DEALER in the percentages indicated below. DEALER warrants there will be no change affecting more than 50% of the ownership interest of DEALER, nor will there be any other change in the ownership interest of DEALER which may affect the managerial control of DEALER without CMC's prior written approval.

Name	Voting Stock	Non-Voting Stock	Partnership Interest	Active Yes/No
________	____%	____%	____%	____
________	____%	____%	____%	____
________	____%	____%	____%	____
________	____%	____%	____%	____
________	____%	____%	____%	____
Total	____%	____%	____%	

4 SALES LOCALITY

DEALER shall have the non-exclusive right, subject to the provisions of this Agreement, to purchase from CMC those new specified CMC vehicles, vehicle parts, accessories and other CMC products for resale at the DEALER'S facilities and location described in the Dealership Facilities and Location Addendum, attached hereto and incorporated herein by reference. DEALER will actively and effectively sell and promote the retail sale of CMC vehicles, vehicle parts and accessories in DEALER'S Sales Locality. As used herein, "Sales Locality" shall mean the area designated in writing to DEALER by CMC from time to time as the territory of DEALER'S responsibility for the sale of CMC vehicles, vehicle parts and accessories, although DEALER is free to sell said products to customers wherever they may be located. Said Sales Locality may be shared with other CMC dealers as CMC determines to be appropriate.

5 ADDITIONAL TERMS AND PROVISIONS

The additional terms and provisions set forth in the document entitled "Chrysler Motors Corporation Sales and Service Agreement Additional Terms and Provisions" marked "Form 88CMC," as may hereafter be amended from time to time, constitute a part of this Agreement with the same force and effect as if set forth at length herein, and the term "this Agreement" includes said additional terms and provisions.

6 FORMER AGREEMENTS, REPRESENTATIONS OR STATEMENTS

This Chrysler Motors Corporation Chrysler Sales and Service Agreement and other documents, (or their successors as specifically provided for herein) which are specifically incorporated herein by reference constitute the entire agreement between the parties relating to the purchase by DEALER of those new specified CMC vehicles, parts and accessories from CMC for resale; and it cancels and supersedes all earlier agreements, written or oral, between CMC and DEALER relating to the purchase by DEALER of Chrysler vehicles, parts and accessories, except for (a) amounts owing by CMC to DEALER, such as payments for warranty service performed and incentive programs, or (b) amounts owing or which may be determined to be owed, as a result of an audit or investigation, by DEALER to CMC due to DEALER'S purchase from CMC of vehicles, parts, accessories and other goods or services, or (c) amounts DEALER owes to CMC as a result of other extensions of credit by CMC to DEALER. No representations or statements, other than those expressly set forth herein or those set forth in the applications for this Agreement submitted to CMC by DEALER or DEALER'S representatives, are made or relied upon by any party hereto in entering into this Agreement.

7 WAIVER AND MODIFICATION

No waiver, modification or change of any of the terms of this Agreement or change or erasure of any printed part of this Agreement or addition to it (except the filling in of blank spaces and lines) will be valid or binding on CMC unless approved in writing by the President or a Vice President or the National Dealer Placement Manager of Chrysler Motors Corporation.

8 AMENDMENT

DEALER and CMC recognize that this Agreement does not have an expiration date and will continue in effect unless terminated under the limited circumstances set forth in Paragraph 28. DEALER and CMC further recognize that the passage of time, changes in the industry, ways of doing business and other unforeseen circumstances may cause CMC to determine that it should amend all Chrysler Motors Corporation Chrysler Sales and Service Agreements. Therefore, CMC will have the right to amend this Agreement to the extent that CMC deems advisable, provided that CMC makes the same amendment in Chrysler Motors Corporation Chrysler Sales and Service Agreements generally. Each such amendment will be issued in a notice sent by certified mail or delivered in person to DEALER and signed by the President or a Vice President or the National Dealer Placement Manager of Chrysler Motors Corporation. Thirty-five (35) days after mailing or delivery of such notice to DEALER, this Agreement will be deemed amended in the manner and to the extent set forth in the notice.

9 ARBITRATION

Any and all disputes arising out of or in connection with the interpretation, performance or nonperformance of this Agreement or any and all disputes arising out of or in connection with transactions in any way related to this Agreement (including, but not limited to, the validity, scope and enforceability of this arbitration provision, or disputes under rights granted pursuant to the statutes of the state in which DEALER is licensed) shall be finally and completely resolved by arbitration pursuant to the arbitration laws of the United States of America as codified in Title 9 of the United States Code, §§1-14, under the Rules of Commercial Arbitration of the American Arbitration Association (hereinafter referred to as the "Rules") by a majority vote of a panel of three arbitrators. One arbitrator will be selected by DEALER (DEALER'S arbitrator). One arbitrator will be selected by CMC (CMC'S arbitrator). These arbitrators must be selected by the respective parties within ten (10) business days after receipt by either DEALER or CMC of a written notification from the other party of a decision to arbitrate a dispute pursuant to this Agreement. Should either CMC or DEALER fail to select an arbitrator within said ten-day period, the party who so fails to select an arbitrator will have its arbitrator selected by the American Arbitration Association upon the application of the other party. The third arbitrator must be an individual who is familiar with business transactions and be a licensed attorney admitted to the practice of law within the United States of America, or a judge. The third arbitrator will be selected by DEALER'S and CMC'S arbitrators. If said arbitrators cannot agree on a third arbitrator within thirty (30) days from the date of the appointment of the last selected arbitrator, then either DEALER'S or CMC'S arbitrator may apply to the American Arbitration Association to appoint said third arbitrator pursuant to the criteria set forth above. The arbitration panel shall conduct the proceedings pursuant to the then existing Rules.

Notwithstanding the foregoing, to the extent any provision of the Rules conflict with any provision of this Paragraph 9, the provisions of this Paragraph 9 will be controlling.

CMC and DEALER agree to facilitate the arbitration by: (a) each party paying to the American Arbitration Association one-half (½) of the required deposit before the proceedings commence; (b) making available to one another and to the arbitration panel, for inspection and photocopying all documents, books and records, if determined by the arbitration panel to be relevant to the dispute; (c) making available to one another and to the arbitration panel personnel directly or indirectly under their control, for testimony during hearings and prehearing proceedings if determined by the arbitration panel to be relevant to the dispute; (d) conducting arbitration hearings to the greatest extent possible on consecutive business days; and (e) strictly observing the time periods established by the Rules or by the arbitration panel for the submission of evidence and of briefs.

Unless otherwise agreed to by CMC and DEALER, a stenographic record of the arbitration shall be made and a transcript thereof shall be ordered for each party, with each party paying one-half (½) of the total cost of such recording and transcription. The stenographer shall be state-certified, if certification is made by the state, and the party to whom it is most convenient shall be responsible for securing and notifying such stenographer of the time and place of the arbitration hearing(s).

If the arbitration provision is invoked when the dispute between the parties is either the legality of terminating this Agreement or of adding a new CMC dealer of the same line-make or relocating an existing CMC dealer of the same line-make, CMC will stay the implementation of the decision to terminate this Agreement or add such new CMC dealer or approve the relocation of an existing CMC dealer of the same line-make until the decision of the arbitrator has been announced, providing DEALER does not in any way attempt to avoid the obligations of this Paragraph 9, in which case the decision at issue will be immediately implemented.

Except as limited hereby, the arbitration panel shall have all powers of law and equity, which it can lawfully assume, necessary to resolve the issues in dispute including, without limiting the generality of the foregoing, making awards of compensatory damages, issuing both prohibitory and mandatory orders in the nature of injunctions and compelling the production of documents and witnesses for pre-arbitration discovery and/or presentation at the arbitration hearing on the merits of the case. The arbitration panel shall not have legal or equitable authority to issue a mandatory or prohibitory order which: (a) extends or has effect beyond the subject matter of this Agreement, or (b) will govern the activities of either party for a period of more than two years; nor shall the arbitration panel have authority to award punitive, consequential or any damages whatsoever beyond or in addition to the compensatory damages allowed to be awarded under this Agreement.

The decision of the arbitration panel shall be in written form and shall include findings of fact and conclusions of law.

It is the intent and desire of DEALER and CMC to hereby and forever renounce and reject any and all recourse to litigation before any judicial or administrative forum and to accept the award of the arbitration panel as final and binding, subject to no judicial or administrative review, except on those grounds set forth in 9 USC §10 and §11. Judgment on the award and/or orders may be entered in any court having jurisdiction over the parties or their assets. In the final award and/or order, the arbitration panel shall divide all costs (other than attorney fees, which shall be borne by the party incurring such fees and other costs specifically provided for herein) incurred in conducting the arbitration in accordance with what the arbitration panel deems just and equitable under the circumstances. The fees of DEALER'S arbitrator shall be paid by DEALER. The fees of CMC's arbitrator shall be paid by CMC.

10 SIGNATURE

This Agreement becomes valid only when signed by the President or a Vice President or the National Dealer Placement Manager of Chrysler Motors Corporation and by a duly authorized officer or executive of DEALER if a corporation; or by one of the general partners of DEALER if a partnership; or by DEALER if an individual.

IN WITNESS WHEREOF, the parties hereto have signed this Agreement which is finally executed at

______________________________, Michigan, in

triplicate, on ______________________________.

SPECIMEN

____
(DEALER - Firm Name)

By ______________________________
(Individual Duly Authorized to Sign)

____
(Title)

CHRYSLER MOTORS CORPORATION

By ______________________________

____
(Title)

Chrysler
Motors
Corporation

SALES AND SERVICE AGREEMENT

ADDITIONAL TERMS AND PROVISIONS

CHRYSLER MOTORS

FORM 88CMC

Document 7-1. (*continued*)

INDEX

1

Chrysler Motors Corporation
SALES AND SERVICE AGREEMENT
ADDITIONAL TERMS AND PROVISIONS

The following additional terms and provisions apply to and are part of the Chrysler Motors Corporation Sales and Service Agreement(s) to which Dealer is a signatory:

11 SELLING, SERVICE, COMPLIANCE, FACILITIES AND LOCATION, FINANCES, PERSONNEL AND SIGNAGE

(a) SELLING

DEALER shall use its best efforts to promote energetically and sell aggressively and effectively at retail (which includes lease and rental units) each and every model of CMC vehicles identified in the aforementioned Motor Vehicle Addendum and CMC vehicle parts, accessories and other CMC products and services, to private and fleet customers in DEALER'S Sales Locality. DEALER will sell the number of new CMC vehicles necessary to fulfill DEALER'S Minimum Sales Responsibility for each passenger car line or truck line represented by the vehicles listed on the Motor Vehicle Addendum, as defined below.

DEALER'S Minimum Sales Responsibility for each such line will be determined as follows:

From time to time, but at least once a year for each such line, CMC will compute the ratio of the number of new CMC passenger cars and/or trucks registered in the most recent whole or partial calendar year-to-date period for which registration figures are available in the CMC Sales Zone in which DEALER is located to the total number of new passenger cars or, if CMC deems it appropriate, the total number of those new passenger cars or trucks which CMC, in its sole discretion, determines to be competitive with any or all of its passenger cars or trucks so registered in that Zone during the same period. The ratio thus obtained will be applied to the comparable category of the total number of new passenger cars or competitive passenger cars and/or trucks, as appropriate, registered during the same period in DEALER'S Sales Locality. The resulting number will be DEALER'S Minimum Sales Responsibility for each of said lines during this same period, subject to adjustment as described below.

Upon DEALER'S written request, CMC may adjust DEALER'S Minimum Sales Responsibility, if appropriate in CMC's judgment, to take into account extraordinary local conditions to the extent, in CMC's opinion, such conditions are beyond DEALER'S control and have affected DEALER'S sales performance differently from the sales performance of other new vehicle dealers in DEALER'S Sales Locality or other like vehicle line CMC dealers in the Sales Zone in which DEALER is located.

If DEALER'S Sales Locality is shared by one or more other CMC dealer(s) of the same line, DEALER'S Minimum Sales Responsibility for such line will be the number of new vehicles DEALER must sell in order to achieve DEALER'S fair share of the Minimum Sales Responsibility for all such CMC dealers in the Sales Locality. The Minimum Sales Responsibility for the total CMC dealers of the same line in the Sales Locality will be determined by using the same method described above in this Paragraph 11(a). CMC will determine DEALER'S fair share by assessing the relative importance of DEALER'S immediate area of influence as compared with the Sales Locality as a whole.

3

FORM 88CMC

This assessment will then be converted to a percentage which will represent DEALER'S fair share of the Minimum Sales Responsibility for the Sales Locality.

Registration figures used in these computations will be new vehicle registrations as reported by any recognized reporting organization selected by CMC. If vehicle registration data is not reasonably available, CMC may use other records, generally accepted in the industry, for the purpose of determining motor vehicle purchases and to establish DEALER'S Minimum Sales Responsibility. To the extent that registration figures or other records generally accepted in the automotive industry for purposes of determining motor vehicle purchases are not reasonably available for purposes of considering any of the factors specified herein, CMC may rely on other records and data developed by CMC that reasonably depict purchases of motor vehicles in an applicable area to establish DEALER'S Minimum Sales Responsibility.

(b) SERVICE

DEALER shall service CMC vehicles actively and effectively and provide and maintain, for servicing CMC vehicles, adequate facilities equipped with the basic tools common to the trade and with special tools and equipment peculiar to CMC products and necessary for servicing and repairing specified CMC vehicles properly, efficiently and competitively. DEALER shall comply with parts, service and warranty guides established by CMC from time to time, make a sincere effort to satisfy service customers, and render prompt, efficient and courteous service to all owners or lessees of all CMC vehicles regardless of where such vehicle was purchased or leased. DEALER shall perform all pre-delivery and road-ready services recommended by CMC on new CMC vehicles DEALER sells.

DEALER shall, at all times during this Agreement, meet its minimum service satisfaction requirements by maintaining a rating on Chrysler Motors Corporation's Customer Satisfaction Index, Prep-It-Right and Deliver-It-Right evaluations (as determined by Chrysler Motors Corporation from time to time, based upon surveys conducted of DEALER'S customers) which is equal to or greater than the average Customer Satisfaction Index, Prep-It-Right and Deliver-It-Right ratings for the national Sales Level Group (as those groups are determined by CMC from time to time) in which DEALER is included. CMC will review, at least once a year, DEALER'S performance under the Customer Satisfaction Index and DEALER'S Prep-It-Right and Deliver-It-Right ratings.

DEALER shall supply to all purchasers from DEALER of new CMC vehicles a copy of CMC's appropriate new vehicle warranty; make such certifications and verifications of CMC owners' odometer readings, maintenance service performance, and other matters as may be required under the terms of the CMC vehicle warranty and as CMC may from time to time otherwise prescribe; and provide owners of CMC vehicles all warranty service and campaign inspections or corrections to which they may be entitled in accordance with the policies and procedures set forth in Chrysler Motors Corporation's Warranty Policy and Procedure Manual and in bulletins and documents relating to service that CMC may, from time to time, supply to DEALER. The provisions of said Warranty Policy and Procedure Manual, including any revisions thereto which shall be furnished to DEALER by CMC from time to time, constitute a part of this Agreement with the same force and effect as if set forth in its entirety herein.

DEALER shall comply with all policies, procedures, directives and rulings of the CMC Customer Arbitration Board.

CMC has placed its trust and confidence in the integrity and fidelity of DEALER and, therefore, CMC shall compensate DEALER for services claimed to have been performed by DEALER under CMC's warranties or campaign inspections and corrections if claimed in accordance with CMC's then current policies and procedures described above. DEALER agrees to comply with all such policies and procedures including, but not limited to, policies and procedures relating to the keeping of books and records respecting claims DEALER may make for compensation for service DEALER performs under CMC's warranties or campaign inspections and corrections. DEALER

4

agrees that CMC may inspect DEALER'S books and records regarding any warranty service or other claims for compensation DEALER may submit to CMC. CMC may charge DEALER'S account for claims which have been disallowed as a result of such inspection.

DEALER shall perform all warranty, pre-delivery, road-ready, campaign inspections and corrections, and other services hereunder as an independent contractor and not as the agent of CMC and shall assume responsibility for and hold CMC harmless from, all claims (including, but not limited to, claims resulting from the negligent or willful acts or omissions of DEALER) against CMC arising out of or in connection with DEALER'S performance of such service.

If DEALER modifies any CMC vehicle or installs on any CMC vehicle any equipment, part or accessory that has not been supplied or approved by CMC, or sells any CMC vehicle which has been modified after leaving the possession, custody or control of CMC, or sells a non-Chrysler Motors Corporation service contract in connection with the sale of any CMC vehicle, DEALER shall disclose to the customer in writing that the modification, equipment, accessory or part is not supplied or approved by CMC and is not included in warranties furnished by CMC or, in the case of a service contract, the coverage is not provided by Chrysler Motors Corporation, its parent, subsidiaries or its affiliates. DEALER will write such disclosure on the purchase order and on the customer's bill of sale. Notwithstanding the foregoing, DEALER may not use parts which have not been authorized by CMC in performing repairs under CMC warranties.

(c) COMPLIANCE

DEALER shall comply with all applicable federal, state and local laws, rules or regulations in the operation of the dealership.

(d) FACILITIES AND LOCATION

(i) DEALER'S Responsibilities

DEALER shall provide facilities for the sale and service of CMC products and related activities ("Dealership Operations") at the location set forth in the aforementioned Dealership Facilities and Location Addendum. The entire Dealership Facilities including, but not in limitation of the foregoing, new and used vehicle display area, salesrooms, service area, parts and accessories area, building exterior and grounds will be satisfactory to CMC as to appearance and layout, and will be maintained and used as set forth in the Dealership Facilities and Location Addendum. DEALER shall at all times maintain the Dealership Facilities so that they are of adequate capacity to accommodate DEALER'S total vehicle sales volume and are relatively equivalent in their attractiveness, level of maintenance, overall appearance and use to those facilities maintained by DEALER'S principal competitors.

DEALER shall conduct its Dealership Operations only from the dealership location and dealership facilities above mentioned and in the manner and at least during the hours usual in the trade in DEALER'S Sales Locality. DEALER shall not, except as provided for in subparagraph 11(d)(ii) hereunder, either directly or indirectly, establish any place or places of business for the conduct of its Dealership Operations other than at the Dealership Facilities and Dealership Operations location as set forth in the Dealership Facilities and Location Addendum.

If all of the Dealership Facilities are not at the same location, DEALER shall not utilize any separate portion of the Dealership Facilities for the conduct of any Dealership Operations other than as specified in the current Dealership Facilities and Location Addendum. The Dealership Facilities and Location Addendum shall identify any other purposes for which the Dealership Facilities are to be used and the actual space and areas to be allocated for such purposes.

(ii) Changes in Facilities or Location

DEALER shall not make any change in the location of Dealership Operations or make any change in the area and use of Dealership Facilities without the prior written approval of CMC. Any written approval of a change in the location or in the area or use of Dealership Facilities shall be valid only

5

if in the form of a new Dealership Facilities and Location Addendum or a separate written agreement signed by DEALER and one of the authorized representatives of CMC identified in Paragraph 10 hereinabove.

(e) FINANCES

DEALER shall maintain and employ in connection with DEALER'S business such net working capital, net worth, and wholesale credit and retail financing arrangements necessary for DEALER to carry out successfully DEALER'S undertakings pursuant to this Agreement and in accordance with guides therefor as may be issued by CMC from time to time. At no time shall DEALER'S net working capital be less than the amount specified in the Minimum Working Capital Agreement executed in conjunction with this Agreement and incorporated herein by reference, or the amount thereafter established by any superseding Minimum Working Capital Agreement.

(f) PERSONNEL

DEALER shall employ in accordance with the volume of DEALER'S business such number of competent technicians in DEALER'S repair shops as may be required to assure prompt, satisfactory and competitive customer service for all owners of CMC vehicles who may request such service from DEALER. In particular and without limitation to the generality of the foregoing, DEALER shall cause its service personnel to receive such training from time to time required by CMC to maintain their technical expertise to render competent customer service, including the use of improved methods of repair, or the repair of new parts or systems, developed by CMC.

Failure to comply with the service training requirements of the immediately preceding subparagraph of this Paragraph 11(f) may result in suspension of deliveries of CMC vehicles until DEALER complies with such training requirements. Protracted failure to comply with such training requirements may result in termination of this Agreement pursuant to Paragraph 28 hereunder. The immediately foregoing sentence shall not be construed as in any way limiting the general applicability of Paragraph 28 to any of the other provisions of this Paragraph 11.

DEALER shall employ and maintain for its retail business a number of trained and competent new and used motor vehicle sales, lease, service, parts and general management personnel that are sufficient for DEALER to carry out successfully all of DEALER'S undertakings in this Agreement. In particular and without limitation of the generality of the foregoing, DEALER shall cause its sales personnel to receive such training from time to time as may be required by CMC to maintain their sales expertise to render satisfactory sales.

(g) SIGNAGE

DEALER shall display and maintain brand signs, fascia and other signage in compliance with the policies and guidelines of Chrysler Motors Corporation's Dealership Identification Program, including any modification or revisions to such policies and guidelines, which shall from time to time be furnished to DEALER by CMC.

12 ADVERTISING

CMC, in promoting the sale and lease of its products by DEALER and other CMC dealers, shall seek to advertise in the most effective manner to develop public interest and confidence in its dealers and products.

DEALER shall engage in advertising and sales promotion programs and shall use effective showroom displays to help fulfill DEALER'S responsibility to promote CMC products and services vigorously and aggressively. In advertising in support of DEALER'S selling, leasing and servicing CMC products, DEALER shall advertise only in a manner that will develop customer confidence in DEALER and CMC products and shall not use any advertising tending to mislead or deceive the public or violate any applicable federal, state or local laws, rules or regulations, nor shall DEALER disparage CMC or any company, or products of such company, directly involved in the manufacture of CMC vehicles. DEALER shall discontinue any advertising that CMC may find to be injurious to CMC's business or likely to deceive the public

6

or violative of any applicable federal, state or local laws, rules or regulations.

DEALER shall at all times be a member in good standing of the Dealer Advertising Association, for the lines set forth in the Motor Vehicle Addendum, which covers a geographical area that encompasses, in whole or significant part, DEALER'S Sales Locality and which has been approved by CMC.

13 REPORTS, RECORDS AND BUSINESS SYSTEMS

DEALER shall submit to CMC for confidential use by CMC and its affiliates, in such manner, in such form, and at such times as CMC may reasonably request, complete and accurate reports of sales and stocks of new and used vehicles on hand and other reports, including monthly financial statements and operating reports.

DEALER shall use and keep accurate and current at all times a uniform accounting system and will follow accounting practices, satisfactory to CMC, which will enable CMC to develop comparative information in order, among other things, to provide business management assistance to dealers for the mutual benefit of DEALER and CMC. DEALER agrees that CMC may at any time for confidential use inspect DEALER'S books and records to determine whether they are kept in such manner that the data shown in them can be used in CMC's business management assistance to dealers, to assess DEALER'S financial condition, and to verify invoices or other claims DEALER may render to CMC. CMC may, during the course of such inspection, make copies of such books and records and retain such copies for CMC's confidential use.

DEALER shall maintain an electronic data storage, transmission and communication system in the manner and form required from time to time by CMC.

CMC and its affiliates shall not, without approval of DEALER, disclose the contents of DEALER'S financial records to persons not a party or an affiliate of a party to this Agreement except when required by compulsory process from a court, government agency or arbitrator, or when CMC, in its discretion, considers it appropriate to disclose said financial records in an adjudicatory or arbitration proceeding involving the parties to this Agreement.

14 ORDERS

CMC shall ship specified CMC vehicles, parts and accessories to DEALER only on DEALER'S order.

DEALER shall submit to CMC, in the manner and form required by CMC, current orders for CMC vehicles, parts and accessories, and estimates of DEALER'S future vehicle requirements at such times and for such periods as CMC reasonably may request for the mutual benefit of all CMC dealers and CMC. All orders are subject to acceptance by CMC, which acceptance may be in whole or in part. CMC shall not be obligated to accept any order from DEALER for any reason including, but not limited to, default of DEALER on any obligation to CMC.

Except as otherwise allowed by this Agreement, CMC shall use its best efforts to fill accepted orders for specified CMC vehicles, parts and accessories. Notwithstanding the foregoing, in the event that demand exceeds supply of specified CMC vehicles, DEALER acknowledges that CMC has the right to allocate such supply in any reasonable manner CMC deems fit in any geographical market.

15 DELIVERY

CMC may deliver specified CMC vehicles by rail, truck, boat or any other means of transport, or deliver them for driveaway, endeavoring, when exceptional circumstances arise and the cost is not increased, to meet DEALER'S preference as to mode of transportation. CMC may deliver specified CMC vehicles to a carrier that CMC selects, for shipment to DEALER at DEALER'S place of business or to the city or town where DEALER'S place of business is located (or to the nearest practicable unloading point) "to CMC's order, notify DEALER," or may deliver such vehicles at any other point that CMC may establish.

CMC may deliver parts and accessories to DEALER by delivering them to a carrier that CMC selects

7

for shipment to the city or town where DEALER'S place of business is located, or by delivering them to DEALER at any point that CMC may establish.

16 ACCEPTANCE OF SHIPMENTS

If DEALER requests diversion of CMC products shipped to DEALER or if CMC is required to divert any CMC products because DEALER fails, refuses or is unable to accept delivery of such products, or if there is a failure to pay as required for the products that DEALER has ordered, or a failure to accept C.O.D. shipments of products DEALER has ordered, CMC may divert the shipments and charge DEALER the demurrage, transport, storage and other expense arising by reason of any such diversion.

17 OTHER CHARGES

DEALER shall be responsible for and will pay any and all charges for demurrage, storage or other charges accruing after arrival of shipment at the distribution point established by CMC.

18 DELAY OR FAILURE TO FILL ORDERS

CMC shall not be liable for delay or failure to fill orders that have been accepted, where such delay or failure is the result of any event beyond the control of CMC including, but not in limitation of the generality of the foregoing, any law, regulation or administrative or judicial order, or any acts of God, wars, riots, wrecks, fires, strikes, lockouts, other labor troubles, embargoes, blockades, delay or failure of any other supplier or carrier of CMC to deliver or make delivery of CMC products, or any material shortage or curtailment of production, including those due to economic conditions, or any discontinuance of manufacture or sale of products by CMC or its suppliers. Furthermore, CMC will not be liable for delay or failure to fill orders when such delay or failure is pursuant to any provision under this Agreement.

19 OPTION TO REPURCHASE DAMAGED VEHICLES

DEALER shall notify CMC if any new and unused CMC vehicle in DEALER'S possession has sustained major damage as defined in the Warranty Policy and Procedure Manual. To preserve the quality and value of new CMC vehicles ordered for the public, CMC shall have the option to divert such a vehicle prior to delivery to DEALER or repurchase from DEALER all or any of such vehicles at a price equal to the net purchase price paid by DEALER to CMC. DEALER agrees to assign its rights under any insurance contract related to the repurchased CMC vehicles to CMC. CMC shall make appropriate payment for repurchased CMC vehicles directly to any lien holder or, if there is no lien, directly to DEALER.

20 CLAIMS FOR DAMAGE OR SHORTAGE

CMC shall not be liable for loss of or damage to CMC products sold hereunder occurring after delivery thereof to DEALER, DEALER'S agent, or a carrier within the North American Continent for shipment to DEALER, as provided in Paragraph 15 of this Agreement. Should any products sold under this Agreement be delivered in damaged condition or with shortages, claims for said damages or shortages shall be made in accordance with CMC's then current policies and procedures. To the extent required by law, DEALER shall notify the purchaser of a vehicle of any damage sustained by such vehicle prior to sale. DEALER shall indemnify and hold CMC harmless from any liability resulting from DEALER'S failure to so notify such purchasers.

21 PRICES, CHARGES, TERMS OF PURCHASE AND PAYMENT

CMC shall notify DEALER from time to time of the prices, charges and terms of purchase for products sold under this Agreement and shall charge DEALER for such products according to the prices, charges and terms of purchase in effect at the date of shipment. CMC reserves the right, without prior notice, to change prices, charges and

8

terms of purchase for any product sold under this Agreement.

DEALER shall pay CMC for products sold under this Agreement in lawful money of the United States of America by such method and/or in such manner as CMC may announce from time to time or approve in writing, with collection charges, if any, added.

If not included in the price, DEALER shall pay all excise or other taxes which may be levied on the products purchased hereunder or on the sale, shipment, ownership or use thereof. Further, DEALER certifies as of the date of each purchase hereunder that all products purchased hereunder are purchased for resale, retail lease or demonstration purposes.

22 CHANGE IN PRICE

Should CMC reduce the wholesale price at factory of any CMC vehicle (not including accessories and optional equipment) of a particular yearly model, line and body style then currently in production, CMC shall refund to DEALER in cash or by a credit against DEALER'S indebtedness to CMC, for each new, unused and unsold CMC vehicle (not including demonstrators) of that particular model, line and body style that at the time of the reduction is in DEALER'S stock or in transit to DEALER, an amount equal to the difference between the reduced wholesale price and the wholesale price paid to CMC by DEALER.

If, at the time of the official model introduction date (as determined by CMC) of a new yearly model, CMC announces a wholesale price of any CMC vehicle (not including accessories and optional equipment) of any particular body style and line of the new model which is below the wholesale price of a vehicle of the same body style and line of the discontinued yearly model, CMC shall refund to DEALER in cash or by credit against DEALER'S indebtedness to CMC an amount equal to the difference between the reduced wholesale price and the wholesale price of the same body style and line of the discontinued yearly model. Such refund will apply only to new, unused and unsold CMC vehicles (not including demonstrators) of the particular body style and line of the discontinued yearly model that on the official model introduction date (as determined by CMC) of the new yearly model is in DEALER'S stock or in transit to DEALER, unless CMC determines that the line or particular body style of the new yearly model is so changed in size, design, equipment, specifications or price as, for all practical purposes, to make the line a new and different line or to make the particular body style a new and different body style of the discontinued yearly model.

Notwithstanding the provisions of the two paragraphs immediately above, in any case where items considered standard equipment on a current vehicle or on a vehicle of the discontinued yearly model are not included as standard equipment on the corresponding vehicle with a reduced wholesale price or on the corresponding vehicle of the new model, any wholesale price decrease resulting from the exclusion of such standard equipment will not be included in any refund under this Paragraph 22.

In order to qualify for a refund in either case set forth above, DEALER must make a written claim, supported by adequate evidence, within thirty (30) days of the effective date of the reduction in price or the official model introduction date of the new yearly model.

Should CMC increase the wholesale price of any CMC vehicle, said price increase will not apply to an order submitted to CMC by DEALER prior to the date the notification of such price increase was issued if the order was submitted for the specific purpose of fulfilling a valid and legitimate purchase agreement between DEALER and a retail purchaser and if such an order was properly identified in the manner required by CMC and was delivered to the ordering retail purchaser.

23 SALE AND SUPPLY OF PARTS

DEALER shall not represent, sell, offer for sale or use in repairing CMC vehicles, parts which are represented as new or remanufactured Chrysler Corporation, CMC, or Mopar parts or parts which are represented to be manufactured or produced by any company directly involved in the manufacture of the vehicles specified in the Motor Vehicle

9

Addendum to this Agreement, unless such parts are in fact manufactured, remanufactured or designed for or by Chrysler Corporation, CMC, Mopar or a company directly involved in the manufacture of said specified vehicles and are properly identified as Chrysler Corporation, CMC, Mopar parts or parts of said directly involved companies with the respective consent of each of the aforementioned organizations.

DEALER at all times shall keep on hand in DEALER'S place of business the number and assortment of Chrysler Corporation, CMC or Mopar parts that in CMC's judgment is necessary to meet the service requirements of DEALER'S CMC customers and to meet all of DEALER'S obligations under this Agreement.

24 COLLECTION OF INDEBTEDNESS

CMC may apply to any amount owed by DEALER to CMC or to any of CMC's affiliates any credit owing to DEALER by CMC or any of its affiliates. As used in this Agreement, "affiliate" means Chrysler Corporation and any of its subsidiaries or their subsidiaries, or any other corporation, partnership or other legal entity which has an ownership interest in CMC or any corporation, partnership or other legal entity in which CMC has an ownership interest, or any subsidiary thereof.

Should DEALER assign its right to amounts owed to DEALER by CMC to any third party, prior to executing such an assignment DEALER shall notify such third party of CMC's first priority right to such credits.

25 TITLE

Title to products CMC sells to DEALER hereunder and risk of loss will pass to DEALER on delivery of the products to DEALER, DEALER'S agent, or the carrier, whichever occurs first. However, CMC retains a lien for payment on the products so sold until paid for in full, in cash. CMC will receive negotiable instruments only as conditional payment.

26 WARRANTY AND INDEMNIFICATION FOR PRODUCT LIABILITY LITIGATION

(a) WARRANTY

CMC's warranty on new CMC vehicles, as in effect from time to time, will be as set forth in Chrysler Motors Corporation's Warranty Policy and Procedure Manual. CMC shall supply sufficient copies of CMC's then current CMC vehicle warranty to DEALER to permit DEALER, in accordance with DEALER'S obligation under Paragraph 11 of this Agreement, to provide a copy to each purchaser from DEALER of a new CMC vehicle. EXCEPT FOR THE CMC WARRANTY, THERE ARE NO OTHER EXPRESS OR IMPLIED WARRANTIES MADE OR DEEMED TO HAVE BEEN MADE TO ANY PERSON BY CMC APPLICABLE TO PRODUCTS SOLD UNDER THIS AGREEMENT. THE CMC WARRANTY WILL BE EXPRESSLY IN LIEU OF ANY OTHER WARRANTY, EXPRESS OR IMPLIED, INCLUDING BUT NOT LIMITED TO, ANY IMPLIED WARRANTY OF MERCHANTABILITY OR FITNESS FOR A PARTICULAR PURPOSE; AND THE REMEDIES SET FORTH IN SUCH WARRANTY WILL BE THE ONLY REMEDIES AVAILABLE TO ANY PERSON WITH RESPECT TO PRODUCTS SOLD HEREUNDER. CMC neither assumes nor authorizes any other person, including DEALER, to assume for CMC any other obligation or liability in regard to such products.

(b) INDEMNIFICATION FOR PRODUCT LIABILITY LITIGATION

If a product liability lawsuit is filed naming DEALER as a defendant and it is determined that the bodily injury or property damage alleged by the plaintiff was caused solely by a design defect or a defect created by CMC in the manufacture or assembly of a CMC vehicle, part or accessory, which latter defect was not reasonably susceptible of discovery by DEALER in either DEALER'S new car preparation or subsequent servicing during the warranty period, then CMC shall indemnify and hold DEALER harmless from losses, damages and

10

expenses, including reasonable attorneys' fees, resulting from such product liability lawsuit. As used in this Paragraph 26(b), a "product liability lawsuit" shall mean a lawsuit seeking damages for bodily injury or property damage allegedly sustained in a motor vehicle accident, and which injury or damage is alleged to have been caused in any part by a defect in the design, manufacture or assembly of a CMC vehicle, part or accessory.

Whenever DEALER intends to request CMC to indemnify DEALER with respect to a product liability lawsuit, DEALER shall, within five (5) business days after service of the complaint, notify CMC in writing and shall provide at that time copies of any pleadings which may have been served, together with all information then available regarding the circumstances giving rise to such product liability lawsuit. Any such notices shall be sent by certified mail to the attention of the Office of the General Counsel, Chrysler Motors Corporation, Post Office Box 1919, Detroit, Michigan 48288 or such other address as CMC may designate in writing to DEALER. Upon such request for indemnification, CMC shall have the option, upon reasonable notice to DEALER, to retain counsel and assume full control over the defense of the lawsuit. If CMC is prevented by DEALER from exercising this option, CMC's obligation hereunder to indemnify DEALER shall be rendered null and void and be of no force or effect.

(c) REPAIR/REPLACE REQUIREMENTS

This provision shall apply if DEALER is located in a state which has in effect or hereafter adopts or enacts any law or regulation imposing liability on a motor vehicle manufacturer, importer, distributor and/or dealer for sale of a vehicle presumed under such law or regulation to be defective by reason, *inter alia*, of repeated unsuccessful attempts to repair such vehicle within a specified period of time or by reason of such vehicle being unavailable and out of service to the purchaser for a specified period of time.

DEALER shall make a good faith effort to immediately notify CMC in writing of the existence of any vehicle which may become subject to such law or regulation prior to a presumption of liability arising under such law or regulation from the inability to repair or correct a nonconformity or condition of a vehicle.

27 CHANGE OF MODELS, PARTS AND ACCESSORIES DECLARED OBSOLETE OR DISCONTINUED

CMC at any time may discontinue any or all models, lines or body styles and may revise, change or modify their construction or classification. All DEALER orders for specified CMC vehicles shall refer to models, lines and body styles in production at the time CMC receives the orders unless DEALER specifies otherwise. CMC at any time may declare obsolete or discontinue any or all parts, accessories and other merchandise. CMC may act under this Paragraph 27 without notice and, except as set forth in Paragraph 22 of this Agreement, without any obligation to DEALER by reason of DEALER'S previous purchases.

28 TERMINATION

(a) DEALER may terminate this Agreement on not less than thirty (30) days written notice.

(b) CMC may terminate this Agreement on not less than sixty (60) days written notice for the following reasons:

(i) the failure of DEALER to fully perform any of DEALER'S undertakings under Paragraph 11(a) of this Agreement or failure of DEALER to meet its minimum service satisfaction requirements set forth in Paragraph 11(b) of this Agreement within one hundred and eighty (180) days after notification by CMC that DEALER has not fully performed the aforementioned undertakings, obligations or requirements, or

(ii) the failure of DEALER to perform fully any of DEALER'S undertakings or obligations as set forth in this Agreement including, but without limiting the generality of the foregoing, the undertakings and obligations set forth in Paragraphs 11(b) through 11(g) or Paragraphs 12, 13, 14, 23, 26(c) or 35 of this Agreement, or

11

(iii) the death of any person listed in Paragraph 2 of this Agreement (other than the death of DEALER if DEALER is a sole proprietorship) or the failure of any such person so listed to continue active and substantial personal participation in the management of the Dealership Operation as required by Paragraph 2, or

(iv) a misrepresentation of or change, whether voluntary or by operation of law, in the ownership if DEALER is an individual or of the ownership interests listed in Paragraph 3 of this Agreement resulting in a transfer of control or majority interest in the capital stock or partnership interest of DEALER, unless CMC has given prior written approval to such change, or

(v) any material misrepresentation by any of DEALER'S owners or executives as to any fact relied upon by CMC in entering into this Agreement, or

(vi) a disagreement, dispute or controversy between or among principals, partners, managers, officers or stockholders of DEALER that, in the opinion of CMC, may adversely affect the operation, management or business of DEALER, or

(vii) the conviction of DEALER, or a partner, principal stockholder, officer or manager of DEALER of any crime that in CMC's opinion may affect adversely the operation or business of DEALER or the name, goodwill or reputation of Chrysler Corporation, CMC, CMC products or DEALER, or

(viii) failure of DEALER to pay any indebtedness of DEALER to CMC in accordance with the applicable terms and conditions required by CMC, or

(ix) impairment of the reputation or financial standing of DEALER or any of DEALER'S owners or executives or discovery by CMC of any facts existing prior to or at the time of signing this Agreement which, in CMC's opinion, tend to impair such reputation or financial standing, or

(x) any submission by DEALER to CMC of a false or fraudulent application or claim, or any claim or statements in support thereof, for payment including, but not limited to, pre-delivery inspection or adjustments, warranty repairs, special policy or campaign adjustments or repairs performed by DEALER, sales incentives, parts compensation, or any other discount, allowance, refund or credit under any plan, provision or other program offered by CMC, whether or not DEALER offers or makes to CMC or CMC seeks or obtains from DEALER restitution of any payments made to DEALER on the basis of any such false or fraudulent application, claim or statement, or

(xi) conduct by DEALER which, in DEALER'S dealings with customers or the public, is fraudulent or constitutes a deceptive or unfair act or practice, or

(xii) DEALER'S failure to comply with requirements set forth in the National Traffic and Motor Vehicle Safety Act of 1966 or any other legislation or regulation pertaining to safety, air pollution or noise control which may be imposed on automobile dealers or with reasonable requests of CMC made in conjunction with action being taken on its part to comply with the aforementioned statutory or regulatory requirements, or

(xiii) the notification of termination or termination, for any reason, of any other Chrysler Motors Corporation Dealer Agreement(s) which may be in effect between DEALER and Chrysler Motors Corporation, or

(xiv) the failure of DEALER to comply fully with the policies, procedures, directives and rulings of the CMC Customer Arbitration Board, or

(xv) CMC offers a new Sales and Service Agreement to all of its dealers selling the line(s) of vehicles set forth on the Motor Vehicle Addendum.

Termination by CMC will not be effective unless the President or a Vice President or the National Dealer Placement Manager of Chrysler Motors Corporation signs the notice.

(c) Notwithstanding the provisions above, this Agreement will terminate automatically without notice from either party on:

12

(i) the death of DEALER, if DEALER is a sole proprietorship, or

(ii) an attempted or actual assignment or transfer of this Agreement or an attempted or actual transfer of a substantial portion of dealership assets by DEALER without the prior written consent of CMC, or

(iii) an assignment by DEALER for the benefit of creditors, or

(iv) the insolvency of DEALER, or the preparation of any petition by or for DEALER for voluntary institution of any proceeding under the Bankruptcy Act or under any State insolvency law, whether or not such petition is ever filed; or the involuntary institution against DEALER of any proceeding under the Bankruptcy Act or under any State insolvency law which is not vacated within ten (10) days from the institution thereof; or the appointment of a receiver or other officer having similar powers for DEALER or DEALER'S business which is not removed within ten (10) days from his/her appointment; or any levy under attachment, execution or similar process which is not within ten (10) days vacated or removed by payment or bonding, or

(v) the discontinuance by CMC of the production or distribution of all CMC vehicles listed on the Motor Vehicle Addendum, or

(vi) the failure of DEALER to fully conduct its Dealership Operations for seven (7) consecutive business days, or

(vii) the loss, termination or expiration of any license or permit required by law for DEALER to perform DEALER'S obligations under this Agreement or otherwise conduct business as a new vehicle dealer for CMC products.

Termination of this Agreement will cancel all unfilled orders for vehicles, parts and accessories.

The obligations of the parties to this Agreement as set forth in Paragraphs 9, 21, 24, 26(a), 26(b), 29, 30, 31 and 35 shall remain in full force and effect after the effective date of termination.

29 REPURCHASE OBLIGATIONS UPON TERMINATION

Except when termination of this Agreement will be followed by CMC issuing to DEALER, or to DEALER'S successors, assigns, heirs or devisees, a new agreement of any sort for the sale and service of CMC vehicles, including, but not in limitation of the generality of the foregoing, such an agreement with a term of limited duration, CMC agrees to buy and DEALER agrees to sell, free and clear of any liens and encumbrances, within ninety (90) days after the effective date of any termination under Paragraph 28:

(a) All new, unused and unsold specified CMC vehicles (not including demonstrators), unmodified and in good, undamaged condition, of the yearly model current at the effective date of termination that were purchased by DEALER from CMC and that are on the effective date of termination the property of and in the possession, custody and control of DEALER. The repurchase price will be the dealer net invoice price at the time of DEALER'S purchase of each such vehicle from CMC, less any applicable rebates, incentive payments, adjustments or allowances paid or credited by CMC to DEALER. CMC shall not be required to repurchase CMC vehicles built on DEALER'S special order to other than CMC standard specifications.

(b) All new, unused and undamaged CMC parts that are priced and identified as eligible for return in Chrysler Motors Corporation's then current parts lists and that were purchased by DEALER from CMC and are on the effective date of termination the property of and in the possession, custody and control of DEALER, at current listed prices (exclusive of transportation charges). CMC shall add to such current listed prices (exclusive of transportation charges) an allowance of five percent (5%) of such prices for packing and crating by DEALER and a credit for transportation charges paid by DEALER to ship such parts to the destination CMC designates. CMC shall subtract from such current listed prices (exclusive of transportation charges) all maximum allowable discounts and the cost of any necessary refinishing, reconditioning or repacking to restore the parts to their original

13

saleable condition, and CMC's cost of determining whether such parts are free and clear of all liens and encumbrances. Prior to purchase by CMC, DEALER shall deliver the parts (tagged and inventoried in accordance with CMC's instructions) for inspection F.O.B. at any point CMC may designate. CMC's determination of the quantity and value of the parts returned will be conclusive unless DEALER notifies CMC in writing within 15 days of receiving the check or statement of account for such parts returned of any error made in such determination.

(c) All new, unused and undamaged CMC accessories or accessories packages for the yearly model current at the effective date of termination, complete as supplied to and purchased by DEALER from CMC during the twelve (12) months immediately preceding the effective date of termination and that are on the effective date of termination the property of and in the possession, custody and control of DEALER at the prices then applicable (less maximum allowable discounts) and current at the effective date of termination, exclusive of transportation charges. CMC shall add to such currently applicable prices an allowance of five percent (5%) of such prices (less maximum allowable discounts) for packing and crating by DEALER and a credit for transportation charges paid by DEALER in shipping such accessories to the destination CMC designates. CMC shall subtract from such currently applicable prices (less maximum allowable discounts) the cost of necessary refinishing, reconditioning or repackaging of such accessories or accessories packages to restore them to their original salable condition and CMC's cost of determining whether such accessories or accessories packages are free and clear of all liens and encumbrances. Prior to purchase by CMC, DEALER will deliver the accessories or accessories packages, tagged and inventoried in accordance with CMC's instructions, for inspection F.O.B. at any point CMC may designate. CMC's determination of the quantity and value of the accessories or accessories packages returned will be conclusive unless DEALER notifies CMC in writing within 15 days of receiving the check or statement of account for such accessories or accessories packages returned of any error made in such determination.

(d) All signs of a type required by CMC belonging to DEALER, showing the name "Chrysler Motors Corporation" or one of the designated trade names applicable only to CMC products or CMC's affiliated companies. CMC shall pay to DEALER for such signs the fair market value or the price for which DEALER purchased such signs, whichever is lower. CMC shall have the right, upon termination of this Agreement, to enter DEALER'S premises peacefully and remove all such signs.

(e) Special tools (in complete sets), of a type recommended by CMC, adapted only to the servicing of CMC vehicles and purchased by DEALER during the thirty-six (36) months immediately preceding the effective date of termination at a price and under terms and conditions to be agreed upon by CMC and DEALER.

CMC will pay DEALER for any items purchased pursuant to this Paragraph 29 within ninety (90) days of CMC's receipt and acceptance of said items, subject to Paragraph 24 of this Agreement.

30 DISPOSITION OF DEALER'S PREMISES

On termination of this Agreement by CMC on sixty (60) days' written notice pursuant to Paragraph 28 hereof, except when termination results because DEALER'S facilities have been closed for seven (7) consecutive business days or from a person named in Paragraph 2 of this Agreement ceasing to participate in the management of DEALER, CMC shall take the following action respecting DEALER'S premises as defined below (herein called the Premises), if DEALER so requests, and provided that DEALER has paid to CMC all monies owing to CMC:

(a) If, on DEALER'S receipt of notice of termination, DEALER owns the Premises:

CMC shall assist DEALER in effecting an orderly and equitable disposition of the Premises by a sale or lease. If necessary to effect such disposition, CMC, at its option, within a reasonable time shall lease the Premises from DEALER for at least one (1) year or purchase the Premises, or cause them

14

to be leased or purchased, on fair and equitable terms. In such event, DEALER and CMC shall agree on the value or rental value of the Premises for the purpose of either a sale or lease. If DEALER and CMC are unable to so agree, each shall appoint a disinterested qualified real estate appraiser and the two so appointed will agree on the value or rental value of the Premises, as the case may be. If the two appraisers are unable to agree, they shall select a third disinterested qualified real estate appraiser who shall determine such value. The value or rental value so determined shall be final and binding on both DEALER and CMC. If one or more appraisals are necessary, DEALER and CMC shall share equally the cost of such appraisals.

(b) If, on DEALER'S receipt of notice of termination, DEALER is leasing the Premises:

CMC shall assist DEALER in effecting an orderly and equitable disposition of DEALER'S leasehold interest in the Premises. If necessary to effect such disposition, CMC, at its option, within a reasonable time, for the remainder of the lease or for twelve (12) months, whichever period is shorter, shall (1) sublet the Premises from DEALER, or (2) take an assignment of the lease of the Premises from DEALER, or (3) pay DEALER monthly or otherwise, as the parties may agree, the lower of the rental specified in the lease or the fair rental value of the Premises determined in the manner provided in (a) above; provided, however, that DEALER may receive such payments under only one dealer agreement with CMC or Chrysler Corporation or any of their affiliates or subsidiaries.

(c) If DEALER owns part of the Premises and leases part of them, section (a) above will apply to the part owned and section (b) above to the part leased.

CMC shall have no obligation to DEALER under this Paragraph 30 if, after receipt of notice of termination, (1) DEALER in any way encumbers the Premises or DEALER'S interest in them or takes any other action respecting the Premises that would adversely affect any of CMC's obligations under this Paragraph 30, or performance thereof, or (2) DEALER receives and refuses a bona fide offer to purchase, lease or sublet all or substantially all of the Premises at a price and on terms that CMC believes are fair, or (3) DEALER'S lease of the Premises or part thereof is continued, renewed or extended by DEALER'S act or failure to act, or (4) DEALER fails or refuses to use DEALER'S best efforts to sell, lease or sublease the Premises or to notify CMC of any offer to buy, lease or sublease the Premises; or if, after the effective date of termination of this agreement, (a) the Premises or part thereof are used or occupied by anyone for any purpose, or (b) DEALER, if a proprietor, or any of the persons named in Paragraph 3 of this agreement is in the business of selling and/or servicing new or used motor vehicles in the Sales Locality referred to in this agreement or the general area surrounding it, or (c) DEALER, if a proprietor, or any of the persons named in Paragraph 3 of this agreement occupies or could, in CMC's opinion, occupy all or substantially all of the Premises for any business in which one or more of them engages.

"Premises" as used in this Paragraph 30 means the place or places of business in the Sales Locality (1) that DEALER uses exclusively to carry out DEALER'S obligations in selling and servicing new products under this agreement or jointly under this and any other agreement or agreements with CMC on the date of DEALER'S receipt of notice of termination and (2) are set forth in the Dealership Facilities and Location Addendum (Addenda).

To receive CMC's assistance as set forth in this Paragraph 30, DEALER must have operated continuously as a CMC dealer for the twelve (12) months immediately preceding the effective date of termination and must have given CMC a written request for such assistance within thirty (30) days after DEALER'S receipt of the notice of termination of this Agreement. On receipt of such request from DEALER, CMC will initiate compliance with its obligations under this Paragraph 30. If under section (b) above CMC elects to make monthly payments, then DEALER shall make written application for them on such forms and at such times as CMC reasonably may require. If DEALER requests assistance under this Paragraph 30, then CMC, at all reasonable times, shall have full access to the Premises and DEALER'S books and records pertaining to the Premises.

15

31 TRANSACTIONS AFTER TERMINATION

After the effective date of termination, if CMC, in its discretion, elects to fill retail orders of DEALER or otherwise transacts business related to the sale of CMC products with DEALER, all such transactions will be governed by the same terms that this Agreement provides, so far as those terms are applicable. Notwithstanding any such transactions, CMC shall not be deemed to have waived or rescinded the termination or have renewed this Agreement.

32 SUCCESSORS TO DEALER

On termination of this Agreement by reason of the death of DEALER if he is an individual, or on termination by CMC because of the death of any of the persons named in Paragraph 2 of this Agreement if DEALER is a partnership or corporation:

(a) If DEALER had so requested in writing (signed by DEALER if he is an individual or by those persons representing a majority of the ownership interest in DEALER if DEALER is a partnership or corporation), delivered to CMC during the lifetime of such decedent, CMC shall offer a Chrysler Motors Corporation Sales and Service Agreement (limited to a two-year term) to any person DEALER has nominated in such written request to CMC as the person DEALER desires to continue DEALER'S business after such death, provided that such nominated person has demonstrated operating qualifications satisfactory to CMC in the course of active, substantial and continuing participation in the management of DEALER'S organization, and possesses or is able to acquire within a reasonable time after such death, capital and facilities that are satisfactory to CMC, and will be able to exercise as much control over the operations and affairs of the dealership as the deceased exercised. Such Chrysler Motors Corporation Sales and Service Agreement shall be limited to a term of two (2) years and subject to earlier termination as provided therein. At least ninety (90) days before the expiration of the two (2) year term referred to above, CMC shall determine if the person granted said two (2) year agreement possesses the required capital and facilities and has satisfactorily performed the obligations under said two (2) year agreement. This determination will be based on said person's performance during the aforementioned two-year period to qualify for the standard Chrysler Motors Corporation Sales and Service Agreement then in effect. If CMC determines that said person possesses all such qualifications, then CMC shall offer such standard agreement to said person.

(b) CMC shall, if DEALER has not nominated a successor under this Paragraph 32 and has not named a person whose surviving spouse may hold a financial interest under Paragraph 33, review the qualifications of any remaining person named in Paragraph 2 of this Agreement. If any such person possesses operating qualifications satisfactory to CMC and possesses or is able to acquire within a reasonable time facilities and capital necessary to qualify as a CMC dealer, CMC shall offer such person a Chrysler Motors Corporation Sales and Service Agreement or Term Sales and Service Agreement, as CMC deems appropriate. If more than one such person qualifies, CMC will select the person or persons to whom an agreement will be offered.

33 SURVIVING SPOUSE'S FINANCIAL INTEREST

On termination of this Agreement by reason of the death of DEALER, if an individual, or on termination by CMC because of the death of any of the persons named in Paragraph 2 of this Agreement if DEALER is a partnership or corporation, the surviving spouse of the person who died may hold a financial interest in any successor dealership, provided that the following conditions are met:

(a) Prior to the death referred to above, DEALER had delivered to CMC a notice in writing signed by all the persons named in Paragraph 2 of this Agreement naming the deceased person (who must also be named in Paragraph 2 of this Agreement) as the person whose surviving spouse may hold the financial interest. DEALER may

16

name only one person but may, on written notice to CMC, signed as above, change the person named.

(b) Within sixty (60) days of the date of such death, the surviving spouse executes with the person or persons who will be named in Paragraph 2 of the CMC Sales and Service Agreement between CMC and the successor dealership a written agreement in which the surviving spouse agrees not to participate in any way in the management or operation of the successor dealership. Such agreement shall be delivered to CMC within fifteen (15) days after it has been signed by both parties. Notwithstanding the immediately foregoing provisions of this Paragraph 33(b), such an agreement not to participate need not be made if CMC has approved the surviving spouse as a person to be named in Paragraph 2 of the CMC Sales and Service Agreement between CMC and the successor dealership.

Nothing contained herein will obligate CMC to enter into a sales and service agreement with the surviving spouse or any person not otherwise acceptable to CMC or require CMC to continue this or any other agreement with the surviving spouse or any other person for any period of time beyond the time when CMC would have a right to terminate such an agreement in accordance with the terms thereof.

"Successor dealership" as used in this Paragraph 33 means a dealership (1) that qualifies for and enters into a Chrysler Motors Corporation Sales and Service Agreement with CMC, (2) that possesses and has the right to use the physical assets and organization that remain after the death first referred to in this Paragraph 33, and (3) in which the surviving spouse retains or acquires the financial interest as referred to above.

34 SALE OF DEALERSHIP ASSETS OR OWNERSHIP INTERESTS

CMC acknowledges that DEALER may at any time negotiate for the sale of its assets, and any of the owners of DEALER may at any time negotiate the sale of their ownership interests in DEALER, with any purchaser on such terms as may be agreed upon by them and the prospective purchaser. Any such sale, however will not create any obligation of CMC to do business with any such purchaser.

DEALER acknowledges that, in connection with any such sale to any such purchaser, this Agreement is not assignable without the written consent of CMC. If the proposed purchase and sale arrangement contemplates or is conditioned upon the prospective purchaser being granted by CMC an agreement similar to this Agreement, DEALER shall provide CMC written notice thereof prior to any completion or closing of the transactions contemplated by such purchase and sale arrangement and the prospective purchaser shall apply to CMC, on forms provided by CMC for such an agreement. In order that CMC can determine whether effective dealership operations will result if the prospective purchaser's application is approved, CMC may, in processing the application, without liability to DEALER or any such owners, counsel with the prospective purchaser regarding any matters including, but not limited to, matters relating to the investments in the proposed dealership operations, the management and the facilities that may be required by CMC.

If DEALER or such owners have notified CMC, and the prospective purchaser has made application as provided above, CMC shall consider and process such application, together with the applications of any others for such an agreement, in accordance with its established procedures and CMC shall not unreasonably withhold its approval of such an application. Any such approval shall be conditioned upon payment in full by DEALER of all DEALER'S obligations to CMC, which payment shall be made at CMC's option on or before the sale to the prospective purchaser. If CMC decides not to continue authorized dealership operations at DEALER'S premises, however, no such application will be considered or processed by CMC and CMC shall so notify DEALER or such owners and the prospective purchaser.

Notwithstanding the foregoing provision of this Paragraph 34, even if the prospective purchaser of DEALER'S assets or ownership interests in DEALER meets CMC's qualifications for appointment as a dealer, CMC may, at its discretion, offer

17

to purchase DEALER'S assets or ownership interest in DEALER on the same terms as said qualified prospective purchaser. If CMC makes such an offer, DEALER shall sell the dealership assets to CMC on the aforementioned same terms. However, if CMC has not made such an offer within fifteen (15) business days after CMC's receipt of the afformentioned application and all necessary information, CMC shall be deemed to have declined to offer to purchase DEALER'S assets or ownership interests in DEALER. Additionally, DEALER may request in writing that CMC predetermine whether a proposed purchaser would be acceptable to CMC prior to entering into an agreement to sell DEALER'S assets or ownership interests. If such a request is made, CMC shall make such determination. If CMC determines that the proposed purchaser is acceptable to CMC, CMC shall decline to make an offer to purchase such assets or ownership interest. Such determination of acceptability and declination will not act to deny CMC its right not to approve the proposed purchase and sale arrangement as set forth above.

35 USE OF TRADE NAMES, TRADEMARKS, LOGOS, ETC.

DEALER may use in DEALER'S corporate, firm or trade name in a manner CMC approves in writing any trade name applicable to those CMC products set forth in the Motor Vehicle Addendum. DEALER shall discontinue immediately the use of any such trade names in DEALER'S corporate, firm or trade name when CMC so requests in writing and DEALER shall take such steps as may be necessary or appropriate, in CMC's opinion, to change such corporate, firm or trade name so as to eliminate any trade name of CMC products therefrom.

Except as specifically allowed herein, DEALER shall not use, in any manner, the trademarks, trade names, insignias or the like of CMC, its divisions, affiliates or subsidiaries without CMC's explicit and prior written consent. DEALER shall discontinue immediately any and all use of any such trademark, trade name, insignias or the like when CMC so requests in writing.

On termination of this Agreement, DEALER shall discontinue immediately using any trade names applicable to CMC vehicles or other products in DEALER'S corporate, firm or trade name or using any trade names, trademarks or insignias adopted or used by CMC or its divisions, affiliates or subsidiaries, and will take such steps as may be necessary or appropriate, in CMC's opinion, to change such corporate, firm or trade name so as to eliminate any trade names applicable to CMC products therefrom, and will discontinue using any signs, stationery or advertising containing any such trade names, trademarks or insignias or anything else that might make it appear that DEALER is an authorized dealer for CMC vehicles or products.

36 DEALER IS NOT AGENT

This Agreement does not create the relationship of principal and agent between CMC and DEALER, and under no circumstances is either party to be considered the agent of the other.

37 INABILITY TO PERFORM

In addition to any other exemption from liability specifically provided for in this Agreement, neither DEALER nor CMC will be liable for failure to perform its part of this Agreement when the failure is due to fire, flood, strikes or other labor disputes, accident, war, riot, insurrection, acts of government, governmental regulation or other circumstances beyond the control of the parties.

38 ASSIGNMENT

DEALER may not assign or transfer this Agreement, or any part hereof, or delegate any duties or obligations under this Agreement without the written consent of CMC, executed by the President or a Vice President or the National Dealer Placement Manager of Chrysler Motors Corporation.

39 NON-WAIVER

The waiver by either party of any breach or violation of or default under any provision of this Agreement will not operate as a waiver of such

18

provision or of any subsequent breach or violation thereof or default thereunder.

40 SEVERABILITY

If any provision of this Agreement should be held invalid or unenforceable for any reason whatsoever or to violate any law of the United States, the District of Columbia or any State, this Agreement is to be considered divisible as to such provision, and such provision is to be deemed deleted from this Agreement or, in the event that it should be held to violate only the laws of the District of Columbia or of any State, to be inapplicable within the territory thereof, and the remainder of this Agreement will be valid and binding as if such provision were not included herein or as if it were included herein only with respect to territories outside of such District or State, as the case may be.

41 TITLES

The titles appearing in this Agreement have been inserted for convenient reference only and do not in any way affect the construction, interpretation or meaning of the text.

42 INTERPRETATION

In the event of a dispute hereunder, the terms of this Agreement shall be construed in accordance with the laws of the State of Michigan.

43 VENUE

Although it is the intent of the parties that all disputes between them be resolved pursuant to the arbitration provisions set forth in Paragraph 9 of this Agreement, in the event that a dispute should arise between the parties which is determined to be nonarbitrable, only the Federal District Court for the Eastern District of Michigan shall be deemed to have venue, to the extent that federal subject matter jurisdiction exists, or the Michigan Circuit Court for the County of Oakland shall be deemed to have venue, if there is no federal subject matter jurisdiction. The parties hereby waive any objection to the aforesaid venue; provided, however, that nothing within this paragraph should be construed as a waiver of the parties' preeminent right to the arbitration of disputes arising between them.

44 NOTICES

Unless otherwise specifically required by the terms of this Agreement, any notice required or permitted under this Agreement must be in writing and will be sufficient if delivered personally, or sent through the United States mail system, postage prepaid, addressed, as appropriate, either to DEALER at the place of business designated in this Agreement, or at such other address as DEALER may designate in writing to CMC, or to Chrysler Motors Corporation at Post Office Box 857, Detroit, Michigan 48288 or such other address as CMC may designate in writing to DEALER.

19

Document 7-1. (*continued*)

MOTOR VEHICLE ADDENDUM
To
Chrysler Motors Corporation
SALES AND SERVICE AGREEMENT

____
Dealer Firm Name

____
City State

As of the effective date of this Motor Vehicle Addendum to the Chrysler Motors Corporation Sales and Service Agreement between Dealer and Chrysler Motors Corporation, Dealer, as an authorized Chrysler Motors Corporation dealer, has a non-exclusive right to purchase the following new models of Motor Vehicles:

This Motor Vehicle Addendum shall remain in effect unless and until superseded by a new Motor Vehicle Addendum furnished Dealer by Chrysler Motors Corporation.

Effective Date: ________________

CHRYSLER MOTORS CORPORATION

By ______________________________
Signature

____
Title

SPECIMEN

Arbitration Election Addendum DAP-28 (Rev. 4-89)

Paragraph 9 of the ______________________________
Sales and Service Agreement(s) (Paragraph 7 if this is a Term Sales and Service Agreement), currently in effect, provides for mandatory binding arbitration of all disputes. By this Addendum, DEALER is given the option of excluding such arbitration from the Agreement(s).

If DEALER desires to have all disputes submitted to arbitration as set forth in the Agreement(s), DEALER should check the box next to the word "YES".

If DEALER does not want to have all disputes submitted to arbitration as set forth in the Agreement(s), DEALER should check the box next to the word "NO". By checking the "NO" box and signing this form, the arbitration provision is deemed to be excluded from the Agreement(s).

☐ YES, DEALER elects to have all disputes submitted to arbitration.

☐ NO, DEALER elects not to submit disputes to arbitration.

JEEP EAGLE SALES CORPORATION

____
(DEALER FIRM NAME)

By ______________________________
(SIGNATURE)

____
(DBA)

____
(TITLE)

____
(CITY) (STATE)

____
(DATE)

By ______________________________
(INDIVIDUAL DULY AUTHORIZED TO SIGN)

CHRYSLER MOTORS CORPORATION

____
(TITLE)

By ______________________________
(SIGNATURE)

Five Digit Code# ______________________________

____
(TITLE)

SPECIMEN

____
(DATE)

**NOTICE OF SALES LOCALITY DESCRIPTION
TO
CHRYSLER MOTORS CORPORATION
SALES AND SERVICE AGREEMENT(S)**

Effective ____________________________ , DEALER will have the non-exclusive right, subject to the provisions of the Chrysler Motors Corporation Sales and Service Agreement(s), to purchase from CMC for resale at retail (which includes lease and rental units) such new CMC vehicles as are described in the Motor Vehicle Addendum to DEALER'S Chrysler Motors Corporation Sales and Service Agreement(s), and parts and accessories therefor, in the following communities and/or areas of which some or all may be defined by census tracts as defined by the U.S. Department of Commerce or by the service areas of the U.S. Post Office Stations servicing said communities and/or areas which will constitute DEALER'S Sales Locality.

STATE	COUNTY	CITY	STATE	COUNTY	CITY	STATE	COUNTY	CITY

The above Sales Locality is hereby designated as the territory of DEALER'S responsibility for the sale of CMC vehicles and vehicle parts and accessories therefor, and will be used by CMC to determine DEALER'S Minimum Sales Responsibility (MSR) and to measure DEALER'S sales performance in relation to such MSR, and to evaluate DEALER'S performance pertaining to other matters relating to DEALER'S operations.

The Sales Locality described above will continue to be employed for the foregoing purposes until changed by written notice to DEALER.

Chrysler Motors Corporation

By: ____________________

(Dealer Firm Name) (DBA Name)

Title: ____________________

(City) (State)

SPECIMEN

CHRYSLER MOTORS

Chrysler Motors Corporation
Chrysler Center

December 31, 1988

TO: ALL CHRYSLER, PLYMOUTH AND/OR DODGE DEALERS OPERATING UNDER CHRYSLER MOTORS CORPORATION'S STANDARD OR TERM SALES AND SERVICE AGREEMENT(S)

Pursuant to Paragraph 8 of Chrysler Motors Corporation's standard Chrysler, Plymouth and/or Dodge Sales and Service Agreement(s) or Paragraph 6 of Chrysler Motors Corporation's Term Sales and Service Agreement, as the case may be, please be advised that Chrysler Motors Corporation has deemed it advisable to amend certain terms and provisions contained in the booklet entitled "Chrysler Motors Corporation Sales and Service Agreement Additional Terms and Provisions" (marked "Form 88CMC") as follows:

1. Paragraph 11(b). Service. The second paragraph of Paragraph 11(b) is modified to read as follows (the underlined portion setting forth the new provisions):

> After six (6) quarters of operation, including operation under any preceding CMC Dealer Agreement, DEALER shall, at all times during this Agreement, meet its minimum service satisfaction requirements by maintaining a rating on Chrysler Motors Corporation's Customer Satisfaction Index, Prep-It-Right and Deliver-It-Right evaluations (as determined by Chrysler Motors Corporation from time to time, based upon surveys conducted of DEALER'S customers) which is equal to or greater than the average Customer Satisfaction Index, Prep-It-Right and Deliver-It-Right ratings for the national Sales Level Group (as those groups are determined by CMC from time to time) in which DEALER is included within DEALER'S Sales Zone (as said Sales Zone is determined by CMC from time to time). CMC will review, at least once a year, DEALER'S performance under the Customer Satisfaction Index and DEALER'S Prep-It-Right and Deliver-It-Right ratings.

2. Paragraph 14. Orders. The last sentence of the second paragraph of Paragraph 14, "Orders," is deleted. The deleted sentence read as follows: "CMC shall not be obligated to accept any order from DEALER for any reason including, but not limited to, default of DEALER on any obligation to CMC."

3. Paragraph 26. Warranty and Indemnification for Product Liability Litigation; Subparagraph (b): Indemnification for Product Liability

12000 Chrysler Drive
Highland Park MI 48288-0857

December 31, 1988
Page 2

Litigation. The first sentence of the second paragraph of Paragraph 26(b) is modified to read as follows:

> Whenever DEALER intends to request CMC to indemnify DEALER with respect to a product liability lawsuit, DEALER shall file with the court an appropriate response which will prevent a default judgment from being taken against DEALER, and DEALER shall, within thirty (30) business days after service of the complaint, notify CMC in writing and shall provide at that time copies of any pleadings which may have been served, together with all information then available regarding the circumstances giving rise to such product liability lawsuit.

4. Paragraph 28. Termination. Paragraphs 28(b)(i) and (vii) are modified to read as follows:

> (i) in accordance with CMC's ordinary and customary procedures, upon the failure of DEALER to fully perform any of DEALER'S undertakings under Paragraph 11(a) of this Agreement or failure of DEALER to meet its minimum service satisfaction requirements set forth in Paragraph 11(b) of this Agreement within one hundred and eighty (180) days after notification by CMC that DEALER has not fully performed the aforementioned undertakings, obligations or requirements, or

* * *

> (vii) the conviction of DEALER or any individual named in Paragraph 2 or 3 herein of any crime that, in CMC's opinion, may affect adversely the operation or business of DEALER or the name, goodwill or reputation of Chrysler Corporation, CMC, CMC products, or Dealer, or

5. Paragraph 34. Sale of Dealership Assets. The last paragraph of Paragraph 34, "Sale of Dealership Assets or Ownership Interests," is modified to read as follows (the underlined portion setting forth the new provisions):

> Notwithstanding the foregoing provision of this Paragraph 34, even if the prospective purchaser of DEALER'S assets or ownership interests in DEALER meets CMC's qualifications for appointment as a dealer, CMC may, at its discretion, offer to purchase DEALER'S assets or ownership interest in DEALER on the same terms as said qualified prospective purchaser. If CMC makes such an offer, DEALER shall sell the dealership assets to CMC on the aforementioned same terms. However, if CMC has not made such an offer within fifteen (15) business days after CMC's receipt of the aforementioned application and all necessary information, CMC shall be deemed to have declined to offer

December 31, 1988
Page 3

to purchase DEALER'S assets or ownership interests in DEALER. Within fifteen (15) days after CMC has communicated its offer to purchase DEALER'S assets or ownership interest in DEALER, as described above, DEALER may withdraw, by written notification to CMC, its proposal to sell said assets or ownership interest to any purchaser, in which case CMC's aforementioned offer to purchase will be null and void. Additionally, DEALER may request in writing that CMC predetermine whether a proposed purchaser would be acceptable to CMC prior to entering into an agreement to sell DEALER'S assets or ownership interests. If such a request is made, CMC shall make such determination. If CMC determines that the proposed purchaser is acceptable to CMC, CMC shall decline to make an offer to purchase such assets or ownership interest. Such determination of acceptability and declination will not act to deny CMC its right not to approve the proposed purchase and sale arrangement as set forth above.

6. Paragraph 40. Severability. The following paragraph is added at the end of the current Paragraph 40, "Severability":

Notwithstanding the foregoing, when, in the absence of this Paragraph 40, Federal law would otherwise be deemed to preempt a state law which purports to limit or prohibit any right, obligation or duty under any provision of this Agreement, then this Paragraph 40 shall not be construed to delete any such provision of this Agreement and the parties hereto will be subject to the terms of such provision as if such a state law did not exist.

7. Paragraph 43. Venue. Paragraph 43, "Venue", is hereby deleted from all Chrysler, Plymouth and Dodge Sales and Service Agreements and Term Sales and Service Agreements.

These amendments will be effective ninety (90) days after the date hereof.

Please retain this letter with your sales agreement papers.

Sincerely,

CHRYSLER MOTORS CORPORATION

M. Joswick

M. Joswick
National Dealer Placement Manager

552WSH/vlb

LICENSE AGREEMENT

THIS AGREEMENT, effective as of the last day of execution hereof, made at Detroit, Michigan, U.S.A., between Licensee, a corporation of the State of Delaware, having a place of business at Detroit, Michigan, hereinafter referred to as "Licensee" and Licensor, a corporation of the State of Delaware, and having a place of business at Southfield, Michigan, hereinafter referred to as "Licensor;"

WITNESSETH:

WHEREAS, Licensor is the owner of United States Patent No. __________, entitled "_____________________________", issued ______________, 19___, hereafter referred to as "Licensed Patent;" and

WHEREAS, Licensee is desirous of obtaining certain rights under said patent;

NOW, THEREFORE, the parties hereto agree as follows:

ARTICLE I - DEFINITIONS

(a) The term "Licensee," as used herein shall include Licensee and any present or future United States or Canadian entities owned or controlled, directly or indirectly, by Licensee.

(b) The term "Licensed Products" as used herein, shall mean __________ covered by the claims of the Licensed Patent.

ARTICLE II - THE GRANT

(a) Licensor hereby grants Licensee a nonexclusive, nontransferable license under the Licensed Patent from its date of issue to make, use and sell Licensed Products.

(b) It is understood that Licensed Products which Licensee makes under this license can be incorporated in and supplied as service parts for products manufactured in the United States and Canada and exported by any foreign country free and clear of any further obligations to Licensor.

ARTICLE III - ROYALTIES AND PAID-UP LICENSES

(a) Licensee shall pay Licensor a royalty of fifteen (15) cents for each Licensed Product sold after _____________.

(b) When accumulated royalties paid by Licensee to Licensor hereunder for Licensed Products sold for products made by Licensee total one million ($1,000,000.00) Dollars, the license granted under ARTICLE II shall be paid-up and irrevocable for licensed Products sold for products made by Licensee.

(c) When accumulated royalties paid by Licensee to Licensor hereunder for Licensed Products sold for products made by third parties together with the royalties of paragraph (b) of this Article total one million, seven hundred fifty thousand ($1,750,000.00) Dollars, the license granted under ARTICLE II shall become fully paid-up and irrevocable.

ARTICLE IV - REPORTS

Licensee shall furnish written reports to licensor within thirty (30) days after the first of January, April, July and October of each year during which royalties are due hereunder setting forth separately the number of Licensed Products sold under paragraphs (b) and (c) of ARTICLE III hereof during the preceding three months and the royalties due thereon. Each report shall be accompanied with a remittance covering the royalties then due and shall be addressed to ________________
____. The first such report shall cover the period from ____________ to ____________.

ARTICLE V - RECORDS

Licensee shall keep accurate records in sufficient detail to enable the royalties payable by Licensee hereunder to be determined and agrees to permit said records to be examined from time to time during the life of this agreement and for one (1) year thereafter by a duly designated independent certified public accountant during usual business hours to the extent necessary to verify the reports and payments required hereunder.

The parties hereto have executed this agreement in duplicate through their duly authorized officers on the date set forth below.

LICENSEE

By: ______________________
Title: ______________________
Date: ______________________

LICENSOR

By: ______________________
Title: ______________________
Date: ______________________

2

8

Bulk Sales

§8.1 THE TRAP

Bulk sales law is probably anachronistic; it rests on assumptions that are no longer valid. Yet, bulk sales law is still alive. At this writing, the Uniform Commercial Code's sponsoring agencies have approved two new approaches to bulk sales. One is to abolish the bulk sales law altogether — a suggestion that no state has yet adopted. The other is to revise the law somewhat.

The effect of the bulk sales law is to make certain buyers of goods in bulk liable for the debts of the seller to the extent that those goods remain in the buyer's hands. The effect of the law is quite startling. Before the sale, the seller's creditors have no interest in the seller's goods, but after the sale, the goods, in the hands of the usually innocent buyer, are subject to the creditors' claims. Figure 8-1 illustrates the operation of the bulk sales law.

In short, the bulk sales rule fashions a trap for unwary bulk sale buyers, and, in all probability, for the buyer's lawyer who fails to advise her client properly.

Figure 8-1. Bulk Sale Trap

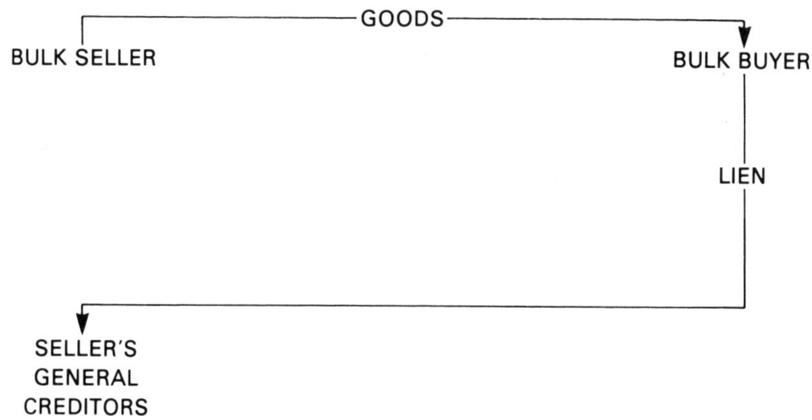

§8.2 THE SETTING

In the past, there were unscrupulous merchants who engaged in fraudulent practices common enough that the law took notice of them. The practices consisted of selling inventory out of the ordinary course of business in bulk, sometimes for less than a valuable consideration, and then disappearing or setting up a new business, all without paying unsecured creditors. The assumption of the proponents of bulk sales laws was that unsecured creditors of the bulk seller relied on his stock of merchandise and were caught off guard when he sold out quickly denying them an opportunity to attach his merchandise and protect themselves. That assumption is probably invalid today, when unsecured creditors tend not to rely on their debtor's stock in trade. The modern unsecured creditors generally are open account sellers (the merchant's inventory suppliers), utilities, and the like and may also include nontrade creditors such as taxing authorities and tort victims. To the extent that the merchant's unsecured creditors rely, they rely on the debtor's credit rating, not on the fact that it has shelves full of merchandise. Taxing authorities and tort claimants are classic examples of nonreliance creditors. It may be safe to say that they never rely on the debtor's stock in trade and that it is no surprise to them when the debtor sells out quickly. Concern for tort victims postdates the bulk sales laws in any event. That concern cannot justify their existence ab initio but may serve to justify them now. The nervous unsecured creditor has a plethora of devices now, e.g., security interests, especially purchase-money security interests, personal guaranties, and letters of credit, under which she can obtain security cheaply. Unsecured creditors remain unsecured because they are not interested in incurring the expense or going to the trouble of (1) discerning which customers' can and should give them security and (2) getting the security. Tort victims' recovery is usually a matter for liability insurance.

Thus, the bulk sales law is with us in most jurisdictions, and commercial lawyers need to understand the way it can trap their clients.

§8.3 THE TRANSACTION

Given the assumption on which the original bulk sales laws rested, those laws usually restricted their application to bulk sellers of inventory and to sellers that were substantially engaged in sales out of inventory. Hardware stores, retail clothing establishments, feed sellers, drapers, and dry goods stores were the kind of establishment that might be the subject of the fraudulent sellout and that the law covered. Barber shops, restaurants, and hotels were not covered, since their sales primarily involved services with the sale of goods as a subsidiary consideration. Certainly no utility that sold electricity to a barber shop relied on the barber's stock of combs and hair tonic.

Yet the bulk sales law took on a life of its own and came to cover equipment sales when they were accompanied by bulk sales of inventory, and in some jurisdictions the law has been expanded to cover bulk sales by service enterprises.

Generally, the bulk sales laws do not apply unless there is a sale of more than half of the seller's inventory, but once the sale reaches that threshold, the rules apply to the equipment that the buyer purchases as well as the inventory. Thus, when an employee of a trendy jeans outlet buys the business from his boss, if he fails to comply with the bulk sales law, he takes the inventory and the equipment (shelving, mannequins, and cash register) subject to the claims of the seller's creditors. Similarly, the assistant manager of a restaurant who purchases the business from the retiring restaurant owner may, depending on the state's version of the bulk sales law, take the small inventory of food and the like (salt and pepper, coffee, ketchup, paper towels), and the equipment (ovens, refrigerators, silverware, tables, and chairs) subject to claims arising out of the seller's unpaid telephone bill, the amount she owed her wine distributor, and the dry cleaner's bill for linen napkins and tablecloths.

§8.4 THE "CURE"

Generally, though the versions of Article 6, both in its scope and its implementation, vary as the various states have adopted it, the bulk sales statutes require the bulk buyer to notify all creditors of the impending bulk sale. Note that, in most jurisdictions, the statute does not require the bulk buyer to reserve a portion of the purchase price for the unsecured creditors, it only requires notice, so that, theoretically, the creditors can take steps (unspecified in the statute) to protect themselves. Note also, that all creditors, including categories that have not relied on the seller's stock in trade, or on any of his assets for that matter, are entitled to notice. In brief, the bulk sales law has become a **fraudulent conveyance** statute that applies against innocent buyers. It does not matter that the buyer fails to give the notice by virtue of innocent neglect. The bulk sales law imputes fault to the buyer and renders the subject of her purchase hostage to her neglect or fraud, as the case may be.

The bulk buyer cannot give the notice unless she has a list of the creditors. The statute requires the buyer to ask the seller for a sworn list. It does not matter that the seller gives the buyer an incomplete list. If the buyer notifies all of the creditors listed and unless the buyer knows or has good reason to believe that the list is incomplete, the buyer takes the goods free and clear of the claims.

§8.5 CONCLUSION

You may conclude from this discussion that the bulk sales law is a bad idea. It does not really protect creditors very much, since they often can do little to protect themselves without considerable transaction costs. The creditor can hire a lawyer and get a judgment or some kind of prejudgment relief, but that kind of action can rarely be obtained prior to consummation of the sale, given the fact that the notice might be given only ten days before the sale and is generally not available without proof of fraud — a notoriously difficult proof problem. The law also rests on the questionable assumption that the creditor is looking to the seller's inventory, even though few unsecured creditors, if any, rely on inventory these days and even though the statute frequently covers sellers of services who have little inventory to start with. The major effect of the law, in the view of some, is to catch the unwary buyer and permit the creditors to collect from an honest party as a matter of fortuity. Those problems with the bulk sales law aside, it remains a problem for the lawyer who represents the buyer in bulk.

9

Leasing

§9.1 DISTINGUISHING THE NONLEASE

This chapter deals with **leases** but does not deal with a common transaction that parties frequently refer to as a "lease," that is, the lease-purchase transaction. For a variety of reasons, installment sellers that want to hold "title" to the goods that are the subject of a sale will designate the transaction a "lease" when in law the arrangement is a secured transaction. It is not always easy to draw the line between the "true" lease and the secured transaction disguised as a lease. Article 2A of the Uniform Commercial Code and the modifications that the Code's sponsoring agencies adopted to the Article 1 definition of *security interest* cause the distinction to turn on the economic realities of the transaction rather than its form or the intent of the parties.

In general, if the lease and any extensions or renewals comprise the entire useful life of the property, or if the lessee must buy the property or has the option to buy the property at the termination of the lease period for a nominal consideration, the lease is in reality a secured transaction, not a lease. In leases with significant tax consequences, the parties must review Internal Revenue Service guidelines to determine the nature of the transaction. Part II deals generally with secured transactions; this chapter deals with the true lease.

§9.2 THE CONSUMER LEASE

In the simplest lease, familiar to any consumer, the lessor is an enterprise in the business of leasing equipment for a day or a few days. Travelers who lease automobiles for a week or less, the weekend gardener who leases a tiller for a Saturday afternoon, and the bride's parents who rent a green and white striped tent for a reception usually enter into this kind of short-term lease.

In recent years automobile leasing by dealers to consumers has become popular. These closed-end lease transactions assume that some consumers (and some businesses) prefer to lease new vehicles for fixed periods at charges that approximate the cost of the vehicle, less its value at the termination of the lease, plus interest charges. Document 9-1 is such an automobile lease.

§9.3 EQUIPMENT LEASING

Of much greater commercial importance than these consumer rentals is the equipment lease. Today, users of industrial equipment are more likely to lease than purchase it. Purchasers of equipment in this multi-billion-dollar industry tend to be finance companies, banks, and their leasing subsidiaries or the leasing subsidiary of the equipment manufacturer itself.

There are a number of reasons that parties may want to enter into an equipment lease. First, some equipment leases are short-term arrangements under which the goods revert to the lessor at a time when they retain significant commercial value and can be leased again to other lessees. In these situations, it is less expensive for the lessee to enter into a short-term lease than to purchase equipment, use it for a brief time, and then let it sit idle or resell it. Second, equipment leases for longer terms often cover equipment that is subject to quick obsolescence by virtue of the fast pace of innovation in an industry. Third, sometimes the lessee is unsure that he wants to keep the equipment and enters into the lease in order to maintain his options to return the equipment after the initial lease term. Fourth, tax considerations may enter into the true lease transaction. Lessors with high gross revenues may want to retain ownership of equipment in order to reduce tax liabilities through investment tax credits or accelerated depreciation rules currently unavailable under federal law but formerly important tax considerations. Lessees that face unprofitable futures might prefer to lease property rather than own it, so that the lessor can enjoy the tax advantages and pass them on, or at least part of them on, to the lessee in the form of reduced lease payments. Finally, some lessees will enter into an equipment lease under which the lessor must maintain the equipment, so that the lessee, who may not have the expertise or trained personnel to undertake that maintenance, can avoid the cost of investing in that expertise or personnel. This kind of lease is often referred to as a service lease.

In all of these transactions, the parties must take care that the arrangement is a true lease and not a secured transaction. Ultimately, a lessee enters into a lease because he needs the equipment but does not want to buy it.

Note that in the lease situation, the lessor is using the lease to market products. An automobile dealer, for example, may sell a new car to a business enterprise and buy it back each year as part of a trade for a new purchase, or the dealer can lease a new vehicle each year to its customer. In both cases, the customer enjoys the use of a new car for a year, and the dealer must dispose of the used car at the end of the year. In the sale transaction, the dealer takes the car in trade; in the lease transaction, the car reverts to it when the lease expires. In both cases, the dealer disposes of the used car through its used-car lot or through its used-car broker.

Similarly, a computer manufacturer that markets products directly to businesses can use equipment leases to effect distribution. Often, under such a lease, when the manufacturer develops a modified product, the lessee will terminate the lease of the old product and enter into a new lease of the upgraded product. The manufacturer knows that if it does not keep its product competitive, the lessee will terminate and go with a competitor. The lessee knows that he will not be stuck with obsolete equipment. Some leases are "net" leases, that is, they provide that the lessee will pay all costs of maintaining, insuring, and servicing the equipment. Document 9-2 is an example of an equipment lease that might arise in these transactions.

Document 9-1. Automobile Lease

Lease Account No. ________ **Net (Closed End) Lease** Lease Date (Delivery Date) ________

Lessor — Name and Address	Lessee (and Co-Lessee) — Name and Address (include County and Zip Code)
SPECIMEN	

By signing this Lease, the Lessee (including any Co-Lessee) leases from the Lessor the following Vehicle under the agreements in this Lease. The Lessee understands that the Lessor will assign this Lease to Ford Motor Credit Company ("Ford Credit").

New or Used	If Used Mileage	Year and Make	Series	Body Style	No Cyl	If Truck GVW	Vehicle Identification Number

INCLUDING: ☐ Radio ☐ Air Conditioner ☐ Automatic Transmission ☐ Power Steering ☐ ________ ☐ ________

USE ☐ Personal ☐ Commercial ☐ Agricultural ☐

Vehicle Insurance: The Lessee must insure the Vehicle for the term of this Lease and give Ford Credit evidence of the insurance. This insurance must protect the Lessee and Ford Credit with (i) comprehensive fire and theft insurance if the Vehicle is a car, or fire, theft and combined additional coverage if the Vehicle is a truck, with a deductible amount of not more than **$500;** (ii) collision and upset insurance with a deductible amount of not more than **$500;** and (iii) automobile liability insurance with limits of not less than **$100,000** for any one person for bodily injury or death, **$300,000** for any one accident for bodily injury or death, and **$25,000** for property damage. The Lessor may buy the insurance if the Lessee does not, but the Lessor does not have to do so. If the Lessor buys the insurance, the Lessee must pay back to the Lessor the cost of the insurance. If the cost of the insurance increases during the term of this Lease, the Lessee will pay the increase. The Lessor either will bill the Lessee for the cost or increase the monthly payment to cover the cost.

If a charge for insurance is shown in Item (3)(a) opposite, the Lessor will try to get the coverage checked below:

☐ Collision ($________ Deductible)
☐ Comprehensive ($________ Deductible)
☐ Fire, Theft and Combined Additional Coverage ($________ Deductible)
☐ Liability Insurance with limits of: (a) $________ bodily injury per person, $________ bodily injury per accident, or (b) $________ single limit.
☐ Other ________

The Lessor, however, is not responsible if he cannot do so. If the Lessor cannot get any insurance, the Lessee must get it. The Lessee assigns to Ford Credit any monies paid under the insurance, by whomever obtained. The Lessee authorizes Ford Credit to receive or collect any money paid under the insurance, endorse checks or drafts relating to the payment, cancel the insurance or settle or release any claim with respect to the insurance. Whether or not the Vehicle is insured, the Lessee must still make lease payments for the Vehicle during the term of this Lease if the Vehicle is lost, damaged or destroyed. Unless shown above, vehicle insurance and/or LIABILITY INSURANCE IS NOT PROVIDED BY LESSOR.

Life and Disability Insurance: Life and disability insurance are not required to enter into this Lease and will not be provided unless you sign below.

Life Insurance ________ Insurer $________ Premium

________ Insured(s) $________ Initial Amount of Coverage

________ Insured's Signature(s)

Disability Insurance ________ Insurer $________ Premium

________ Insured $________ Amount of Monthly Coverage

Amounts payable monthly under Item (3) opposite are not covered by disability insurance.

________ Insured's Signature

Life and disability insurance are for the term of this Lease. The coverages are shown in a notice or agreement given to you this date.

Vehicle Maintenance and Operating Costs: The Lessee will provide and pay for all gas, oil and anti-freeze for the Vehicle. The Lessee will keep the Vehicle in good order and see that all needed repairs are made. All service and repairs will be done when needed but at least as often as set forth in the owner's manual. If the space below is filled in, the Lessor will provide and pay for the service set forth. The work to be done and the place where it is to be done will be set forth in a separate agreement or in coupons that the Lessor will give to the Lessee.

____
____
____
____
____

Warranty: The Vehicle is covered by any extended warranty or service contract described in this Lease and the following, if checked.

☐ Standard new vehicle warranty provided by the manufacturer or distributor of the Vehicle.
☐ ________

EXCEPT AS EXPRESSLY PROVIDED UNDER THIS LEASE, THE LESSOR MAKES NO PROMISE AS TO THE MERCHANTABILITY, SUITABILITY OR FITNESS FOR PURPOSE OF THE VEHICLE. This means that there is no promise that the Vehicle will be fit for use for any particular purpose or even that it will be fit for the normal purpose for which a vehicle is used.

Assignment: When this Lease is signed by the Lessee and the Lessor, the Lessor will assign it to Ford Credit. The Lessee must then make all payments under this Lease to Ford Credit. **The Lessee agrees that Ford Credit will not have to make any repairs to or maintain the Vehicle, get any insurance or perform any other service that the Lessor has agreed to perform under this Lease.** The Lessee will look only to the Lessor for these services. The Lessee shall have no right to assign this Lease or any interest herein or in the Vehicle or to sublease the Vehicle without the prior written consent of Lessor and Ford Credit.

(1) **Initial Charges**
(a) Capitalized Cost Reduction $
(b) Trade-In Allowance $
(c) Refundable Security Deposit $
(d) Refundable Reconditioning Reserve $
(e) Advance Monthly Payment (1st month) $
(f) Registration Fees $
(g) Certificate of Title Fee $
(h) ________ $
(i) ________ $
(j) ________ $
Total Payment Due at Inception $________ (1)

(2) **Basic Monthly Payment**
(a) Monthly Payment $
(b) Use or Lease Tax $
$________ (2)

(3) **Other Charges Payable Monthly**
(a) Vehicle Insurance $
(b) Maintenance $
(c) ________ $
(d) ________ $
(e) ________ $
$________ (3)

(4) **Total Monthly Payment** (Sum of (2) & (3)) $________ (4)

(5) **Term of this Lease:** ____ months, starting on the date of this Lease. (See termination provisions on back of this Lease)

(6) **Payment Schedule:** The Lessee agrees to pay ____ payments of $________. The first payment is due on the date of this Lease. The rest of the payments are due on the ____ day of each month during the term of this Lease, starting with the month of ________, 19 ____. All amounts that the Lessee must pay under this Lease and that are not in the Total Monthly Payment will be paid directly by the Lessee, or if paid by the Lessor, the Lessee agrees to pay back the Lessor promptly.

(7) **Total of Basic Monthly Payments** ((2) multiplied by (5)) $________ (7)

(8) **Total of Monthly Payments** ((4) multiplied by (5)) $________ (8)

(9) **Total of Other Charges Payable to Lessor**
(a) ________ $
(b) ________ $
$________ (9)

(10) **Fees and Taxes:** Total estimated amount to be paid by the Lessee during the term of this Lease for official fees, registration, certificate of title, license fees and taxes. $________ (10)

(11) **Insurance:** See opposite for types and amounts of insurance. If insurance is to be obtained by the Lessor, the total premium cost during the term of the Lease for insurance is (a) $________ for life insurance; (b) $________ for disability insurance and (c) estimated at $________ for vehicle insurance. $________ (11)

(12) **Excess Mileage Charge:** At the end of this Lease, the Lessee will pay to the Lessor **$0.**__ per mile for each mile in excess of ____ miles. The Lessor and the Lessee believe that this will be the maximum mileage that the Vehicle will be driven over the term of this Lease. If the Lease is terminated prior to the scheduled lease end, the excess mileage charge will be figured on a pro rata basis.

(13) **Late Charge:** The Lessee will pay a late charge on each payment that is not made within **10** days after it is due. The charge is **7.5%** of the payment or **$50.00**, whichever is less.

(14) **Lease Only — No Option to Purchase:** This Lease is one of leasing only. The Lessee does not have an option to buy the Vehicle.

(15) **Lease Charges** $________ (15)

(16) **Lease Residual Value** $ (16)

(17) **Other Agreements:** The Lessee promises to keep the agreements on the front and back of this Lease.

The LESSOR accepts this Lease. The Lessor assigns this Lease to FORD MOTOR CREDIT COMPANY under the Assignment on the back of this Lease.

Lessor: ________

By: ________ Title: ________

SPECIMEN

NOTICE TO THE LESSEE: (1) Do not sign this Lease before you read it or if it has any blank space to be filled in. (2) You have the right to get a filled-in copy of this Lease. The Lessee states that he has been given a filled-in copy of this Lease at the time he signs it and notice of the assignment of this Lease by the Lessor to Ford Credit.

Lessee: ________

By: ________ Title: ________

Co-Lessee: ________

FC 16956 JUN 87 **NOTICE: SEE OTHER SIDE FOR IMPORTANT INFORMATION** **ORIGINAL**

Printed with the permission of Ford Motor Credit Company.

Document 9-1. *(continued)*

OTHER AGREEMENTS

(18) **Excess Wear and Tear:** The Lessee will pay the cost of all repairs to the Vehicle that are not the result of normal wear and tear. These costs include, but are not limited to, the cost necessary to:

(i) replace any tire not part of a matching set of four or any tire which has less than **1/8** inch of remaining tread;

(ii) repair all mechanical defects;

(iii) repair or replace all dented, scratched, chipped, rusted or mismatched body panels, paint or vehicle identification items; all dented, scratched, rusted, pitted, broken or missing trim and grill work; all scratched, cracked, pitted or broken glass; all faulty window mechanisms; all broken or burned out lights; all electronic malfunctions; all interior rips, stains, burns or worn areas; and all damage which would be covered by collision or comprehensive insurance whether or not such insurance is actually in force.

(19) **Return of the Vehicle:** At the end of this Lease, the Lessee will return the Vehicle to the Lessor's address shown on the reverse side or to such other place as Ford Credit may direct. If the Lessee keeps possession of the Vehicle past the end of the Lease Term, the Lessee shall continue to pay the monthly lease payments (Item 4 on reverse side). That payment shall not permit the Lessee to keep the Vehicle. The Lessee also shall pay to the Lessor any damage which the Lessor may have because the Lessee failed to return the Vehicle at lease end.

(20) **Termination:** This Lease shall terminate upon (i) the end of the term of this Lease, (ii) the return of the Vehicle to the Lessor and (iii) the payment by the Lessee of all amounts owed under this Lease. The Lessor may terminate this Lease if the Lessee defaults under this Lease.

(21) **Voluntary Early Termination:** This Lease may be terminated by the Lessee before the end of the term if the Lessee is not in default under this Lease, gives Ford Credit and the Lessor **10** days written notice, delivers the Vehicle to the Lessor and pays to Lessor at once the following: (a) an early termination fee of **$200**, (b) the difference, if any, between the Adjusted Balance Subject to Lease Charges and the Realized Value of the Vehicle, and (c) all other amounts then due under this Lease. The Adjusted Balance Subject to Lease Charges will be figured by reducing the Balance Subject to Lease Charges each month by the difference between the Monthly Payment (Item 2(a) on reverse side) and the part of the Lease Charges (Item 15 on reverse side) earned in that month on an actuarial basis. The Balance Subject to Lease Charges shall be calculated by adding the Lease Residual Value (Item 16 on reverse side) to the Lease Depreciation. The Lease Depreciation shall be calculated by subtracting (y) the Lease Charges (Item 15 on reverse side) from (z) the amount of the Monthly Payments (Item 2(a) on reverse side) multiplied by the Lease term in months (Item 5 on reverse side). The Realized Value of the Vehicle shall mean the fair market wholesale value of the Vehicle agreed to by the Lessor and the Lessee. If the Lessee and the Lessor do not agree on the value of the Vehicle, the Lessee may obtain, within **10** days and at his own expense, from an independent third party agreeable to the Lessor and Ford Credit, a professional appraisal of the wholesale value of the Vehicle which could be realized at sale. The appraised value shall then be used as the actual value. If the value of the Vehicle is not determined by agreement or appraisal, the Realized Value shall be the net amount received by Ford Credit upon the sale of the Vehicle at wholesale.

(22) **Termination — Life Insurance:** Upon the death of the insured, if life insurance described on the reverse side is in effect and is payable, this Lease shall continue and any Co-Lessee shall not have to pay amounts becoming due under Item 2 on the reverse side after the date of the death of the insured. If there is not a Co-Lessee, the estate of the Lessee may designate an individual, reasonably satisfactory to Ford Credit, to assume this Lease. Such individual must execute a document in the form provided by Ford Credit agreeing to perform all of the Lessee's obligations under the Lease, except the payment of amounts becoming due under Item 2 on the reverse side after the date of the death of the insured.

(23) **Loss or Destruction of Vehicle:** If the Vehicle is lost or destroyed and the Lessee is not in default under this Lease, the Lessee may provide a substitute vehicle, satisfactory to Ford Credit, and continue this Lease. Any insurance proceeds paid with respect to the Vehicle shall be applied to the purchase of the substitute vehicle. If the Lessee does not provide a substitute vehicle, the Lessee shall pay to Ford Credit the difference, if any between (a) the sum of (i) the Adjusted Balance Subject to Lease Charges (see Item 21 above) and (ii) all other amounts then due under this Lease and (b) the amount of insurance proceeds received by Ford Credit for the Vehicle.

(24) **Default:** If the Lessee fails to make any payment under this Lease when it is due, or if the Lessee fails to keep any other agreement in this Lease, the Lessor may terminate this Lease and take back the Vehicle. The Lessor may go on the Lessee's property to retake the Vehicle. Even if the Lessor retakes the Vehicle, the Lessee must still pay at once the sum of (a) the difference, if any, between the Adjusted Balance Subject to Lease Charges (see Item 21 above) and net amount received by Ford Credit upon the sale of the Vehicle at wholesale and (b) all other amounts then due under this Lease. The Lessee must also pay all expenses paid by the Lessor to enforce the Lessor's rights under this Lease, including reasonable attorney's fees as permitted by law, and any damages caused to the Lessor because of the Lessee's default. The Lessor may sell the Vehicle at public or private sale with or without notice to the Lessee.

(25) **Taxes:** The Lessee will pay all sales, use and other taxes, and all fees and charges, that are levied on the Vehicle during the term of this Lease. The Lessee will also pay all taxes that are charged to the Lessor by reason of the Lessor's interest in the Vehicle except for income taxes.

(26) **Title:** The Vehicle will be titled in the name of Ford Credit. It will be registered as directed by Ford Credit. The Lessee will pay the title and registration costs.

(27) **Vehicle Use:** The Lessee will obey all laws in using the Vehicle. The Lessee will not use or permit the use of the Vehicle (i) outside the state where the Vehicle was first titled and/or registered for more than **30** days without the Lessor's and Ford Credit's prior written consent, (ii) outside of the United States, except in Canada or Mexico if such use does not exceed **30** days or (iii) as a public or private carrier. The Lessee shall not place any sign or mark on the Vehicle unless the Lessor agrees to it. If the Lessor agrees, the Lessee will pay the cost to remove the sign or mark and all needed repairs that are caused by the removal.

(28) **Indemnity:** The Lessee will indemnify the Lessor and Ford Credit from any loss or damage to the Vehicle or its contents during the term of this Lease. The Lessee will also indemnify the Lessor and Ford Credit from all claims, losses and costs arising out of the use or condition of the Vehicle. The Lessee will pay all fines imposed on the Vehicle or on any driver of the Vehicle during the term of this Lease. If the Lessee fails to pay the fines and the Lessor pays, the Lessee will pay the Lessor a **$20.00** administration charge, where permitted by law, for each time the Lessor must pay a fine, in addition to any fine or penalty imposed.

(29) **Security Deposit:** Any security deposit held by the Lessor under this Lease may be used to pay all costs that the Lessee should pay under this Lease but does not.

(30) **Reconditioning Reserve:** Any reconditioning reserve held by the Lessor under this Lease may be used to pay the cost of reconditioning the Vehicle that the Lessee should pay under this Lease but does not.

(31) **General:** This Lease sets forth all of the agreements of the Lessor and the Lessee for the lease of the Vehicle. There is no other agreement. The only way this Lease can be changed is by a new lease signed by Ford Credit. The law that will apply to this Lease is the law of the state where the Lessor's place of business is, as set forth on the front of this Lease. If that law does not allow any of the agreements in this Lease, the ones that are not allowed will be void. The rest of this Lease will still be good.

GUARANTY

To cause the Lessor to lease the Vehicle to the Lessee, the person(s) who signs below as a "Guarantor" guarantees payment of this Lease. This means that if the Lessee fails to pay any money that is owed on this Lease, the Guarantor will pay it when asked. The Guarantor agrees to be bound even if one or more other persons guaranty payment of this Lease. He or she also agrees to be bound even if the Lessor does one or more of the following: (a) gives the Lessee more time to pay one or more payments, or (b) gives a release in full or in part to any of the other Guarantors, or (c) releases any security. The Guarantor also states that he or she has received a completed copy of the Lease and this Guaranty at the time of signing.

Guarantor: ______________ Address ______________

SPECIMEN

Guarantor: ______________ Address ______________

ASSIGNMENT

For valuable consideration, LESSOR hereby assigns, sells, transfers and sets over unto FORD MOTOR CREDIT COMPANY ("Ford Credit") all of Lessor's right, title and interest in and to the Lease and the Vehicle described therein, and Ford Credit is hereby authorized to do every act and thing necessary to collect and discharge the obligations arising out of or incident to the Lease and this assignment. To induce Ford Credit to accept the assignment of the Lease, Lessor warrants that: the Lease, and Guaranty, if any, are genuine, legally valid and enforceable and arose from the lease of the Vehicle; the Lease was complete in all respects and Lessor made all disclosures required by law prior to the execution thereof by Lessee; Lessee is not a minor, has capacity to contract and paid all amounts included in Item (1) of the Lease with his own funds; the signature of Lessee is genuine, the Vehicle is as described in the Lease and has been delivered to and is in the possession of Lessee; title to the Lease and the Vehicle is vested in Lessor free and clear of all liens and encumbrances and Lessor has the right to sell and assign the same; and all statements made by or on behalf of Lessee and furnished to Ford Credit by Lessor are true to the best of Lessor's knowledge and belief and Lessor knows of no fact or circumstance which would impair the validity or value of the Lease. The Lessor also warrants that the Lease was assigned to Ford Credit prior to the use of the Vehicle by Lessee. The Lease is assigned to Ford Credit under Ford Credit's Red Carpet Lease — WOR or Residual Purchase Plan identified below ("the Plan") and is subject to the terms and conditions thereof and the agreements and undertakings of Lessor contained in the Red Carpet Lease — WOR or Residual Purchase Dealer Application executed by Lessor with respect to the Plan; provided that in the event of a breach of any of the foregoing warranties, without regard to Lessor's knowledge or lack of knowledge with respect thereto or Ford Credit's reliance thereon, Lessor shall repurchase the Lease from Ford Credit for the full amount then unpaid whether the Lease shall then be, or not be, in default. Lessor agrees that the lease-end residual value of the Vehicle is as set forth in Item (16) on the face of the Lease.

In the event Lessee desires to obtain a voluntary early termination of the Lease, Lessor agrees to perform certain services for Ford Credit at no charge. Lessor will make a good faith effort to reach agreement with the Lessee as to fair market wholesale value of the Vehicle and, if agreement is reached, pay that amount to Ford Credit. Lessor also will attempt to collect from the Lessee and pay to Ford Credit any amount due from the Lessee in connection with the early termination. Lessor will prepare, sign, and attempt to obtain the signature of the Lessee on a vehicle condition report in such form as Ford Credit may require. If the Vehicle is to be disposed of by Ford Credit, Lessor agrees to store the Vehicle for up to thirty (30) days. Such storage shall be without cost to Ford Credit and Lessor shall exercise the same degree of care with respect to the Vehicle as he would with his own property.

The Lessor agrees that this assignment shall be subject to the Plan initialled below:

☐ Residual Purchase Plan

☐ Without Recourse (WOR) Plan

The Lessee states that he has been given a filled-in copy of this Lease at the time he signs it and notice of the assignment of this Lease to Ford Credit.

Lessee: ______________ Co-Lessee: ______________

FC 16956 JUN 87

NOTICE: SEE OTHER SIDE FOR IMPORTANT INFORMATION

UNISYS FINANCE CORPORATION
MASTER EQUIPMENT LEASE AGREEMENT

LEASE AGREEMENT No. ____________________

DATE: ____________________

LESSEE: ____________________

LESSEE'S PRINCIPAL PLACE OF BUSINESS: ____________________

SPECIMEN

Lease Agreement, made as of the above date, between UNISYS FINANCE CORPORATION, a Michigan corporation ("Lessor"), having as a mailing address One Unisys Place, Detroit Michigan 48232, and the Lessee named above ("Lessee"), having its principal place of business located at the address set forth above.

1. **LEASE AGREEMENT:** Lessor hereby leases to Lessee and Lessee hereby rents from Lessor all the machinery, equipment and other personal property ("Equipment") described in Equipment Lease Schedule(s) related hereto which are or may from time to time be executed by Lessor and Lessee ("Schedules"), upon the terms and conditions set forth herein as supplemented by the terms and conditions set forth in the appropriate Schedule identifying such items of Equipment. Equipment is to be used for business and commercial purposes and not for personal, family or household use. THE EQUIPMENT DESCRIBED IN EQUIPMENT LEASE SCHEDULE(S) RELATED HERETO DOES NOT INCLUDE SYSTEM SOFTWARE OR ANY OTHER PROGRAM PRODUCTS. ANY SUCH SOFTWARE OR PROGRAM PRODUCTS SHALL BE SUBJECT TO A SEPARATE LICENSING AGREEMENT BETWEEN LESSEE AND UNISYS CORPORATION. Whenever reference is made herein to this "Lease" it shall be deemed to include each of the various Schedules identifying all items of Equipment, all of which together with this lease agreement constitute one undivided lease of the Equipment, and the terms and conditions of which are incorporated herein by reference. Lessor assumes no liability and makes no representation as to the treatment by Lessee of this Lease, the Equipment or the rental payments or other payments hereunder for financial statement or tax purposes.

2. **TERM:** The obligations under this Lease shall commence as of the date hereof provided this Lease is accepted in writing by Lessor and shall end upon full performance and observance of each and every term, condition and covenant set forth in this Lease and any extensions thereof (the "Lease Term"). **The rental term of the Equipment listed in a Schedule shall commence upon the date of acceptance of the Equipment by Lessee (the "Acceptance Date") and shall continue for the number of months set forth in such Schedule, beginning with the first month commencing after the Acceptance Date,** unless such term has been extended or otherwise modified in writing and signed by Lessor and Lessee (the "Rental Term"). This Lease cannot be cancelled or terminated by Lessee except as expressly provided herein.

3. **RENTAL PAYMENTS:** Lessee shall pay rent to Lessor for the Equipment in the monthly amounts specified in the applicable Schedule. **Rent shall be payable in such amounts in advance on the first day of each month during the Rental Term, plus, in the case of the first such rental payment, 1/30th of the amount of the applicable monthly rent for each day from and including the Acceptance Date to and excluding such first rental payment date.** Rent shall be payable at the mailing address of Lessor set forth above. Rental payments made by check will be accepted subject to collection.

At Lessee's request, Lessor may advance for Lessee's benefit software license fees and/or service fees incidental to the delivery, installation and/or operation of the Equipment. If such fees are advanced by Lessor, the monthly rental payable by Lessee to Lessor shall include an additional amount to cover repayment of such fees.

4. **DELIVERY AND INSTALLATION:** Lessee will select the type, quantity and supplier of each item of Equipment designated in the appropriate Schedule, and in reliance thereon such Equipment will then be ordered by Lessor from such supplier, or Lessor will accept an assignment of an existing purchase order therefor. Lessor shall have no liability for any delay in delivery or failure by the supplier to deliver any Equipment or to fill any purchase order or meet the conditions thereof. Lessee, at its expense, will pay all transportation, packing, taxes, duties, insurance, installation, testing and other charges in connection with the delivery, installation and use of the Equipment. As soon as practicable after receipt of the Equipment, Lessee shall furnish Lessor with a written statement acknowledging receipt of the Equipment in good operating condition and repair, and accepting it as satisfactory in all respects for the purposes of this Lease. Completion and signature of such statement by any employee, partner or agent of Lessee having authority in the premises or having managerial, supervisory, or procurement duties with respect to equipment of the same general type as the Equipment leased hereunder shall constitute acceptance of such Equipment on behalf of Lessee.

Lessee understands and agrees that neither manufacturer, seller or supplier, nor any salesman or other agent of manufacturer, seller or supplier, is an agent of Lessor. No salesman or agent of manufacturer, seller or supplier is authorized to waive or alter any term or condition of this Lease, and no representation as to Equipment or any other matter by manufacturer, seller or supplier shall in any way affect Lessee's duty to pay the rental payments and perform its other obligations as set forth in this Lease.

5. **WARRANTIES:** LESSOR, NOT BEING THE MANUFACTURER, SELLER OR SUPPLIER OF THE EQUIPMENT, OR THE AGENT OF THE MANUFACTURER, SELLER OR SUPPLIER, MAKES NO WARRANTY, REPRESENTATION OR COVENANT, EXPRESS OR IMPLIED, AS TO ANY MATTER WHATEVER, INCLUDING BUT NOT LIMITED TO: THE MERCHANTABILITY OF THE EQUIPMENT OR ITS FITNESS FOR ANY PARTICULAR PURPOSE, THE DESIGN OR CONDITION OF THE EQUIPMENT, THE QUALITY OR CAPACITY OF THE EQUIPMENT, THE WORKMANSHIP IN THE EQUIPMENT, COMPLIANCE OF THE EQUIPMENT WITH THE REQUIREMENT OF ANY LAW, RULE, SPECIFICATION OR CONTRACT PERTAINING THERETO, PATENT INFRINGEMENT, OR LATENT DEFECTS. Lessee accordingly agrees not to assert any claim whatsoever against Lessor based thereon. Lessee further agrees, regardless of cause, not to assert any claim whatsoever against Lessor for any direct, indirect, consequential, incidental or special damages or loss, of any classification, including, without limitation, any lost profits. Lessor shall have no obligation to install, erect, test, adjust, service, or maintain the Equipment. Lessee shall look solely to the manufacturer, seller and/or supplier for any and all claims related to the Equipment. LESSEE LEASES THE EQUIPMENT "AS IS". NOTWITHSTANDING THE FOREGOING, LESSEE'S OBLIGATIONS TO PAY THE RENTALS OR OTHERWISE UNDER THIS LEASE SHALL BE AND ARE ABSOLUTE AND UNCONDITIONAL.

Lessor hereby acknowledges that the warranties of the manufacturer, seller and/or supplier of the Equipment, if any, are for the benefit of both Lessor and Lessee.

6. **TITLE TO AND LOCATION OF EQUIPMENT:** Title to each item of Equipment leased hereunder shall remain with Lessor at all times and Lessee shall have no right, title or interest therein except as expressly set forth in this Lease. Lessee, at its expense, will protect and defend Lessor's title to the Equipment and will keep the Equipment free and clear from any and all claims, liens, encumbrances and legal processes of Lessee's creditors and other persons. All items of Equipment shall at all times be and remain personal property notwithstanding that any such Equipment may now or hereafter be affixed to realty.

The Equipment shall be delivered to the location specified in the Schedule with respect thereto and shall not thereafter be removed from such location without the written consent of Lessor. Without limitation of the foregoing, Lessee shall not permit the Equipment or any part thereof to be removed outside the United States. Lessor shall be permitted to display notice of its ownership of the Equipment by affixing to each item of Equipment an identifying stencil or plate or any other indicia of ownership. Lessee agrees to affix to each item of Equipment, in a reasonably prominent place, such indicia of Lessor's ownership if requested and supplied by Lessor. Lessee will not alter, deface, cover or remove such ownership identification.

7. **TAX BENEFITS:** Lessee acknowledges that unless otherwise agreed by Lessor, Lessor intends to claim all available tax benefits of ownership with respect to the Equipment (the "Tax Benefits"), including, but not limited to cost recovery deductions as provided in Section 168 of the Internal Revenue Code of 1986, as amended (the "Code") with respect to each item of Equipment for each of Lessor's taxable years during the Rental Term. Notwithstanding anything herein to the contrary, if Lessor shall not be entitled to, or shall be subject to recapture of, the Tax Benefits, as a result of any act, omission or misrepresentation of Lessee, Lessee shall pay to Lessor upon demand an amount or amounts sufficient to reimburse Lessor for such loss, together with any related interest and penalties, based on the highest marginal corporate income tax rate prevailing during the Lease Term, regardless of whether Lessor or any member of a consolidated group of which Lessor is also a member is then subject to any increase in tax as a result of such loss of Tax Benefits.

8. **USE OF EQUIPMENT, INSPECTION AND REPORTS:** During the Rental Term, Lessee shall be entitled to quiet enjoyment of the Equipment and may possess and use the Equipment in accordance with this Lease, provided that Lessee is in compliance in all respects with the terms of this Lease and that such possession and use are in conformity with all applicable laws, any insurance policies, and any installation requirements (including environmental specifications) or

No. 3029509 REV. 6/87

warranties of the manufacturer, seller and/or supplier with respect to the Equipment. Lessee shall provide all permits and licenses, if any, necessary for the installation and operation of the Equipment. Lessor shall have the right, upon reasonable prior notice to Lessee and during regular business hours, to inspect the Equipment at the premises of Lessee or wherever the Equipment may be located. Lessee shall promptly notify Lessor of all details arising out of any change in location of the Equipment, any alleged encumbrances thereon or any accident allegedly resulting from the use or operation thereof or any claim relating thereto. Lessee shall be responsible for the removal of its data and information contained in or accompanying any Equipment being returned or repossessed and Lessor shall have no responsibility for any data or information remaining in or accompanying any returned or repossessed Equipment.

9. **FURTHER ASSURANCES:** Lessee shall execute and deliver to Lessor upon Lessor's request such instruments and assurances as Lessor deems necessary for the confirmation or perfection of this Lease and Lessor's rights hereunder including but not limited to corporate resolutions, opinions of counsel and financing statements. In furtherance thereof, Lessor may file or record this Lease or a financing statement with respect thereto so as to give notice to any interested parties. Lessor is authorized to file a financing statement signed only by Lessor in accordance with the Uniform Commercial Code or signed by Lessor as Lessee's attorney in fact. Any such filing or recording shall not be deemed evidence of any intent to create a security interest under the Uniform Commercial Code.

10. **RISK OF LOSS:** Lessee shall bear the entire risk of any item of Equipment being lost, stolen, destroyed or otherwise rendered permanently unfit or unavailable for use from any cause whatsoever (hereinafter called an "Event of Loss") after its delivery to Lessee. If an Event of Loss shall occur with respect to any item of Equipment, Lessee shall promptly and fully notify Lessor thereof. On the rental payment date following such notice Lessee shall pay to Lessor an amount equal to the rental payment or payments due and payable for such item of Equipment on such date plus a sum equal to the Stipulated Loss Value (as hereinafter defined) of such item as of the date of such payment. Upon the making of such payment by Lessee regarding any item of Equipment, the rental for such item shall cease to accrue, the Rental Term as to such item shall terminate and (except in the case of loss, theft or complete destruction) Lessor shall be entitled to recover possession of such item in accordance with the provisions of Paragraph 23 hereof. Provided that Lessor has received the Stipulated Loss Value for any item of Equipment, Lessee shall be entitled to the proceeds of any recovery in respect of such item from insurance or otherwise. The Stipulated Loss Value for an item of Equipment as of any date of payment thereof shall be an amount equal to the present value of all future monthly rental payments with respect to such item, discounted at the rate of 12% per annum to such date of payment, plus 12 times the monthly rental payment with respect to such item of Equipment as set forth in the applicable Schedule.

11. **INSURANCE:** Lessee, at its own expense, shall throughout the Rental Term insure each item of Equipment against all risks and in an amount at least equal to the Stipulated Loss Value thereof (or such greater amount as shall be reasonably required by Lessor), with carriers acceptable to Lessor, under a policy or policies containing a loss payable endorsement in favor of Lessor and its successors and assigns, and affording to Lessor and its successors and assigns such additional protection as Lessor and its successors and assigns shall reasonably require. Lessee shall further at its expense maintain in effect throughout the Rental Term a policy or policies of comprehensive public liability and property damage insurance in form and amount and with carriers satisfactory to Lessor. All such insurance shall name Lessor and its successors and assigns as additional insureds. The policies shall provide that they may not be cancelled or altered without at least 30 days prior written notice to Lessor or its successors and assigns. Lessee shall deliver to Lessor copies or other evidence satisfactory to Lessor of each insurance policy and each renewal thereof. Failure of Lessor to request evidence of such insurance policies or renewals, or otherwise to verify the existence of such insurance, shall not constitute a waiver of the requirements hereof. Lessor shall have the right, on behalf of itself and Lessee, to make claim for, receive payment of, and execute and endorse all documents, checks or drafts received in payment for loss or damage under said insurance policies.

12. **MAINTENANCE AND REPAIRS:** Lessee shall, at its expense, maintain each item of Equipment and all additions, attachments and accessories with respect thereto, in good repair, condition and working order, but shall not be responsible for normal wear and tear or depreciation resulting from the authorized use thereof. Lessee shall, at its own expense, enter into and keep in force during the Rental Term a maintenance agreement to maintain, service and repair the Equipment. Unless otherwise agreed in writing by Lessor, such maintenance agreement will be with the manufacturer of the Equipment. Lessor shall have the right to approve such maintenance agreement, and Lessee shall furnish Lessor with an executed copy of such maintenance agreement. Lessee, without the prior written consent of Lessor, shall make no modifications or alterations to any item of Equipment except engineering changes suggested by the manufacturer. Lessee shall make no repair, addition or attachment with respect to any item of Equipment which interferes with the normal and satisfactory operation or maintenance thereof, or creates a safety hazard. Lessee shall, at its own expense and within a reasonable period of time, replace all parts of Equipment that may become worn out, lost, destroyed or otherwise rendered permanently unfit for use, with appropriate new replacement parts. Lessee shall not take any action which might result in the creation of a mechanic's or materialman's lien with respect to any item of Equipment. All modifications, repairs, alterations, replacement parts, additions and attachments, at any time made or placed in or upon the Equipment shall become part of the Equipment and shall be the property of Lessor, provided, however, that Lessee shall retain ownership of and shall have the option of removing any addition or attachment which has been paid for or otherwise provided by Lessee, so long as the Equipment shall have been restored to its original condition, normal wear and tear excepted.

13. **TAXES:** Lessee shall timely pay all assessments, license fees, taxes (including sales, use, excise, personal property, ad valorem, stamp, documentary and other taxes) and all other governmental charges, fees, fines or penalties whatsoever, whether payable by Lessor or Lessee, on or relating to the Equipment or the use, registration, rental, shipment, transportation, delivery, ownership or operation thereof, and on or relating to this Lease, provided, however, that the foregoing shall not include any federal, state or local income or franchise taxes of Lessor.

14. **LESSOR'S PERFORMANCE OF LESSEE'S OBLIGATION:** If Lessee shall fail to duly and promptly perform any of its obligations under this Lease with respect to the Equipment, Lessor may, at its option, perform any act or make any payment which Lessor deems necessary for the maintenance and preservation of the Equipment and Lessor's title thereto, including but not limited to payments for satisfaction of liens, repairs, taxes, levies and insurance. All expenses incurred by Lessor in performing such acts and all such payments made by Lessor together with late charges as provided in Paragraph 15 below, and any reasonable legal fees incurred by Lessor in connection therewith, shall be additional rent under this Lease and payable by Lessee to Lessor on demand. The performance of any act or payment by Lessor as aforesaid shall not be deemed a waiver or release of any obligation or default on the part of Lessee.

15. **LATE CHARGES:** Should Lessee fail to duly pay any part of any rental payment or other sum to be paid to Lessor under this Lease (including, but not limited to, any amounts due as a result of Lessor's exercise of its remedies under Paragraph 25 hereof) within ten days of the date on which such amount is due hereunder, then Lessee shall pay late charges on such delinquent payment from the tenth day after the due date thereof until paid (both dates inclusive), at the rate of 20% per annum or the highest rate permitted by law, whichever is less.

16. **INDEMNIFICATION:** Lessee assumes liability for, and hereby agrees to indemnify, protect and keep harmless Lessor and its successors and assigns and their respective agents, employees, officers, directors, parents, subsidiaries and stockholders from and against any and all liabilities, obligations, losses, damages, injuries, claims, demands, penalties, actions, costs and expenses (including reasonable attorney's fees), of whatsoever kind and nature, arising out of the use, condition (including, but not limited to, latent and other defects and whether or not discoverable by Lessee or Lessor), operation, ownership, selection, delivery, leasing or return of any item of Equipment, regardless of where, how and by whom operated, or any failure on the part of Lessee to accept the Equipment or otherwise to perform or comply with any conditions of this Lease. The indemnities and assumptions of liabilities and obligations herein provided for shall continue in full force and effect notwithstanding the expiration or termination of any Rental Term or the Lease Term. Lessee is an independent contractor and nothing contained in this Lease shall authorize Lessee or any other person to operate any item of Equipment so as to incur or impose any liability or obligation for or on behalf of Lessor.

17. **NO OFFSET:** This Lease is a net lease. ALL RENTAL PAYMENTS SHALL BE PROMPTLY PAID BY LESSEE IRRESPECTIVE OF ANY SET-OFF, COUNTERCLAIM, RECOUPMENT, DEFENSE OR OTHER RIGHT WHICH LESSEE MAY HAVE AGAINST LESSOR, OR THE MANUFACTURER, SELLER AND/OR SUPPLIER OF THE EQUIPMENT OR ANY OTHER PARTY.

18. **PURCHASE OPTION:** Lessee shall have no option to purchase or otherwise acquire title or ownership of any item of Equipment unless (a) the terms of such purchase option are set forth in or annexed to the Schedule relating to such item of Equipment, (b) if there is any such purchase option, and Lessee is not in default under this Lease, any such purchase option can only be exercised as to any item of Equipment by Lessee's written notice to Lessor, at Lessor's address set forth above, not earlier than 120 days prior to the end of the Rental Term with respect to such item of Equipment nor later than 60 days prior to the end of such

-2-

Document 9-2. (*continued*)

Rental Term and (c) the purchase price shall be payable on the last day of the Rental Term or on such later date as Lessor and Lessee may agree. Any purchase option price stated as "fair market value" ("FMV") for any item of Equipment shall be determined on the basis of, and shall be equal in amount to, the value which would obtain in an arm's-length transaction between an informed and willing buyer-user and an informed and willing seller under no compulsion to sell and, in such determination, costs of removal of the items of Equipment from their location of current use shall not be a deduction from such value. On the date of such purchase, Lessee shall pay to Lessor in cash the purchase price for such item of Equipment and Lessor shall transfer to Lessee without recourse or warranty, express or implied, Lessor's interest in such Equipment, "AS IS", in its then condition and location. In the event Lessee purchases any item of Equipment, Lessee shall be responsible for all applicable sales, use, excise, personal property, ad valorem, stamp, documentary and other applicable taxes.

19. **RENEWAL:** If a renewal rental is set forth in any Schedule relating to any item of Equipment, Lessee may, at its option, renew the lease thereof for a period of 12 or more months by giving Lessor written notice of such renewal and the term thereof not less than 60 days before the expiration of the Rental Term or the then current renewal thereof, provided that such renewal option is not exercisable if Lessee is in default under this Lease. In the event of such renewal, the lease of such Equipment shall continue on the same terms and conditions as set forth herein and such renewal term shall be treated as a Rental Term hereunder, provided however, that the rental payments for such Equipment shall be in the amount of the renewal rent as provided for in the applicable Schedule. If Lessee fails to return any item of Equipment at the end of the Rental Term or any renewal thereof, and does not exercise its renewal option or purchase option as aforesaid, then, without limiting any of the rights or remedies of Lessor hereunder, the lease of such Equipment shall automatically be renewed from month to month with rent payable monthly at the monthly rate applicable during the Rental Term, and all other obligations of Lessee under this Lease shall continue during the period of such month to month rental.

20. **ADVANCE RENTALS; SECURITY DEPOSIT:** Any advance rentals paid by Lessee to Lessor shall be applied to initial rental payments coming due under this Lease. A security deposit shall be due upon acceptance by Lessor of each Schedule providing therefor in the amount specified in such Schedule. The security deposit shall be non-interest bearing and shall be security for the full payment and performance of all terms, conditions and obligations of Lessee under this Lease. Such deposit shall not excuse the performance at the time and in the manner prescribed of any obligation of Lessee or prevent or cure default thereof. Lessor may, but shall not be required to, apply such security deposit toward discharge of any overdue obligation of Lessee. The portion of the security deposit received by Lessor in connection with acceptance of a particular Schedule shall be refunded to Lessee, provided that Lessee has fully complied with and discharged all its obligations under such Schedule and is not and has not been in default under this Lease.

21. **ASSIGNMENT BY LESSEE:** Without Lessor's prior written consent, Lessee may not, by operation of law or otherwise, (a) assign, transfer, pledge, hypothecate or otherwise dispose of this Lease or any interest therein or (b) sublet or lend the Equipment or permit the Equipment to be used by anyone other than Lessee or Lessee's employees, provided however, that Lessee may allow third parties under Lessee's supervision to use the Equipment so long as Lessee shall retain uninterrupted possession and control of the Equipment.

22. **ASSIGNMENT BY LESSOR:** Lessor may assign, sell or encumber all or any part of this Lease, the Equipment and the rental payments hereunder, including the rights under this Lease, the Equipment and the rental payments relating to any individual Schedule hereto. In the event of any such assignment of rental payments hereunder and written direction by Lessor to Lessee, Lessee shall unconditionally pay directly to any such assignee all rentals and other sums due or to become due under this Lease. THE RIGHTS OF ANY SUCH ASSIGNEE SHALL NOT BE SUBJECT TO ANY DEFENSE, COUNTERCLAIM OR SET-OFF WHICH LESSEE MAY HAVE AGAINST LESSOR. Notwithstanding the foregoing, any such assignment (a) shall be subject to Lessee's right to possess and use the Equipment so long as Lessee is not in default under this Lease and (b) shall not release any of Lessor's obligations hereunder or any claim which Lessee has against Lessor.

23. **RETURN OF EQUIPMENT:** Upon expiration or termination of the Rental Term with respect to any item of Equipment, unless Lessee shall have duly exercised any renewal or purchase option with respect thereto, Lessee will at its own risk and expense deliver such items of Equipment to such place or places within the United States as shall be designated by Lessor in writing, for such disposition as Lessor may determine. All Equipment so delivered by Lessee to Lessor will be in the same condition as when first delivered to Lessee, reasonable wear and tear resulting solely from authorized use thereof excepted.

24. **EVENTS OF DEFAULT:** Lessee shall be in default under this Lease upon the happening of any of the following events or conditions ("Events of Default"), unless such Event of Default shall have been specifically waived by Lessor in writing:

(a) Default by Lessee in payment of any installment of rent or any other indebtedness or obligation now or hereafter owed by Lessee to Lessor under this Lease or otherwise or in the performance of any obligation, covenant or liability contained in this Lease or any other agreement or document with Lessor, and the continuance of such default for 10 consecutive days after written notice thereof by Lessor to Lessee, or (b) any warranty, representation or statement made or furnished to Lessor by or on behalf of Lessee proves to have been false in any material respect when made or furnished, or (c) actual or attempted sale, lease or encumbrance of any of the Equipment, or the making of any levy, seizure or attachment thereof or thereon, or (d) dissolution, termination of existence, discontinuance of Lessee's business, insolvency, business failure, failure to pay debts as they mature, or appointment of a receiver of any part of the property of, or assignment for the benefit of creditors by Lessee, or the commencement of any proceedings under any bankruptcy, reorganization or arrangement laws by or against Lessee, or (e) any Event of Default (as herein defined) shall have occurred with respect to any guarantor of this Lease.

25. **REMEDIES OF LESSOR:** Upon the occurrence of any Event of Default and at any time thereafter, Lessor may, without any further notice, exercise one or more of the following remedies as Lessor in its sole discretion shall elect: (a) terminate the Rental Term and all of Lessee's rights hereunder as to any or all items of Equipment; (b) personally, or by its agents, take immediate possession from Lessee of any or all items of Equipment wherever found and for this purpose enter upon Lessee's premises where any item of Equipment is located and remove such item of Equipment without notice or process of law and free from all claims of any nature whatsoever by Lessee, (c) proceed by appropriate court action or actions to enforce performance by Lessee of its obligations hereunder or to recover damages for the breach hereof (which damages shall, without limitation, consist of (i) all accrued and unpaid rentals, (ii) the present value of all future rentals due hereunder, (iii) all late charges, (iv) all of Lessor's costs and expenses incurred in connection with the enforcement of this Lease, (v) the amount of any Tax Benefits lost by Lessor by reason of Lessee's default hereunder, and (vi) any other damages caused by Lessee's default hereunder) or pursue any other remedy available to Lessor at law or in equity or otherwise, (d) declare all unpaid rentals and other sums payable hereunder during the term hereof to be immediately due and payable without any presentment, demand or protest (all of which hereby are expressly waived by Lessee), and (e) cause Lessee, at its sole cost and expense, to promptly return any or all items of Equipment to Lessor in the condition referred to in the last sentence of Paragraph 23 of this Lease.

A termination of any Rental Term on account of any Event of Default hereunder shall occur only upon written notice by Lessor to Lessee and only with respect to such item or items of Equipment as Lessor specifically elects to terminate in such notice. Except as to such item or items with respect to which there is a termination of the Rental Term, this Lease shall continue in full force and effect and Lessee shall be obligated to perform all acts and to pay all rental payments and other amounts required under this Lease.

No right or remedy herein conferred upon or reserved to Lessor is exclusive of any right or remedy herein or at law or in equity or otherwise provided or permitted, but each shall be cumulative of every other right or remedy given hereunder or now or hereafter existing at law or in equity or by statute or otherwise, and may be enforced concurrently therewith or from time to time.

26. **DISPOSITION OF EQUIPMENT:** In the event Lessor repossesses the Equipment, Lessor may, without any obligation whatsoever on the part of Lessor to do so, (a) lease the Equipment, or any portion thereof, in such manner, for such time and upon such terms as Lessor may determine or (b) sell the Equipment, or any portion thereof, at one or more public or private sales, in such manner, and at such times and upon such terms as Lessor may determine.

In the event that Lessor leases any such Equipment, any rentals received by Lessor for the Remaining Lease Term(s) (the period ending on the date when the Rental Term of this Lease for the Equipment would have expired if an Event of Default had not occurred) for such Equipment shall be applied to the payment (in the following order) of (i) all costs and expenses (including reasonable attorney's fees) incurred by Lessor in retaking possession of, and removing, storing, repairing, refurbishing and leasing such Equipment, and (ii) the rentals for the remainder of the Rental Term and all other sums then remaining unpaid under this Lease, including, without limitation, late charges payable under Paragraph 15 hereof. The balance of such rentals, if any, shall be applied first to reimburse Lessee for any

-3-

sums previously paid by Lessee to Lessor as damages described in subparagraphs (c)(ii), (iv) and (v) of Paragraph 25 hereof, and any remaining amounts shall be retained by Lessor. All rentals received by Lessor for the period commencing after the expiration of the Remaining Lease Term(s) shall be retained by Lessor. Without limiting any other rights or remedies of Lessor hereunder, Lessee shall pay to Lessor upon demand any amount by which the sum of the amounts referred to in clauses (i) and (ii) above shall exceed the aggregate rentals received by Lessor under such leases for the respective Remaining Lease Term(s) applicable to the Equipment covered by such leases.

In the event that Lessor shall sell or otherwise dispose of (other than pursuant to a lease) any such Equipment, the proceeds thereof shall be applied to the payment (in the following order) of (i) all costs and expenses (including reasonable attorney's fees) incurred by Lessor in retaking possession of, and removing, storing, repairing, refurbishing and selling or otherwise disposing of such Equipment, (ii) the rentals accrued under this Lease but unpaid up to the time of such sale or other disposition, (iii) any and all other sums (other than rentals) then owing to Lessor by Lessee hereunder, including, without limitation, late charges payable under Paragraph 15 hereof, and (iv) the Stipulated Loss Value of such Equipment determined as of the date of such sale or other disposition as provided herein. The balance of such proceeds, if any, shall be applied first to reimburse Lessee for any sums previously paid by Lessee to Lessor as damages described in subparagraphs (c)(ii), (iv) and (v) of Paragraph 25 hereof, and any remaining amounts shall be retained by Lessor. Without limiting any other rights or remedies of Lessor hereunder, Lessee shall pay to Lessor upon demand any amount by which the sum of the amounts referred to in clauses (i) through (iv) above shall exceed the aggregate proceeds received by Lessor in connection with the sale or disposition of the Equipment.

27. **COSTS:** Lessee shall pay Lessor all costs and expenses, including reasonable attorney's fees, incurred by Lessor in enforcing any of the terms, conditions or provisions of this Lease.

28. **SEVERABILITY:** Any provision of this Lease which is prohibited or unenforceable in any jurisdiction shall, as to such jurisdiction, be ineffective to the extent of such prohibition or unenforceability, without invalidating the remaining provisions hereof. To the extent permitted by applicable law, Lessee hereby waives any provision of law which prohibits or renders unenforceable any provision hereof in any respect.

29. **NOTICES:** All notices, reports, and other documents provided for herein shall be deemed to have been given or made when received or when mailed, postage prepaid, or delivered to a telegraph or cable company, addressed to Lessor or Lessee at their respective addresses set forth above or such other addresses as either of the parties hereto may designate in writing to the other from time to time for such purpose.

30. **AMENDMENTS AND WAIVERS:** This instrument and the Schedules executed by Lessor and Lessee constitute the entire agreement between Lessor and Lessee with respect to the Equipment and the subject matter of this Lease. No term or provision of this Lease may be changed, waived, amended or terminated except by a written agreement signed by both Lessor and Lessee, except that Lessor may insert the serial number of any item of Equipment after delivery thereof. No waiver of or delay or omission in the exercise of any right or remedy herein provided or otherwise available to Lessor shall impair, affect or be construed as a waiver of its rights thereafter to exercise the same. Any single or partial exercise by Lessor of any right hereunder shall not preclude any other or further exercise of any right hereunder.

31. **CONSTRUCTION:** This Lease shall in all respects be governed by and construed in accordance with the laws of the State of Michigan. The titles of the sections of this Lease are for convenience only and shall not define or limit any of the terms or provisions hereof. Time is of the essence of this Lease in each of its provisions.

32. **PARTIES:** The provisions of this Lease shall be binding upon, and (subject to the limitations of Paragraph 21 hereof) shall inure to the benefit of, the assigns, representatives and successors of Lessor and Lessee. If there is more than one Lessee named in this Lease, the liability of each shall be joint and several.

LESSEE HEREBY ACKNOWLEDGES THAT IT HAS READ AND UNDERSTANDS THIS AGREEMENT.

IN WITNESS WHEREOF, Lessor and Lessee have each caused this Lease to be duly executed as of the date first above written.

LESSEE ______________________________

By ______________________________
(Signature and Title)

By ______________________________
(Signature and Title)

(Must be Signed by Authorized Corporate Officer, Partner or Proprietor)

Accepted as of the date first above written at Lessor's principal place of business in the State of Michigan set forth below:

UNISYS FINANCE CORPORATION

By ______________________________
(Signature and Title)

____
(Address)

____

SPECIMEN

-4-

Document 9-2. (*continued*)

UNISYS FINANCE CORPORATION

LEASE SCHEDULE

MASTER EQUIPMENT LEASE AGREEMENT NO. ____________________

DATE OF LEASE AGREEMENT: ____________________

LEASE SCHEDULE NO. ____________________

DATE OF LEASE SCHEDULE: ____________________

LESSEE: ____________________

1. DESCRIPTION OF THE EQUIPMENT:

Quantity	Style	Description of Units of Equipment	Monthly Rent	Serial Numbers (If available)

2. EQUIPMENT LOCATION: ____________________

To be used with Lease Agreement No. 3029509

Form No. 3029517 Rev. 1/87

Document 9-2. *(continued)*

3. RENTAL TERM: ________ months.

4. MONTHLY RENTAL PAYMENT: $____________.

5. AMOUNT OF ADVANCE RENTAL PAYMENTS: $____________.

6. SECURITY DEPOSIT: $____________.

7. RENEWAL OPTION: ____.

8. PURCHASE OPTION: ____.

9. THIS SCHEDULE AND ITS TERMS AND CONDITIONS ARE HEREBY INCORPORATED BY REFERENCE IN THE ABOVE MASTER EQUIPMENT LEASE AGREEMENT. LESSEE PERMITS LESSOR TO INSERT SERIAL NUMBERS OF EQUIPMENT WHEN DETERMINED BY LESSOR. THE EQUIPMENT LISTED IN ITEM 1 DOES NOT INCLUDE SYSTEM SOFTWARE OR ANY OTHER PROGRAM PRODUCTS. ANY SUCH SOFTWARE OR PROGRAM PRODUCTS SHALL BE SUBJECT TO A SEPARATE AGREEMENT BETWEEN LESSEE AND UNISYS CORPORATION.

LESSEE

____

By ____________________________________
(Signature and Title)

By ____________________________________
(Signature and Title)

(Must be signed by Authorized Corporate Officer, Partner, or Proprietor)

LESSOR

Accepted as of the date of this Schedule at Lessor's principal place of business in the State of Michigan set forth below:

UNISYS FINANCE CORPORATION

By ____________________________________
(Signature and Title)

____
(Address)

____

UNISYS FINANCE CORPORATION

One Unisys Place
Detroit, MI 48232

CERTIFICATE OF ACCEPTANCE

LESSEE OR BUYER ____________________

EQUIPMENT LEASE OR CONDITIONAL SALES CONTRACT ("AGREEMENT") NUMBER .... ____________________

SCHEDULE NUMBER .... ____________________

THE UNDERSIGNED ACKNOWLEDGES THAT:

1. The Equipment and products described in the above-referenced Schedule are delivered, installed, available for use and are placed in service as of the Acceptance Date indicated below.
2. Such Equipment and products are in good operating condition and repair and are accepted as satisfactory in all respects for the purpose of the Agreement.
3. The undersigned will commence payment in accordance with the provisions of the Agreement, beginning on the Acceptance Date noted below.

Acceptance Date: x____________________

Authorized Signature: x____________________

SPECIMEN

Name Typed or Printed: x____________________

Title: x____________________

Form No. 3029525 Rev 7/87

10 Construction Contracts

§10.1 THE INDUSTRY

The construction industry involves an ever-larger number of players as its activity becomes increasingly complex. Few industries embrace as many different processes, services, and products as this one, which comprises simple activity such as repairing a leaky garage roof and complex activity such as constructing a space center or a nuclear power facility. In most cases, the transaction begins when a purchaser, whom the industry generally calls the "owner," decides to buy construction services and, usually, materials. In any reasonably complex construction, the owner must express her requirements in some fashion. Unlike many sales transactions, construction sales are often unique or nearly so. This year's automobile assembly facility, for example, will be different from last year's, for innovation in the automobile industry, as in most competitive industries, continues at a considerable pace. In specifying their requirements, owners often seek the help of architects and engineers, and their specifications are recorded in excruciating detail.

Construction activity also differs from other sales in that it frequently requires a long period of time between the day the owner specifies what he wants and the day of completion when he finally gets what he ordered.

Finally, the construction industry itself consists of hundreds of separate industries. In even the simplest home construction contract, there will be excavators, masons, carpenters, plumbers, electricians, roofers, and painters, whose suppliers will include equipment rental companies, lumberyards, pipe and fitting suppliers, hardware wholesalers, window manufacturers, insulation producers, and the like.

In short, construction activity is not akin to the assembly line. Contractors cannot always rely on timely deliveries, weather, subsoil conditions, the absence of strikes or work disputes, the availability of skilled workers, the adequacy of materials supply, steady prices during construction, continued fiscal health among subcontractors, and the absence of specification changes by the owner. The **prime contractor,** the contractor that agrees to complete the project in accordance with the owner's drawings and specifications, engages subcontractors, who may engage their own subcontractors to perform portions of the work. In such cases, subcontractors and their subsubcontractors may be working on a number of projects at one time. Delays on one project will tend to force delays on the subcontractor's other projects, since his employees (construction workers and management personnel) can only work on one project at a given time. One subcontractor's delays, furthermore, tend to delay everyone else. The pipe fitters cannot install pipe until the structural steel is in place; the carpet installers cannot lay the carpet while the painters are at work. One might marvel that anything ever gets built, and some owners might complain that during the period of construction, they wondered whether their project would ever see completion.

In fact, the system, ragged and complex as it is, works pretty well, but it is not always simple, and there are lots of traps and sometimes unhappy results.

§10.2 THE PLANNING PHASE

While an owner often knows what she wants her project to do, e.g., carry traffic over a gully, generate electricity, or house a tool and die works' expanded operation, she frequently does not know what it takes to achieve her desired objectives. Most commercial owners engage inside or outside construction experts, engineers, architects, and designers to create the specifications and drawings that will guide the construction of the facility. The product of this planning can be quite voluminous, so bulky and difficult to reproduce that often when the parties reach the bidding stage, potential bidders have to visit the owner's or the architect's premises to view the drawings, which may easily number in the hundreds, and specifications, which may easily comprise thousands of pages. Such drawings and specifications will include the dimensions of each doorway and window, the location of every power outlet for the plant's assembly area, the grades of plywood for interior and exterior surfaces, the diameter of steel reinforcing rods in the concrete footings, and the glazing compound for the windows.

Contracts with engineers, designers, and architects have been standardized to some extent. The American Institute of Architects, for example, publishes standard contract forms. Document 10-1 is one of them that illustrates a contract between an owner and a contractor.

§10.3 THE BIDDING PHASE

After the owner and its architects, engineers, and other designers have completed the drawings and specifications for the project, it is time to let the contract. While some owners may act as their own "general" contractor, most owners, especially small and medium-sized commercial enterprises without engineering or construction experience, will let the entire construction contract to a general contractor who will subcontract those portions of the project that he is not equipped to perform. The general contractor, for example, might have his own excavation equipment, carpenters, sheet metal workers, and laborers but will subcontract the mechanical work (plumbing, heating, and electrical) and some of the specialized work, such as the roofing, painting, and landscaping. At other times the prime contractor will subcontract all of the work, except for some general supervisory operations.

In government construction projects, the bidding procedure is usually governed by statute and regulations, and any failure on the part of a bidder to comply with the governing rules will render the bid unacceptable to the owner. In private projects, the owner has more leeway in soliciting bids. He might, for example, negotiate face-to-face with a single contractor or a few contractors and let the work on the basis of a cost-plus arrangement or at a fixed price for the completed work. He might invite sealed bids from a number of designated contractors or might open the bidding to contractors in general. Owners must take some care in specifying the terms of the bidding procedure. If, for example, the owner wants to reserve the right to reject the lowest bid if the reputation or financial integrity of a bidder is unsatisfactory, the invitation for bids should say so. Usually, the owner will want to accept the lowest bid and will want to insure fairness in the bidding process in order to attract bidders. The greater the number of responsible bidders, the greater the chance that the bids will be competitive and that the owner will enjoy the full benefit of that competition.

The general contractor, or prime contractor, cannot submit its bid to the owner until it knows what it will take to satisfy subcontractors. The prime contractor will solicit bids from its potential subcontractors in advance of submitting its bid to the owner. The prime contractor will require its subcontractors to leave their bids open until it knows whether it will

Figure 10-1. Construction Contract Model

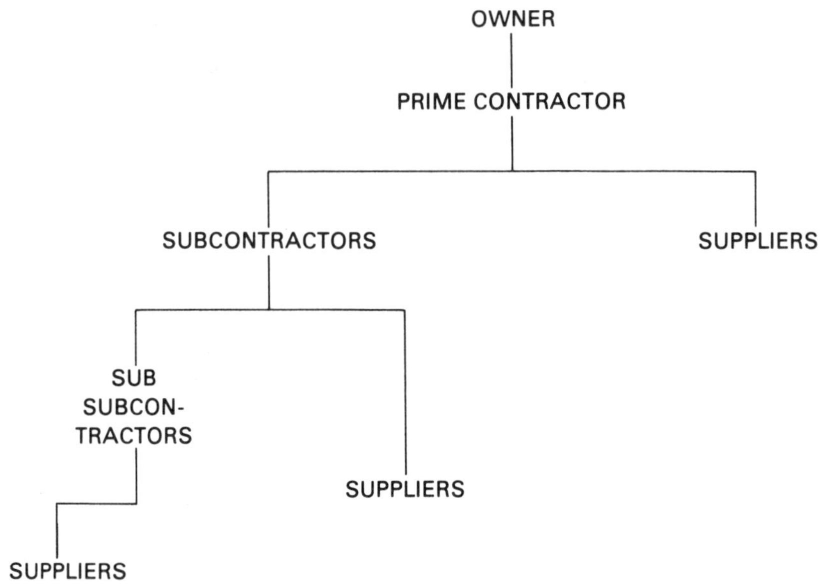

have the job and so that it can quickly accept the subcontractors' bids and thereby bind them.

After the owner notifies the prime contractor that it has been awarded the job, the prime contractor notifies its subcontractors. In a small building construction project, for example, at the time the bids are accepted, the overall transaction is illustrated by Figure 10-1.

Included in that diagram are the many suppliers from whom subcontractors will purchase materials and supplies for the project. Supply of some materials may be sufficiently scarce or price sensitive that subcontractors assure themselves of sources before bidding, but other materials are in abundant supply and do not justify the transaction costs in obtaining bids and the fixed price that results in the bidding process.

§10.4 THE ROLE OF THE BONDING COMPANY OR OTHER GUARANTOR

By insisting on bonds or their equivalent from bidders, prime contractors, subcontractors, and owners have reduced their exposure to risks of nonperformance. In the case of bids, for example, owners run the risk that a bidder might submit a bid and then, either because he no longer values the deal or is in financial difficulties, be unable to secure the necessary bonds or refuse to enter into the contract after the owner accepts the bid. In that case, the owner must either accept the next-lowest bid, which may be significantly higher than the lowest bid, or relet the contract. The reletting process will take time, may occur after word of the prior bid has become public, and will result in delay and higher costs for the project. Failure of the winning bidder to enter into the contract and post the required payment and performance bonds is a serious blow to the owner's interests, and she can prevent some of the loss by looking to a bond in a liquidated amount and conditioned on such a breach by the successful bidder. For similar reasons, prime contractors and subcontractors will seek **bid bonds** from their subcontractors. Document 10-2 is a sample bid bond.

The risk of nonperformance or misperformance does not confine itself to the bidding stage of the construction transaction. After the parties begin to perform, there is the danger that one or more of them will default. As a hedge against that eventuality, the owner may require the prime contractor and all subcontractors to obtain **payment** and **performance bonds**. These bonds require the bonding company to perform the insured contractor's work in the event of default and to pay any subcontractor or supplier whom the defaulting contractor fails to pay. Companies that issue performance bonds do not perform the work of the defaulting contractor but hire another contractor to do the work. Document 10-3 is a performance and material payment bond.

Lately, some contractors have been complaining that the cost of bonds, especially bid bonds, is too great and that they sometimes cannot obtain them even when they are financially responsible. Since most large construction projects call for bid bonds, a contractor that cannot obtain a bid bond or its equivalent will have to go out of business. Some owners have agreed to permit bidders to use letters of credit issued by commercial banks in lieu of the fidelity company's bid bond. There are two significant differences between the letter of credit and the bond. First, letters of credit are the primary obligation of the issuer, while bonds are secondary obligations, and second, a letter of credit issuer pays funds to the beneficiary, while the bond issuer, depending on the nature of the bond, may perform or may hire another contractor to perform an obligation of a defaulting contractor.

§10.5 THE PERFORMANCE PHASE

The owner must supervise performance of the construction contract. It would be wasteful to wait until the project is complete to determine whether the contractors have complied with the drawings and specifications, and, as any first-year law student knows, the courts are reluctant to force a contractor to rip a building apart to replace one brand of pipe with another. The owner, furthermore, must make periodic payments to his contractors. Construction companies are not sufficiently capitalized that they can finance the construction project. Banks and other short-term lenders traditionally serve that function. Contractors cannot perform on credit for very long periods. By delaying payments to their subcontractors and suppliers, contractors can usually perform on credit for a week or two or perhaps a little longer, but, during the performance of the contract, they must be paid frequently.

The owner will engage a manager, perhaps the architect or a firm specializing in the business, to supervise the construction at the job site. That supervision will include the keeping of records of material delivered to the site and work performed. The supervisor must determine that the materials delivered conform to the specifications and that the work done is also conforming. If the materials and work are conforming, the supervisor will authorize payment at the end of the payment interval. If everything goes according to plans, at the end of a payment period, each subcontractor will submit an application for payment to the contractor. Accompanying that application will be a statement of work done by the prime contractor and subcontractors. The owner then applies to the lender or the lender's agent, typically a title company, for an advance under the construction loan.

Under the law of most jurisdictions, persons who supply goods or services that are incorporated into real estate have a lien on that real estate and on the funds due under a contract for the construction of the improvement. In order to insure that those liens do not cloud the title and impair its mortgage, the construction lender will insist that each application be accompanied by partial lien waivers, executed by the subcontractors and their suppliers. The contractor will ask the job supervisor to approve the applications. The owner will then submit all of the applications to the construction lender, who will pay the face amounts of the applications, less any retainage specified in the contracts. Usually, the owner has the right to retain 10 percent of each application, the retainage to be paid when all of the work is satisfactorily completed. At that point, the owner or the construction lender's agent will require final lien waivers from the contractors. Document 10-4 is a final lien waiver form.

THE AMERICAN INSTITUTE OF ARCHITECTS

AIA Document A101

Standard Form of Agreement Between Owner and Contractor

where the basis of payment is a

STIPULATED SUM

1987 EDITION

THIS DOCUMENT HAS IMPORTANT LEGAL CONSEQUENCES; CONSULTATION WITH AN ATTORNEY IS ENCOURAGED WITH RESPECT TO ITS COMPLETION OR MODIFICATION.

The 1987 Edition of AIA Document A201, General Conditions of the Contract for Construction, is adopted in this document by reference. Do not use with other general conditions unless this document is modified.

This document has been approved and endorsed by The Associated General Contractors of America.

AGREEMENT

made as of the day of in the year of Nineteen Hundred and

BETWEEN the Owner:
(Name and address)

and the Contractor:
(Name and address)

The Project is:
(Name and location)

The Architect is:
(Name and address)

The Owner and Contractor agree as set forth below.

ARTICLE 1
THE CONTRACT DOCUMENTS

The Contract Documents consist of this Agreement, Conditions of the Contract (General, Supplementary and other Conditions), Drawings, Specifications, Addenda issued prior to execution of this Agreement, other documents listed in this Agreement and Modifications issued after execution of this Agreement; these form the Contract, and are as fully a part of the Contract as if attached to this Agreement or repeated herein. The Contract represents the entire and integrated agreement between the parties hereto and supersedes prior negotiations, representations or agreements, either written or oral. An enumeration of the Contract Documents, other than Modifications, appears in Article 9.

ARTICLE 2
THE WORK OF THIS CONTRACT

The Contractor shall execute the entire Work described in the Contract Documents, except to the extent specifically indicated in the Contract Documents to be the responsibility of others, or as follows:

ARTICLE 3
DATE OF COMMENCEMENT AND SUBSTANTIAL COMPLETION

3.1 The date of commencement is the date from which the Contract Time of Paragraph 3.2 is measured, and shall be the date of this Agreement, as first written above, unless a different date is stated below or provision is made for the date to be fixed in a notice to proceed issued by the Owner.

(Insert the date of commencement, if it differs from the date of this Agreement or, if applicable, state that the date will be fixed in a notice to proceed.)

Unless the date of commencement is established by a notice to proceed issued by the Owner, the Contractor shall notify the Owner in writing not less than five days before commencing the Work to permit the timely filing of mortgages, mechanic's liens and other security interests.

3.2 The Contractor shall achieve Substantial Completion of the entire Work not later than

(Insert the calendar date or number of calendar days after the date of commencement. Also insert any requirements for earlier Substantial Completion of certain portions of the Work, if not stated elsewhere in the Contract Documents.)

, subject to adjustments of this Contract Time as provided in the Contract Documents.

(Insert provisions, if any, for liquidated damages relating to failure to complete on time.)

ARTICLE 4
CONTRACT SUM

4.1 The Owner shall pay the Contractor in current funds for the Contractor's performance of the Contract the Contract Sum of Dollars ($), subject to additions and deductions as provided in the Contract Documents.

4.2 The Contract Sum is based upon the following alternates, if any, which are described in the Contract Documents and are hereby accepted by the Owner:

(State the numbers or other identification of accepted alternates. If decisions on other alternates are to be made by the Owner subsequent to the execution of this Agreement, attach a schedule of such other alternates showing the amount for each and the date until which that amount is valid.)

4.3 Unit prices, if any, are as follows:

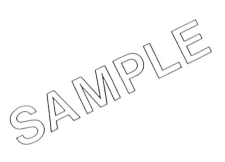

ARTICLE 5
PROGRESS PAYMENTS

5.1 Based upon Applications for Payment submitted to the Architect by the Contractor and Certificates for Payment issued by the Architect, the Owner shall make progress payments on account of the Contract Sum to the Contractor as provided below and elsewhere in the Contract Documents.

5.2 The period covered by each Application for Payment shall be one calendar month ending on the last day of the month, or as follows:

5.3 Provided an Application for Payment is received by the Architect not later than the day of a month, the Owner shall make payment to the Contractor not later than the day of the month. If an Application for Payment is received by the Architect after the application date fixed above, payment shall be made by the Owner not later than days after the Architect receives the Application for Payment.

5.4 Each Application for Payment shall be based upon the Schedule of Values submitted by the Contractor in accordance with the Contract Documents. The Schedule of Values shall allocate the entire Contract Sum among the various portions of the Work and be prepared in such form and supported by such data to substantiate its accuracy as the Architect may require. This Schedule, unless objected to by the Architect, shall be used as a basis for reviewing the Contractor's Applications for Payment.

5.5 Applications for Payment shall indicate the percentage of completion of each portion of the Work as of the end of the period covered by the Application for Payment.

5.6 Subject to the provisions of the Contract Documents, the amount of each progress payment shall be computed as follows:

5.6.1 Take that portion of the Contract Sum properly allocable to completed Work as determined by multiplying the percentage completion of each portion of the Work by the share of the total Contract Sum allocated to that portion of the Work in the Schedule of Values, less retainage of percent (%). Pending final determination of cost to the Owner of changes in the Work, amounts not in dispute may be included as provided in Subparagraph 7.3.7 of the General Conditions even though the Contract Sum has not yet been adjusted by Change Order;

5.6.2 Add that portion of the Contract Sum properly allocable to materials and equipment delivered and suitably stored at the site for subsequent incorporation in the completed construction (or, if approved in advance by the Owner, suitably stored off the site at a location agreed upon in writing), less retainage of percent (%);

5.6.3 Subtract the aggregate of previous payments made by the Owner; and

5.6.4 Subtract amounts, if any, for which the Architect has withheld or nullified a Certificate for Payment as provided in Paragraph 9.5 of the General Conditions.

5.7 The progress payment amount determined in accordance with Paragraph 5.6 shall be further modified under the following circumstances:

5.7.1 Add, upon Substantial Completion of the Work, a sum sufficient to increase the total payments to percent (%) of the Contract Sum, less such amounts as the Architect shall determine for incomplete Work and unsettled claims; and

5.7.2 Add, if final completion of the Work is thereafter materially delayed through no fault of the Contractor, any additional amounts payable in accordance with Subparagraph 9.10.3 of the General Conditions.

5.8 Reduction or limitation of retainage, if any, shall be as follows:

(If it is intended, prior to Substantial Completion of the entire Work, to reduce or limit the retainage resulting from the percentages inserted in Subparagraphs 5.6.1 and 5.6.2 above, and this is not explained elsewhere in the Contract Documents, insert here provisions for such reduction or limitation.)

Document 10-1. (*continued*)

ARTICLE 6
FINAL PAYMENT

Final payment, constituting the entire unpaid balance of the Contract Sum, shall be made by the Owner to the Contractor when (1) the Contract has been fully performed by the Contractor except for the Contractor's responsibility to correct nonconforming Work as provided in Subparagraph 12.2.2 of the General Conditions and to satisfy other requirements, if any, which necessarily survive final payment; and (2) a final Certificate for Payment has been issued by the Architect; such final payment shall be made by the Owner not more than 30 days after the issuance of the Architect's final Certificate for Payment, or as follows:

ARTICLE 7
MISCELLANEOUS PROVISIONS

7.1 Where reference is made in this Agreement to a provision of the General Conditions or another Contract Document, the reference refers to that provision as amended or supplemented by other provisions of the Contract Documents.

7.2 Payments due and unpaid under the Contract shall bear interest from the date payment is due at the rate stated below, or in the absence thereof, at the legal rate prevailing from time to time at the place where the Project is located.

(Insert rate of interest agreed upon, if any.)

(Usury laws and requirements under the Federal Truth in Lending Act, similar state and local consumer credit laws and other regulations at the Owner's and Contractor's principal places of business, the location of the Project and elsewhere may affect the validity of this provision. Legal advice should be obtained with respect to deletions or modifications, and also regarding requirements such as written disclosures or waivers.)

7.3 Other provisions:

ARTICLE 8
TERMINATION OR SUSPENSION

8.1 The Contract may be terminated by the Owner or the Contractor as provided in Article 14 of the General Conditions.

8.2 The Work may be suspended by the Owner as provided in Article 14 of the General Conditions.

Document 10-1. (*continued*)

ARTICLE 9
ENUMERATION OF CONTRACT DOCUMENTS

9.1 The Contract Documents, except for Modifications issued after execution of this Agreement, are enumerated as follows:

9.1.1 The Agreement is this executed Standard Form of Agreement Between Owner and Contractor, AIA Document A101, 1987 Edition.

9.1.2 The General Conditions are the General Conditions of the Contract for Construction, AIA Document A201, 1987 Edition.

9.1.3 The Supplementary and other Conditions of the Contract are those contained in the Project Manual dated and are as follows:

Document	Title	Pages

9.1.4 The Specifications are those contained in the Project Manual dated as in Subparagraph 9.1.3, and are as follows:
(Either list the Specifications here or refer to an exhibit attached to this Agreement.)

Section	Title	Pages

9.1.5 The Drawings are as follows, and are dated   unless a different date is shown below:
(Either list the Drawings here or refer to an exhibit attached to this Agreement.)

Number	Title	Date

9.1.6 The Addenda, if any, are as follows:

Number	Date	Pages

Portions of Addenda relating to bidding requirements are not part of the Contract Documents unless the bidding requirements are also enumerated in this Article 9.

9.1.7 Other documents, if any, forming part of the Contract Documents are as follows:

(List here any additional documents which are intended to form part of the Contract Documents. The General Conditions provide that bidding requirements such as advertisement or invitation to bid, Instructions to Bidders, sample forms and the Contractor's bid are not part of the Contract Documents unless enumerated in this Agreement. They should be listed here only if intended to be part of the Contract Documents.)

This Agreement is entered into as of the day and year first written above and is executed in at least three original copies of which one is to be delivered to the Contractor, one to the Architect for use in the administration of the Contract, and the remainder to the Owner.

OWNER	CONTRACTOR
(Signature)	*(Signature)*
(Printed name and title)	*(Printed name and title)*

THE AMERICAN INSTITUTE OF ARCHITECTS

AIA Document A310

Bid Bond

KNOW ALL MEN BY THESE PRESENTS, that we
(Here insert full name and address or legal title of Contractor)

as Principal, hereinafter called the Principal, and
(Here insert full name and address or legal title of Surety)

a corporation duly organized under the laws of the State of
as Surety, hereinafter called the Surety, are held and firmly bound unto
(Here insert full name and address or legal title of Owner)

as Obligee, hereinafter called the Obligee, in the sum of

Dollars ($),

for the payment of which sum well and truly to be made, the said Principal and the said Surety, bind ourselves, our heirs, executors, administrators, successors and assigns, jointly and severally, firmly by these presents.

WHEREAS, the Principal has submitted a bid for
(Here insert full name, address and description of project)

NOW, THEREFORE, if the Obligee shall accept the bid of the Principal and the Principal shall enter into a Contract with the Obligee in accordance with the terms of such bid, and give such bond or bonds as may be specified in the bidding or Contract Documents with good and sufficient surety for the faithful performance of such Contract and for the prompt payment of labor and material furnished in the prosecution thereof, or in the event of the failure of the Principal to enter such Contract and give such bond or bonds, if the Principal shall pay to the Obligee the difference not to exceed the penalty hereof between the amount specified in said bid and such larger amount for which the Obligee may in good faith contract with another party to perform the Work covered by said bid, then this obligation shall be null and void, otherwise to remain in full force and effect.

Signed and sealed this day of 19

(Witness) — (Principal) (Seal)

(Title)

(Witness) — (Surety) (Seal)

(Title)

THE AMERICAN INSTITUTE OF ARCHITECTS

AIA Document A311

Performance Bond

KNOW ALL MEN BY THESE PRESENTS: that

(Here insert full name and address or legal title of Contractor)

as Principal, hereinafter called Contractor, and,

(Here insert full name and address or legal title of Surety)

as Surety, hereinafter called Surety, are held and firmly bound unto

(Here insert full name and address or legal title of Owner)

as Obligee, hereinafter called Owner, in the amount of

Dollars ($),

for the payment whereof Contractor and Surety bind themselves, their heirs, executors, administrators, successors and assigns, jointly and severally, firmly by these presents.

WHEREAS,

Contractor has by written agreement dated 19 , entered into a contract with Owner for

(Here insert full name, address and description of project)

in accordance with Drawings and Specifications prepared by

(Here insert full name and address or legal title of Architect)

which contract is by reference made a part hereof, and is hereinafter referred to as the Contract.

PERFORMANCE BOND

NOW, THEREFORE, THE CONDITION OF THIS OBLIGATION is such that, if Contractor shall promptly and faithfully perform said Contract, then this obligation shall be null and void; otherwise it shall remain in full force and effect.

The Surety hereby waives notice of any alteration or extension of time made by the Owner.

Whenever Contractor shall be, and declared by Owner to be in default under the Contract, the Owner having performed Owner's obligations thereunder, the Surety may promptly remedy the default, or shall promptly

1) Complete the Contract in accordance with its terms and conditions, or

2) Obtain a bid or bids for completing the Contract in accordance with its terms and conditions, and upon determination by Surety of the lowest responsible bidder, or, if the Owner elects, upon determination by the Owner and the Surety jointly of the lowest responsible bidder, arrange for a contract between such bidder and Owner, and make available as Work progresses (even though there should be a default or a succession of defaults under the contract or contracts of completion arranged under this paragraph) sufficient funds to pay the cost of completion less the balance of the contract price; but not exceeding, including other costs and damages for which the Surety may be liable hereunder, the amount set forth in the first paragraph hereof. The term "balance of the contract price," as used in this paragraph, shall mean the total amount payable by Owner to Contractor under the Contract and any amendments thereto, less the amount properly paid by Owner to Contractor.

Any suit under this bond must be instituted before the expiration of two (2) years from the date on which final payment under the Contract falls due.

No right of action shall accrue on this bond to or for the use of any person or corporation other than the Owner named herein or the heirs, executors, administrators or successors of the Owner.

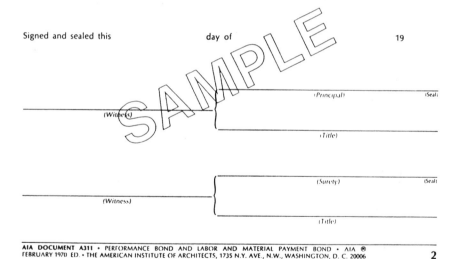

Signed and sealed this day of 19

(Principal) (Seal)

(Witness)

(Title)

(Surety) (Seal)

(Witness)

(Title)

THE AMERICAN INSTITUTE OF ARCHITECTS

AIA Document A311

Labor and Material Payment Bond

THIS BOND IS ISSUED SIMULTANEOUSLY WITH PERFORMANCE BOND IN FAVOR OF THE OWNER CONDITIONED ON THE FULL AND FAITHFUL PERFORMANCE OF THE CONTRACT

KNOW ALL MEN BY THESE PRESENTS: that

(Here insert full name and address or legal title of Contractor)

as Principal, hereinafter called Principal, and,

(Here insert full name and address or legal title of Surety)

as Surety, hereinafter called Surety, are held and firmly bound unto

(Here insert full name and address or legal title of Owner)

as Obligee, hereinafter called Owner, for the use and benefit of claimants as hereinbelow defined, in the amount of

(Here insert a sum equal to at least one-half of the contract price) Dollars ($),

for the payment whereof Principal and Surety bind themselves, their heirs, executors, administrators, successors and assigns, jointly and severally, firmly by these presents.

WHEREAS,

Principal has by written agreement dated 19 , entered into a contract with Owner for

(Here insert full name, address and description of project)

in accordance with Drawings and Specifications prepared by

(Here insert full name and address or legal title of Architect)

which contract is by reference made a part hereof, and is hereinafter referred to as the Contract.

AIA DOCUMENT A311 • PERFORMANCE BOND AND LABOR AND MATERIAL PAYMENT BOND • AIA ®
FEBRUARY 1970 ED. • THE AMERICAN INSTITUTE OF ARCHITECTS, 1735 N.Y. AVE., N.W., WASHINGTON, D. C. 20006 3

LABOR AND MATERIAL PAYMENT BOND

NOW, THEREFORE, THE CONDITION OF THIS OBLIGATION is such that, if Principal shall promptly make payment to all claimants as hereinafter defined, for all labor and material used or reasonably required for use in the performance of the Contract, then this obligation shall be void; otherwise it shall remain in full force and effect, subject, however, to the following conditions:

1. A claimant is defined as one having a direct contract with the Principal or with a Subcontractor of the Principal for labor, material, or both, used or reasonably required for use in the performance of the Contract, labor and material being construed to include that part of water, gas, power, light, heat, oil, gasoline, telephone service or rental of equipment directly applicable to the Contract.

2. The above named Principal and Surety hereby jointly and severally agree with the Owner that every claimant as herein defined, who has not been paid in full before the expiration of a period of ninety (90) days after the date on which the last of such claimant's work or labor was done or performed, or materials were furnished by such claimant, may sue on this bond for the use of such claimant, prosecute the suit to final judgment for such sum or sums as may be justly due claimant, and have execution thereon. The Owner shall not be liable for the payment of any costs or expenses of any such suit.

3. No suit or action shall be commenced hereunder by any claimant:

a) Unless claimant, other than one having a direct contract with the Principal, shall have given written notice to any two of the following: the Principal, the Owner, or the Surety above named, within ninety (90) days after such claimant did or performed the last of the work or labor, or furnished the last of the materials for which said claim is made, stating with substantial accuracy the amount claimed and the name of the party to whom the materials were furnished, or for whom the work or labor was done or performed. Such notice shall be served by mailing the same by registered mail or certified mail, postage prepaid, in an envelope addressed to the Principal, Owner or Surety, at any place where an office is regularly maintained for the transaction of business, or served in any manner in which legal process may be served in the state in which the aforesaid project is located, save that such service need not be made by a public officer.

b) After the expiration of one (1) year following the date on which Principal ceased Work on said Contract, it being understood, however, that if any limitation embodied in this bond is prohibited by any law controlling the construction hereof such limitation shall be deemed to be amended so as to be equal to the minimum period of limitation permitted by such law.

c) Other than in a state court of competent jurisdiction in and for the county or other political subdivision of the state in which the Project, or any part thereof, is situated, or in the United States District Court for the district in which the Project, or any part thereof, is situated, and not elsewhere.

4. The amount of this bond shall be reduced by and to the extent of any payment or payments made in good faith hereunder, inclusive of the payment by Surety of mechanics' liens which may be filed of record against said improvement, whether or not claim for the amount of such lien be presented under and against this bond.

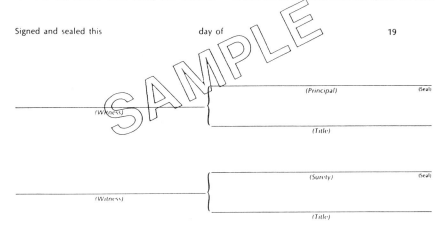

Signed and sealed this day of 19

	(Principal) (Seal)
(Witness)	
	(Title)
	(Surety) (Seal)
(Witness)	
	(Title)

CAM CONSTRUCTION ASSOCIATION OF MICHIGAN

Form No. LL0016

FULL UNCONDITIONAL WAIVER

My/our contract with ....
(other contracting party)

to provide ....

....

for the improvement of the property described as: ....

....

....

....

having been fully paid and satisfied, all my/our construction lien rights against such property are hereby waived and released.

....

BY: ....
(signature of claimant)

Address: ....

....

Telephone: ....

SPECIMEN

Signed on: ....
(date)

DO NOT SIGN BLANK OR INCOMPLETE FORMS. RETAIN A COPY.

THE CONSTRUCTION ASSOCIATION OF MICHIGAN EXPRESSLY DISCLAIMS ANY LIABILITY FOR CHANGES MADE TO THIS FORM BY LEGISLATIVE ENACTMENTS OR JUDICIAL DECISIONS.

PART I
GLOSSARY

Acceleration — in installment obligations, the right of the obligee, in certain circumstances, to declare all installments due. [The obligee will invariably insist on the right to accelerate payment obligations in the event of the obligor's default on one payment. In an installment promissory note, for example, the holder will want to declare the full balance due upon the default of the maker on one payment. Otherwise, the obligee of an installment obligation must wait until each installment is due before it can bring an action against the defaulting obligor.]

Acceptance — a negotiable instrument that is payable a stated period of time after its "acceptance." [In the **documentary draft** transaction, a seller draws a **draft** on the buyer. If the sales contract between the buyer and the seller calls for credit, the buyer will have a number of days, say 60, to pay the draft. When the seller's agent, usually a collecting bank, presents the draft to the buyer, the buyer will signal its undertaking to pay the draft upon maturity by signing the draft on its face. That signature is an act of acceptance and the negotiable draft becomes a negotiable acceptance.] (*See also* **banker's acceptance, trade acceptance.**)

Agreement — the bargain of the parties in fact. (*Compare* **contract.**)

Allowance — credit due a buyer for returns, damages to delivered goods, and short shipments.

Arbitrage — the practice of buying in one market and selling in another. [If the price of a commodity, for example, in New York is higher than the price of the same commodity in California, arbitrageurs will buy in California and sell in New York. Sometimes a seller will attempt to maintain price differentials by restricting resales of its commodities in a particular market. If *A* sells to *B* in the North with an understanding that *B* will not sell in the South, *A* will be able to charge higher prices in the South than *B* charges its customers in the North only so long as C, an arbitrageur, does not learn of the price disparity. Once C learns the facts, he will buy from *B* and resell in the South at a price lower than *A* is charging.]

Attornment — acknowledgment of another's rights in property. [In feudal times, a tenant recognized a new landlord by attorning — the act of acknowledging that the tenant held the real estate through the lord. The concept of attorning survived to some extent in **bailments**, by virtue of the fact that the law treated as significant a **bailee's** acknowledgment that he held for a new owner. To a degree, notice to a bailee has displaced attornment. It is not necessary in general for the bailee to attorn, notice to the bailee being sufficient.]

Bailee — one who takes possession of goods and holds or transports them for another. [Bailees may, in turn, bail goods with a third party, a sub-bailee, or may hold goods that are transferred from the original bailor to a second full or part owner, such as a secured party.]

Bailment — delivery of property by the **bailor** to an agent, the **bailee**, for storage, transport, service, or other purpose. [It is sometimes difficult to distinguish a bailment from a sale. Common bailments include personal property leases, storage arrangements with commercial warehouses, and shipment by common carrier.] (*See also* **bill of lading** and **warehouse receipt**.)

Bailor — one who delivers goods to a **bailee** for storage, transport, services, or other purposes. (*See* **bailment**.)

Banker's acceptance — an acceptance made by a bank, rather than by a merchant. (*Compare* **trade acceptance**.)

Basing Point Pricing System — determining price to include the cost of shipment from a base point even though shipment may be from a different point.

Bill of exchange — synonym for **draft**. [The term derives from the earliest function of the draft as a medieval instrument of international trade that served, in part, to exchange one currency for another. The term survives in England and other common law jurisdictions.]

Bill of lading — a **document of title** issued by a carrier evidencing a contract of carriage of the goods and setting out delivery terms.

Bid bond — undertaking of a surety company to pay a percentage of the contractor's bid to the owner if the owner accepts the contractor's bid and the contractor does not enter into the construction contract and supply **performance** and **payment bonds.**

Bond — an undertaking whereby one party (1) acts as surety for another's obligation to a third party or (2) agrees to hold a party free from loss. (*See also* **bid bond**, **performance bond**, **payment bond**.)

Boot — in a trade, something given in addition to the item traded.

Broker — middleman that undertakes to sell frequently odd lots and usually not on a continuing basis. [Brokers may represent any number of sellers in an industry or in related industries. Brokers usually do not take title to the goods they sell for their principals but "broker" the merchandise, real estate, or securities. Often, brokers do not even take possession of the property they sell but traditionally bring together sellers and buyers that do not regularly do business with each other. Sellers of odd lots and distress merchandise and occasional sellers often resort to brokers. Owners of real estate and securities traditionally use brokers to find buyers, and, conversely, buyers of real estate and securities use brokers to find sellers.]

Bulk sale — traditionally, a sale of more than one-half of inventory out of the ordinary course of business. [Bulk sales are extraordinary, and they attract the attention of the law because they were used at times in the past as a method to avoid creditors' claims. A merchant that had obtained credit on the strength of his inventory might sell out in bulk, abscond with the sale proceeds and leave his reliance creditors with nothing. The advent of credit reporting agencies, audited financial statements, and filing systems have largely put an end to the bulk sale fraud. Today's creditors rarely extend credit on the strength of a merchant's stock in trade. The Bulk Sales Law, Article 6 of the Uniform Commercial Code, survives in most jurisdictions, nonetheless, and the notion of a bulk sale is still important to the extent that it is not a sale in ordinary course, so that the bulk sale buyer does not qualify for the favored treatment of the **buyer in ordinary course**.]

Buyer in ordinary course — a buyer who buys out of inventory in good faith and without knowledge that his purchase is in violation of the ownership interest of a third party. [The advantage of buyer in ordinary course status lies in the **good-faith purchase** doctrine, that is, the notion that the buyer in ordinary course takes free and clear of most claims and defenses.]

Cartel — a horizontal combination of independent sellers or producers for the purpose of restricting output and increasing prices.

Cashier's check — a **check** drawn by a bank on itself. [The act of the bank's drawing on itself raises conceptual questions. Some courts view the cashier's check as an "accepted" item, since it contains the signature of the drawee, just as an acceptance does. Other courts see the cashier's check more in the nature of a promissory note. The commercial advantage of the cashier's check over the regular check is the fact that it involves the undertaking of the bank, which cannot stop payment, except in unusual circumstances. The cashier's check reduces significantly the risks of insufficient funds and of stopped payment.]

Cash sale — sale not on credit. [In every sale, the seller, consciously or unconsciously, decides whether (1) he will deliver on the credit of the buyer's promise to pay or (2) insist on delivery against payment. The former is a **credit sale**; the latter is a **cash sale.** To some extent, there is always a measure of trust on both sides of a sale. If the seller hands the goods to the buyer, while the buyer fills out a check, the seller has, in a sense, entered into a credit transaction. By the same token, the buyer that hands cash to the seller as the seller prepares to hand the buyer goods has extended credit to the seller by prepaying. As a matter of commercial and legal necessity, the law and merchants have distinguished these substantially contemporaneous transactions from those in which payment or delivery is deferred. Payment by a check postdated by a single day creates a credit sale. The distinction between cash and credit sales is important. Mercantile fairness demands that the credit seller shoulder the risks inherent in his decision to trust the buyer and that he not be able to shift the risk to innocent third parties that rely on appearances created by the seller's delivery of merchandise to the buyer. Yet, the law, in order perhaps to encourage the use of certain negotiable instruments and to reward transactions that are regular, treats the seller that takes a check that is not postdated, i.e., a check that is payable on demand, as a cash sale.] (*Compare* **credit sale.**)

Caveat emptor — "let the buyer beware." [The rule that the buyer should beware originated in the **security of property** concept that the buyer could take no greater interest in the property sold than the seller enjoyed. The first crack in the caveat emptor doctrine was the **good-faith purchase** exception to security of property.]

Certified check — check drawn by a customer on his bank and accepted by the bank, the act of acceptance constituting certification. [The commercial advantages of the certified check are that it virtually eliminates the risks of insufficient funds and stopped payment.] (*See also* **cashier's check.**)

Channel of distribution — method of marketing products. [Each seller must decide which method of distributing its goods is most efficient. Large firms may seeks economies through **vertical integration**. Smaller firms may use **direct sales** efforts, **distributors, manufacturers' agents**, or a combination of these and other distribution methods.]

Chattel — item of personal property.

Check — a **negotiable instrument**, being an order (i.e., a **draft**) drawn on a bank and payable on demand. [Formerly, some checks were "counter" checks that permitted a depositor to use a blank check supplied by a merchant. With the advent of reader sorter machines in the bank collection system and the need for microencoded ink character recognition (MICR) symbols that the reader sorter equipment reads, preprinted checks with symbols that route the check during the collection process and that identify the drawee bank and the drawer's account became indispensable. At that point, the counter check disappeared. There are a number of items in the bank collection system that are "near checks." The thrift industry in the 1970s introduced the **negotiable order of withdrawal** and the share draft. While these items are not technically checks (since they are not drawn on banks), they generally function as checks do, and most courts seem inclined to treat them as such. Current efforts at legislative reform are catching up with these financial industry innovations.]

Chose in action — right to bring an action to enforce an obligation. [At early common law, prompted by fears of fraudulent claims, courts were adamant in their opposition to the alienability of a chose in action. Only the original obligee could maintain the action. That view unduly inhibited the marketability of obligations (notes, **drafts, bonds,** etc.), and eventually, after a long struggle and with the prodding of the legislature, the courts abandoned it.]

Claim — an assertion of a property interest. [The true owner of goods that brings an action to recover them from a thief is making a claim. By the same token, a secured party that sues for the value of security that has been disposed of by a third party is making a claim. Causes of action in replevin and conversion are classic claims. One of the benefits of **good-faith purchase** status is that it cuts off the claims that arise most often.]

Coase Theorem — the theorem that in a world without **transaction costs**, regardless of the legal allocation of risks, contracting parties will opt for a **pareto optimal** risk allocation.

Commission merchant — similar to a **broker**, except that the commission merchant traditionally does take delivery from its seller and may store and transport the merchandise and sell in its own name.

Commodities exchange — organization of merchants or brokers that trade usually at a given location commodities represented by contracts or other documents.

Consignment — seller's delivery of goods to buyer for resale with the understanding that **title** will remain in seller and buyer will return to seller any goods that are not resold. [The law has some difficulty distinguishing true consignments from disguised inventory financing arrangements.]

Consumer — any party that uses up, rather than resells, services, raw materials, or products. [A utility company consumes raw materials and uses motor vehicles. In the broad sense, the utility is a consumer. The concept is often used more narrowly to cover individuals who are using goods or services for personal, family, or household purposes. It is important for commercial law to maintain the distinction between the consumer and the nonconsumer and especially between the consumer and the **merchant**. Law fashioned to meet the exigencies of the merchant setting often does not suit the consumer setting, and, conversely, law fashioned to protect consumers often does not suit the market place's needs for celerity and certainty.]

Contract — legal obligation that arises from the **agreement** of the parties. [The distinction between *agreement* and *contract* is a basic Llewellynism grounded in the Uniform Commercial Code and in the dogma of legal realism — the jurisprudence he, in his role as chief reporter, enshrined in much of the Uniform Commercial Code.]

Cost — a nebulous and often troublesome concept in sales transactions relating to the expenses incurred by a seller in producing a product or service. [Buyers sometimes agree to buy on a seemingly simple "cost plus basis." In fact, there are significant difficulties in computing the cost of a manufactured or processed commodity or of services. Allocation of overhead is frequently the subject of dispute. Tooling-up costs and labor costs are very much subject to the whim of the manufacturer, unless the sales contract specifies matters in great detail. By making short production runs at times when employees are working at overtime rates and by using raw materials and parts that are the highest priced of those items in inventory, a producer can pass high costs on to its cost plus buyer. Even the most scrupulous seller and buyer will find themselves at odds over cost allocations as cost accountants themselves frequently disagree over those allocations.]

Credit sale — sale not for cash. [When a seller delivers goods or provides services without substantially contemporaneous payment, it has extended credit to the buyer, and the law frequently imposes burdens on it. The act of extending credit is not commercially unreasonable and, in fact, is economically desirable. There inheres in the credit transaction the risk of the buyer's default, and the law generally takes account of that reality by depriving the seller of certain rights that the cash seller, who has not extended credit, still enjoys.] (*Compare* **cash sale.**)

Dating — the practice of extending the time for payment beyond the customary credit period. [In the brass industry, for example, foundries that serve as parts **vendors** may sell on 30-day credit terms. If a brass parts buyer's business is seasonal, it may not be able to pay within 30 days, and the foundry may extend the time for payment to 60 or 90 days. EOM (end of month) dating is the practice, common in some industries, of having the credit term start at the end of the month in which purchases are made. Under EOM dating, a 30-day credit term will begin to run at the end of the month. Buyers who purchase at the beginning of a month will have more than 30, perhaps as many as 60 days, before payment is due.]

Death of contract — the idea that formal contract rules, especially the Statute of Frauds, the perfect tender rule, and the doctrine of consideration, are unimportant relics that courts largely ignore in deed, if not in word. [In reaction to the formalism that characterized contract law in the eighteenth and nineteenth centuries, courts began in this century and to some extent in the last to relax the enforcement of contract provisions and even to challenge the notion that contracts needed consideration to be binding. By invoking estoppel in all its guises, opening the parol evidence rule and the Statute of Frauds to numerous exceptions, inferring "missing terms," fashioning unconscionability and bad-faith defenses and standards, and generally rendering contract enforcement problematic and uncertain, courts have, in the words of Professor Grant Gilmore, given the death to contract. While Gilmore generally applauded this retreat from formalism, the development left commercial parties with serious problems. The issue in contract drafting became one not so much of spelling out the agreement but of predicting whether the courts would enforce the agreement as written. Merchants and business people have adapted in a number of ways. They have, in many cases, deprived the courts of jurisdiction by agreeing to commercial arbitration. To some extent, they have modified the contractual relationship by introducing commercial specialties such as standby letters of credit and first demand guaranties. It is axiomatic, furthermore, that they have increased their prices to cover the cost of doing business with contractual uncertainties.]

Dealer — a retailer, the last seller in the **channel of distribution**.

Defense — legal argument excusing nonpayment or other nonperformance of a contract or other obligation. [Defenses become important in commercial and contract law when the obligee transfers the **chose in action** to a third party. If that third party enjoys **good-faith purchase** protection, it takes free of commercial defenses, that is, personal defenses, but takes subject to real defenses. The law of each state determines which defenses are real and which personal, but it is the law in all jurisdictions that the good-faith purchaser takes free of the defenses of failure of consideration and fraud in the inducement. Since these two defense are the defenses that arise most commonly in commercial transactions, by protecting the good-faith purchaser from them, the doctrine of good-faith purchase provides significant protection. Real defenses usually cover such matters as incompetence, fraud in the execution, illegality, and the like, i.e., defenses arising out of rather uncommon settings.]

Delivery terms — terms in a sales contract that specify the place, time, and manner of delivery of goods or services. (*See also* **Price terms**.)

Demand — in economics, the quantity of a product that will be sold at a given price.

Demand curve — in economics, graph on which the *y* axis is the price and the *x* axis is the quantity of **demand**. (*Compare* **Supply curve**.)

Derivation principle — the first rule of conveyancing law, a synonym for the **shelter principle**, based on the notion that the taker derives all of his rights from the transferor. (*See also* **nemo dat rule**.)

Direct sales — sales by a manufacturer or other supplier to its customers without using a **commission merchant, manufacturer's agent,** or the like.

Discount —

(1) reductions in the price, usually by virtue of early payment, volume purchase, or early order. [In an open account sale, for example, sellers might offer 60-day credit terms with a 5 percent discount

for payment within 30 days. Seasonal businesses, anxious to even out their production schedules, increase cash flow during slow periods, and reduce inventory costs, will offer special discounts to customers that place orders early in the season or off season. Many manufacturers offer discounts to special customers, such as **OEM** or fleet buyers. Sometimes, sellers in an industry publish their price lists and give trade discounts off the list price. Trade discounts are determined by the market, and the trade discount arrangement is designed to obviate the need to republish price lists.]

(2) purchase of **dealer** paper at a price below face. [Formerly, banks performed an important function called the "discount function," which consisted of taking a merchant's paper (obligations, usually promissory notes, of the merchant's customers) and collecting it. When the bank took the paper, it paid less than par, i.e., less than the face value of the paper. The difference between par and the amount the bank paid was the discount. Today, banks and other lenders discount retail installment contracts and receivables for dealers and sometimes discount a seller's time draft.]

Distributor — enterprise that buys from manufacturers, transports, stores, and resells to **original equipment manufacturers,** governmental units, mining, transportation, communications, retailers, and similar firms. [Distributors are **wholesalers**. Distributors that deal in products that are not sold at retail are sometimes called "industrial distributors."]

Documentary draft — a **draft** accompanied by a **document of title**. [The documentary draft arises in the documentary draft transaction and the letter of credit transaction. Usually the document that accompanies the draft will be a **bill of lading** or a **warehouse receipt**.]

Document of title — document issued by or to a **bailee** involving the carriage or storage of goods. [The most common documents of title are the **bill of lading, the warehouse receipt**, and the **delivery order**, of which the first two also serve as a contract between the **bailor** and the bailee. Documents of title may be negotiable or nonnegotiable. In the former case, they generally stand for the goods; in the latter they do not.] (*See also* **bailment, documentary draft, negotiability**.)

Draft — an instrument, usually negotiable in form, by which the drawer of the draft orders the drawee to pay the payee. ["Sight" drafts are payable on demand, i.e., "at sight." "Time" or "usance" drafts are payable a period of time after presentment or date, i.e., "at usance." Drafts arise in the **letter of credit** transaction and the **documentary draft** transaction. A **check** is a draft drawn on a bank and payable on demand.]

Drop shipping — delivery of goods not to buyer but, at buyer's request, to buyer's subpurchaser. [Frequently manufacturers or other suppliers will enter into contracts with buyers, such as **group buyers**, that do not take delivery of the merchandise. The buyer, who has located a sub-buyer, will direct the supplier to deliver to the sub-buyer, that is, to drop ship to the sub-buyer. Drop shipping is a common practice, and its significance to the supplier can be overemphasized. The typical seller will treat drop shipment instructions as ordinary delivery instructions, and courts should not, though they sometimes do, attach significance to the drop shipping arrangement.]

EDI (*See* **electronic data interchange.**)

Elasticity — in economics, the direct response of one factor (e.g., price or supply) to the increase or decrease of another factor. [When demand or supply tends to react to price or income change, that demand or supply is said to be elastic. If, for example, the demand for French wine tends to increase as the price decreases or tends to increase as income increases, the demand for French wine is elastic. (In the first case "price elastic," in the second case "income elastic.") If the demand for bread does not decrease when the price increases or does not decrease when income decreases, the demand for bread is inelastic. Similarly, the supply of some agricultural commodities is inelastic, that is, when the price decreases, the supply may increase; while the supply of oil is traditionally seen to be elastic, since the supply of oil will usually increase as the price increases.]

Electronic data interchange — technological development, much ballyhooed of late, that permits information to be transmitted by computer technology. [Commercial activity is often subject to documentation, thanks in no small part to us lawyers. That documentation slows the process. It may take three days for a purchase order to travel by mail from Boston to San Francisco and three days for the order acknowledgment to get back. It takes seconds for information to be transmitted by computers using satellite and telephone communications systems. Buyers and sellers with access to electronic date interchange (EDI) systems can often conclude a **contract** in seconds, rather than days. EDI systems may be quite sophisticated. SWIFT, an international bank communication system, for example, uses switching centers, so that banks need access SWIFT only and need not have direct access to the hundreds of banks in the system. The switching center, acting like the hub of a hub-and-spoke system, can relay information from any sender to any bank connected to the system. Part III explains EDI in the Payments System, and Chapter 27 of that Part explains SWIFT.]

Ex ante — before the fact. [In many executory contract situations, a party will attempt to take full advantage of the benefits accorded him under the contract at the outset (ex ante) but to deprive the other party of the benefits of the arrangement later (**ex post**).]

Ex post — after the fact. (*Compare* **ex ante**.)

Express warranty — obligation relating to the nature of goods or services imposed on a party, usually a seller, by virtue of terms in the agreement between the parties. (*Compare* **implied warranty**.)

Externalities — consequences of economic activity that are not included in the cost of that activity. [If the cost of pollution from a garbage incinerator is borne by the residents in the vicinity of the incinerator rather than those who produce the garbage or use the steam generated by the incinerator, the pollution costs are externalities.]

Fabricator — manufacturing enterprise that takes a manufactured product and refashions it. [An aluminum fabricator, for example, takes aluminum ingots produced by a mill that refines bauxite (aluminum ore) into ingots. The fabricator takes the ingots and makes aluminum products, such as framing for storm doors and windows.]

Factor — formerly, a merchant that holds and sells the goods of others, today usually called a **commission merchant**. [For many centuries until the beginning of this one, manufacturers would use a factor to market their goods away from the place of manufacture, and agricultural producers would use factors to market their produce in the cities. A New York manufacturing firm would deliver merchandise to a factor who would transport the goods to Tennessee, for example, and sell them to retailers. Tennessee farmers would deliver grain to factors who would transport them to New Orleans, for example, and sell them to exporters or mills. Today, the term *factor* usually refers to finance companies that buy and collect or lend against receivables. The literature sometimes refers to the selling agent as the "old factor" and the company that finances receivables as the "new factor."] (*See also* **supercargo**.)

Finisher — an enterprise that takes a product and transforms it in some way. A textile finisher, for example, buys materials produced by a mill and, using dyes, creates patterns and colors in the product.]

Fixed cost — cost that does not increase with increases in sales. The cost of heating a manufacturing facility is a fixed cost, since it does not increase as productivity increases. (*Compare* **variable cost**.)

Forward contract — agreement for the sale of a specific quantity of goods or securities at an agreed-upon price, delivery and payment to be made at a subsequent date. (*See also* **futures contract**.)

Franchise — the right to market a manufacturer's goods or to use a trade name or mark in a designated territory, often on an exclusive basis. [When an organization grants special marketing privileges, such as an exclusive territory and the use of marks or names, to a buyer, the arrangement is termed a franchise, the buyer being the franchisee and the seller the franchisor.]

Fraudulent conveyance — the third rule of conveyancing law under which the taker receives less than his transferor. [Under this third rule of conveyancing law, **security of property** and the **good-faith purchase** doctrine being the first two, in order to serve some public policy, usually one against fraud, the taker receives fewer rights than his transferor enjoyed in the property. If, for example, Transferor holds goods free and clear of any **claims** but owes money to Creditor, and if Transferor conveys to Transferee in a fashion that offends a fraudulent conveyancing statute or common law fraudulent conveyancing rule, Transferee takes the property subject to Creditor's claims. In short, even though Transferor held the property free of Creditor's claims, Transferee takes subject to them.]

Futures contract — agreement to sell a commodity or security at a future date. [A grain producer may enter into a contract in June with a local elevator to sell his corn for delivery and payment in October. The elevator will obtain the price of October corn from a commodity exchange and will immediately, unless the elevator is speculating, resell the contract on the exchange. The producer, in turn, has locked the elevator in at the agreed-upon price. Futures contracts have been the subject of litigation when the price of the commodity rises or falls dramatically after the parties enter into the contract. As a general rule, courts have recognized that parties entering into futures contracts assume that the buyer bears the risk of a falling market and the seller of a rising market and have enforced the contracts despite dramatic price fluctuation.]

Good-faith purchase — the second rule of conveyancing law, to the effect that a taker receives greater rights in the property transferred than the transferor enjoyed. [Conveyancing law has three basic rules: (1) the **security of property** principle, (2) the good-faith purchase principle, and (3) the doctrine of **fraudulent conveyance**. Under the first rule of conveyancing law, the transferee receives everything that his transferor had to convey, under the second he receives more, and under the third he receives less. Good-faith purchase is rooted in the market's need to provide for free movement of goods. By protecting the good-faith purchaser, the second principle of conveyancing permits the honest **purchaser** who acts in the ordinary course of business to give value without inquiring as to the transferor's **title**, that is, he cuts off **claims**. The one exception to the protection afforded the good-faith purchaser arises when he takes from a thief, for the thief cannot give the good-faith purchaser good title. The good-faith purchase doctrine also protects the purchaser from **defenses**. When the good-faith purchaser takes a **chose in action,** he generally cuts off those defenses of the obligor on the chose that arise by virtue of failure of consideration or fraud in the inducement.]

Gray market — market for goods in violation of some resale restrictions. [Some strong manufacturers will require their distributors to purchase periodically a minimum number of units or volume of product. A distributor that cannot sell all of the units or the volume at its customary price faces the problem of selling below that price or selling to distributors that are not authorized distributors of the manufacturer. Often, the authorized distributor is unwilling to cut its price. Once it does so, it becomes difficult to enforce the customary price. The distributor, therefore, resorts to the unauthorized distributors who comprise the gray market.]

Gresham's law — the principle that when bad money competes with good money in circulation, debtors will hoard the good money and pay their debts with the bad money, that is, the principle that bad money drives out good money. [The term now has a broader meaning and applies whenever lower standards in an industry drive out higher standards by putting the party that maintains the high standards at a competitive disadvantage.]

Guaranty — usually, a secondary obligation, contingent on default of the principal obligor. [A guarantor of principal's debt undertakes to pay the debt if principal fails to pay it when due. In some areas of commerce, there are primary guarantees. These undertakings, often issued by banks or other financially strong institutions, serve to guarantee the obligation of a principal but are payable not on the principal's default but on the presentation of documents.]

Hedging — the practice of matching sales and purchases in order to reduce market risks. [In order to protect themselves against price fluctuation, parties that deal in commodities and that are not willing to speculate will match one purchase or sale with another purchase or sale. For example, an Iowa propane gas **wholesaler** that knows it will need product in February may buy February propane on the futures market. If the price has risen in February when the wholesaler needs the propane, it will purchase locally at the higher price but make a profit on the futures contract, which it will sell on the exchange. The wholesaler might not take delivery of the propane under the futures contract because the delivery point under the contract could be in Houston. On August 1, a manufacturer of corn meal will buy corn from a seller to make into product and agree at the same time to sell the same quantity of corn at the same price to a buyer on August 30, the day the corn meal will be ready for market. If the price of corn increases, the manufacturer will not enjoy any profit on the corn, since it will have to buy corn in the market to fill its contract to sell on August 30. If, on the other hand, the price of corn falls, the manufacturer will have avoided the loss on his meal, which will now sell at a lower price given the drop in the raw material cost. Even though the manufacturer will not be able to sell its meal at a price that reflects its cost, it will make money on the August 30 sale, since it will buy at market (low) and sell at the contract price (high). Hedging will occur whenever there is a recognized market. The practice is common in the securities industry and in banking as well as the commodities markets.]

Indemnity agreement — primary undertaking of the indemnitor to hold the indemnitee harmless from losses. [A buyer of goods, for example, may need to take delivery of them from a carrier before the buyer has obtained the **bill of lading** covering them. The buyer will ask the carrier to release the goods against an indemnity agreement, which the buyer will obtain from a financially strong institution.]

Identification — determination that certain goods will be used to satisfy a contract of sale. [By designating certain goods to a contract for sale the seller alone or the buyer and seller together have identified the goods. Identification is a critical time in the sales transaction. It is the first moment at which the buyer has an interest in the goods. That interest is an insurable interest and a **special property**.]

Implied warranty — obligation imposed by the law on a party, usually a seller, relating to the nature of goods or services. [The implied warranty arises even though the parties' agreement is silent as to warranties and may survive efforts by the obligor to disclaim the warranty if the disclaimer fails to meet statutory requirements.] (*Compare* **express warranty**.)

Indenture — (1) agreement between the obligor on bonds or debentures and the holders of those obligations; (2) a real estate deed to which there are two parties, rather than simply a grantor.

Installment — partial performance or payment. [Sales contracts frequently call for delivery of goods or services in discrete increments over a period of time. Also, sales contracts and other obligations sometimes call for payment in increments.]

Invoice — a record of the charges and a description of the goods or services provided by the seller and rendered to the buyer. [In lay parlance, the invoice is the seller's bill for goods sold or services rendered.]

Jobber — middleman in the **channel of distribution** who traditionally buys from a manufacturer, distributor, or importer, often in small or odd lots, and resells to **dealers** or other retailers.

Kaldor-Hicks efficiency — notion that the reallocation of resources is efficient if society in the aggregate is better off, without regard for the fact that one party may be made worse off by that reallocation. [Kaldor-Hicks efficiency differs, then, from **pareto** efficiency, which does not favor reallocation that makes one person worse off.] (*Compare* **Pareto optimal**.)

Lease — agreement for the use of property under which the lessor permits the lessee to use the property in return for a stipulated rent. [Real estate and equipment are the most common subjects of leases. Equipment leases may be true leases or disguised sales contracts with a security interest reserved to the seller.] (*See also* **net lease**.)

Leaseback (*See* **sale and leaseback**.)

Letter of credit — an undertaking, usually issued by a bank, in favor of a beneficiary and on behalf of the issuer's customer, to honor **drafts** or demands for payment, often on the condition that they be accompanied by other documents.]

Limited partnership — partnership made up of one or more general partners and a number of limited partners. [The limited partnership is a device used to syndicate real estate developments, oil and gas exploration, equipment leasing ventures, and the like. The general partner is the syndicator or a cognate that plans the venture and carries it out. The limited partners are usually just investors with only their investment at risk.]

Liquidated — determined, fixed. [A **claim** is liquidated when there is no bona fide dispute over the amount due, though there may be a dispute over the validity of the claim itself.]

Lock box — collection facility that permits a collecting bank or other party to intercept a payee's mail, remove **checks** or other instruments, and collect them. [Corporations with widespread sales face the problem of consolidating their funds efficiently. The lock box assists the company's comptroller in that process by permitting the company to collect payments at diverse locations and deposit them at nearby banks, thereby reducing float and making the funds available for the company's cash needs more quickly.]

Loss leader — merchandise sold by a retailer at a loss in order to attract customers for other merchandise.

Manufacturers' agent — independent enterprise that represents two or more manufacturers, usually of related products, and services customers on a continuing basis. [Unlike **wholesalers** and **distributors**, manufacturers' agents generally do not purchase and store merchandise, except for samples, and do not provide repair or maintenance service.]

Manufacturers' representative (*See* **manufacturers' agent**.)

Manufacturers' sales branch — a vertical extension of the manufacturer's operation involved in wholesaling and, therefore, different from manufacturers' **direct sales** operations. [Sometimes the branch will not stock merchandise but operates solely as a sales office and not as a wholesaler.]

Marginal cost — increase or decrease in a producer's total cost of production by producing one more unit, i.e., the cost of the last item produced. [Theoretically, marginal cost determines the rate of production, since producers should increase production as long as doing so reduces the marginal cost and should reduce production when doing so decreases marginal cost. In normal economic times, most producers do not reach optimum output, the point at which marginal cost equals the average cost of producing a unit and at which the producer's profits are maximized per unit of production. For some producers, however, and in times of shortages, for many producers, production has reached a level that makes further economies of scale impossible. Such producers, if they increase production, will lose more on the increase than they make, because, for example, they have to hire additional workers who will not be utilized efficiently or because they have to add warehouse or shipping capacity that will not be used efficiently.]

Market overt — market in which purchasers take free of **claims**. [For a long time the merchants of England had chafed under the **security of property** rule that made it necessary for buyers to investigate the **title** of their sellers or bear the risk that the title was defective. Eventually, they established the notion of market overt, whereby sales made at designated places and at designated times were not subject to the security of property notion but to the doctrine of **good-faith purchase**. Eventually the term came to include all sales that benefit from good-faith purchase.]

Market value — a nebulous concept that assumes that property has an inherent value abstract from any actual sales price. [From time to time it is necessary to determine the value of property without selling it. If the property is similar to that traded on a recognized market, market value is the same as market price. If A holds 100 shares of common stock in X Corporation, whose common stock is traded publicly on the New York Stock Exchange, the market value of A's stock is computed by using the price at which X Corporation common trades on the exchange. As the market price goes up or down, the market value of A's stock goes up or down. This perfectly rational concept has given rise to an irrational myth — the idea that property that is not traded in a recognized market still has market value and that some expert can determine it. There are times when it is imperative that the law determine property values without a sale. In eminent domain cases, for example, the parties and perhaps ultimately the court, must place a value on the property that the state takes. Similarly, it is necessary to place a value on property for property tax purposes. The use of experts who give their opinions in those cases (nontransaction situations) should not give rise to the mistaken notion that their opinions are more than that — opinions. Opinions of market value are not market price. Unfortunately, courts have often been seduced into thinking that because the law recognizes those opinions in nontransaction situations, the law is justified in assuming that those opinions are the equivalent of market price. In some cases, for example, courts will hear testimony of market price and conclude that the contract price is unfair or unrealistic or unconscionable and therefore unenforceable. In fact, contract prices agreed to in arms length settings are the market price, the opinions of the experts are usually the source of the unrealistic prices.]

Materialman — in the construction industry, a subcontractor of the **prime contractor** or another subcontractor that agrees to supply materials for the project. (*See also* **mechanic's lien.**)

Mechanic's lien — claim against property and, sometimes, against funds due for work done on or materials supplied for construction of improvements to real estate or personal property.

Mercantile agency — generally, a credit reporting agency that sometimes also does collections. [The advent of mercantile agencies made open account selling possible. Dun & Bradstreet and TRW are two of the larger mercantile agencies.]

Merchant — person or entity that deals in goods or services of a kind or holds itself out as having expertise peculiar to the goods or services or to whom such expertise may be attributed by virtue of its engagement of a merchant. [The merchant is often held to a higher standard than the nonmerchant. Much of the tension in commercial law today results when (1) parties attempt to enforce against nonmerchants rules fashioned for the market place and (2) courts apply to merchants rules whose proper application should be limited to situations involving consumers or other nonmerchants. The distinction between merchants and nonmerchants does not resolve all of the difficulty, since the line between the two is often blurred. Most commentators prefer a broad reading of the term *merchant.*]

Money order — **draft** usually on or payable at a bank, sold by the bank to a customer who pays cash for the draft and uses it in lieu of a **check.** [The postal service also sells money orders.]

Moral hazard — unintended consequence, consisting of an incentive to behave in an economically inefficient fashion, usually arising out of a system designed to allocate losses. [If a system permits *A* at no cost to himself to incur costs for *B*, the system poses a moral hazard. Casualty insurance is an efficient device for spreading casualty losses, but it poses the moral hazard that one party owning an asset that she cannot sell will fake an accident, that is, the existence of the insurance may create the moral hazard that owners will destroy their property. Similarly, the existence of liability insurance may lead parties to act with less care, since the losses their carelessness produces are covered by insurance. Welfare benefits provided by the state can yield similar moral hazards.]

Negotiability — in negotiable instruments law, the **good-faith purchase** rule. [Under the doctrine of negotiability, the holder in due course and a person having the rights of a holder in due course cut off **claims** and **defenses**.]

Negotiable order of withdrawal — a customer's order, widely adopted by the thrift industry, for transferring deposits. [Traditionally, thrift industry deposits were not demand deposits, that is, they were not available to the depositor by **draft** or **check**. With the advent of deregulation in the banking and thrift industries, thrifts initiated competition with commercial banks by offering thrift customers the negotiable order of withdrawal and its ability to transfer deposits (financial institution credits) to third parties.]

Nemo dat rule — the principle that a taker by voluntary conveyance cannot take more than his transferor had to convey. [This is a corollary of the **security of property** principle. It is an old idea, rooted in logic, that one cannot give what one does not have. It comes from a Latin maxim: *nemo dat quod non habet*.]

Net — said of an amount calculated by subtracting charges of one kind or another. [List prices and specified prices in a contract are often subject to adjustments for discounts, returned merchandise, and the like. Rents specified in a lease are subject to similar adjustments for taxes, maintenance charges, and insurance. Net prices and net rents are prices and rents so adjusted.]

Net lease — lease under which the lessee pays property taxes, insurance, and maintenance costs, sometimes referred to as a "triple net" lease.

Net net — said of any arrangement that involves more than one netting process. [If, for example, a settlement system is "netted" it is bilateral, so that each party to the system nets against the other. If the system calls for all parties to settle with a central party, the netting takes two steps for two parties to net against each other. They each net against the central party. CHIPS (*see* Chapter 27) involves net net settlements, since the CHIPS switch acts as a central clearing agent.]

Nominal — said of prices and interest rates expressed in figures that do not reflect inflation or deflation. [Nominal prices or interest rates may be misleading. The nominal interest rate on a bond may be 10 percent over one year, but inflation will make the *real* interest rate something below 10 percent. A seller may list a nominal price for merchandise but with various discounts may never charge that price.]

OEM (*See* **original equipment manufacturer**.)

Operating lease — an equipment lease under which the lessor services the equipment and, sometimes, agrees to update the equipment in the event of product improvements. [Users of high technology equipment are often reluctant to make large investments in equipment that may have a long useful life but that might become obsolete as a consequence of improvements made by the manufacturer. The operating lease is a device manufacturers and users have implemented to give the manufacturer greater accessibility to the market and the user more security in the event the manufacturer improves its product.]

Opportunity cost — cost incurred when a person chooses one activity over another. [Law students not only pay tuition and expenses while they go to law school, they also incur an opportunity cost — the loss of income they would have earned had they entered the workforce full time instead of attending law school.]

Option — the right to obligate another to perform, usually, a contract for sale. [In the securities industry, the right to require another to sell is called a *call option;* the right to require another to buy a *put option.* Options also frequently arise in real estate transactions.]

Order acknowledgment — the seller's indication that it has accepted the buyer's offer to purchase. (*Compare* **purchase order.**)

Original equipment manufacturer — designation sellers give to their buyers that take the sellers' product and incorporate it into a new product. [A manufacturer of hose, for example, may sell to distributors, retailers, and industrial and household consumers that use the hose as a discrete product. The seller may also have a customer that uses the hose, say, in a washing machine or motor vehicle that it manufactures for sale. The seller would refer to this customer as an original equipment manufacturer and would often make special discounts and other sales terms available to it.] (*See also* **vendor.**)

Ostensible ownership — the concept that possession of personal property connotes ownership. [In personal property law, **title** is not a matter of record and may be difficult to determine. To some extent, the concept of possession has supplanted the concept of title: "Possession is nine points of the law." The law recognizes, furthermore, that possession often raises reasonable expectations on the part of third parties. A true owner, for example, will not be heard to say that he owns the horse he delivered to a horse merchant at a horse auction, if the merchant sells the animal to a **good-faith purchaser**. The merchant has ostensible title to the horse and gives good title to the buyer.]

Overhead — costs that are not directly related to the production of a product or the provision of services. [Insurance and taxes are part of a manufacturer's overhead; raw material expenses are generally not.]

Pareto optimal — in **welfare economics,** said of the allocation of property that has achieved the maximum efficiency of distribution, i.e., when no change in that allocation can benefit one person without damaging another. [If under allocation A every one is as well off as under allocation *B* and at least one party is better off, allocation *A* is pareto superior to allocation *B*.] (*Compare* **Kaldor-Hicks efficiency**.)

Payable-through draft — **draft** drawn on someone other than a bank and payable through the bank that, rather than paying the item, presents it to the person on which it is drawn. [Self-administered insurance plans use payable-through drafts. An employer providing insurance to its employees, for example, will draw a draft on the insurance company for the amount of an employee's loss. When the payable-through bank presents the payable-through draft to the insurance company, the company will check to see that the draft is in order. If it is, the insurance company will authorize payment of the draft. Credit unions use payable-through drafts as their share drafts.]

Payment bond — surety company's undertaking to pay all suppliers and subcontractors in the event the purchaser of those supplies or services does not pay for them. [In real estate construction, owners are concerned that the **prime contractor** may complete the work but not pay all of the suppliers or subcontractors. The owner will insist that the prime contractor obtain a payment bond to insure that there are no liens on the property.] (*See also* **performance bond**.)

Performance bond — surety company's undertaking to complete performance of a contract in the event the obligor fails to perform. [In the construction industry, owners traditionally require contractors to supply a performance bond. In the event of the contractor's default, the surety company engages another contractor to complete the work.] (*Compare* **payment bond**.)

Prepaying buyer — buyer that pays the seller in advance of delivery of goods or services. [In the simplest transaction of sale, the seller delivers the goods against the buyer's payment of the price. The demands of modern commerce do not always permit simple sales transactions, and sellers frequently sell on credit. On the rare occasion, the seller and the buyer will agree upon prepayment. Such prepayment raises questions concerning the buyer's rights in the goods. Some courts have concluded that the prepaying buyer is a **buyer in ordinary course**; others have taken the position that the prepaying buyer is really a lender who has no interest in the goods other than an unperfected security interest. Generally, the prepaying buyer should bear the risks his prepayment creates, but courts and commentators do not always agree.]

Present value — the value today of a future payment or payments. [Present value is computed by discounting the future payment in a calculation that presumes the rate of interest (compounded) on funds over the period in question. To compute, for example, the present value of $10,000 to be paid ten years from today, it is necessary to assume an interest rate that the discounted sum will earn that will yield $10,000 of principal and interest in ten years. If the assumed rate is 10 percent per year, the present value will be $6,145; if the assumed rate is 5 percent per year, the present value will be $7,722.]

Price elasticity — the degree to which price is a direct function of demand or supply. [When the demand for a product (e.g., imported wine) increases and decreases as the price decreases and increases, the demand is price elastic. If the demand for a product (e.g., bread) remains relatively steady in the face of price changes, the demand is price inelastic. If supply of a product (e.g., oil) increases and decreases with increases and decreases in price, the supply is price elastic; if supply of the product remains steady when prices increase or decrease (or even increases when prices decrease as in the case of agricultural commodities), the supply is price inelastic.]

Price terms — terms in a sales contract that describe the financial compensation of the seller and also may include discount, credit, and method of payment terms. [The shipment terms "C.I.F." and "C&F" are price terms. They determine the remuneration that the buyer must provide to the seller. "F.O.B." and "F.A.S." are **delivery terms**.]

Prime contractor — in the construction industry and under government contracts, the contractor that enters into a contract with the owner of the project or the government. [Contractors who enter into contracts with the prime contractor to do portions of the prime contractor's work are subcontractors.]

Progress payments — in the construction industry and under other contracts, especially government contracts, payments by the owner to the contractor periodically for work done.

Purchase — transfer by voluntary conveyance. [As a general rule, in contract and commercial law, a voluntary conveyance is a purchase transaction. Buyers, donees, and secured parties are purchasers. Some purchasers, such as secured parties and buyers, are purchasers for value. Some purchasers, such as secured parties or mortgagees, are purchasers of less than the full interest. The law also distinguishes between the **good-faith purchaser** and the purchaser who takes out of the ordinary course (such as the buyer under a **bulk sale**) or with notice of title infirmities. Persons who take by involuntary conveyance are not purchasers. A buyer at a sheriff's sale and a lien creditor are not purchasers, since they take their interest in property by operation of law rather than by voluntary transfer.]

Purchase order — the form in which the buyer customarily makes its offer to purchase the seller's goods or services. [In many industries, seller's publish price lists. Potential purchasers take information from the price list and incorporate it into a purchase order. Traditionally, the purchase order was in writing, but often parties take purchase orders by telephone or **EDI**. Some sellers confirm the purchase arrangement with an order acknowledgment. In the fast pace of domestic sales, the paperwork may lag behind performance. When a sales office is busy, the sales manager may be more concerned about getting orders shipped than about getting the papers out. Lawyers, of course, are always more concerned about the papers. That is one of the reasons that the president of a company is usually more respectful of his sales vice president than he is of his lawyer.]

Regression analysis — in statistics, the determination of the extent to which a dependent variable relates to an independent variable. [For example, a manufacturer may want to know whether rainfall in a geographic area is related to sales of irrigation equipment in that area. The process of determining the relationship between rainfall (the independent variable) and sales (the dependent variable) is regression analysis. If the relationship is perfect and direct, the correlation coefficient is 1, that is, a 100 percent increase in rainfall yields a 100 percent increase in product sales. The coefficient is -1 if an increase in rainfall yields an identical decrease in sales. If there is no correlation between rainfall and sales, the coefficient is 0.]

Reinsurance — that part of an insurance risk that one insurance company transfers to a second company (the reinsurer). [Reinsurance is the insurance analogue to the banking industry's practice of transferring parts of loans, i.e., loan participations.]

Requirements contract — sales agreement under which the buyer agrees to take all of its need for a product from the seller. [When a buyer wants to protect itself against shortages and price increases, it may agree to give an exclusive contract to a supplier by promising to purchase all of its requirements from that single supplier. If the contract fixes a price, the arrangement deprives the buyer of any advantage it might realize if the market price of the product supplied goes down. The quantity term of a requirements contract is open, and disputes sometimes arise if the buyer's needs for the product increase dramatically. Sometimes, the price term remains open in a requirements contract. In that case, the buyer is attempting to assure itself of a source of supply but does not have any protection against a rising market.]

Resale price maintenance — the manufacturer (or supplier) practice of specifying the prices above or below which a customer may not sell products.

Risk — the possibility of loss. [There are many kinds of risk, and parties frequently allocate risks in their contracts. Among the kinds of risk that may be allocated are risk of accidental loss, exchange rate fluctuation, political upheaval, insolvency, market increases or decreases, material shortages, unforeseen developments, and litigating in a foreign jurisdiction. Unhappily, some courts do not understand that commercial, as opposed to consumer, parties almost always allocate risk in their contract, and those courts are wont to reallocate the risks based on the courts' views of what is fair.]

RISK (*See* **retail installment sales contract** in Part II Glossary.)

Sale and leaseback — arrangement under which the owner of property, usually real estate or equipment, sells the property to a party that leases it back to the original owner.

Security of property — the first rule of conveyancing law, the principle that a party may transfer an interest in property freely. [The first and necessary corollary of this rule law is the **shelter principle** — the idea that the taker receives all of the transferor's interest. The second and equally necessary corollary is the idea that the taker receives no greater rights than those of the transferor. This is the **nemo dat rule**. The net effect of the two corollaries is that the taker will receive exactly the same interest that the transferor enjoyed. It is important to bear in mind that the first principle of conveyancing law with its two corollaries is the starting point in any conveyancing analysis. If the transaction does not qualify for treatment under the second (the **good-faith pur-**

chase principle) or third (the **fraudulent conveyance** principle) rules, the first rule always applies.]

Selling agent — an independent enterprise similar to the **manufacturer's agent** but with more authority for determining prices and other sales terms with its customers and often with the exclusive right to handle the entire production output of the manufacturer.

Shelter principle — a corollary to the first rule of conveyancing law (**security of property**) — the notion that the transferee obtains exactly the same interest that the transferor conveyed. [Under the first corollary, the shelter principle, the taker enjoys all of the interests in the property conveyed that the transferor enjoyed. Under negotiable instruments law, for example, a transferee from a holder in due course generally will have the rights of a holder in due course, even though the transferee does not itself meet the requisites for holder in due course status. Similarly, a buyer in ordinary course, having bought without notice of **claims**, usually cuts off those claims and can convey that power to its transferee even though the transferee knows of the claims at the time it takes. The shelter principle has an important obverse feature. Just as the taker under the shelter principle takes every thing that the transferor enjoyed, so he can take no more. This feature is the **nemo dat** principle.]

Special property — an interest in property, but not **title** and not a security interest. [When goods are **identified** to a contract for sale, the buyer has a special property in them. That special property is not the same as title; it is something less than title. It is an interest that gives the buyer rights in the goods. That is not to say that the buyer's rights by virtue of the special property are superior to those of the seller or some third party. They may not be. The fact that a buyer has a special property in goods under a contract for sale, for example, even though it arises before the time for delivery, does not relieve the buyer from its obligation to pay the seller the price.]

Specialty — at early common law, a contract under seal. [Bonds, for example were usually under seal. They needed no consideration to be binding, and the paper itself, the bond, rather than any underlying promise, was the source of the obligation. The term "specialty" has developed to encompass any obligation embodied in an instrument that is independent of the transaction out of which it arises. **Letters of credit** are said to be specialties because they are peculiarly independent of the transactions out of which they arise. To some extent, negotiable instruments are specialties. With the **death of contract**, courts have declined to enforce contractual obligations vigorously, and the distinction between **contracts** and specialties has taken on a significance that it did not have at early common law or even as recently as the beginning of this century. As commercial parties became aware of the imprecision that courts had given to contractual undertakings and the slow, painful, and often unpredictable process that attended the enforcement of contracts, those parties (primarily merchants and bankers) began to rely increasingly on tools of international trade that had retained their commercial rigor. The letter of credit and the first demand guaranty, both of which are arguably specialties, have grown in importance as a consequence of these developments and of the commercial need for undertakings that can be enforced with celerity and certainty. Regrettably, courts are not always inclined to observe the distinction, so that the death of contract may be followed by the death of specialty.]

Specialty manufacturer — a manufacturer that fabricates goods, often machinery, at the request and to the specifications of the buyer. [The specialty manufacturer is often a rather small concern relative to the buyer and may be thinly capitalized.]

Speculating — buying and selling in the hope of being able to profit from changes in market price. [While most buyers and sellers buy and sell in connection with their activity in a line of commerce in a fashion that reduces the risk of price fluctuation, some buyers and sellers are speculators, that is, they buy and later sell with a view at the outset of playing the market. While a grain elevator, for example, may buy and sell grain, it usually **hedges** in a way to reduce the risk of price decreases, realizing that such hedging wipes out any profit that might accrue because of price increases. The grain speculator, on the other hand, buys grain when it thinks the price will go up and sells grain, usually on the futures market, when it suspects that the price will go down. Some observers feel that speculators are an unworthy branch of the **merchant** profession. In fact, speculators play a critical role in stabilizing prices. By virtue of their willingness to play the market, other buyers and sellers are able to **hedge** and to find sources of supply and outlets for product when otherwise there would be limited sources and outlets. To some extent, nearly all merchants must speculate, since they can never protect themselves completely from the vagaries of the market, but the existence of speculators renders market vagaries more manageable.]

Spot market — over-the-counter market (i.e., one conducted by telephone or similar wire communication) for commodities that are bought and sold for cash and immediate delivery. (*Compare* **futures contract**.)

Spot delivery — immediate delivery.

Statement — summary of periodic activity of a customer's account.

Supercargo — formerly, a ship's captain that took on merchandise and transported it, often from port to port, looking for a buyer. [**Title** to the goods remained in the seller, the supercargo being an agent. The arrangement might have misled creditors of the supercargo if it had not been clear that his authority over the goods entrusted to him included the power to sell them but not to borrow against them, i.e., the supercargo had no power to "mortgage" the goods.] (*See also* **factor.**)

Supply curve — graph on which price is the *y* axis and quantity of supply is the *x* axis. (*Compare* **demand curve.**)

Telex — telecommunications device that permits communication, often internationally by translating telephonic signals into words and printing them on a receiving machine. [Often, the parties refer to the message as printed by the telex machine as a "telex."]

Teller's check — an official check, i.e., one issued by a financial institution, rather than a **merchant** or **consumer.**

Title — the notion of property ownership and its concomitant, the power to exclude others from its use or possession. [Title is a metaphysical concept embedded in the psychology of the individual, as any witness to sibling or schoolyard disputes can attest. It is difficult to imagine that the title notion did not antedate sophisticated legal systems. Primitive jurisprudence may give ownership to the strong and take it from the weak, but the concept of title is nonetheless present. Karl Llewellyn, the chief reporter for the Uniform Commercial Code, felt that the law, especially sales law, was burdening the title concept too much. He argued against deciding issues of risk of loss and the like on the basis of title and fashioned a statute that largely dethroned that ancient concept. Whether he succeeded in depriving courts and lawyers of a notion that is as much psychological as legal and that may be stronger than any legislative enactment remains to be seen.]

Trade acceptance — an **acceptance** on which the acceptor is a merchant rather than a bank. (*See also* **banker's acceptance.**)

Transaction costs — costs incurred in order to effect a transaction as opposed to the cost of the goods themselves. [If a buyer spends $5,000 to learn of the location of goods that he needs and to arrange the contract for their purchase and then pays $100,000 to the seller for the goods, the transaction costs are $5,000.]

Turnkey project — a project sold to a customer with the understanding that the seller will set it up so that the buyer can walk in and operate the project. [A seller of car wash equipment may offer a turnkey operation to its customers who would expect to be able to operate the car wash without start-up costs after the seller installs the equipment.]

Tying — marketing practice whereby the seller refuses to sell the tying product (presumably an attractive product) unless the buyer agrees to buy the tied product (presumably a less-competitive product). [Sometimes the tying seller does not require the buyer to buy the tied product but insists that the buyer promise not to buy the tied product from anyone else. Motion picture distributors, for example, might "block-book" their products by requiring movie houses to take less attractive films in order to get the box office successes.]

Umbrella rule (*See* **shelter principle**.)

Usance (*See* **draft**.)

Variable cost — expense that varies directly with activity. [For a taxicab company, the cost of fuel would be a variable cost.] (*See* **fixed cost**.)

Vendor — firm that supplies parts to a manufacturer. [A company that makes lighting fixtures, for example, may need brass fittings and plastic parts for its product. Because the manufacturer does not have brass foundry or plastic extrusion capabilities, it will order the fittings and the plastic parts from parts suppliers that it will refer to as its "vendors."] (*See also* **original equipment manufacturer**.)

Vertical integration — consolidation of various operations from supplying to manufacturing, distribution, and sales. [In order to achieve economies, some concerns do not use independent entities in the **channel of distribution** but provide their own wholesale and retail functions. This vertical integration of the firm can extend forward into sales and distribution or backward into raw material supply and parts vending. Vertical integration is distinct from horizontal integration, the merging of competitors or of potential competitors.]

Voucher — usually, a receipt evidencing payment.

Warehouse receipt — **document of title** issued by a commercial **bailee** of goods and specifying the terms of the **bailment** and of the redelivery of the goods. [Warehouse receipts may be negotiable or nonnegotiable. In the former case, they are said to stand for the goods.]

Warranty (*See* **express warranty** and **implied warranty.**)

Warranty disclaimer (*See* **implied warranty.**)

Welfare economics — theory of economic analysis based on the assumption that the economic system should maximize human welfare.

Wholesaler — firm that buys merchandise, usually from one or more manufacturers, stores the merchandise, and resells it to **retailers**, other wholesalers, or **distributors**. [Wholesalers often perform financing and product service functions and in some industries do product research for their customers. Wholesalers may enjoy exclusive territories and may agree to exclusive distribution arrangements.]

PART I
TABLE OF DOCUMENTS

PART I
BIBLIOGRAPHY

Akroyd, R., A Guide to Contracting for the Sale of Goods (1984).
Barron's Dictionary of Finance and Investment Terms (2d ed. 1987).
Brown, H., Franchising Realities and Remedies (1978).
Chandler, A., The Visible Hand (1977).
Diamond, W., Distribution Channels for Industrial Goods (1963).
Dolan, J., The Law of Letters of Credit (2d ed. 1991).
Friedlander, M. & G. Gurney, Handbook of Successful Franchising (1981).
Garner, B., A Dictionary of Modern Legal Usage (1987).
Gilmore, G., The Ages of American Law (1977).
Gilmore, G., The Death of Contract (1974).
Glickman, G., 15 Business Organizations — Franchising (1987).
Guild, I. & R. Harris, Forfaiting (1986).
Hamilton, R., Fundamentals of Modern Business (1989).
Hayutin, D., Distributing Foreign-Produced Products in the United States (1988).
Henson, D., The Law of Sales (1985).
Johnson, J. & D. Wood, Contemporary Physical Distribution and Logistics (3d ed. 1986).
Joseph, W., Professional Service Management (1983).
Keating, W., Franchising Adviser (1987).
McLaughlin, G., Letters of Credit (1985).
Mills, P., Managing Service Industries (1986).
Miller, M., Miller's Comprehensive GAAP Guide 1986 (8th ed. 1985).
Molloy, Law and Economics: A Comparative Approach to Theory and Practice (1990).
Mooney, Personal Property Leasing: A Challenge, 36 Bus. Law. 1605 (1981).
Nordhaus, R., Patent License Agreements (1986).
Pines, H., 1987-88 Patent Law Handbook (1987).
Pohly, L., Limited Partnerships (1986).
Polinsky, M., An Introduction to Law and Economics (2d ed. 1989).
Posner, R., Economic Analysis of Law (3d ed. 1986).
Rosenberg, R. & M. Bedell, Profits from Franchising (1969).
Rosenfeld, C., The Law of Franchising (1970).

Schmitthoff, C., Export Trade (8th ed. 1986).
Schneider, G., Patents, Trademarks, and Copyrights, 25 West's Legal Forms (2d ed. 1986).
Siegfried, S., Introduction to Construction Law (1987).
Sloan, H. & A. Zurcher, Dictionary of Economics (5th ed. 1970).
Stern, L. & A. El-Ansary, Marketing Channels (2d ed. 1982).
Stern, W. & T. Eovaldi, Legal Aspects of Marketing Strategy: Antitrust and Consumer Protection Issues (1984).
Sweet, J., Sweet on Construction Industry Contracts: Major AIA Documents (1987).
Wallach, G., The Law of Sales Under the Uniform Commercial Code (1986 & Supps.).
Watson, A., Finance of International Trade (2d ed. 1981).

PART II

SECURED LENDING

11 Introduction

§11.1 SUBJECT MATTER

Part II (Secured Lending) deals with those transactions that generally fall within the coverage of the traditional law school course on secured transactions, that is, with activity governed by Article 9 of the Uniform Commercial Code.

Discussion of that activity must include consideration of unsecured lending in order to place secured lending in context and to contrast the two kinds of lending activity. One of the problems these days in academic literature and to some extent in the cases is the failure to pay enough attention to the distinction between the secured and unsecured lender. The secured lender is, in fact, if not in the theory of some law teachers, a very different animal from the lender that intentionally does not take security.

Before we treat the various secured transactions, it is also important to consider (1) the ways financial institutions and **commercial** sellers extend credit and (2) the complex process they traditionally utilize in making the decision to lend or not to lend.

§11.2 SOME HISTORY OF COMMERCIAL LENDING

Over the last century, commercial lending has changed dramatically, but for present purposes it is enough to know that in the recent past there were five basic lenders: (1) financing sellers, (2) **commercial banks,** (3) **finance companies,** (4) **small loan companies,** and (5) **thrifts**.

Financing sellers traditionally extended credit in two ways. As credit reporting became more and more reliable, they began to sell enormous amounts of **goods** and services on open **account,** that is, **short-term,** unsecured credit (30, 90, or 120 days, typically). Some sellers granted longer credit terms but took a discrete **security interest** in the goods they sold. This security interest is the **purchase-money security interest** to which commercial law often accords favored treatment. These two practices continue and probably comprise the greatest single category of commercial credit in the economy today. Note that only one of them involves secured lending; that one, moreover, is significantly less in volume than unsecured, open account credit.

Commercial banks traditionally targeted large industrial corporations and the **middle market** as sources for commercial bank loans. These loans were generally unsecured, but they involved **negative pledges,** that is, the borrower agreed not to grant security interests to any other lender or even to borrow from any other lender, with some exceptions, such as for purchases on open account. The net effect of the arrangements was to give the bank a favorable position in the event of bankruptcy, since other creditors were usually few in number with relatively low credit balances, and, in any event, the risk of insolvency was generally small for the all-important reason that commercial banks did not lend to marginal operations. Only the good credit risk, the industrial corporation with a healthy balance sheet or the strong mid-level company with personal guaranties from wealthy individuals could get a bank loan.

There were exceptions to this pattern, and commercial banks, especially the larger ones in major financial centers, did engage in a significant amount of secured lending, most notably in connection with self-liquidating loans. These usually involved transactions that gave rise to valuable paper: **documents of title,** corporate securities, and the like.

The conservative nature of the commercial banker and his appetite for safe loans left considerable room for the more adventurous lender. Commercial finance companies targeted the territory of the borrower who could not satisfy the commercial banker but who often did have assets to collateralize the obligation and who would pay a somewhat higher rate of interest for credit than the bank charged. This is the area where secured lending advanced considerably. At first, the loans tended to be against discrete items of **collateral,** such as a loan to **purchase** a given shipment of merchandise or to buy a specific piece of **equipment**. Eventually, the finance companies saw the benefit of revolving loans and **revolving collateral.** They granted loans to purchase **inventory** or equipment and took a security interest in that collateral as it existed at the time of the loan and as it was augmented or altered thereafter. Commercial bankers operated within the confines of a theory of banking under which each loan had to be self-liquidating, that is, each loan had a schedule of payments reducing the loan balance to zero over a fixed period of time. Finance companies advanced the notion that loan payments should be a matter subject to the debtor's cash flow, not preordained payment schedules of short-term lending custom. In brief, the signal advances in secured lending occurred in the commercial finance sector, not in the commercial bank sector of the lending industry.

Eventually, even before the advent of **deregulation** in the financial institutions industry, commercial bankers discovered the profitability of entering into secured lending. To some extent events forced them to venture into secured lending. First, they lost much of the industrial market when large borrowers were able to squeeze **financial intermediaries** such as banks out of the picture by borrowing directly from investors. Today, a national retailer may not seek credit from a bank but directly from the investing public. By asking a brokerage house to underwrite its offering of short-term notes (30-, 60-, or 90-day **paper**), for example, a large, well-regarded enterprise is able to market its notes (**commercial paper**) at lower rates of interest than banks would charge the same borrower. This method of borrowing removes the financial intermediary, the bank, and thereby saves the borrowing corporation money. By eliminating the bank, the borrower eliminates the bank's charges from the borrower's cost of raising funds.

Second, commercial bankers realized that secured loans were often as good as the unsecured loans they were accustomed to making and that such loans were often as profitable or more profitable than the unsecured loans they had traditionally made.

At the same time that bankers entered the asset-based lending field, they began to exploit the **consumer** market with installment loans. These loans are also secured, usually by the goods that the consumer has purchased.

One effect of this transformation of commercial banking has been a significant decline in the number of finance companies, with many of them now owned by commercial banks. The unique product of today's commercial finance company is often not its willingness to lend against collateral (banks are willing to do that) but its willingness to lend to the marginal borrower at higher rates and also to lend quickly, sometimes without first obtaining collateral. Thus in a curious way, finance companies now sometimes make unsecured loans, which later become secured.

Thrifts have not figured prominently in personal property secured lending, and small loan companies have restricted their activity to small consumer transactions. Until recent deregulation, thrifts were forbidden by law from making commercial loans. They could lend to consumers only in connection with certain types of activity and were required by law to confine the bulk of their loans to real estate financing.

Although many of those strictures no longer apply to the thrift industry, savings institutions, as of this writing, have not acquired the expertise to make them feel comfortable in the commercial-lending area. This lack of confidence is subsiding, however, and the arrival of thrifts in the commercial-lending area may be a matter of time. To some extent commercial lending by thrifts has already begun. With much of the thrift industry presently in the throes of fiscal and regulatory turmoil, no one can be certain what that industry will look like in the future.

Small loan companies traditionally have made loans for consumer purchases or emergencies. These institutions usually take a purchase-money security interest in the appliances and the like that their customers buy. Small loan companies also take security interests in a consumer's furniture and other personal property. The small loan companies' share of the consumer market is relatively small.

Credit unions have a long history of making secured consumer loans and have done so at generally attractive interest rates. Automobile and home appliance financing have been an important part of their business.

§11.3 DECIDING TO LEND

The decision to lend is usually the culmination of a subtle, complex evaluation process. Parents lending to their children do not customarily take security, neither do utility companies that provide services on credit to most customers, but the reasons for these decisions not to take security are obviously different. By the same token, the decisions of the bank loan officer to grant unsecured credit to Company A, to grant credit to Company *B* only on a secured basis, and to deny credit to Company C may rest on judgments that are difficult to ascertain and to explain. This discussion of that process is necessarily summary and may have the unfortunate effect of misleading someone. Some courts have been misled in rendering judgments against lenders, under **lender liability** theories, because the lenders themselves could not adequately explain the process. In fact, it is true that the same loan officer may extend credit to one person without security and deny it to a similarly situated person who offers security (or extend a loan's term in the first case and deny it in the second), and in each case the decision may be rational and justified, though difficult to articulate.

There are instances when the law emphatically interdicts that process. It would not matter for example, that persons who are divorced and have not remarried are statistically less likely to repay their loans than persons who have not been divorced or who have been divorced but are remarried. If those statistics are true, and this is not to say that they are, the law forbids lenders from taking marital status into account in making loan decisions. Similarly, other factors such as race, national origin, sex, religion, and residential location may be proscribed by state or federal law, no matter that they might, on a statistical basis, be relevant considerations.

Experience suggests, moreover, that the most compelling consideration is not whether the borrower provides the lender with security but whether, on the whole, the lender judges that the borrower will repay the loan. The existence of security is but one among many factors on which that judgment rests. True, in some cases, the existence of security is determinative. If a borrower grants a bank a security interest in a $100,000 United States treasury obligation, virtually any loan officer will authorize a $50,000 loan, if the interest rate is fair. Yet, some loan officers will balk at such a loan, if, say, the borrower is of unsavory character or one who has been unpleasant in prior business dealings. Lenders are not yet public utilities obliged to serve the public, and the federal courts have not found a constitutional right to borrow.

In the vast majority of loan transactions the strongest factor militating in favor of making a loan is the credit history of the borrower. Most lenders are not interested in foreclosing on collateral. They find **foreclosure** distasteful. Bankers are financial people; they deal with audited balance sheets and reports; they are interested in economic indicators and community trends. In short, they are comfortable at what nonbankers view as paper shuffling. They are not comfortable and are not interested in liquidating securities or grain futures contracts, let alone used factory equipment or (God forbid) hogs. Lawyers for defaulting borrowers often use that feature of the loan officer's personality in order to exact concessions from the lender. "Just lend us another $500,000, and we will make this loan good." It is an important fact of commercial lending that lenders resist the conclusion that they have made a bad loan. When a borrower is in financial difficulty, loan officers often feel helpless and regret that circumstances have transformed what starts out as a quite cheerful and optimistic relationship into a tense, adversarial one.

Commercial lenders victimized by the defaulting borrower's hard times exculpate themselves with the maxim: "No loan is bad when it is made." Loans go bad, but they start out good.

That maxim hints at an important facet of commercial lending that the commentators have overlooked. While it is true that lenders are profit maximizers and are at the same time risk averse, and while the economists and their imitators in the world of legal scholarship can create models to track those forces, they cannot track the very personal judgments that can be so compelling in loan decisions, especially in the all-important (for this is the locus of lender liability lawsuits) middle market. An economic model is incomplete unless it takes into account the fact that no loan officer enjoys walking past the desks of his colleagues to the water cooler the day after his loan to yesterday's wunderkind, who is today's notorious bankrupt, goes sour.

"He cheats on his wife." "He wears white shoes." "He is too ready to buy the drinks." "He is not ready enough to buy lunch." "He has halitosis." "He buys too many toys," i.e, sporty car, power boat, etc. "Never lend to a ______ [insert "plumber," "lawyer," "salesman," or other category of business person that has burned the loan officer in the past]."

These may not sound like good reasons to deny credit (or to refuse credit extensions) to someone who has collateral and a history of earnings, but these are typical of the factors a loan officer considers. Ultimately, and especially in the middle market where secured lending predominates, the controlling consideration is the judgment of the loan officer or of the **loan committee** that the prospective borrower will repay the loan, and that judgment is often the product of years of experience, personal taste, and personal views of the world. In short, the loan officer's judgment may be visceral — a fact that troubles senior loan vice presidents who rely on their loan officers' abilities to generate good loans, not bad ones, and courts, all of whom would like to see lenders justify their decisions with objective standards. Those who would like to change these facts of commercial lending should consider changing the law of gravity.

§11.4 FUNCTION OF COLLATERAL

Lenders take collateral for one reason: to secure repayment of the loan. Lenders can use the collateral in two ways. First, in the event of **default,** they can sell the collateral and apply the proceeds to the loan balance. Second, they can use the threat of foreclosure to get the borrower's attention and induce her to resume payments or otherwise attend to her obligations under the **loan agreement**. A few commercially squeamish courts and commentators find something odious about the second use of collateral. Such conduct is oppressive, it forces people to do something they do not want to do, to allocate their resources in a fashion contrary to their wishes. Such conduct also resembles the habits of the loan shark and evokes images of beefy enforcers threatening to break legs or of unscrupulous bankers in the classic western eyeing the family ranch or the favor of the rancher's daughter.

There is no excuse for the practices of loan sharks and the villains of Hollywood fiction, but efforts by secured lenders to use their security to enforce the terms of the loan agreement are, though not always dainty, quite harmless and, in fact, socially and economically beneficial. The defaulting borrower, at the least, raises the cost of credit to the nondefaulter and, at worst, endangers the credit system and the economy that rests upon it. Those few who object to the use of threats under **security agreements** are really objecting to secured credit, not to particular practices.

There are some who candidly acknowledge their objections to secured credit either on these grounds or on theories of efficiency. It is not our purpose to address the challenge on the latter grounds here. As to the former, there can be no doubt that a market economy can exist without secured lending, but that is not to admit that the same number of people and the same class of people will have access to credit under a system that does not allow it as will have access to credit in a system that does. The raison d'être of secured lending is not to enhance the power of lenders. Ultimately, it is to increase the availability of credit to people who would otherwise not have it.

§11.5 BANK REGULATION AND STRUCTURE

It is helpful in studying secured lending to understand a little about bank regulation. Commercial banks are now a primary source of secured lending. Unlike credit sellers, commercial banks are heavily regulated. For a number of reasons, that regulation is rather Byzantine. First, under the American dual banking system, we have both state and federally chartered banks, with the result that there are federal and state regulators for the two types. The federal agency that regulates **national associations,** i.e., national banks, is the **Comptroller of the Currency**. State regulators go under a variety of names, such as the Superintendent of Banking in New York and the Director of the Financial Institutions Bureau in Michigan.

In addition, because most state banks and all national banks must be insured, the **Federal Deposit Insurance Corporation** has important regulatory functions and is the primary federal regulator for state chartered banks that are not members of the Federal Reserve. The **Federal Reserve Board** is the chief federal regulator for state banks that are members of the Federal Reserve.

Under the Bank Holding Company Act, the Federal Reserve Board is also the regulator of **bank holding companies,** that is, corporations that own the stock of commercial banks, referred to as their *operating subsidiaries*. The **Office of Thrift Supervision** (OTS) acts as chief regulator of **savings and loan associations**. The FDIC also exercises such functions in its new role of insurer of thrift deposits. The **National Credit Union Administration** (NCUA) is the chief regulator of federal credit unions.

The net effect of this crisscrossing of bank regulation can be complex and problematic. For example, if a bank holding company owns several operating subsidiaries, some of which may be state **nonmember banks,** some national banks, and some state member banks, the lawyers for the holding company will deal with the Federal Reserve Board as regulator of the state member banks and the holding company, the Comptroller of the Currency as regulator of the national banks, the FDIC as regulator of the state nonmember banks, and a state agency as regulator of state banks.

Some holding companies exploited a loophole in the definition of *bank* in the Bank Holding Company Act by organizing nonbank banks that were not subject to any bank regulators until Congress put a moratorium on the practice. The chief executive officer of Chase Manhattan Bank, N.A. (a national bank as the letters "N.A." for "National Association" indicate) has suggested that his bank could compete better against the insurance and securities industries, the biggest competitors of banks today, if Chase dissolved as a bank and became a business corporation. In that event, it would not have to deal with regulatory strictures against bank and bank holding company activity in the securities and insurance fields.

The traditional commercial bank allocates its activities among various departments. A typical bank might be organized into (1) operations, (2) commercial loans, (3) installment loans, (4) trust department, and (5) international banking. The operations division handles payments and **collections** (the payment system) and administrative tasks. **Installment loan departments** are the source of consumer loans in the bank. The international bank department, if there is one, deals with international collections and payments and with letters of credit.

The banking industry divides banks into three categories: money center banks, regionals, and country banks, all of which usually engage in commercial lending of one sort or another. With the advent of a relaxation of the laws against interstate banking, interstate acquisitions have created the super-regional bank. Some banks have traditionally emphasized retail banking, that is, dealing with small business enterprises or consumers; while other banks, fewer in number, have emphasized wholesale banking, that is, dealing with other, usually smaller, banks, with multinational corporations and the like. Regional and money-center banks usually combine retail and wholesale banking.

§11.6 EXCLUSIONS

The material in this part does not deal with real estate financing, except to the marginal extent that it deals with **fixtures,** and does not generally deal with consumer lending, except in purchase-money cases. Real estate lending is a subject for another book. Nonpurchase-money consumer borrowing is seldom secured now, though many consumers borrow against home equity or **pledge** stock in order to raise money for home improvements, tuition, medical expenses, and other extraordinary consumer expenses.

12

The Basic Loan Agreement and the Working Capital Loan Concept

§12.1 INTRODUCTION

Prior to the adoption of the Uniform Commercial Code, the varied history of secured lending and the disparate origins of such lending yielded a mélange of secured lending practices and terminology. The signal achievement of the Code project was to standardize much of the practice, though a few vagaries survive. It is important for the student of secured transactions *law* to study that law with an eye to those features and to study that law in discrete fashion. In other words, the study should proceed along the lines of the various kinds of financing, e.g., inventory, accounts, equipment, and **dealer**. By the same token, our study here, the study of secured lending *practices* uses the same approach by devoting separate chapters to those kinds of secured lending and the various practices that arise in them. This chapter deals with a few important, basic premises of good secured lending.

§12.2 NEED FOR THE LOAN AGREEMENT

The first, basic premise is the notion that most secured loan transactions, especially those involving a secured lender rather than a secured seller, should commence with a well-crafted loan agreement. There may be a tendency for the law teacher and the student to overemphasize in the study of secured transactions the note, security agreement, and **financing statement** — the **documents** that the Code defines and governs. Surely, secured lending documentation is incomplete until the parties consider whether those documents are necessary and, if so, until they are properly drafted and executed; nothing in this book suggests the contrary. In fact, the lawyer's role in secured lending is often clerical, just as it is in most other areas of the law.

The importance of those documents should not overshadow the importance of the loan agreement, which addresses the general relationship between lender and borrower and does far more than the note, the security agreement, and the financing statement are designed to do.

§12.3 PROMISSORY NOTE

Having said that the note, the security agreement, and the financing statement generally do not, by themselves, satisfy the needs of **loan documentation,** we must add that sometimes the **promissory note** does indeed perform the general function of the loan agreement by specifying in detail the relationship between the parties. Negotiable-**instruments** law renders that approach problematic, since under that law, a note with "excess baggage" is not negotiable. It is either a curious tribute to the conservative nature of bank lenders or evidence of the power of tradition that most institutional lenders continue to take negotiable promissory notes from their borrowers. In a former era, banks negotiated their borrowers' notes, that is, they indorsed them to **correspondent banks** or other holders. The acceptability of those notes related directly to their negotiability, since the correspondent that took a negotiable note was a holder in due course who took free of **claims** and of important commercial defenses. Today, commercial banks generally do not negotiate their notes, except in some evolving areas of export finance. (*See* Section 20.9) Virtually all of the notes that are executed in the domestic commercial loan industry sit in the files of the original lender and are never transferred to anybody. The one important exception to this domestic practice arises when a bank becomes insolvent. In that event, another bank or the Federal Deposit Insurance Corporation may acquire the failed bank's portfolio of promissory notes.

There is a considerable body of federal law that protects the FDIC in those situations, and it is probably fair to say that the FDIC does not need the benefit of the Code's holder-in-due-course rules. Perhaps the purchasing banks do need it, however. In any event, the practice of taking promissory notes in negotiable form survives in the banking industry. Document 12-1 illustrates a bank negotiable promissory note form.

§12.4 FORM OF LOAN AGREEMENT

While many institutional lenders will prepare form loan agreements for certain types of recurring transactions, some loan agreements will be tailored to the specific loan transaction. Document 12-2 is a standard form that a bank might use in connection with a number of loans. Note that in the loan agreement, there is no request for a security agreement, the loan in that case being an unsecured loan. Such unsecured loan agreements are not unusual in commercial banking, where, traditionally, banks make unsecured loans to good credit risks. Document 12-3 is the kind of note a bank might take under a working capital loan agreement. This note will bear a face amount equal to the full amount of the loan commitment. If the borrower's **line of credit,** for example, is $1 million, the note will be for that amount. The note stipulates, however, that the sum due under it is not the face amount, but the amount of all advances, less payments, plus interest.

§12.5 THE WORKING CAPITAL LOAN CONCEPT

At this point it is time to introduce the idea of the working capital loan. Much commercial lending relates to the type of collateral that the lender takes. The law of secured lending and the industry itself reflect that fact. The rules for purchase-money security interests in inventory are different from purchase-money security interests in other commercial collateral, for example.

In a similar way account lending can differ, depending on the nature of the account lender. Generally, lenders against accounts fall into one of three categoris: banks, finance companies that lend against the accounts, and finance companies that buy the accounts (**factors**). Bankers that use accounts to secure the working capital loan will let the borrower collect the accounts and use the proceeds as he sees fit. The borrower may use the proceeds to pay off a portion of the loan or may use them to pay taxes and insurance. The commercial finance industry traditionally has been tougher in lending against accounts, may monitor them closely, and may insist that payments by the **account debtors** be used to reduce the loan balance. Some finance companies "buy" accounts, that is, they take the accounts and collect them themselves. In both of the latter cases, the lender is lending against discrete accounts and is not making a working capital loan. The bank's loan against accounts, however, is typical of the working capital loan.

Sometimes, especially in equipment lending, the loan is self-liquidating, that is, there is a set payment schedule that commences with the loan balance in the loan amount, gradually reduces the loan principal to zero,

Figure 12-1. Cash Need Graph

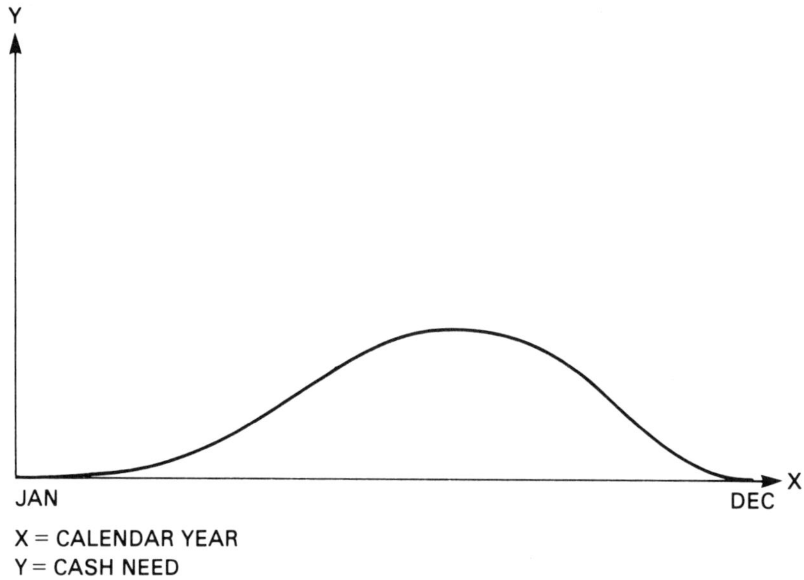

and does not exceed the life of the equipment. That type of loan is not a working capital loan either.

The working capital loan is more general in its treatment of the borrower and more flexible in meeting the borrower's cash needs. Under the working capital loan, the parties assume that the borrower will need capital during a period, often one calendar year, and that he will draw on the line of credit with the bank and will make repayments of principal from time to time during that period. In a business that has seasonal sales that peak in June, for example, the borrower may draw on the line all during the spring, as it builds inventory. During that period, expenses for raw materials, parts, payroll, and utilities will be relatively high, and cash flow will be relatively low. After June, those costs will diminish, and cash flow will increase as customers begin paying for deliveries. In this ideal illustration, the borrower's annual cash needs will resemble a sine curve over the course of the year as Figure 12-1 illustrates.

Typically, the working capital loan agreement will require the borrower to reduce its principal balance to zero at one time during the business cycle. The requirement reflects the fact that banks are short-term lenders and do not take an equity position in their borrower's business, that is, they lend to a company, they do not buy an interest in the company.

§12.6 FURTHER LOAN DOCUMENTATION

In a loan transaction, there will be any number of documents in addition to the agreement. Corporate certificates, opinions of counsel, and various schedules are common examples. In addition, there is usually a separate promissory note and, in secured loan transactions, a security agreement and a financing statement.

Frequently, as chapters in this Part illustrate, security agreements are peculiar to the kind of collateral involved. Sometimes, a general security agreement will suffice. Document 12-4 is an example of a general security agreement.

In any security agreement, it is critical to identify the parties with care and to obtain the signature of the "debtor." The description of the collateral is also a matter for careful attention.

The financing statement, the document that the lender files in the public records as a notice to the world of its security interest, also calls for care. Courts are disposed to challenge the sufficiency of such documents if they do not identify the parties correctly or if the description of the collateral is in any way insufficient. The most common errors are in the designation of the "debtor." Lawyers and bankers should be aware that the law recognizes certain entities and does not recognize others. Individuals, corporations, partnerships, trusts, and estates have legal names. The lawyer or lender that fills out a financing statement without verifying the legal name of a borrower does so at its peril. Financing statement forms are prescribed by state variations of the Code and usually take the form of Document 12-5.

§12.7 POLICING

In any loan setting, the lender must take steps to protect itself from the consequences of the borrower's default. In asset-based loans, that policing often requires the lender to keep current on the status of the borrower's inventory or accounts and, in particular, current on the value of such collateral — a difficult task.

Some working capital loans are secured; some are not. In the unsecured loan the lender relies primarily on the creditworthiness of its borrower. The borrower establishes that creditworthiness primarily through its credit history and through its financial statements. Lenders in these cases must know whether there are any material adverse changes in the financial posture of the borrower. In the best of all possible worlds, the lender perceives adverse trends before debilitating changes occur.

There are a number of steps that lenders take in monitoring the financial health of borrowers that do not give security. First, lenders will insist on periodic statements certified by independent **auditors**. The audits that generate audited financial statements are usually time-consuming and expensive for the borrower, who pays for them. They also arrive at the desk of the loan officer several months after the fact. An audit that covers a fiscal year ending on September 30, for example, might not be completed until the following February. The information in these audits is invaluable to the sophisticated loan officer, who may spot problems before the borrower's corporate officers are aware of them or at least before they are prepared to admit to their bank that they are aware of them.

In addition to the certified audit, it is customary for the lender to require the borrower to submit unaudited financial information on a periodic basis, probably monthly or quarterly. Loan officers might be particularly concerned with the age of accounts receivable and accounts payable and with inventory values. These financial records are generated internally by the borrower and are therefore less reliable than those prepared by independent certified public accounting firms. Internally prepared statements usually must be certified by a financial officer of the borrower, and the criminal sanctions that attend the false certification of information to a federally insured financial institution give them a measure of reliability.

In addition to these statements, loan officers rely on credit information agencies and legal newspapers that report on litigation, bankruptcies, name changes, and other activity that may spell financial difficulty for a borrower. Nothing, however, will substitute for a bank loan officer that consistently monitors industry activity. A loan officer with responsibility for agricultural lending is every bit as concerned about commodity prices and weather predictions as the farmers is.

Michigan
National
Bank

PROMISSORY NOTE
(Time or Term Loan)

Note No. ____________________

Amount $ ____________________ ____________________, Michigan

Due Date ____________________ Dated: ____________________

FOR VALUE RECEIVED the undersigned, jointly and severally (the "Borrower"), promise to pay to the order of ____________________ ____________________, a ____________________

(Full Proper Bank Name)

(the "Bank"), at Bank's office set forth below or at such other place as Bank may designate in writing, the principal sum of ____________________ ____________________ Dollars

($ ____________________), together with interest as hereinafter provided, all in lawful money of the United States of America.

The unpaid principal balance of this promissory note ("Note") shall bear interest computed upon the basis of a year of 360 days for the actual number of days elapsed in a month, at a rate of interest (the "Effective Interest Rate") which is equal to:
(COMPLETE ONE:)

(1) ____________ percent (________ %) per annum.

(2) ____________ percent (________ %) per annum in excess of that rate of interest established by ____________________ as its ____________________ rate (the "Index"), as such Index may vary

(the "Designee Bank")

from time to time. Borrower understands and agrees that the Effective Interest Rate payable to Bank under this Note shall be determined by reference to the Index, and not by reference to the actual rate of interest charged by the Designee Bank to any particular borrower(s). If the Index shall be increased or decreased the Effective Interest Rate under this Note shall be increased or decreased by the same amount, effective the day of each increase or decrease in the Index. If at any time the Designee Bank shall abandon the use and quotation of the rate of interest used as the Index for this Note, the Index shall be Bank's own Prime Rate of interest. Principal and interest shall be paid to Bank as follows:
(COMPLETE ONE:)

(1) On ____________, 19 ____. (Single Payment)

(2) Consecutive payments of $ ____________ ☐ plus interest ☐ including interest (if neither of the foregoing boxes is checked, the payment stated above shall be "plus interest") accrued to the date of such payment, commencing on the ____________ of ____________, 19 ____, and continuing on the ________ day of each ____________ thereafter, until the Due Date, upon which date the entire unpaid principal balance of this Note and all accrued and unpaid interest shall be due and payable to Bank in full.

Borrower expressly assumes all risks of loss or delay in the delivery of any payments made by mail, and no course of conduct or dealing shall affect Borrower's assumption of these risks. If Bank shall determine that the Effective Interest Rate under this Note is, or may be, usurious or otherwise limited by law, the unpaid balance of this Note, with accrued interest at the highest rate then permitted shall, at the option of the Bank, become immediately due and payable

☐ This Note may be prepaid, in full or in part, at any time, without any prepayment fee. All partial prepayments shall be applied against the last accruing installment or amount due under this Note and no partial prepayments shall affect the obligation of Borrower to continue making all payments specified in this Note until the entire unpaid principal and all accrued interest shall have been paid in full.

☐ Upon prepayment of this Note, Borrower agrees to pay Bank that prepayment fee stated in the Prepayment Addendum attached to this Note.

Upon the occurrence of any of the following events of default, Bank, at its option and without notice to Borrower, may declare the entire unpaid principal balance of this Note and all accrued interest, together with all other indebtedness of Borrower to Bank, to be immediately due and payable: (a) Borrower's failure to pay any installment of principal or of interest when due; (b) any breach by Borrower of any warranty, representation, covenant, term, or condition stated in any loan agreement, security agreement, mortgage or other agreement executed in connection with this Note; (c) the death, dissolution or termination of existence of Borrower; (d) if Borrower is generally not paying debts as such debts become due; (e) the commencement of any proceedings under any bankruptcy or insolvency laws by or against Borrower; (f) if any other indebtedness of Borrower to the Bank or to any other creditor shall become due and remain unpaid after acceleration of the maturity or after the maturity stated; (g) if any writ of attachment, garnishment, execution, tax lien, or similar process shall be issued against any property of Borrower; or (h) Borrower's business shall be sold to, or merged with, any other business, individual, or entity.

Upon the occurrence of any event of default, the unpaid principal balance of this Note shall bear interest at a rate which is two percent (2%) greater than the Effective Interest Rate otherwise applicable. If any payment under this Note is not paid within ten (10) days after the date due, then, at the option of the Bank, a late charge of not more than four cents ($0.04) for each dollar of the installment past due may be charged by Bank. In addition to any other security interests granted, Borrower grants Bank a security interest in all of Borrower's bank deposits, instruments, negotiable documents, and chattel paper which at any time are in the possession or control of Bank, and after the occurrence of any event of default Bank may apply its own indebtedness or liability to Borrower or to any guarantor in payment of any indebtedness due under this Note.

Acceptance by Bank of any payment in an amount less than the amount then due shall be deemed an acceptance on account only, and Borrower's failure to pay the entire amount due shall be and continue to be an event of default. Borrower and all guarantors hereof do hereby jointly and severally waive presentment for payment, demand, notice of nonpayment, notice of protest or protest of this Note, and Bank diligence in collection or bringing suit, and hereby consent to any and all extensions of time, renewals, waivers, or modifications as may be granted by Bank with respect to payment or any other provisions of this Note, and to the release of any collateral or any part thereof with or without substitution. The liability of the Borrower under this Note shall be absolute and unconditional, without regard to the liability of any other party. Borrower agrees to pay all of Bank's costs incurred in the collection of this Note, including reasonable attorney fees. This Note shall be deemed to have been executed in, and all rights and obligations hereunder shall be governed by, the laws of the State of Michigan.

This Note is secured by (CHECK WHERE APPLICABLE):

☐ Security Agreement dated ____________, 19 ____ ☐ Loan Agreement dated ____________, 19 ____

☐ Real Estate Mortgage dated ____________, 19 ____ ☐ Guaranty dated ____________, 19 ____

☐ Other ____________________

Reference is hereby made to the document(s) and agreement(s) described above for additional terms and conditions relating to this Note.

Borrower Address: BORROWER

____________________ ____________________

____________________ ____________________

SPECIMEN

Bank Address: ____________________

____________________ ____________________

____________________ ____________________

Tax I.D. or Social Security No.

10016 (12/88)

WHITE - BANK ORIGINAL YELLOW - BANK PROCESSING COPY PINK - CUSTOMER COPY

Printed with the permission of Michigan National Corporation.

BUSINESS LOAN AGREEMENT
(SHORT FORM)

The undersigned ______________________________ (NAME OF BORROWER)

a ______________________ SPECIMEN ______________________, with its chief executive offices located

at ______________________________ (ADDRESS)

(the "Borrower") has requested from ______________________________ (FULL PROPER BANK NAME)

of ______________________________, Michigan ("Bank") and Bank agrees to make, or has made, the loan(s) described below (the "Loans") under the terms and conditions set forth in this Business Loan Agreement ("Agreement").

I. LOANS:

The following Loan(s) and any amendments, extensions, renewals or refinancing thereof are subject to this Agreement:

	TYPE OF LOAN	INTEREST RATE	NOTE AMOUNT	NOTE MATURITY DATE	LOAN DATE
A.					
B.					

Purpose of Loan(s) listed above:

A. ______________________________

B. ______________________________

Unless otherwise specified, any previous Business Loan Agreements are superceded by this Agreement.

II. BORROWER'S REPRESENTATIONS AND WARRANTIES.

Borrower represents and warrants to Bank, all of which representations and warranties shall be continuing and shall survive the execution of this Agreement until all of the Indebtedness is fully paid to Bank and Borrower's obligations under this Agreement and the Related Documents are fully performed, as follows:

A. **Borrower's Existence and Authority.** Borrower is a ______________________ (Sole proprietorship/partnership/corporation) and the person or persons executing this Agreement have full power and complete authority to execute this Agreement and all Related Documents.

B. **Nature of Borrower's Business.** The nature of Borrower's business is: ______________________.

C. **Financial Information.** All Financial Information provided to Bank has been prepared and will continue to be prepared in accordance with generally accepted accounting principles (GAAP), consistently applied, and fully and fairly present the financial condition of the Borrower, and there has been no material adverse change in Borrower's business, Property, or condition (financial or otherwise) since the date of the Borrower's latest Financial Statements.

D. **Title and Encumbrances.** Borrower owns and has good title to all of its Property, including the Collateral, and there are no liens or encumbrances on any of the Property, including the Collateral, except as have been disclosed to Bank in writing prior to the date of this Agreement and as are identified and listed in an attachment to this Agreement (the "Permitted Encumbrances"). Borrower agrees that Borrower shall not obtain further loans, leases, or extensions of credit from any of the parties identified in the said Permitted Encumbrances list without Bank's prior written consent.

E. **No Litigation/No Misrepresentations.** There are no pending suits or proceedings pending before any court, government agency, arbitration panel, or administrative tribunal, or, to Borrower's knowledge, threatened against Borrower, which may result in any material adverse change in the business, Property or financial condition of Borrower, and all representations and warranties in this Agreement and the Related Documents are true and correct and no material fact has been omitted.

F. **Environmental Compliance.** No part of the Property is classified or classifiable as hazardous waste under Federal and Michigan environmental laws and regulations, and Borrower (and all Obligors) agree to indemnify and hold Bank harmless from any and all violations by Borrower of any Federal or Michigan environmental laws and regulations.

III. AFFIRMATIVE COVENANTS.

As of the date of this Agreement and continuing until the Borrower's obligations under this Agreement and the Related Documents are fully performed and the Indebtedness is fully repaid to Bank, Borrower shall at all times:

A. **Financial Requirements.**
1. Requirements: ______________________________

B. **Books and Reports.**
1. Furnish to Bank, in form acceptable to Bank: [ ] management prepared and certified [ ] certified public accountant prepared [ ] **compiled** [ ] **reviewed** [ ] **audited** Financial Statements within __________ days after the end of each [ ] **month** [ ] **quarter** [ ] **six months** [ ] **fiscal year.**
2. Furnish to Bank, in form satisfactory to Bank, within __________ days after the end of each Borrower's fiscal [ ] **month** [ ] **quarter** [ ] **year** [ ] **compiled** [ ] **reviewed** [ ] **audited** Financial Statements prepared by certified public accountants acceptable to Bank.
3. Promptly furnish to Bank such other information and reports concerning the Borrower's business, Property, and financial condition as are provided to Borrower's owners, or as Bank shall request, and permit Bank to inspect, confirm, and copy Borrower's books and records at any time during Borrower's normal business hours.

C. **Notice of Adverse Events.** Promptly notify Bank in writing of any litigation, governmental proceeding, default or any other occurrence which may have a material adverse effect on Borrower's business, Property or financial condition.

D. **Maintain Business Existence and Operations.** Do all things necessary to keep in full force and effect Borrower's corporate, partnership or proprietorship existence, as the case may be, and to continue its business described in Paragraph II B. as presently conducted, and maintain its present business status. Borrower shall not change its corporate, partnership or proprietorship existence, nor sell or merge Borrower's business, in whole or in part, without the prior written consent of Bank.

E. **Insurance.**
Maintain adequate fire and extended risk coverage, business interruption, workers compensation, public liability and such other insurance coverages as may be required by law or as may be required by Bank. All insurance policies shall be in such amounts, upon such terms, and be in form acceptable to Bank, and shall be carried with insurers acceptable to Bank. Borrower shall provide evidence satisfactory to Bank of all insurance coverages and that the policies are in full force and effect, and all insurance coverages upon any Property which is Collateral for any of Borrower's Indebtedness to Bank, shall name Bank as a loss payee and shall be endorsed to require thirty (30) days advance written notice to Bank of any cancellation of coverage. If Borrower fails to maintain insurance as provided in this Agreement, such failure shall be an Event of Default and Bank may obtain the insurance but shall have no obligation to do so; and all amounts so expended by Bank shall be added to the Indebtedness or shall be payable on demand, at Bank's option.

10027 (12/86)

F. **Payment of Taxes.** Promptly pay all taxes, levies and assessments due all local, State and Federal agencies. Except to the extent that Borrower has established a cash reserve therefore and is actively pursuing a tax appeal, any failure by Borrower to promptly pay any taxes, levies and assessments due shall be an Event of Default.

G. **Use of Proceeds; Purpose of Loans.** Use the proceeds of the Loans only for Borrower's business described in Paragraph II B, and for those purposes stated in Paragraph I.

H. **Maintenance of Records; Change in Place of Business or Name.** Keep all of its books and records at the address set forth above in this Agreement, and shall give the Bank prompt written notice of any change in its principal place of business, in the location of Borrower's books and records, in Borrower's name, and any change in the location of the Collateral.

I. **Workers Compensation Insurance.** At all times during the term of this Agreement and until the Indebtedness shall have been fully repaid, maintain workers' compensation insurance as required by law unless Borrower is qualified and duly authorized by law to self-insure with respect to its workers' compensation liability and is not otherwise prohibited by this Agreement from doing so.

IV. NEGATIVE COVENANTS.
Until all of Borrower's obligations under this Agreement and the Related Documents are fully performed and the Indebtedness is fully repaid, Borrower shall not:

A. **Investment In Fixed Assets.** Invest in fixed assets in excess of $_____________ in any 12 month period, without the prior written consent of Bank.

B. **No Borrowings, Guarantees, or Loans.** Borrow money or act as a guarantor of any loan or other obligation of others, or lend any money to any person. Any sale of Borrower's accounts receivable shall be deemed the borrowing of money.

C. **Liens and Encumbrances; Transfer of Assets.** Mortgage, assign, hypothecate, or encumber in any way any of its Property to any person except to Bank, nor sell, transfer, or assign any Property except in the ordinary course of Borrower's business.

D. **Salary Limitations.** During the term of this Agreement and until all Indebtedness is repaid to Bank, the annual total of all salaries, bonuses, fringe benefits, and all other monetary compensation paid by Borrower to the following officers, directors, or employees shall not exceed the following limitations:

Name	Limitation
____________________	$ ____________________
____________________	$ ____________________

V. EVENTS OF DEFAULT.
The occurrence of any of the following events shall constitute an Event of Default under this Agreement.

A. **Failure to Pay Amounts Due.** If any principal or interest on any Indebtedness to Bank is not paid when due.

B. **Misrepresentation; False Financial Information.** If any warranty or representation of the Borrower in connection with or contained in this Agreement, or if any Financial Statements now or hereafter furnished to the Bank by or on behalf of the Borrower, are false or misleading in any material respect.

C. **Noncompliance with Bank Agreements.** If the Borrower shall fail to perform any of its obligations and covenants under, or shall fail to comply with any of the provisions of this Agreement or any other agreement with the Bank, including but not limited to the Related Documents.

D. **Other Lender Default.** Any non-Bank indebtedness of Borrower matures or is declared to be due and payable prior to the stated maturity thereof.

E. **Judgments; Attachments; Garnishments; Tax Liens.** If there shall be entered against Borrower or any other Obligor, any judgment which materially affects Borrower's or the Obligor's business, Property or financial condition, or if any tax lien, levy, writ of attachment, garnishment, execution or smiliar writ shall be issued against the Collateral or which materially affects Borrower's business, Property or financial condition, and which remains unpaid, unstayed on appeal, undischarged, unbonded, or undismissed for a period of thirty (30) days after the date thereof.

F. **Business Merger, Suspension, Bankruptcy.** If Borrower or any other Obligor shall sell or merge Borrower's business to or with any other business; shall voluntarily suspend transaction of its business; shall not generally pay debts as they mature; shall make a general assignment for the benefit of creditors; or shall file or have filed against Borrower any reorganization or liquidation under the Bankruptcy Code or under any other state or federal law for the relief of debtors which is not discharged within thirty (30) days after filing; or a receiver, trustee or custodian shall be appointed for the Borrower or any Obligor.

G. **Material Adverse Change.** Any material adverse change in the Borrower's business, Property or financial condition has occurred or is imminent; if the full performance of the obligations of any Obligor is materially impaired; or if the Collateral and its value or the Bank's rights with respect thereto are materially impaired in any way.

H. **Authority to Charge Interest Rate Adversely Affected.** If Bank shall determine that the Loan(s) interest rate is usurious, or is otherwise unlawful or limited in any way, including but not limited to Bank's right to periodically adjust the agreed upon rate of interest or the method of adjustment.

I. **Non-Compliance with Worker's Compensation Laws.** If Borrower fails to comply with any workers' compensation law, regulation, administrative rule, directive or requirement; has its workers' compensation insurance terminated or cancelled for any reason; or, if applicable, has its self-insurance certification revoked or should such certification lapse for any reason.

VI. REMEDIES ON DEFAULT.

A. **Acceleration/Set-off.** Upon the occurrence of any Event of Default, the Loan(s) and all Indebtedness to Bank may, at the option of Bank, be declared to be immediately due and payable, and Bank shall have the right to apply any or all of Borrower's or any Obligor's bank accounts or any other property held by Bank, against any Indebtedness of Borrower to Bank.

B. **Remedies; No Waiver.** The remedies provided for in this Agreement are cumulative and not exclusive, and Bank may exercise any remedies available to it at law or in equity and as are provided in the Related Documents or other agreement between Borrower and Bank. No delay or failure of Bank in exercising any right, remedy, power or privilege under this Agreement or the Related Documents shall affect that right, remedy, power or privilege, nor shall any single or partial exercise preclude the exercise of any other right, remedy, power or privilege. No delay or failure of Bank to demand strict adherence to the terms of this Agreement shall be deemed to constitute a course of conduct inconsistent with the Bank's right at any time, before or after any Event of Default, to demand strict adherence to the terms of this Agreement or the Related Documents.

VII. CROSS-COLLATERALIZATION/CROSS-DEFAULT.
Borrower agrees that all of the Collateral is security for the Loan(s) and for all other Indebtedness of Borrower to Bank, whether or not such Indebtedness is related by class or kind, and whether or not contemplated by the parties at the time of executing each evidence of Indebtedness. Any Borrower default under the terms of any Indebtedness to Bank shall constitute an Event of Default under this Agreement.

VIII. MISCELLANEOUS.

A. **Compliance with Bank Agreements.** Borrower acknowledges that Borrower has read and understands this Agreement, the Related Documents, and all other agreements between Borrower and Bank, and Borrower agrees to fully comply with all the agreements.

B. **Expenses.** Borrower agrees to pay all of Bank's expenses incidental to perfecting Bank's security interests and liens, all insurance premiums, Uniform Commercial Code search fees, and all fees incurred by Bank for audits, inspection, and copying of Borrower's books and records. Borrower also agrees to pay all costs and expenses of Bank in connection with the enforcement of the Bank's rights and remedies under this Agreement, the Related Documents, and any other agreeement between Borrower and Bank, and in connection with the preparation of any amendments, modifications, waivers or consents with respect to this Agreement, including reasonable attorney fees.

C. **Further Action.** Borrower agrees, from time to time, upon request of Bank, to make, execute, acknowledge, and deliver to Bank such further and additional instruments, documents, and agreements, and to take such further action as may be required to carry out the intent and purpose of this Agreement and the repayment of the Loan(s).

D. **Governing Law/Partial Illegality** This Agreement and the Related Documents shall be interpreted, and the rights of the parties hereunder shall be determined under, the laws of the State of Michigan. Should any part, term, or provision of this Agreement be adjudged illegal or in conflict with any law of the United States or State of Michigan, the validity of the remaining portion or provisions of the Agreement shall not be affected.

E. **Writings Constitute Entire Agreement; Modifications Only in Writing.** This Agreement together with all other written agreements between Borrower and Bank, including but not limited to the Related Documents, constitute the entire agreement of the parties and shall be interpreted in harmony one with the others. None of the parties shall be bound by anything not expressed in writing, and this Agreement can not be modified except by a writing executed by Borrower and by the Bank. This Agreement shall inure to the benefit of and shall be binding upon all of the parties to this Agreement and their respective successors, estate representatives, and assigns, provided, however, that Borrower can not assign or transfer its rights or obligations under this Agreement without Bank's prior written consent.

F. **Headings.** All section and paragraph headings in this Agreement are included for reference only and do not constitute a part of this Agreement.

G. **Term of Agreement.** Unless superseded by a later Business Loan Agreement, this Agreement shall continue in full force and effect until all of Borrower's obligations to Bank are fully satisfied and the Loan(s) and Indebtedness are fully repaid.

IX. DEFINITIONS.

The following words shall have the following meanings in this Agreement:

A. **"Collateral"** shall mean that property which Borrower and any other Obligor has pledged, mortgaged, or granted Bank a security interest in, wherever located and whether now owned or hereafter acquired, together with all replacements, substitutions, proceeds and products thereof.

B. **"Base Rate" or "Prime Rate"** shall mean that variable rate of interest from time to time established by the Designee Bank as its prime commercial lending rate.

C. **"Event of Default"** shall mean any of the events described in Section V of this Agreement and in the Related Documents.

D. **"Financial Statements"** shall mean all balance sheets, earnings statements, and other financial information (whether of the Borrower, or an Obligor) which have been, are now, or are in the future furnished to Bank.

E. **"GAAP"** shall mean "generally accepted accounting principles" consistently applied as set forth from time to time in the Opinion of the Accounting Principles Board of the American Institute of Certified Public Accountants and the Financial Accounting Standards Board, or which have other substantial authoritative support.

F. **"Indebtedness"** shall mean all Loans and indebtedness of Borrower to the Bank, including but not limited to, Bank advances for payments of insurance, taxes, any amounts advanced by Bank to protect its interest in the Collateral, overdrafts in deposit accounts with Bank, and all other indebtedness, obligations and liabilities of Borrower to Bank, whether matured or unmatured, liquidated or unliquidated, direct or indirect, absolute or contingent, joint or several, due or to become due, now existing or hereafter arising.

G. **"Michigan National Bank Prime Rate"** shall mean that variable rate of interest so designated and from time to time established by Michigan National Corporation as the Michigan National Bank prime commercial lending rate.

H. **"Obligor"** shall mean any person having any obligation to Bank, whether for the payment of money or otherwise, under this Agreement or under the Related Documents, including but not limited to any guarantors of Borrower's Indebtedness.

I. **"Permitted Encumbrances"** shall mean that list of existing secured parties or mortgagee identified in a list attached to this Agreement.

J. **"Property"** shall mean all of Borrower's (or other Obligor's, as applicable) assets, whether tangible or intangible, real or personal.

K. **"Related Documents"** shall mean any and all documents, promissory notes, security agreements, leases, mortgages, guarantys, pledges, and any other documents or agreements executed in connection with this Agreement. The term shall include both documents existing at the time of execution of this Agreement and documents executed after this date of this Agreement.

X. ADDITIONAL PROVISIONS.

____

____

IN WITNESS WHEREOF, the parties have executed this Agreement on this ______ day of ______________, 19____.

Witnesses: **BORROWER**

____

SPECIMEN

BANK

By: ______________________________

Its: ______________________________

AGREEMENT OF GUARANTORS

By executing this Agreement each Guarantor: (1) acknowledges and agrees that the Guarantor has completely read and understands this Agreement; (2) consents to all of the provisions of this Agreement relating to Borrower; (3) agrees to furnish such financial information to Bank concerning the Guarantor as Bank shall reasonably request; (4) agrees to all of those portions of this Agreement which apply to Guarantor; (5) acknowledges and agrees that this Agreement has been freely executed without duress and after an opportunity was provided to Guarantor for review of this Agreement and the guaranty agreement by legal counsel of Guarantor's choice; and (6) that the Bank has provided Guarantor with a copy of this Agreement, the Guaranty, and such other related documents as the Guarantor has requested.

Witnesses:

____

(ADDRESS)

____

(ADDRESS)

Document 12-3. Promissory Note

PROMISSORY NOTE
(Line of Credit)

Note No. ______________

$ ______________ ______________, Michigan

Due Date: ______________ Dated: ______________

FOR VALUE RECEIVED, on the Due Date, the undersigned, jointly and severally, (the "Borrower"), promise to pay to the order of

______________ a ______________ (the "Bank"),
(Full Proper Bank Name)

at its office set forth below or at such other place as Bank may designate in writing, the principal sum of ______________

______________ Dollars ($) or such lesser sum as shall have been advanced by Bank to Borrower under the loan account hereinafter described, plus interest as hereinafter provided, all in lawful money of the United States of America. The unpaid principal balance of this promissory note ("Note") shall bear interest computed upon the basis of a year of 360 days for the actual number of days elapsed in a month, at a rate of interest (the "Effective Interest Rate") which is equal to:

(COMPLETE ONE:)

(1) ______________ percent (______ %) per annum.

(2) ______________ percent (______ %) per annum in excess of that rate of interest established by ______________

______________ (the "Designee Bank") as its ______________ rate (the "Index"), as such index may vary from time to time. Borrower understands and agrees that the Effective Interest Rate payable to Bank under this Note shall be determined by reference to the Index and not by reference to the actual rate of interest charged by the Designee Bank to any particular borrower(s). If the Index shall be increased or decreased, the Effective Interest Rate under this Note shall be increased or decreased by the same amount, effective upon the day of each increase or decrease in the Index. If at any time, the Designee Bank shall abandon the rate of interest used as the Index for this Note, the Index shall be the Bank's own Prime Rate of interest.

Interest on all principal amounts advanced by Bank from time to time and unpaid by Borrower shall be paid on the ______________ day of ______________, 19____, and on the ______ day of each ______________ thereafter.

Advances of principal, repayment, and readvances may be made under this Note from time to time, but Bank, in its sole discretion, may refuse to make advances or readvances hereunder during any period(s) this Note is in default. All advances made hereunder shall be charged to a loan account in Borrower's name on Bank's books, and Bank shall debit to such account the amount of each advance made to, and credit to such account the amount of each repayment made by, Borrower. From time to time, Bank shall furnish Borrower a statement of Borrower's loan account, which statement shall be deemed to be correct, accepted by, and binding upon Borrower, unless Bank receives a written statement of exceptions from Borrower within ten (10) days after such statement has been furnished.

This Note may be paid in full or in part at any time without payment of any prepayment fee or penalty. All payments received hereunder shall, at the option of the Bank, first be applied against accrued and unpaid interest and the balance against principal. Borrower expressly assumes all risks of loss or delay in the delivery of any payments made by mail, and no course of conduct or dealing shall affect Borrower's assumption of these risks. If Bank shall determine that the Effective Interest Rate under this Note is, or may be, usurious or otherwise limited by law, the unpaid balance of this Note, with accrued interest at the highest rate then permitted by law, shall at the option of the Bank become immediately due and payable.

Unless this Note is due upon demand, in which case the provisions of this paragraph shall not apply, upon the occurrence of any of the following events of default, Bank, at its option and without notice to Borrower, may declare the entire unpaid principal balance of this Note and all accrued interest, together with all other indebtedness of Borrower to Bank, to be immediately due and payable: (a) Borrower's failure to pay any installment of principal or of interest when due; (b) any default by Borrower under any loan agreement, security agreement, mortgage, or other agreement excuted in connection with this Note; (c) the death, dissolution, or termination of existence of Borrower; (d) if Borrower is generally not paying its debts as such debts become due; (e) the commencement of any proceedings under any bankruptcy or insolvency laws by or against Borrower; (f) if any other indebtedness of Borrower to the Bank or to any other creditor shall become due and remain unpaid after acceleration of the maturity or after the maturity stated: (g) if any writ of attachment, garnishment, execution, tax lien, or similar process shall be issued against any property of Borrower; (h) Borrower's business shall be sold to, or merged with, any other business, individual, or entity.

Upon the occurrence of any event of default or upon non-payment of this Note after demand, the unpaid principal balance of this Note shall bear interest at a rate which is two percent (2%) greater than the Effective Interest Rate otherwise applicable. If any payment under this Note is not paid within ten (10) days after the date due, at the option of the Bank a late charge of not more than four cents ($.04) for each dollar of the installment past due may be charged by Bank. In addition to any other security interest granted, Borrower hereby grants Bank a security interest in all of Borrower's bank deposits, instruments, negotiable documents, and chattel paper which at any time are in the possession or control of Bank, and after the occurrence of any event of default, Bank may apply its own indebtedness or liability to Borrower or to any guarantor to any indebtedness due under this Note. Borrower agrees to pay all of the Bank's costs incurred in the collection of this Note, including reasonable attorney fees.

Acceptance by Bank of any payment in an amount less than the amount then due shall be deemed an acceptance on account only, and Bank's acceptance of any such partial payment shall not constitute a waiver of Bank's right to receive the entire amount due. Borrower and all guarantors of this Note do hereby jointly and severally waive presentment for payment, demand, notice of non-payment, notice of protest or protest of this Note, and Bank diligence in collection or bringing suit, and do hereby consent to any and all extensions of time, renewals, waivers or modifications as may be granted by Bank with respect to payment or any other provisions of this Note, and to the release of any collateral or any part thereof, with or without substitution. The liability of the Borrower under this Note shall be absolute and unconditional, without regard to the liability of any other party. This Note shall be deemed to have executed in Michigan, and all rights and obligations hereunder shall be governed by the laws of the State of Michigan.

This Note is secured by: (CHECK WHERE APPLICABLE):

☐ Security Agreement dated ______________, 19 ____ ☐ Real Estate Mortgage dated ______________, 19 ____

☐ Guaranty dated ______________, 19 ____ ☐ Loan Agreement dated ______________, 19 ____. ☐ Other ______________

Reference is hereby made to the agreement(s) and document(s) described above for additional terms and conditions relating to this Note.

Borrower Address BORROWER

______________ ______________

______________ ______________

SPECIMEN ______________

Bank Address ______________

______________ ______________
Tax ID or Social Security No.

____

10015(3/87) ©1987 Michigan National Corporation

WHITE-BANK ORIGINAL YELLOW-BANK PROCESSING COPY PINK-CUSTOMER COPY

SECURITY AGREEMENT

(General)

I. The parties to this agreement are as follows:

Debtor:________________________________

Secured Party:________________________________

II. The Debtor for valuable consideration, receipt whereof is hereby acknowledged, hereby transfers to the Secured Party a security interest in the following property and any and all additions and accessions thereto:

SPECIMEN

III. The Collateral has been acquired and is used by the Debtor (or will be acquired and will be used) primarily for the purpose checked below:

☐ Equipment used in business. ☐ Consumer goods (personal, family or household goods).

If checked here ☐, the Collateral will be acquired with proceeds of loans from the Secured Party which may disburse the proceeds thereof directly to the Seller.

IV. The Collateral will be kept at________________________________
(No. and Street)

____
(City or Town) (County) (State)

and the record owner of said premises is________________________________.

Debtor agrees to promptly notify Secured Party of any change in the location of the Collateral and that Debtor will not remove the Collateral from said State without the written consent of the Secured Party.

V. The aforesaid security interest shall secure the obligations evidenced by notes described as follows:

Date________________Amount________________________________
and shall secure the payment of any and all indebtednesses and liabilities whatsoever of the Debtor to the Secured Party, whether now existing or hereafter arising, together with all costs and expenses of Secured Party in respect of or connected with any of the indebtedness or Collateral.

VI. Debtor at its expense will keep and maintain in force such insurance in such amounts covering loss or damage to the Collateral, including extended coverage, as is usually and customarily carried by owners of like property or as may be requested by Secured Party, including loss payable clauses if demanded.

VII. Debtor hereby warrants and covenants that except for the security interest granted hereby Debtor is, or to the extent that this agreement states that the Collateral is to be acquired after the date hereof, will be, the owner of the Collateral free from any adverse lien, security interest or encumbrance and that Debtor will defend the Collateral against all claims and demands of all persons at any time claiming the same or any interest therein.

VIII. If any or all of the Collateral has been or is to be attached to real estate, Debtor on demand of Secured Party shall furnish the Secured Party with a disclaimer or disclaimers signed by all persons having an interest in the real estate (including landowners, mortgage holders, and lessees) disclaiming any interest in the Collateral prior to the interest of the Secured Party.

IX. Debtor will pay on demand all costs and expenses of filing and recording, including the costs of any searches deemed necessary by Secured Party, to establish and determine the validity and the priority of the security interest of the Secured Party and also all other claims and charges which in the opinion of Secured Party might prejudice, imperil or otherwise affect the Collateral or its security interest therein. At its option, Secured Party may discharge taxes, liens or security interests or other encumbrances at any time levied or placed on the Collateral, may pay for insurance on the Collateral and may pay for the maintenance and preservation of the Collateral. Debtor agrees to reimburse Secured Party on demand for any payment made, or any expense incurred by Secured Party pursuant to the foregoing authorization.

X. Debtor will keep the Collateral free from any adverse lien, security interest or encumbrance and in good order and repair and will not waste or destroy the Collateral or any part thereof. Debtor will not use the Collateral in violation of any statute or ordinance. Secured Party may examine and inspect the Collateral at any time, wherever located.

XI. In the event the Debtor fails to pay when due any installment of interest or principal of any indebtedness secured by this Security Agreement, or in the event the Debtor violates any term of this Security Agreement, or in the event the Secured Party in good faith deems itself insecure either as to the payment of the obligations secured by this agreement, as to the Debtor's ability to perform this Security Agreement, or as to the sufficiency of the collateral securing the indebtedness, then the Debtor shall be in default of this Security Agreement and the Secured Party may proceed in accordance with law. In furtherance of and not in limitation of the foregoing, in the event of default, the Secured Party shall have the right to take immediate possession of the Collateral, and for that purpose may pursue the same wherever it may be found and may enter any of the Debtor's premises, with or without force or process of law, wherever said Collateral may be, or be supposed to be, and search for the same, and if found, may take possession of and remove and sell the Collateral or any part thereof at public or private sale. Unless the Collateral is perishable or threatens to decline speedily in value or is of a type customarily sold on a recognized market, the Secured Party will give the Debtor reasonable notice of the time and place of any public sale or of the time after which any other intended disposition is to be made. The requirement of reasonable notice shall be met if such notice is mailed, postage prepaid, to the Debtor at the address given herein or if none to any address in the Secured Party's files, at least five days before the time of sale or other disposition. Expenses of retaking, holding, preparing for sale, selling or the like shall include Secured Party's reasonable attorney's fees and legal expenses. Out of the money arising from such sale, Secured Party may retain all costs and charges for pursuing, searching for, retaking, removing, keeping, storing, advertising and selling such Collateral, together with the amount due and unpaid upon any notes held by it, accounting to the Debtor for any surplus.

XII. No default shall be waived by Secured Party except in writing and no waiver of any default shall operate as a waiver of any other default or of the same default on a future occasion. All rights of Secured Party hereunder shall be cumulative and shall inure to the benefit of itself, its successors and assigns; and all obligations of Debtor shall bind legal representatives and successors. If there is more than one Debtor, all undertakings, warranties and covenants made by the Debtor and all rights, powers and authorities given to or conferred on the Secured Party shall be made or given jointly and severally.

Dated:________________, 19__ __. Signed:________________

________________ ________________

________________ ________________
Address Debtor

FORM UCC-1

STATE OF MICHIGAN

UNIFORM COMMERCIAL CODE FINANCING STATEMENT

(Approved by the Secretary of State and Michigan Association of Registers of Deeds)

INSTRUCTIONS:

1. TYPE OR PRINT All information required on this Form.
2. **If filing is made with the Secretary of State, send the WHITE copies to the Secretary of State, Lansing, Michigan. If filing is made with the Register of Deeds, send the YELLOW copies to the Local Register of Deeds. Retain the PINK copies for files of secured party and debtor.**
3. Enclose filing fee.
4. IF ADDITIONAL SPACE IS NEEDED for any items on this Form, continue the items on separate sheets of paper (5" x 8"). One copy of these additional sheets should accompany the WHITE Forms, and one copy should accompany the YELLOW Forms. USE PAPER CLIPS to attach these sheets to the Forms (DO NOT USE STAPLES, GLUE, TAPE, ETC.) and indicate in Item 1 the number of additional sheets attached.
5. At the time of filing, the filing officer will return acknowledgement. At a later time, the secured party may date and sign the termination legend and use acknowledgement copy as a termination statement.
6. Both the WHITE and YELLOW Filing Officer copies must have original signatures. Only the debtor must sign the financing statement, and the signature of the secured party is not necessary, except that the secured party alone may sign the financing statement in the following 4 instances: Please specify action in Item 7 below.
   (1) Where the collateral which is subject to the security interest in another state is brought into Michigan or the location of the debtor is changed to Michigan.
   (2) "For proceeds if the security interest in the original collateral was perfected."
   (3) The previous filing has lapsed.
   (4) For collateral acquired after a change of debtor name etc., and a filing is required under MCLA 440.9402 (2) and (7); MSA 19.9402 (2) and (7).

1. No. of additional sheets	Liber	Page	For Filing Officer (Date, Time, Number, and Filing Office)
2. Debtor(s) (Last Name First) and address(es)	3. Secured Party(ies) and address(es)		
4. Name and address(es) of assignee(s) (if any)	CHECK [x] if applicable 5. ☐ Products of collateral are also covered. 6. ☐ Collateral was brought into this state subject to a security interest in another jurisdiction.		

7. This financing statement covers the following types (or items) of property:

____

________________ ________________

________________ by: ________________

Signature(s) of Debtor(s) (Signature of Secured Party or Assignee of Record)

SECRETARY OF STATE COPY

Order by Form B411 Rev. 1/80 From Doubleday Bros. & Co., Kalamazoo, Mich. 49002 FINANCIAL PRINTERS

13 The Financing Seller

§13.1 INTRODUCTION

Banks and finance companies are major participants in secured lending, and the secured transaction that involves them is customarily a three-party transaction, which Figure 13-1 illustrates.

There is, however, another category of secured lender that also plays a major role in secured lending. This secured lender is the seller of goods, and in two significant ways the security interest of the secured seller differs from the security interest of the secured lender. First, the sales transaction is two-party, not three-party. Second, in the secured sales transaction, we normally think of the seller as "retaining" a security interest, while in the three-party secured transaction, the debtor "grants" the security interest to the **secured party**. In addition, in the sales secured transaction, the documentation is somewhat simpler. There is no need for a loan agreement here. This "loan" (or extension of credit) is discretely related to a single item or a designated group of items — the products that the seller is selling to the debtor. The security agreement in these cases is usually part of the sales agreement, which itself contains the payment terms, there being no promissory note. Document 2-2 in Chapter 2 includes a security agreement arising out of a sales transaction, and Figure 13-2 illustrates the two-party nature of this secured transaction.

Retailers generate a great volume of secured seller transactions, and those sellers fall into one of two categories. The first is the credit plan

Figure 13-1. Three-Party Secured Transaction

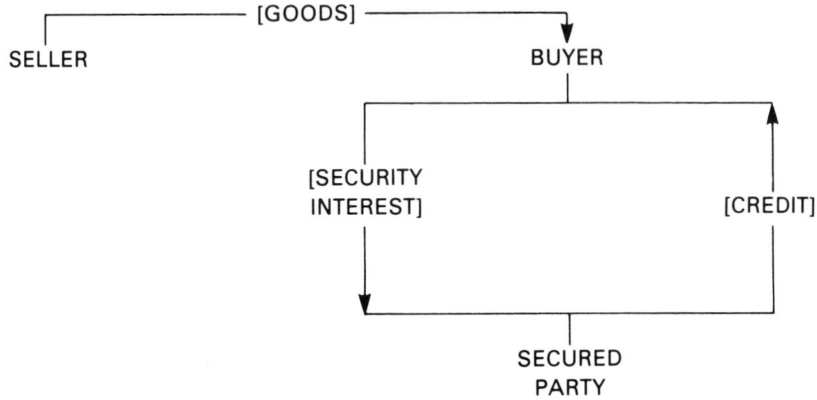

seller that takes a security interest in all merchandise sold on credit under a "charge-account" arrangement. Traditionally, department stores and larger retailers have engaged in this kind of consumer credit transaction. The second category involves credit granted in connection with a single purchase. These transactions usually arise out of big ticket sales, that is, sales of home appliances, automobiles, and the like.

There are other sellers, usually of business or manufacturing equipment, that finance the buyer's purchase, but some of them are really lenders. Equipment financing, for example, will frequently take the form of a finance lease that is in reality a security agreement. The lessor in those cases, may be the equipment manufacturer but often will be a finance company that is a subsidiary of the manufacturer or of a bank holding company. Section 13.4 below discusses indirect equipment financing generally, and Chapter 18 deals with equipment financing at greater length.

§13.2 SECURED TRANSACTIONS AND CHARGE-ACCOUNT SALES

Many revolving charge accounts do not entail any security agreement. If the retailer is satisfied with the credit history of a customer, the retailer

Figure 13-2. Two-Party Secured Transaction

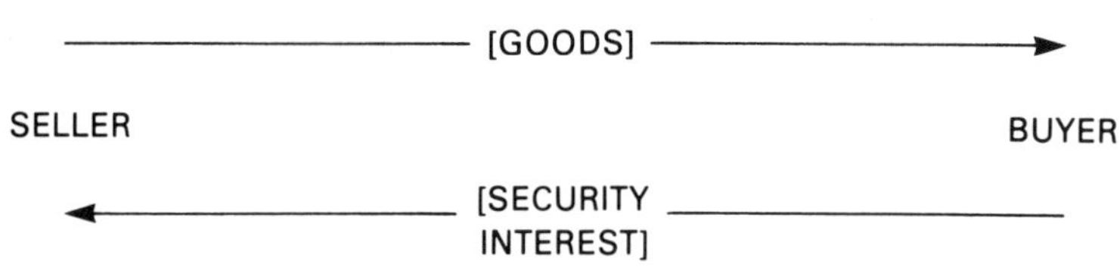

Figure 13-3. Revolving Credit-Account Balance

	FEB.	MAR.	APR.	MAY	JUN.	JUL.
JAN. SALE ($10)	5.00	3.33	2.50	1.66	0.83	-0-
FEB. SALE ($10)		6.67	5.00	3.34	1.67	-0-
MAR. SALE ($10)			7.50	5.00	2.50	-0-

ALLOCATION OF
$5 MONTHLY PAYMENT

	FEB.	MAR.	APR.	MAY	JUN.
JAN. SALE	5.00	1.67	0.83	0.84	0.83
FEB. SALE		3.33	1.67	1.66	1.67
MAR. SALE			2.50	2.50	2.50

will accept charges and bill monthly, usually with a service charge for bills that are not paid promptly. Although direct retailer secured lending is diminishing as a source of consumer credit relative to all sources, some retailers who are unwilling to extend credit on that basis at all or are unwilling to extend it to some customers grant credit to such customers only if they can do so on a secured basis.

Efforts by retailers to secure revolving credit accounts have fostered some controversy. Usually, the retailer uses a **cross-collateralization** provision in the agreement whereby all goods purchased secure all of the debt. Retailers have given that provision expanded effect by providing that the buyer's periodic payments shall be allocated ratably among the principal balances due on each purchase. Assume, for instance, that a consumer acquires a videocassette recorder in January and a refrigerator in June, and that the balance due in August is $500 on the VCR and $1,000 on the refrigerator. Under these revolving charge account provisions, the retailer will allocate one-third of the August payment to the VCR balance and two-thirds of the payment to the refrigerator balance. The effect of the arrangement is to leave a small balance owing on an early purchase, thereby insuring that the security interest in that item will continue and that it will retain its purchase-money character.

Because of the Code's **perfection** rules and restrictions on the ability to use **consumer goods** as collateral, the purchase-money nature of the security interest is important to the retailer. Figure 13-3 illustrates this attempt to retain purchase-money status as to each item of collateral.

Consumer advocates and some courts have objected to these arrangements as unconscionable. It does not require a great deal of sophistication to realize quickly that retailers take security interests in these cases not because used consumer goods are valuable collateral that will fetch good prices in the used furniture market: Retailers use these security agreements for their ad terrorem effect.

Figure 13-4. Consumer Sale (Retail Installment Sales Contract)

It is a hot summer day, the unemployed parent of small children hears the doorbell. At the door are two burly gentlemen in green uniforms. "We come to get the fridge," one of them announces, and it occurs to the parent that perhaps the proceeds of the welfare check on the kitchen table should go to the department store instead of the grocer. In one case, a department store sought to repossess a shower curtain and children's toys among other items a welfare mother had acquired over a period of months.

Some have argued that the creditor practices in question are a concomitant of poverty and not the consequences of merchant greed. These commentators contend that if these agreements are not enforceable, poor people will not be able to obtain credit or will pay more for that credit. They also point out that security provisions make it easier for retailers to collect from those buyers who can afford to pay but who prefer to default and let the rest of the consuming public share the loss. Document 13-1 is a revolving credit agreement with security provisions that conspicuously omit the offensive provisions.

§13.3 CONSUMER PAPER

In secured transactions law, **consumer paper** is a far more important source of credit than revolving charge account agreements. In a typical transaction, an automobile dealer enters into a credit sale with a customer who grants the dealer a purchase-money security interest in the subject of the sale. Document 13-2 is an automobile retail sales contract with such a security interest, and Figure 13-4 illustrates this frequent consumer purchase transaction.

Automobile dealers are not financial institutions and cannot carry the volume of **chattel paper** that they generate. It would not be unusual for a dealer's volume of paper generated in a given year to exceed its assets by a factor of ten or more. Only a financial institution can afford to finance such paper, and automobile dealers, as well as other merchandisers that generate chattel paper, "sell" that paper to a bank or finance company or arrange the loan for the institutional lender by using loan documents supplied by the lender itself. Chapter 18 discusses chattel-paper financing. For now it suffices to compare the chattel-paper financing transaction, illustrated in Figure 13-5, with the simple sales transaction of Figure 13-4.

Figure 13-5. Discounting the Risk

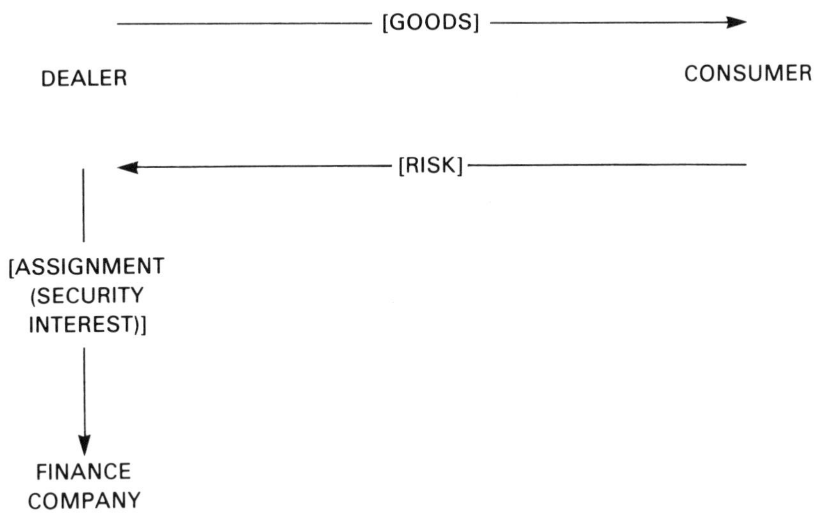

§13.4 EQUIPMENT FINANCING

Some manufacturers and dealers of industrial or farm equipment engage in the same kind of financing that automobile dealers and other retailers use. The equipment dealers sell on credit and retain a purchase-money security interest in the equipment they sell. That security agreement often appears in the form of a lease. They then discount the paper (the lease) to a financial institution. Other equipment sellers, especially some manufacturers, use leasing companies to finance equipment sales. These transactions take one of two forms. First, the manufacturer can lease the equipment directly to its customer. In this case, the manufacturer will then finance the lease by transferring it to a financial institution. In other cases, the buyer will approach a financial institution's leasing company subsidiary, ask the leasing company to buy the equipment, and lease it from the company.

In all of these lease transactions, the law distinguishes true leases from finance leases. The former are not secured transactions; the latter are. Chapter 19 discusses equipment leasing.

§13.5 POLICING

Financing sellers tend to engage in minimal policing. While security agreements in this kind of financing traditionally contain clauses that make it an instance of default to "remove the collateral from the jurisdiction," most financing sellers will not learn that the goods are gone until the buyer defaults. In commercial equipment financing, sellers may take more sophisticated steps to ensure that the collateral is not moved, that it is properly maintained, and that it is insured adequately. In connection with this last concern, sellers may insist that the buyer provide evidence of insurance from the company providing it, sometimes with the requirement that the insurer notify the seller in advance of any policy cancellation.

In all events, of course, removal of the goods and failure to maintain and insure them must be instances of default, which give the seller the right to proceed against the collateral under the foreclosure provisions of the agreement and Article 9.

SEARS, ROEBUCK AND CO. SEARSCHARGE SECURITY AGREEMENT

On all charges to my SearsCharge account, I agree to the following:

1. **OPTION TO PAY IN FULL EACH MONTH TO AVOID FINANCE CHARGES.** I have the right each month to pay the total balance on my account. If I do so within 30 days (28 days for February statements) of my billing date, no **Finance Charge** will be added to the account for that month. The billing date will be shown on a statement sent to me each month. The total balance on my billing date will be called the New Balance on my monthly statement.
2. **OPTION TO PAY INSTALLMENTS PLUS A FINANCE CHARGE.** If I do not pay the total balance in full each month, I agree to make at least a minimum payment within 30 days (28 days for February statements) of the billing date shown on my monthly statement.
3. **MINIMUM MONTHLY PAYMENTS.** The required minimum monthly payment is based on the highest New Balance on the Account. It will increase when charges are added to the account. It will not decrease until the entire New Balance is paid in full.

When the "Highest New Balance" Reaches:	The Minimum Monthly Payment will be:
$ .01 to $ 10.00	Balance
10.01 to 250.00	$10.00
250.01 to 300.00	11.00
300.01 to 350.00	12.00
350.01 to 410.00	13.00
410.01 to 470.00	14.00
470.01 to 540.00	15.00
Over 540.00–	1/36th of highest balance

rounded to the next higher whole dollar amount.

I can always pay more than the minimum monthly payment.

4. **FINANCE CHARGE.** If I do not pay the total Balance within 30 days (28 days for February statements) of the monthly billing date, a **Finance Charge** will be added to the account for the current monthly billing period. The ***FINANCE CHARGE*** will be either a minimum of 50¢ if the Average Daily Balance is $28.50 or less, or a periodic rate of 1.75% per month ***(ANNUAL PERCENTAGE RATE*** of 21%) on the Average Daily Balance.
5. **HOW TO DETERMINE THE AVERAGE DAILY BALANCE.** Sears will determine each day's outstanding balance in the monthly billing period and divide the total of these daily balances by the number of days in the monthly billing period. The result is the Average Daily Balance. Sears will include the current month's charges but will not include unpaid Finance or Insurance Charge(s), if any, when determining a daily balance. All payments and other credits will be subtracted from the previous day's balance.
6. **FAILURE TO MAKE MINIMUM PAYMENT.** If I do not make at least the minimum required monthly payment when due, Sears may declare my entire balance immediately due and payable.
7. **SECURITY INTEREST IN GOODS.** Sears has a security interest under the Uniform Commercial Code in all merchandise charged to the account. If I do not make payments as agreed, the security interest allows Sears to repossess only the merchandise which has not been paid in full. Upon my default, Sears may charge me reasonable attorneys' fees. I am responsible for any loss or damage to the merchandise until the price is fully paid. Any payments I make will first be used to pay any unpaid Insurance or Finance Charge(s), and then to pay for the earliest charges on the account. If more than one item is charged on the same date, my payment will apply first to the lowest priced item.
8. **CHANGE OF TERMS – CANCELLATION.** Sears has the right to change any terms or part of this agreement by sending me a written notice. Sears also has the right to cancel this agreement as it relates to future purchases. I agree to return all credit cards to Sears upon notice of such cancellation.
9. **STATE OF RESIDENCE CONTROLS TERMS.** All terms of this agreement are controlled by the laws of my state of residence.
10. **CHANGE OF RESIDENCE.** If I change my residence, I will inform Sears. Sears has the right to transfer the account to a unit servicing my new residence. If I move to another state, the account, including any unpaid balance, will be controlled by the credit terms which apply to Sears credit customers in my new state of residence. Sears will provide me with a written disclosure of any new terms, including the amount and method of calculating the **Finance Charge**.
11. **AUTHORIZED BUYERS.** This agreement controls all charges made on the account by me or any person I authorize to use the account.
12. **CREDIT INVESTIGATION AND DISCLOSURE.** Sears has the right to investigate my credit, employment and income records, to verify my credit references and to report the way I pay this account to credit bureaus and other interested parties.
13. **WAIVER OF LIEN ON DWELLING.** Sears gives up any right to retain or acquire any lien which Sears might be automatically entitled to by law on my principal dwelling. This does not apply to a lien created by a court judgment or acquired by a filing as provided by statute.
14. **ACCOUNT SUBJECT TO APPROVAL OF SEARS CREDIT SALES DEPARTMENT.** This agreement and all charges on the account are subject to the approval of Sears Credit Sales Department. The agreement will be considered approved when Sears delivers a Sears credit card or other notice of approval to me.
15. **ASSIGNMENT OF ACCOUNT–PROTECTION OF BUYER'S RIGHTS.** I understand this account may be sold or assigned by Sears to another creditor without further notice to me. If so, the notice below, which is required by Federal law, is intended to protect any claim or right I have against Sears.

NOTICE: ANY HOLDER OF THIS CONSUMER CREDIT CONTRACT IS SUBJECT TO ALL CLAIMS AND DEFENSES WHICH THE DEBTOR COULD ASSERT AGAINST THE SELLER OF THE GOODS OR SERVICES OBTAINED PURSUANT HERETO OR WITH THE PROCEEDS HEREOF. RECOVERY HEREUNDER BY THE DEBTOR SHALL NOT EXCEED AMOUNTS PAID BY THE DEBTOR HEREUNDER.

16. **ERRORS OR INQUIRIES ON MONTHLY STATEMENTS.**
NOTICE: SEE ACCOMPANYING STATEMENT FOR IMPORTANT INFORMATION REGARDING YOUR RIGHTS TO DISPUTE BILLING ERRORS.

NOTICE TO BUYER: DO NOT SIGN THIS AGREEMENT BEFORE YOU READ IT OR IF IT CONTAINS ANY BLANK SPACES. YOU ARE ENTITLED TO AN EXACT COPY OF THE PAPER YOU SIGN. YOU HAVE THE RIGHT TO PAY IN ADVANCE THE FULL AMOUNT DUE.

SEARS, ROEBUCK AND CO.

RECEIPT OF A COPY OF THIS AGREEMENT IS ACKNOWLEDGED.

SPECIMEN

(Customer's Signature) (Date)

(Please Print Name)

(Address) (City) (State) (Zip Code)

(Account Number)

14421-051 Illinois Rev. 11/88
Sears Forms Management

Document 13-2. Vehicle Retail Installment Sales Contract

ACCT. NO. ______ | **MICHIGAN VEHICLE RETAIL INSTALMENT CONTRACT** | DATE ______

Buyer (and Co-Buyer) Name and Address (Include County and Zip Code)	**CREDITOR (Seller Name and Address)**

You, the Buyer (and Co-Buyer, if any), may buy the vehicle described below for cash or on credit. The cash price is shown below as "Cash Price". The credit price is shown below as "Total Sale Price". By signing this contract, you choose to buy the vehicle on credit under the agreements on the front and back of this contract.

New or Used	Year and Make	Series	Body Style	No. Cyl.	If Truck Ton Capacity	Vehicle Identification Number	Use For Which Purchased
							☐ Personal ☐ Agricultural ☐ Commercial ☐ ______

INCLUDING: ☐ Radio ☐ Air Conditioner ☐ Automatic Transmission ☐ Power Steering ☐ ______ ☐ ______

ITEMIZATION OF AMOUNT FINANCED

(1) Cash Price .... $ ______(1)
(2) Down Payment
Cash Down Payment .... $ ______
Trade-in: ______ (Year And Make) $ ______ (Gross Allowance) $ ______ (Amount Owing) .... $ ______
Total Down Payment .... $ ______(2)
(3) Unpaid Cash Price Balance (1 minus 2) .... $ ______(3)
(4) Amounts Paid on Your Behalf
To Insurance Companies for (See A. & B. below)
Vehicle Insurance (Term ______ Months (Estimate)) .... $ ______
Credit Life Insurance (for term of contract) .... $ ______
Credit Disability Insurance (for term of contract) .... $ ______
______ (Term ______ Months (Estimate)) .... $ ______
To Public Officials (i) for license ($ ______), title ($ ______),
& registration ($ ______) fees $ ______;
(ii) for filing fees $ ______;
(iii) for taxes (not in Cash Price) $ ______ .... $ ______
To ______ for ______ .... $ ______
To ______ for ______ .... $ ______
To ______ for ______ .... $ ______
Total .... $ ______(4)
(5) Amount Financed (3 plus 4) .... $ ______(5)

Amount Financed (The amount of credit provided to you or on your behalf) .... $ ______
FINANCE CHARGE (The dollar amount the credit will cost you) .... $ ______
ANNUAL PERCENTAGE RATE (The cost of your credit as a yearly rate) .... ______ %
Total of Payments (The amount you will have paid when you have made all scheduled payments) .... $ ______
Payment Schedule — Your payment schedule will be:

☐	Number of Payments	Amount of Each Payment	When Payments are Due
	______	$ ______	monthly starting
	1 Final	$ ______	______, 19__
☐			

Total Sale Price (The total price of your purchase on credit, including your downpayment of $______) $ ______
Prepayment: You may be entitled to a refund of part of the Finance Charge if you pay off your debt early.
Late Payment: You must pay a late charge on each payment made more than 10 days late. The charge is 2 per cent of the part of the payment that is late or $50.00, whichever is less.
Security Interest: You are giving a security interest in the vehicle being purchased.
Contract: Please see this contract for additional information on security interest, nonpayment, default, the right to require repayment of your debt in full before the scheduled date and prepayment refund.

INSURANCE

A. Vehicle Insurance:

You are required to insure the vehicle. If a charge is shown below, the Creditor will try to buy the coverages checked for the term shown. Coverages will be based on the cash value of the vehicle at the time of loss but not more than the limits of the policy.

☐ Comprehensive ☐ Fire-Theft-Combined Additional Coverage ☐ Term ______ Months (Estimate)
☐ $ ______ deductible collision ☐ Towing and Labor Premium $ ______

VEHICLE INSURANCE MAY BE OBTAINED FROM A PERSON OF YOUR CHOICE

B. Credit and Other Optional Insurance:

CREDIT LIFE, CREDIT DISABILITY AND OTHER OPTIONAL INSURANCE ARE NOT REQUIRED TO OBTAIN CREDIT AND WILL NOT BE PROVIDED UNLESS YOU SIGN AND AGREE TO PAY THE PREMIUM

☐ Credit Life ______ (Insurer) ______ (Insured(s)) $ ______ (Premium) ______ (Signature(s))

☐ Credit Disability ______ (Insurer) ______ (Insured) $ ______ (Premium) ______ (Signature)

Credit Life and Credit Disability insurance are for the term of the contract. The amount and coverages are shown in a notice or agreement given to you on this date.

☐ ______ (Type of Insurance) ______ (Insurer) ______ (Term) $ ______ (Premium) ______ (Signature)

Warning: The insurance afforded hereunder does not cover liability for injury to persons or damage to property of others unless so indicated hereon.

Notice to buyer. Do not sign this contract in blank. You are entitled to 1 true copy of the contract you sign without charge. Keep it to protect your legal rights.

Buyer Signs ______ **(Co) Buyer Signs** ______

Buyer acknowledges receipt of an exact copy of this contract at the time of signing.

Buyer Signs ______ **(Co) Buyer Signs** ______

SEE BACK FOR ADDITIONAL AGREEMENTS

By signing below, the Seller accepts this contract.

Seller ______ SPECIMEN By ______ Title ______

Assignment: If no other Assignee is named in a separate assignment attached to this contract the Seller assigns it to Ford Motor Credit Company under the Assignment on the back of this contract.

Seller ______ By ______ Title ______

FC 17621 NOV 87 Previous editions may be used
FOR SELLER'S USE ONLY KEY I KEY G ORIGINAL

Printed with the permission of Ford Motor Credit Company.

Document 13-2. *(continued)*

ADDITIONAL AGREEMENTS

A. **Payments and Summary Notice**: You must make all payments when they are due. You may prepay your debt at any time. If you prepay in full, you will get a refund of part of the Finance Charge. The refund will be figured by the sum of the digits method. The Creditor may keep a minimum finance charge of $15.00. There will be no refund if it is less than $1.00. If the vehicle is repossessed, you will not have the right to reinstate this contract unless the Creditor agrees.

B. **Security Interest**: You give the Creditor a security interest in the vehicle, in all parts or other goods put on the vehicle, in all money or goods received for the vehicle and in all insurance premiums financed for you. This secures payment of all amounts you owe in this contract. It also secures your other agreements in this contract.

C. **Use of Vehicle — Warranties**: You must take care of the vehicle, and obey all laws in using it. You may not sell or rent the vehicle, and you must keep it free from the claims of others. **In this contract, there is no promise as to the merchantability, suitability or fitness for purpose of the vehicle.** You may receive a separate warranty on the vehicle.

D. **Vehicle Insurance**: You must insure yourself and the Creditor against loss or damage to the vehicle. The type and amount of insurance must be approved by the Creditor. The Creditor may buy the insurance if you do not but he does not have to do so. If the Creditor buys the insurance, he will insure both you and himself, if possible. Otherwise, he will insure only himself. In either case, you must pay back to the Creditor what he pays for the insurance plus interest at the highest rate allowed by law. If the Creditor insures only himself, you will not have insurance. **Whether or not the vehicle is insured, you must pay for it if it is lost, damaged or destroyed.**

If a charge for vehicle insurance is shown on the front, the Creditor will try to buy the coverages checked for the term shown. The Creditor is not liable though if he cannot do so. If these coverages cost more than the amount shown for insurance, the Creditor may buy them for a shorter term or he may give you credit for the amount shown. If he cannot buy any insurance, he will give you credit for the amount shown. The credit will be made to the last payments due, if allowed by law.

E. **Late Charge**: You will have to pay a late charge on each payment made more than ten days late. The charge is shown on the front. You must also pay any cost paid by the Creditor to collect any late payment, as allowed by law. Acceptance of a late payment or late charge does not excuse your default or mean that you can keep making payments after they are due. The Creditor may take the steps set forth below if there is any default.

F. **Default**: If you fail to make any payment when it is due, or if a bankruptcy petition is filed by or against you, or if you fail to keep any other agreement in this contract, the Creditor may require you to pay at once all remaining payments less a refund of part of the Finance Charge. He may repossess (take back) the vehicle too. He may also take goods found in or on the vehicle when repossessed and hold them for you.

If the vehicle is taken back, he will send you a notice. The notice will state that you may redeem (buy back) the vehicle. It will also show the amount needed to redeem. You may redeem the vehicle up to the time the Creditor sells it or agrees to sell it. If you do not redeem the vehicle, it will be sold.

The money from the sale, less allowed expenses, will be used to pay the amount still owed on this contract. Allowed expenses are those paid as a direct result of having to retake the vehicle, hold it, prepare it for sale and sell it. Lawyers' fees and legal costs permitted by law are allowed too. If there is any money left (a surplus), it will be paid to you. If the money from the sale is not enough to pay off this contract and costs, you will pay what is still owed to the Creditor.

G. **General**: Any change in this contract must be in writing and signed by you and the Creditor. The law of Michigan applies to this contract. If that law does not allow all of the agreements in this contract, the ones that are not allowed will be void. The rest of this contract will still be good.

NOTICE
ANY HOLDER OF THIS CONSUMER CREDIT CONTRACT IS SUBJECT TO ALL CLAIMS AND DEFENSES WHICH THE DEBTOR COULD ASSERT AGAINST THE SELLER OF GOODS OR SERVICES OBTAINED PURSUANT HERETO OR WITH THE PROCEEDS HEREOF. RECOVERY HEREUNDER BY THE DEBTOR SHALL NOT EXCEED AMOUNTS PAID BY THE DEBTOR HEREUNDER.

Used Motor Vehicle Buyers Guide. If you are buying a used vehicle with this contract, federal regulations may require a special Buyers Guide to be displayed on the window of the vehicle. **THE INFORMATION YOU SEE ON THE WINDOW FORM FOR THIS VEHICLE IS PART OF THIS CONTRACT. INFORMATION ON THE WINDOW FORM OVERRIDES ANY CONTRARY PROVISIONS IN THE CONTRACT OF SALE.**

GUARANTY

To cause the Seller to sell the vehicle described on the front of this contract to the Buyer, on credit, each person who signs below as a "Guarantor" guarantees the payment of this contract. This means that if the Buyer fails to pay any money that is owed on this contract, each one who signs as a guarantor will pay it when asked. Each person who signs below agrees that he will be liable for the whole amount owed even if one or more other persons also signs this Guaranty. He also agrees to be liable even if the Creditor does one or more of the following: (a) gives the Buyer more time to pay one or more payments, or (b) gives a release in full or in part to any of the other Guarantors, or (c) releases any security. Each Guarantor also states that he has received a completed copy of this contract and this Guaranty at the time of signing.

Guarantor ______________________ Address ______________________

Guarantor ______________________ Address ______________________

ASSIGNMENT

The seller (hereinafter called Seller) named on the face of the within contract (hereinafter called the Contract) sells, assigns and transfers to Ford Motor Credit Company (hereinafter called Ford Credit) Seller's entire right, title and interest in and to the Contract and the property (hereinafter called the Property) described therein and authorizes Ford Credit to do every act and thing necessary to collect and discharge obligations arising out of or incident to the Contract and this Assignment. In order to induce Ford Credit to accept assignment of the Contract, Seller warrants that: the Contract, and guaranty, if any, are genuine, legally valid and enforceable and arose from the sale of the Property; the Property is as represented to the buyer (hereinafter called Buyer) named therein who was quoted both a total sale price and a lesser cash price; the Contract was complete in all respects and Seller made all disclosures required by law, and in the manner required by law, prior to the execution thereof by Buyer; Buyer is not a minor, has capacity to contract and paid the downpayment stated in the Contract with his own funds; all statements made by or on behalf of Buyer and furnished to Ford Credit by Seller are true to the best of Seller's knowledge and belief, and Seller has no knowledge of any fact that would impair the validity or value of the Contract; title to the Property is vested in Seller free of all liens and encumbrances and Seller has the right to assign said title; and a certificate of title to the Property showing a lien or encumbrance for the benefit of Ford Credit or Seller has been or will be applied for forthwith if permitted by law. If there is any breach of any of the foregoing warranties, without regard to Seller's knowledge or lack of knowledge with respect thereto or Ford Credit's reliance thereon, Seller hereby agrees unconditionally to purchase the Contract from Ford Credit, upon demand, for the full amount then unpaid whether the Contract shall then be, or not be, in default. Seller further agrees that in the event Buyer or any other person makes a claim against Ford Credit alleging facts which, if true, would constitute a breach of any of the foregoing warranties, Seller shall assume the defense of such claim and shall indemnify and save Ford Credit harmless from all loss, cost and expense arising therefrom. In addition, this Assignment includes the provisions of the paragraph initialed below by Seller; provided, that if none of the paragraphs below has been initialed by Seller, this Assignment shall include the provisions of the paragraph below entitled "Repurchase". The liability of Seller shall not be affected by any extension, renewal or other change in the time of payment of the Contract, or any change in the manner, place or terms of payment thereof, or the release, settlement or compromise of or with any party liable for the payment thereof or the release or non-perfection of any security thereunder. Ford Credit shall not be bound to exhaust its recourse against Buyer or any other person or any security Ford Credit may at any time have before being entitled to payment from Seller hereunder. Seller waives notice of the acceptance of this Assignment and notices of non-payment and non-performance of the Contract and any other notices required by law and waives all setoffs and counterclaims. This Assignment shall become effective upon delivery of the Contract to Ford Credit or upon Ford Credit's payment of the purchase price therefor, whichever first occurs.

☐ Initial — "WITHOUT RECOURSE" This Assignment of the Contract is and shall be without recourse against Seller, except as otherwise provided by the terms of the Ford Credit Retail Plan in effect at the time this Assignment becomes effective.

☐ Initial — "REPURCHASE" Seller guarantees payment of the full amount remaining unpaid under the Contract and covenants if default be made in payment of any instalment thereunder to pay the full amount then unpaid to Ford Credit, upon demand, except as otherwise provided by the terms of the Ford Credit Retail Plan in effect at the time this Assignment becomes effective.

☐ Initial — "LIMITED REPURCHASE" Seller guarantees payment of the full amount remaining unpaid under the Contract and covenants if default be made in payment of any instalment thereunder to pay the full amount then unpaid to Ford Credit, upon demand, except as otherwise provided by the terms of the Ford Credit Retail Plan in effect at the time this Assignment becomes effective, provided, that if Buyer satisfactorily pays the number of instalments under the Contract specified in the Ford Credit Retail Plan, this Assignment shall thereafter be without recourse against Seller, except as otherwise provided by the terms of the Ford Credit Retail Plan in effect at the time this Assignment becomes effective.

☐ Initial — "PARTIAL GUARANTY" Notwithstanding the terms of the Ford Credit Retail Plan, Seller unconditionally guarantees payment of the full amount remaining unpaid under the Contract, and agrees to purchase the Contract from Ford Credit, upon demand, for the full amount then unpaid whether the Contract shall then be, or not be, in default; provided, that at the time of any such demand by Ford Credit, Seller may, at his election, pay to Ford Credit the sum of $ ____________ in consideration of being released from such guaranty obligation, and in such event, this Assignment of the Contract is without recourse against Seller, except as otherwise provided by the terms of the Ford Credit Retail Plan in effect at the time this Assignment becomes effective.

☐ Initial — "LIMITED TERM REPURCHASE" Seller guarantees payment of the full amount remaining unpaid under the Contract, and covenants if default be made in payment of any instalment thereunder to pay the full amount then unpaid to Ford Credit, upon demand, except as otherwise provided by the terms of the Ford Credit Retail Plan in effect at the time this Assignment becomes effective, provided, that if Buyer satisfactorily pays each of the first ________ instalments coming due under the Contract, this Assignment shall thereafter be without recourse against Seller, except as otherwise provided by the terms of the Ford Credit Retail Plan in effect at the time this Assignment becomes effective.

☐ Initial — "FULL GUARANTY" Notwithstanding the terms of the Ford Credit Retail Plan, Seller unconditionally guarantees payment of the full amount remaining unpaid under the Contract and agrees to purchase the Contract from Ford Credit, upon demand, for the full amount then unpaid whether the Contract shall then be, or not be, in default.

☐ Initial — "FORD DEALER RETAIL TRUCK FINANCE PLAN" Except for breach of any of the foregoing warranties this Assignment shall be governed by the "Ford Dealer Retail Truck Financing Agreement" heretofore executed by Ford Credit and Seller.

☐ Initial — "FORD FLEET TRUCK FINANCE PLAN" Except for breach of any of the foregoing warranties this Assignment shall be governed by the "Truck Fleet Sales Financing Agreement" between Ford Credit and Ford Motor Company, dated September 19, 1960, and a "Dealer Truck Financing Agreement" between Seller and Ford Motor Company.

FC 17621 NOV 87 Previous editions may be used

14

Pledges (Especially of Securities)

§14.1 INTRODUCTION

Because we know something about ancient systems of collateral and because we see them re-created in the financial markets and on the schoolyard, we can guess with some assurance of accuracy that the pledge is the oldest security device. The Code of Hammurabi, the Roman legal system, and medieval practices testify to the effectiveness of using the pledge of valuable "property" (sometimes a slave or child) to secure performance of an obligation. To twentieth-century minds, it is curious that ancient legal systems did not always accept the notion that the pledgor had the right to redeem his property. Ancient minds, it seems, did not distinguish transfers for a limited purpose from outright transfers. Fortunately, commercial law has advanced since those days. Today, debtors cannot pledge their grandmothers to secure a debt, and the right of redemption is secure.

Ancient as it may be, the pledge is still very much alive and is an important facility for certain secured transactions. In effect, the pledge serves two purposes: First, under the Uniform Commercial Code, it gives the secured party a perfected security interest, and second, it deprives the debtor of the ability to dispose of the collateral that is the subject of the pledge.

In ancient times, for example, a Celtic base client might desire to borrow a bull from a neighboring king. The king would agree to the loan for a fee, perhaps paid in advance, but was concerned that the base client might not return the bull. In order to secure the base client's promise, the parties would agree that the client's eldest son would stay with the king until the base client returned the bull. The son, in effect, was the collateral for the base client's promise, and the delivery of him to the king was a pledge. Note that in this secured transaction, the king is probably not interested in the son per se, though he might sell him as a slave in the event of the base client's default. The crucial feature of the transaction is not the value of the son to the king, the lender, but to the base client, the borrower, who would probably make heroic effort to return the bull rather than lose his first born into slavery. That feature of the pledge does not survive in most modern commercial transactions, since much collateral is fungible, but it is still inherent in the pledge transaction. Some lenders are not above taking advantage of it. Although the law would not permit parties to pledge their children today, there are pledges involving collateral more valuable to the borrower than to the lender.

§14.2 POSSESSION

Possession is an essential requirement of the pledge. Generally, Article 9, the secured transactions article in the Uniform Commercial Code, renders the pledgee's security interest perfected and does away with the requirement of a written security agreement only so long as the pledgee remains in possession. That possession may be by an agent of the secured party, but the agent must be under the control of the secured party, not the borrower, and the borrower itself cannot act as that agent.

Frequently, goods are in the possession of a bailee. Raw materials and agricultural commodities may be stored in warehouses, elevators, or storage tanks. By notifying the bailee of the secured party's interest, the parties can create a pledge under Article 9, the notice serving to make the bailee the agent of the secured party rather than that of the owner-borrower.

In the event the secured party loses possession of the goods, his security interest usually expires. Generally, the loss of possession renders him unperfected, if not unsecured. In those narrowly limited cases where surrender of possession does not destroy the security interest, Article 9 permits many third party purchasers of the collateral to take free of the lender's security interest and thereby deprives the lender of its collateral.

Because **general intangibles** and accounts are intangible by definition,

Figure 14-1. Simple Pledge

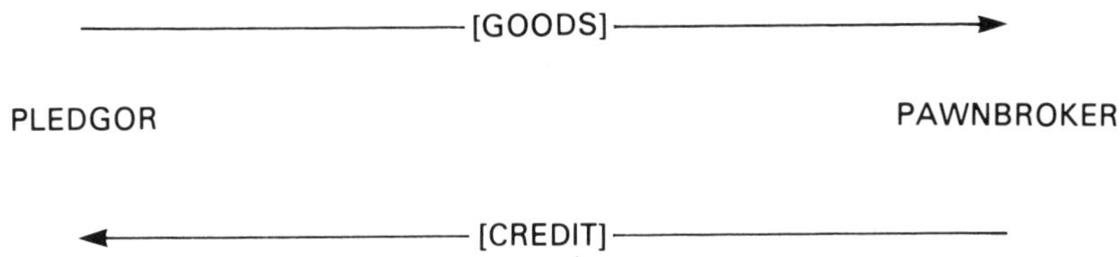

Article 9 does not permit security interests in them to be created or perfected by possession. In these two cases, there is nothing to possess.

§14.3 COMMON PLEDGE TRANSACTIONS

Pledges usually arise when the lender is unwilling to let the borrower remain in possession of the collateral. Often, these are commercially marginal situations that do not arise with much frequency. If Uncle Charlie is going to lend money to his profligate nephew and take a security interest in the nephew's gold watch, Charlie may be well advised to make his security interest possessory rather than to rely on a written security interest. Even though Article 9 generally protects the secured party's interest by stipulating that it follows the goods into the hands of purchasers, the problem of finding the collateral is often sufficient reason to insist that the secured party retain possession of it. Pawnbrokers are frequent users of the pledge. Security interests in art objects, coins, jewels, and precious metals often take the form of a pledge. Figure 14-1 is a simple pledge transaction.

In some cases, the pledge is essential. Generally, the Code does not permit security interests in money, certificated securities, or negotiable instruments except by pledge. The theory of the Code drafters was that such collateral is so readily accepted by transferring possession that it would be impossible to render a nonpossessory security interest effective. Curiously, some negotiable paper (negotiable documents of title) can be the subject of a nonpossessory security interest.

Under the Code, the beneficiary of a letter of credit can create a security interest in the credit, but the secured party will be perfected only if it takes possession of the credit instrument. Such **assignments,** as they are called, of letters of credit are not uncommon in import financing. Chapter 19 discusses the use of letters of credit to finance imports and exports.

One of the more common pledge transactions arises when an owner of valuable stock seeks to borrow for a short time. Stock certificates, because they are negotiable, are attractive collateral, and although banks and other lenders are constrained somewhat by federal regulations in the amount that they can lend against stock, the pledge of a stock certificate

Figure 14-2. Sale of Securities

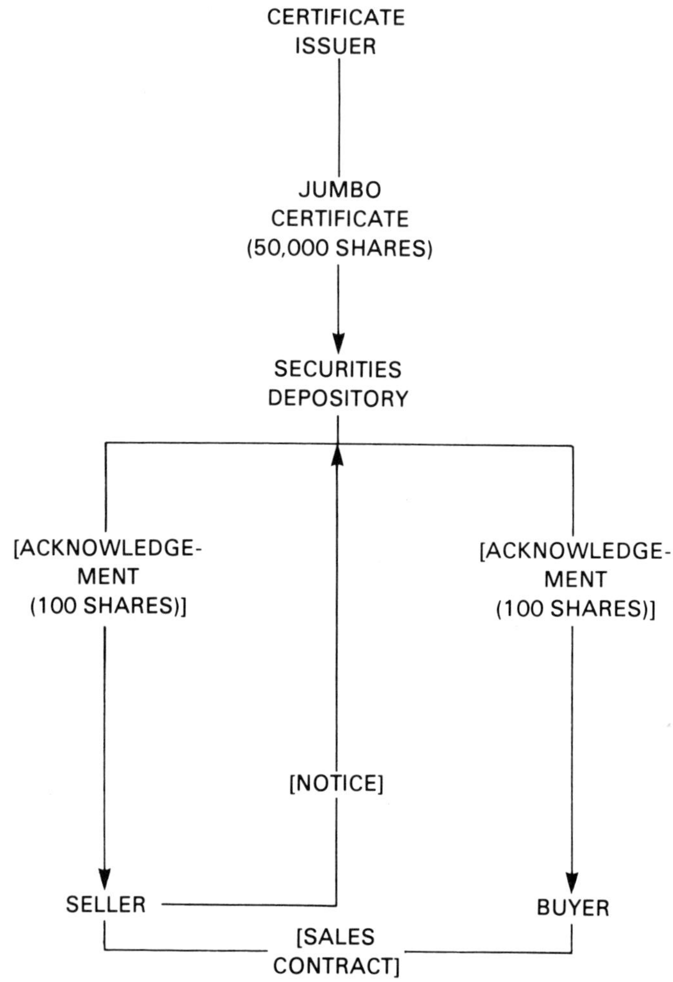

is a quick, easy way to secure a short-term personal loan or even a business loan.

In the stock pledge, the parties assume that the borrower will repay the loan and that the lender will return the certificate to the borrower. For that reason, the borrower will not indorse the stock certificate. Were she to do that, upon payment of the loan and redelivery of the certificate to her, she would hold a certificate in "bearer" form — a dangerous way to hold securities. Bearer certificates can be negotiated by a thief. Document 14-1 is a copy of a stock certificate. Note the signature line provided on the reverse side for the registered owner's indorsement.

The pledgee, however, wants the stock in a form that will permit quick sale in the event of the borrower's default. An unindorsed stock certificate will not do the job. The corporation's registered agent will not issue a new certificate to the pledgee's buyer until there is an indorsement. Buyers are unwilling to pay for an unindorsed certificate.

The parties have worked out an arrangement under which the borrower grants the pledgee a power of attorney to indorse the certificate in the event of default. In fact, the power of attorney is usually executed in blank and without date, so that anybody can sign the back of the certificate, and in the event of a sale, the bank or its buyer will forward both the unindorsed certificate and the blank stock power to the registered agent when requesting a new certificate. Document 14-2 is a stock power form.

§14.4 BUYING SECURITIES ON MARGIN

The securities industry has fashioned a system of bailments that is consistent with these rules and has avoided the nuisance and cost of transferring millions of stock certificates in that fast-paced industry. Under this system, a depository institution holds jumbo certificates covering, say, 100,000 shares of IBM common stock. A small investor that owns 100 shares of IBM common will not have possession of a certificate covering those shares, rather, his broker (ABC Co.) holds the depository institution's acknowledgment that of the 100,000-share jumbo certificate it holds, 100 shares belong to the broker, who, in turn, acknowledges that it holds the 100 shares for the investor. Figure 14-2 illustrates a sale of securities in this setting.

This system fits neatly into the pledge concept as codified in the Code. Assume, as is often the case, that the investor desires to buy the stock on margin, that is, she wants to pay only 50 percent of the purchase price in cash and to borrow the balance under her customer agreement with the broker. Given the demands and traditions of the securities industry, the broker is willing to lend the unpaid balance to its customer, but only on the condition that it have adequate security. The broker, therefore, takes a security interest in the shares. Figure 14-3 illustrates the pledge in a margin purchase transaction.

§14.5 REPLEDGES

Brokers that finance their customers' purchases of securities on margin face significant credit needs and generally turn to commercial banks to satisfy them. At the end of each business day, the broker's bank determines the amount by which the broker's checks or wire transfers exceed the broker's deposits and generates a loan to cover the deficit, if any. The bank, of course, must take security to protect itself, and the obvious collateral is the investors' stock in which the broker has taken a security interest. Under the customer agreement between the broker and its client and under the Code, such practice is proper and efficient. The rights of the broker in the

Figure 14-3. Pledge to Broker (Margin Purchase)

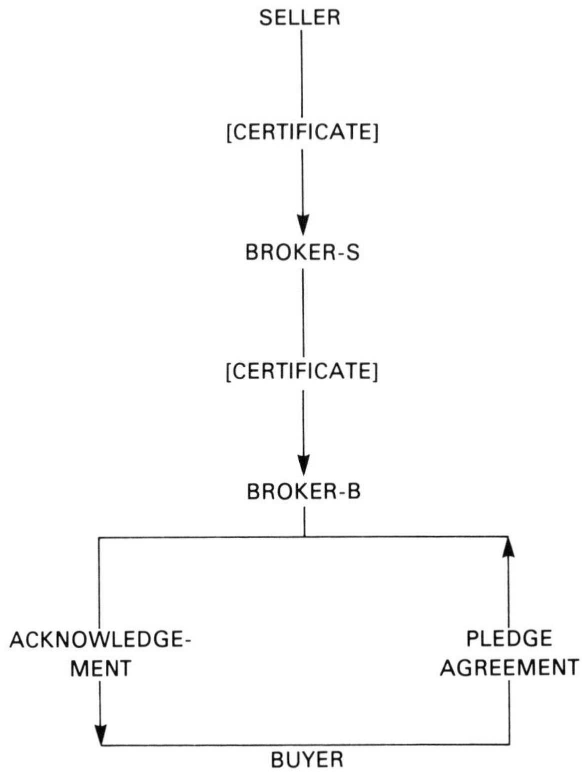

stock are limited, of course, by the amount of the customer's debt, and there may be a problem if the broker defaults on its loan with the bank and the bank takes the IBM stock to satisfy that debt. In some cases, that will be a risk investors who buy on margin take, but securities investor insurance, issued by an agency of the federal government, covers most losses. As for losses not covered by such insurance, investors may be well advised to evaluate the financial strength of their brokers. Figure 14-4 illustrates the repledge transaction.

§14.6 REPURCHASE AGREEMENTS

In the securities and banking industries it is common to borrow on securities under a **repurchase agreement.** Under this agreement, referred to in the industry as a **repo,** the owner of a security enters into a contract with a lender to "sell" the security at a given price and to "repurchase" it at another price, say, 30 days later. Its form notwithstanding, the arrangement is a secured transaction, and the difference between the two prices is the interest the "seller," i.e., the borrower, is paying the "buyer," i.e., the lender. Often, at the end of the loan period, the parties will extend the

Figure 14-4. Repledge

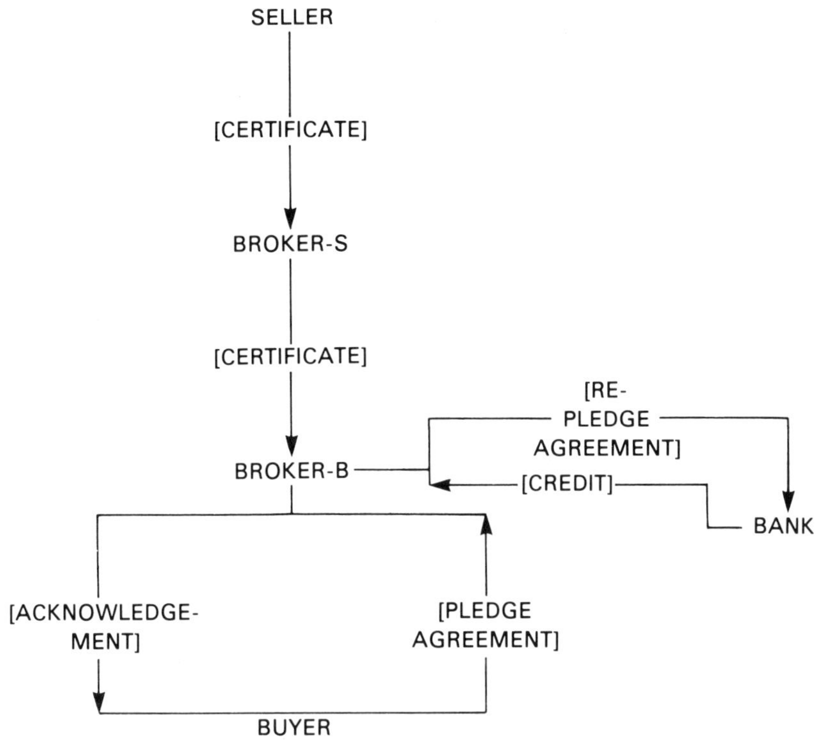

term of the loan by agreeing to roll the repo over for another 30 or 60 days.

The buyer under a repo agreement may take physical possession of the security in order to effect its security interest, but it may also use the bailment system referred to above. Under that system, the buyer will ask the seller to provide notice of the transfer under the repo agreement to the depository institution bailee. In a sophisticated transaction, the purchaser under the repo agreement may want to borrow on its interest under the agreement. This arrangement is a repledge. The transaction requires two notices to the bailee of the jumbo certificate. The repo transaction is illustrated in Figure 14-5.

§14.7 FIELD WAREHOUSING

Another traditional form of pledge by bailment is the **field warehouse.** Under this method of inventory financing, the secured party, through its field warehouse agent, holds the debtor's inventory. Although the primary purpose of the arrangement is to prevent an inventory borrower from selling collateral out from under the secured party, conceptually, the arrangement is a pledge.

Figure 14-5. Repurchase Agreement

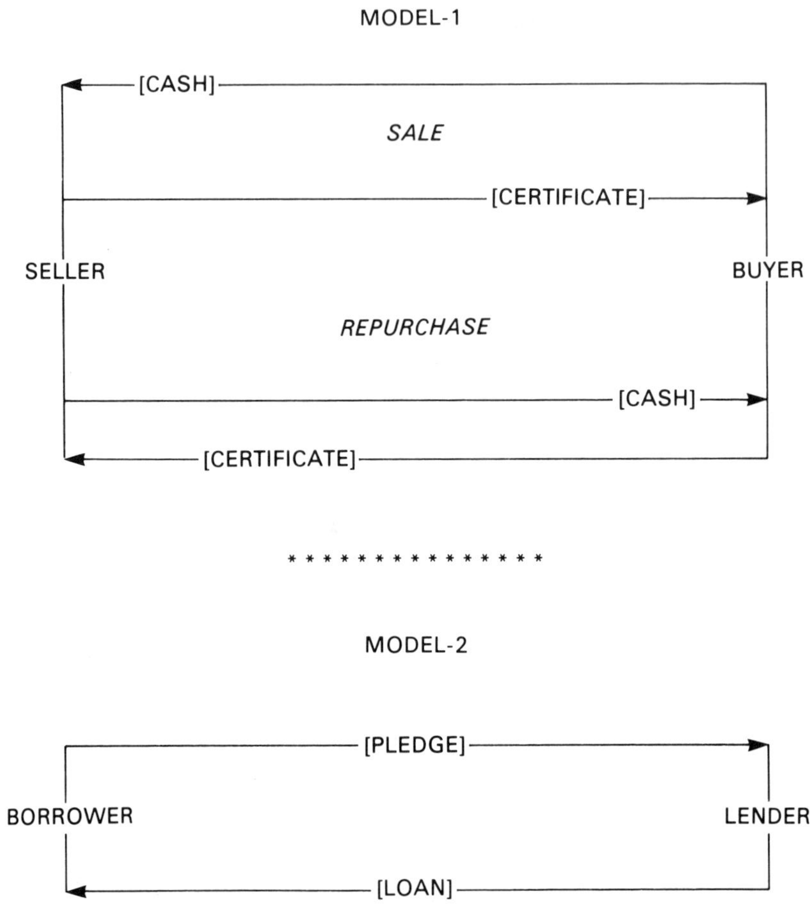

In a classic instance of field warehousing, a manufacturer of automobile parts will sell to an automobile dealer's service operation on credit taking a security interest in the parts. Under the Code, customers of the dealer who purchase parts in the ordinary course of business will take the parts free of the manufacturer's security interest. Unless the dealer is financially strong, the manufacturer faces the risk that it will not have any collateral to resort to in the event of the dealer's failure to pay the manufacturer: The dealer may have sold all the parts.

The field warehouse provides a policing mechanism that reduces the manufacturer's exposure. Under the arrangement, the dealer "leases" a portion of its premises to a field warehouse company. The field warehouse may have an office in San Francisco but no warehousing facilities other than the premises it leases in the field from dealers such as the one in question. Under the lease, the warehouse may pay only a dollar a year in rent. When the manufacturer ships parts in satisfaction of the dealer's purchase orders, it directs the shipment to the field warehouse representative, a bonded employee of the field warehouse (and probably the dealer's parts manager) with instructions that the goods not be delivered to the

Figure 14-6. Field Warehouse

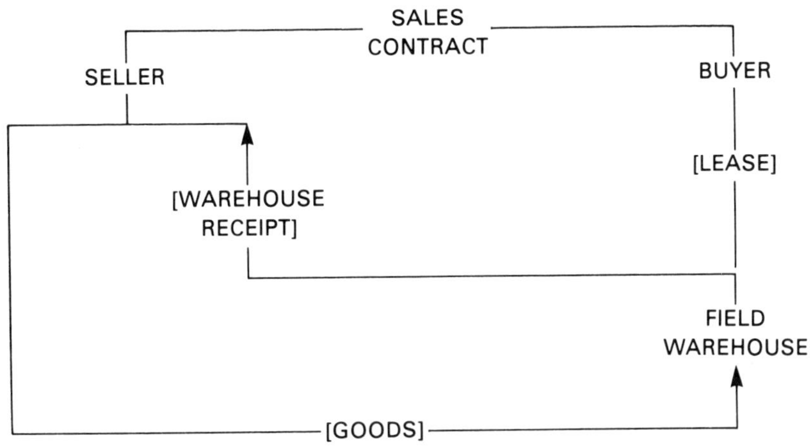

dealer without manufacturer authorization. An efficient operation uses nonnegotiable documents of title to effect that authorization, as Section 32.4 explains. Figure 14-6 illustrates the field warehouse transaction.

Field warehousing suffered a number of reverses in the 1980s. Lenders have been successful at holding the field warehouse liable when the borrower circumvents the warehouse's security and sells or otherwise removes the collateral. At least one national field warehouse has entered bankruptcy as a consequence of adverse judgments in such circumstances. Some experienced field warehousing personnel prefer to offer inventory control services that do not involve taking possession of the collateral. It may be, therefore, that field warehousing is largely a thing of the past, but commercial practices have a tendency to reappear at the very time academics pronounce them finished. The idea remains a good one. Perhaps in an era when courts and juries are less inclined to find everyone liable to everyone for everything, the field warehouse will reappear.

§14.8 SECURITY AGREEMENTS IN GENERAL

Although Article 9 does not require a written security agreement for secured transactions created by pledging collateral, the well-advised secured party will insist on a security agreement. In some cases, there may be a dispute over the nature of the lender's possession. If the nephew in the example mentioned above defaults on his repayment obligation, he may dispute the right of Charlie to sell the watch. At that point, Charlie will have to prove that he held the watch as security and not for some other reason. In addition, security agreements can spell out the rights of the parties that are not delineated in the Code and can alter the Code's allocation of rights and responsibilities. Document 12-4 in Chapter 12 is a general form security agreement that can be used to cover pledged collateral.

§14.9 NOTICE TO BAILEE

In many pledge situations, the parties will effectuate the change of possession by notice to a bailee that is holding the goods. In the field warehouse transaction, a dealer or manufacturer may have inventory stored with an independent bailee, such as a terminal warehouse. A vegetable oil refinery, for instance, may have grain stored in elevators located on the midwestern prairie or may have processed oil stored in tank farms next to rail facilities. If the operators of the elevators or the tank farms have not issued negotiable documents of title, notice to them of a lender's security interest will perfect that interest. The theory of the arrangement is that the notice serves to change the status of the bailee from agent of the vegetable oil company to agent of the lender and to transfer possession of the grain or the oil to the lender.

Similarly, a second secured party will use notice to effect a transfer of possession. If an owner of a security has pledged the security with First National Bank and if the owner wants to grant a second security interest to Second National Bank, there is no convenient way for both secured parties to hold the security. The Code permits the second secured party to notify the first secured party of the second security interest. That notice is supposed to render the first secured party a bailee for the second secured party. Figure 14-7 illustrates the transaction.

Figure 14-7. Two Pledges, One Bailee

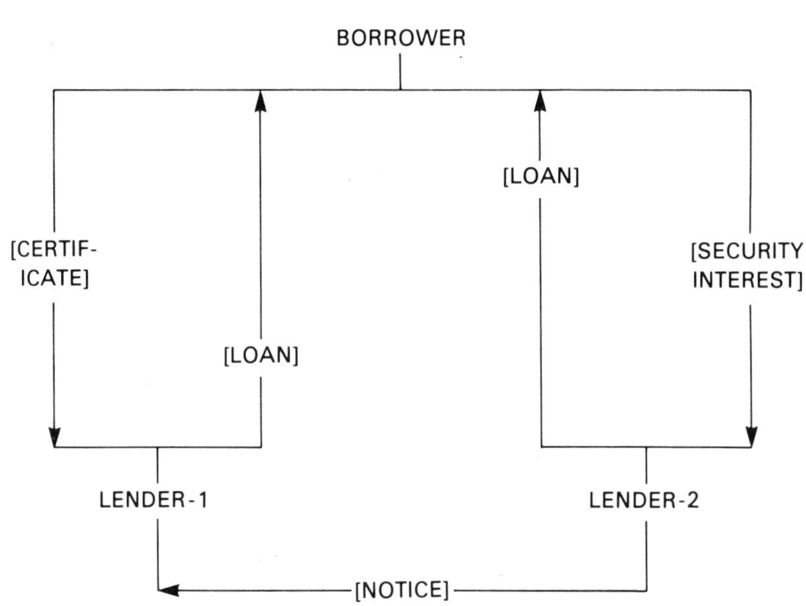

The same kind of arrangement is used in import financing with letters of credit, whereby second secured parties will use notice to the holder of the credit to effect their vicarious possession. Chapter 19 discusses import and export financing.

The law in this area is not altogether clear. Some commentators have cast doubt on the efficacy of these notices to first secured parties and question whether the first secured party cannot release the collateral to the debtor despite the notice. Out of concern that the courts might accept those arguments, some second secured parties have obtained acknowledgments from the first secured party that it holds the collateral for the second secured party.

§14.10 UNCERTIFICATED SECURITIES

Just as the securities dealers invented the concept of the jumbo certificate and the securities depository in order to do away with the transfer of paper in their industry, so corporate and government borrowers saw the advantage of recording the ownership of equity and debt securities by book entry rather than by the issuance of certificates or **bonds.** Many corporations now offer owners of common stock the option of having the stock issued to the owner or of having the ownership recorded on the books of the issuing corporation, with a notice to the owner. The federal government has created a similar system of recording the ownership of Treasury securities,

Figure 14-8. Book-Entry Security Interest

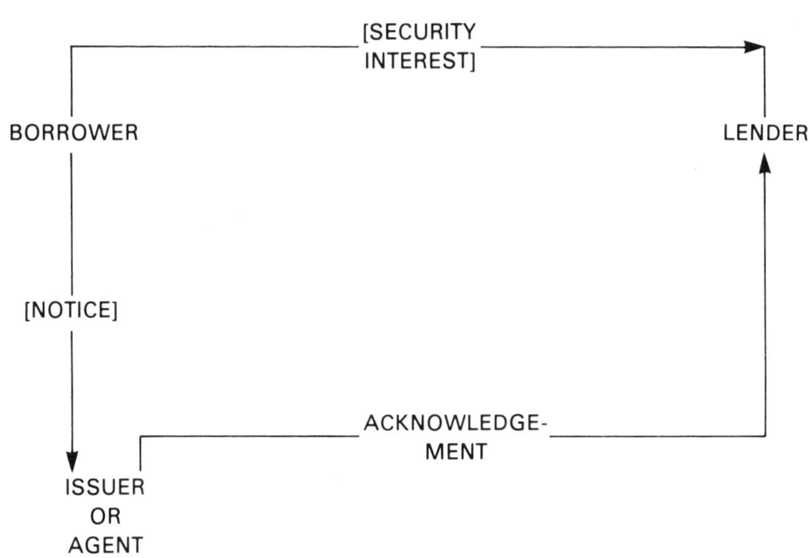

which are no longer issued in paper form. There is no method of transferring possession of such intangible interests, and the practice of notifying the issuer is the method the Code fashions for effecting a security interest in such certificateless securities. Significantly, the Code refers to this notice as an instruction to register a "pledge" of the intangible. Figure 14-8 illustrates the transaction.

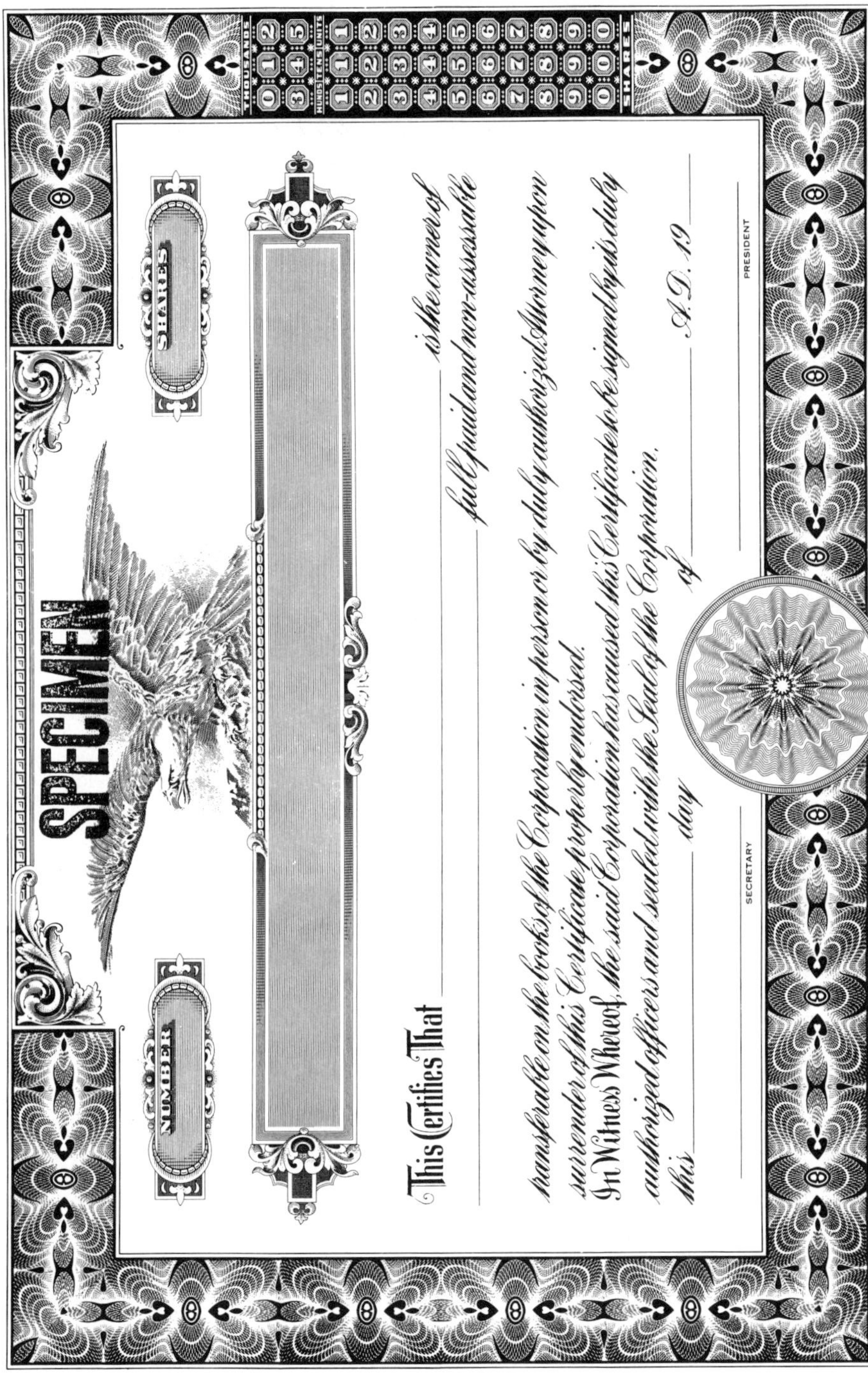
NUMBER

SHARES

SPECIMEN

This Certifies That ______ is the owner of ______ full paid and non-assessable

transferable on the books of the Corporation in person or by duly authorized Attorney upon surrender of this Certificate properly endorsed.

In Witness Whereof, the said Corporation has caused this Certificate to be signed by its duly authorized officers and sealed with the Seal of the Corporation.

this ______ day of ______ A.D. 19__

SECRETARY

PRESIDENT

© DWIGHT & M H JACKSON 205 W RANDOLPH STREET DIV OF CORPORATION SUPPLY CO CHICAGO ILLINOIS 60606

Printed with the permission of Dwight & M.H. Jackson, a Division of Corporation Supply Co.

Document 14-1. (*continued*)

For Value Received, *hereby sell, assign and transfer unto* ______________________________

______________________________ *Shares represented by the within Certificate, and do hereby irrevocably constitute and appoint*

______________________________ *Attorney to transfer the said Shares on the books of the within named Corporation with full power of substitution in the premises.*

Dated ____________________ *19* ____

In presence of

______________________________ ______________________________

NOTICE: THE SIGNATURE TO THIS ASSIGNMENT MUST CORRESPOND WITH THE NAME AS WRITTEN UPON THE FACE OF THE CERTIFICATE IN EVERY PARTICULAR, WITHOUT ALTERATION OR ENLARGEMENT, OR ANY CHANGE WHATEVER

THIS SPACE IS NOT TO BE COVERED IN ANY WAY

Document 14-2. Stock Power

ASSIGNMENT SEPARATE FROM SECURITY

DEAN WITTER REYNOLDS INC.

For Value Received, the undersigned hereby sell(s), assign(s), and transfer(s) to

____

IF STOCK, COMPLETE THIS PORTION

__________ shares of the __________ stock of ______________________

represented by Certificate No(s) ______________________

standing in the name of the undersigned on the books of said Corporation.

IF BOND, COMPLETE THIS PORTION

one bond of the ______________________

in the principal amount of $ __________, No(s) __________

standing in the name of the undersigned on the books of said Corporation.

The undersigned does (do) hereby irrevocably constitute and appoint ______________________

______________________ Attorney to transfer the said stock(s), bond, or debenture(s),

as the case may be on the books of said Corporation with full power of substitution in the premises.

OFFICE	ACCOUNT NO.	A.E.
RECEIPT NO.		

Signed ______________________

SPECIMEN

Signed ______________________

Dated ______________________

DWR-8304 (2-82)

Reprinted with the permission of Dean Witter Reynolds, Inc.

15

Financing Accounts (Including Factoring)

§15.1 INTRODUCTION

Most sales in the commercial sector of the economy, that is, nonconsumer sales, are on open account. Under that kind of sale, which Chapter 3 discusses in some detail, the commercial seller holds the obligation of an account debtor, the buyer to whom it sold on open account. For a period of from 30 to 60 or 90 days, depending on the industry and the relative bargaining strengths of the parties, the seller has sold the goods but has no cash to show for it. It has depleted its inventory, reduced the value of the collateral securing its inventory loan, but has no money to pay its suppliers, employees, and other creditors.

Yet, the seller has something of significant value. Because cautious sellers make their open account sales only after checking the credit records of their buyers and because those credit records are reliable, virtually all open account buyers pay, and most of them pay on time. There are exceptions. Some sellers are less risk averse than others, and some sell in markets that are problematic. Lenders can familiarize themselves with a seller's industry and practices and are willing to make a judgment about the predictability that a seller's accounts will become cash within a short period of time. These lenders take accounts as security and provide an enormous amount of credit in the economy.

In addition, any business that seeks **working capital loans** may confront a request from its bank for as much collateral as the bank can get. Since accounts are frequently one of the biggest assets that a borrower will own, working capital lenders will often insist that they have a security interest in that property.

Generally, account lenders fall into three categories. First are those lenders that are particularly interested in accounts. These lenders, usually finance companies, utilize considerable expertise and familiarity with an industry in the course of their lending operations and often exercise tight control over the activity of the borrower. It is not unusual, for example, for a finance company lending against accounts to keep daily records of the payments received by the borrower from the account debtors or to maintain a lock box — a device under which payments from account debtors find their way into the finance company's bank account.

The second lender, usually a commercial bank, is interested in the accounts incidentally. It takes a security interest in the accounts because it is the best security to protect the loan. A working capital lender lends to undercapitalized businesses, i.e., enterprises that cannot function without secured borrowing. The lender makes the loan because it is secured by an interest in the most valuable asset of the enterprise, the accounts. These accounts are often more valuable than all the rest of the enterprise's assets combined. They are, furthermore, self-liquidating, that is, it is not necessary to look for purchasers of them, they generate funds in the normal course. Finally, accounts are almost always short term and, therefore, match the life of the loan of the commercial lender, who is a short-term lender.

This second kind of account lender will often have nothing to do with the accounts unless the borrower defaults, while the finance company may be intimately involved in the evaluation of the account debtors' creditworthiness and in the collection of the accounts.

The third kind of account lender is the factor. In this transaction, which the law treats as a loan secured by the accounts, the parties think of the transaction as a sale of the accounts by the commercial seller to the factor. Factors are intimately involved in evaluating the credit strength of the account debtors whose obligations they purchase. Often the factor gives the commercial seller preapproved credit limits for accounts and reserves the right to reject new accounts from account debtors who have defaulted. Factors, moreover, typically purchase accounts **without recourse,** that is, the factor agrees to pay for the account even though the account debtor fails to pay the factor. The first two account lenders described above usually take the accounts **with recourse,** that is, on the understanding that if the account debtor does not pay, the commercial seller will take the account back from the lender and suffer the loss.

Figure 15-1. Account Financing

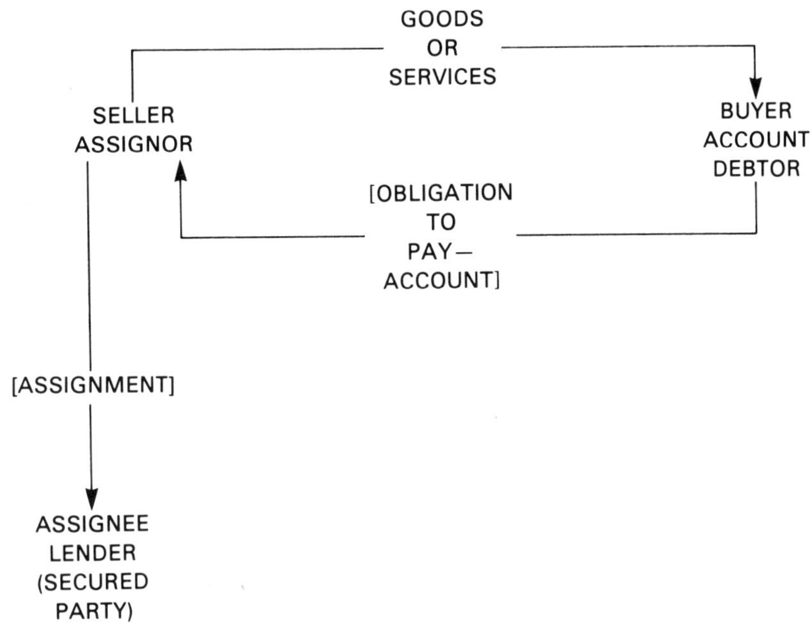

§15.2 THE TRANSACTION

Account receivable financing is essentially a three-party transaction that begins with the borrower's sale of goods or services on credit to a buyer whom we call the *account debtor*. When the seller decides to become a borrower and to use the accounts as security for its loan, it must transfer the accounts to the lender. Traditionally, secured transactions law has called that transfer an assignment and has designated the borrower as the **assignor** and the lender as the **assignee**. Figure 15-1 illustrates the transaction.

§15.3 REVOLVING ACCOUNTS

While it is possible for a seller to borrow against or sell accounts separately or in a specified bulk, many account lenders take a security interest in accounts that revolve. As a seller sells more product or services and collects sums due on outstanding accounts, it creates new accounts and extinguishes old ones. Under a revolving account loan agreement, the collateral changes daily, and the body of accounts that are due the seller at any given moment in time secure the loan debt. Document 15-1 is a security agreement used in connection with revolving account financing. In Figure 15-1, the batch of accounts changes constantly and may turn over completely in a 30- or 60-day period.

§15.4 DISCRETE ACCOUNT FINANCING

Some borrowers will borrow against a specific batch of accounts or against a single account. This kind of borrowing may occur if the seller is not ordinarily in the practice of financing its accounts. There are costs in borrowing, and many businesses conclude that they can evaluate credit and collect accounts with their internal credit and collections departments at less cost than having a factor perform those processes for them. Yet, these businesses may find themselves, from time to time, with cash-flow problems and may use their accounts to secure short-term borrowing.

§15.5 FACTORING

The factor, the third of the account lenders described in Section 15.1 above, is more prevalent in some industries than in others. In those industries, notably the garment industry, manufacturers are often small and yet are faced with the problem of selling to numerous buyers located, perhaps, all over the country. The cost of maintaining credit information on a national industry as widespread and full of recent entries as the retail clothing industry would impose a serious burden on small garment manufacturers. It is economically efficient and, therefore, not surprising that in such an industry certain account financers undertake to evaluate and collect a seller's accounts. Factors, the name these industries have given to the finance company that performs these functions, traditionally "buy" accounts from their customers, notify the account debtors (the buyers from the manufacturers), and collect the accounts by instructing the account debtors to make payment directly to the factor.

Factors, given their size and their access to credit information, are in a position to evaluate the accounts they purchase, which they usually purchase on a without recourse basis. By evaluating the credit strength of the various buyers, the factor determines the value to it of a given manufacturer's accounts and will price them accordingly. Some manufacturers may sell their accounts at a small discount; others may have to pay a larger discount.

Note that these transactions involve discrete accounts and differ somewhat from the revolving account arrangement described above. That is not to say that the factoring industry is unwilling to engage in revolving account financing. It is, but the traditional factoring arrangement involves the transfer of discrete accounts.

It is worth mentioning that in the last century and the early parts of this one, sales representatives of manufacturers that sold merchandise on behalf of the manufacturer often called themselves "factors." The term survives to some extent in commercial literature and even in some legislation, but the "old" factor and the "new" factor described here perform distinctly different commercial functions. For a number of reasons, "new" factors, though still important and profitable in some industries, are declining in number. "Old" factors have disappeared from the commercial scene.

§15.6 SALE OR SECURED TRANSACTION

Secured transactions law, as the Uniform Commercial Code delimits it, does not distinguish between accounts that the factor or other lender buys and accounts it lends against. In a fashion similar to that which the Uniform Commercial Code accords transfers of chattel paper, discussed in Chapter 17, Article 9 defines a security interest to include generally all sales of accounts. It does not matter that the parties think of the transfer as a sale, or that they intend it to be a sale, or that the transfer is with or without recourse. Article 9 applies in all these events, and the lender will have to satisfy the requirements of the article in order to create and perfect a security interest.

§15.7 POLICING

The pitfalls of account lending arise in two ways. First, the lender runs the risk that the seller has fraudulently created the accounts. Accounts are, by definition, intangible. The lender cannot see them and must rely first on the borrower's sales records and on the **warranty** that is traditionally part of the security agreement. That warranty is a representation that the accounts exist and that there are no defenses to the account debtor's obligation to pay. Cautious lenders will insist on a certified audit of the borrower's records periodically and will conduct unannounced audits of their own from time to time. Those audits consist of independent verification of the existence and the amount of outstanding accounts and are effected by asking the various accounts, by mail or telephone, to acknowledge such facts.

By virtue of the fact that secured lending law permits borrowers to finance their accounts without notifying the account debtor, there is always a risk that the debtor will make payments to the borrower-seller after the lender has acquired the accounts. Sometimes, those payments cause no problems. If the lender and the borrower agree that the borrower is to collect the accounts and remit the proceeds to the lender, payments by the account debtor to its seller will be consistent with the parties' understanding.

Sometimes, the lender chooses to collect the accounts itself. If the lender is unsure of the borrower's financial integrity, the lender is unwilling to let the borrower collect the accounts. At other times, the borrower is not equipped to collect the accounts, and the factor is selling its collection services when it acquires an interest in the accounts. In that case, the factor will not want the account debtors to pay the borrower-seller. Secured transactions law protects all parties concerned by putting the risks in these cases on the lender until it notifies the account debtor. Prior to that notice, the account debtor's payments to the borrower-seller will discharge the account debtor pro tanto. After notice to the account debtor of the assignment of the account, payments to the borrower-seller will not discharge the account debtor.

If the borrower is reluctant to let its customers know that it is financing its accounts, it may be able to negotiate an agreement under which the lender does not notify the account debtors until there is a default by the borrower. There will not be any notice to the account debtors in the event the lender does not want to collect the accounts. Working capital lenders often take a security interest in the borrower's accounts but have no interest in collecting them. In these cases of non-notice borrowing, lenders will reserve the right to notify the account debtors in the event of default by the borrower. After such notice, the account debtors must make their payments directly to the lender.

§15.8 DEALER RESERVE

It is not uncommon in the financing of any third-party obligations such as account and chattel-paper financing for the lender to insist on a reserve account, commonly referred to as a dealer's reserve account. The terms of the arrangement can be negotiated to fit the needs of the parties. Usually, the arrangement calls for the lender to collect the accounts and to reserve a portion of the collections in the separate reserve account. The amounts allocated to the account are charged against the borrower's portion of the collections. If, for example, the arrangement between the borrower and the lender calls for the lender to pay the borrower 95 percent of the face amount of each account, the **dealer reserve** provision may stipulate that 1 percent of that 95 percent will not be paid to the borrower but will be credited to the dealer reserve until the reserve account has accumulated to an agreed-upon figure. After that accumulation, the lender will remit the full 95 percent to the borrower. In the event of default on an account, the lender will debit the reserve account by an amount equal to the lender's loss and will then recommence the practice of crediting the account with 1 percent of future accounts financed until the reserve balance is restored to the specified figure.

§15.9 INVOICE STANDBY LETTER OF CREDIT

Remember that accounts are an asset of the borrower that it wants to make attractive to the lender. To the extent that the lender views the accounts as valuable, it will take them more readily. There are ways in which the dealer can enhance the attractiveness of its accounts. In earlier times, it would take a negotiable instrument from the buyer and negotiate it to the bank or finance company, which took free of claims and defenses under the holder-in-due-course doctrine. To some extent, the dealer could achieve the same effect with chattel paper and the rules that the law fashioned for chattel-paper financing. (Section 17.1 in this Part discusses these efforts to enhance the attractiveness of the dealer's customer obligations.)

In the international setting, parties have used trade acceptances and banker's acceptances to achieve much the same effect. These acceptances are negotiable instruments, and, if they are the obligations of creditworthy enterprises, they generally find a ready buyer in the money markets. Chapter 4 and Chapter 19 explain trade and banker's acceptances in this setting, and Chapter 20 discusses banker's acceptances as a medium of financing goods in general.

Accounts are not so easily marketed. First, they are not free from defenses in the underlying sales transaction. Generally, under the Uniform Commercial Code, the account debtor may assert against the assignee of an account all of the defenses it has against the assignor, unless the account debtor expressly agrees otherwise — an unusual commercial arrangement. In addition, factors or other assignees of accounts must assume that a certain number of them are due from parties that will encounter financial difficulties, with the consequences of those difficulties: late payment or bankruptcy (i.e., no payment). Dealers have some incentive, therefore, to reduce the number of or potential for defaults and thereby make their accounts more attractive.

One device that dealers have been using of late is the invoice **standby letter of credit.** Under this device, a seller will insist that all of its accounts or select accounts (those with poorer credit ratings) may not purchase on open account unless they post a standby letter of credit securing their open account obligations. Such buyers must obtain from their banks or other financial institution a standby letter of credit that is payable against the seller's draft accompanied by the invoice and the seller's certification that it has not been paid.

A pipe and pipe fittings distributor, for example, may be selling to contractors on 60-day open account terms, that is, under terms that permit the contractor to take delivery of the pipe and pay for it 60 days after the date of the invoice. The distributor will need to finance the accounts with his factor, bank, or finance company, but the financer may not like the

Figure 15-2. Invoice Standby to Distributor

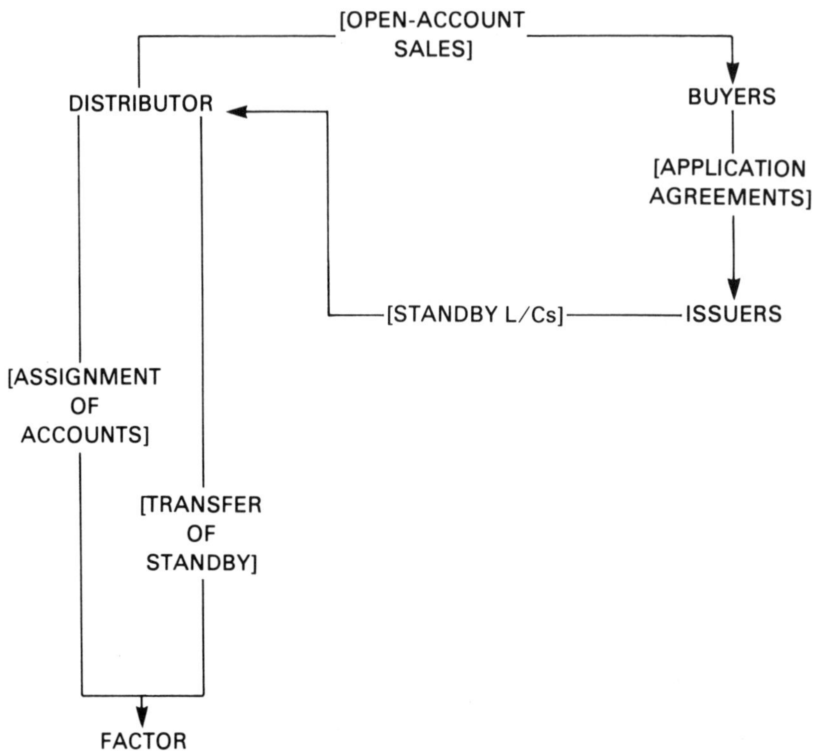

accounts. Contractors have serious cash-flow problems. If work on a project is delayed by bad weather, labor difficulties, or the like, payments tend to be late. The finance company, therefore, may subject the accounts to heavy discount.

The distributor can enhance the accounts with the standby device. First, the distributor will ask his open-account buyers to have their banks issue the standby credits. The credits may be issued directly to the distributor with the right to transfer them to the finance company or they may be issued to the finance company in the first instance. In the former case, the transaction is illustrated by Figure 15-2, in the latter by Figure 15-3. Document 3-6 in Chapter 3 is an Invoice Standby Letter of Credit used by the automobile industry.

Once the buyers cause the credits to issue, the distributor will proceed to sell them on open account, and the factor will take the accounts at an attractive discount rate. In the event of default by one of the buyers, the beneficiary of the credit (either the distributor or the finance company) will draw a draft on the issuer of the credit and present it to the issuer with the overdue invoice and the appropriate certification. Upon that presentation, the issuer will pay the draft, thereby making the account good.

Parties have fashioned a variation of the invoice standby under which

Figure 15-3. Invoice Standby to Factor

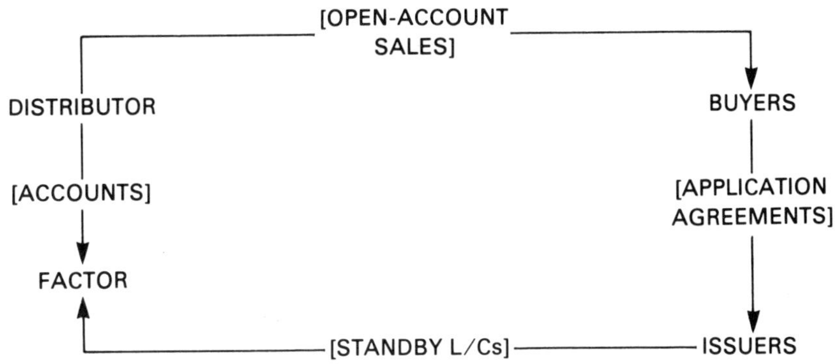

buyers themselves initiate use of the device. In the garment industry, for example, an industry with many sellers and many buyers, it is traditional for garment manufacturers to sell on open account and to factor those accounts, as Section 15.5 of this chapter explains. There are times, however, when the factor will refuse to accept certain accounts. If Ace Clothiers, Inc., is a poor credit risk in the eyes of the factors, garment manufacturers will not want to sell to Ace because the factors will not take an account arising from sales to Ace.

In these circumstances, Ace might approach its bank and ask the bank to issue a standby letter of credit in favor of the factor, payable against the factor's draft and its certificate that it holds accounts from Ace's suppliers that Ace has not paid according to the industry's open account terms.

Note that in both of these invoice-standby situations, the standby letter of credit may never be drawn on. If the account debtors (the contractors who purchase the pipe in the first example and Ace Clothiers in the second) pay their open account obligations, there will be no need for the assignee of the accounts to draw. The standby is itself a form of collateral that enhances the value of the accounts. Note also that the standby in these cases is an efficient device because it puts the bank issuer (a party that knows the creditworthiness of the account debtor and that has taken collateral or guaranties to secure its obligation under the standby) at risk in the place of the assignee, who does not know enough about the account debtor and is not in a position easily to obtain collateral or guaranties from the account debtor.

SECURITY AGREEMENT

THIS AGREEMENT, made and entered into on ______________________________ 19_____, by and between ______________________________ (FULL PROPER BANK NAME), of ______________________________, Michigan,

hereinafter called "Bank," and ______________________________, ______________________________ of ______________________________ State of ______________________________, hereinafter called "Borrower."

WITNESSETH

WHEREAS, it is contemplated that Borrower may from time to time request loans or advances from the Bank and that the Bank may, at its election, comply with any such request, in whole or in part.

NOW, THEREFORE, for and in consideration hereof, the parties hereto agree as follows:

1. **GRANT OF SECURITY INTEREST.** Borrower hereby grants to Bank a continuing security interest in the Collateral described in Paragraph No. 2 below to secure the repayment of all loans and advances (including all renewals and extensions thereof) from Bank to Borrower and all obligations of any and every kind and nature heretofore, now or hereafter owing from Borrower to Bank, however incurred or evidenced, whether primary, secondary, contingent or otherwise, whether arising under this Agreement, under any other security agreements, promissory notes, guaranties, mortgages, leases, instruments, documents, contracts or similar agreements heretofore, now or hereafter executed by Borrower and delivered to Bank, or by oral agreement or created by operation of law (hereinafter collectively called "Liabilities") plus all interest, costs, expenses and reasonable attorney fees, which may be made or incurred by Bank in the disbursement, administration and collection of said Liabilities, and in the protection, maintenance and liquidation of the Collateral. All statements of account rendered by Bank to Borrower relating to Borrower's Liabilities, including all statements of principal, interest, expenses and costs owing by Borrower to Bank, shall be presumed correct and accurate and constitute an account stated between Borrower and Bank unless within thirty (30) days after mailing thereof to Borrower, Borrower shall deliver to Bank by registered or certified mail addressed to Bank at its principal place of business, written objection thereto specifying the error or errors, if any, contained in any such statement. This Agreement shall be and become effective when, and continue in effect as long as any Liabilities of Borrower to Bank are outstanding and unpaid. Borrower will not sell, assign, transfer, pledge, alienate or otherwise dispose of or encumber any Collateral to any third party while this Agreement is in effect without the prior written consent of Bank.

It is the true, clear, and express intention of the Debtor that the continuing grant of this security interest remain as security for payment and performance of the Liabilities, whether now existing, or which may hereinafter be incurred by future advances, or otherwise, and whether, or not, such Liabilities are related to the transaction described in this Agreement, by class, or kind, or whether or not contemplated by the parties at the time of the granting of this security interest. The notice of the continuing grant of this security interest therefore shall not be required to be stated on the face of any document representing any such Liability, nor otherwise identify it as being secured hereby, and if such Liability shall remain, or become that of less than all of the Debtors herein, any Debtor not liable therefore hereby expressly hypothecates his, her, its, or their ownership interest in the Collateral to the extent required to satisfy said Liability, without restriction, or limitation. Any such Liability shall be deemed to have been made pursuant to Section 9-204(5) of the Uniform Commerical Code.

2. **COLLATERAL.** The Collateral covered by this Agreement is all the Borrower's property described below, where an "X" or check mark has been placed in the box applicable thereto, which it now owns or shall hereafter acquire or create, immediately upon the acquisition or creation thereof, and includes, but is not limited to, any items listed on any schedule or list attached hereto.

- ☐ A. **Accounts.** Accounts, Documents, Chattel Paper, Instruments, Contract Rights, General Intangibles, Choses in Action, including any right to any refund of any taxes heretofore or hereafter paid to any governmental authority (all of which are hereinafter individually and collectively referred to as "Accounts"), regardless of whether any such Accounts are acceptable or unacceptable to Bank or whether any such Accounts have been scheduled to Bank on any schedule or list attached hereto or otherwise given to Bank.
- ☐ B. **Inventory.** All Inventory and Goods, including but not limited to, raw materials, work in process, finished goods, tangible property, stock in trade, wares and merchandise used in or sold in the ordinary course of business, including Goods whose sale, lease or other disposition by Borrower has given rise to any Accounts, and which Goods have been returned to, or repossessed by or stopped in transit by Borrower.
- ☐ C. **Equipment.** All Equipment, including all machinery, furniture, furnishings and vehicles, together with all accessions, parts, attachments, accessories, tools and dies, or appurtenances thereto, or appertaining, attached, kept, used, or intended for use in connection therewith, and all substitutions, improvements and replacements thereof and additions thereto.
- ☐ D. **Fixtures.** All fixtures, whether now or to be hereafter attached, to the following described real property. See Attached Exhibit ______________
- ☐ E. **All Assets.** All assets set forth in Paragraphs 2.A. through 2.D., inclusive.
- ☐ F. **Specific.** The following specific property, together with all related rights:

For each and every type of property described in Paragraph No. 2 and which constitutes Collateral, the proceeds, and proceeds of hazard insurance and eminent domain or condemnation awards of all the foregoing described properties or interests in properties, including all products of, and accessions to, such properties or interests in properties are also part of the Collateral. In addition, any and all deposits or other sums at any time credited by or due from Bank to Borrower and any and all Instruments, Documents, Policies and Certificates of Insurance, Securities, Goods, Accounts Receivables, Choses in Action, Chattel Paper, Cash, Property and the proceeds thereof (whether or not the same are Collateral or proceeds thereof hereunder) owned by Borrower or in which Borrower has an interest, which are now or at any time hereafter in possession or control of Bank or in transit by mail or carrier to or from Bank or in possession of any third party acting on Bank's behalf, without regard to whether Bank received the same in pledge, for safekeeping, as agent for collection or transmission or otherwise, or whether Bank has conditionally released the same (excluding, nevertheless, any of the foregoing assets of the Borrower which are now or at any time hereafter in possession or control of Bank under any written trust agreement wherein Bank is trustee and Borrower is trustor) shall be Collateral.

Notwithstanding statements hereinabove to the contrary, if none of the boxes in this Paragraph No. 2 are checked, it is hereby agreed and understood that the Borrower grants the Bank a security interest in all his assets, as if the box adjacent to "E. All Assets" had been checked.

The properties and interest in properties described in this Paragraph No. 2 are sometimes hereinafter individually and collectivelly referred to as the "Collateral."

3. **PERFECTION OF SECURITY INTEREST.** Borrower shall execute and deliver to Bank, concurrently with Borrower's execution of this Agreement and at any time or times hereafter at the request of Bank (and pay the cost of filing or recording same in all public offices deemed necessary by Bank), all financing statements, continuation financing statements, assignments, certificates of title, applications for vehicle titles, affidavits, reports, notices, schedules of Accounts, designations of Inventory, letters of authority and all other documents that Bank may reasonably request, in form satisfactory to Bank, to perfect and maintain Bank's security interests in the Collateral, in order to fully consummate all of the transactions contemplated hereunder. Borrower shall make appropriate entries on its books and records disclosing Bank's security interests in the Collateral.

4. **WARRANTIES.** Borrower warrants and agrees that while any of the Liabilities remain unperformed and unpaid: (a) Borrower is the owner of the Collateral free and clear of all liens or security interests, except Bank's security interest and any other lien or security interest set forth in Paragraph No. 10, and all Chattel Paper constituting Collateral evidences a perfected security interest in the goods covered by it, free from all other liens or security interests, other than those set forth in Paragraph No. 10, and no financing statement, other than the Bank's is on file covering the Collateral or any of it, and if inventory is represented or covered by documents of title, Borrower is the owner of the documents, free of all liens and security interests other than Bank's security interest, the lien or security interest of any other creditor named in Paragraph No. 10, and warehousemen's charges, if any, are not delinquent; (b) the address of Borrower's principal office is as set forth above, while the addresses of Borrower's other places of business where Collateral is now or may in the future be located, if any, are set forth in a schedule attached hereto and made a part hereof by reference, and Borrower's business locations shall not be changed without the prior written consent of Bank, and Borrower further warrants that the Collateral, wherever located, is covered by this Agreement; (c) the Collateral will not be used, nor will Borrower permit the Collateral to be used, for any unlawful purpose, whatever; (d) Borrower will neither change its name, form of business entity, nor address of its principal office without giving written notice thereof at least ten (10) days prior to the effective date of such change, and Borrower agrees that all documents, instruments, and agreements demanded by Bank in response to such change shall be prepared, filed, and recorded at Borrower's expense prior to the effective date of such change; (e) each Account, Contract Right and Chattel Paper constituting Collateral is genuine and enforceable against the account debtor according to its terms, and it, and the transaction out of which it arose, comply with all applicable laws and regulations, and the amount represented by Borrower to Bank as owing by each account debtor is the amount actually owing and is not subject to setoff, credit, allowance or adjustment except any discount for prompt payment, nor has any account debtor returned the goods or disputed his liability; (f) no payment on any Account or Chattel Paper constituting Collateral is more than 60 days overdue, or such other number of days as set forth in Paragraph No. 10; there has been no default according to the terms of any such Collateral, and no step has been taken to foreclose the security interest it evidences or otherwise enforces its payment; (g) Borrowers shall at all times maintain the Collateral in first-class condition and repair; (h) the execution and delivery of this Agreement and any instruments evidencing Liabilities will not violate nor constitute a breach of Borrower's Articles of Incorporation, By-Laws, Partnership Agreement, or any agreement or restriction of any type whatsoever to which Borrower is a party or is subject; (i) all financial statements and information relating to Borrower delivered or to be delivered by Borrower to Bank are true and correct and prepared in accordance with generally accepted accounting principles consistently applied, and there shall be no changes made in the Borrower's accounting system without written notice to and prior approval of same by the Bank, and also there has been no material adverse change in the financial condition of Borrower since the submission of any such financial information to Bank; (j) there are no actions or proceedings which are threatened or pending against Borrower which might result in any material adverse change in Borrower's financial condition or which might materially affect any of Borrower's assets; (k) Borrower has duly filed all federal, state, and other governmental tax returns which Borrower is required by law to file, and will continue to file same during such time as any of the Liabilities hereunder remain owing to Bank, and all such taxes required to be paid have been paid in full; and (l) Borrower will indemnify and hold the Bank harmless against claims of any persons or entities not a party to this Agreement concerning disputes arising over the Collateral, including but not limited to, reasonable attorney fees, court costs, expenses, and other charges relating thereto.

10025 (2/85)

Document 15-1. (*continued*)

5. **INSURANCE, TAXES, ETC.** Borrower shall (a) pay promptly all taxes, levies, assessments, judgments, and charges of any kind upon or relating to the Collateral, to Borrower's business, and to Borrower's ownership or use of any of its assets, income, or gross receipts; (b) at its own expense, keep and maintain all of the Collateral fully insured against loss or damage by fire, theft, explosion and other risks in such amounts, with such companies, under such policies and in such form as shall be satisfactory to Bank, which policies shall expressly provide that loss thereunder shall be payable to Bank as its interest may appear (and the Bank shall have a security interest in the proceeds of such insurance and may apply any such proceeds which may be received by it toward payment of Borrower's Liabilities, whether or not due, in such order of application as Bank may determine); and (c) maintain at its own expense public liability and property damage insurance in such amounts, with such companies, under such policies and in such form as shall be satisfactory to Bank, and, upon Bank's request, shall furnish Bank with such policies and evidence of payment of premiums thereof. If Borrower at any time hereafter should fail to obtain or maintain any of the policies required above or pay any premium in whole or in part relating thereto, or shall fail to pay any such tax, assessment, levy, or charge or to discharge any such lien, claim, or encumbrance, then Bank, without waiving or releasing any obligation or default of Borrower hereunder, may at any time hereafter (but shall be under no obligation to do so) make such payment or obtain such discharge or obtain and maintain such policies of insurance and pay such premiums, and take such action with respect thereto as Bank deems advisable. All sums so disbursed by Bank, including reasonable attorney fees, court costs, expenses, and other charges relating thereto, shall be part of Borrower's Liabilities, secured hereby, and payable upon demand, together with interest thereon at the rate provided in the Liabilities, to the extent allowed by law.

6. **DEALING WITH ACCOUNTS OR INVENTORY.**

A. If Paragraph No. 2(A) or 2(E) hereof is checked, Borrower hereby assigns to Bank full title to the Accounts. The Bank is hereby entitled to and has all the ownership, title, rights, securities and guaranties of Borrower in respect thereto, and in respect to the property evidenced thereby, including the right of stoppage in transit. Bank hereby grants Borrower a revocable license to act upon and deal with such Accounts in a commercially reasonable manner until such time as Bank, in its sole and absolute discretion, terminates this license in any manner it may choose. Bank may notify any debtors of this assignment of Accounts and collect the same; thereafter all payments on Account received by Borrower shall be as agent of and for Bank and Borrower shall transmit to Bank, on the day of receipt thereof, all original checks, drafts, acceptances, notes and other evidence of payment received in payment of or on account of Accounts, including all cash monies similarly received by Borrower. Until such delivery, Borrower shall keep all such remittances separate and apart from Borrower's own funds, capable of identification as the property of Bank, and shall hold the same in trust for Bank. All items or amounts which are delivered by Borrower to the Bank on account of partial or full payment or otherwise as proceeds of any of the Collateral shall be deposited to the credit of a deposit account (hereinafter called the "Collateral Deposit Account") of Borrower with the Bank, as security for payment of the Liabilities. Borrower shall have no right to withdraw any funds deposited in the Collateral Deposit Account. The Bank may, from time to time, at its discretion, and shall upon request of Borrower made not more than once in any week, apply all or any of the then balance representing collected funds, in the Collateral Deposit Account, toward payment of the Liabilities, whether or not then due, in such order of application as the Bank may determine, and the Bank may, from time to time, in its discretion, release all or any of such balance to Borrower. Borrower, if in default in the performance of any of the provisions of this Agreement, upon demand will open all mail only in the presence of a representative of Bank, who may take therefrom any remittance on Accounts assigned to Bank. Bank or its representatives is authorized to endorse, in the name of Borrower, any item, howsoever received by the Bank, representing any payment on or other proceeds of any of the Collateral and may endorse or sign the name of Borrower to Accounts, invoices, assignments, financing statements, notices to debtors, bills of lading, storage receipts, or other instruments or documents in respect to Accounts or the property covered thereby requested by Bank. Borrower shall promptly give Bank copies and all Accounts, to be accompanied by such information and by such documents or copies thereof as Bank may require. Borrower shall maintain such records with respect to Accounts and the conduct and operation of its business as Bank may request, and shall furnish Bank all information with respect to Accounts and the conduct and operation of its business, including balance sheets, operating statements and other financial information, as Bank may request.

B. If Paragraph No. 2(B) or 2(E) hereof is checked, until such time as the Bank shall notify Borrower of the revocation of such power and authority, Borrower (a) may only in the ordinary course of its business, at its own expense, sell, lease, or furnish under contracts of service any of the inventory normally held by Borrower to such purpose, (b) may use and consume any raw materials, the use and consumption of which is necessary in order to carry on Borrower's business, and (c) shall, at its own expense, endeavor to collect, as and when due all amounts due with respect to any of the Collateral, including the taking of such action with respect to such collection as the Bank may reasonably request or, in the absence of such request, as Borrower may deem advisable. A sale in the ordinary course of business does not include a transfer in partial or total satisfaction of a debt.

7. **INFORMATION.** Borrower shall permit Bank or its agents upon reasonable request to have access to, and to inspect, all the Collateral and Bank may from time to time verify Accounts, inspect, check, make copies of, or extracts from the books, records, and files of Borrower, and Borrower shall make same available at any time for such purposes. In addition, Borrower shall promptly supply Bank with financial and such other information concerning its affairs and assets as Bank may request from time to time.

8. **DEFAULT.**

A. The occurrence of any of the following events shall constitute a Default (as such term is used herein): (a) the non-payment, when due, of any amount payable on any of the Liabilities, or any extension or renewal thereof, or the failure to perform any agreement of the Borrower contained herein; (b) any statement, representation, or warranty of the Borrower herein or in any other writing at any time furnished by the Borrower to the Bank is untrue in any respect as of the date made; (c) any Obligor (which term, as used herein, shall mean the Borrower and each other party primarily or secondarily liable on any of the Liabilities) becomes insolvent or unable to pay debts as they mature or makes an assignment for the benefit of creditors, conveys any assets to a trustee for the benefit of Obligor's creditors, conveys substantially all of its assets, or any proceeding is instituted by or against any Obligor alleging that such Obligor is insolvent or unable to pay debts as they mature or a petition of any kind is filed under the Federal Bankruptcy Act by or against such Obligor; (d) entry of any judgment against any Obligor or order of attachment, execution, sequestration, or other order in the nature of a writ is levied on the Collateral; (e) death of any Obligor who is a natural person, or of any partner of any Obligor which is a partnership; (f) dissolution, merger or consolidation or transfer of a substantial part of the property of any Obligor which is a corporation or a partnership; (g) Borrower fails to pay the full amount of any tax, fee or assessment due and owing to any federal, state or local governmental authority; or (h) the Bank feels insecure for any other reason whatsoever.

B. Whenever a Default shall exist, the Note and all other Liabilities may (notwithstanding any provisions thereof), at the option of the Bank, and without demand or notice of any kind, be declared, and thereupon immediately shall become due and payable, and the Bank may exercise from time to time any rights and remedies, including the right to immediate possession of the Collateral, available to it under applicable law. Bank shall have the right to hold any property then in or upon said Collateral at time of repossession not covered by this Security Agreement until return is demanded in writing by the Borrower. Borrower agrees, in case of Default, to assemble, at its expense, all the Collateral at a convenient place acceptable to the Bank and to pay all costs of the Bank of collection of Liabilities, and enforcement of rights hereunder, including reasonable attorney fees and legal expenses, including participation in bankruptcy proceedings, and expense of locating the Collateral and expenses of any repairs to any realty or other property to which any of the Collateral may be affixed or be a part. If any notification of intended disposition of any of the Collateral is required by law, such notification, if mailed, shall be deemed reasonably and properly given if sent at least (7) seven days before such disposition, postage prepaid, addressed to the Borrower either at the address shown on the reverse side of this Agreement, or at any other address of the Borrower appearing on the records of the Bank.

C. BORROWER AGREES THAT THE BANK SHALL, IN THE EVENT OF ANY DEFAULT, HAVE THE RIGHT TO PEACEFULLY RETAKE ANY OF THE GOODS. BORROWER WAIVES ANY RIGHT IT MAY HAVE, IN SUCH INSTANCE, TO A JUDICIAL HEARING PRIOR TO SUCH RETAKING.

9. **GENERAL.** Time shall be deemed of the very essence of this Agreement. Except as otherwise defined in this Agreement, all terms in this Agreement shall have the meanings provided by the Michigan Uniform Commercial Code. Bank shall be deemed to have exercised reasonable care in the custody and preservation of any Collateral in its possession if it takes such action for that purpose as Borrower requests in writing, but failure of Bank to comply with any such request shall not of itself be deemed a failure to exercise reasonable care, and failure of the Bank to preserve or protect any rights with respect to such Collateral against any prior parties or to do any act with respect to the preservation of such Collateral not so requested by Borrower shall not be deemed a failure to exercise reasonable care in the custody and preservation of such Collateral. Any delay on the part of Bank in exercising any power, privilege, or right hereunder, or under any other instrument executed by Borrower to Bank in connection herewith shall not operate as a waiver thereof, and no single or partial exercise thereof, or the exercise of any other power, privilege, or right shall preclude other or further exercise thereof, or the exercise of any other power, privilege, or right. The waiver by Bank of any default by Borrower shall not constitute a waiver of any other or subsequent defaults, but shall be restricted to the default so waived. If any part of this Agreement shall be contrary to any law which Bank might seek to apply or enforce, or should otherwise be defective, the other provisions of this Agreement shall not be affected thereby, but shall continue in full force and effect. All rights, remedies, and powers of Bank hereunder are irrevocable and cumulative, and not alternative or exclusive, and shall be in addition to all rights, remedies, and powers given hereunder or in or by any other instruments or by the Michigan Uniform Commercial Code, or any laws now existing or hereafter enacted.

This Agreement has been delivered in Michigan, and shall be construed in accordance with the laws of the State of Michigan. Whenever possible each provision of this Agreement shall be interpreted in such manner as to be effective and valid under applicable law, but if any provision of this Agreement shall be prohibited by or invalid under applicable law, such provision shall be ineffective to the extent of such prohibition or invalidity, without invalidating the remainder of such provisions of this Agreement. Any part of this Agreement determined to be prohibited by or invalid under applicable law shall be replaced by Bank, in its sole and absolute discretion, with a similar provision which shall not suffer such prohibition or invalidity and yet grant Bank such rights and remedies as are necessary to recover any and all monies due and owing, or to become due and owing pursuant to any of the Liabilities. The rights and privileges of the Bank hereunder shall inure to the benefit of its successors and assigns and this Agreement shall be binding on all heirs, executors, administrators, assigns, and successors of Borrower.

10. **SPECIAL PROVISIONS.** See Attached Exhibit ______

In addition to the provisions herein, this Agreement includes ______ pages of attachments labelled ______________ This Agreement and the attachments or exhibits, however designated, if any, together with the Liabilities shall constitute the complete Agreement between the parties hereto and may not be amended except in a writing executed by the party to be charged with such amendment.

IN WITNESS WHEREOF, the parties hereto execute this Agreement on the date and year first above written.

BANK

____
(FULL PROPER BANK NAME)

Address ______________________________

____

By ______________________________

Its ______________________________

BORROWER

____

By ______________________________

____

By ______________________________

Its ______________________________

By ______________________________

Its ______________________________

SPECIMEN

16

Inventory Lending (Including Automobile Dealer Financing)

§16.1 INTRODUCTION

Inventory, the stuff that the commercial seller sells in the ordinary course of its business, is an important asset but one that is illiquid. Concrete sellers may have large supplies of gravel next to barge terminals they replenish during the winter months when the road-building industry is quiet. During February, the owner of that gravel cannot pay suppliers, employees, and other creditors with gravel, though the gravel is valuable and will be a reliable source of income to the gravel company when the spring thaw permits its customers to resume their profitable activity.

Sometimes, a business enterprise will hold assets that are more valuable in the hands of another. A manufacturer's accounts, for example, may be more valuable to a factor that can collect them efficiently than to the manufacturer who cannot use the accounts to pay bills. Inventory, however, is almost always more valuable to the borrower than to its secured creditor. Farina in the hands of a pasta manufacturer is more valuable than farina in the hands of a banker; newborn hogs are more valuable in the hands of a farmer than in the hands of a finance company. Pasta companies know how to make pasta; bankers do not. Farmers can feed young hogs and bring them to market; finance company executives cannot imagine themselves engaging in such activity (in a three-piece suit?). Bankers have to hire strangers to load and unload gravel. The gravel company owner probably can run an augur or a front-end loader herself.

Thus, inventory is problematic collateral in part because it is illiquid. There is a second problem with inventory collateral: It is difficult to value. Gravel close to the site of heavy road building activity next summer is far more valuable than gravel situated far from that activity: It is expensive to haul gravel. Parts for the automotive industry will lose their value when automobile manufacturers change dimensions on original equipment or change design so that the parts no longer have any use.

For these reasons, inventory financing poses a challenge to the inventory financer. It must value the inventory carefully and evaluate the competence of the borrower to transform inventory into dollars. This is not an easy task, and one consequence of it is that borrowers do not enjoy much **leverage** when they are borrowing against inventory. The cautious lender may not loan more than 50 percent of the value an independent audit accords inventory.

The inventory financer assumes many disguises. Sellers who retain security interests in goods they sell on credit comprise a significant part of the inventory financing picture. Working capital lenders who take a security interest in all or a substantial part of a firm's assets often hold a security interest in inventory and often contribute cash for inventory acquisition. This chapter deals with these secured lenders peripherally and concentrates on the lender that makes enabling loans to an enterprise that will use the proceeds to acquire inventory. Some industries, especially the automobile industry, call these lenders "floorplanners," since they lend against inventory that is on the showroom floor. Figures 16-1 and 16-2 illustrate these inventory-loan transactions.

§16.2 INVENTORY DEFINITION

The Code defines the term *inventory* broadly. In a manufacturing operation the term encompasses raw materials, work in process, and finished goods. In a wholesale or retail operation, it includes stock in trade, supplies used by the business, and goods held for lease. Curiously, the Code does not include a farming operation's inventory in the definition, such inventory

Figure 16-1. Secured Seller

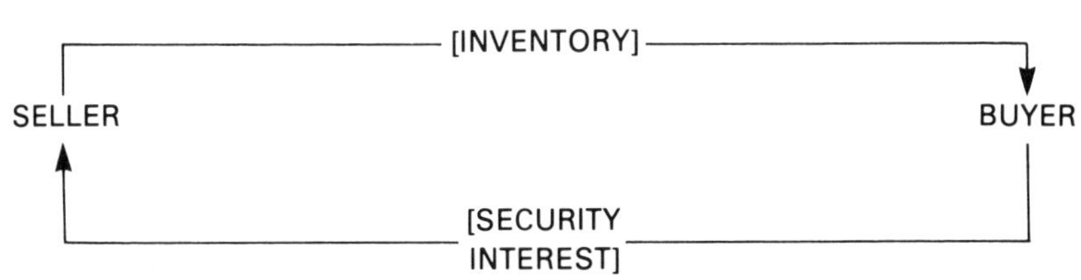

Figure 16-2. Inventory Lender

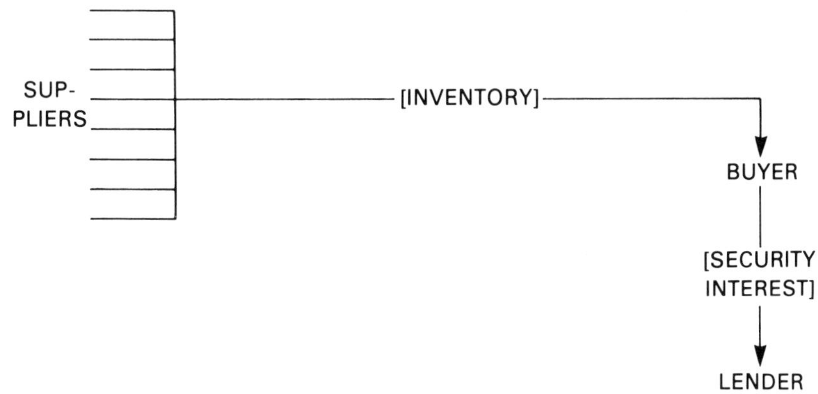

falling within a separate Code classification: **farm products**. In this chapter, we will include farm products as part of the "inventory" category.

§16.3 BORROWER SPECIFIC

In any secured transaction, the lender must learn about its borrower's business in order to evaluate the chattel paper, equipment, accounts, and general intangibles that it is taking as security for the repayment of its loan advances. Generally, however, no category of collateral challenges the loan officer as much as inventory financing does in confronting the valuation problem. Wire rods have a market value, but the ability of a steel fabricator to resell wire rods that it cannot use because of falling demand for steel fabrication can be easy and inexpensive or difficult and costly depending on location, market conditions, and other factors. Finished goods inventory is a notoriously difficult category of inventory to evaluate. A manufacturer may have obsolete product in its warehouse or may have parts from vendors that retain only salvage value.

Inventory control is another problem that loan officers must confront. Even though a lender takes large amounts of collateral as security, the health of the loan and the prospects of repayment correlate directly with the health of the borrower's business. Large inventories may reflect the health of a going concern. They may also reflect the ill-advised purchase of too much inventory or the consequences of falling sales. The value of inventory in the hands of a going concern will drop precipitously if that concern suddenly finds itself in the bankruptcy court. At distress sales, inventory of the highest quality often yields pitiful prices.

In any commercial-loan transaction, but particularly in inventory-loan transactions, loan officers must be in a position to know the borrower's industry and business practices in order to determine the quality of the collateral and the status of the loan.

§16.4 AUTOMOBILE DEALER FINANCING

Automobile manufacturers, both domestic and foreign, enjoy a measure of bargaining strength in relation to the dealers that comprise their network of buyers. The manufacturers have exploited their market and financial strength to exact from dealers a cash-sale arrangement whereby dealers must pay in cash for all goods shipped to the dealer.

Typically, the arrangement involves a local bank, though manufacturer owned finance companies may play the bank role, in which the bank issues to the manufacturer a standby letter of credit. Under the credit, which often goes by other names, such as "standby payment authorization," the manufacturer ships vehicles to the dealer and immediately forwards invoices, shipping documents, and certificates of origin to the dealer's bank. Under the standby credit, if the documents are in order, the bank must pay the invoices promptly and does so, often, before the vehicles arrive at the dealer's showroom. Document 3-6 in Chapter 3 is a standby covering such an arrangement.

The dealer's bank is willing to issue the standby only if the dealer's obligation to reimburse the bank is clear and is secured. In virtually all cases, the vehicles themselves will comprise the bank's security, and the application agreement between the bank and the dealer when it applies for the letter of credit will spell out the dealer's reimbursement obligation. Contemporaneously, the dealer will enter into a floorplan agreement, which grants a security interest in the vehicles to the bank. Document 16-1 is a floorplan agreement.

Briefly, the manufacturer sells, i.e., transfers title to, the vehicles to the dealer. Simultaneously, the dealer grants a security interest to the bank. The bank pays for the vehicles, thereby generating the loan that the security interest secures. Figure 16-3 illustrates the transaction.

§16.5 PROCEEDS

Frequently, especially in floorplanned loans, borrowers satisfy inventory loans out of the proceeds they receive upon the sale of the inventory. Floorplanning is the financing of big-ticket items of inventory. To an extent, it is usually discrete financing, that is, the lender expects the borrower to pay off that portion of the loan balance that was generated for the dealer to purchase the item of inventory. If a bank pays $12,000 to an automobile manufacturer when the manufacturer ships the vehicle to the dealer, the bank will expect the dealer to pay off that loan when the dealer sells that vehicle. That is not to suggest that floorplans are devoid of cross-collateralization provisions. In fact, floorplan agreements such as the one set out in Document 16-1 typically provide that all collateral secures all

Figure 16-3. Floorplanning with Standby

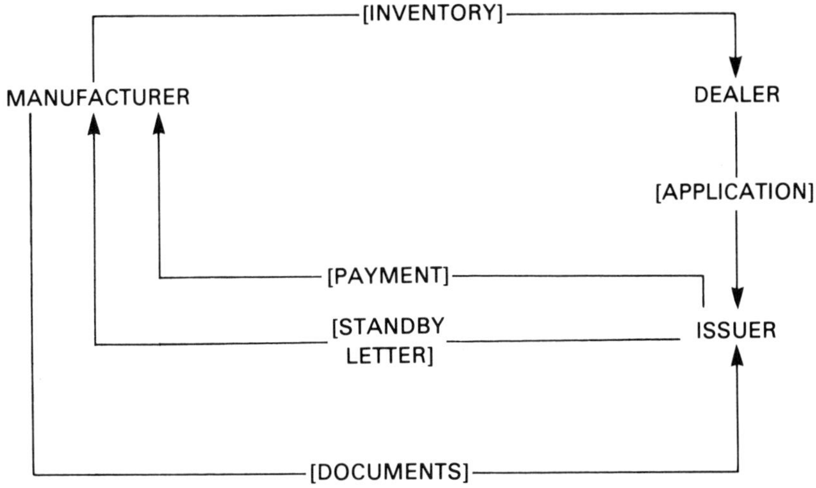

advances. Nonetheless, the bank and the dealer understand, and the floorplan agreement provides, that the dealer will pay the bank upon sale of the vehicle.

For dealers that sell for cash, those payments are not difficult, but many dealers of big-ticket items such as automobiles or large home appliances will not receive cash from their customers upon the sale of inventory. Sometimes, the dealer will sell for cash, either when the customer is a cash buyer or when the customer obtains credit from his own financial institution. Many buyers finance their motor vehicle purchases directly through their own credit union or bank and use the proceeds of the loan from financial institutions to pay the dealer cash. In those cases, the dealer will pay the bank the amount it advanced to purchase the vehicle from the manufacturer plus **finance charges** and will retain the rest.

Most of the time, however, automobile dealers do not receive much cash upon the sale of a vehicle but receive proceeds in the form of either a small cash down payment or a trade-in vehicle (or both) and a **retail installment sales contract**. In these cases, the dealer must use the retail installment sales contract (chattel paper) to generate cash to pay the bank. The dealer can generate that cash by transferring the chattel paper to a second financial institution or to the bank itself. That transfer is itself a secured transaction, since the Code makes all transfers of chattel paper secured transactions whether they are outright sales of the paper or merely the transfer of the paper for the purpose of securing an advance. Generally, Chapter 18 discusses chattel-paper financing. Figure 16-4 illustrates the transaction when the floorplanner takes the paper.

If the dealer transfers the chattel paper to a third party, say a finance company, the finance company makes an advance to the dealer who pays off the bank's loan. Figure 16-5 illustrates this transaction.

Significantly, the Code gives the floorplanner an automatic security

Figure 16-4. Chattel Paper to Floorplanner

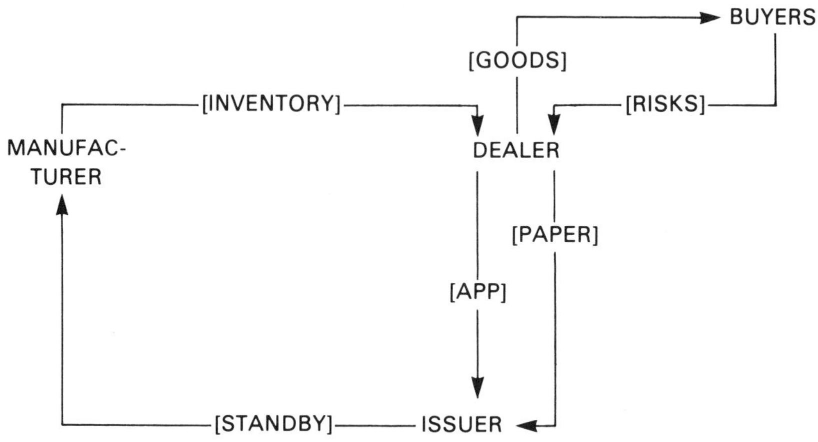

interest in the proceeds received by the dealer (and by any other borrower that grants the bank a security interest in inventory) upon the sale, exchange, or other disposition of the inventory. It is quite easy, however, for third parties to cut off the bank's security interest in those proceeds. The finance company in Figure 16-5, for example, that takes chattel paper from the dealer and makes an advance to the dealer will probably defeat the bank's interest. Floorplanners must take some precautions to prevent the dealer who faces financial exigencies from depriving them of their collateral or its proceeds — a process that is strikingly easy for the less-than-honest

Figure 16-5. Chattel Paper to Third Party

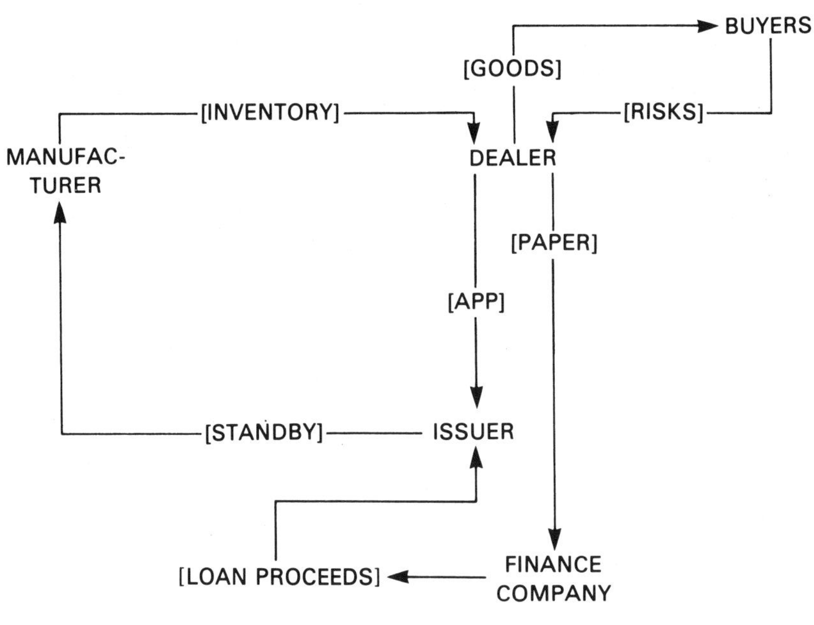

dealer. If such a dealer sells inventory to a customer for cash, he can pocket the proceeds. If he sells to a customer under a retail installment sales contract, he can discount the paper with the finance company and pocket the proceeds of the transfer. Eventually, of course, the floorplanner will catch up with this rogue, but by that time he may have sold a million dollars' worth of collateral and be sunning himself in the South Seas.

Some inventory lenders, such as those that finance manufacturing concerns and some farming operations, will confront collateral that changes. Raw materials become work in process, which becomes finished goods. Heifers in a cattle feedlot operation become mature, and dairy cows give milk and have offspring. The carefully drafted security agreement will anticipate these collateral changes and will define the collateral in such a way that the security agreement extends to original collateral as modified by accessions or manufacturing processes and to the products and natural increase of livestock.

§16.6 POLICING

Floorplanners and other inventory lenders face unique problems in policing their collateral. Under the Uniform Commercial Code, most buyers out of inventory will take the goods free of the inventory lender's security interest. The floorplanner that has a security interest in 100 motor vehicles on a dealer's lot may be surprised the day after the George Washington's Birthday sale to find that there are only 25 vehicles on the lot and no proceeds in the dealer's office. Floorplanners typically make unannounced visits to the dealer's showroom to make spot or complete checks of inventory. By comparing serial numbers and counting vehicles or home freezers, a loan officer's checkers can determine quickly whether the dealer is "out of trust," that is, whether the dealer has sold inventory without accounting to the lender for the proceeds. In the event a dealer is in default under the loan agreement or the security agreement, the floorplanner may have an officer on the dealer's premises to witness the opening of mail (in order to take the checks) and to sit in on **closings** with the dealer's customers (in order to take the down payments and the retail installment sales contracts). Floorplan security agreements traditionally spell out the floorplanner's rights to take such action.

Often, lenders do not rely solely on the floorplan agreement but also take a "trust receipt" from the dealer at the time the manufacturer delivers merchandise to the dealer. The trust receipt has the advantage of listing the items of merchandise separately and facilitates the lender's policing of the transaction. Note that it is in fact a security agreement. It takes its name from the old Uniform Trust Receipts Act, which Article 9 of the Code replaces.

In any inventory-loan transaction, the lender must review inventory values periodically to insure that the value of the inventory is sufficient to secure repayment of the loan. Most loan agreements require the borrower to submit financial statements periodically that include inventory evaluations. Loan officers must be able to determine whether those statements are reliable. In the case of audited statements, certified public accountants will explain their evaluation of the inventory. Such auditors make spot checks to determine whether inventory is obsolete, whether the market for it has fallen, and whether it is in fact there. Audits go through the stage when the auditors climb up into the warehouse and go through the dusty bins to make sure the borrower is not claiming to own inventory that it has already sold. Computer technology has aided inventory control and auditing to an extent by permitting sellers to make records of sales as they are made and to generate computer printouts that auditors can review and verify. The auditing process is not perfect, and the inventory loan officer will have to know a good deal about the borrower's business and its integrity before he can sleep without worrying that his inventory collateral is insufficient. Some secured lenders hire their own auditors. A dealer may be tempted, when cash is short, to sell one of its cars "out of trust," that is, to sell the car and not remit the proceeds to the floorplanner. When the lender's auditors arrive and start checking the serial number of every vehicle on the dealer's floor and lot, that sale out of trust will become a matter of concern to the lender. It may prompt the lender to ask the dealer for the keys to the dealership, that is, a sale out of trust may prompt the lender to **accelerate** the dealer's note and close the dealer down.

MOTOR VEHICLE FLOOR PLANNING AGREEMENT

THIS AGREEMENT, made the ______ day of ______________, 19 ____, between ____, hereinafter called Dealer, whose address is ____, and , a Michigan Banking Corporation, whose address is , Detroit, Wayne County, Michigan, hereinafter called the Bank;

WITNESSETH:

WHEREAS, Dealer is engaged in the business of buying and selling new motor vehicles and wishes the Bank to finance his purchase of motor vehicles from ____________________________________, hereinafter called Manufacturer; and

WHEREAS, the Bank is willing to lend to Dealer the wholesale cost of such new motor vehicles, up to the amount of $ ____________________ at any one time outstanding (except as such ceiling may be exceeded on a temporary basis by mutual consent of the parties hereto) upon receipt of a security interest in such motor vehicles and on the terms hereinafter set forth;

IT IS AGREED:

1. The Bank is authorized to pay invoices issued or drafts drawn by Manufacturer for the wholesale price of such motor vehicles, provided such invoices and/or drafts contain a statement describing the motor vehicles purchased by Dealer and evidencing in a form satisfactory to the Bank that title has passed to Dealer.

2. In consideration of the Bank's commitment to make each such payment to Manufacturer, Dealer will execute and deliver to the Bank a Demand Note and Grant of Security Interest in the annexed form, in the same amount and bearing the same date as such payment, granting to the Bank a security interest in the motor vehicles for which the Bank has made such payment and the chattel paper and proceeds arising from the sale or other disposition of such vehicles and the proceeds of any hazard insurance covering such motor vehicles. Such demand notes are further secured pursuant to the terms and conditions of each and every Security Agreement, Continuing Collateral Mortgage and/or other security arrangement, assignment or pledge which has been or will hereafter be executed by the Dealer in favor of the Bank. Upon default thereunder or hereunder, the Bank may exercise any one or more of the rights and remedies granted by each said Security Agreement, Continuing Collateral Mortgage and/or other security arrangement, assignment or pledge or given to a mortgagee or other secured party under applicable law.

3. Dealer hereby authorizes and empowers

and

each of them severally, to execute such notes and Grants of Security Interest in Dealer's name. The power of attorney hereby conferred on the above-named employees of the Bank may be revoked only by personal delivery of a notice in writing to the President or a Vice President of the Bank, and otherise, shall continue in full force until dissolution of Dealer. At the Bank's request, Dealer will execute in his proper name Notes and Grants of Security Interest to be substituted for those executed under this power of attorney.

4. Dealer shall have possession of the motor vehicles covered by such Grants of Security Interest for the purpose of sale at retail in the ordinary course of business. Dealer at once will report to the Bank in writing all sales of such motor vehicles and will segregate the proceeds of sale from his other assets, holding them in trust for the Bank and will discharge such trust within twenty-four hours by paying over to the Bank in cash the wholesale cost of each motor vehicle so sold, to be credited on the principal balance of the related Note and Grant of Security Interest. If Dealer defaults in the payment of any such note or fails to perform any provision of this agreement, the Bank shall be entitled forthwith to take possession of all unsold motor vehicles and all proceeds of sale and to dispose of them according to law.

5. Such notes shall bear interest at the rate set forth therein, payable on or before the fifteenth day of each month thereafter, computed from the date of payment by the Bank to the Manufacturer on the average daily balance owing on such loans during the preceding month.

6. Dealer will keep the motor vehicles covered by such Grants of Security Interest at all times insured against loss or damage by fire, theft and collision, in manner and amount and by insurers satisfactory to the Bank, with loss payable to the Bank as its interest may appear.

7. Dealer will keep carefully and in good order the motor vehicles covered by such Grants of Security Interest, without waste, and free from encumbrance other than such Grants of Security Interest and will not use them or remove them from his address above stated and will not remove them or permit them to be removed from the State of Michigan for any purpose without the written consent of the Bank.

8. Dealer will permit the Bank by its agents, at any time during business hours, to enter his premises, inspect and inventory his stock of motor vehicles and inspect and make copies of his books and records.

- 2 -

9. This agreement shall bind and inure to the benefit of the parties, their representatives, heirs, devisees, successors and assigns.

10. If Dealer is a partnership or corporation, the pronouns and relative words shall be read as if written in the neuter form.

11. Dealer will promptly execute and deliver to Bank whatever Financing Statements and other documents may in the opinion of the Bank be necessary to comply with the requirements of the Uniform Commercial Code, being Act No. 174 of the Michigan Public Acts of 1962, as amended; and the Bank shall at all times have all of the rights and remedies now or hereafter provided therein for the holder of a security interest.

12. Bank may terminate its commitment hereunder at any time, at its sole discretion, by giving notice of such termination to Dealer.

IN WITNESS WHEREOF, Dealer and the Bank have executed this Security Agreement the day and year first above written.

WITNESS: ______________________
Dealer

______________________ By ______________________
Its ______________________

By ______________________
Its ______________________

WITNESS: By ______________________
Its ______________________

______________________ By ______________________
Its ______________________

17

Chattel-Paper Financing (Including Automobile Paper Financing)

§17.1 INTRODUCTION

Secured lending is a direct function of the valuable assets of a business. Borrowers with no assets have a hard time getting any credit and, by definition, cannot get secured credit, not having any collateral to act as security. One of the challenges that faces secured lenders and borrowers is to render the borrowers' assets something that the "market" will accept. A borrower with valuable Etruscan art objects may have a more difficult time obtaining credit than someone with IBM stock of the same value. Exotic assets may have a market, but lending institutions are not familiar with them and are less willing to take them as collateral.

In short, the secured loan is a device for making an illiquid asset liquid. A firm cannot pay taxes and payroll with its accounts or equipment, but it can pay them with the loan proceeds that these assets generate in a secured-loan transaction.

In a medium-sized and small business, one of the single biggest assets of the enterprise will be the sums owed to the business by its customers. Various customary industry practices and distinctions fashioned by the Uniform Commercial Code as a consequence of those practices have distinguished those sums owed to the company into a number of classes. The broadest might be called "accounts receivable." These are the sums due from sales on open account. Chapter 15 deals with the financing of accounts.

The second category of sums due covers sums reflected in pieces of paper that are recognized in financial markets. In the past, sellers often took promissory notes from their credit buyers and "discounted" the notes with a financial intermediary (usually the local bank), which marketed them to other banks. That practice has largely fallen into disuse, except in forfaiting, a practice used in export financing.

There is, however, a kind of "paper" embodying a buyer's obligation to pay a seller that has survived in modern commercial law. That paper consist of two parts: (1) an obligation to pay the purchase price and (2) an interest in the goods that are the subject of the sale. Commercial law calls this paper *chattel paper,* the first word in the term reflecting the property interest feature of the device, the second word being an ancient commercial-law term referring to an obligation to pay money embodied in a piece of paper.

Chattel paper is readily accepted in financial markets. Banks and finance companies consider it an attractive medium of investment. Traditionally, it has paid relatively high rates of interest.

When a financial institution takes chattel paper from a dealer, there will be many debtors, so that the risk is spread nicely. This spreading of the risk coupled with the American ethic of paying one's bills and with the fact that chattel paper includes an interest in the goods sold has kept losses at an attractive level. Recently, banks and finance companies have been able to package their chattel paper as security for bonds, which they sell in the financial markets. In short, chattel paper is a rich source for secured borrowing, and the dealer that generates it usually has little trouble finding a financial institution that will take it.

There are two kinds of chattel paper that are important collateral in the economy: retail installment sales contracts and leases.

The retail installment sales contract usually arises out of the consumer purchase of a big-ticket item such as a snowblower, washing machine, or automobile. Because the consumer desires to pay for the item over a period of time, the retailer provides credit but retains a purchase-money security interest in the sold goods. For an illustration of a retail installment sales contract, see Document 2-2 in Chapter 2.

Automobile retail installment sales contracts comprise a significant portion of the chattel paper in the economy. They arise out of the dealer's sale of an item with a significant price. Most buyers under these contracts are consumers or small businesses. Document 13-2 in Chapter 13 is an example of an automobile retail installment sales contract.

The equipment leasing industry is the source of most chattel paper in lease form. Some of these leases are **lease purchase** arrangements, that is, they are disguised security agreements. Here, the parties create a lease for various business reasons, but the law regards the transaction as a sale with the "lessor" as a secured party and the "lessee" as the buyer-owner of the

Figure 17-1. Chattel-Paper Financing

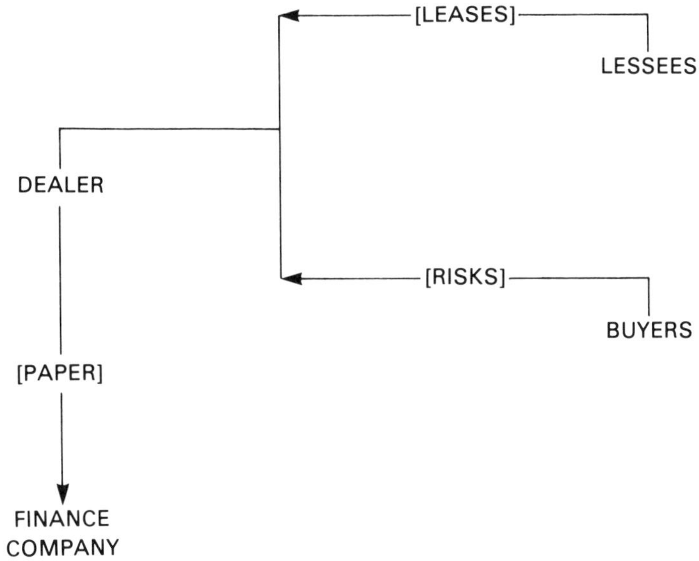

goods. Others leases are true leases, that is, the law regards the lessee as one with a leasehold interest but no more.

Whatever their nature (true lease or disguised security agreement) all leases are chattel paper for purposes of the financing that this chapter describes. Chapter 9 describes leasing. Documents 17-1 and 17-2 are illustrations of chattel paper in the form of the lease purchase of equipment (i.e., the disguised security agreement) and the true equipment lease respectively.

Taken together, leases and retail installment sales contracts comprise an enormous amount of consumer and commercial borrowing that requires a significant allocation of credit. Figure 17-1 illustrates chattel-paper financing in which an automobile dealer is marketing its product under true, short-term leases and under retail installment sales contracts, and Document 17-3 is an example of an agreement between a bank and a dealer for the dealer's sale to the bank of its chattel paper.

§17.2 RELATIONSHIP TO INVENTORY

The sale or lease of inventory is the event that gives rise to chattel paper. Selling inventory is the business of the borrower, a dealer, or other retailer. When the dealer sells inventory, it receives proceeds. In some industries, notably the automotive and appliance industries, retailers do not sell for cash. They sell on credit under arrangements whereby the buyers give the dealer paper. That paper, usually retail installment sales contracts or leases is the most common type of chattel paper that is the subject of this chapter.

In the hands of the retailer, the sale of inventory acts as a process of substituting inventory assets (e.g., automobiles) into paper assets (chattel paper), and the inventory lender may confront the paper lender in a contest over the collateral, which the inventory lender claims as proceeds from the sale of its collateral and the paper lender claims as security for a loan it made against the paper. The Code has a definite set of rules for determining the priorities between the two lenders.

The relationship between inventory lenders and paper lenders has another important dimension. An enterprise engaged in retail sales usually turns its inventory over in a short period. Traditionally, chattel paper runs for terms longer than the period it takes the retailer to exhaust a supply of inventory. The dollar amount of chattel paper that a retailer generates is usually considerably more than the dollar amount of the retailer's inventory. Lenders that are interested in increasing their loans will be more inclined to engage in chattel-paper lending than in inventory lending. The relatively high rate of interest on chattel paper and the remarkably low rate of default by the widely dispersed obligors on such paper enhance that inclination. Often, the lure of chattel-paper profits drives lenders to finance the retailer's inventory, sometimes at quite competitive inventory lending rates, and the bank that makes a retailer an inventory secured loan often insists that the retailer offer its chattel paper to the bank. At other times, the retailer may be able to shop for a chattel-paper financer accepting the best bid of competing lenders.

In short, chattel paper in the form of retail installment contracts and leases comprises a significant source of collateral for retailers and equipment manufacturers. So attractive is such collateral that many lenders will finance a retailer's inventory in order to have the chattel paper that the retailer generates. In fact, at times lenders will pay a premium to dealers for their chattel paper. They will pay more than the face amount of the contracts they acquire from the retailer.

§17.3 THE COLLATERAL

It is a peculiarity of secured transactions law that chattel paper is collateral (1) when the dealer, as we call the retailer, borrows against it and (2) when the dealer sells it outright to a bank or finance company. The law cannot distinguish these transactions easily and treats them both as secured transactions, the intent of the parties and the form of the transaction notwithstanding. Sometimes, dealers transfer their paper to banks or finance companies without recourse. In those cases, if the account debtor, the obligor on the paper, i.e., the buyer or lessee, defaults, the finance company takes the loss and has no recourse against the dealer. In other cases, the transfer is "with recourse." In those cases, the dealer must repurchase from the finance company those contracts or leases on which the account debtor defaults.

Under the Code, it does not matter whether the chattel paper transferee takes the paper with or without recourse. In both cases, the transfer is a secured transaction subject to the rules of Article 9. Chattel paper in the hands of the transferee is always collateral.

It is not the only collateral. In the original chattel paper transaction, that between the dealer and its customer, if the transaction is a sale, the customer grants a security interest to the dealer. That security interest is explicit in the retail installment sales contract. It is implicit in the lease sale transaction where the lease is a disguised security agreement. The security interest created by those security agreements is in the equipment or other goods that are the subject of the lease or the installment sale.

In brief, chattel-paper financing involves two kinds of collateral. One is paper collateral — the chattel paper, a valuable obligation of the account debtor to make the payments he has promised to make. The history of chattel-paper financing evidences the value of that obligation, which traditionally bears relatively high rates of interest and experiences low default rates. The second kind of collateral is durable — the automobile or refrigerator or industrial equipment that is the subject of the sale or lease. This collateral is also valuable, though often less so than the account debtor's obligation to pay the full purchase price. In the event of default, however, the value of the account debtor's obligation becomes questionable, and the holder of the chattel paper will resort to a used automobile or a used metal stamping machine that may retain sufficient value to satisfy part or all of the balance due on the finance company's investment in the paper. Figure 17-2 illustrates the various collateral involved in the chattel-paper transaction.

§17.4 POLICING

It does not take the imagination of a great swindler or a dealer with pressing cash needs to conclude that he can obtain that cash with a little creativity. Normally, a dealer takes paper to its lender periodically, perhaps in the morning of each business day and asks the lender to credit the dealer's account in the face amount of the paper delivered or in the face amount, less a discount or plus a premium, as the general relationship between the parties requires. Although the dealer's assignment form on the chattel paper and the agreement governing the dealer-lender relationship usually includes an express warranty by the dealer that the chattel paper is genuine, such warranties do not always deter business people that are facing financial ruin.

Hope springs eternal in the human breast and never more so than in

Figure 17-2. The Collateral in Dealer-Paper Financing

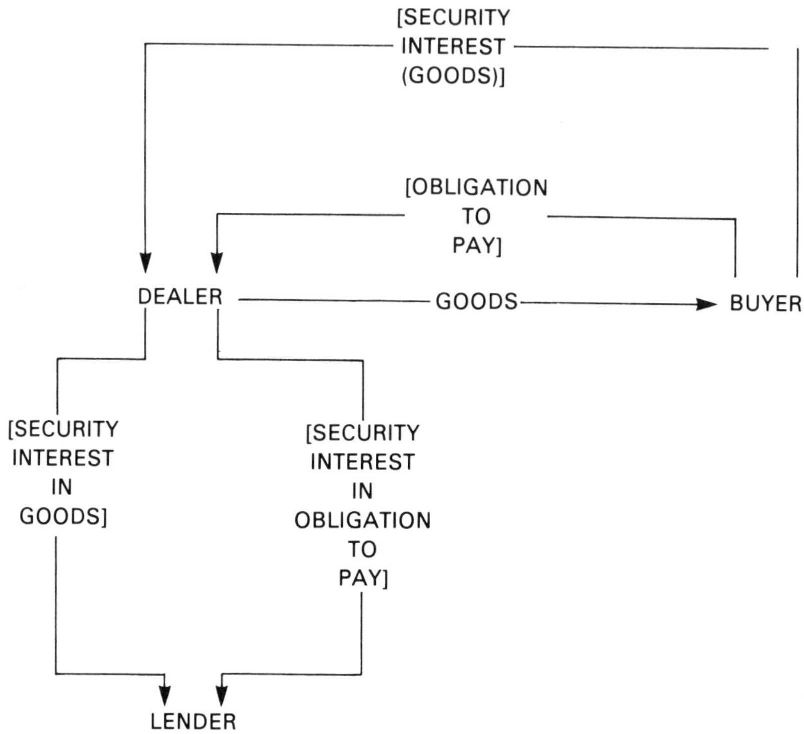

the breast of the dealer who thinks that he can turn the corner next week and repay the money he is planning to steal this week.

Lenders must be aware of the danger in chattel-paper financing that the dealer is in a position to create chattel paper when there are no sales or leases to back the paper. The cautious lender will make periodic checks of account debtors, especially in non-notice situations, where the dealer collects from the account debtor and remits to the lender. Even in notice financing situations, where the lender undertakes to notify the account debtors that their obligations have been assigned and to make payments directly to the lender, there is the possibility that the dealer can practice fraud for a brief period of time. Ultimately, the fraud will unravel, but the time it takes to do so may be sufficient to cost the lender considerably.

These fraud risks prompt lenders who take chattel paper from thinly capitalized operations or dealers that have a poor credit history to take additional collateral or personal guaranties and to maintain considerable dealer reserve accounts.

§17.5 DEFENSES

Remember that the reason the dealer takes chattel paper from its customers is to enhance the attractiveness of the obligation in the financial market.

The dealer could sell on open account, but the fact is that banks and finance companies are much less inclined to buy an automobile dealer's accounts when they consist of significant consumer obligations that are not secured by the property the consumer purchased. When the obligation is secured by the snowblower or automobile, however, financial institutions are more interested and will pay the dealer more money for the obligation.

Long ago, dealers learned that if they could abstract the buyer's obligation from the sales transaction, financial institutions were even more interested in the paper. To abstract an obligation is to render it independent of the transaction out of which it arises. The promissory note that was a common device for financing receivables up until 75 years ago was a negotiable instrument. Under the law, most purchasers of that paper, i.e., the banks that bought it from the dealer, were holders in due course who held the paper free from claims and defenses arising out of the sales transaction.

To a significant extent, the law created similar treatment for holders of chattel paper. In fact, the earliest kind of chattel paper, which has now largely disappeared, was a promissory note and a security agreement together. When the dealers put the two documents into a single document (the retail installment sales contract), the paper lost its negotiability, but the legislatures fashioned an abstraction rule that put the holder of the chattel paper in much the same position that the holder in due course had occupied. The holder of the paper took free of the defenses.

Unfortunately, this legal abstraction concept, which, one might argue, made credit more readily available to the consumer, was often the subject of abuse. Chattel-paper history bears witness to fraudulent practices. Fly-by-night retailers, many of them door-to-door, high-pressure sales organizations took retail installment sales contracts or negotiable instruments from consumers in return for overpriced or shoddy merchandise. In a manner that took full advantage of the commercial doctrines of good-faith purchase and holder in due course, these retailers then discounted their paper with finance companies or bank installment loan departments. The effect of the two commercial doctrines was to render the holder of the paper free of any defenses that the consumer had under the contract with the unconscionable retailer. All too often, the aluminum siding started to fall off, the vacuum sweeper failed after two months of use, or the consumer suddenly realized that he had entered into subscriptions to purchase $100 per month worth of magazines or dancing lessons for life. At that point, the holder of the paper was able to say that the consumer's only remedy was against the retailer, who by then was in the next county if not the next state.

By virtue of a combination of judge-made doctrines, state consumer-protection rules, and Federal Trade Commission regulations, the law has eliminated most of those unethical and socially harmful practices by preventing assignees of consumer paper from cutting off the consumer's defenses. Today, when a consumer buys shoddy merchandise from a dealer, he can assert his right of recoupment in the transaction with the dealer against the finance company that buys the paper from the dealer. There is still room in commercial law for some purchasers of paper to raise the argument that they take free of defenses. Outside the consumer setting, a rule abstracting the paper from the underlying transaction makes sense, and much financing of industrial equipment purchases benefits from these rules that raised so many problems in the consumer context.

Ford Motor Credit Company

EQUIPMENT LEASE-PURCHASE AGREEMENT

Lease No. ____________________

Lessee: (Name and Address)

Lessor: Ford Motor Credit Company
The American Road
P.O. Box 1729, Rm. 2729
Dearborn, MI 48121

Lessor agrees to lease to Lessee and Lessee agrees to lease from Lessor, the Equipment described in any Schedule A now or hereafter attached hereto ("Equipment") in accordance with the following terms and conditions of this Lease-Purchase Agreement ("Lease").

1. TERM. This Lease will become effective upon the execution hereof by Lessor. The term of this Lease will commence on the date the Equipment is accepted pursuant to Section 3 hereunder and, unless earlier terminated as expressly provided for in this Lease, will continue until the expiration date set forth in Schedule A attached hereto ("Lease Term").

2. RENT. Lessee agrees to pay to Lessor or its assignee the Lease Payments, including the interest portion, equal to the amounts specified in Schedule A. The Lease Payments will be payable without notice or demand at the office of the Lessor (or such other place as Lessor or its assignee may from time to time designate in writing), and will commence on the first Lease Payment Date as set forth in Schedule A and thereafter on the subsequent dates set forth in Schedule A. Any payments received later than ten (10) days from the due date will bear interest at the highest lawful rate from the due date. Except as specifically provided in Section 5 hereof, the Lease Payments will be absolute and unconditional in all events and will not be subject to any set-off, defense, counterclaim, or recoupment for any reason whatsoever including, without limitation, any failure of the Equipment to be delivered or installed, any defects, malfunctions, breakdowns or infirmities in the Equipment or any accident, condemnation or unforeseen circumstances. Lessee reasonably believes that funds can be obtained sufficient to make all Lease Payments during the Lease Term and hereby covenants that it will do all things lawfully within its power to obtain, maintain and properly request and pursue funds from which the Lease Payments may be made, including making provisions for such payments to the extent necessary in each budget submitted for the purpose of obtaining funding, using its bona fide best efforts to have such portion of the budget approved and exhausting all available administrative reviews and appeals in the event such portion of the budget is not approved. It is Lessee's intent to make Lease Payments for the full Lease Term if funds are legally available therefor and in that regard Lessee represents that the use of the Equipment is essential to its proper, efficient and economic operation. Lessor and Lessee understand and intend that the obligation of Lessee to pay Lease Payments hereunder shall constitute a current expense of Lessee and shall not in any way be construed to be a debt of Lessee in contravention of any applicable constitutional or statutory limitation or requirement concerning the creation of indebtedness by Lessee, nor shall anything contained herein constitute a pledge of the general tax revenues, funds or monies of Lessee.

3. DELIVERY AND ACCEPTANCE. Lessee, or if Lessee so requests, Lessor, will cause the Equipment to be delivered to Lessee at the location specified in Schedule A ("Equipment Location"). Lessee will pay all transportation and other costs, if any, incurred in connection with the delivery and installation of the Equipment. Lessee will accept the Equipment as soon as it has been delivered and is operational. Lessee will evidence its acceptance of the Equipment by executing and delivering to Lessor a Delivery and Acceptance Certificate in the form provided by Lessor.

4. DISCLAIMER OF WARRANTIES. Lessee acknowledges and agrees that the Equipment is of a size, design and capacity selected by Lessee, that Lessor is neither a manufacturer nor a vendor of such equipment, and that LESSOR HAS NOT MADE, AND DOES NOT HEREBY MAKE, ANY REPRESENTATION, WARRANTY, OR COVENANT, EXPRESS OR IMPLIED, WITH RESPECT TO THE MERCHANTABILITY, CONDITION, QUALITY, DURABILITY, DESIGN, OPERATION, FITNESS FOR USE, OR SUITABILITY OF THE EQUIPMENT IN ANY RESPECT WHATSOEVER OR IN CONNECTION WITH OR FOR THE PURPOSES AND USES OF LESSEE, OR ANY OTHER REPRESENTATION, WARRANTY, OR COVENANT OF ANY KIND OR CHARACTER, EXPRESS OR IMPLIED, WITH RESPECT THERETO, AND LESSOR SHALL NOT BE OBLIGATED OR LIABLE FOR ACTUAL, INCIDENTAL, CONSEQUENTIAL, OR OTHER DAMAGES OF OR TO LESSEE OR ANY OTHER PERSON OR ENTITY ARISING OUT OF OR IN CONNECTION WITH THE USE OR PERFORMANCE OF THE EQUIPMENT AND THE MAINTENANCE THEREOF. Lessor hereby assigns to Lessee during the Lease Term, so long as no Event of Default has occurred hereunder and is continuing, all manufacturer's warranties, if any, expressed or implied with respect to the Equipment, and Lessor authorizes Lessee to obtain the customary services furnished in connection with such warranties at Lessee's expense. Lessee's sole remedy for the breach of any such manufacturer's warranty shall be against the manufacturer of the Equipment, and not against Lessor, nor shall such matter have any effect whatsoever on the rights and obligations of Lessor with respect to this Lease, including the right to receive full and timely payments hereunder. Lessee expressly acknowledges that Lessor makes, and has made, no representations or warranties whatsoever as to the existence or the availability of such warranties of the manufacturer of the Equipment.

5. NON-APPROPRIATION OF FUNDS; NON-SUBSTITUTION. Notwithstanding anything contained in this Lease to the contrary, in the event no funds or insufficient funds are appropriated and budgeted or are otherwise unavailable by any means whatsoever in any fiscal period for Lease Payments due under this Lease, Lessee will immediately notify the Lessor or its assignee of such occurrence and this Lease shall terminate on the last day of the fiscal period for which appropriations were received without penalty or expense to Lessee of any kind whatsoever, except as to the portions of Lease Payments herein agreed upon for which funds shall have been appropriated and budgeted or are otherwise available. In the event of such termination, Lessee agrees to peaceably surrender possession of the Equipment to Lessor or its assignee on the date of such termination, packed for shipment in accordance with manufacturer specifications and freight prepaid and insured to any location in the continental United States designated by Lessor. Lessor will have all legal and equitable rights and remedies to take possession of the Equipment. Notwithstanding the foregoing, Lessee agrees (i) that it will not cancel this Lease under the provisions of this Section if any funds are appropriated to it, or by it, for the acquisition, retention or operation of the Equipment or other equipment performing functions similar to the Equipment for the fiscal period in which such termination occurs or the next succeeding fiscal period thereafter, and (ii) that it will not during the Lease Term give priority in the application of funds to any other functionally similar equipment. This paragraph will not be construed so as to permit Lessee to terminate this Lease in order to acquire or lease any other equipment or to allocate funds directly or indirectly to perform essentially the same application for which the Equipment is intended.

6. CERTIFICATION AND AUTHORIZATION. Lessee represents, covenants and warrants that it is a state, or a political subdivision thereof, or that Lessee's obligation under this Lease constitutes an obligation issued on behalf of a state or political subdivision thereof, such that any interest derived under this Lease will qualify for exemption from Federal income taxes under Section 103 of the Internal Revenue Code. Lessee further warrants that this Lease represents a valid deferred payment obligation for the amount herein set forth of a Lessee having legal capacity to enter into the same and is not in contravention of any Town/City, District, County, or State statute, rule, regulation, or other governmental provision. In the event that a question arises as to Lessee's qualification as a political subdivision, Lessee agrees to execute a power of attorney authorizing Lessor to make application to the Internal Revenue Service for a letter ruling with respect to the issue. Lessee agrees that (i) it will do or cause to be done all things necessary to preserve and keep the Lease in full force and effect, (ii) it has complied with all bidding

CI 57915 Jun 85

requirements where necessary and by due notification presented this Lease for approval and adoption as a valid obligation on its part, and (iii) it has sufficient appropriations or other funds available to pay all amounts due hereunder for the current fiscal period.

7. TITLE TO EQUIPMENT; SECURITY INTEREST. Upon acceptance of the Equipment by Lessee hereunder, title to the Equipment will vest in Lessee subject to Lessor's rights under this Lease, provided, however, that (i) in the event of termination of this Lease by Lessee pursuant to Section 5 hereof; (ii) upon the occurrence of an Event of Default hereunder, and as long as such Event of Default is continuing; or (iii) in the event that the purchase option has not been exercised prior to the Expiration Date, title will immediately vest in Lessor or its assignee without any action by Lessee and Lessee shall immediately surrender possession of the Equipment to Lessor. In order to secure all of its obligations hereunder, Lessee hereby (i) grants to Lessor a first and prior security interest in any and all right, title and interest of Lessee in the Equipment and in all additions, attachments, accessions, and substitutions thereto, and on any proceeds therefrom, (ii) agrees that this Lease may be filed as a financing statement evidencing such security interest, and (iii) agrees to execute and deliver all financing statements, certificates of title and other instruments in form satisfactory to Lessor necessary or appropriate to evidence such security interest.

8. USE; REPAIRS. Lessee will use the Equipment in a careful manner for the use contemplated by the manufacturer for the Equipment and shall comply with all laws, ordinances, insurance policies and regulations relating to, and will pay all costs, claims, damages, fees and charges arising out of its possession, use or maintenance. Lessee, at its expense will keep the Equipment in good working order and repair and furnish all parts, mechanisms and devices required therefor.

9. ALTERATIONS. Lessee will not make any alterations, additions or improvements to the Equipment without Lessor's prior written consent unless such alterations, additions or improvements may be readily removed without damage to the Equipment.

10. LOCATION; INSPECTION. The Equipment will not be removed from, or if the Equipment consists of rolling stock, its permanent base will not be changed from the Equipment Location without Lessor's prior written consent which will not be unreasonably withheld. Lessor will be entitled to enter upon the Equipment Location or elsewhere during reasonable business hours to inspect the Equipment or observe its use and operation.

11. LIENS AND TAXES. Lessee shall keep the Equipment free and clear of all levies, liens and encumbrances except those created under this Lease. Lessee shall pay, when due, all charges and taxes (local, state and federal) which may now or hereafter be imposed upon the ownership, leasing, rental, sale, purchase, possession or use of the Equipment, excluding however, all taxes on or measured by Lessor's income. If Lessee fails to pay said charges, and taxes when due, Lessor shall have the right, but shall not be obligated, to pay said charges and taxes. If Lessor pays any charges or taxes, Lessee shall reimburse Lessor therefor.

12. RISK OF LOSS; DAMAGE; DESTRUCTION. Lessee assumes all risk of loss of or damage to the Equipment from any cause whatsoever, and no such loss of or damage to the Equipment nor defect therein nor unfitness or obsolescence thereof shall relieve Lessee of the obligation to make Lease Payments or to perform any other obligation under this Lease. In the event of damage to any item of Equipment, Lessee will immediately place the same in good repair with the proceeds of any insurance recovery applied to the cost of such repair. If Lessor determines that any item of Equipment is lost, stolen, destroyed or damaged beyond repair, Lessee, at the option of Lessor, will either (a) replace the same with like equipment in good repair, or (b) on the next Lease Payment date, pay Lessor: (i) all amounts then owed by Lessee to Lessor under this Lease, including the Lease Payment due on such date, and (ii) an amount equal to the applicable Concluding Payment set forth in Schedule A. In the event that Lessee is obligated to make such payment with respect to less than all of the Equipment, Lessor will provide Lessee with the pro rata amount of the Lease Payment and the Concluding Payment to be made by Lessee with respect to the Equipment which has suffered the event of loss.

13. PERSONAL PROPERTY. The Equipment is and will remain personal property and will not be deemed to be affixed or attached to real estate or any building thereon. If requested by Lessor, Lessee will, at Lessee's expense, furnish a waiver of any interest in the Equipment from any party having an interest in any such real estate or building.

14. INSURANCE. Lessee, will, at its expense, maintain at all times during the Lease Term, fire and extended coverage, public liability and property damage insurance with respect to the Equipment in such amounts, covering such risks, and with such insurers as shall be satisfactory to Lessor, or, with Lessor's prior written consent may self-insure against any or all such risks. In no event will the insurance limits be less than the amount of the then applicable Concluding Payment with respect to such Equipment. Each insurance policy will name Lessee as an insured and Lessor or its assigns as an additional insured, and will contain a clause requiring the insurer to give Lessor at least thirty (30) days prior written notice of any alteration in the terms of such policy or the cancellation thereof. The proceeds of any such policies will be payable to Lessee and Lessor or its assigns as their interests may appear. Upon acceptance of the Equipment and upon each insurance renewal date, Lessee will deliver to Lessor a certificate evidencing such insurance. In the event that Lessee has been permitted to self-insure, Lessee will furnish Lessor with a letter or certificate to such effect. In the event of any loss, damage, injury or accident involving the Equipment, Lessee will promptly provide Lessor with written notice thereof and make available to Lessor all information and documentation relating thereto.

15. INDEMNIFICATION. Lessee shall indemnify Lessor against, and hold Lessor harmless from, any and all claims, actions, proceedings, expenses, damages or liabilities, including attorney's fees and court costs, arising in connection with the Equipment, including, but not limited to, its selection, purchase, delivery, possession, use, operation, rejection, or return and the recovery of claims under insurance policies thereon. The indemnification arising under this paragraph shall continue in full force and effect notwithstanding the full payment of all obligations under this Lease or the termination of the Lease Term for any reason.

16. ASSIGNMENT. Without Lessor's prior written consent, Lessee will not either (i) assign, transfer, pledge, hypothecate, grant any security interest in or otherwise dispose of this Lease or the Equipment or any interest in this Lease or the Equipment or (ii) sublet or lend the Equipment or permit it to be used by anyone other than Lessee or Lessee's employees. Lessor may assign its rights, title and interest in and to this Lease, the Equipment and any documents executed with respect to this Lease and/or grant or assign a security interest in this Lease and the Equipment, in whole or in part and Lessee's rights will be subordinated thereto. Any such assignees shall have all of the rights of Lessor under this Lease. Subject to the foregoing, this Lease inures to the benefit of and is binding upon the heirs, executors, administrators, successors and assigns of the parties hereto. Lessee covenants and agrees not to assert against the assignee any claims or defenses by way of abatement setoff, counterclaim, recoupment or the like which Lessee may have against Lessor. Upon assignment of Lessor's interests herein, Lessor will cause written notice of such assignment to be sent to Lessee which will be sufficient if it discloses the name of the assignee and address to which further payments hereunder should be made. No further action will be required by Lessor or by Lessee to evidence the assignment, but Lessee will acknowledge such assignments in writing if so requested.

17. EVENT OF DEFAULT. The term "Event of Default," as used herein, means the occurrence of any one or more of the following events: (i) Lessee fails to make any Lease Payment (or any other payment) as it becomes due in accordance with the terms of the Lease, and any such failure continues for ten (10) days after the due date thereof; (ii) Lessee fails to perform or observe any other covenant, condition, or agreement to be performed or observed by it hereunder and such failure is not cured within twenty (20) days after written notice thereof by Lessor; (iii) the discovery by Lessor that any statement, representation, or warranty made by Lessee in this Lease or in writing ever delivered by Lessee pursuant hereto or in connection herewith is false, misleading, or erroneous in any material respect; (iv) proceedings under any bankruptcy, insolvency, reorganization or similar legislation shall be instituted against or by Lessee, or a receiver or similar officer shall be appointed for Lessee or any of its property, and such proceedings or appointments shall not be vacated, or fully stayed, within twenty (20) days after the institution or occurrence thereof; or (v) an attachment, levy or execution is threatened or levied upon or against the Equipment.

18. REMEDIES. Upon the occurrence of an Event of Default, and as long as such Event of Default is continuing, Lessor may, at its option, exercise any one or more of the following remedies: (i) by written notice to Lessee, declare an amount equal to all amounts then due under the Lease, and all remaining Lease Payments due during the Fiscal Year in effect when the default occurs to be immediately due and payable, whereupon the same shall become immediately due and payable; (ii) by written notice to the Lessee, request Lessee to (and Lessee agrees that it will), at Lessee's expense, promptly return the Equipment to Lessor in the manner set forth in Section 5 hereof, or Lessor, at its option, may enter upon the premises where the Equipment is located and take immediate possession of and remove the same; (iii) sell or lease the Equipment or sublease it for the account of Lessee, holding Lessee liable for all Lease Payments and other payments due to the effective date of such selling, leasing or subleasing and for the difference between the purchase price, rental and other amounts paid by the purchaser, lessee or sublessee pursuant to such sale, lease or sublease and the amounts payable by Lessee hereunder; and (iv) exercise any other right, remedy or privilege which may be available to it under applicable laws of the state of the Equipment Location or any other applicable law or proceed by appropriate court action to enforce the terms of the Lease or to recover damages for the breach of this Lease or to rescind this Lease as to any or all of the Equipment. In addition, Lessee will remain liable for all covenants and indemnities under this Lease and for all legal fees and other costs and expenses, including court costs, incurred by Lessor with respect to the enforcement of any of the remedies listed above or any other remedy available to Lessor.

19. PURCHASE OPTION. Upon thirty (30) days prior written notice from Lessee to Lessor, and provided that there is no Event of Default, or an event which with notice to lapse of time, or both, could become an Event of Default, then existing, Lessee will have the right to purchase the Equipment on the Lease Payment dates set forth in Schedule A by paying to Lessor, on such date, the Lease Payment then due together with the Concluding Payment amount set forth opposite such date. Upon satisfaction by Lessee of such purchase conditions, Lessor will transfer any and all of its right, title and interest in the Equipment to Lessee as is, without warranty, express or implied, except that the Equipment is free and clear of any liens created by Lessor.

20. NOTICES. All notices to be given under this Lease shall be made in writing and mailed by certified mail, return receipt requested, to the other party at its address set forth herein or at such address as the party may provide in writing from time to time. Any such notice shall be deemed to have been received five days subsequent to mailing.

21. SECTION HEADINGS. All section headings contained herein are for the convenience of reference only and are not intended to define or limit the scope of any provision of this Lease.

22. GOVERNING LAW. This Lease shall be construed in accordance with, and governed by the laws of, the state of the Equipment Location.

23. DELIVERY OF RELATED DOCUMENTS. Lessee will execute or provide, as requested by Lessor, such other documents and information as are reasonably necessary with respect to the transaction contemplated by this Lease.

24. ENTIRE AGREEMENT; WAIVER. This Lease, together with the Delivery and Acceptance Certificate and other attachments hereto, and other documents or instruments executed by Lessee and Lessor in connection herewith, constitute the entire agreement between the parties with respect to the lease of the Equipment, and this Lease shall not be modified, amended, altered, or changed except with the written consent of Lessee and Lessor. Any provision of this Lease found to be prohibited by law shall be ineffective to the extent of such prohibition without invalidating the remainder of the Lease. The waiver by Lessor of any breach by Lessee of any term, covenant or condition hereof shall not operate as a waiver of any subsequent breach thereof.

IN WITNESS WHEREOF, the parties have executed this Agreement as of the ______ day of ______________ 19_____

LESSEE:

By: ______________________________

Title: ______________________________

SPECIMEN

LESSOR: FORD MOTOR CREDIT COMPANY

By: ______________________________

Title: ______________________________

OPINION OF COUNSEL

With respect to that certain Equipment Lease-Purchase Agreement (Lease) dated ______________________ by and between Ford Motor Credit Company and the Lessee, I am of the opinion that: (i) the Lessee is a tax exempt entity under Section 103 of the Internal Revenue Code; (ii) the execution, delivery and performance by the Lessee of the Lease have been duly authorized by all necessary action on the part of the Lessee; (iii) the Lease constitutes a legal, valid and binding obligation of the Lessee enforceable in accordance with its terms and all statements contained in the Lease and all related instruments are true; (iv) Lessee has sufficient monies available to make all payments required to be paid under the Lease during the current fiscal year of the Lease, and such monies have been properly budgeted and appropriated for this purpose in accordance with State law; and (v) the Uniform Commercial Code of the state where the Equipment is located and/or the certificate of title laws of such state will govern the method of perfecting Lessor's security interest in the Equipment.

____
Attorney for Lessee

Ford
Credit

Ford

LEASE AGREEMENT
(Net Lease)

FC 17939 OCT 88

Printed with the permission of Ford Motor Credit Company.

LEASE AGREEMENT
(Net Lease)

SPECIMEN

____________________________ of ____________________________
(Lessee's Name) (Street Address)

____ ("Lessee"),
(City, State & Zip)

a ____________________________________ organized under the laws of the State of
(Entity)

__________________, hereby leases from Ford Motor Credit Company, a Delaware corporation ("Lessor"), and Lessor hereby leases to Lessee, vehicles (hereinafter called "Leased Vehicles") designated and described from time to time in one or more Supplements ("Supplement(s)") hereto for use in lease service upon the following terms and conditions:

1. USAGE. All Leased Vehicles shall be leased by Lessee for use in Lessee's business in accordance with all applicable governmental and insurer requirements and limitations. All Leased Vehicles shall be inspected, prepared and equipped by Lessee in a manner approved by Lessor. No Leased Vehicle shall be removed from the United States.

2. TERM. The term of lease as to each Leased Vehicle shall be as designated in the applicable Supplement. The lease of a Leased Vehicle shall expire on the later of (a) the date specified in the Supplement therefor, or (b) the date on which such Leased Vehicle is returned to Lessor in an acceptable condition in accordance with Paragraph 10 hereof.

3. LEASE CHARGE. (a) The monthly lease charge for each Leased Vehicle shall be based on the lease rate for such Leased Vehicle set forth in the Supplement applicable to such Lease Vehicle. Lessee shall pay the monthly lease charge to Lessor for each Leased Vehicle in the amounts and on the dates set forth in the Supplement(s) to this Lease Agreement. In the event any monthly or other lease charges hereunder are not paid promptly when due, Lessee shall pay to Lessor, as an additional lease charge, interest on such overdue payment from the due date of such payment at a rate equal to the lesser of (i) 15% per annum or (ii) the maximum rate permitted by applicable law.

   (b) Lessor understands that Lessee may receive from manufacturers and vendors of the Leased Vehicles volume discounts, fleet rebates and dealer holdbacks ("Dealer Incentives") with respect to the Leased Vehicles, and Lessor has agreed that Lessee may retain any and all Dealer Incentives Lessee may receive as a result of leasing such Leased Vehicles with no duty to account to Lessor for such Dealer Incentives, except as may otherwise be agreed by the parties under a separate agreement.

   (c) At the commencement of the term of lease for a Leased Vehicle, the Lessee shall pay to Lessor in respect of such Leased Vehicle a refundable security deposit ("Security Deposit") equal to one monthly lease charge (rounded upwards, if necessary, to the nearest $25.00). Such Security Deposit shall be held by Lessor as security for Lessee's obligations hereunder and may be set-off against such obligations to the extent Lessee fails to perform such obligations. Any remaining amount of a Security Deposit for a Leased Vehicle shall be refunded or credited to Lessee, without interest, upon the termination or expiration of the lease of such Leased Vehicle, provided Lessee's obligations hereunder in respect of such Leased Vehicle have been fully performed.

4. REGISTRATION AND TAXES. Lessee shall, at Lessee's own expense, register, title and license each Leased Vehicle in the manner prescribed by Lessor so as to maintain Lessor's ownership and insurable interest in the Leased Vehicle and forward such title to Lessor at ____________________________
   ____.

   Lessee shall provide to Lessor any documentation pertaining to a Leased Vehicle as Lessor may from time to time request. Lessee shall be responsible for determining taxes due and shall pay all such taxes and other charges and expenses whatsoever with respect to each Leased Vehicle, and file all reports attendant thereto.

5. OPERATING EXPENSES, MODIFICATIONS. (a) Lessee shall pay, or provide for the payment of, all operating expenses of each Leased Vehicle, including without limitation, gasoline, oil, grease, antifreeze, adjustments and repairs (except those covered by Ford Motor Company's warranty and policy adjustments), and storage, fines, towing and servicing.

   (b) Lessee shall not make any additions, alterations or modifications to any Leased Vehicle; provided, however, that Lessee may make additions to a Leased Vehicle so long as Lessee obtains Lessor's prior written consent and such additions are readily removable without any damage to the Leased Vehicle. Any dealer installed modifications, alterations

1

or additions, the cost of which are included in the Capitalized Cost of a Leased Vehicle, as set forth in the Supplement therefor, shall be the property of Lessor.

6. RISK OF LOSS, MAINTENANCE AND INSPECTION. Lessee shall bear, and indemnify Lessor against, any damage, loss, theft or destruction of each Leased Vehicle and shall maintain and repair each Leased Vehicle in accordance with manufacturer requirements and recommendations. Lessee shall permit representatives of Lessor to inspect each Leased Vehicle from time to time at reasonable intervals.

7. INSURANCE. Lessee shall provide, or cause to be provided, on each Leased Vehicle during the lease term thereof insurance with coverage and amounts not less than $ __________ bodily injury per person and $ __________ bodily injury per accident, $ __________ property damage, and collision and comprehensive coverages, subject to deductibles not greater than $ __________. Lessee shall cause each insurance policy issued pursuant to this Paragraph 7 to provide that (i) Lessor, as owner and Lessor of the Leased Vehicles, shall be insured as its interest may appear and (ii) if such policy shall be cancelled or materially changed for any reason, such insurer will promptly notify Lessor, and such cancellation or change will not be effective as to Lessor for 20 days after receipt by Lessor of such notice. Lessee shall deliver to Lessor copies of each insurance policy required by this Paragraph 7 upon execution hereof and copies of each renewal policy not less than 30 days prior to the expiration of the original policy or preceding renewal policy, as the case may be, and the Lessee shall deliver to Lessor receipts or other evidence that the premiums thereon have been paid. Lessee shall bear the entire risk of the Leased Vehicle being lost, destroyed, damaged or otherwise rendered permanently unfit or unavailable for use. Lessee, at Lessee's own expense, shall provide, or cause to be provided, any other insurance and post any bonds required by any governmental authority with respect to the operation of any Leased Vehicle. All such insurance shall protect Lessor, Lessee, any other person having an interest in the Leased Vehicle (if desired) and, except for any additional blanket liability insurance, any person leasing or driving the Leased Vehicle with valid permission. If any claim is made or action commenced for personal injury or death or property damage in connection with any Leased Vehicle, Lessee shall promptly notify Lessor, any other person known to have an interest in the Leased Vehicle and the insurance carrier thereof and furnish each of them with a copy of each process and pleading received in connnection therewith and diligently defend against such claim or action and/or cooperate in the defense thereof. Lessee shall promptly furnish to the insurance carrier a report of any accident involving a Leased Vehicle on the form furnished by such carrier.

8. PERFORMANCE BY LESSOR. If Lessee shall fail for any reason to perform any provision hereof to be performed by Lessee, Lessor may (but shall not be obligated to) perform the same without relieving Lessee of its obligation in respect thereof and Lessee shall reimburse Lessor upon demand for any costs and expenses incurred by Lessor in connection with such performance.

9. INDEMNITY. Lessee shall indemnify and hold Lessor, its agents and employees, harmless against any and all losses, claims, damages or expenses (including attorney's fees) connected with or arising out of the use, condition (including, without limitation, defects, whether or not discoverable by Lessor or Lessee) or operation of each Leased Vehicle. Lessee shall promptly notify Lessor of any such claim.

10. RETURN OF LEASED VEHICLE. Upon the expiration or termination of the lease of any Leased Vehicle, at Lessee's sole expense, Lessee will return each Leased Vehicle to a reasonable location designated by Lessor. Each Leased Vehicle upon its return shall be in good working order and operating condition and shall meet the conditions set forth in Exhibit I hereto, ordinary wear and tear expected. Unexpired license plates shall be returned with each Leased Vehicle where required. In all other jurisdictions, Lessee will promptly destroy or promptly effect transfer of the unexpired license plates from returned Leased Vehicles. The monthly lease charges or fair market monthly rentals, as the case may be, will continue for any Leased Vehicle not returned in accordance with this Paragraph 10.

As used herein "ordinary wear and tear" will be determined in accordance with the following:

(1) Exterior. Paint chips or nicks, regardless of the amounts prevailing on any particular panel, paint scrapes, scratches and scuff marks which have not penetrated through to the sheet metal surface, nicked or scratched bright metal, and bumper and wheel cover scratches, scuffs and minor dents shall be considered ordinary wear and tear.

(2) Interior. Soiled upholstery and carpeting and small nicks and dents in the body panels will be considered ordinary wear and tear. Rips, tears, splits, stains or burns on, or missing, headliner, seat cushions, backrests, door trim, carpets, padded dash or trunk trim will not be considered ordinary wear and tear. Vehicles on which soft trim panels have been replaced or carpet burns have been repaired will be accepted as long as such replacement or repair is not evident.

(3) Glass. Broken, missing, chipped, pitted, cracked or discolored glass will not be considered ordinary wear and tear.

2

(4) Tires. Each Vehicle must be returned with four matching tires and standard factory spare, all of which must have no less than 4/32 inch tread remaining. White side wall scrapes, scuffed white walls and normal tire repairs will be considered ordinary wear and tear. Lessee will replace any tire not meeting these requirements with a tire meeting these requirements and matching the other tires as to size, width, tread design, and white wall design and size. Matching tire brands is not required.

If Lessor has not received the Leased Vehicle title pursuant to Paragraph 4 hereof to permit sale of such Leased Vehicle or such Leased Vehicle is not returned in the manner or condition required by this Paragraph 10, Lessee will pay Lessor the then applicable Early Termination Value (as defined below) and Lessor will transfer all of its rights and title and interest in such Leased Vehicle to Lessee.

11. EXCESS MILEAGE CHARGE. Upon the expiration of the lease of a Leased Vehicle, Lessee will pay to Lessor $________ per mile for each mile in excess of ________ miles and less than ________ miles and $________ per mile for each mile in excess of ________ miles that the Leased Vehicle has been driven. Lessor and Lessee believe that this will be the maximum mileage that the Leased Vehicle will be driven over the term of the lease. If the lease of a Leased Vehicle is terminated prior to the expiration thereof, the excess mileage charge will be determined on a pro rata basis.

12. LOSS OF LEASED VEHICLE. In the event that the Leased Vehicle suffers a total loss or is stolen prior to the end of its lease term, Lessee shall pay the monthly lease charge for the month in which such loss or theft occurs and the applicable early termination value ("Early Termination Value") for such Leased Vehicle determined by Lessor at the commencement of the lease for such Leased Vehicle in accordance with Lessor's procedures with respect thereto in effect at such time and set forth in a schedule maintained by Lessor. The Early Termination Value for a Leased Vehicle applicable for a particular month during the term of the lease of such Leased Vehicle will be set forth in a statement corresponding to such month provided to Lessee by Lessor. Such statements will be provided to Lessee each month during the term of the lease of such Leased Vehicle. To the extent of payment by the Lessee pursuant to this Paragraph 12, any insurance proceeds shall be for the account of Lessee.

13. TERMINATION. (a) Lessor may terminate this Lease Agreement at any time with respect to any or all of the Leased Vehicles by written notice to Lessee upon the occurrence of any of the following events of default: (i) failure to pay any monthly lease charge or any other sum payable to Lessor hereunder, or (ii) failure or refusal by Lessee to perform any other provision hereof to be performed by Lessee, or (iii) the filing of any petition by or against Lessee under any bankruptcy or insolvency law or the making by Lessee of any assignment for the benefit of creditors or the appointment of any trustee or receiver for all or any part of Lessee's business or assets or the assignment (voluntary or involuntary) of Lessee's interest in any Leased Vehicle or the attachment of any lien or levy on any Leased Vehicle (unless such petition, assignment, appointment or attachment is withdrawn or nullified within two days). Upon such termination, the Leased Vehicle(s) shall be delivered to Lessor by Lessee in the manner and condition required by Paragraph 10 hereof and Lessee shall pay to Lessor the amounts provided for in Paragraph 14(c) hereof. If Lessee fails to return the Leased Vehicle(s), Lessor may repossess the same at any time wherever the same may be located and may enter upon the premises of Lessee for the purpose of repossessing the Leased Vehicle(s), and shall hold the same when so repossessed free and clear of this Lease Agreement and any rights of Lessee therein.

(b) Upon notice to Lessee, which shall be effective immediately upon receipt thereof, Lessor may at any time, at its sole discretion, terminate Lessee's right to lease additional Leased Vehicles under this Lease Agreement.

14. EARLY TERMINATION. (a) Lessee may terminate the lease of any Leased Vehicle prior to the expiration of the term thereof by giving Lessor 30 days prior written notice of its election to terminate such lease. The effective date of such termination shall be the date on which such Leased Vehicle is returned to Lessor in the manner and condition required by Paragraph 10 hereof.

(b) Lessor shall sell the Leased Vehicle within a reasonable period of time after its return. The sale may be public or private and with or without notice to Lessee, shall be at wholesale, and shall be for cash payable in full upon delivery of the Leased Vehicle and its title papers to purchaser.

(c) Within ________ days after written notice from Lessor, Lessee shall pay Lessor (i) the monthly lease charge for the month in which the termination occurs, (ii) any other monthly or other lease charges, including excess mileage charges then due and owing, and (iii) an amount equal to the applicable Early Termination Value of such Leased Vehicle on the effective date of termination less the Net Proceeds (as defined below) from the sale of such Leased Vehicle. "Net Proceeds" shall mean the amount received on a sale of the Leased Vehicle less all expenses incurred by Lessor in selling the Leased Vehicle and all debts incurred by Lessee which, if not paid, might constitute a lien on the Leased Vehicle or a liability of Lessor.

15. FORCE MAJEURE AND NO CONSEQUENTIAL DAMAGES. Lessor shall not be liable for any failure or delay in delivering any Leased Vehicle ordered for lease pursuant to this Lease Agreement, or for any failure to perform any provision thereof, resulting from fire or other casualty, riot, strike or other labor difficulty, governmental regulation or restriction, or any cause beyond Lessor's control. IN NO EVENT SHALL LESSOR BE LIABLE FOR ANY INCONVENIENCES, LOSS OF PROFITS OR ANY OTHER CONSEQUENTIAL, INCIDENTAL OR SPECIAL DAMAGES RESULTING FROM ANY DEFECT IN OR ANY THEFT, DAMAGE, LOSS OR FAILURE OF ANY LEASED VEHICLE, AND THERE SHALL BE NO ABATEMENT OF SET-OFF OF MONTHLY LEASE CHARGES BECAUSE OF THE SAME.

16. ASSIGNMENT; SUBLEASE. Neither this Lease Agreement nor any right hereunder may be assigned by Lessee, in whole or in part, without the prior written consent of Lessor. Lessee will not, without the prior written consent of Lessor, sublease or otherwise deliver, transfer or relinquish possession of a Leased Vehicle. If Lessor so consents to a sublease of a Leased Vehicle (i) the term of such sublease (including any renewal term) shall not extend beyond the term of lease for such Leased Vehicle provided herein, (ii) such sublease shall prohibit any further subleasing by the sublessee, (iii) such sublease shall provide that the rights of any sublessee thereunder shall be subject and subordinate to the terms of this Lease Agreement and rights and interests of Lessor in such Leased Vehicle, including, without limitation, the right of Lessor to repossess such Leased Vehicle and to avoid such sublease upon any repossession, (iv) Lessee shall remain primarily liable hereunder for the performance of all the terms of this Lease Agreement to the same extent as if such sublease had not occurred, (v) such sublease shall contain appropriate provisions for the maintenance and insurance of such Leased Vehicle, (vi) such sublease shall provide that it is assigned to Lessor for security purposes and (vii) such sublease shall provide that Lessor shall be permitted to proceed directly against the sublessee to enforce the sublessee's obligations thereunder. The review or approval by Lessor of a sublease agreement shall not constitute a waiver of any of the foregoing conditions or an ackowledgement that any of such conditions have been met.

17. NO WARRANTIES. LESSEE ACKNOWLEDGES THAT LESSOR IS NOT THE MANUFACTURER, THE AGENT OF THE MANUFACTURER, OR THE DISTRIBUTOR OF THE LEASED VEHICLES HEREUNDER. LESSOR MAKES NO WARRANTY OR REPRESENTATION, EXPRESS OR IMPLIED AS TO THE FITNESS, SAFENESS, DESIGN, MERCHANTABILITY, CONDITION, QUALITY, CAPACITY OR WORKMANSHIP OF THE LEASED VEHICLES NOR ANY WARRANTY THAT THE LEASED VEHICLES WILL SATISFY THE REQUIREMENTS OF ANY LAW OR ANY CONTRACT SPECIFICATION, AND AS BETWEEN LESSOR AND LESSEE, LESSEE AGREES TO BEAR ALL SUCH RISKS AT ITS SOLE RISK AND EXPENSE. LESSEE SPECIFICALLY WAIVES ALL RIGHTS TO MAKE CLAIM AGAINST LESSOR AND ANY LEASED VEHICLE FOR BREACH OF ANY WARRANTY OF ANY KIND WHATSOEVER AND AS TO LESSOR, LESSEE LEASES THE LEASED VEHICLES "AS IS." IN NO EVENT SHALL LESSOR BE LIABLE FOR SPECIAL, INCIDENTAL, OR CONSEQUENTIAL DAMAGES, WHATSOEVER OR HOWSOEVER CAUSED.

18. NOTICES. Any notice required or permitted by this Lease Agreement shall be in writing and given by personal delivery or sent by United States mail, postage prepaid, addressed to the intended recipient (to Lessee at its address first above written or to Lessor at ______________________________
______________________________).

19. NO IMPLIED WAIVERS. The waiver by either party of, or failure to claim, a breach of any provision of this Lease Agreement shall not be deemed to be a waiver of any subsequent breach or to affect in any way the effectiveness of such provision.

20. MISCELLANEOUS. This Lease Agreement shall constitute the entire agreement between the parties and may not be changed except by an instrument in writing, signed by the party against whom the change is to be enforced. This Lease Agreement is a Michigan agreement and shall be governed by and construed in accordance with the laws of the State of Michigan. In the event that any court determines that this Lease Agreement is not a lease, then Lessee hereby grants to Lessor a security interest in the Leased Vehicles together with all accessions, replacements and substitutions thereto or therefor and the proceeds thereof.

21. WAIVER OF DEFENSES. Lessee's obligations to Lessor under the terms of this Lease Agreement shall not be subject to any reduction, abatement, defense, counterclaim, set off or recoupment which Lessee may now or hereafter claim against Lessor.

4

Document 17-2. *(continued)*

22. FEDERAL INCOME TAX INDEMNITY. In determining its Federal income tax liability, Lessor expects to claim with respect to each Leased Vehicle deduction for accelerated cost recovery provided in Section 168 of the Internal Revenue Code of 1986, as amended. If Lessor loses this tax benefit or is subject to recapture of this tax benefit as a result of an act, omission, or misrepresentation of Lessee or any sublessee, Lessee shall pay Lessor an amount which, after deduction of any Federal income tax applicable thereto, is sufficient to reimburse Lessor for the loss of this tax benefit, plus the amount of any interest or penalties with respect thereto, within 30 days after written notice by Lessor to Lessee of a loss or disallowance of the tax benefit or 30 days prior to the time Lessor pays the additional tax, interest, or penalties, whichever occurs later. This indemnity shall be refunded to the extent that Lessor realizes a Federal income tax benefit as a result of an event which has given rise to an indemnity payment. In dealing with the Internal Revenue Service concerning a matter which may give rise to an indemnity payment under this paragraph, Lessor shall use reasonable efforts to make payment of the indemnity unnecessary, and, at Lessee's expense, shall exhaust such administrative remedies available as Lessor shall deem reasonable and necessary. Lessee's sole remedy for Lessor's failure to comply with the preceding sentence shall be relief from the indemnity required by this paragraph.

23. INSPECTION; FINANCIAL STATEMENTS. During normal business hours, Lessor and its authorized representatives may inspect each Leased Vehicle and the books and records of Lessee relative thereto. Lessor shall have no duty to make any such inspection and shall not incur any liability or obligation by reason of making or not making any such inspection. In addition, at the request of Lessor, Lessee shall furnish Lessor any financial statements of Lessee, including, without limitation, balance sheets and income statements.

IN WITNESS WHEREOF, the parties have duly executed this agreement this ________ day of ______________, 19____.

LESSOR

FORD MOTOR CREDIT COMPANY

By: ______________________________

Title: ______________________________

LESSEE

By: ______________________________

Title: ______________________________

SPECIMEN

Rev. 12/87

5

Exhibit I

Minimum Vehicle Standards

Leased Vehicles returned to Lessor pursuant to Paragraph 10 must meet the following conditions/standards:

1. No body damage in excess of $100.
2. New air filter, oil filter and oil change as recommended in the Ford Service Maintenance Guide.
3. Sound mechanical operating condition.
4. No frame, fire or water damage (any Leased Vehicles returned with such damage will be treated as a loss under Paragraph 12 of the Lease).
5. No severe body damage which has been poorly repaired.
6. No glass damage.
7. All tires must have 4/32″ tread remaining, including the spare, and all tires must meet Ford original equipment standards and must be matched.
8. No carpet or upholstery damage, including burns and stains.
9. All original factory equipment as noted on the factory invoice must be on the vehicle. Missing parts (bodyside moldings, wheel covers, spare tires, etc.) are to be replaced before the car is returned. All parts must meet Ford original equipment standard.

DEALER AGREEMENT

DRAFT

This Dealer Agreement ("Agreement") entered into on this ______ day of ______________, 19__, by and between ______________________________ of ______________________________, Michigan _____ (the "Dealer") and MICHIGAN NATIONAL BANK, a national banking association with offices located at ____________________, ________________, Michigan _____.

- R E C I T A L S -

WHEREAS Dealer is a ______________________________ with its chief executive offices located at the above address and is engaged in selling at retail ______________________________ (hereinafter called the "Goods"); and

WHEREAS from time to time Dealer sells Goods on credit, taking back a security interest in the Goods from the purchaser of the Goods (the "Chattel Paper"); and

WHEREAS Dealer has requested Bank to purchase Chattel Paper from Dealer from time to time, and Bank is agreeable to the purchase of Dealer's said Chattel Paper under the terms and conditions set forth in this Agreement; and

NOW THEREFORE in consideration of the above recitals of fact and the several representations, warranties, and agreements hereinafter set, Dealer and Bank AGREE AS FOLLOWS:

AGREEMENTS OF DEALER

1. Use of Bank Approved Forms. Dealer acknowledges and agrees that all Chattel Paper sold to Bank under this Agreement must be on Bank approved forms.

2. Representations and Warranties. In addition to the specific warranties and representations made to Bank upon sale of each Chattel Paper, Dealer warrants to Bank as follows, which warranties shall be deemed to be continuing and shall survive the termination of this Agreement:

(a) That the sale of Goods under which the Chattel Paper arose was in all respects a bona fide sale in the ordinary course of Dealer's business;

(b) That all facts set forth in the Chattel Paper are accurate, true and complete, including but not limited to the name and address of the consumer purchaser, the description of the Goods sold, the total sale price, down payment, and amount financed;

(c) That the Goods described in the Chattel Paper were in good working order and condition on the date of sale;

Printed with the permission of Michigan National Corp.

were not violative of any Uniform Commercial Code warranties of merchantability or fitness for a particular purpose, express or implied; and the true condition and market value of the Goods was not misrepresented to the consumer purchaser(s) thereof nor to Bank;

(d) That Dealer had good and unencumbered title to the Goods sold at the time of sale; that the Goods were subject to no lien, claim, encumbrance or security interest except the security interest granted under the Chattel Paper; and the Goods are fully and accurately described in the Chattel Paper;

(e) That the Chattel Paper was actually executed by the consumer purchaser(s) therein named and all signatures appearing thereon are genuine; the said purchaser(s) of the Goods is a resident of the State of Michigan and was of full legal age and capacity to enter into the Chattel Paper agreements; and, possession of the Goods has been delivered by Dealer to the consumer purchaser(s) named in the Chattel Paper;

(f) Dealer is in compliance with all relevant laws, rules, and regulations of the United States of America and of the State of Michigan, including but not limited to the Truth In Lending Act, Equal Credit Opportunity Act, Federal Trade Commission Act, Consumer Credit Protection Act, the Michigan Consumer Protection Act, and the several Michigan Retail Installment Sales Acts;

(g) Dealer has no knowledge of any fact which would impair the validity or enforceability of the Chattel Paper, and no representations or agreements of any kind, either written or oral, have been made between Dealer and the consumer purchaser(s) of the Goods named in the Chattel Paper other than those expressed in or specifically referred to in the Chattel Paper;

(h) Dealer has not previously sold nor encumbered any Chattel Paper sold to Bank under this Agreement, and has delivered the originals of the Chattel Paper to Bank on all Chattel Paper purchased by Bank;

(i) That the security interest granted in the Goods by the consumer purchaser(s) of the Goods is a first priority purchase money security interest under Article 9 of the Michigan Uniform Commercial Code;

(j) The partner, officer or other representative of Dealer executing this Agreement and all drafts, documents and agreements relating to this Agreement and the Chattel Paper sales herein described, is fully and completely authorized to enter into said Agreement and all of said related documents, papers, and agreements, and Dealer shall be fully bound thereon.

- 2 -

3. Draft System. Dealer acknowledges and agrees that all Chattel Paper purchased by Bank from Dealer shall be purchased by Dealer's drafting upon Bank using a sight draft provided to Dealer by Bank, an example of which sight draft is attached hereto as Exhibit "A" (the "Draft" or, collectively, the "Drafts"). Dealer further acknowledges and agrees with Bank that:

(a) All blank Draft forms provided to Dealer by Bank are the property of Bank and shall be promptly returned to Bank upon request;

(b) The blank Draft forms are potentially negotiable for purposes outside the intent of this Agreement, and Dealer agrees: (1) to at all times keep the Drafts in a safe and secure place and under sufficient safekeeping methods and procedures to preclude the theft or unauthorized use of the Drafts; (2) to indemnify and hold Bank harmless against any Bank loss caused or related to Dealer's failure or neglect to implement adequate security, safekeeping, and audit procedures concerning the Drafts; (3) to allow Bank's representatives access to Dealer's unused Drafts supply for purposes of Bank's audit of same during Dealer's normal business hours.

(c) All Drafts will be presented to Bank only as set forth in the Dealer Operating Procedures ("DOP") set forth in Exhibit "B" attached hereto.

4. Procedures for Sale of Chattel Paper. For any and all Chattel Paper sold to Bank under this Agreement, Dealer agrees to strictly and fully comply with each and all of the Dealer procedures set forth in the DOP attached hereto as Exhibit "B", and Dealer specifically acknowledges and agrees with Bank that Dealer's failure to strictly and fully follow and comply with the DOP may result in Bank's return to Dealer unpaid of Drafts and Chattel Paper presented for Bank purchase, Dealer's repurchase of the Chattel Paper as subsequently provided, or Bank's termination of this Agreement. Dealer further agrees that the DOP can be amended by Bank at any time by Bank's mailing or delivery to Dealer of an amended DOP, which amended DOP will be effective upon Dealer's receipt.

5. Dealer Agreement to Repurchase Upon Breach of Warranty. Dealer agrees with Bank that upon the breach of any Dealer representation or warranty made in Paragraph 2. above or Dealer's breach of any representation or warranty made to Bank in the Chattel Paper, Dealer shall, at Bank's sole option, repurchase the Chattel Paper affected by said breach for the full unpaid indebtedness owing on the Chattel Paper by the consumer purchaser(s), plus interest at the rate specified in the Chattel Paper to the repurchase date. Upon Bank's discovery of any such breach of Dealer representations or warranties, Bank shall give written notice to Dealer of the claimed breach of representation or warranty, identifying the breach and the Chattel Paper to which the breach is applicable, and within ten

- 3 -

(10) days after the date of Bank's said notice of breach, Dealer shall either fully cure, to Bank's and its counsel's satisfaction, said breach, or shall deliver to Bank, by certified or cashier's check, the unpaid indebtedness shown on Bank's books for the Chattel Paper affected by said breach to, as aforesaid, the repurchase date, in exchange for Bank's concurrent reassignment to Dealer of the Chattel Paper identified in Bank's notice letter.

6. Repurchase of Non-Conforming Chattel Paper. Dealer agrees that it shall immediately repurchase from Bank, at the price paid by Bank plus __________%, any Chattel Paper upon which the Bank has paid a Dealer's Draft and the Chattel Paper is found by Bank not to be in conformity with the DOP. Dealer may resubmit to Bank any Chattel Paper which is repurchased by Dealer due to Dealer's non-conformity with the DOP once the non-conformity is fully corrected by Dealer. Bank shall notify Dealer by telephone of any non-conforming Chattel Paper and Dealer agrees to repurchase the said non-conforming Chattel Paper by certified or cashier's check by not later than the close of Bank's next business day following the day said Bank telephone call is made to Dealer.

7. Chattel Paper Encumbrances. Dealer agrees with Bank that for so long as this Agreement shall be in effect Dealer shall not grant security interests in its Chattel Paper to any financial institution, person or entity other than Bank.

8. Further Action. Dealer agrees to take such further action, do such further things, and execute such further documents and agreements concerning the Chattel Paper as are consistent with the sale of Dealer's Chattel Paper to Bank within the intents and purposes of this Agreement and the DOP.

9. Other Agreements of Dealer.

____

____

____

____

AGREEMENTS OF BANK

10. Purchase of Dealer's Chattel Paper. Upon those terms and under those conditions set forth in this Agreement and under the DOP, Bank agrees to purchase Chattel Paper from Dealer from time to time in an amount of up to but exceeding a maximum of $____________________ in unpaid Chattel Paper balances on Bank's books.

11. Chattel Paper Purchase Price. Bank agrees to pay to Dealer for all Chattel Paper purchased by Bank ______________ (____%) of the Amount Financed (as set forth in the Chattel

- 4 -

Paper), provided, however, that Bank may adjust said Chattel Paper purchase price upward and downward, from time to time upon thirty (30) days advance written notice to Dealer. Bank's payment of the said Chattel Paper purchase price shall be effected by Bank's honor of the Draft drawn by Dealer on Bank on each Dealer Chattel Paper sale and Bank purchase.

12. Additional Agreements of Bank.

____

____

____

____

MUTUAL AGREEMENTS

13. Agreement Termination. Dealer and Bank each agree with the other that this Agreement may be terminated by either party at any time and for any reason upon ten (10) days advance written notice by the party desiring to terminate, mailed to the other at the address above stated or at such other address as either party shall subsequently notify the other in writing, provided however, that any such termination shall not affect in any way the representations, warranties and agreements made to Bank by Dealer as to Chattel Paper sold to Bank prior to the termination of this Agreement.

14. Governing Law. This Agreement, the Chattel Paper and the DOP shall be interpreted and the rights of the parties shall be determined under the laws of the State of Michigan.

15. Writings Constitute Entire Agreement. This Agreement supersedes all prior agreements between the parties, written or oral, and together with the written documents executed by the parties upon Dealer's sale of the Chattel Paper to Bank, constitutes the entire agreement of the parties. The parties do further agree, each with the other, that this Agreement can be modified or amended only by a further writing signed by both parties. This Agreement shall inure to the benefit of and shall be binding upon the parties and their respective successors, estate representatives and assigns, except this Agreement can not be assigned by Dealer without Bank's prior written consent.

IN WITNESS WHEREOF the parties have executed this Agreement on date first above written.

DEALER

____

WITNESSES: a ____________________________

________________________ By: ________________________

________________________ Its: ________________________

- 5 -

BANK

MICHIGAN NATIONAL BANK,
a national banking association,

______________________ By:______________________

______________________ Its:______________________

0808I66A014

SPECIMEN

- 6 -

18

Equipment Financing

§18.1 UNIQUE FEATURES OF EQUIPMENT LENDING

Generally, equipment financing differs from inventory and account financing in two respects. First, it is uncommon for an equipment financer to rely heavily on **after-acquired property,** though equipment financers may take a security interest in such property.

The equipment loan, however, is often discrete. It relates to a single piece of equipment or a number of pieces acquired at the same time in connection with plant expansion or improvements. Thus, if a manufacturer needs $4 million to purchase equipment in order to increase capacity, it may borrow that sum under an arrangement whereby the lender takes a security interest in that new equipment alone and receives payment over a prescribed schedule for a definite period. At the end of the period, the loan balance will be zero, and the lender will release its security interest. Such a loan is discretely related to the collateral and is quite different from the revolving loans that are common in account and inventory financing described in Chapters 15 and 16 respectively. Equipment security interests are much less likely to revolve than security interests in inventory and accounts. By virtue of the discrete nature of the equipment loan, the debtor tends to reduce it to zero and not to take it back up. Later advances are less frequent than in inventory and account financing.

Also, in many cases, equipment stands as supplemental security. The working capital lender, for example, will usually take a security interest in the borrower's equipment, but the security interest in the equipment is often secondary to that in the inventory and accounts. Working capital lenders may want security interests in a borrower's equipment, so that in the event of default, the lender may sell the business as a going concern, rather than piecemeal.

By virtue of its discrete nature and the lack of after advances and after-acquired property, the equipment loan usually forbids the debtor to sell the collateral, and the parties, unlike the parties to the farm loan, take the prohibition seriously. Chapter 22 explains the traditional prohibition of sale in the farm-loan transaction.

The second major difference between the revolving inventory and account loans and the equipment loan is that equipment financing usually involves an enabling loan, that is, the loan most often relates to the acquisition of equipment. Consequently, equipment financers are quite often purchase-money secured parties.

Equipment secured parties include sellers and their subsidiaries as well as financial institutions and subsidiaries of financial institutions. Some equipment security agreements are more general than others. In a transaction involving large sums, the security agreement may be transaction specific, that is, drafted for that single transaction. At other times, industries will fashion security agreements for one kind of collateral or another. Document 18-1 is a security agreement covering an aircraft.

§18.2 LEASE FINANCING

For a variety of reasons, many equipment lenders style themselves lessors of the equipment. In fact, there is considerable confusion in the law over the demarcation between a true lease, which is not a secured transaction, and a finance lease, which is.

Sometimes an enterprise with a capital asset will find it attractive for tax or **liquidity** purposes to sell the asset to a bank or other financial institution or investor and lease it back. Under this sale and leaseback the lessee sells the asset, say, a metal stamping machine, to a bank. The payment the seller receives under the sale provides the seller with cash, that is, with liquidity. By virtue of the sale, the seller has transformed an illiquid asset, a machine, into a liquid asset, cash, that it can use to meet payroll, tax, insurance, and other obligations. Also, the seller is now a lessee, and generally it can deduct the payments it makes to the bank under the lease.

§18.3 FIXTURES

Equipment lenders face knotty problems when non-Code law renders the equipment a fixture. Under real estate law, fixtures pass with the real estate, so that a sale, mortgage, or other encumbrance of the real estate affects the secured party's interest in the equipment. Equipment lenders often take warranties from their borrowers to the effect that the equipment will not become a fixture, but that warranty gives the lender only a cause of action if the borrower breaches. The lender would rather have its equipment. To some extent, the Code gives the secured party a method of protecting itself by making a fixture filing in the office where real estate transactions are recorded. That relief is somewhat illusory, however, since the fixture filing rules require the secured party to search the real estate records for a description (somewhat abbreviated) of the real estate and sometimes for the identity of the record owner. Document 18-2 is a form for a fixture filing.

AIRCRAFT SECURITY AGREEMENT

This Security Agreement ("Agreement") is made this ________________ day of ________________, 19____,

by and between ________________________________
(Borrower's Name)

of the ________________, County of ________________, State of ________________,

(the "Borrower") and ________________________________
(FULL PROPER BANK NAME)

of ________________, County of ________________, State of ________________, (the "Bank").

WHEREAS Borrower has borrowed or is about to borrow from Bank the principal sum of ________________

Dollars ($ ________________) ("the Loan") under the terms and conditions stated in a certain promissory note dated

________________, 19____ ("the Note"), and as stated in this Agreement and any separate loan agreement; and

WHEREAS Borrower has agreed to secure the repayment of the Loan and Note and any and all renewals, extensions, modifications, amendments, and refinancings thereof together with any and all other loans and obligations of Borrower to Bank, by granting Bank first priority security interests in Borrower's personal property in this Agreement described; and

NOW THEREFORE, Borrower and Bank **AGREE AS FOLLOWS:**

1. GRANT OF SECURITY INTEREST. Borrower hereby grants Bank a continuing security interest in the collateral described is Paragraph 2. below, to secure the repayment of the Loan and Note (including all renewals, refinancings, and extensions) and any and all other obligations of any and every kind and nature heretofore, now, or hereafter owing from Borrower to Bank and however incurred or evidenced, whether primary, secondary, contingent or otherwise, whether arising under this Agreement or under any other security agreements, promissory notes, guarantys, mortgages, leases, instruments, documents, contracts or agreements heretofore, now, or hereafter executed by Borrower (hereinafter collectively called "the Liabilities") together with all interest, costs and expenses and reasonable attorneys fees made or incurred by Bank in the disbursement, administration, and collection of the Liabilities, and in the protection, maintenance, and liquidation of the Collateral, including without limitation all of Bank's costs and expenses incurred in locating or repossesion of the Collateral, returning the Collateral to the situs designated by the Bank, and all costs of repairing, rehabilitating, insuring and storing the Collateral.

2. COLLATERAL. The "Collateral" in which Borrower here grants Bank security interests is all of Borrower's personal property described in A. through F. below, now owned or hereafter acquired and wherever located, together with all proceeds thereof and the proceeds of all insurance policies and awards concerning the Collateral.

A. Aircraft Description.

Year	Manufacturer	Model	FAA Reg. No.	Serial No.

B. Aircraft Equipment. The following described radio, avionics, radar, and, navigation equipment, affixed to or used in conjunction with the above described aircraft, and all other equipment, accessories and accessions now or hereafter attached thereto or used in connection therewith, and all substitutions and replacements thereof:

____

____

____

____

C. Aircraft Engine(s) (When 750 H/P or more)

Manufacturer	Model	Serial No.

D. Log Books. All log books and maintenance records for the aircraft and engines described above (all of which property described in Paragraph 2. A. through D. is hereinafter collectively called the "Aircraft").

E. Insurance. All policies of insurance and rights in and to the foregoing described Aircraft, interests in the Aircraft, and all proceeds thereof and any and all deposits or other sums at any time credited by or due from Bank to Borrower, and all instruments, securities, chattel paper, negotiable property and the proceeds thereof in the possession or control of Bank or in transit by mail or carrier to or from Bank (excluding any of the foregoing property of Borrower which is in the possession or control of Bank under any written trust agreement wherein Bank is the trustee and Borrower is the settlor).

F. Other Property: ________________________________

____

____

3. WARRANTIES. To induce Bank to make the Loan, Borrower represents and warrants to Bank as follows, all of which warranties shall be continuing for so long as any of the Liabilities remain unpaid or unperformed:

A. Citizenship. Borrower is a citizen of the United States as defined in the Federal Aviation Act of 1958, as amended (hereinafter called the "Act"), and the Aircraft will at all times be and remain duly registered under the Act and will not be registered under the laws of any other country;

B. Borrower's Existence and Authority. Borrower is a ________________________________
(Sole proprietorship/partnership/corporation)
in good standing and validly existing under the laws of the State of ________________, and the person(s) executing this Agreement have full power and complete authority to execute this Agreement, the Note, and all related documents and agreements.

C. Financial Information. All financial information provided to Bank has been prepared and will continue to be prepared in accordance with generally accepted accounting principles (GAAP), consistently applied, and fully and fairly present the financial condition of Borrower, and there has been no material adverse change in Borrower's business, property, or condition (financial or otherwise) since the date of Borrower's latest financial statements provided to Bank.

D. Title and Encumbrances. Borrower owns and has good title to the Collateral, and there are no liens or encumbrances on any part of the Collateral.

E. No Litigation. There are no suits or proceedings pending before any court, government agency, arbitration panel, or administrative tribunal, or to Borrower's knowledge, threatened against Borrower, which may result in any material adverse change in the business, property or financial condition of Borrower.

F. No Misrepresentations. All representations and warranties made in this Agreement and in the related documents are true and correct and no material fact has been omitted.

G. Taxes. Borrower has filed all Federal, State and local tax returns which Borrower is required by law to file, and all such taxes required to be filed are current and have been paid in full.

H. Non-Violative. Borrower's execution of the Note, this Agreement, and all related documents and agreements pertaining to the loan or the Liabilities does not violate nor constitute a breach of Borrower's articles of incorporation or bylaws if Borrower is a corporation, nor, if Borrower is a partnership, violate any provision of the partnership agreement, nor does Borrower's execution of the Note, this Agreement, and said related documents and agreements constitute a breach of any other agreement to which Borrower is a party or is subject.

4. AFFIRMATIVE CONVENANTS. For so long as the Loan and Note shall be unpaid and any of the Liabilities shall be unpaid or unperformed, Borrower specifically convenants and agrees with Bank that Borrower **shall:**

A. Aircraft Maintenance. Maintain, service, repair, overhaul, and test the Aircraft so as to keep the Aircraft in good operating condition and at all times in such operating condition as is necessary to enable the airworthiness certification of the Aircraft to be maintained in good standing under the Act, and maintain or cause to be maintained all records, logs, and other materials required to be maintained on the Aircraft by the Federal Aviation Administration (hereinafter referred to as the "FAA") or by any other governmental authority (domestic or foreign) having jurisdiction;

B. Aircraft Base. Base the Aircraft at ________________________________
and at no other location without the Bank's prior written consent;

C. Payment/Agreement Observance. Promptly pay to the Bank all sums due under the Loan and Note, promptly pay and perform all of the Liabilities, and at all times strictly observe and perform the requirements of this Agreement and any related agreements;

D. Aircraft Damage. Immediately inform the Bank, in writing, of any damage to, destruction of, or confiscation of the Collateral or any part thereof;

E. Other Liens. At all times keep the Collateral free and clear of any and all non-Bank security interests, liens, and claims of any and every kind, and immediately advise Bank in writing of the pendency of any proceeding, action, suit, claim or occurrance concerning the Collateral or which affects or may affect Borrower's continued possession of the Collateral.

F. Inspection. Permit the Bank or its agent, to enter upon Borrower's or Borrower's agents' premises to permit the inspection of the Collateral and the inspection and copying of Borrower's records pertaining thereto (including specifically the Aircraft log books and maintenance records.)

G. Compliance With Law. At all times to strictly observe, obey, and comply with all applicable Federal, State, and local statutes, ordinances and regulations, including by illustration, but not limitation, the Act.

5. NEGATIVE COVENANTS. For so long as the Loan and Note are unpaid and any of the Liabilities remain unpaid or unperformed, Borrower specifically covenants and agrees with Bank that unless Bank shall have given its prior written consent, Borrower **shall not:**

A. Registration. Register the Aircraft under the laws of any foreign country;

B. Sale, Leasing, Use. Sell, lease, assign, or transfer the Collateral or any part thereof to any other person, party or entity, for any purpose, nor allow the Collateral at any time to pass out of Borrower's possession and control, nor at anytime use the Aircraft for skydiving or for hire;

C. Illegal Purposes. Use or permit the Aircraft to be used at any time for any illegal purpose;

70037 (9/86)

Document 18-1. (*continued*)

D. Removal From United States. Remove the Aircraft from the continental United States of America or the base specified above for a period exceeding thirty (30) days;

E. Maintenance and Operation. Maintain, use, or operate the Aircraft in violation of any airworthiness, or any other rule, regulation, or order of the FAA, or in violation of any airworthiness certificate, license, or registration relating to the Aircraft, nor at any time permit the Aircraft to be flown or otherwise operated by any person not having the minimum number of pilot hours, license, and certification required by the FAA and under the insurance coverages described subsequently in this Agreement.

F. Insurance. Borrower shall at all times, at its own expense, maintain in effect with insurers satisfactory to Bank, all risk (including ground and flight) aircraft hull insurance with respect to the Aircraft for not less than the full unpaid amount of the Loans and Note, and, if the Borrower shall operate the Aircraft in any area of actual or threatened hostilities, war risk (including, without limitation, hijacking, air piracy, confiscation, and expropriation by governments) aircraft hull insurance with respect to the Aircraft in such amount; all risks (including, without limitation, fire, transit and extended coverage) insurance with respect to any engine when not installed on the Aircraft in an amount not less than the full insurable value of such engine, and public liability and property damage insurance with respect to the Aircraft in amounts satisfactory to the Bank. All such policies of insurance shall (1) insure the interests of the Borrower and the Bank as their respective interest may appear; (2) provide that if the insurers cancel such insurance for any reason whatsoever, or if the same is allowed to lapse for nonpayment of premium, the insurer(s) shall give Bank not less than thirty (30) days notice of such cancellation or lapse; and (3) provide that in respect of the interest of Bank in such policies, the insurance shall not be invalidated by any action or inaction of the Borrower or any other person and shall insure Bank's interests regardless of any breach or violation by the Borrower of any warranties, declarations or conditions contained in such policies. All such policies carried shall be made payable to Bank. Borrower shall either deliver to the Bank the policies here required or shall arrange for delivery to Bank of approprate certifications from insurance underwriters of recognized standing certifying to Bank that the insurance coverages here required have been placed in effect. Borrower hereby authorizes the Bank to receive the proceeds of any insurance loss, and at the option of the Bank, to apply such proceeds toward either the repair of the Aircraft or the payment of the Loan and Note and any of the Liabilities secured hereby.

The Bank is hereby appointed attorney-in-fact for the Borrower with respect to any and all insurance policies covering the Collateral, whether Bank is or is not named as loss payee in such policies, to make proof of loss, settle or compromise claims, and to receipt for any sums collected under such policies. Borrower shall not adjust, settle, or compromise any loss or claim with Borrower's insurance carrier without the prior written consent of the Bank. Any injury to or loss of the Collateral from whatever cause shall not release Borrower from payment of the Loan and Note and any Liabilities due Bank under this or any other agreement. The Borrower agrees to use the Collateral only for the purposes and in the manner set forth in the application(s) for the various insurance policies required to be obtained by Borrower. If Borrower at any time fails to obtain or maintain the insurance coverage required above or pay any insurance premium due, the Bank, without waiving or releasing the default of Borrower hereunder, may at any time (but without obligation to do so) made such payment and obtain and maintain such policies of insurance, pay such premiums, and take such action with respect thereto as Bank deems advisable. All sums disbursed by Bank pertaining to the Collateral, including but not limited to insurance premiums, attorney fees, court costs, expenses, and all other fees, charges, costs, and expenses relating thereto, shall be part of Borrower's Liabilities secured hereby and shall be payable upon demand, and upon nonpayment by Borrower shall bear interest at the highest interest rate specified in the Note.

7. EVENTS OF DEFAULT. Upon the occurrence of any of the following events of default, Bank, at its sole option and without notice to Borrower, may declare the entire unpaid principal balance of the Loan and Note and all accrued interest, together with all other Liabilities of Borrower to Bank, to be immediately due and payable: (a) Borrower's failure to promptly pay any installment of principal or of interest under the Loan and Note when due; (b) any breach by Borrower of any warranty, representation, covenant, term, or condition stated in this Agreement and any other loan agreement, security agreement, mortgage or other agreement executed in connection with the Loan and Note; (c) the death, dissolution or termination of existence of Borrower; (d) if Borrower is generally not paying debts as such debts become due; (e) the commencement of any proceedings under any bankruptcy or insolvency laws by or against Borrower; (f) if any other indebtedness of Borrower to Bank or to any other creditor shall become due and remain unpaid after the maturity thereof; (g) if any writ of attachment, garnishment, execution, tax lien, or similar process shall be issued against any property of Borrower; (h) Borrower's business shall be sold to, or merged with, any other business, individual, or entity; (i) Borrower shall at any time and for any reason lose possession of the Aircraft.

Whenever any one or more of the above events of default shall exist, the Bank shall be entitled to exercise all of its legal rights and remedies, including the right to immediate possession of the Collateral, and shall be entitled to setoff against the Liabilities any of Borrower's deposit accounts with Bank. Borrower agrees, in case of default, to assemble the Collateral at its expense, at a place acceptable to the Bank, and to pay all of Bank's cost of collection of the Note and Liabilities and enforcement of the Bank's rights hereunder, including reasonable attorney fees, Bank's costs in locating, taking, returning, repairing, keeping, storing, insuring and selling the Collateral, and paying all liens, if any, having priority over the Bank's lien. In case of any deficiency upon sale of the Collateral, Borrower shall immediately pay such deficiency to the Bank. If any notification of intended disposition of the Collateral is required by law, such notification shall be deemed reasonably and properly given if sent at least 7 days before such dispostion, postage prepaid, addressed to Borrower at the address shown in this Agreement.

8. INDEMNIFICATION. Borrower agrees to at all times indemnify the Bank and its directors, officers, employees and agents, from and against any and all liabilities, obligations, losses, damages, penalties, actions, suits, costs, legal fees, expenses, and disbursements of any and every kind and nature as are imposed on, incurred by, or asserted against the Bank, its directors, officers, employees and agents which in any way arise out of or are related to the Aircraft and any other item of Collateral, the transactions contemplated hereby, or the use, possession, maintenance, operation, condition, sale, registration, ownership, lease or other disposition of the Aircraft and any other item of Collateral, including, without limitation, any and all claims or penalties arising from any violation of the laws of any country or political subdivision thereof and any loss of or damage to any property or the death or injury of any person.

9. LEGAL PROCESS. Borrower consents and agrees that any legal proceeding brought by the Bank against Borrower with respect to the Loan and Note, this Agreement, or the Liabilities, may be brought in any Michigan court of competent jurisdiction or in the United States District Court for the Eastern District of Michigan, and Borrower hereby irrevocably accepts and consents with regard to any such action or proceeding, to both the jurisdiction of the aforesaid courts and venue therein.

10. GENERAL. Except as otherwise defined in this Agreement, all terms in this Agreement shall have the meanings provided by the Act, rules, and regulations, and by the Michigan Uniform Commercial Code as either is amended from time to time. Any delay on the part of the Bank in exercising any power, privilege, or right hereunder, under the Note, or under any other instrument or agreement executed by Borrower, shall not operate as a waiver thereof, and no single or partial exercise or the exercise of any other power, privilege, or right shall preclude other or further exercise thereof, or the exercise of any other power, privilege or right. The waiver by Bank of any default by Borrower shall not constitute a waiver of any subsequent defaults. All rights, remedies, and powers of Bank hereunder are irrevocable and cumulative, and not alternative or exclusive, and shall be in addition to all rights, remedies, and powers given hereunder or by any other instruments, documents, and agreements with Borrower or by the Act or the Michigan Uniform Commercial Code.

This Agreement has been delivered in Michigan, and shall be construed in accordance with the laws of the State of Michigan. Whenever possible each provision of this Agreement shall be interpreted in such manner as to be effective and valid under all applicable law, but if any provision of this Agreement shall be prohibited by or invalid under applicable law, such provision shall be void or ineffective to the extent of such prohibition or invalidity only, without invalidating the remainder of such provision or the remaining provisions of this Agreement. The rights and privileges of the Bank hereunder shall inure to the benefit of its successors and assigns and this Agreement shall be binding on all heirs, executors, administrators, assigns, and successors of Borrower, but this Agreement is not assignable by Borrower.

This Agreement may only be modified by a writing which specifically refers to this Agreement and which is signed by the Bank, the Borrower and any other party charged with the changes expressed in such modification. Any notices required to be given hereunder or at law shall be deemed served if such notice is in writing, addressed to the parties hereto at the last known address of such party and deposited in the United States mail postage prepaid.

Borrower acknowledges and agrees with Bank that this Agreement, the Note, and all of the other documents and agreements referenced herein are the entire agreement between the parties, and that there are no other agreements, written or oral, express or implied, and Borrower acknowledges receipt of a true and complete copy of this Agreement and such other documents, instruments, and agreements as Borrower shall have requested from Bank on or prior to the date of this Agreement.

11. ADDITIONAL PROVISIONS.

IN WITNESS WHEREOF, the parties have executed this Agreement on the date above written.

SPECIMEN

BANK	BORROWER
______________________ (FULL PROPER BANK NAME)	______________________ (BORROWER'S NAME)
Address: ______________________	Address: ______________________
______________________	By: ______________________
By: ______________________	Its: ______________________
Its: ______________________	and
	By: ______________________
	Its: ______________________

STATE OF ______________________)
) SS
COUNTY OF ______________________)

The foregoing instrument was acknowledged before me on this ________ day of ______________________, 19____, by

______________________ (NAME(S))

the ______________________ (TITLE(S)) of ______________________

on behalf of the ______________________ (PARTNERSHIP/CORPORATION)

____
Notary Public
My Commission Expires: ______________________

NOTARIAL SEAL

1. No. of additional sheets			State Billing Account No.	For Filing Officer (Date, Time, Number, and Filing Office) **DO NOT WRITE IN THIS SPACE**
2. Debtor(s) Last name first, address(es) Soc. Sec. No. — Tax I.D. No.		3. Secured Party(ies) and address(es)		

4. This financing statement covers the following types (or items) of property:
(Describe)________________________

a. The goods are to become fixtures on ☐
b. The above described timber is standing on ☐
c. The goods are crops growing or to be grown on ☐
d. The above described minerals or the like (including oil and gas) are to be extracted from the wellhead or minehead of the well or mine located on ☐
e. The above described accounts include accounts resulting from the sale of minerals or the like (including oil and gas) to be extracted from the well head or minehead of the well or mine located on ☐

(Describe real estate): ________________________

NAME AND ADDRESS OF ASSIGNEE

And this financing statement is to be recorded in the real estate records, if 1 of the above boxes is checked (if the debtor does not have an interest of record) the name of the record owner is________________________

5.

Check if covered: ☐ Products of collateral

____
SIGNATURE OF DEBTOR

____
SIGNATURE OF DEBTOR

by: ________________________
SIGNATURE OF SECURED PARTY OR ASSIGNEE OF RECORD

Secretary of State Copy

RIEGLE PRESS, FLINT, MICH.

19

Financing Imports and Exports

§19.1 IMPORT TRANSACTIONS

For a long time, a few major banks in New York dominated the import business. They issued up to 90 percent of the commercial letters of credit in the United States, had a lock on international banking, and formed an efficient little group of competitors. All that has changed.

Although New York continues to be an important center of international trade and banking, the import business has dispersed throughout the country, so that money-center banks in other parts of the country and many regional banks are significant players in export and import trade.

Many importers specialize in imports. A fabricator in Kansas City may need a quantity of specialty steel manufactured in Italy. The fabricator will often find it cost-effective to approach a metals importer that has contacts with Italian suppliers. The fabricator will place an order through the importer, who will arrange the transaction with the foreign supplier.

A small chain of souvenir shops may seek new products from abroad. An importer of manufactured goods from the Pacific Rim will be able to present the chain with lines of merchandise. This importer will probably arrange to import some goods before it has found buyers for them.

In both cases, the importers will need to turn the goods around quickly, for the importers are buying the goods or financing them, in effect,

Figure 19-1. Importing Specialty Steel

with their customers' money, as the following sections explain. Figures 19-1 and 19-2 illustrate these import transactions.

Other importers import for themselves. Automobile manufacturers import parts; computer hardware manufacturers import chips; large chain retailers import garments. In each of these cases, the importer buys from foreign vendors for its own account and resells directly in the domestic market, often with considerable delay. Figure 19-3 illustrates this kind of import transaction.

These importers for their own account generally are able to hold the goods they import, unlike the first group of small, thinly capitalized importers who must turn the goods over in a short time. Unlike the small import operation that may deal in large quantities of valuable merchandise and commodities and that is most often in need of financing, the larger importer for its own account may arrange its import financing as part of its overall inventory borrowing.

§19.2 EXPORT TRANSACTIONS

We can differentiate exporters in much the same way we differentiated importers, that is, those that export for themselves and those that export for others. Automobile manufacturers, oil refiners, and grain companies often export their own product to buyers that they locate in foreign markets. Smaller manufacturers, coal producers, and some farming operations will rely on brokers who find customers in foreign countries and handle the export arrangements.

Sometimes the exporter will purchase the commodity or goods from the domestic seller; sometimes it serves as a broker bringing the parties

Figure 19-2. Importing for Wholesale

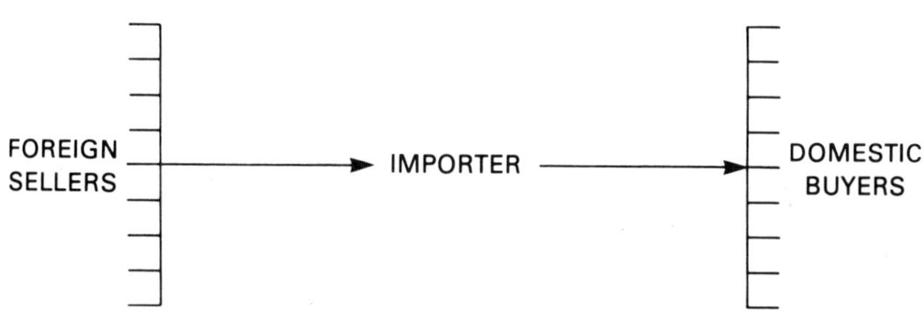

Figure 19-3. Chain Importer

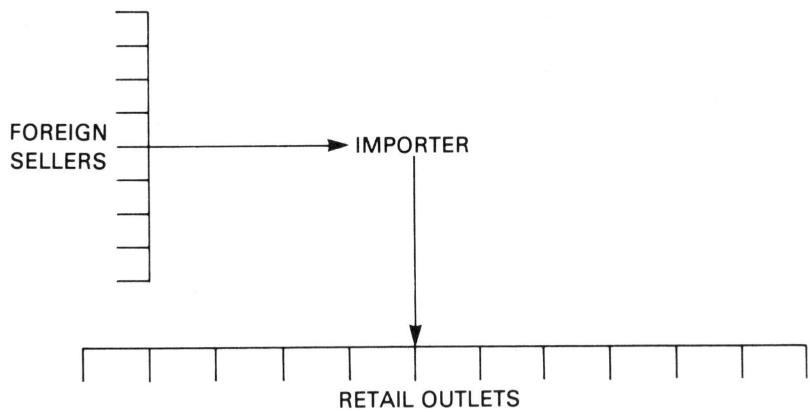

together. To the extent that an automobile manufacturer buys parts from domestic vendors, incorporates them into a finished product, and exports that product, it serves as an exporter of the vendor's goods. Most export financing occurs in cases where the exporter buys the product from the domestic producer, finds a foreign buyer, and arranges for the financing and transport of the goods overseas. Figure 19-4 illustrates this transaction.

§19.3 THE COMMERCIAL LETTER OF CREDIT IN THE IMPORT TRANSACTION

More than 85 percent of import transactions into the United States are supported by a commercial letter of credit. In this transaction, a credit issuer, usually the buyer's commercial bank, issues a letter of credit in favor of the foreign seller. The credit obliges the issuing bank to honor the seller's drafts if they are accompanied by certain documents. Usually, commercial credits call for a commercial invoice, a document of title (most often a negotiable bill of lading), and various certificates of origin, insurance, and

Figure 19-4. Exporting

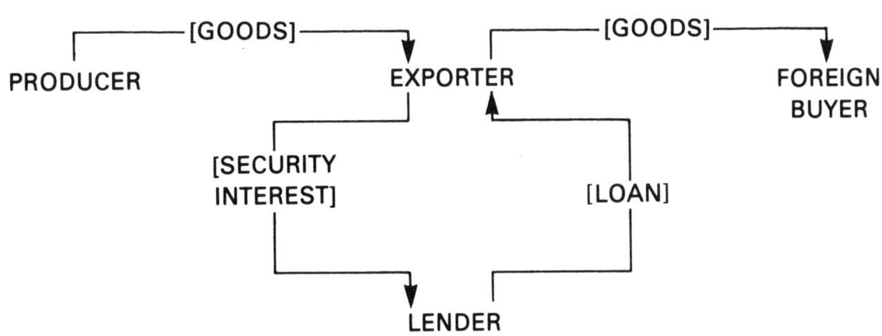

inspection. When the foreign seller ships its goods, it obtains the necessary documents, forwards them to the paying bank, which may be the issuer or its foreign correspondent, and receives payment while the goods are still en route.

The arrangement facilitates the import transaction in a number of ways. First, the foreign seller gets its money before it surrenders control of the goods, since as long as it holds the bill of lading, it controls the goods. Second, the buyer, through its bank, the issuer, does not pay for the goods until it gets control of them (through transfer of the bill of lading) and until it is satisfied (through the certificates) that the goods conform.

If an Atlanta buyer needs petrochemicals, for example, it may ask a New York importer to find the product and arrange for its shipment to Atlanta. The importer will enter into a contract of sale with, say, a Dutch refinery and will have a New York bank issue its credit in favor of the refinery. Probably, the New York bank will ask its Amsterdam correspondent to advise or confirm the credit. Under the arrangement, the refinery will take the documents to the Amsterdam bank and receive payment promptly, usually within three days. If the Amsterdam bank determines that the documents are not in order, it must return them immediately to the refinery. In most cases, the documents will be acceptable, and the bank will pay. The Amsterdam bank will then seek reimbursement from the New York bank, which will debit the importer's account.

Figure 19-5 illustrates this import transaction with the correspondent bank. Document 19-1 is a typical import letter of credit issued by a domestic bank. Chapter 5 provides further discussion of the commercial letter of credit and illustrations of the various documents in the transaction. Chapter 35 discusses the use of the bill of lading in the import transaction.

Figure 19-5. Import Letter of Credit

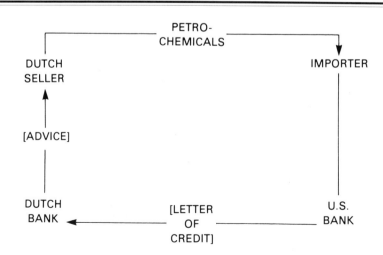

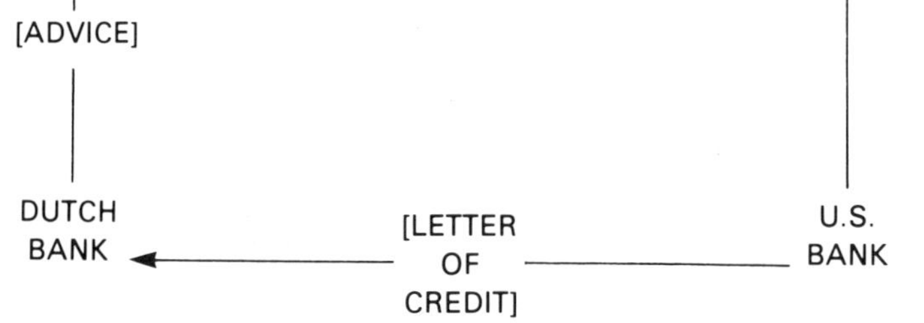

§19.4 THE COMMERCIAL LETTER OF CREDIT IN THE EXPORT TRANSACTION

In the export transaction the domestic bank's role is that of correspondent of a foreign issuer. If a U.S. grain producer exports to Bangladesh through a Chicago grain broker, the broker will be the beneficiary of a credit issued by a bank in Dacca. The broker will insist that the Dacca bank's credit be advised or, more probably, confirmed by a Chicago bank. When the grain is loaded on a vessel in Chicago, the carrier will issue the bill of lading to the broker, who assembles the other documents and presents them to the Chicago bank for payment. Figure 19-6 illustrates the transaction.

§19.5 NEED FOR FINANCING (IMPORTS)

The common need for financing imports occurs when the importer is a broker. A metals broker, for example, will import 100 tons of chrome from Africa for a number of small manufacturers in the home appliance, automobile parts, and kitchenware industries. Although the broker may have purchasers for all of the chrome at favorable prices, the broker must pay the African seller of the chrome before it arrives in, say, Seattle. Under the letter of credit that the Seattle bank issues in favor of the African

Figure 19-6. Export Transaction

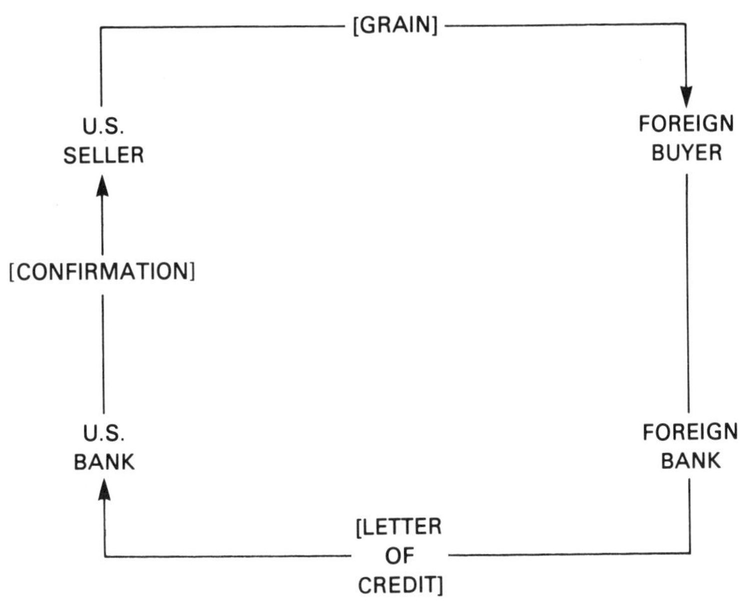

seller, the bank's correspondent in Italy or Switzerland, where many African sellers do their banking, must pay the seller as soon as it presents the documents.

Assuming that the goods were loaded on board on May 1, the seller may have its documents at the Zurich counter of the paying bank by May 4. The goods are still on the ocean-going vessel and may not arrive in Seattle until May 14. In the meantime, the Seattle bank has paid the Swiss bank and seeks to debit the metal broker's account, but the account does not contain enough to cover the charges. It would be extraordinary and inefficient for a metals broker, a middleman, to have the kind of capital necessary to import this chrome, the bauxite from Venezuela it is buying for an aluminum foundry, the tin ore from Ecuador for its smelter client, and the copper from southeast Asia for its specialty manufacturer's account. Rather, the broker and the Seattle bank fashion an arrangement whereby the resale transactions and the commodities themselves finance the import transaction.

Under this arrangement, the issuing bank, that is, the Seattle bank that issues the letter of credit, takes a security interest in the commodity. It effects that interest, usually, through the bill of lading. As long as the bill is negotiable, the issuer's possession of it, under the Code, makes it the party with first crack at the goods. By insisting in the letter of credit that it will not pay the seller unless the seller presents negotiable bills of lading indorsed in blank or to the order of the issuer, the issuer knows that once it pays, it will hold the goods through the negotiable bill.

Sometimes, the parties do not use a negotiable bill of lading. If, for example, the goods are shipped by air and arrive at the broker's city before the mail can get the bill of lading to the issuer, it makes no sense to use a negotiable bill. (Carriers will not release goods subject to a negotiable bill without surrender of the bill.) In the case of air shipments, therefore, the parties use a nonnegotiable air bill. In the case of shipment by nonnegotiable bills or in circumstances where there are no bills of lading, the issuing bank must insist that the broker grant the bank a security interest in the goods. The agreement between the issuer and the broker, the application agreement, normally contains the grant of a security interest.

In either of these arrangements, the bank is secure and will make an advance, i.e., a loan, when it reimburses the foreign bank that paid the seller. Instead of debiting the buyer's checking account for the amount reimbursed, the issuer generates a loan and increases the broker's principal loan balance.

Often the bank takes a security interest both ways. It insists on negotiable bills, and it takes a security agreement in the application agreement. If the broker enters into these transactions on a frequent basis, as it probably would, the bank takes a **blanket security interest.**

Despite all of its efforts to use the subject matter of the sale as security for its advances, the bank faces a hiatus in its security when the broker ships the goods to its customer. Generally, the Code protects these customers, so that once they pay for the goods or take negotiable documents of title covering them, they cut off the bank's security interest. The bank cannot rely on negotiable bills, for example, once it surrenders them to the broker, as it must when the goods arrive in Seattle. The broker needs the bills in order to take delivery from the ocean carrier and arrange shipment on a domestic carrier to the ultimate buyer. Once the bank surrenders the bills, it puts the broker in position to resell them to a good-faith purchaser or to take delivery from the ocean carrier and resell the goods to the customer without accounting to the bank for the proceeds. In either event, an honest buyer will defeat the bank's security interest.

Banks are generally willing to take the risk inherent in delivery of the bills to the broker and in letting the broker have possession of the goods. First, the bank knows the broker and trusts him. Second, the bank is financing other imports and can look to other commodities in the event the broker defaults on one transaction. The security agreements generally provide that each shipment secures all advances the bank makes, whether for the shipment in question or other shipments. In the event the broker's credit is weak, the bank can take steps to arrange shipment of the goods to the ultimate purchaser itself and thereby guard against misappropriation of the proceeds, or the bank can insist on a commercial letter of credit from the buyer in a back-to-back letter of credit transaction.

§19.6 NEED FOR FINANCING (EXPORTS)

Export financing can assume a number of forms, but all of them are essentially account financing. In the classic case, the exporter sells its goods under a foreign bank's commercial letter of credit that calls for time drafts. Under this arrangement, the foreign buyer has exacted credit terms from the domestic seller. If the exporter and the foreign buyer agree, for example, on 90-days' credit, the seller's drafts will be payable 90 days after the date of the acceptance, or the shipment, or some other ascertainable date. When the exporter present its drafts to the paying bank, that bank will accept them, that is, will sign them and thereby undertake to pay them when they come due. The acceptor returns these banker's acceptances to the exporter who now holds valuable paper that it can discount in the money markets. Often the paying bank itself will discount the acceptances for the exporter.

Acceptances that are eligible under Federal Reserve Board regulations are called "eligible acceptances" and are a prime medium of investment. Most acceptances that (1) arise under export transactions involving commodities and (2) have a life of not more than 180 days will be eligible. They provide the exporter with readily marketable paper that attracts investors at a small discount. Document 20-1 in Chapter 20 is a banker's acceptance. That chapter discusses those acceptances in general.

§19.7 FORFAITING AND SIMILAR ARRANGEMENTS

Just as most law professors had decided that the negotiable promissory note had outlived its usefulness, international sellers and their banks devised a new practice to which the negotiable note is indispensable.

The practice is called *forfaiting,* and its purpose is to enhance the attractiveness of a foreign buyer's obligation to pay the exporter. The reason for that enhancement, of course, is to make the obligation more attractive in the financial markets so that the exporter may provide credit to the foreign buyer and yet obtain funds promptly.

In a forfaiting transaction, an exporter of twelve shipments of beef to Germany over the next twelve months, for example, might want to make 90-day credit terms available to her buyer. She could, of course, resort to the commercial-letter-of-credit transaction described in Section 19.4 of this chapter and use a 90-day time draft that will result in a 90-day banker's acceptance — a medium of investment that is highly attractive in the financial markets. That method entails expenses that the buyer may be unwilling to incur, however. If the buyer is strong enough, he will insist on the 90-day credit terms and refuse to obtain the letter of credit.

In that case, the seller might be able to arrange a forfait with a bank. The seller will ship the beef against the buyer's promissory notes for the purchase price of each shipment. After each shipment, the seller will hold a negotiable instrument executed by the buyer payable to the seller's order. The seller will indorse the note to the forfaiting bank, which will take it at a discount and enforce it against the buyer when it comes due.

The beauty of the arrangement for the seller is that under a forfait, the bank will permit the seller to indorse "without recourse." That indorsement means that the seller does not guarantee payment of the note in the event the buyer defaults.

The first bank to take the notes under the forfait may not hold them until maturity but has the option of negotiating them to subsequent holders. In some transactions, notes arising from a forfait will change hands many times before maturity when the holder presents them to the buyer through the banking chain for payment.

In the forfait transaction, the holders of the notes may look only to the buyer and indorsers subsequent to the seller for payment. Usually, therefore, the buyer is a concern of sound financial repute. Significantly, of course, the holders are holders in due course and are unconcerned about the underlying transaction. If the beef turns out to have too many hormones to satisfy the German customs inspectors, the buyer may not want it and may have a defense to payment in the underlying transaction of sale with the seller. That defense, however, is unavailable to the buyer when the holder sues him on the notes. Thus the negotiable nature of the note renders it attractive to the financial institutions and other investors who take it and who provide the credit for the export transaction.

There are a number of variations to the financing of foreign obligations arising from exports. Under one of them, the seller ships on open account and finances its accounts with a bank. The bank is willing to take the accounts because the accounts are insured. That insurance may extend to commercial risk (i.e., the risk that the buyer will not pay) or political risk (i.e., the risk of war, political upheaval, or exchange-control problems in the importing country). These subsidized arrangements have the same effect on the marketability of the seller's receivables that negotiable promissory notes have — they enhance the attractiveness of the obligation.

7

☐ This refers to our preliminary teletransmission advice of this credit.

IRREVOCABLE LETTER OF CREDIT NO. DATE OF ISSUE: May 1, 1990	APPLICANT Buyer Co. (Buyer Co.'s address)
ADVISING BANK REFERENCE NO.:	BENEFICIARY Seller Co. (Seller Co.'s address)
DATE AND PLACE OF EXPIRY August 1, 1990 Los Angeles, CA	AMOUNT $XX,XXX.XX

Credit available with this office
by ☐ sight payment ☐ deferred payment [XX] acceptance ☐ negotiation
against presentation of the documents detailed below and your draft(s) at 90 days' sight
drawn on us

DOCUMENTS REQUIRED:

1. Commercial invoice in triplicate
2. Clean, on-board ocean bill of lading, to our order
3. Marine insurance policy
4. Certificate of origin

SPECIMEN

We hereby issue this Documentary Credit in your favour. It is subject to the Uniform Customs and Practice for Documentary Credits, 1983 revision, ICC Publication No. 400, and engages us in accordance with the terms thereof. The number and the date of the credit and the name of our bank must be quoted on all drafts required. If the credit is available by negotiation, each presentation must be noted on the reverse of this advice by the bank where the credit is available.

All documents to be forwarded in one cover, by airmail, unless otherwise stated above. Negotiating bank charges, if any, are for account of beneficiary. The advising bank is requested to notify the credit to the beneficiary without adding their confirmation.

This document consists of 1 signed page(s)	AUTHORIZED COUNTERSIGNATURE	AUTHORIZED SIGNATURE

Please examine this instrument carefully. If you are unable to comply with the terms or conditions, please communicate with your buyer to arrange for an amendment. This procedure will facilitate prompt handling when documents are presented.

FX-1311 2-86

20 Banker's Acceptances

§20.1 UNDERSTANDING THE DEVICE

The banker's acceptance is a commercial bank product or "facility," as they say, that arises in a number of transactions. In many ways the product is unique, and its unique features make it difficult to position the device in the commercial law curriculum.

The banker's acceptance is a negotiable instrument, yet it is not altogether clear what kind of instrument it is. The acceptance begins life as a draft, when a drawer creates (or "utters") it. It may travel through the hands of a number of parties in that form until ultimately the drawee, a bank, accepts it. That acceptance transforms the item from an instrument with no one primarily liable on it into an instrument on which a bank (usually one of a few strong banks that are involved in the acceptance market) has signaled its primary undertaking to pay the instrument. At that point, the item is much more akin to a promissory note or certificate of deposit than it is to a draft.

Once transformed into a banker's acceptance, the item usually becomes a prime medium for investment in the money market. There are about 400 banks involved in banker's acceptances and a small number of dealers who buy and sell these acceptances. Thus, unlike most negotiable instruments today, which usually serve as media of payment, the banker's acceptance becomes a medium of investment, something in the nature of a security.

Notwithstanding its nature as a payment mechanism and as an investment product, the description of the device is in the secured lending section of this book. The decision to place it here rests on the fact that today the banker's acceptance grows primarily out of the financing of goods. From a pedagogical standpoint, it is best to think of the device in terms of a financing device. That said, it is important to bear in mind that the beauty of the device is that although banks use it to get funds to their borrowers, they do not have to use any of their own funds. Because the device is so attractive in the money market, the bank can obtain funds from third parties contemporaneously with the creation of the acceptance. Thus the banker's acceptance is a classic facility for intermediation. Banks create the acceptance, give credit to their borrowing customers, and contemporaneously draw credit from the investing public.

The procedure is not only quick; it is also inexpensive. Traditionally, only banks of good credit repute have engaged in the creation of banker's acceptances, and investment brokers have been able to rely on the acceptances and to represent them to their customers as sound investments.

Much of the literature confines itself to discussion of the regulations that govern banker's acceptances and ignores the important fact that they often arise out of a transaction in goods.

§20.2 EXPORT TRANSACTIONS

Chapters 5 and 20 explain in some detail the way in which parties may use a letter of credit in the export of goods. This section will concentrate on the draft in that transaction, the way that draft becomes a banker's acceptance, and the way the exported goods or commodities become security for the bank's obligation on the acceptance.

Recall that in the time letter of credit transaction, the exporter agrees to sell goods to a foreign buyer on credit terms. An exporter of U.S. citrus concentrate to Japan, for example, might agree with its Japanese buyer that payment will be due 90 days after the issuance of the bill of lading covering the shipment of the concentrate to Japan. The exporter will agree to that arrangement only if the buyer causes its bank to issue a time letter of credit in favor of the exporter. Under the terms of the sales contract, moreover, the exporter will insist that the credit be confirmed by a Los Angeles bank.

The confirmation will require the exporter to obtain a negotiable ocean bill of lading covering the concentrate and to present it (and probably other documents) to the confirming bank in Los Angeles with a time draft payable 90 days after the date of the bill.

Once it has the confirmation in hand, the exporter will arrange for the shipment of the goods, obtain the bill of lading, and take the bill and the draft to the Los Angeles bank. Document 4-5 is a time draft such as the one the exporter would prepare.

When the exporter presents the documents to the bank, its document examiner will determine whether they are in order. If they are, the bank will sign the draft on its face and thereby "accept" it, transforming the draft into a banker's acceptance. Document 20-1 is a banker's acceptance.

At that point, the parties must decide what to do with the acceptance. It is, at that moment, the property of the exporter, but the exporter probably does not want it. It wants money to pay the growers who sold it the concentrate and to pay other creditors. A likely customer for the acceptance is the acceptor itself. The Los Angeles bank may have funds it wants to invest in an acceptance, knowing that the acceptance is liquid, that is, that it is readily marketable. The bank will be satisfied that it can sell the acceptance quickly if there is a need for funds. In case the bank wants the acceptance, it will take it from the exporter at a discount. The bank computes the discount by applying the current interest rate to the face amount of the acceptance for 90 days.

Sometimes the bank will take the acceptance only momentarily and immediately rediscount it in the money market through one of a small number of banker's acceptance dealers who broker acceptances among other financial institutions and investors.

Ultimately, the acceptance may pass through a number of parties' hands before it comes due on the ninetieth day. On that day, the holder will present the acceptance to the Los Angeles bank, which will honor it by payment.

Note that the Los Angeles bank is on the hook for a considerable period of time here, and as you might suspect, it will want some security for its undertaking. Admittedly, the bank expects to be reimbursed by the Tokyo bank, the Japanese buyer's bank that opened the credit that the Los Angeles bank confirmed. The U.S. exporter got its money, less the interest charges, when the bank discounted the acceptance, but during the 90 days, the Japanese seller is sitting on its money, as it has the right to do under the sales contract, which gave it 90-day terms and under the reimbursement agreement that it negotiated with its bank when it asked it to open the letter of credit. If all goes according to plan, of course, the Los Angeles bank will pay the holder of the acceptance on maturity, the Tokyo bank will reimburse the Los Angeles bank, and the Japanese buyer will reimburse the Tokyo bank. During the 90-day interim, however, the Los Angeles bank has created a liability for itself, and under sound banking practices, it must have security for the undertaking.

The citrus concentrate is the security. As long as the bank holds the negotiable bill of lading, the bank knows that it will be able to resort to the concentrate if it is not reimbursed. In the unlikely event, then, that the Tokyo bank does not reimburse, the Los Angeles bank will cause its

Tokyo agent to surrender the bill of lading to the ocean carrier or to a warehouse at the dock in Yokohama where it has been stored since the ship docked, take delivery of the concentrate, sell it, and forward the proceeds to Los Angeles. If the Tokyo bank does reimburse, the Los Angeles bank will deliver the document to the Tokyo bank, which will hold it until the Japanese buyer reimburses it. Upon that reimbursement, the Tokyo bank will deliver the bill to the Japanese buyer, who will then be in a position to take delivery of the merchandise.

There are variations in the transaction. If the Japanese buyer wants the concentrate before the 90 days have expired, he can put his own bank in funds or can grant his own bank a security interest in the concentrate or in other collateral. In those events, the Japanese bank will be able to buy the bill of lading from the Los Angeles bank and deliver it to the buyer, who will then be able to take delivery of the goods.

§20.3 IMPORT TRANSACTIONS

The banker's acceptance in the import transaction is similarly secured by the goods that are being imported. In the import situation, a New York importer might arrange to buy polypropylene granules from a Frankfurt, Germany, seller. Under the sales agreement, the importer has obtained 180-day credit terms but has agreed to pay by letter of credit. Importer causes its New York bank to issue the credit in favor of the German seller, payable against the seller's 180-day time draft. The draft is payable 180 days after the New York bank accepts it.

The seller will prepare the documents required by the letter of credit, including a negotiable bill of lading covering the granules. When the New York bank's document examiner determines that the documents are in order, it accepts the draft and creates the banker's acceptance.

The New York bank holds the bill as security for its obligation on the acceptance. When the 180 days have passed, the holder of the acceptance presents it for payment, and the New York bank pays. By that time, however, the importer probably has resold the granules and has something of value to give the bank either in reimbursement for its payment to the holder of the acceptance or as replacement security for the bank's advance.

In order to effect that resale, it may be necessary for the importer to obtain delivery of the bill of lading or the granules. In that case, the New York bank might be willing to surrender the bill, but usually it does so only if it has other collateral from the importer. In any event, in the short term, the imported goods serve as collateral for the bank's undertaking on the acceptance.

§20.4 STORED COMMODITIES

There may be times when a broker holds commodities (sugar, for example) that she does not want to sell and that she desires to use as collateral for a loan. The broker may need the sugar to fill a contract in a month, but she needs cash now. The broker could simply grant a lender a security interest in the commodity and take a simple inventory loan, as Chapter 16 describes. There may be times, however, when acceptance financing yields more attractive interest charges. In this case, the borrower draws a time draft, say one payable 30 days after sight. She presents the draft to the bank for acceptance accompanied by a negotiable warehouse receipt covering the sugar. Document 32-1 is an example of a negotiable warehouse receipt. The bank knows that the warehouse will not deliver the sugar to anyone who does not surrender the receipt. In effect, then, the bank's possession of the receipt is possession of the sugar. Under the Uniform Commercial Code, the bank has a perfected security interest in the sugar.

Once the bank accepts the time draft, the broker has an attractive investment medium that investors who know nothing about the sugar market are willing to buy. When the 30 days elapse, the holder of the acceptance presents it to the bank and receives payment. If the broker does not reimburse the bank for its payment, the bank sells the receipt to someone who wants the sugar or takes the receipt to the warehouse, receives the sugar, and resells it or uses it for lemonade at the next board meeting.

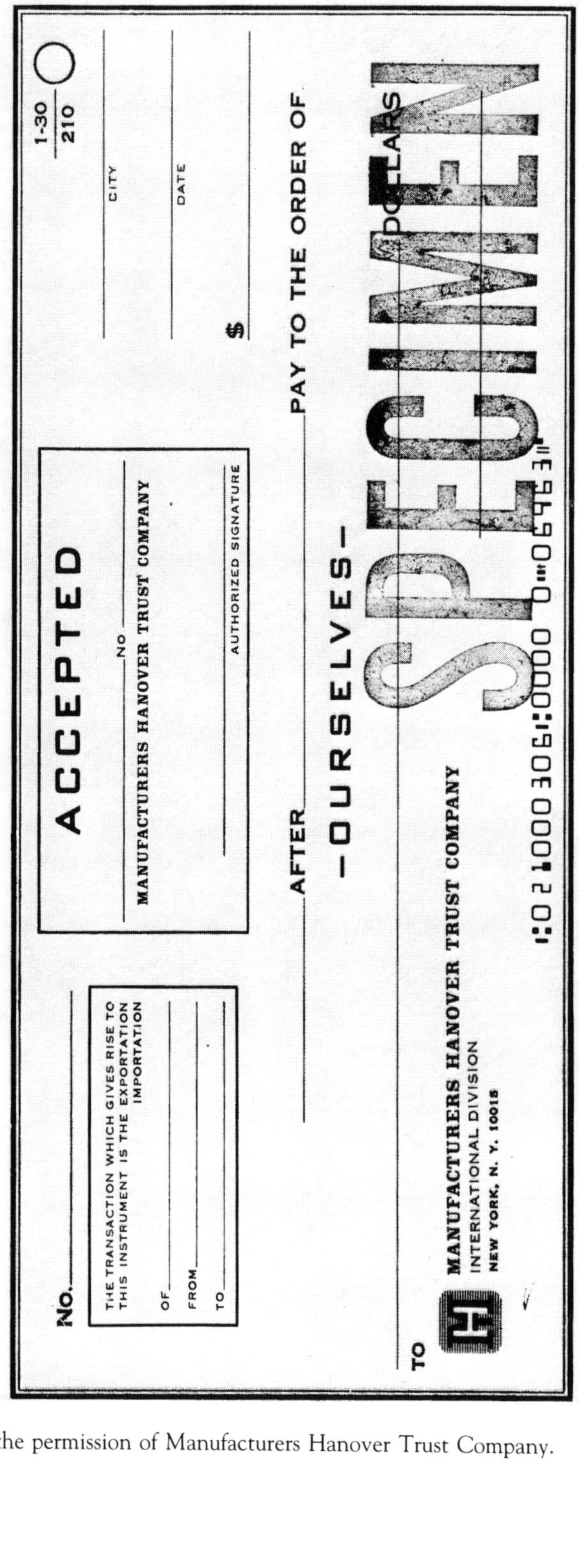

1-30
210

CITY

DATE

$

PAY TO THE ORDER OF

DOLLARS

AFTER

-OURSELVES-

ACCEPTED

NO

MANUFACTURERS HANOVER TRUST COMPANY

AUTHORIZED SIGNATURE

NO.

THE TRANSACTION WHICH GIVES RISE TO THIS INSTRUMENT IS THE EXPORTATION IMPORTATION

OF

FROM

TO

TO

MANUFACTURERS HANOVER TRUST COMPANY
INTERNATIONAL DIVISION
NEW YORK, N. Y. 10015

SPECIMEN

1716 4835

Printed with the permission of Manufacturers Hanover Trust Company.

21 Financing the Farmer

§21.1 INTRODUCTION

The United States has had a curious romance with the farm producer. The American Gothic image of the proud and proper farm couple standing with a pitchfork before the white frame dwelling and the myth of the sturdy yeoman farmer working the fields from dawn to dusk prevail even today. American politicians, it seems, never tire of advancing the cause of the family farm, and the popular myths enhance their efforts.

In fact, of course, the American farmer is a business person. Producers of the overwhelming majority of agricultural commodities in this country are university-trained people, sophisticated in the sciences of agronomy, animal husbandry, and the like. Farmers frequently sell under futures contracts and other complicated marketing arrangements that they monitor on their computer terminals or those of their brokers. They finance their operations with the help of the vast private and government-subsidized credit industry. Many of them test their soil scientifically and irrigate with computer-devised equipment and programs. Others raise and breed hogs in antiseptic environments. Agriculture is a big, complicated business. The people who engage in it are not hayseeds. Their investment in land and equipment matches that of many medium-sized enterprises. In short, agricultural production is a business much like any other business.

History, the large number of marginal farms, and the American romance with the farm myth leave a different impression, however, and different practices, different financing institutions, and even different legal rules differentiate farm lending from much of the rest of the lending sector.

§21.2 GOVERNMENT ROLE

There is perhaps one significant difference between the small agricultural enterprise and the small or medium-sized commercial establishment. When the farm economy is in trouble, the government and the public perceive it as a national problem that must be addressed. However efficient it may be from an economic standpoint, the political price of letting family farms be sold at bankruptcy auction is one the U.S. is not willing to pay.

In the lean years that inevitably confront the cyclical agricultural sector, the federal government has responded with a wide array of special legislation that includes significant efforts to provide credit to agriculture. Among the legislative creatures that these efforts have spawned are the **Farm Credit System,** the Commodity Credit Corporation, and the **Farmers Home Administration.** In addition, the Small Business Administration makes special loans to farmers.

The Farm Credit System finances its operations through the sale of bonds in the capital markets. For personal property lending purposes, the System consists of twelve Federal Intermediate Credit Banks that lend to over 400 **production credit associations** (federally chartered loan institutions that lend directly to farmers, often on a secured basis) and twelve Banks for Cooperatives that lend to agricultural cooperatives. The Commodity Credit Corporation makes loans to farmers for storage and grain-drying equipment and makes nonrecourse price-support loans secured by stored commodities that are the Corporation's only source of loan repayment. Finally, the Farmers Home Administration, often referred to as the farm lender of last resort, makes **direct loans** to or insures commercial bank loans for farmers that cannot obtain credit anywhere else.

Recently, the government has begun making payment to farmers under the numerous farm subsidy programs in certificates rather than in cash. Farmers buy and sell commodity certificates, which are negotiable in form. At present, certificates cannot be subject to a security interest under state law. Federal regulations render them free of any encumbrance, though some courts have found them to be proceeds of collateral and, therefore, subject to a lender's security interest. Some commentators suggest that they can be transferred to lenders as security, presumably if the secured party takes possession as a transferee. The area is not free from doubt, but the use of the certificates has subsided with the reduction in government surpluses occasioned by recent droughts.

§21.3 FARM INVENTORY

Under the Uniform Commercial Code, farmers do not have inventory. They have farm products, and the inventory **priority** and purchase-money rules do not apply to them. Purchasers from farmers, moreover, do not enjoy the full protection that buyers in ordinary course normally enjoy under the Code, though federal law has changed that rule somewhat. Farm lenders are aware of these anomalies in the Code treatment of agricultural activity and take advantage of them. Security agreements covering crops and livestock, for example, almost always forbid the farmer to sell collateral without the prior approval of the lender. Document 21-1 is such a security agreement. Such prohibition is the exception in nonfarm sectors of the economy. In actual practice, the farm lender almost never objects if the farmer sells the collateral and accounts for the proceeds. Only when the proceeds disappear does the lender argue that the sale was unauthorized and that, under the rules of the Code, the buyer or, in some cases, the auctioneer, is liable in conversion.

§21.4 FARM BUYERS

In the usual course of business, farmers market their grain and livestock either through the federal government or, in private markets, through brokers and large buyers: grain companies, slaughterhouses, and elevators. Although the farmer is clearly a business person, his operation, even with significant investments in real estate and equipment, is relatively small, especially in relation to the larger operations to whom he sells his product. This picture (small sellers, big buyers) is a reversal of the paradigmatic sales transaction (big sellers, small buyers) in other sectors of the economy. The effect of the disparity in size is a disparity in bargaining strength, and farm sellers are usually not in a position to bargain with their buyers over sales terms, which may be fixed by distant exchanges.

The result in many grain and livestock transactions is to leave the farm seller unprotected. Livestock sellers, for example, normally cannot sell for cash, since the price of the livestock cannot be computed until the animals are slaughtered, dressed, and graded. The rancher, then, must wait one or more days after delivery of his cattle for a check. He has, in effect, made a credit sale, and he has done so without retaining any security interest in the goods: He is an **unsecured creditor**. The Packers and Stockyards Act and similar legislation in many states provide, however, that the livestock seller and sometimes the grain seller as well have a super **lien** that defeats the rights of the buyer and the buyer's creditors, if the seller is not paid.

Figure 21-1. A Super Lien

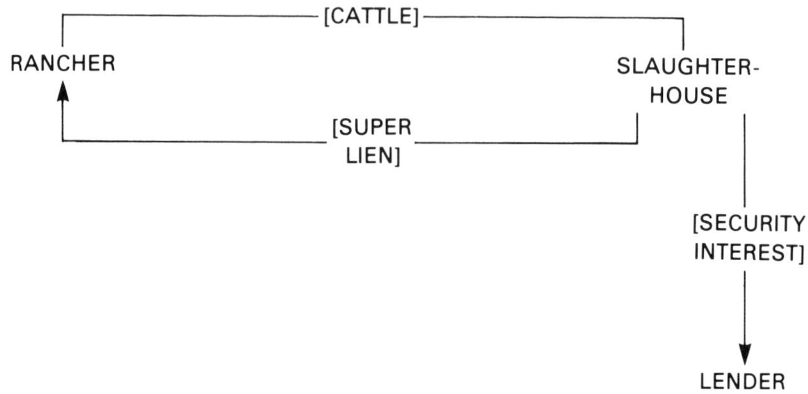

Creditors of buyers from farm sellers must take these super liens into account. The inventory lender of a slaughterhouse, for example, cannot rely on the slaughterhouse's inventory of beef or hogs without considering that much of the inventory is not paid for and, therefore, subject to the statutory seller's super lien. Figure 21-1 illustrates the super-lien setting.

§21.5 FARM LENDERS

Three enterprises play the most significant role in personal property farm lending: (1) commercial banks; (2) production credit associations; and (3) the Commodity Credit Corporation, which acts through local committees of the Agricultural Stabilization and Conservation Service (ASCS).

The role of commercial banks in farm lending is not, on the surface, altogether different from that role in nonfarm lending. The banks take loan applications, subject the loan to their credit-review process, and document the transaction with a promissory note, security agreement, and financing statement. The security agreement generally contains a prohibition against sale.

A significant feature of farm lending is that the banks frequently can avail themselves of the benefits of the farm credit system — a vast array of federally supported and subsidized loans and guarantees implemented by a number of government agencies. In the typical case, the agency is the Farmers Home Administration (FmHA), and the service it performs is one of guaranteeing the farmer's loan for an amount equal to a percentage (often 90 percent) of the loan balance.

Under the agreement, if the farmer defaults, the bank that made the loan assigns all of its interest in it and in the security interest that secures it to the FmHA, which then pays the bank 90 percent of the loan balance. Figure 21-2 illustrates the FmHA loan-guaranty arrangement.

Figure 21-2. Loan Guaranty

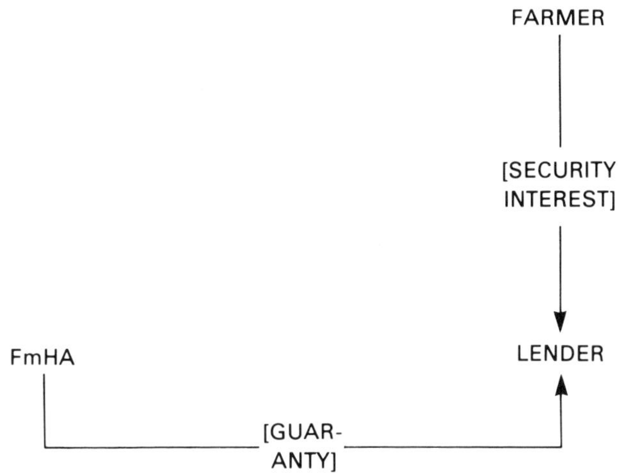

Production Credit Associations, incorporated under federal law, are in the nature of mutual organizations, that is, they are owned by their borrowers. Traditionally, the board of a PCA consists of the leading farmers in the farm community. The Federal Intermediate Credit Banks provide the PCA with the funds. The PCA lends the funds directly to the farmer and takes a security interest to secure the loan. PCA loan documentation does not differ from the typical loan documentation of a commercial bank that is acting as a secured lender. PCAs know the rules of agricultural lending. They nearly always provide in their security agreement that the farmer may not sell his crops or livestock without the PCA's prior written approval, but the PCAs in practice rarely enforce the provision ex ante.

The Commodity Credit Corporation (CCC) also makes agricultural loans, but its lending function is secondary to its function as the branch of the federal government that provides price support for agricultural commodities. Under the CCC program, a farmer will store grain with an elevator, receive the support price from the CCC in the form of a loan, and hold the commodity until the price improves or until the farmer decides to sell. Upon the sale, the CCC receives the proceeds first, to the extent of its loan, and the farmer receives the balance, if any. If the market price never exceeds the support price (used in funding the loan), the CCC takes the crop in satisfaction of the loan debt and has no recourse against the farmer.

Rather than storing the product in its own facility, the CCC may take and perfect a security interest in one of two ways. First, it can take a negotiable warehouse receipt from an elevator, cotton gin, or other bailee and hold the document until the farmer finds a buyer. At that point, the CCC must release the document to the farmer or to the buyer in order to permit the sale to close. Figure 21-3 illustrates the entire transaction.

Figure 21-3. Commodity Credit Corporation Loan

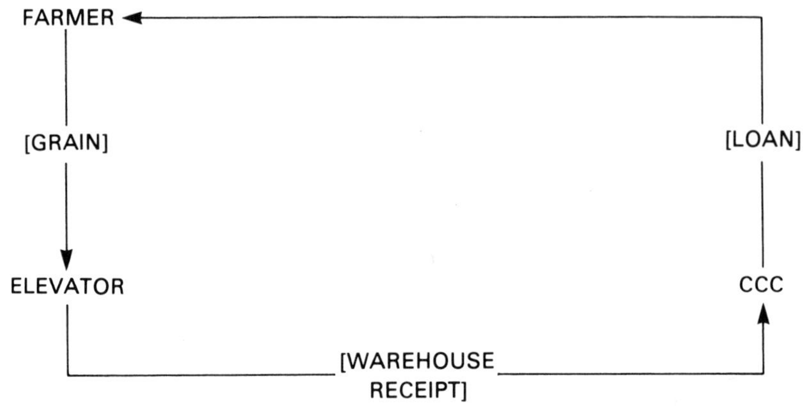

Alternatively, the CCC either can ask the farmer to have the bailee issue nonnegotiable receipts directly to the CCC or can notify the bailee of the CCC's security interest. Either method constitutes perfection under the Code.

PRODUCTION CREDIT ASSOCIATION SECURITY AGREEMENT

1. CREATION OF SECURITY INTEREST.

For value received, the undersigned Debtor grants to Production Credit Association of ______ (Secured Party hereinafter referred to as "PCA") a security interest in the property described opposite the box(s) checked in Section 2 and in Debtor's PCA stock and participation certificates ("Collateral"), to secure the payment and performance by Debtor of all Debtor's obligations. "Obligations" shall mean (a) all loans, advances, liabilities, and amounts owing by Debtor to PCA at any time, whether representing existing or future credit granted by PCA to Debtor, to Debtor and another, or to another guaranteed or endorsed by Debtor; and (b) to the extent not prohibited by law, all costs and expenses, including attorneys' fees and legal expenses, incurred or paid by PCA in the preservation or enforcement of its rights under this Agreement.

2. DESCRIPTION OF COLLATERAL.

Except as otherwise stated herein, the Collateral includes the following designated property, whether now owned or hereafter acquired, and all proceeds of such property. All Collateral (except any covered under Section 2.4) is covered regardless of whether it is classified under the Uniform Commercial Code as equipment, farm products or inventory and regardless of whether or not such classification changes.

☐ 2.1 All equipment, motor vehicles and fixtures, all accessions thereto, and all spare parts and special tools for such equipment.

☐ 2.2 All livestock and poultry and the young of such livestock and poultry.

☐ 2.3 The following products of livestock and poultry: ______

☐ 2.4 All accounts arising from the sale, lease, or other disposition of other Collateral (but Debtor is authorized to sell, lease, or dispose of Collateral only to the extent stated in Section 3 hereof).

☐ 2.5 All crops growing or to be grown by Debtor, and the products of all such crops, on real estate described as:

☐ 2.6 All: harvested and processed crops not covered under other sections of this Agreement (whether or not produced by Debtor); feed; seed; fertilizer, insecticides, herbicides and other agricultural chemicals; and other supplies.

☐ 2.7 Property specifically described here and on any Addendum hereto.

3. RESTRICTIONS ON DISPOSITION OF COLLATERAL BY DEBTOR.

3.1 GENERAL RESTRICTION. DEBTOR MAY NOT SELL, LEASE OR OTHERWISE DISPOSE OF ANY COLLATERAL UNLESS SPECIFICALLY AUTHORIZED IN SECTION 3.2 OR IN A SEPARATE WRITING SIGNED BY PCA, OR IN AN ADDENDUM HERETO.

3.2 Collateral Which May be Sold, Leased or Expended. Subject to any conditions stated in Sections 3.3 and 3.4 and to PCA's continuing security interest in all proceeds and accounts arising from permitted disposition of Collateral, Debtor, before default, may in a commercially reasonable manner, (a) market milk, (b) market eggs, (c) use feed and crops or products thereof as feed for Debtor's livestock and poultry, and (d) sell or lease any other Collateral listed here:

______

______

______

3.3 Required Livestock Herd Size. ☐ If checked here, then, notwithstanding any rights given Debtor herein to dispose of livestock, such disposition shall not reduce the size of Debtor's livestock herds below the following specified number of head. [Debtor represents that such herd(s) is/are presently maintained]:

Type	Breed	Number	Age	Other

3.4 Conditions for Disposition. Debtor's right to dispose of Collateral listed in Section 3.2 is further conditioned upon the following restrictions, if any:

______

______

______

______

______

3.5 Termination of Debtor's Right to Dispose of Collateral. PCA reserves the right, in its sole discretion, to revoke or modify any permission granted herein to Debtor to dispose of Collateral.

4. WARRANTIES AND AGREEMENTS. Debtor warrants and agrees that:

4.1 Ownership. Debtor is the owner of Collateral free of all liens, encumbrances and security interests, except PCA's security interest and the following exceptions, if any:

4.2 Records. Debtor shall keep and maintain permanent records of all material information relating to the acquisition, maintenance, identification and disposition of all Collateral, in a form acceptable to PCA. PCA shall have the right to examine and copy such records at any reasonable time and place. Debtor's records are kept at Debtor's residence. Debtor shall not remove any of the Collateral or Debtor's records of accounts from the state of Debtor's present residence.

4.3 Address and Location. Debtor's residence (registered or main office if Debtor is a corporation or partnership) is at the address to the left of Debtor's signature. If all Collateral is not at such address, its location is:

______

4.4 Change of Address. Debtor shall immediately advise PCA in writing of any change in Debtor's address, the location of Collateral, and of any changes in the location of Debtor's records described in Section 4.2 of this Agreement.

THIS AGREEMENT INCLUDES ALL THE PROVISIONS ON THE REVERSE SIDE. DEBTOR ACKNOWLEDGES RECEIPT OF AN EXACT COPY OF THIS AGREEMENT.

Dated: ______, 19__ ______ (Debtor)

Address: ______ [See Section 4.3] * ______

County: ______ ______ (Debtor)

* ______

*Type or Print Name Signed Above

SPECIMEN

PCA 449 Revised 11/78

ORIGINAL PCA COPY

5. COLLECTIONS

5.1 **Verification and Notification.** PCA may verify accounts constituting Collateral in any manner and Debtor shall assist PCA in so doing. PCA may at any time and Debtor shall, upon request of PCA, notify the account debtors to make payment directly to PCA and PCA may enforce collection of, settle, compromise, extend or renew the indebtedness of such account debtors. Unless account debtors are otherwise notified, Debtor, as agent of PCA, shall make collections on the accounts.

5.2 **Deposit with PCA.** When required by PCA, all proceeds of Collateral received by Debtor shall be held by Debtor upon an express trust for PCA, shall not be commingled with any other funds or property of Debtor and shall be turned over to PCA in precisely the form received (but endorsed by Debtor, if necessary for collection) not later than the third business day following the date of receipt. All proceeds of Collateral received by PCA directly or from Debtor shall be applied against the Obligations in such order and at such time as PCA shall determine.

6. ADDITIONAL PROVISIONS.

6.1 **Maintenance of Collateral.** Debtor shall: care for the Collateral and not permit its value to be impaired; keep it free from all liens, encumbrances and security interests (other than those created or expressly permitted by this Agreement); defend it against all claims and legal proceedings by persons other than PCA; pay and discharge when due all taxes, license fees, levies and other charges upon it; not permit it to become a fixture or an accession to other goods except as specifically authorized in writing by PCA; and not permit it to be used in violation of any applicable law, regulation or policy of insurance. Loss of or damage to the Collateral shall not release Debtor from any of the Obligations.

6.2 **Insurance.** Debtor shall keep the Collateral and PCA's interest in it insured under policies with such provisions, for such coverages, in such amounts and by such insurers as shall be satisfactory to PCA fom time to time, and shall furnish evidence of such insurance satisfactory to PCA and at the request of PCA shall have PCA specifically named in an appropriate loss payable clause endorsed on such insurance policy. Debtor assigns (and directs any insurer to pay) to PCA the proceeds of all such insurance and any premium refund and authorizes PCA to endorse in the name of Debtor any instrument for such proceeds or refunds and, at the option of PCA, to apply such proceeds and refunds to any unpaid balance of the Obligations, whether or not due, and/or to restoration of the Collateral, returning any excess to Debtor. PCA is authorized, in the name of Debtor or otherwise, to make, adjust and settle claims under any credit insurance financed by PCA or any insurance on the Collateral, or cancel the same after the occurrence of an event of default.

6.3 **Inspection of Collateral.** PCA is authorized to examine the Collateral wherever located at any reasonable time or times; and Debtor shall assist PCA in making any such inspection.

6.4 **Maintenance of Security Interest.** To the extent permitted by law, Debtor shall pay all expenses and, upon request, take any action reasonably deemed advisable by PCA to preserve the Collateral or to establish, determine priority of, perfect, continue perfected, terminate or enforce PCA's interest in it or rights under this Agreement.

6.5 **Authority of PCA to Perform for Debtor.** If Debtor fails to perform any of Debtor's duties set forth in this Agreement or in any evidence of or document relating to the Obligations, PCA is authorized, in Debtor's name or otherwise, to take any such action including without limitation signing Debtor's name or paying any amount so required (including the payment of any insurance premium, tax, lien, or other charge or cost for the protection or preservation of the Collateral) and the cost shall be one of the Obligations secured by this Agreement and shall be payable by Debtor upon demand with interest at the current loan rate of PCA from the date of payment by PCA.

6.6 **Default.** The occurrence of any of the following events shall constitute a default by Debtor:

A. Nonperformance. If Debtor fails to pay when due the principal or interest due on any of the Obligations, or if Debtor fails to perform, or rectify the breach of any warranty or other undertaking by Debtor in this Agreement or in any evidence of or other document relating to the Obligations;

B. Unauthorized Disposition of Collateral. If Debtor disposes of Collateral and such disposition is not expressly permitted by PCA under this Agreement;

C. Inability to Perform. If Debtor or a surety for any of the Obligations dies or ceases to exist; or if the Debtor shall admit in writing the inability to pay its debts, or shall have made a general assignment for the benefit of creditors, or shall have been adjudicated bankrupt, or shall have filed a voluntary petition in bankruptcy or for reorganization or to effect a plan or other arrangement with creditors, or shall have filed an answer to creditor's petition or other petition filed against it (admitting the material allegations thereof) for an adjudication of bankruptcy or for reorganization; or if a petition in bankruptcy or for reorganization or to effect a plan or other arrangement with creditors shall be instituted against the Debtor and the petition shall remain undismissed for a period of sixty (60) days; or if Debtor shall have applied for or consented to the appointment of a receiver, or trustee, or custodian for any of its property or assets, or such a receiver or trustee or custodian or similar officer shall be appointed without the application or consent of Debtor and such appointment shall continue undischarged for a period of sixty (60) days;

D. Misrepresentation. If any warranty or representation made to induce PCA to extend credit to Debtor, under this Agreement or otherwise, is false in any material respect when made;
or

E. Insecurity. If any other event occurs which causes PCA, in good faith, to deem itself insecure.

6.7 **PCA's Rights and Remedies Upon Default.** If default occurs, then all of the Obligations of Debtor shall, at the option of PCA and without any notice or demand, become immediately payable and PCA shall have all rights and remedies for default provided by the Uniform Commercial Code, as well as any other applicable law and as provided in any evidence of or other document relating to the Obligations. With respect to such rights and remedies on default the following shall apply when permitted by applicable law:

A. Repossession. PCA may take possession of the Collateral without notice or hearing, which Debtor waives;

B. Assembling Collateral. PCA may require Debtor to assemble the Collateral and to make it available to PCA at any convenient place designated by PCA;

C. Notice of Disposition. Written notice, when required by law, sent to any address of Debtor shown on the first page of this Agreement or to any new address given by Debtor to PCA as required herein, at least 10 calendar days (counting the day of sending) before the date of a proposed disposition of the Collateral is reasonable notice;

D. Expenses and Application of Proceeds. Debtor shall reimburse PCA for any expense incurred by PCA in protecting or enforcing its rights under this Agreement, including, to the extent not prohibited by law, reasonable attorneys' fees and legal expenses and all expenses of taking possession, holding, preparing for disposition, and disposing of the Collateral. After deduction of such expenses, PCA may apply the proceeds of disposition to the Obligations in such order and amounts as it elects;
and

E. Application. PCA may apply the proceeds of Debtor's PCA stock and participation certificates to the Obligations in such order and at such times as PCA shall determine.

PCA may waive any default without waiving any other subsequent or prior default by Debtor.

6.8 **Non-Liability of PCA.** PCA has no duty to protect, insure or realize upon the Collateral. Debtor releases PCA from any liability for any act or omission relating to the Obligations, the Collateral or this Agreement, except PCA's willful misconduct.

6.9 **PCA Stock.** Debtor shall acquire and maintain PCA stock or participation certificates in the amount required by the Farm Credit Act of 1971 and the PCA By-Laws from time to time.

6.10 **Wisconsin Performance Deposit.** If Debtor has a right to redeem any Collateral under Section 425.208, Wisconsin Statutes, and Debtor exercises that right, the performance deposit tendered by Debtor shall not bear interest while held by PCA.

6.11 **Persons Bound.** The Obligations hereunder of all Debtors under this Agreement are joint and several. This Agreement benefits PCA, its successors and assigns, and binds the Debtor(s) and their respective heirs, personal representatives, successors and assigns.

6.12 **Agency.** Unless and until PCA is prospectively notified in writing by Debtor to the contrary, PCA may rely upon the following:

A. In the event Debtors are two or more individuals, the act or signature of any one of them shall bind all hereunder.

B. In the event Debtor is a partnership, each partner is fully authorized to act for the partnership in all matters governed by this Agreement.

C. In the event Debtor is a corporation, each officer is fully authorized individually to act for and bind the corporation in all matters governed by this Agreement.

6.13 **Interpretation.** The validity, construction and enforcement of this Agreement are governed by the laws of the state in which Debtor has its principal business. All terms not otherwise defined have the meanings assigned to them by the Uniform Commercial Code.

USDA-FmHA
Form FmHA 449 34
(Rev. 2-88)
Type of Loan: ______________
Applicable 7 C.F.R. Part 1980
Subpart ______________

LOAN NOTE GUARANTEE

	State
	County
	Date of Note
Borrower	FmHA Loan Identification Number
Lender	Lender's IRS ID Tax Number
Lender's Address	Principal Amount of Loan $

The guaranteed portion of the loan is $ ______________ which is ______________ (______________ %)

percent of loan principal. The principal amount of loan is evidenced by ______________ note(s) (includes bonds as appropriate) described below. The guaranteed portion of each note is indicated below. This instrument is attached to note ______________ in the face amount of $ ______________ and is number ______________ of ______________.

LENDER'S IDENTIFYING NUMBER	*FACE AMOUNT*	*PERCENT OF TOTAL FACE AMOUNT*	*AMOUNT GUARANTEED*
	$	%	$
TOTAL	$ ______________	100%	$ ______________

In consideration of the making of the subject loan by the above named Lender. the United States of America, acting through the Farmers Home Administration of the United States Department of Agriculture (herein called "FmHA"), pursuant to the Consolidated Farm and Rural Development Act (7 U.S.C. 1921 et. seq.), the Emergency Livestock Credit Act of 1974 (7 U.S.C. note preceding 1961, P.L. 93-357 as amended), the Emergency Agricultural Credit Adjustment Act of 1978 (7 U.S.C. note preceding 1921, P.L. 95-334), or Title V of the Housing Act of 1949 (42 U.S.C. 1471 et. seq.) does hereby agree that in accordance with and subject to the conditions and requirements herein, it will pay to:

A. Any Holder 100 percent of any loss sustained by such Holder on the guaranteed portion and on interest due (including any loan subsidy) on such portion.

B. The Lender the lesser of 1. or 2. below:

1. Any loss sustained by such Lender on the guaranteed portion including:
   a. Principal and interest indebtedness as evidenced by said note(s) or by assumption agreement(s), and
   b. Any loan subsidy due and owing, and
   c. Principal and interest indebtedness on secured protective advances for protection and preservation of collateral made with FmHA's authorization, including but not limited to, advances for taxes, annual assessments, any ground rents, and hazard or flood insurance premiums affecting the collateral, or

2. The guaranteed principal advanced to or assumed by the Borrower under said note(s) or assumption agreement(s) and any interest due (including any loan subsidy) thereon.

If FmHA conducts the liquidation of the loan, loss occasioned to a Lender by accruing interest (including any loan subsidy) after the date FmHA accepts responsibility for liquidation will not be covered by this Loan Note Guarantee. If Lender conducts the liquidation of the loan, accruing interest (including any loan subsidy) shall be covered by this Loan Note Guarantee to date of final settlement when the Lender conducts the liquidation expeditiously in accordance with the liquidation plan approved by FmHA.

Definition of Holder.

The Holder is the person or organization other than the Lender who holds all or part of the guaranteed portion of the loan with no servicing responsibilities. Holders are prohibited from obtaining any part(s) of the guaranteed portion of the loan with proceeds from any obligation, the interest on which is excludable from income, under Section 103 of the Internal Revenue Code of 1954, as amended (IRC). When the Lender assigns a part(s) of the guaranteed loan to an assignee, the assignee becomes a Holder only when Form FmHA 449-36, "Assignment Guarantee Agreement," is used.

Definition of Lender.

The Lender is the person or organization making and servicing the loan which is guaranteed under the provisions of the applicable Subpart 7 CFR of Part 1980. The Lender is also the party requesting a loan guarantee.

U.S. GOVERNMENT PRINTING OFFICE: 1988-554-052/60014-FmHA-88 *Position 2* FmHA 449-34 (Rev. 2-88)

Document 21-2. (*continued*)

CONDITIONS OF GUARANTEE

1. Loan Servicing.

Lender will be responsible for servicing the entire loan, and Lender will remain mortgagee and/or secured party of record not withstanding the fact that another party may hold a portion of the loan. When multiple notes are used to evidence a loan, Lender will structure repayments as provided in the loan agreement. In the case of Farm Ownership, Soil and Water, or Operating Loans, the Lender agrees that if liquidation of the account becomes imminent, the Lender will consider the Borrower for an Interest Rate Buy-down under Exhibit C of Subpart B of 7 CFR, Part 1980, and request a determination of the Borrower's eligibility by FmHA. The Lender may not initiate foreclosure action on the loan until 60 days after a determination has been made with respect to the eligibility of the Borrower to participate in the Interest Rate Buydown Program.

2. Priorities.

The entire loan will be secured by the same security with equal lien priority for the guaranteed and unguaranteed portions of the loan. The unguaranteed portion of the loan will not be paid first nor given any preference or priority over the guaranteed portion.

3. Full Faith and Credit.

The Loan Note Guarantee constitutes an obligation supported by the full faith and credit of the United States and is incontestable except for fraud or misrepresentation of which Lender or any Holder has actual knowledge at the time it became such Lender or Holder or which Lender or any Holder participates in or condones. If the note to which this is attached or relates provides for payment of interest on interest, then this Loan Note Guarantee is void. In addition, the Loan Note Guarantee will be unenforceable by Lender to the extent any loss is occasioned by the violation of usury laws, negligent servicing, or failure to obtain the required security regardless of the time at which FmHA acquires knowledge of the foregoing. Any losses occasioned will be unenforceable to the extent that loan funds are used for purposes other than those specifically approved by FmHA in its Conditional Commitment for Guarantee. Negligent servicing is defined as the failure to perform those services which a reasonably prudent lender would perform in servicing its own portfolio of loans that are not guaranteed. The term includes not only the concept of a failure to act but also not acting in a timely manner or acting in a manner contrary to the manner in which a reasonably prudent lender would act up to the time of loan maturity or until a final loss is paid.

4. Rights and Liabilities.

The guarantee and right to require purchase will be directly enforceable by Holder notwithstanding any fraud or misrepresentation by Lender or any unenforceability of this Loan Note Guarantee by Lender. Nothing contained herein will constitute any waiver by FmHA of any rights it possesses against the Lender. Lender will be liable for and will promptly pay to FmHA any payment made by FmHA to Holder which if such Lender had held the guaranteed portion of the loan, FmHA would not be required to make.

5. Payments.

Lender will receive all payments of principal, or interest, and any loan subsidy on account of the entire loan and will promptly remit to Holder(s) its pro rata share thereof determined according to its respective interest in the loan, less only Lender's servicing fee.

6. Protective Advances.

Protective advances made by Lender pursuant to the regulations will be guaranteed against a percentage of loss to the same extent as provided in this Loan Note Guarantee notwithstanding the guaranteed portion of the loan that is held by another.

7. Repurchase by Lender.

The Lender has the option to repurchase the unpaid guaranteed portion of the loan from the Holder(s) within 30 days of written demand by the Holder(s) when: (a) the borrower is in default not less than 60 days on principal or interest due on the loan or (b) the Lender has failed to remit to the Holder(s) its pro rata share of any payment made by the borrower or any loan subsidy within 30 days of its receipt thereof. The repurchase by the Lender will be for an amount equal to the unpaid guaranteed portion of principal and accrued interest (including any loan subsidy) less the Lender's servicing fee. The Loan Note Guarantee will not cover the note interest to the Holder on the guaranteed loan(s) accruing after 90 days from the date of the demand letter to the Lender requesting the repurchase. Holder(s) will concurrently send a copy of demand to FmHA. The Lender will accept an assignment without recourse from the Holder(s) upon repurchase. The Lender is encouraged to repurchase the loan to facilitate the accounting for funds, resolve the problem, and to permit the borrower to cure the default, where reasonable. The Lender will notify the Holder(s) and FmHA of its decision.

8. FmHA Purchase.

If Lender does not repurchase as provided by paragraph 7 hereof, FmHA will purchase from Holder the unpaid principal balance of the guaranteed portion together with accrued interest (including any loan subsidy) to date of repurchase less Lender's servicing fee, within thirty (30) days after written demand to FmHA from Holder. The Loan Note Guarantee will not cover the note interest to the Holder on the guaranteed loan(s) accruing after 90 days from the date of the original demand letter of the Holder to the Lender requesting the repurchase. Such demand will include a copy of the written demand made upon the Lender. The Holder(s) or its duly authorized agent will also include evidence of its right to require payment from FmHA. Such evidence will consist of either the original of the Loan Note Guarantee properly endorsed to FmHA or the original of the Assignment Guarantee Agreement properly assigned to FmHA without recourse including all rights, title, and interest in the loan. FmHA will be subrogated to all rights of Holder(s). The Holder(s) will include in its demand the amount due including unpaid principal, unpaid interest (including any loan subsidy) to date of demand and interest (including any loan subsidy) subsequently accruing from date of demand to proposed payment date. Unless otherwise agreed to by FmHA, such proposed payment will not be later than 30 days from the date of demand.

The FmHA will promptly notify the Lender of its receipt of the Holder(s)'s demand for payment. The Lender will promptly provide the FmHA with the information necessary for FmHA determination of the appropriate amount due the Holder(s). Any discrepancy between the amount claimed by the Holder(s) and the information submitted by the Lender must be resolved before payment will be approved. FmHA will notify both parties who must resolve the conflict before payment by FmHA will be approved. Such conflict will suspend the running of the 30 day payment requirement. Upon receipt of the appropriate information, FmHA will review the demand and submit it to the State Director for verification. After reviewing the demand the State Director will transmit the request to the FmHA Finance Office for issuance of the appropriate check. Upon issuance, the Finance Office will notify the office servicing the borrower and State Director and remit the check(s) to the Holder(s).

9. Lender's Obligations.

Lender consents to the purchase by FmHA and agrees to furnish on request by FmHA a current statement certified by an appropriate authorized officer of the Lender of the unpaid principal and interest then owed by Borrowers on the loan and the amount including any loan subsidy then owed to any Holder(s). Lender agrees that any purchase by FmHA does not change, alter or modify any of the Lender's obligations to FmHA arising from said loan or guarantee nor does it waive any of FmHA's rights against Lender, and that FmHA will have the right to set-off against Lender all rights inuring to FmHA as the Holder of this instrument against FmHA's obligation to Lender under the Loan Note Guarantee.

10. Repurchase by Lender for Servicing.

If, in the opinion of the Lender, repurchase of the guaranteed portion of the loan is necessary to adequately service the loan, the Holder will sell the portion of the loan to the Lender for an amount equal to the unpaid principal and interest (including any loan subsidy) on such portion less Lender's servicing fee. The Loan Note Guarantee will not cover the note interest to the Holder on the guaranteed loans accruing after 90 days from the date of the demand letter of the Lender or FmHA to the Holder(s) requesting the Holder(s) to tender their guaranteed portion(s).

a. The Lender will not repurchase from the Holder(s) for arbitrage purposes or other purposes to further its own financial gain.

b. Any repurchase will only be made after the Lender obtains FmHA written approval.

c. If the Lender does not repurchase the portion from the Holder(s), FmHA at its option may purchase such guaranteed portions for servicing purposes.

11. Custody of Unguaranteed Portion.

The Lender may retain, or sell the unguaranteed portion of the loan only through participation. Participation, as used in this instrument, means the sale of an interest in the loan wherein the Lender retains the note, collateral securing the note, and all responsibility for loan servicing and liquidation.

12. When Guarantee Terminates.

This Loan Note Guarantee will terminate automatically (a) upon full payment of the guaranteed loan; or (b) upon full payment of any loss obligation hereunder; or (c) upon written notice from the Lender to FmHA that the guarantee will terminate 30 days after the date of notice provided the Lender holds all of the guaranteed portion and the Loan Note Guarantee(s) are returned to be cancelled by FmHA.

13. Settlement.

The amount due under this instrument will be determined and paid as provided in the applicable Subpart of Part 1980 of Title 7 CFR in effect on the date of this instrument.

14. Loan Subsidy.

*In addition to the interest rate of the note attached hereto, FmHA will pay a loan subsidy of ________ percent per year. Payments will be made annually.

15. Notices.

All notice and actions will be initiated through the FmHA ________

for ________ (State) with mailing address at the date of this instrument:

____

____

UNITED STATES OF AMERICA
Farmers Home Administration

By: ________

Title: ________

SPECIMEN

____
(Date)

Assumption Agreement by ________ dated ________, 19__

Assumption Agreement by ________ dated ________, 19__

**If not applicable delete paragraph prior to execution of this instrument.*

U.S. GOVERNMENT PRINTING OFFICE: 1988-554-052/60014-FmHA-88 *Position 2* FmHA 449-34 (Rev. 2-88)

PART II
GLOSSARY

Acceleration — the act of declaring all installments of an installment obligation due. [In the event of a **default** under the **loan agreement** or the **security agreement,** a secured lender usually has the right to declare all obligations due immediately. This power to accelerate the debt of the borrower is essential to the secured party, who otherwise would have to wait until the maturity date under a term loan or until each of the installment dates under an installment loan before proceeding against the collateral.]

Acceptance corporation — a **finance company**.

Account — right to payment, for the sale of goods or for services, not evidenced by **paper**.

Account debtor — the obligor on **paper** or an **account** that is assigned to a lender. [When a **dealer** discounts a **retail installment sales contract** to a lender, the consumer buyer is the account debtor. When a seller grants a lender a security interest in the seller's **accounts,** the seller's buyers, the obligors on the account (usually for sold goods or services) are the account debtors.]

Add-on interest — interest computed at a nominal rate multiplied by the original principal balance without allowance for prior payments of principal, often expressed in language such as the following: "$4 per hundred per year." (*Compare* **annual percentage rate, discount interest rate.**)

After-acquired property — collateral acquired by the borrower after the date of the **security agreement**. [Under the **floating lien** of many security agreements, especially those involving **inventory** and **accounts,** the creditor's **security interest** will attach to the property owned by the debtor at the time he enters into the agreement and to property acquired thereafter. Such security agreements may describe the collateral as property "now owned or hereafter acquired."]

Annual Percentage Rate — nominal rate of interest expressed in a percentage computed on the basis of an annual rate applied to a declining principal balance to yield the finance charge. (*Compare* **add-on interest, discount interest rate.**)

APR (*See* **annual percentage rate.**)

Asset-backed issue — issuance of obligations that are secured by assets such as consumer related receivables. (*See* **asset securitization.**)

Asset-based lender — traditionally, a **finance company** or other lender that takes a **security interest** in property of the borrower and relies on that interest as an important potential source for repayment of the loan.

Asset securitization — practice of selling, usually in the **secondary market,** obligations that are secured by collateral, such as mortgages, automobile loans, or credit-card receivables.

Assignee — in secured lending, the transferee of **paper** or **accounts** from a **dealer** or other seller. (*See also* **assignment, assignor.**)

Assignment — in secured lending, the transfer of **paper** or **accounts** to a lender by a **dealer** or other seller. (*See also* **assignee, assignor.**)

Assignor — in secured lending, the seller who transfers **paper** or **accounts** to a lender. (*See also* **assignee, assignment.**)

Attachment — the secured lending concept that describes the creation of the **security interest.** [Under the Uniform Commercial Code, a security interest is not enforceable until it has attached. The Code spells out the requirements for attachment and the rules for determining the time that attachment occurs — a time that may be crucial for determining the priorities of conflicting claims to the same collateral.]

Auditor — in secured lending, independent accountant that audits, reviews, or compiles information concerning the financial status of the borrower and, in the first case, certifies its financial statements.

Balloon — the last payment in a loan that is repayable in a number of installments, the last of which is relatively large and equals the unpaid principal balance. [A balloon loan is in essence an agreement to finance the obligation for a short term only with the understanding that the borrower will have to refinance the obligation by "financing the balloon" at the time the balloon payment comes due.] (*Compare* **bullet note.**)

Bank holding company — business corporation that owns one or more commercial banks.

Basis point — a measure of interest, being .01 percent, that is, one percent of one percent.

Blanket security interest — **security interest** that covers all or virtually all of the borrower's personal property. [Often, especially in the financing of middle-market operations, secured lenders insist that they have a security interest in all of the borrower's property. They take a blanket security interest and make a **broad form filing** that effectively ties up all of the borrower's assets. The lender's insistence on that arrangement may strike some as overreaching, but the request for a blanket security interest is usually reasonable and efficient. In loans that are marginal, that is, where the value of the collateral is questionable, the credit history of the borrower is relatively weak, or the borrower's business prospects are problematic, lenders may be unwilling to make a loan unless they know that, in the event of default, they will have unfettered control of the borrower's assets. For example, in the event of default, the secured creditor will want the option of selling the borrower's business as a going concern or piecemeal, whichever in the judgment of the lender will yield the greater return. If the lender does not have a security interest in some of the borrower's assets, or if another secured party has a prior position with respect to some of those assets, the lender loses one of its options or must negotiate with a third party (the other lender) before acting. By respecting the right of a borrower to grant blanket security interests, commercial law increases the marginal borrower's prospects of obtaining financing.] (*See also* **working capital lending.**)

Bond — evidence of an obligation to pay interest and principal, sometimes secured by assets of the obligor, say, real estate (in the case of a corporate bond) or by designated revenues (in the case of a municipal bond).

Book entry security — a certificateless security, that is, a corporate or governmental obligation that is evidenced not by the issuance of a bond, debenture, or promissory note but by a "book entry," i.e., by a computer record reflected in a paper record that is only a receipt or acknowledgment and is not itself the obligation. [Book entry obligations are not reified in a piece of paper.]

Broad form filing — **financing statement** that covers all or virtually all of the borrower's personal property. [In order to protect its **blanket security interest,** a secured lender must file a financing statement that covers all of the borrower's assets. The broad form filing is such a financing statement and merits enforcement as an indispensable part of the blanket-security-interest arrangement.]

Bullet note — **promissory note** with principal and interest payable in a single designated payment at maturity. (*See also* **balloon.**)

C & I Loans — commercial and industrial loans.

Cashier — an officer of a bank, the analogue to the business corporation's secretary.

Chapter 7 — describing a form of bankruptcy relief for a debtor under which the debtor's debts are discharged and its assets liquidated.

Chapter 11 — describing a form of bankruptcy relief under which the debtor is reorganized with a view to keeping the debtor in business. [Chapter 11 proceedings are often unsuccessful, in which case, the debtor is liquidated under Chapter 7.]

Chattel lease — security agreement disguised as a lease. (*See also* **lease purchase agreement.**)

Chattel mortgage — type of security agreement under pre-Code chattel mortgage statutes, the term sometimes still being used to refer to a security agreement covering goods.

Chattel paper — usually, a **retail installment sales contract** or a lease.

Claim — in secured transactions, an assertion of a property interest. [The notion is akin to the claims that prospectors make in Hollywood westerns and is essentially different from the claims that law students deal with in tort courses. The common law fashioned a number of writs or causes of action by which a claimant could proceed. Among them are trover, replevin, and (most important) conversion. Conversion is an important commercial remedy. It is, of course, a strict liability cause of action, and it is a claim. When commercial law decides that a purchaser in good faith cuts off claims, it prevents these claimants from asserting such claims against the purchaser.]

Closing — the exchange of documents and funds that are the subject of the **loan agreement.**

Collateral — the goods or other property in which the borrower conveys an interest to the lender under the **security agreement**.

Collection agency — firm that specializes in the collection of delinquent **accounts**.

Collections — in secured lending, the activity of pursuing delinquent **accounts**.

Commercial — pertaining to business as opposed to **consumer** activity.

Commercial bank — traditionally, a "full service" financial institution that accepts time and demand deposits, provides payments and collections services, a trust department, and commercial and consumer loans. (*Compare* **thrift** and **finance company**.)

Commercial loan officer — bank employee that has authority to make commercial loans, that obtains that authority from the **loan committee** in some cases, and that attends to the loan documentation, the loan closing, and, in some cases, workouts and loan collections.

Commercial paper — short-term (not usually longer than nine months) **promissory notes** issued by large borrowers who borrow directly from investors rather than from financial intermediaries.

Comptroller of the Currency — primary regulator of nationally chartered banks (national associations).

Consumer — pertaining to sales or loans for personal, family, or household purposes.

Consumer goods — goods used primarily for personal, family, or household purposes. [Goods that lay people may consider consumer goods may not be such for purposes of secured lending. A refrigerator, for example, in the kitchen of a homemaker would be consumer goods. The same refrigerator in the kitchen of a restaurant would be **equipment** and on the showroom floor of an appliance store would be **inventory**.]

Consumer paper — generic term for paper usually generated by **dealer** sales to consumers, now generally confined to **retail installment sales contracts** and leases.

Contract right — in secured lending, a concept (rendered archaic by the 1972 revisions to Article 9) referring to the right to payment under a contract for the sale of goods or services before the seller has performed. [Contract rights are now generally **accounts** or **general intangibles.**]

Correspondent bank — bank with which another bank maintains a relationship that may involve corresponding account balances, referral of business, loan participations, and the routing of checks for collection. [**Nonmember banks,** for example, will use a correspondent that is a member of the **Federal Reserve System** when the nonmember bank wishes to avail itself of the System's collection apparatus.]

Cosigner — one who signs a borrower's obligation in order to provide a guaranty to the lender or credit seller. [The term comes from negotiable-instruments practices, which sometimes involved a requirement that an obligor, say, the maker of a note, obtain a cosignature by a second obligor, usually someone of strong credit repute.]

Credit bureau — firm that maintains credit records on individuals and firms in a given area and discloses credit information for a fee.

Credit department — that part of a financial institution that analyzes the credit information relating to a potential borrower.

Credit enhancement — said of any effort to increase the acceptability of an obligation in the market. [This is an old concept that merchants and bankers seem to rediscover from time to time. In the earliest of commercial transactions, we read of the merchant who could not obtain credit because his paper was not marketable. A trader whose credit repute in seventeenth-century London, for example, was not widely known and favorable could not get other traders and merchants to accept his promissory notes and drafts. The new entrant was forced to take measures to increase the attractiveness of his paper. He did so generally by obtaining the signature on the paper or elsewhere of someone who enjoyed the requisite financial reputation. He could obtain the signature of an accommodation party (a cosigner), or he could ask the drawee of his draft to announce in advance his willingness to accept (a virtual acceptance or letter of credit). These practices of enhancing the paper of the borrower exist today. The consumer borrower frequently obtains a cosigner in order to render his promissory note acceptable to a lender. Corporations that borrow directly from investors through the financial markets often use **standby letters** of credit, credit insurance, or **securitization** to enhance the marketability of their **commercial paper** or **bonds.**]

Credit reporting agency — a form of **credit bureau**. [In addition to credit bureaus, there are commercial credit reporting agencies, such as Dun & Bradstreet and TRW that secure credit information from firms and their creditors and make it available to subscribers.]

Cross-collateralization — using collateral to secure more than one advance, so that, for example, collateral granted to the lender to secure an **inventory** loan will also secure loans made against **accounts**.

Dealer — any retailer that sells on credit and generates **accounts** or **paper**.

Dealer reserve — in **consumer-paper** borrowing **with recourse,** lenders frequently insist that a small percentage of the sums collected on the paper be allocated to a reserve account that will be used to satisfy consumer defaults.

Debenture — unsecured, interest-bearing obligation of business or municipal corporation.

Default — failure on the part of an obligor to fulfill a legal obligation. [It is essential that a **loan agreement** spell out with some specificity those events that constitute default and give the lender the right to **accelerate** the debt and to proceed against the collateral. As a general rule, the default provision is broadly drawn, so that breach of any **warranty** or **negative covenant** or default on any other obligation to the lender will give the lender such rights.]

Deposit liability — obligation of financial institution to repay sums to depositors. [In banking, deposits are liabilities of the bank; loans are the bank's assets.]

Deregulation — generally, the process of breaking down the legal barriers that distinguish the banking, **thrift,** insurance, securities, and other components of the financial services industry.

Direct loan — loan made directly to a borrower, rather than indirectly by acquiring his obligation from a **dealer**. [In dealer financing, the lender can buy the **consumer paper** from the dealer and indirectly lend money to the consumer, or the dealer can send the consumer to the lender to arrange a **direct loan**.]

Discount interest rate — rate of interest applied to principal balance of loan and collected at the time of the loan closing. In a $100 loan for one year at 4 percent discount, the lender will disburse $96 to the borrower and collect $100 in loan payments. (*Compare* **add-on interest,** and **annual percentage rate.**)

Discrete lending — lending against a single asset or single group of assets, usually with the idea that the asset is sufficient to serve as collateral for the debt. [While some lenders engage in **working capital** lending and take security interests in **revolving collateral,** there are still many instances of lending against a discrete item of collateral. Banks and **equipment** leasing companies, for example, often enter into finance leases under which the only security they have in the event of the lessee's default is the leased equipment. Similarly, lenders or credit sellers that take purchase-money security interests from consumer borrowers are engaging in discrete lending.] (*See also* **floating lien, revolving collateral, working capital loan.**)

Disintermediation — movement of funds out of **banks** and **thrifts** (**financial intermediaries**), an economic phenomenon that occurs when it is more efficient for investors to lend directly to borrowers rather than to utilize financial intermediaries such as banks and thrifts.

Document — in secured lending, (1) a **document of title** or (2) papers executed in connection with the documentation of the loan, e.g., **promissory note, security agreement, financing statement.**

Document of title — generally, a bill of lading or other transport document or a warehouse receipt.

Dragnet clause — provision in a **security agreement** that defines broadly the obligations secured by the debtor's property, so that, for example, the property secures not only the advance made at the time of the loan transaction in question but also any future advances and all other obligations due from the debtor to the **secured party**.

Equipment — usually, office or production machinery but also any goods that do not fall within the Article 9 definitions of **consumer goods, farm products,** and **inventory**.

Estoppel certificate — certificate by a creditor often used in connection with a loan closing certifying the amount of the debt as of the date and time of the closing.

Factor — in secured lending, a lender that takes **accounts** from a **dealer,** manufacturer, or other seller and collects them.

Factoring — the practice of conveying an interest in accounts receivable to a party that collects the accounts.

Farm credit system — broad structure of federally subsidized organizations that generally service the agricultural sector of the economy and that includes the **Farmers Home Administration** and **Production Credit Associations**.

Farmers Home Administration — federal agency that insures loans made to farmers and that acquires the loans in the event of the borrower's default. **FmHA** loan officers, who are located in rural areas, are often intimately involved in loan decisions and loan documentation.

Farm products — usually, crops and livestock but, in both cases, only as long as they are in the possession of a person engaged in farming operations, i.e., in the possession of a farmer.

Federal Deposit Insurance Corporation — primary federal regulator of state **nonmember banks,** insurer of bank and thrift deposits, and receiver for failed banks and thrifts.

Federal Housing Finance Board — supervisory authority for the system of **Federal Home Loan Banks**.

Federal Reserve Bank — privately owned (by member financial institutions) bank that comprises one of the twelve federal reserve banks in the **Federal Reserve System**. [**Member Financial Institutions** utilize the federal reserve banks as sources of credit and as the primary vehicle for the presentation and collection of checks and wire transfers of funds.]

Federal Reserve Board — the central bank of the United States, that is, the federal agency charged with the primary role in shaping and effecting government economic policy, and the federal regulator of **bank holding companies** and state chartered banks that are members of the **Federal Reserve System**.

Federal Reserve System — system of 12 regional **federal reserve banks** and their 24 branches, governed by the **Federal Reserve Board.**

Field warehousing — form of secured **inventory** loan under which an independent warehouse in the field, i.e., at the borrower's place of business, takes control of the inventory and permits sales of it only upon authorization from the lender.

Finance charge — cost of credit, including interest, points, and other charges. (*See also* **time price differential.**)

Finance company — traditionally, an **asset-based lender** that would make loans that were, for whatever reason, unattractive to **commercial banks.** [Finance companies pioneered **consumer** lending by taking **consumer paper** from **dealers.** Large manufacturers have their own finance companies, such as Chrysler Credit Corp. and General Motors Acceptance Co., which may be larger, in terms of assets, than the largest U.S. commercial banks. Finance companies have been strong in **equipment** and lease financing as well. At the present time, many finance companies are subsidiaries of **bank holding companies.**]

Financial intermediary — an institution that accepts funds from investors and lends them to borrowers. [Bank depositors have invested their money in checking accounts and various kinds of time deposit accounts. When the bank lends those funds to borrowers, it is engaging in the classic role of financial intermediation. **Thrifts,** brokers, **investment bankers,** and insurance companies are also financial intermediaries.]

Financing buyer — buyer that prepays a portion of the purchase price in order to enable the seller to obtain raw materials or supplies necessary to fill the buyer's order. [Sometimes the prepaying buyer takes a **security interest** in the **goods,** at other times it argues that it has an interest in the goods as a buyer of them.]

Financing statement — short document identifying the "debtor" and the **"secured party"** and the collateral in which the debtor has granted or plans to grant the **security interest.** [The secured party files the **financing statement** in the office of a public official.]

Fixed rate — rate of interest that does not vary throughout the life of the loan.

Fixture — a vague concept: Personal property, not including building materials incorporated into a building on the real estate, that has become, by virtue of its affixation to the real estate or real estate improvements, under the real estate law of the jurisdiction, part of the real estate.

Floating lien — **security interest** that extends to **after-acquired property.** [When lenders make **working capital loans** or finance **inventory** or **accounts,** it is inconvenient for them to lend against discrete items of collateral. It is more efficient to permit the borrower to grant such lenders a security interest in collateral "now owned or hereafter acquired." Such a security interest "floats," that is, it attaches to new inventory or **equipment,** as those items are acquired by the borrower and to new accounts as the sale of goods and services gives rise to them.]

Forbearance agreement — agreement between lender and borrower executed in the event of borrower default under which (1) lender agrees not to exercise default rights and (2) borrower undertakes to comply with certain duties in addition to those set out in the **loan agreement.**

Foreclosure — **secured party's** exercise of its rights under the **security agreement** to resort to the borrower's property. [When a secured party forecloses on the collateral to satisfy the borrower's debt, it may take the collateral in satisfaction of the debt or may sell it.]

General intangible — any property interest that does not fall into one of the specific categories of property described in Article 9 (**goods, accounts, chattel paper, documents, instruments,** or money), *e.g.*, an inheritance, sums due under a copyright license, the right to have stock issue under a preincorporation agreement.

Goods — in secured lending, personal property, which falls into one of four classifications: **consumer goods, equipment, farm products,** and **inventory.**

Grace period — period during which a defaulting party may cure the **default.** [In the event of default under a **loan agreement** or a **security agreement,** the borrower would like to have a period of time during which the lender may not proceed against the collateral or otherwise enforce its **security interest** while the borrower attempts to cure the default. For example, most loan agreements stipulate that it is an event of default for a borrower to be late with an interest payment. If, because of a misdirected wire transfer or an error in mail delivery, an interest payment is late, a healthy borrower will be able to cure the default promptly and will want the right to do so. Many creditors will refuse to grant any grace period in the loan agreement or security agreement. In the event of default, delay is problematic for the secured party. A grace period of one week or even two days may seriously imperil the value of collateral. Such creditors are not without constraint, since the duty of good faith in the enforcement of the agreement stands as a general barrier to overreaching creditor conduct.]

Indirect loan — loan made by a financial institution not directly to the borrower but by acquiring the borrower's obligation from a **dealer.** [In dealer financing, when the dealer refers the customer to the lender to arrange the financing, the loan is direct; when the dealer sells on credit and then discounts or finances the **paper** with a lender, the lender has made an indirect loan to the purchaser.]

Installment loan department — in a **commercial bank,** the department that generally deals with **consumer** as opposed to **commercial** loans.

Installment loan officer — bank employee who makes direct **consumer** loans and who makes **indirect loans** to consumers by acquiring **consumer paper** from **dealers.**

Instrument — usually, a negotiable instrument or a certificated security.

Inventory — **goods** held for sale or lease, including work in process, raw materials, and supplies (such as stationery or gasoline for trucks) used up in the course of the affairs of an enterprise, but not **equipment.**

Investment banker — **financial intermediary** that, among other activity, (1) underwrites the issuance of securities, that is, agrees to purchase securities from the issuer and resell them, itself or through brokers, to the investing public or (2) arranges the sale of securities by the issuer to others.

Lease purchase agreement — **security agreement** disguised as a lease.

Lender liability — a broad term encompassing various causes of action against lenders all of which assume that the lender's unconscionable, bad-faith, or capricious conduct injured the borrower. [Such claims generally arise when the lender refuses to renew a loan or to extend additional credit.]

Leverage — the act of using relatively small equity to generate credit. [There is a measure of tension in any loan situation. The lender tends to seek as much security as it can get, while the borrower will usually try to limit the amount of security it must transfer. In **discrete loan** situations, the first step the lender takes in securing itself is often an insistence that the borrower commit itself significantly to the transaction by investing money of its own. Real estate development lenders, for example, will only lend 80 or 90 percent of the development cost and will insist that the developers come up with the balance as the developer's equity. Similarly, purchase money sellers often require buyers on credit to make a downpayment. These efforts on the part of the lender reflect lender concern that the loan be properly secured. The correlative concern on the part of the borrower is to keep as much property for itself. The borrower's success in that regard is his ability to leverage a small amount of investment or a small amount of collateral into a significant loan. A relatively large loan secured by relatively little collateral or investment is highly leveraged.]

LIBOR (London Interbank Offered Rate) — nominal interest rate large international banks charge each other.

Lien — an interest in property, usually taken, voluntarily or involuntarily, to secure an obligation. [There are a number of property interests in the Uniform Commercial Code: **title,** the **special property,** the **security interest,** and the lien. The last, is a catch-all category that generally includes any property interest that does not fit one of the other categories. Generally, liens, in the catchall sense of the UCC, are possessory, that is, the lienor loses the lien absent possession by itself or its agent. Government liens, such as tax liens, are not possessory. In the broadest sense, of course, liens can be possessory or nonpossessory.] (*See also* **lien creditor.**)

Lien creditor — (1) an unsecured creditor of the borrower who has obtained a judicial **lien** on the borrower's property; (2) under the Bankruptcy Code, the trustee in bankruptcy who has the rights of a hypothetical lien creditor. [By statute or common law writ, creditors may obtain a lien on their debtor's property either simply by obtaining a judgment or, in most states, by causing a state official to seize the property. Such seizure is sometimes symbolic. The sheriff, for example, may simply disable a piece of equipment or lock it up after marking it as having been subjected to levy.]

Line of credit — authorized amount of borrowing against which a borrower may draw, as its cash needs dictate.

Liquidity — measure of ease with which an asset can be converted into cash. [Money-market instruments such as bankers' acceptances or short-term corporate debt instruments with a recognized market are highly liquid. Long-term subordinated debt is not.]

Loan agreement — the entire agreement between the borrower and the lender. [The **security agreement** may be part of the loan agreement.]

Loan committee — committee of bank loan officers and, sometimes, board members that evaluate those loan applications that exceed the loan authority of individual loan officers.

Loan documentation — all of the documents that a loan officer obtains in connection with a loan, including the **promissory note,** loan agreement, security agreement, financing statement, corporate certificate of good standing, corporate resolutions, opinions of counsel, etc.

Loans & discounts — in banking, the department that generally deals with **commercial,** as opposed to **consumer** loans. (*See also* **installment loan department.**)

Long term — said of an obligation whose term exceeds one year. (*Compare* **short term.**)

Mass market — the **consumer** portion of a **commercial bank's** customer base that uses the bank for check writing and personal loan services.

Member financial institution — a financial institution that is a member of the **Federal Reserve System.** [Prior to deregulation, only banks could be members of the system.]

Merchant banker — financial institution, common in foreign countries but unusual in the United States, that engages in some **investment banking** functions and also assists, through counselling and negotiation, and participates in merchant activity such as the buying and selling of commodities, especially in international transactions.

Middle market — that portion of the loan market consisting of medium-sized businesses that presently account for a considerable portion of a commercial bank's secured-loan portfolio.

National association — **commercial bank** chartered under the National Bank Act, a federal statute.

National Credit Union Administration — federal agency that insures and regulates credit unions.

Negative covenants — promises in an agreement by a party under which it undertakes not to engage in certain activity or not to permit certain acts to be taken. [In a **loan agreement,** the creditor will usually secure from the borrower a series of negative covenants, that is, a series of representations that events have not occurred. For example, a lender may insist that the borrower covenant that there are no **liens** on any of its property or that certain financial ratios (e.g., total liabilities to net worth) will not exceed a specified figure. Such covenants survive the loan closing, and if the borrower suffers any of the events to occur, he is in **default** and subject to having the secured debt **accelerated.**]

Negative pledge — promise in the nature of a **negative covenant** under which a borrower agrees not to grant a security interest in designated property or in any of its property to anyone other than the lender in question. [In many **loan agreements** and **security agreements,** secured creditors exact a promise from the borrower not to grant security interests in the same collateral or, perhaps, in any of the debtor's property, without the creditor's prior approval. These negative pledges are not instances of creditor overreaching but are reasonable attempts to put the creditor in a position to obtain the best price for the collateral in the event of the borrower's **default.**]

New value — value given not by virtue of taking a security interest on account of an antecedent debt. [Sometimes, secured lending law distinguishes "value," a concept defined in the Uniform Commercial Code, from "new value." "Value" includes taking security for a preexisting debt. "New value" is anything that would be value under the Code definition other than taking collateral as security for a prior debt.]

Nonmember bank — bank that is not a member of the **Federal Reserve System** and that must use a **Member Financial Institution** in order to avail itself of the benefits of the system.

Office of Thrift Supervision — primary federal regulator of **thrifts.**

Operations officer — employee of a **commercial bank** that is concerned with payments and collections, investment of bank funds, and other administrative duties. (*Compare* **commercial loan officer.**)

Overdraft financing — practice, common in some foreign jurisdictions, of generating loans by honoring overdrafts.

Paper — traditionally, any debt obligation evidenced by a piece of paper, such as a **promissory note,** draft, or installment contract. (*Compare* **account.**)

Participation — a share of a loan. [A lead bank, that is, one that has made a loan commitment to a borrower, may be unwilling or unable to fund the entire loan and will ask other banks to participate in the loan by taking a piece of it and of the collateral that secures it. The lead bank then "participates" out portions of the loan to the participating banks.]

Perfection — the act of rendering a **security interest** superior to any subsequently acquired judicial **lien.** [Once a security interest has become effective, that is, once it has **attached,** third parties need to know whether they are bound by the conveyance. Article 9 of the Uniform Commercial Code uses the concept of perfection to determine the answer to that question. Generally, perfection occurs when there is notice of some kind that will warn the diligent third party that the owner does not hold an uncluttered interest in the property. Article 9 fashions generally clear rules for determining whether perfection has occurred, when it has occurred, and the three means by which it can occur: filing, taking possession, and doing nothing. Perfection rules are also critical in determining the **priority** of competing **secured parties.**]

Pledge — **security interest** effected and perfected by the **secured party's** possession of the collateral. [The oldest secured transaction is probably the pledge. In ancient times, obligors pledged their servants, their first son, or even their royalty as security for repayment of debts or performance of other obligations. Transfer of possession is the essence of the pledge, but the law quickly realized that the transfer can be to the agent of the secured party as well as to the secured party himself. In fact, sometimes the property will be in the possession of a third party, and mere notice to that party or acknowledgment by him will serve to effect the pledge. Two conclusions are inescapable from the premise that the pledge involves a transfer of possession from the owner to the secured party. First, only tangible property can be the subject of a pledge. Second, any retransfer of possession to the owner or other activity that gives the owner power to control the possession of the property destroys the pledge.]

Points — interest charge expressed in terms of a percentage of the loan amount (one percentage point being one point), usually collected at the time of the loan closing.

Prime rate — traditionally, the interest rate banks charge their best customers; now, an indicator against which interest charges on loans are often pegged.

Priority — the concept that one party's rights in property rank ahead of that of another. [In order to avoid uncertainty, the Uniform Commercial Code establishes a wide-ranging scheme for determining the relative positions of each party claiming an interest in collateral. These priority rules often depend on the concepts of **attachment** and **perfection.**]

Private banking — a marketing concept under which a bank reserves special attention (e.g., service at a desk rather than at a teller window) to upper-income customers.

Production credit association — part of the **farm credit system,** a lender that makes federally subsidized loans directly to farmers.

Promissory note — instrument (usually negotiable) signed by the borrower and evidencing a repayment obligation. [If the note is negotiable, the repayment obligation is embodied in the instrument, with significant consequences.]

Purchase — to take by voluntary transfer. [A voluntary conveyance, including transfers by way of sale, gift, or **pledge,** is a transfer by purchase, and one who takes by such voluntary conveyance is a purchaser. Involuntary conveyances, such as transfers by operation of law under judicial **lien** statutes or the Bankruptcy Code are not transfers by way of purchase, and lien creditors and the trustee in bankruptcy are generally not purchasers.]

Purchase-money lender — lender that advances funds to a buyer who uses them to acquire property.

Purchase-money security interest — a **security interest** that secures credit granted in order to enable the borrower to purchase the collateral. [There are two kinds of purchase-money loans: (1) that made by the seller of goods and (2) that made by a lender who advances funds that the borrower uses to purchase the goods.]

Purchase-money seller — seller on credit.

Real-bills banking doctrine — an economic theory that banks will create the proper amount of money only when they make commercial loans that are short-term, self-liquidating loans against goods with market value sufficient to liquidate the loan. [Under this theory of banking, when a loan officer made a loan it was **discrete** and often related to a single piece of equipment or, more probably, a specified quantity of inventory covered by a single sales transaction or a specified document of title. This theory rejects the idea that a borrower's ability to repay a loan depends as much on its value as a going concern with a strong history of good credit and earnings than on the value of a discrete item of collateral. Under the old theory, loans were short term, and the inability of the borrower to repay the loan at maturity was a serious default. Modern bank theorists take a different view. They often see collateral as a secondary source of protection against **default** and see the general financial and managerial competence of the borrower as the primary source of loan repayment. Under this view, borrowers may substitute collateral and may repay their loans, not according to a preordained schedule, but in accordance with cash flow.]

Regulation Z — Federal Reserve Board regulation promulgated under the Consumer Credit Protection Act chiefly governing the advertising and documentation of **consumer** lending.

Repo — (1) a **repurchase agreement** or (2) **equipment** or other property that a lender has repossessed from a defaulting borrower.

Repurchase agreement — a **security agreement** disguised as a sale with an obligation on the part of the seller to repurchase the property that is the subject of the sale, often referred to as a "repo" agreement.

Retail installment sales contract — credit sales contract between a retailer and a **consumer** calling for payment of the purchase price in installments and reserving a **security interest** in the retailer.

Revolving collateral — **collateral (inventory** or **accounts)** that the borrower sells and acquires, usually without the interference of the lender. [When a lender's security agreement includes an **after-acquired property** clause, the collateral revolves. As original inventory, for example, is sold by the borrower, it passes into the hands of buyers free of the security interest, so that the lender loses that collateral. At the same time, the borrower is acquiring new inventory, and the security interest **attaches** to that inventory as soon as the borrower acquires an interest in it.]

Rule of 78s — formula for computing interest rebate to installment borrower who prepays a loan. [The formula assumes that the installments are in equal amounts and that interest payments comprise an increasingly smaller portion of each subsequent payment as the loan balance is reduced by prior payments. Based on those assumptions and using the sum-of-the-digits method, the earned interest in the first month of a one-year loan is $^{12}/_{78}$ths, in the second month $^{11}/_{78}$ths, etc. The sum of the digits 1 through 12 is 78; hence the name of the rule.]

Sale as secured transaction — **secured transaction** disguised as a sale. [Traditionally, many **dealers** entered into transactions with **factors** or other finance companies transferring their **accounts** or **chattel paper** to the factor for **collection**. Those transfers were either **with recourse** or **without recourse.** Sometimes in the with-recourse transfer and most of the time in the without-recourse transfer, the parties considered the transaction a sale of the accounts or chattel paper. At other times, they thought of it as a secured transaction. In order to avoid confusion, the Uniform Commercial Code generally treats transfers of accounts and chattel paper as secured transactions, without distinguishing those that the parties consider a sale from those that the parties consider to be a loan secured by a transfer of collateral.]

Savings and loan association — a **thrift** that traditionally financed home mortgage loans and real estate development.

Savings bank — a **thrift** institution. [The statutes of some states use this term to refer to institutions that are called **savings and loan associations** in most states.]

Secondary market — market in which originating institution sells or wholesales its loans in order to obtain fresh funds to meet borrowers' needs. [For example, **commercial banks** that generate significant volume of automobile loans may sell those loans in the secondary market at rates that yield a profit to the bank and provide the bank with funds.]

Secured party — creditor that has taken a **security interest** in property of the debtor. [A creditor that extends credit on security is referred to under the **security agreement** as the secured party. Secured creditors are often **asset-based lenders** but may also take security in the form of **side guaranties** or **standby letters of credit**. (*Compare* **unsecured creditor**.)

Securitized — said of obligations (**bonds** or notes) that are backed by collateral. [Some large borrowers, including **commercial banks** and **finance companies,** have begun the practice of marketing their loans by packaging them and using them as collateral for bonds or other debt obligations. This practice of, for example, securing paper with automobile loans or **consumer** credit card receivables is called "securitization" or "collateralization."]

Security agreement — a contract of conveyance whereby the borrower grants to the lender an interest in personal property to secure performance of the borrower's obligation to the lender.

Security interest —

(1) (Article 9) — the interest in personal property granted a lender by a borrower in the **security agreement,** an interest created

by agreement, rather than by operation of law. [It is often important in secured lending situations to distinguish the security interest, an Article 9 concept, from other property interests that creditors of the owner may assert. Usually, those other interests will be **liens** of some sort, but they may also be a **seller's right to reclaim** or a nonvoluntary security interest under Article 2 of the Uniform Commercial Code. In secured transactions under Article 9, the security interest is one voluntarily created by a conveyancing agreement called a **security agreement**. The distinguishing features of the security interest are (1) that it results from a voluntary conveyance by the owner (or, in some situations, of the buyer's agreement that the seller retain a security interest) and (2) that it secures a debt, that is, the creditor's interest in the property is limited by the amount of the debt. The "voluntary" feature distinguishes the security interest from most liens, which arise by operation of law. The second limitation distinguishes the security interest from the seller's right to reclaim or **seller's lien,** which gives the seller the right to take the property and keep it. The secured creditor cannot take the property and keep it but must account to the owner for any excess in the value of the property over the amount of the debt.]

(2) (Article 2) — **security interest** created by operation of law, namely, by operation of provisions in Article 2 of the Uniform Commercial Code. [In two instances, Article 2 creates a statutory right in a party, which the Code calls a security interest. This security interest differs from the Article 9 security interest in that it arises not by voluntary conveyance but by operation of law, but it resembles the Article 9 security interest in that it secures an obligation of the owner of the goods and does not give the secured party the right to keep the goods without an accounting. A seller who ships goods under reservation has a security interest in the goods by operation of law to secure payment of the contract price. A buyer who holds nonconforming goods has a security interest in them to secure costs it incurs in connection with the caring of them.]

Seller's lien — **lien** arising (1) by virtue of the seller's right to stop delivery if buyer fails to pay the agreed upon consideration or (2) under provisions of Article 2 codifying common law, antifraud rules that give a defrauded seller rights in goods that it has delivered to the buyer. [In some cases of buyer breach at common law, sellers who had already granted rights in goods to the buyer could reassert an interest in the goods to the point of selling them to a third party free of the buyer's interest. By giving the seller the right to resell in that fashion, the seller's lien became a powerful interest, since it permitted a seller to retain any sales proceeds over and above the loss the seller incurred by virtue of the buyer's breach and relieved the seller of the proof burden of showing that it did not receive a benefit from the buyer's breach.]

Seller's right to reclaim — a manifestation of the **seller's lien,** in this case, arising by virtue of the buyer's fraud. [In some cases involving buyer fraud, the seller's lien extended to goods it had delivered to the buyer. Since liens are almost always possessory in nature, this right is extraordinary and reflects the depth of commercial law's animus toward fraud.]

Short term — said of an obligation whose term is less than one year. (*Compare* **long term.**)

Side guaranty — guaranty given by a party under an agreement that is separate from the primary obligation, i.e., the **promissory note** that the principal debtor executes. [In order to avoid the traps and pitfalls of surety law, most sophisticated lenders no longer take **cosignatures** from parties that lend their credit as security for the debt of the principal borrower but take a side guaranty agreement with strong provisions that generally close the escape routes developed by surety law and that courts have generally, though less often now than formerly, enforce.]

Signature loan — usually, a small unsecured loan made to a borrower with a good credit record upon the signing of a **promissory note.**

Small loan company — **consumer** lender that traditionally made short-term loans in small amounts and took **security interests** in consumer **goods** or in the form of wage assignments. [Now heavily regulated, small loan companies are not an important source of secured credit.]

Standby letter of credit — letter of credit used to secure a repayment or other obligation, often used to enhance the obligation, be it a **promissory note, commercial paper,** or **bond.** [Commercial letters of credit, which arise in sales transactions, provide the model for the standby credit. In the commercial-credit transaction, the seller draws a draft on the credit issuer to obtain payment for goods sold. In the standby credit transaction, the holder of an obligation, such as a promissory note, draws on the standby in the event the obligor **defaults** on the note.]

Subordinating — the act of moving a **claim** or interest from a higher **priority** to a lower one. [At times it may be convenient for a creditor to subordinate itself to the position of a creditor over which it enjoys priority. If for example, a **working capital** lender has taken a **security interest** in all of its borrower's **accounts** and has perfected properly, there is no way that the borrower can grant a second creditor a security interest in those accounts prior to that of the first creditor. The first creditor, however, may not have any objections to the arrangement that the borrower and the second creditor propose and may be content to have the new creditor pump fresh funds into the borrower's enterprise. A small manufacturer may have $400,000 in overdue accounts. Its bank, a working capital lender, advances funds from time to time and feels secure by virtue of its **blanket security interest,** which covers valuable **inventory, equipment,** and current accounts. The manufacturer has located an accounts receivable financer that is familiar with the industry and with these particular accounts and that is willing to "buy" the overdue accounts for $.50 on the dollar but is willing to do so only if it can take them free of the bank's security interest. By entering into a subordination agreement, the bank and the accounts-receivable financer can agree on their relative positions with respect to the overdue accounts.]

Subordination agreement — agreement whereby one creditor agrees to surrender its **priority** over another creditor.

Syndication — selling of obligations to investors. [For a variety of reasons, among them a desire to keep its loan portfolio diversified and to comply with lending limits, a bank will sometimes refuse to make a large loan by itself and will ask other banks to join it in a syndicate. Syndicated loans may take a number of forms. The simplest is the loan **participation** arrangement.]

Thrift — financial institution, such as a savings bank, savings and loan institution, or credit union, that traditionally was limited by law to the making of mortgage loans and some **consumer** loans and that could pay a higher interest rate on deposits than that allowed to **commercial banks,** but that could not accept demand deposits, i.e., checking accounts. [With the advent of deregulation, federal law abolished the deposit interest rate disparity, permitted thrifts to accept demand deposits, and expanded the legitimate area of thrift loan activity to encompass commercial loans. Deregulation notwithstanding, thrifts have largely continued to dominate in the area of real estate lending and have not generally competed in the commercial lending area, though they have offered checking accounts or their equivalent (e.g., share draft or negotiable order of withdrawal accounts). At the present time, thrifts are not subject to regulation by the traditional bank regulators (**FDIC, Comptroller of the Currency,** and **Federal**

Reserve Board) but are part of a different scheme of regulation under the aegis of the **Office of Thrift Supervision** or the **National Credit Union Administration**. The latter insures the deposits of **credit unions**. The **Federal Deposit Insurance Corporation** currently insures the deposits of **savings banks** and **savings and loan associations**.]

Time price differential — difference between the cash price and the credit price. [At times when usury laws prevented the charging of competitive rates for consumer borrowing, merchants invented the concept of the time price differential, which some courts took to be something other than interest and, therefore, not subject to the usury limitation.]

Unsecured creditor — (1) sellers or lenders that extend credit to a buyer or borrower without taking a **security interest** in any property, i.e., nonasset-based lenders; (2) sellers or lenders who attempt to take an interest in the property of the buyer or borrower but who fail to follow the rules of the Uniform Commercial Code and who therefore fail to effect an enforceable security interest. [The former category of creditor probably comprises the single biggest source of short-term credit in the economy and consists of (1) open account sellers of merchandise and (2) public utilities. The creditor without security usually is a party that relies not on the assets of the borrower but on its credit history. Trade creditors, usually open account sellers, generally do not ask for collateral and do not rely on the buyer's assets but look to the buyer's history as a good credit risk. The unsecured creditor is the opposite of the **asset-based lender**. Unsecured parties often complain, after the fact, when assets are unavailable to satisfy their claims. The trustee in bankruptcy, who represents unsecured creditors in a debtor's bankruptcy, attempts to increase the pool of assets that are not subject to security interests in order to augment the bankruptcy dividend that will be paid the unsecured creditors. Unsecured commercial creditors who have not relied on the debtor's assets have convinced some commentators that their claim to those assets in bankruptcy is meritorious. There are some noncommercial creditors that are unsecured. These are mostly tort claimants, whose claims are usually covered by liability insurance.]

Variable rate — said of an interest rate that varies with some indicator, such as the **prime rate** or **LIBOR**. (*Compare* **fixed rate**.)

Warranties — in secured lending, representations by the borrower as to facts usually relating to its financial or legal status. [In a **loan agreement,** the lender will require the borrower to represent as true certain facts that are important to the efficacy of the agreement. A corporate borrower's loan agreement, for example, will include a warranty that all corporate actions necessary to authorize the borrowing have been taken and that the corporation is in good standing in all jurisdictions in which it is authorized to do business. In the event a representation proves to be untrue, the borrower will have breached a warranty, which, in turn, will be an event of **default** under the agreement and permit the lender to **accelerate** the debt and proceed against the collateral.]

With recourse — said of the transfer of **paper** or **accounts** under an agreement that requires the transferor to buy back any paper or account on which the **account debtor** defaults.

Without recourse — said of the transfer of **paper** or **accounts** under an agreement that does not require the transferor to buy back any paper or account on which the **account debtor** defaults.

Working capital lending — lending, usually in the **middle market,** for working capital needs. [With the demise of the **real-bills doctrine of banking,** lenders gradually realized the benefit of letting collateral turn over via the **floating lien** and of letting the borrower draw down on the line of credit to satisfy its credit needs and to pay against the debt balance as cash flow permitted. With some flexible limits, the working capital lender does not concern itself with the borrower's use of loan proceeds, and gives the borrower significant discretion in determining the time to draw against the line of credit and the time to pay off loan principal.]

PART II
TABLE OF DOCUMENTS

PART II
BIBLIOGRAPHY

Benton, D. & J. Douglas, Federal Banking Laws (1987).
Cudworth, E., Equipment Leasing Partnerships (1988).
English, R., Business Contract Forms (1984).
Fraas, Federal Assistance Programs for Farmers: An Outline for Lawyers, 3 Agricultural L.J. 405 (1981-1982).
Gart, A., Handbook of the Money and Capital Markets (1988).
Guild, I. & R. Harris, Forfaiting (1986).
Hamilton, R., Fundamentals of Modern Business (1989).
Hamilton, Securing Creditor Interests in Federal Farm Program Payments, 33 S. Dak. L. Rev. 1 (1988).
Harl, N., Agricultural Law (1986).
Henson, R., Secured Transactions (2d ed. 1979).
Malloy, M., The Corporate Law of Banks (1988).
Meyer, Agricultural Credit and the Uniform Commercial Code: A Need for a Change?, 34 Kan. L. Rev. 469 (1985).
Rasor & Wadley, The Secured Farm Creditor's Interest in Federal Price Supports: Policies and Priorities, 73 Ky. L.J. 595 (1985).
Rice, M., Asset Financing (1989).
Safran, Asset-Based Aircraft Operating Leases, 5 Banking & Fin. L. Rev. 71 (1989).
Sullivan, Changes in the Agricultural Credit Delivery System, Economic Rev. 12 (Jan./Feb. 1990).
Tomczyak, S., Corporate and Commercial Finance Agreements (1984).
U.S. Department of Commerce, A Guide to Financing Exports.
———, Official U.S. and International Financing Institutions (rev. ed. 1985).

PART III

PAYMENTS SYSTEMS

22

Introduction to Payments Systems

§22.1 MOVING MONEY

Payment is the transfer of money, often in execution of a contract for the sale of goods, investment securities, or services. In order to understand the payments system it is necessary to know, then, what money is.

For the purposes of this book, it is best to think of money as a medium that people are willing to accept for the goods, securities, or services that they sell. Sellers accept this medium because they know that they can use it to **purchase** goods, securities, and services from others, that is, they know that other sellers will accept the medium. Coins and federal reserve notes, the greenbacks we carry with us, are obviously such a medium. Less obvious is the fact that **bank** deposits are also money. They are money for the same reason that a dime is money: Sellers will accept them as payment.

Bank deposits are, in the legal metaphor, debts of **depository institutions** and credits of the depositor. When a bank's customer takes cash or a **check** to the bank for deposit, the bank accepts the deposit and becomes the customer's debtor. The customer has loaned the bank the amount of the deposit, usually at interest. The account balance, then, is the amount due from the bank to the customer. The methods that buyers and sellers use to transfer the money described above is the payments system, the subject of Part III.

§22.2 THE NEED FOR PAYMENTS SYSTEMS

In early commercial times, there was little need for a payments system. In the barter transaction, payment occurred through the exchange of goods. As soon, however, as merchants began using cash, a payments system became necessary. Cash attracts brigands and thieves and can become lost or destroyed. Thus, an Italian merchant who purchased tapestries in Belgium did not want to carry specie from his bank in Florence to the fair in Bruge. His medieval bankers developed a rather sophisticated system that made that dangerous and potentially expensive exercise unnecessary: They developed a payments system. Payments systems are as old as money.

Even in today's "cash" sale, such a system is necessary, since many cash sales are by check, and checks require a system for collecting the check proceeds. **Credit sales,** of course, may be satisfied by the payment of cash, but increasingly, cash plays a diminished role in all commercial activity, both "cash" and credit. Today the lines at the utility company payments window and the insurance and rent collector have largely disappeared. They are images from a bygone era.

Today, tenants, insureds, buyers on open account, and other debtors generally pay their creditors not with goods or cash but with deposit credit. The transfer of that credit from the one to the other occurs through the banking system. Although the debtor's credit may be with someone other than a commercial bank, such as a **thrift, credit union,** broker, investment banker, or insurance company, unless the **item** is "on us," the transfer of the credit to the account of the creditor in satisfaction of the debtor's obligation, in the vast majority of cases, will involve the banking system, for nonbank depository institutions usually avail themselves of the banking system when they transfer funds.

§22.3 CREATING MONEY TO MOVE

The deposits that are subject to transfer in this fast-paced system of payments are **demand deposits,** that is, they are funds available to the depositor on demand. The depositor need not wait a period of time after demand, as it must when it desires to withdraw funds on time-deposit. Demand deposits are those that function as cash and are the equivalent of money. These are the deposits economists include in their computation of the nation's money supply.

Banks, since they create deposits (with a bookkeeping or computer entry), create money. They do so subject to constraints imposed by the **Federal Reserve Board,** the nation's central bank, and by market forces. When a farmer asks his local commercial bank for a loan, the bank will grant that loan request only if it decides, after proper credit evaluation, that the farmer can repay the loan. If the farmer is creditworthy, the bank assumes a liability by "creating" a deposit in favor of the farmer. That liability arises by virtue of the bank's undertaking to honor the farmer's checks or withdrawal requests up to the amount of the deposit. At the same time, the bank adds the farmer's note to the asset side of its ledger, the note being his liability to satisfy the loan obligation. Most of the time, the farmer's duty to repay the loan is secured by collateral, e.g., crops, equipment, or livestock. In all events, the effect of the transaction is to increase the money supply, for the farmer will quickly begin to "use" his deposit by writing checks against it or otherwise transferring portions of it to pay taxing authorities, suppliers, feed companies, or his other creditors.

The farmer example illustrates the quainter features of the economy's payment activity. In addition to the 50 billion small collections and payments the system handles each year, are large-dollar payments generated by the securities and banking industries, the government, and by large corporate **payors.** The 50 billion checks **cleared** in the United States annually constitute a small fraction of the dollar transfers that are now effected by wire. **Wire transfers** in the United States exceed $1 trillion per day, the average transfer being in excess of $2 million. Many of these transfers have nothing to do with domestic sales of goods, securities, or services but are the concluding step in acquisitions, international lending, or commercial activity that originates in foreign jurisdictions.

When a German bank purchases eurobonds from a French securities dealer, for example, the parties may effect payment by transferring dollars between accounts at New York **correspondent** banks. **CHIPS,** a wire transfer system fashioned by money-center banks in New York, is designed to facilitate such transfers.

This Part deals with the various payments systems. It begins with the simplest transaction involving a check drawn by a customer on her account at one bank to pay a creditor who maintains an account at the same bank and ends with the international payments that might arise in the securities example between two European parties. In all cases, the problems are similar and the goals are the same — to provide quick, cheap, reliable transfers of funds. The process is at times complicated, is always challenging to the operations people involved, and is moderately fascinating to the nonbanker who watches machines and the human imagination make commercial life easier and safer in a fast-paced payments world.

23 Check Collections

§23.1 IN GENERAL

Although the growth in the use of checks is slowing, by 1990 the check-collection system in the United States will be handling about 52 billion checks per year. Some of those checks clear through a single bank, some through local **clearinghouses,** and some through the national check-collection system maintained by the **Federal Reserve Banks.** In addition, there are now private systems for clearing, though their future is somewhat clouded by recent changes in **funds availability** rules. This chapter discusses the single-bank collection of the "on-us" item, direct presentment, the local clearinghouse, and the federal reserve check-collection system.

Check clearing was originally a manual process, whereby a bank's clerks manually sorted checks drawn "on us" from those that were drawn on clearinghouse members and those that were **transit items,** i.e., checks that had to be mailed or otherwise forwarded to banks in distant communities. Today, **magnetic ink character recognition** (MICR) symbols permit reader-sorter machines to do that sorting and to read the amount of the check and the number of the account on which the check is drawn. Financial institutions preprint checks containing routing information, checking account number, and check number. Thus, when a bank customer receives his checks from the check printer, they are ready for the collection system except for the amount of the check, which amount the customer must enter when he writes the check. When a payee deposits a check, the depositary bank's data-entry clerks read the amount entered by the customer and encode it in MICR symbols on the item before they send it through the reader-sorter machines.

Document 23-1 is a typical check with a preprinted MICR line at the bottom. The first nine MICR symbols are routing and transit digits. The first two of those designate the **Federal Reserve District** in which the **drawee**-payor bank is located. The third digit indicates the proper place within the designated Federal Reserve District. A "1" for the third digit indicates the main office of the Federal Reserve Bank in that district. Any numeral other than a "1" indicates the federal reserve branch that serves the drawee bank. The fourth digit indicates the city (if a main office or branch is indicated) or **regional check processing center** to which the check should be routed. Digits five through eight are unique to the drawee-payor bank. The ninth is an algorithm that the system uses to check the digit regime and guard against counterfeit MICR symbols designed to misroute checks and delay notice of dishonor.

Note that Document 23-1 contains a fractional designation in the upper right-hand corner. The number in the numerator identifies the branch and bank of the customer. In the denominator, the figures indicate the proper federal reserve destination, i.e., whether main office or a branch of a Federal Reserve Bank or a federal reserve regional check processing center. The fractional figures are not machine readable. They are a safety net to permit manual handling of those checks whose MICR lines are accidentally mutilated or otherwise rendered unreadable.

§23.2 THE ON-US TRANSACTION

In the simplest payments system, a debtor seeks to transfer funds held at a depositary institution to a creditor who maintains an account at the same institution. If Smith owes Greengrocer $44, and if Smith and Greengrocer maintain accounts at First National Bank, Smith's payment to Greengrocer is uncomplicated.

First, Smith writes a check in favor of and delivers it to Greengrocer. Second, Greengrocer deposits the check at First National Bank. Immediately, the teller gives a provisional credit to Greengrocer's account. Next, First National's clerk encodes the check with MICR symbols in the amount

Figure 23-1. The On-Us Item

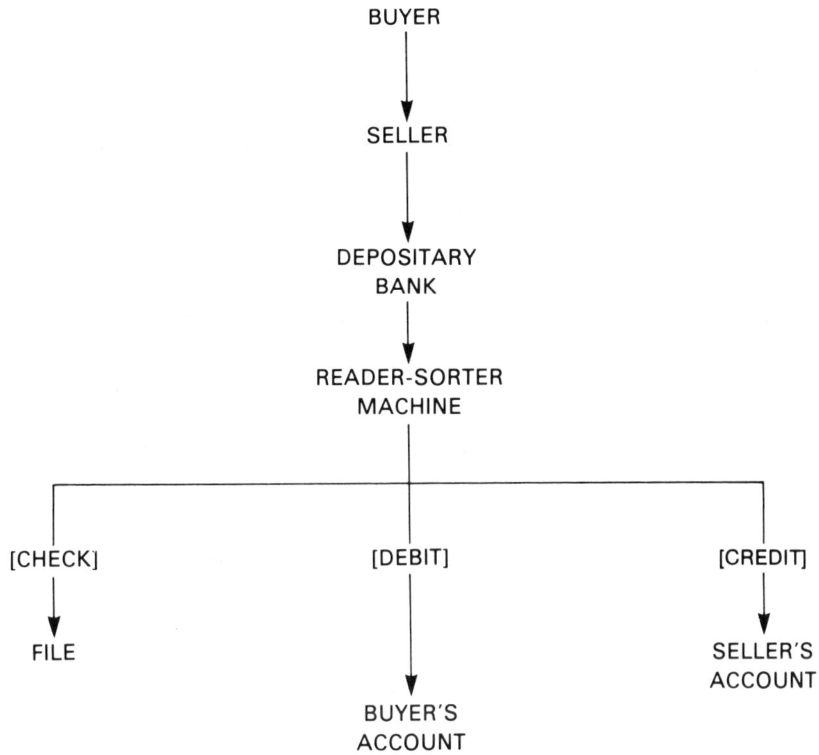

specified by Smith, in this case $44, and runs the check through First National's reader sorter machines.

The machines, having the capability of "reading" the MICR symbols, determine that the account to be charged is that of Smith and that the amount to be charged is $44. The machines then feed that information to First National's computer, which determines whether there are sufficient funds on deposit in Smith's account, and, if so, debits the account. Then the machines route the check to a holding file, where it resides until it is time to forward it to Smith with her periodic statement. Figure 23-1 illustrates the transaction.

§23.3 THE CLEARINGHOUSE

Only 23 percent of checks written in the U.S. are on-us items. Most of the time, Greengrocer, the seller-creditor, will not maintain an account at the bank where Smith, his buyer-debtor, maintains an account. In that event, Smith's payment of Greengrocer becomes more complicated.

In a city with two banks, Smith's bank, First National, and Greengrocer's bank, Second National, would probably maintain a correspondent relationship, that is, each bank would maintain an account with the other. Their corresponding balances would permit them to effect payment of Smith's check in a three-step payment process. When Greengrocer deposits his check at Second National, where he maintains his account, (1) Second will give him a provisional credit, that is, enter a credit of $44 to Greengrocer's account; (2) Second will then debit First's correspondent account in the same amount and will forward the check to First; (3) First will determine that the check is properly payable and will debit Smith's account.

Each day, there will be many checks deposited at First that are drawn on accounts at Second and many checks deposited at Second that are drawn on First. If at the end of the day the corresponding balances are in a state of **net** imbalance one bank will be overdrawn and will have to forward funds to the other or accept a loan from the other. Although there are not many communities with only two banks, there are collections that proceed in this fashion. In international transactions, for example, a foreign bank, say, an English bank, may maintain a dollar-denominated account with a domestic bank. The domestic bank may maintain a pound sterling account with the English bank. Each of these banks, as a depositor, may nominate the other to honor **drafts** to satisfy the depositor's debts. If a customer of the English bank owes dollars to an American concern, for example, he may pay that concern by asking the English bank to draw on its U.S. bank account or to authorize the U.S. concern to draw on that account. In the same way, the U.S. bank may pay pound sterling obligations of its customer through the English bank. Periodically, the banks must settle between themselves.

Similarly, the twelve Federal Reserve Banks, which play a critical role in the **Federal Reserve System's** check-collection service, must settle among themselves. At the end of any given day, one Federal Reserve Bank may be "overdrawn" with respect to another. The Federal Reserve Banks use the interdistrict settlement fund to settle at the end of each day. Section 23.4 discusses the federal reserve check-clearing system. Figure 23-2 illustrates the typical two-bank transaction.

In fact, most people do not live in a community with only two banks, and most local checks, that is, checks drawn on and deposited in banks located in the same community, are paid through an arrangement that dates from the early days of banking called the *clearinghouse.* A clearinghouse is an association of banks that maintain premises for the purpose of getting together to exchange checks or other items drawn on each other. In the classic clearinghouse arrangement, each participant prepares a batch of checks drawn on each other participant and presents the batch with a **cash letter** at the designated meeting time at the clearinghouse premises. Second National will include the Smith check deposited by Greengrocer in the batch Second prepares for the clearinghouse. The cash letter is a summary of the items presented, and the payor banks are concerned, at this point,

Figure 23-2. Local Presentation

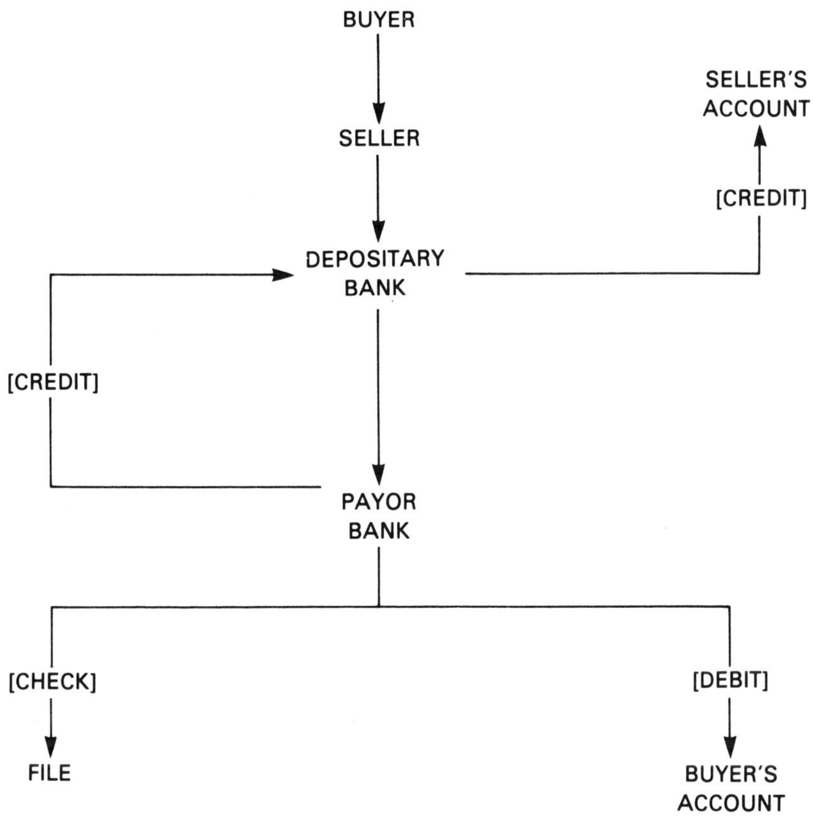

primarily with totals. When the banks submit those cash letters, the clearinghouse can net out all letters from all banks as against all banks, simply by **netting** each bank's position against the clearinghouse. The process yields a net position for each bank. If the net amount of draws on a bank exceeds the net amount of credits in favor of the bank, the bank owes the clearinghouse. If the net draws are less than the net credits, the clearinghouse owes the bank. The bank and the clearinghouse settle through the bank's clearing account, which the clearinghouse will credit or debit, as the case may be.

Members of the clearinghouse could maintain corresponding balances with one another. Under such an arrangement, each pair of banks would settle by making corresponding debits and credits to these mutual accounts. In a community with 20 banks, that arrangement would be complicated and expensive, since banks prefer to invest their money in relatively high-interest-earning loans or other investments than in corresponding balances that earn little or no interest. It is more efficient for the clearinghouse members to use the balances they are required to maintain by law at the local Federal Reserve Bank or federal reserve branch to effect settlements. In fact, the clearinghouse will probably be located on the premises of the Reserve Bank. At the end of the day, the Federal Reserve Bank will debit

Figure 23-3. The Clearinghouse

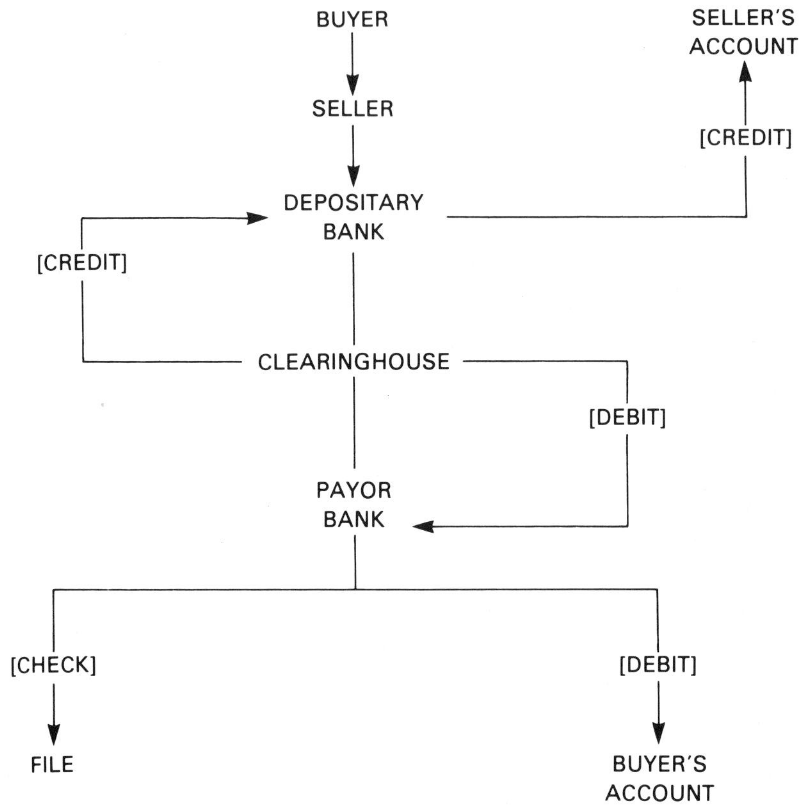

a net debtor bank's account and credit the accounts of its corresponding creditor banks. If, for example, at the end of the day, the cash letter amount that Second presented to First exceeds the cash letter amount First presented to Second, the Federal Reserve Bank will debit First's account and credit Second's in an amount equal to the difference. Under this arrangement, each clearinghouse member need maintain only a single account, that at the Federal Reserve Bank, an account, incidentally, that is available for short-term (usually overnight) loans to the extent that its balance exceeds the bank's reserve requirements. To the extent that a bank's reserves do not suffice to cover the bank's check-clearing volume, the Federal Reserve Bank will require the bank to deposit additional funds into a clearing account. Figure 23-3 illustrates the clearinghouse transaction.

§23.4 THE FEDERAL RESERVE CHECK-CLEARING SYSTEM

Since 1914, the Federal Reserve has provided check-clearing services, first to members of the Federal Reserve and now to all depositary institutions, that is, all institutions, including credit unions and savings institutions that maintain deposits at the Federal Reserve Banks. The system operates, in some respects, like a large clearinghouse, with the Federal Reserve Banks serving as members of the clearinghouse and their depositors playing the role of payors and payees. Access to the system must be through a "depositary institution," i.e., an institution maintaining a clearing account. Individuals cannot route checks directly to a Federal Reserve Bank or branch but must first deposit the check with a depositary institution or with a broker or other institution that maintains a correspondent relationship with a depositary institution.

Since 1972, the Federal Reserve System has had two components. The first involves clearing through the Federal Reserve Banks and their branches. There are 12 Federal Reserve Banks and 25 branches. Usually, a depositary institution will route checks to its local Federal Reserve Bank or branch. That bank or branch follows one of two courses. In the simpler case, the check is drawn on an institution that maintains an account at

Figure 23-4. Through the Federal Reserve

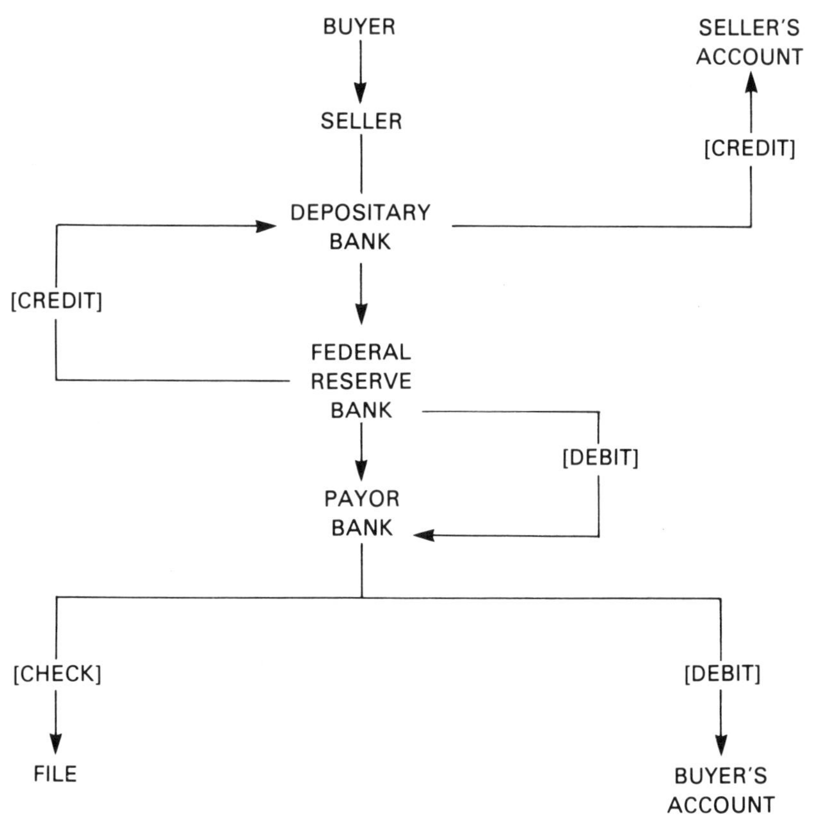

Figure 23-5. The Fed and Depository Institutions

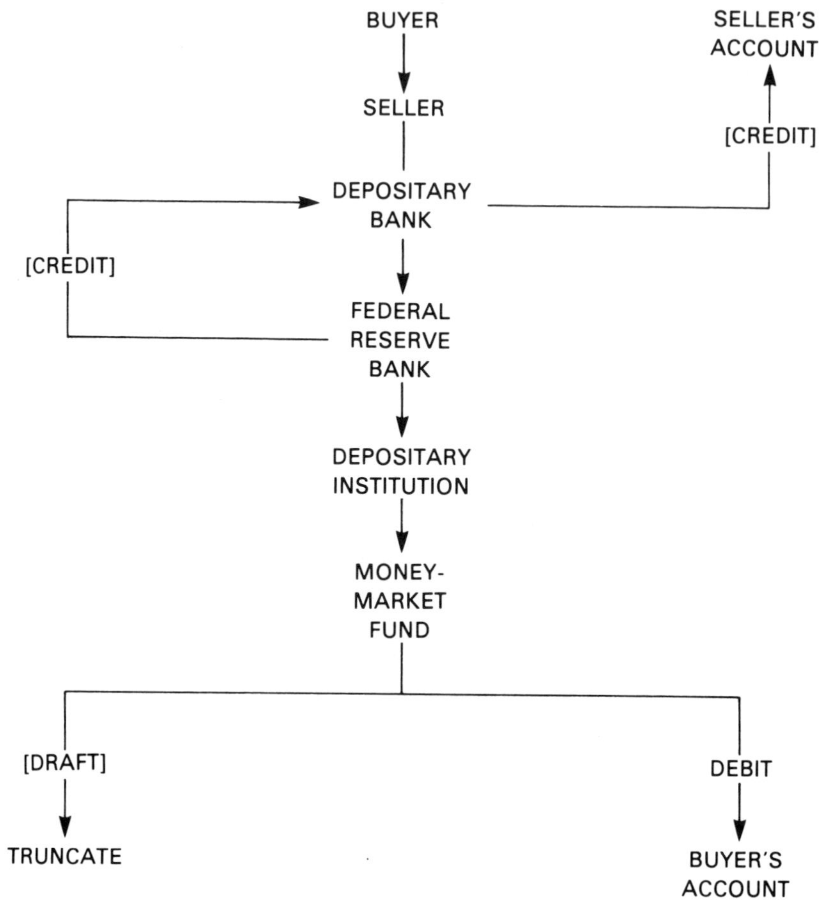

the same bank or branch. The bank or branch can clear that check by crediting the account of the **presenting bank** and debiting the account of the payor bank. In a typical case, Smith will maintain an account at First National Bank, and Greengrocer at Second National Bank, both banks being in the same Federal Reserve District and both being depositary institutions. Figure 23-4 illustrates the collection of the Smith check in such a transaction.

If one or both of the parties to a payment transaction maintains an account at an institution that does not maintain deposits at a Federal Reserve Bank, the transaction requires an additional step. Figure 23-5 illustrates the collection of the Smith check when Smith writes checks on a money-market account with a brokerage firm or other nondepositary institution.

In the more complicated case, the check is drawn on a depositary institution that is in the district of a different branch or bank. In that case, the Federal Reserve Bank or branch that first receives the check must

Figure 23-6. Interdistrict Settlement

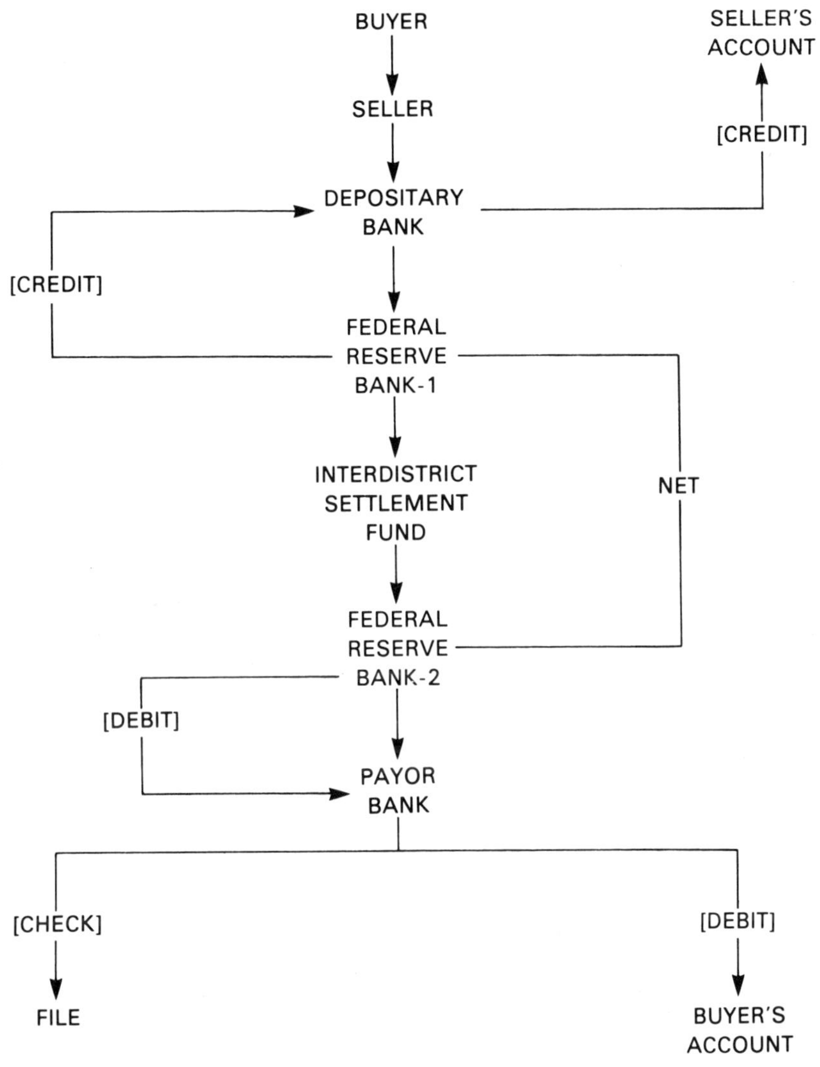

forward it to the other branch or bank. The two Federal Reserve Banks or branches then must settle between themselves. Figure 23-6 illustrates the clearing procedure when First National Bank and Second National Bank are in different districts.

Collection through the Federal Reserve Banks creates the phenomenon of **federal reserve float.** When the Federal Reserve Bank receives an item from the depositary bank, it credits that bank's account according to a federal reserve funds availability schedule. The Reserve Bank does not immediately charge the account of the drawee bank but delays that debit until the checks are delivered to the drawee bank. Because the funds availability schedule sometimes provides for credit to the account of the depositary bank prior to the time that the Federal Reserve Bank debits the account of the drawee-payor bank, there may be a period of time during which the accounts of both banks reflect the amount of a check. That phenomenon is federal reserve float. Until the Federal Reserve Board reformed the system, federal reserve float could aggregate as much as $4 billion in a given day — a significant windfall for the nation's private banks. The reforms have reduced federal reserve float by about 75 percent, and at the present time, the Federal Reserve System charges banks to the extent that they benefit from federal reserve float.

§23.5 REGIONAL CHECK-PROCESSING CENTERS

The second component of the federal reserve clearing system involves regional check-processing centers of which there are now eleven. Regional offices receive from banks in any district checks drawn on banks in the region served by the center. A bank in Sacramento that wants to hasten the collection of a check drawn on a New Jersey bank can avoid the step of depositing the check in the San Francisco Fed by forwarding the check directly to the regional check-processing center in Cranford, New Jersey. That center will give the Sacramento bank, which is a depositary institution, credit to its account at the San Francisco Fed. The processing center then collects the check's proceeds and does so more quickly than the San Francisco Fed would do.

§23.6 INTERDISTRICT SETTLEMENTS AND TRANSPORTATION

Transactions that cross Federal Reserve District lines are not so simple as the interbank transactions that occur once a day at the clearinghouse. The volume of interdistrict transactions among the banks includes many of the 16 billion checks that the system clears each day and of the 165,000 wire transfers that are effected on the average day by the more than 8,000 depositary institutions that use **Fedwire,** the Federal Reserve System's **electronic funds transfer** service. In order to deal with that volume, Federal Reserve Banks utilize an interdistrict settlement fund. That fund is essentially a computerized bookkeeping system that tracks interdistrict transactions and nets them out periodically. The Federal Reserve Banks then settle among themselves by wiring funds over Fedwire, which is explained in Chapter 25.

Interdistrict transportation of checks and drafts is not a problem with wire transfers, which consist of signals transported over telecommunications facilities linking the computers of the various Federal Reserve Banks and branches. Transfer of the more than 16 billion pieces of paper that clear through the Federal Reserve System each year involves considerable transport. The Federal Reserve System has developed an interdistrict transportation system (I.T.S.), which is a hub-and-spoke system. Presently, there are five hubs, one each in Atlanta, Chicago, Cleveland, Dallas, and New York. The system operates to consolidate transportation at the various hubs with collection and distribution along the "spokes," that is, in and out of the hubs to banks in a hub's region. "Inter-region" transport is limited to that between hubs.

§23.7 DIRECT PRESENTMENT

As the previous discussion explains, most of the time, when a depository bank receives an item drawn on a payor that is not a member of the clearinghouse, the bank will resort to the Federal Reserve System's check-collection apparatus. That decision rests in large measure on economics. The Federal Reserve's System is quick and inexpensive. There are times, however, when it makes economic sense for the depository bank to avoid the Federal Reserve's System and, in effect, to create an ad hoc system of its own. If, for example, a New York bank receives, periodically, large-dollar checks drawn on a Los Angeles bank, it may make sense to present the items directly to the Los Angeles bank. The New York bank will arrange to open an account or may already have an account at the Los Angeles bank. When it receives a million dollar check, the New York bank will present the item directly, usually on the day of deposit, by transmitting the item by private messenger service to the counters of the Los Angeles bank prior to the cutoff time for that day under the Los Angeles bank's funds availability schedule. The Los Angeles bank will debit the **drawer's** account and credit the New York bank's account immediately. Thus, the account of the New York bank is augmented by the million dollars on that day.

This crediting of the New York bank's account is not the end of the matter, however. At this point, the New York bank has the funds in Los Angeles, but it cannot use them easily and cannot make them available to its customer, the depositor, whose interests drive the collection efforts in this example. The New York bank, therefore, knowing the Los Angeles bank's cutoff time and knowing that its account with the Los Angeles bank will be credited that day, simultaneous with the presentment in Los Angeles of the check, will order the Los Angeles bank to transfer the funds to New York by Fedwire. That transfer will be effected without delay by the Los Angeles bank, and the net effect of the entire process will be to credit the depositor's account at the New York bank much more quickly than would have been possible if the New York bank had resorted to the Federal

Figure 23-7. Long-Distance Direct Presentation

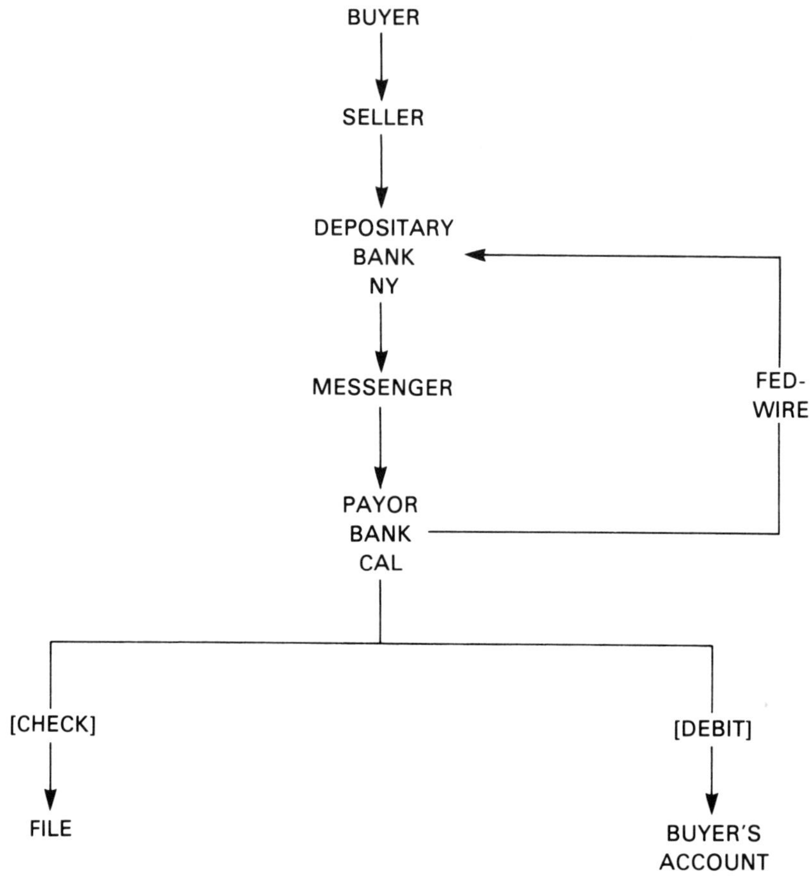

Reserve's system. Figure 23-7 illustrates the direct-presentment arrangement.

§23.8 CASHIER'S CHECKS, CERTIFIED CHECKS, AND OTHER PAYMENT INSTRUMENTS

Checks and drafts are "pull" orders, that is, the party that introduces them into the collection system utilizes them to pull funds from the drawer's account into his own account. The nature of **pull orders** is such that a payee holding one does not know whether the order is good. The drawer may stop payment, the account may be closed, or there may be insufficient funds in the account to pay the item. By virtue of the relatively slow process by which checks clear, furthermore, even though a check does clear, the payees do not always know when it clears, that is, at what point payment has occurred. Even though federal law requires depository institutions to make funds available to a customer within specified time periods, if ultimately the check does not clear, the payee depositor must return the funds to his bank.

These problems with the check-collection system are not serious in most commercial transactions. In many cases, the payee extends credit to his customer, and the check arrives after the seller has delivered the merchandise or provided the services. In some cases, however, sellers are reluctant to part with merchandise or valuable documents without cash or its equivalent.

A seller of real estate, for example, will not deliver a warranty deed, the recording of which will permit the buyer to sell the property to a good-faith purchaser free of the original seller's interest, unless the seller receives cash at the closing. It would be folly for a homeowner to give a buyer a warranty deed in return for a check. The buyer could record the deed, sell the property to an innocent purchaser, and stop payment on the check. The original seller would not have his money, and the innocent purchaser would have the real estate. Similarly, a seller of negotiable securities is not inclined to accept a check in payment for them, because the buyer can take the securities and resell them to a bona fide purchaser who will take them free of the original seller's rights. The bona fide purchaser ends up with the securities, while the seller holds a checked stamped "NSF" or "Payment Stopped."

Sellers are well advised to guard against these eventualities. They are not interested in a claim against the dishonest buyer. He may be insolvent or may have disappeared with the money. Even if he is next door, the prospect of incurring the costs and suffering the headaches of suing him and collecting a judgment is not a happy one.

The **cashier's check** and the **certified check** provide significant protection for any seller that is parting with something of value at a closing. First, the primary obligor on each of these checks is a bank. Solvent bank's do not dishonor their own cashier's checks or certified checks for insufficient funds. If a financial institution becomes insolvent between the time it issues a cashier's check or the time it certifies a check, the federal agencies that insure deposits cover the check up to the insurance limit. Generally, moreover, the law does not permit stop orders against cashier's checks and certified checks.

Document 23-2 is a cashier's check. Note that it is really a two-party instrument, the payee being the first, and the bank being the second in its dual role as drawer and drawee. There is, of course, a third party in the transaction, though it is not a party to the instrument. The person who provides the funds to the bank for the check is the **remitter,** and his name usually appears at the bottom of the check or on the check stub.

Document 23-3 is a certified check. It is a typical check drawn by the bank's customer on his own account, payable to the payee. The certifying bank is the designated drawee, and by certifying, the drawee signals its undertaking to pay the check when it is presented. Certification is the equivalent of **acceptance.** When a bank **accepts** a draft, we call it a **banker's acceptance;** when it accepts a check, we call it certification.

Although there is some sentiment among politicians and consumer advocates for a law or regulation requiring banks to offer checking accounts to poor people, such a mandated government program of "lifeline" banking is not the law at the present time, and there remain some consumers that do not maintain checking accounts. For these people to transfer funds it is necessary to purchase items that can be collected through the bank-collection system.

Bank or postal money orders are instruments that a consumer may purchase and make payable to himself or his creditor. Document 23-4 is a bank money order. There is some controversy over the nature of a bank money order. Some courts view it as the equivalent of a cashier's check, that is, they see the bank money order as a check, which the bank accepts by the act of issuance. Other courts view the bank money order as the bank's promissory note.

Personal and postal money orders, an example of which appears as Document 23-5, differ from bank money orders in that the customer, not the bank, signs the money order. When the postal service or a bank issues a personal money order, the drawer's signature line and the drawee's signature line are blank. A thief of a personal money order that the remitter has not signed can sign his own name to it, and subsequent parties will have a difficult time arguing that the signature is a forgery.

Most authorities seem to agree that a personal money order is analogous to a personal check and that the "owner" of it, that is, the remitter, may stop payment on it. The issue arises when the remitter loses the item before signing it. There is some risk, of course, in signing the instrument in blank, because a thief or finder can fill in his name as payee. Sometimes, however, the remitter will not know the exact name of the payee and cannot complete the instrument at the teller's window.

Traveler's checks are available to a party who may travel in a foreign country or in a part of his own country where checks drawn on his bank will not be readily acceptable. Travelers checks are drawn on the company that issues them and require two signatures of the remitter — one at the time the check issues, and the second at the time the remitter uses the check to purchase goods or services. Document 23-6 is an illustration of a traveler's check.

§23.9 LOCK BOXES

Firms that sell products or services in many states face a problem in consolidating the funds they must collect from their customers. A mail-order business in Massachusetts, for example, does not want its California customers to mail checks drawn on California banks to the house in Massachusetts. Since most California buyers would draw checks on California banks, checks received in Massachusetts would have to be collected by depositing them in the house's Massachusetts bank, which would forward them through the banking chain to California for collection. The mail-order house prefers to have its California customers' checks collected at a bank, say, in California. That bank recovers the checks from a California postal box (the **lock box**) and collects the checks for the mail-order house by indorsing them and sending them to the payor banks. When the payor banks honor the checks, the lock-box bank forwards the proceeds to Massachusetts or notifies the Massachusetts mail-order house that the funds are available. The lock-box system accelerates the collection and thus saves the seller interest charges.

While formerly a nationwide system of lock boxes required twelve separate lock boxes, the standardization of availability schedules and mail deliveries have produced sufficient efficiencies to reduce that number to six or seven. The Internal Revenue Service, however, maintains about 40 lock boxes nationally to collect tax payments quickly.

Wire-transfer technology permits further savings and speed in the collection of checks from widely scattered regions. Banks can use their access to **automated clearinghouses** (ACHs) when they collect items they have gathered from a lock box. One company may operate a system of lock boxes that takes advantage of preprinted payment envelopes and a zip-code program offered by the postal service. Under the program, a seller will include with the invoice to its customers a preprinted envelope that bears a zip code the postal service has reserved for **truncation.** Instead of delivering the mail at the written address, the postal service's sorting machines route the envelope to a processing bank that opens it, takes the customer's check for deposit, and wires funds through the ACH to an account at the payee's bank.

Image processing is a technological innovation that may increase the use of lock boxes. Image processing permits the lock-box bank to capture information from the checks, destroy them, and transmit the information to the various payor banks and to the payee inexpensively by wire.

§23.10 RETURNS

While most checks are paid on the first **presentation,** the drawee-payor bank dishonors some for insufficient funds, stop-payment order, uncollected funds, account closed, and the like. Under federal and state law, the drawee that honors a check is under no duty to give notice of that fact, and the silence that accompanies payment ultimately signals the fact that the depositor's funds are good. When the drawee dishonors, however, it must give notice promptly of that fact, so that the depositary bank will know that the funds are not good.

Under revised check return rules, each **collecting bank** debits the account of the bank to which it sends the check during the forward collection process, and the presenting bank debits the account of the payor bank. Those entries are final, even though the payor bank may ultimately dishonor the check. In the event of dishonor, the payor recoups the money that the presenting bank debited from its account by returning the check to the depositary bank under a system similar to the forward collection process, that is, in the return of the check, each bank debits the account of the bank to which it sends the check, so that ultimately, a returned check is debited to the account of the depositary bank, where it comes to rest. The routing may vary. The banks in the return of the check may not be the banks involved with the forward collection. Sometimes, the payor bank returns the item directly to the depositary bank. In any case, the payor recoups its debit not by reversing the forward collection entries, as in the past, but by recollecting the amount of the check through the return process, which treats the depositary bank as if it were the payor.

Thus, the process of dishonor includes the return of the dishonored item. Absent instructions to the contrary from the owner of the item, the banks are entitled to assume that the owner wants the item back in order to hold secondary parties or to make other collection efforts. Until recently, the return process was largely manual and much slower than the forward progress of the check from the depositary bank to the drawee bank. With the advent of Federal Reserve Board Regulation CC, however, which mandates the availability of deposited funds against short deadlines, the banking system has made serious efforts to hasten the return process. The payor bank will encode the dishonored check or place it in an encoded envelope as if it were a check drawn on the depositary bank. The Federal Reserve System handles such returns as it handles forward collections, and some money center banks offer such return services in competition with the Federal Reserve Banks, just as they compete with the Federal Reserve in the forward collection arena.

Since those efforts include the micro-encoding of the dishonored check or of an envelope containing it with routing symbols, the bank-collection system's reader-sorter machines can handle return items in the same fashion that they handle forward items. Most returns at this time go through the Federal Reserve Banks, but the competition of the commercial banks' marketing their own systems is yielding faster return of dishonored items.

Thus, a payor bank that dishonors an item must take steps to see to its prompt return. First, the dishonoring bank will encode the item itself or an envelope containing the item for return, that is, it will have its data entry clerks encode the MICR symbols of the depositary bank. Next, the dishonoring bank must decide whether to initiate the return by sending the item to the local Federal Reserve Bank or branch or by sending it to a large bank that offers wholesale banking services, including the return of items. The final step in the process occurs when the Federal Reserve Bank or the wholesale bank runs the item through its reader-sorter equipment and effects the automated return of the dishonored item to the bank of first deposit.

§23.11 CHECK-GUARANTY PROGRAMS

Virtually anyone may open a checking account for a small deposit, and the cost of a few printed checks is relatively small. Thus, it is rather easy for unscrupulous individuals to write checks on accounts that are closed or that have insufficient funds to cover the checks that are written. Many check writers issue checks, moreover, and then stop payment on them, either because they are dissatisfied with their purchase or because they never intended to pay for the product or services in the first place. These dishonest or ambivalent individuals arise commonly enough in retail trade to make many retailers reluctant to accept payment by check.

Banks, to which checking accounts serve as a source of deposits, are aware of that retailer reluctance and, anxious to make the checking account attractive to creditworthy customers, have fashioned a facility to deal with the suspicions of the retailer. That facility is the check-guaranty program.

Under a typical check-guaranty program, the bank that accepts checking-account deposits will enter into a contract with retailers under which the retailer may rely on the bank's promise that the checks are good. Banks provide verification of their guaranty by computer or telephone or by virtue of the issuance of a plastic card similar to a credit card. Some bank credit card issuers, in fact, make checks available to cardholders for maximum preauthorized amounts.

§23.12 THE DEPOSITOR AGREEMENT

The array of bank products offered by today's retail bank operation is extensive. Banks now regularly provide **overdraft** protection to their customers, offer them charge cards, **debit cards,** telephone banking, interest bearing accounts, transfer of funds between accounts, and more.

The depositor agreement, which a few short years ago was set forth on a "signature card" small enough to fit into the depositor's wallet, is now a lengthy agreement. To some extent that length is dictated by federal and state disclosure laws. In the past, the depositor agreement often incorporated terms and provisions of the institution's bylaws by reference. Document 23-7 is a typical depositor agreement.

Document 23-1. Check with MICR Symbols

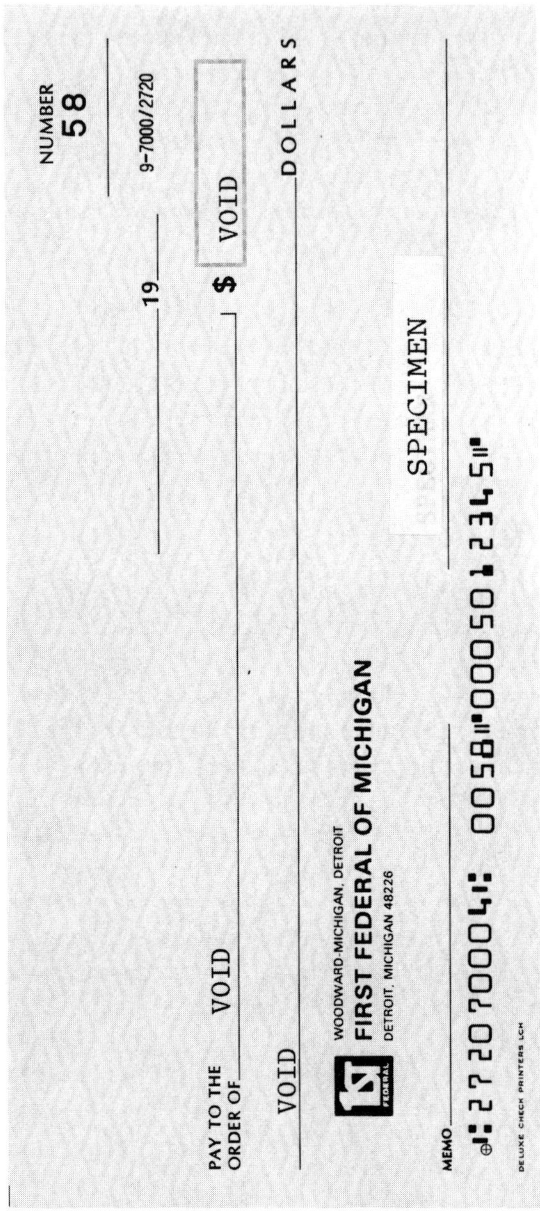

Reprinted with the permission of First Federal of Michigan.

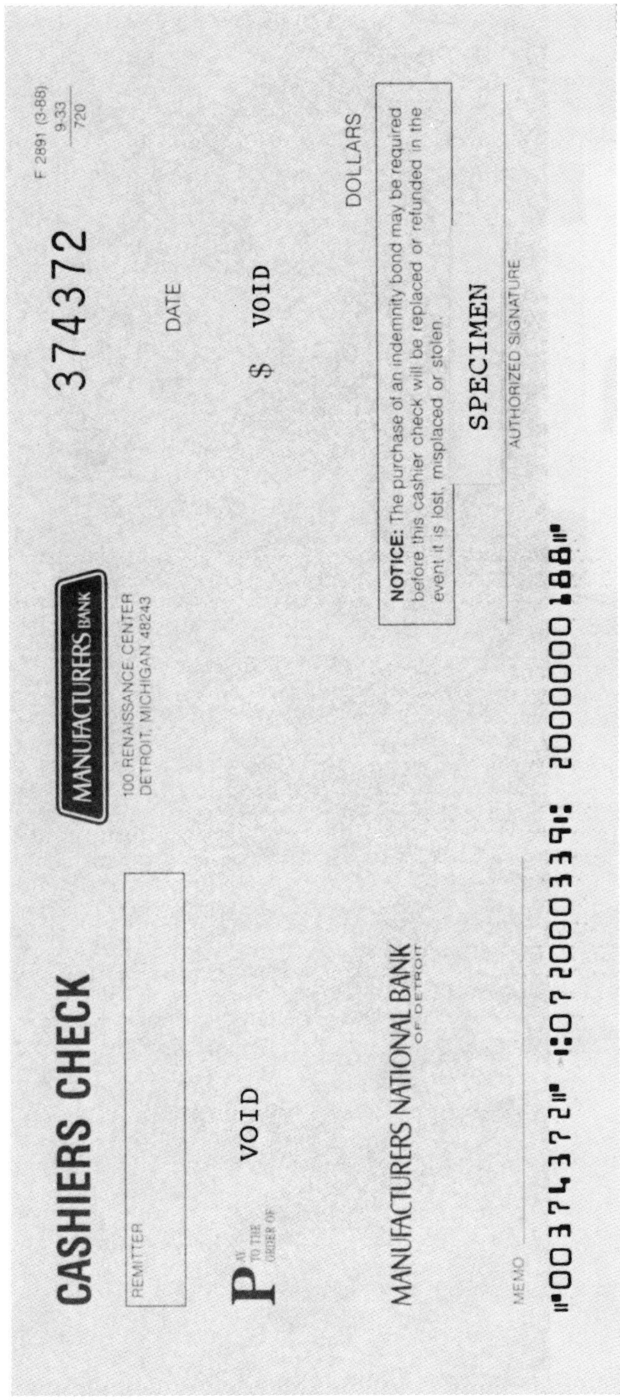

CASHIERS CHECK

MANUFACTURERS BANK

100 RENAISSANCE CENTER
DETROIT, MICHIGAN 48243

374372

F 2891 (3-88)
9-33/720

REMITTER

DATE

PAY TO THE ORDER OF VOID

$ VOID

DOLLARS

MANUFACTURERS NATIONAL BANK
OF DETROIT

NOTICE: The purchase of an indemnity bond may be required before this cashier check will be replaced or refunded in the event it is lost, misplaced or stolen.

SPECIMEN

AUTHORIZED SIGNATURE

MEMO

⑈00374372⑈ ⑆072000339⑆ 2000000188⑈

Printed with the permission of Manufacturers National Bank of Detroit.

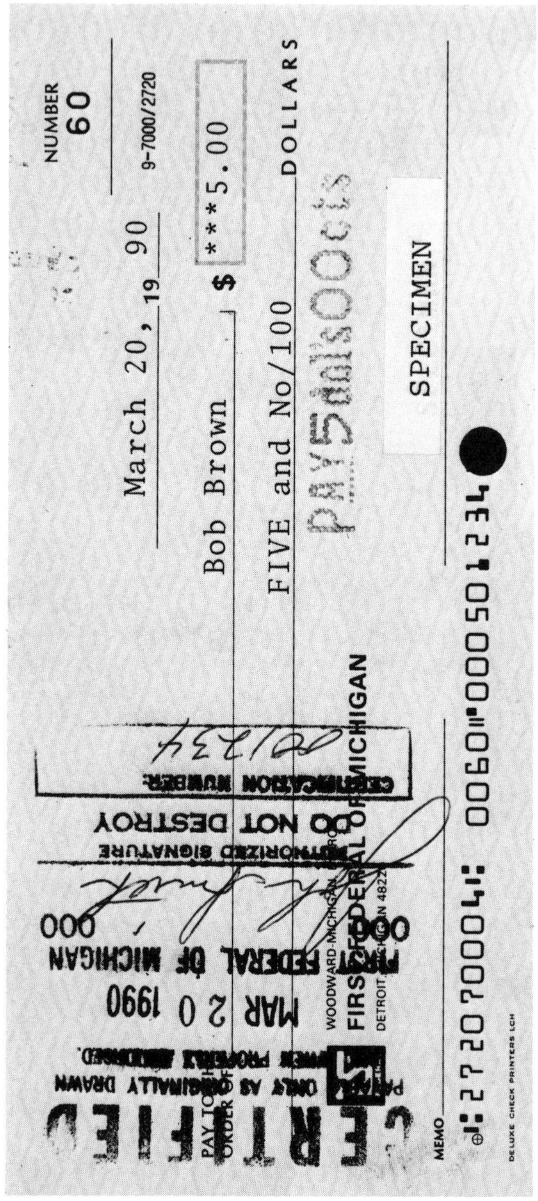

Printed with the permission of First Federal of Michigan.

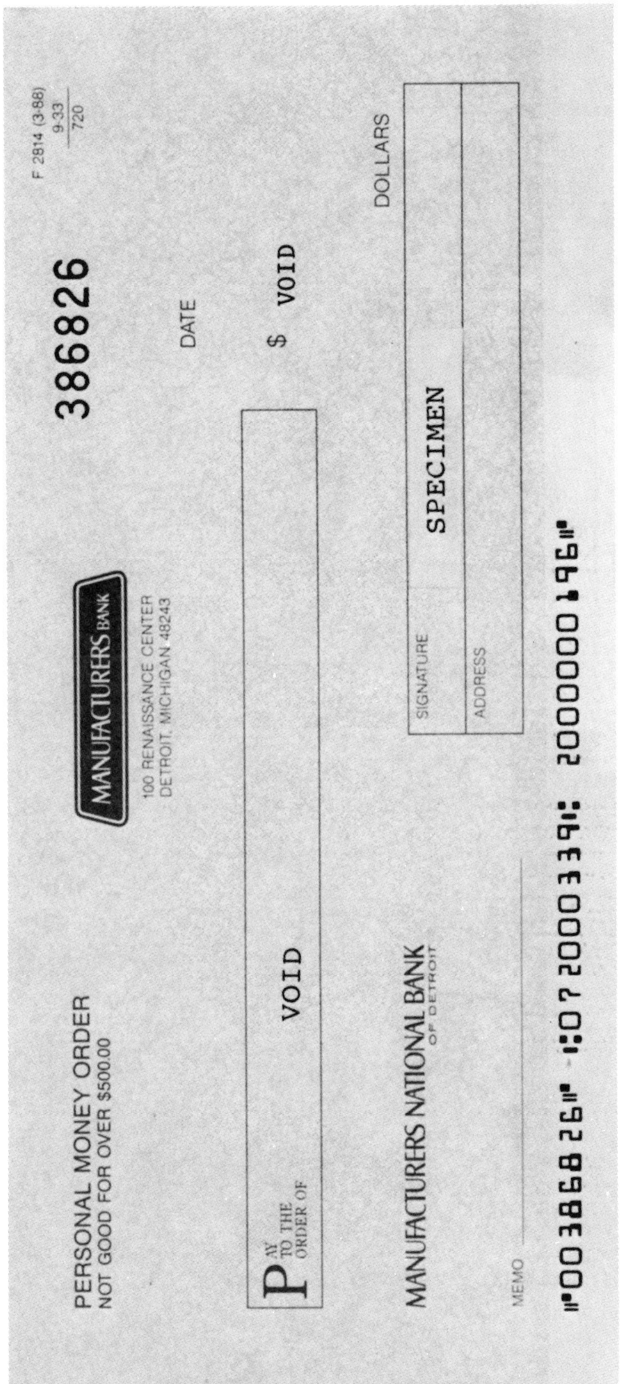

PERSONAL MONEY ORDER
NOT GOOD FOR OVER $500.00

MANUFACTURERS BANK
100 RENAISSANCE CENTER
DETROIT, MICHIGAN 48243

386826

F 2814 (3-88)
9-33
720

DATE

PAY TO THE ORDER OF VOID

$ VOID

DOLLARS

MANUFACTURERS NATIONAL BANK OF DETROIT

SIGNATURE SPECIMEN

ADDRESS

MEMO

⑈00386826⑈ ⑆072000339⑆ 2000000196⑈

Printed with the permission of Manufacturers National Bank of Detroit.

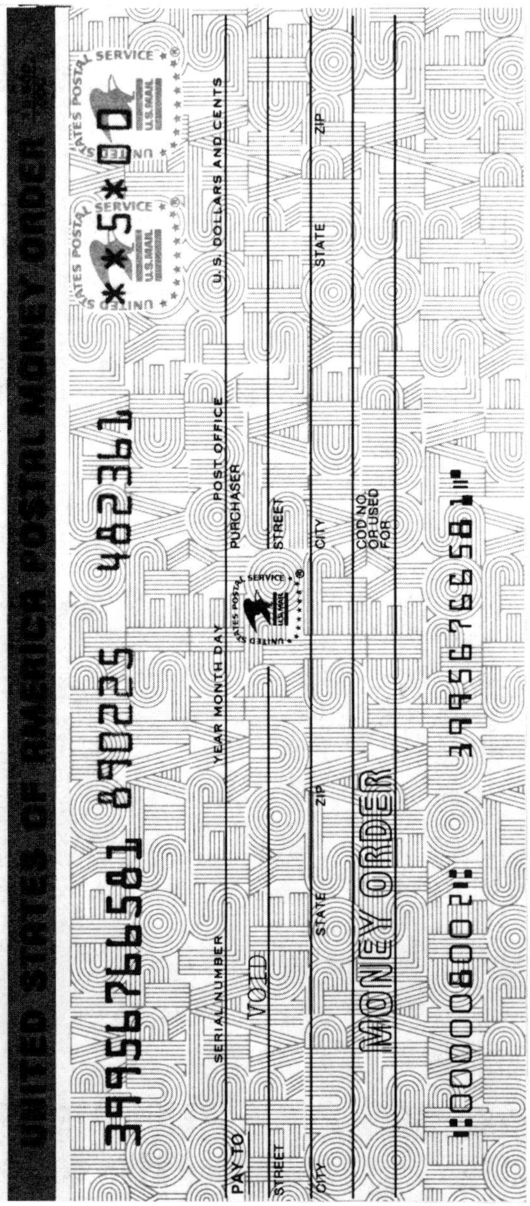

UNITED STATES OF AMERICA POSTAL MONEY ORDER

39956766581 890225 482361 **5*00

SERIAL NUMBER YEAR MONTH DAY POST OFFICE U. S. DOLLARS AND CENTS

PAY TO VOID

PURCHASER

STREET

STREET

CITY STATE ZIP

CITY STATE ZIP

MONEY ORDER

COD NO. OR USED FOR

⑆000008002⑆ 39956766581⑈

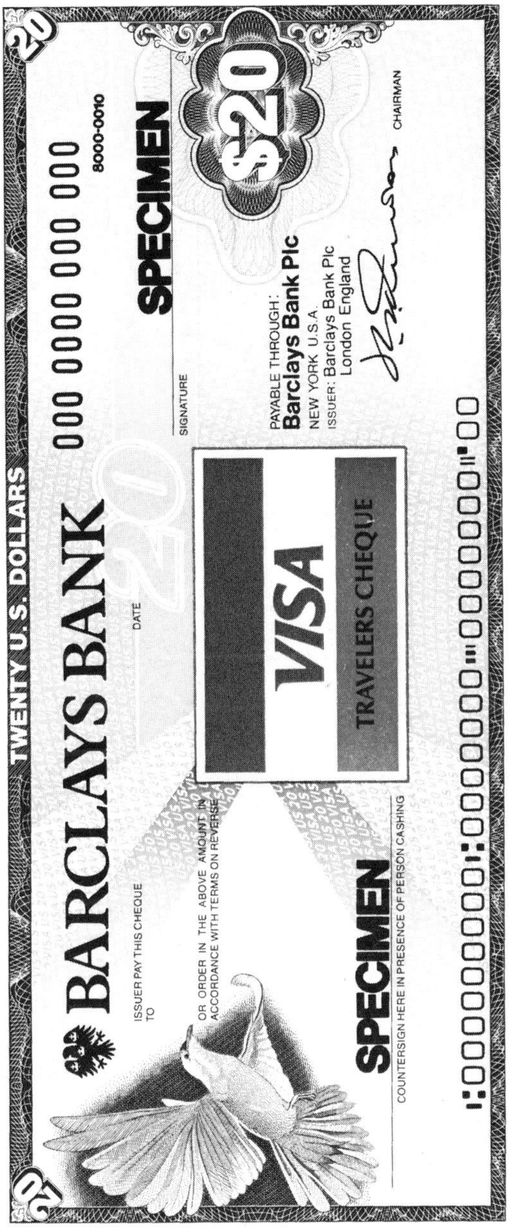

TWENTY U.S. DOLLARS

BARCLAYS BANK

000 0000 000 000

8000-0010

ISSUER PAY THIS CHEQUE TO

DATE

OR ORDER IN THE ABOVE AMOUNT IN ACCORDANCE WITH TERMS ON REVERSE

SIGNATURE

SPECIMEN

$20

VISA

TRAVELERS CHEQUE

PAYABLE THROUGH:
Barclays Bank Plc
NEW YORK U.S.A.
ISSUER: Barclays Bank Plc
London England

CHAIRMAN

SPECIMEN

COUNTERSIGN HERE IN PRESENCE OF PERSON CASHING

Printed with the permission of Barclays Bank Plc.

Document 23-7. Depositor Agreement

MANUFACTURERS NATIONAL BANK OF DETROIT
Rules and Regulations
Retail Deposit Accounts

Personal Checking Account
Statement Savings Account
NOW Interest Checking
Regular Savings Account
ManuFund Money Market Account (Retail)
Basic Checking
Automatic Overdraft Protection

GENERAL RULES FOR ALL ACCOUNTS

1. Depositor opening an account hereunder (herein called "Depositor") agrees to be bound by these Rules and Regulations governing Depositor's accounts with Bank and to be bound by any amendments or modifications or a termination of the Rules and Regulations, after written notice of same shall be sent to Depositor's last known address or upon the posting of such notice in the Main Office and in the lobby of each branch office of Bank.

2. Each Depositor agrees to provide Bank with a signature card, a social security or tax identification number, a corporate resolution, if applicable, and with any other information or documents requested by Bank.

3. Except where inconsistent with any specific provisions hereof, the Rules and Regulations of the Detroit Clearing House Association, the Michigan Automated Clearing House Association, the Michigan Uniform Commercial Code, and such other applicable laws and regulations, as amended from time to time, shall govern and apply to all transactions between the Depositor and Bank under these accounts, where applicable, whether occurring in or outside of the State of Michigan.

4. Rates of interest, methods of computation, interest payment dates, time deposit maturity requirements, deposit and withdrawal amounts, minimum balance requirements, and any service charges for account maintenance, activity or otherwise, shall be determined from time to time by Bank and posted in the lobby of its Main Office and in the lobby of each of its branch offices.

5. Bank reserves the right to limit the amount deposited to Depositor's account and the right to refuse or return all, or any part of, any deposit.

6. Money shall be paid to Depositor by cashiers check or by crediting Depositor's other accounts at Bank, or as ordered by Depositor in form satisfactory to Bank.

7. Bank reserves the right not to pay interest on any fractional part of a dollar on any interest paying account.

8. When Depositor deposits a check or draft drawn on another financial institution into Depositor's account at Bank, there will be a delay before the check or draft reaches the financial institution on which it was drawn and Bank receives payment. Until Bank receives the payment, Bankhas the right to refuse any withdrawal from Depositor's account, by check or otherwise, up to the amount of such check or draft. The number of days that the amount of such check or draft may not be used by depositor will vary depending on the amount and whether the deposited check or draft is drawn on a Detroit financial institution, a Michigan financial institution located outside Detroit or an out-of-state financial institution and shall be in compliance with the regulations of the Federal reserve Board. The Bank's policy will be posted in the lobby of its Main Office and in the lobby of each of its branch offices.

9. The liability of Depositor as endorser or otherwise shall not be affected by failure of Bank to give notice of dishonor or non-payment, nor by certification obtained by Bank for any deposited check. The giving of cash or credit for an item drawn on or payable at Bank shall be provisional, subject to revocation and charging back in the event the item is found not payable for any reason.

10. When an account is in the name of two or more persons, each agrees that it is each Depositor's intention to create a joint tenancy in such account with the right of survivorship, unless otherwise indicated. All sums credited to the account at any time shall be the joint property of each Depositor and may be paid to or on the order of any one of them, whether all other such Depositors be living or not, and the receipt by any one of the Depositors for any such payments so made shall validly and sufficiently discharge and release Bank for that amount. Any check, draft, note or other order for payment of money payable to any one or more of the Depositors may be endorsed "For deposit to the account of within named payee(s)" and deposited in the account by any of the Depositors whether or not the instrument be payable to the Depositor or Depositors so endorsing.

11. Bank may honor a post-dated check or any other order drawn on it before its date.

12. All deposits and withdrawals shall be entered on Bank's records. Depositor shall receive a passbook entry in the case of passbook accounts and a receipt in all other cases. If Depositor's passbook is not available at the time of the deposit or withdrawal, Depositor shall present the passbook as soon as convenient for the purpose of recording said transactions. If the passbook is mislaid, stolen or lost, Depositor must give immediate notice of the fact to Bank.

13. Depositor will be provided with a periodic account statement, except in the case of passbook accounts, which shall set forth all transactions during the statement period, including the current account balance and service charges, if any. Except in the case of transactions which involve an electronic transfer of funds, cancelled negotiable and transferable items may also be provided. Depositor agrees to inspect and compare the statements with the activity evidenced by Depositor's transaction items, checks, drafts, and/or receipts. Any objections to endorsements not made within the limitation period provided by the Michigan Uniform Commercial Code or within fourteen (14) days from date of discovery of such irregularity, whichever date is the earlier, shall be absolutely barred and waived. All other objections to said statement of account, including, but not limited to, any claim of signature irregularity or of any alteration, not made within fourteen (14) days from the receipt of such statement shall be absolutely barred and waived.

14. Depositor having Bank accounts other than Retail Checking or NOW Interest Checking or Statement Savings with the Automatic Overdraft Protection are prohibited from making more than three withdrawals per month by means of preauthorized order or instructions or telephone agreement.

15. Depositor agrees to comply with the Bank's Standard for the endorsement of checks. The Bank reserves the right to refuse to accept a check if the back is not clear and readable or otherwise fails to meet the Banks endorsement standards. The Depositor shall be responsible for any loss to the Bank for any check returned to the Bank because of Depositor's or the payee's failure to comply with the Bank's standards.

F 5416 (9-88)

Document 23-7. *(continued)*

ADDITIONAL RULES FOR REGULAR SAVINGS, STATEMENT SAVINGS AND TIME DEPOSIT ACCOUNTS

In accordance with Federal law and regulation, Statement Savings Accounts, Regular Savings Accounts and Time Deposit Accounts are not transferable, when such accounts are in the name of one or more individuals or a sole proprietorship or a trustee, custodian, agent or other fiduciary (whether or not a natural person), provided the entire interest of such funds is for the benefit of one or more individuals, except if a transfer is made on Bank's books. Notwithstanding the above, such accounts are not prohibited from being pledged as collateral for a loan or from being transferred due to circumstances arising from death, incompetency, marriage, divorce, attachment or otherwise by operation of law.

ADDITIONAL RULE FOR NOW INTEREST CHECKING ACCOUNTS

Depending upon the balance Depositor maintains in the account and the number of checks written per month, Depositor may pay a larger amount in service fees than the amount Depositor will receive in interest, in which case Depositor's principal balance may be reduced, including Statement Savings with the Automatic Overdraft Protection. Depositor shall be provided with a monthly statement.

ADDITIONAL RULE FOR MANUFUND, NOW INTEREST CHECKING, STATEMENT SAVINGS AND REGULAR SAVINGS ACCOUNTS

Bank reserves the right at any time to require Depositor to give notice in writing of an intended withdrawal not less than fourteen (14) days before such withdrawal is made, including Statement Savings with the Automatic Overdraft Protection.

ADDITIONAL RULE FOR STATEMENT SAVINGS ACCOUNTS

Depositor shall receive a quarterly account statement, or, Depositor may request a combined statement that will include all checking account transactions and statement savings account transactions on a monthly account statement.

ADDITIONAL RULES FOR SPECIAL TIME ACCOUNTS

Each deposit to this account shall mature and interest shall be credited on March 1st, June 1st, September 1st, and December 1st following a period of at least three (3) calendar months subsequent to the date of such deposit.

Any deposit or portion thereof not withdrawn at its maturity or within ten (10) days thereafter, shall automatically be renewed for a like period of at least three (3) months.

In the event all or any portion of a deposit is withdrawn prior to its maturity, a substantial penalty, required by Federal law and regulation, may be assessed.

ADDITIONAL RULES FOR AUTOMATIC OVERDRAFT PROTECTION SERVICE

If depositor has requested the Automatic Overdraft Protection ("AOP"), the Bank, upon written request of any of the Depositors, will transfer funds from a designated savings account to a designated checking account. Bank will implement the AOP within five business days from the request. The owners of the designated savings account shall correspond at all times to those of the designated checking account.

Bank will transfer sufficient funds from the designated savings account to the designated checking account to pay items presented for payment. Transfers will consist of an amount necessary to pay all checks up to the balance of the designated savings account. If the designated savings account contains insufficient funds to cover all checks presented, the Bank will transfer an amount down to a one cent balance in a designated savings account to pay as many checks as can be paid with the remaining balance.

Depositor may terminate the AOP by providing Bank with a written request for termination signed by one or more of the Depositors. This request will become effective within five business days after receipt by Bank. When one Depositor terminates the AOP, Bank will not be obligated to notify the other Depositors on the account of the termination. The Bank shall not be responsible for any claim or loss which may arise, either directly or indirectly, from the withdrawal of funds or due to the termination of the AOP, by any one Depositor, which prevents Bank from making further transfers or which may arise from the Bank's, or any other banks', or any other banks' or businesses', failure to accept a check, draft or other instrument issued in connection with the AOP.

The Bank, at its option, may terminate the AOP.

When any of the designated accounts has a zero balance for three consecutive months with no account activity, the AOP will be terminated by Bank with no further notice.

ADDITIONAL RULES FOR MANUFUND ACCOUNTS

Depositor is prohibited from making preauthorized (including automatic) transfers from ManuFund accounts in excess of six per month. No more than three of such transfers may be by check or draft made payable by Depositor to other persons.

Document 23-7. (*continued*)

MANUFACTURERS NATIONAL BANK OF DETROIT
Preauthorized Electronic Funds
Transfer Disclosure Statement

1. **PREAUTHORIZED CREDITS**
If you have arranged to have direct deposits made to your account at least once every sixty (60) days from the same person or Company, you can call Bank to find out whether or not the deposit has been made.

2. **PREAUTHORIZED DEBITS**
If you have requested Bank in advance, to make regular payments from your account, you can stop any of these payments by calling or by writing Bank in time for it to receive your request three (3) business days or more before the payment is scheduled to be made.
Telephone requests must be confirmed in writing and mailed to Bank within fourteen (14) days following each oral request. For each stop payment order made, Bank shall charge you a stop payment fee at Bank's effective rate at such time.
In the event that regular preauthorized payments shall vary in amount, the person who you are going to pay must tell you ten (10) days before each payment when it will be made and how much it will be. (You may choose to get this notice only when the payment would differ by more than a certain amount from the previous payment, or when the amount would fall outside certain limits that you set.)

3. **BANK'S LIABILITY**
If Bank does not properly complete a transfer to or from your account on time or in the correct amount according to its agreement with you, or if you order Bank to stop one of your preauthorized payments three (3) business days or more before such transfer is scheduled, and Bank fails to do so, Bank will be liable for your losses or damages. However, Bank will not be liable in the following circumstances:
(a) If, through no fault of Bank your account does not contain enough money to make the transfer;
(b) If the transfer would go over the credit limit on your overdraft line;
(c) If circumstances beyond Bank's control, such as fire or flood, prevent the transfer, despite reasonable precautions it has taken;
(d) There may be other exceptions.

4. **SERVICE CHARGES**
Bank reserves the right to charge a fee for your preauthorized transfers if Bank's increased costs incurred in maintaining such a service necessitate a fee.
In the event Bank determines that it shall require a fee, such fee will not become effective until thirty (30) days after Bank mails notification to you.

5. **DOCUMENTATION OF TRANSFERS**
For any month in which a preauthorized debit from your account occurs or, at least, quarterly, a statement shall be provided that contains a sufficient description to enable you to identify any transaction made.
If your account(s) is not a passbook account and may only be accessed by preauthorized credits, Bank shall provide you with a quarterly statement.
If you hold a passbook account whereby the only possible transfers are preauthorized credits, Bank shall provide you with a statement but you may bring your passbook to Bank, and Bank will record any electronic deposits that were made to the accounts since the last time you brought the passbook in.

6. **ERROR RESOLUTION PROCEDURES**
If you think your statement is wrong of if you need more information about a transfer listed on your statement, you must call or write Bank no later than sixty (60 days after Bank sent you the FIRST statement on which the problem or error appeared.
Oral complaints or questions must be confirmed in writing within ten (10) business days and must include:
(a) Your name and account number;
(b) The dollar amount of the suspected error;
(c) A description of the error or the transfer in question and an explanation, made as clearly as possible, as to why you believe an error occurred or why you need more information.
An error shall be limited to:
(1) an unauthorized transfer;
(2) an incorrect transfer to or from your account;
(3) the omission from a statement of a transfer to or from your account that should have been included;
(4) a computational or bookkeeping error made by Bank relating to a transfer.
Following notification, Bank will inform you of the results of its investigation within ten (10) business days and will correct any error promptly. (If an oral notification is not confirmed in writing within ten (10) days, Bank may not credit the account.) If Bank needs more time, however, it may take up to forty-five (45) days to investigate a complaint or question, but will provisionally recredit your account within ten (10) business days for the amount believed to be in error, so that you will have the use of the money during the time it takes Bank to complete its investigation.
If Bank decides that no error occurred, it will send a written explanation to you within three (3) business days after it finishes its investigation. You may ask for copies of the documents Bank used in its investigation.

7. **GOVERNING RULES AND REGULATIONS**
All preauthorized electronic fund transactions shall be subject to the laws of the State of Michigan, the United States, the rules and regulations of the Federal Reserve System and Bank's rules and regulations for the respective accounts.

8. **PRONOUNS**
The pronouns and relative words used herein shall be, where appropriate construed singular or plural, and if there is more than one account owner, each agrees to the terms hereof on a joint and several basis.

9. **DISCLOSURES TO THIRD PARTIES**
Bank will not disclose any information to third parties which shall pertain to your accounts, except when necessary to complete transfers, in order to verify the existence and condition of accounts for a third party, such as a credit bureau or merchant, in order to comply, when required, with government agency or court orders, or in accordance with your written instructions.

F 5416 (9-88)

Document 23-7. (*continued*)

10. AMENDMENTS AND TERMINATION
These terms and conditions may be amended or terminated by Bank sending written notice to you at your last known address or by including a written notice with your periodic statement. Any charge, however, will not become effective less than twenty-one (21) days from the date of such notice, in the absence of extenuating circumstances.

11. BANK BUSINESS DAYS
Bank's business days are Monday through Friday. Bank holidays not included.

12. NOTICES TO BANK
All notices to Bank, required under this Agreement, must be given to:
Manufacturers National Bank of Detroit, EFT Desk PO Box 659 Detroit, Michigan 48231 Telephone: (313) 222-5471 (Please call collect if this number is a long distance call for you.)

MANUFACTURERS NATIONAL BANK OF DETROIT
ManuWay Agreement and
Disclosure Statement

By applying for a ManuWay Banking Card (hereinafter called "Card") the ManuWay Cardholder (hereinafter called "Cardholder") does hereby agree to the following terms and conditions:

1. **AVAILABLE TRANSACTIONS.**
Cardholder may use the Card to:
(a) make deposits to and cash withdrawals from Cardholder's Checking, ManuFund or Statement Savings account;
(b) obtain cash advances from Cardholder's credit card account or revolving credit account;
(c) transfer funds from Cardholder's Checking or ManuFund to Statement Savings account, from Statement Savings to Checking or ManuFund, and from credit card or revolving credit account to Checking or ManuFund;
(d) pay bills, including but not limited to instalment loans, revolving credit accounts, mortgage loans and utility payments;
(e) obtain cash and purchase goods or services, including goods or services obtained by placing mail or telephone orders from certain businesses which have agreed to accept the Card (hereinafter called "point-of-sale transactions").

Some of these services may not be available at all terminals.

Access to Statement Savings accounts is limited to those Cardholders who have adopted Bank's combined statement format.

2. **CARDHOLDER'S LIABILITY FOR LOSS OR THEFT.**
Bank shall issue Cardholder a personal identification number without which the Card cannot be used except at staffed, on-premise electronic funds transfer terminals, in which case other identification will be required.

If Cardholder believes the Card has been lost or stolen, Cardholder must tell Bank AT ONCE and can lose no more than **$50.00** if Bank is contacted within two **(2)** business days. If Cardholder does NOT contact Bank within two **(2)** business days and Bank can prove that it could have prevented the loss if Cardholder had contacted it, Cardholder could lose as much as **$500.00**. Also, if Cardholder's monthly statement shows transfers Cardholder did not make and Cardholder does not contact Bank within sixty **(60)** days after the statement was mailed, Cardholder may not get back any money lost after sixty **(60)** days if Bank can prove that it could have prevented the loss if it had been notified in time (these specified time periods shall only be extended under extenuating circumstances).

Telephoning is the best way of keeping possible losses down.

Notice in writing shall be effective and considered given at the time Cardholder deposits the notice in the mail or delivers the notice for transmission by any other means to Bank.

Bank's business days are Monday through Friday; Bank holidays are not included.

The above provisions are NOT applicable to any cash advances or to overdrafts covered by a line of credit that do not result from an electronic funds transfer.

3. **OPTION TO LIMIT CASH WITHDRAWALS.**
Cardholder has the option to limit the total amount of cash which can be withdrawn via the Card from his/her account in a single day. This option includes, but is not limited to, a single daily access per card and Cardholder shall have the option to limit access to one or more specified accounts. Certain terminals may also have limitations regarding the total amount of cash which can be withdrawn in a single day.

4. **DOCUMENTATION OF TRANSFERS.**
Unless the Card is being used in connection with a check guaranty, a check authorization, to obtain information regarding an account balance or to obtain a cash advance from Cardholder's credit card or revolving credit accounts, or a combination of any of the above, the following provisions shall apply:
(a) Each Card transaction shall be accompanied by a receipt at the time of the transaction. If for any reason a receipt is not obtained, Cardholder may request Bank to issue a subsequent receipt. (Some point-of-sale transactions which do not involve an electronic terminal will not be accompanied by a terminal receipt.)
(b) For any month in which a Card transaction occurs or, at least, quarterly, a statement shall be provided that contains a sufficient description to enable Cardholder to identify any transaction made and to enable Cardholder to relate it to the furnished receipt. (Bank may render monthly statements to Cardholder in lieu of a combined statement.) A receipt and/or statement shall be admissible evidence of an account transaction.

5. **BANK'S LIABILITY FOR FAILURE TO MAKE TRANSFERS.**
If Bank does not properly complete a transfer to or from Cardholder's account on time or in the correct amount according to its agreement with Cardholder, Bank will be liable for Cardholder's losses or damages. However, Bank will not be liable in the following circumstances:
(a) if, through no fault of Bank, Cardholder's account does not contain enough money to make a transfer;
(b) if the transfer would go over the credit limit on Cardholder's overdraft line;
(c) if the automated teller machine where Cardholder is making the transfer does not have enough cash;
(d) if the automated teller machine or the terminal system was not working properly and Cardholder knew about the breakdown when Cardholder started the transfer;
(e) if circumstances beyond Bank's control, such as fire or flood, prevent the transfer, despite reasonable precautions it has taken;
(f) there may be other exceptions.

F 5416 (9-88)

6. **ERROR RESOLUTION PROCEDURES.**
If Cardholder thinks his/her statement or receipt is wrong or if Cardholder needs more information about a transfer listed on his/her statement or receipt, Cardholder must call or write Bank no later than sixty **(60)** days after Bank sent Cardholder the FIRST statement on which the problem or error appeared.

Oral complaints or questions must be confirmed in writing within ten **(10)** business days and must include:
(a) Cardholder's name and account number;
(b) the dollar amount of the suspected error;
(c) a description of the error or the transfer in question and an explanation, made as clearly as possible, as to why Cardholder believes an error occurred or why Cardholder needs more information.

An error shall be limited to:
(1) an unauthorized transfer;
(2) an incorrect transfer to or from Cardholder's account;
(3) the omission from a periodic statement of a transfer to or from Cardholder's account that should have been included;
(4) a computational or bookkeeping error made by Bank relating to a transfer;
(5) Cardholder's receipt of an incorrect amount of money from terminal.

Following notification, Bank will inform Cardholder of the results of its investigation within ten **(10)** business days [twenty **(20)** business days in cases of point-of-sale transactions] and will correct any error promptly. (If an oral notification is not confirmed in writing within ten **(10)** business days, Bank may not recredit the accounts.) If Bank needs more time, however, it may take up to forty-five **(45)** days [ninety **(90)** days in cases of point-of-sale transactions] to investigate a complaint or question, but will provisionally recredit Cardholder's account within ten **(10)** business days [twenty **(20)** business days in cases of point-of-sale transactions] for the amount believed to be in error, so that Cardholder will have the use of the money during the time it takes Bank to complete its investigation.

Cardholder's account will not be provisionally recredited when used in connection with the purchase or sale of securities.

7. **FEES.**
Bank reserves the right, without prior notice, to charge a fee for each Card which it issues or reissues under the following circumstances:
(a) if Bank is requested to issue replacements for Card(s) lost, destroyed or misplaced by Cardholder;
(b) if any Card is not used between its date of issuance and date of expiration and Bank is requested by Cardholder to reissue such Card for additional periods.

Bank also reserves the right to assess other charges it may deem necessary in the future. In the event Bank determines that it shall require a fee, such fee will not become effective until thirty **(30)** days after Bank mails notification to Cardholder. Cardholder, however, may terminate this agreement within that thirty **(30)** day period without charge.

8. **OVERDRAFTS.**
Cardholder shall not use the Card to obtain money from an account in excess of the balance then on deposit and Cardholder shall not obtain a cash advance in excess of Cardholder's credit card or revolving credit account limits.

Cardholder agrees to pay upon demand the amount of any overdrafts or any excess over the authorized limits to Cardholder's credit card and revolving credit accounts.

9. **NEW BANKING TRANSACTIONS.**
From time to time Bank may make available to Cardholder other banking transactions that may be accomplished with the use of the Card, and Cardholder agrees that by using the Card for these additional transactions, Cardholder will be bound by this agreement to the same extent as on the transactions now available.

10. **GOVERNING RULES AND REGULATIONS.**
All transactions hereunder shall be subject to the laws of the State of Michigan, the United States, the rules and regulations of the Federal Reserve System and Bank's rules and regulations for the respective accounts.

11. **DISCLOSURES TO THIRD PARTIES.**
Bank will not disclose any information to third parties which shall pertain to Cardholder's accounts, except when necessary to complete transfers, in order to verify the existence and condition of accounts for a third party, such as a credit bureau or merchant, in order to comply, when required, with government agency or court orders, or in accordance with Cardholder's written instructions.

12. **PRONOUNS.**
The pronouns and relative words used herein shall be, where appropriate, construed singular or plural, and if there is more than one Cardholder, each agrees to the terms hereof on a joint and several basis.

13. **AMENDMENTS.**
This agreement may be amended by Bank by sending written notice to Cardholder at Cardholder's last known address or by including a written notice with Cardholder's periodic statement. Any change, however, will not become effective less than twenty-one **(21)** days from the date of such notice, in the absence of extenuating circumstances.

14. **TERMINATION.**
The Card, at all times, shall remain the property of Bank, and Bank may at any time without notice withdraw or revoke its use and may terminate this agreement. Upon demand, Cardholder shall return the Card to Bank.

This agreement may be terminated by Cardholder by delivering the Card to Bank. A termination by either Bank or Cardholder shall not affect prior transactions or existing obligations.

15. **VIOLATIONS BY BANK.**
If Bank violates any of the preceeding provisions, Cardholder may notify the following:

Comptroller of the Currency
Consumers Affairs Division
Washington, DC 20219

16. **NOTICES TO BANK.**
All notices to Bank, required under this agreement, must be given to:

Manufacturers Bank, Electronic Banking Department
P.O. Box 33239
Detroit, Michigan 48232-5239
Detroit area: (313) 222-9764 Out-state: 1-800-572-6620

YOUR ABILITY TO WITHDRAW FUNDS AT MANUFACTURERS NATIONAL BANK OF DETROIT

Our general policy is to make funds from your deposits available to you on the first business day after the day we receive your deposit. At that time, you can withdraw the funds in cash and we will use the funds to pay checks that you have written.

For determining the availability of your deposits, every day is a business day, except Saturdays, Sundays, and federal holidays. If you make a deposit before 4:30 p.m. Monday-Wednesday and 6:00 p.m. Thursday and Friday on a business day that we are open, we will consider that day to be the day of your deposit. However, if you make a deposit after those times or on a day we are not open, we will consider that the deposit was made on the next business day we are open.

Funds received for direct deposit to your account electronically (via the Automated Clearing House) such as Social Security payment or "Direct Deposit of Pay" will be available on the effective payment date.

Please remember that even after we have made funds available to you, you are still responsible for checks you deposit that are returned to us unpaid.

LONGER DELAYS MAY APPLY

In some cases, we will not make all of the funds that you deposit by check available to you on the first business day after the day of your deposit. Depending on the type of check that you deposit, funds may not be available until the seventh business day after the day of your deposit. However, the first $100 of your deposits will be available on the first business day.

If we are not going to make all the funds from your deposit available on the first business day, we will notify you at the time you make your deposit. We will also tell you when the funds will be available. If your deposit is not made directly to one of our employees, or if we decide to take this action after you have left the premises, we will mail you the notice by the day after we receive your deposit.

If you will need the funds from a deposit right away, you should ask us when the funds will be available.

In addition, funds you deposit by check may be delayed for a longer period under the following circumstances:

- We believe a check you deposit will not be paid.
- You deposit checks totaling more than $5,000 on any one day.
- You redeposit a check that has been returned unpaid.
- You have overdrawn your account repeatedly in the last six months.
- There is an emergency, such as failure of communication or computer equipment.

We will notify you if we delay your ability to withdraw funds for any of these reasons, and we will tell you when the funds will be available. They will generally be available no later than the eleventh business day after the day of your deposit.

SPECIAL RULES FOR NEW ACCOUNTS

If you are a new customer, the following special rules may apply during the first 30 days your account is open.

The first $5,000 from a deposit of U.S. Treasury checks will be available on the first business day after the day of your deposit. The excess over $5,000 may be available on the seventh business day after the day of your deposit. Funds from wire transfers into your account will be available on the business day we receive the transfer.

Funds from deposits of cash and the first $5,000 of a day's total deposits of cashier's, certified, teller's, traveler's, and state and local government checks will be available on the first business day after the day of your deposit if the deposit meets certain conditions. For example, the checks must be payable to you and deposited at a staffed facility and you will be required to segregate these checks that are subject to next day availability and to indicate on your regular deposit slip that these special types of checks are being deposited. The excess over $5,000 will be available on the seventh business day after the day of your deposit. If you do not make the deposit in person to one of our employees, the first $5,000 will not be available until the second business day after the day of your deposit.

Funds from all other check deposits will be available on the seventh business day after the day of your deposit.

DEPOSITS AT AUTOMATED TELLER MACHINES (applicable only to retail accounts)

Funds from any deposits (cash or checks) made at automated teller machines (ATMs) we do not own or operate may not be available until the seventh business day after the day of your deposit. This rule does not apply at ATMs that we own or operate. All ATMs that we own or operate are identified as ManuWay machines. Deposits made at ManuWay machines are credited to the account in accordance with the times posted at the machine.

FOR ADDITIONAL INFORMATION

If you would like additional information regarding Regulation CC, please contact your branch office or write to us at:

Manufacturers Bank
P. O. Box 659
Detroit, MI 48231
Attention: Branch Operations

24 Collecting Drafts

§24.1 NONCASH ITEMS

The check-collection system is a highly mechanized program that collects about 50 billion **cash items** a year and does so in a curious way. A check "clears" or is "paid" usually when time passes or when the drawee-payor bank affirmatively decides to pay it. Significantly, however, when the payor decides to pay or when the time limit is reached and the check is paid as a matter of law, the parties that have taken the check do not learn about it. Silence signals payment. Notice occurs only when there is dishonor.

A depositary bank that takes a check for deposit from the payee of the item permits the depositor to use the funds according to a "funds availability schedule." Presumably, the check-collection system is efficient enough that the depositary bank will learn about nonpayment in time to prevent the uncreditworthy customer from withdrawing the uncollected funds.

Some items that pass into the banking system are not cash items and are not subject to the payments apparatus the banking industry has developed for checks. Most noncheck drafts are **noncash items.** A check is a draft drawn on a bank payable on demand. In this chapter and in the parlance of most people familiar with the banking industry, the term "draft" refers to negotiable orders to pay but does not include the check.

Significantly, when the final bank in the chain receives a draft, its obligations are different from the obligations that bank faces when it receives a check. In the check case, the bank must dishonor a check before a deadline (usually midnight of the banking day following the day of receipt) or it becomes responsible for the amount of the check, that is, failure to dishonor by the deadline constitutes payment of the check. When the bank receives a draft, however, its obligation are determined by a number of factors, including the nature of the draft and whether it is drawn on the bank or a third party. "On arrival" drafts, "time" or "usance" drafts, and drafts drawn under letters of credit are subject to payment rules different from those for cash items. Generally, banks handling noncash items must act with due care and diligence and have a reasonable period of time within which to act and a longer period than the law allows for cash items.

§24.2 DEMAND AND TIME DRAFTS

"Demand" or "sight" drafts are payable by the drawee upon presentation. If the bank receives a **sight draft** drawn on Buyer Corp., the bank will notify Buyer of the arrival of the draft and ask Buyer to put the bank in funds. If Buyer fails to do so within the time limits provided, Buyer has dishonored, and the bank must give notice to the prior party in the collection chain. Figure 4-1 illustrates the transaction.

Time drafts differ from demand or sight drafts. The time draft is not payable upon presentation but at a period after a specified date or after sight or on a specified date. It is not unusual, for example, for a time draft to be payable 90 days after date, that is, after the date of the draft itself. It is also quite common for drafts to be payable a given number of days after sight (e.g., "at 90 days' sight"), that is, after presentation. Document 4-5 in Chapter 4 is an example of a time draft.

When the bank receives the time draft, it asks the drawee, the person to whom the order to pay is directed, to "accept" the draft by signing it on its face. The bank then holds the draft or returns it to the drawer or the drawer's agent until it becomes due. When the acceptance is due, the holder will present it again, probably through the banking system, to the drawee, this time for payment.

§24.3 USING THE DRAFT

The draft arises in any number of transactions. Cotton producers have used drafts drawn on their broker buyers with samples of the cotton attached. Used car dealers sometimes wholesale vehicles by attaching certificates of title to drafts drawn on dealer-buyers. In the **documentary draft** transaction, sellers of commodities draw drafts on their buyers and attach a document of title (usually a negotiable warehouse receipt or negotiable bill of lading) to the draft. In the international sale of goods, exporters draw drafts on banks that issue letters of credit supporting the sale. Drafts are quite common in the standby letter of credit transaction. The following transactions illustrate, in the first, the use of a sight draft and, in the second, the use of a time draft.

Automobile dealers take many used vehicles "in trade" that they cannot sell themselves. By virtue of a dealer's location or the nature of its clientele, it cannot sell or prefers not to sell the used vehicles at retail. Such dealers frequently sell their trade-in vehicles to wholesalers who conduct auctions. Buyers at the auctions (used car dealers) may travel from distant points. When a buyer bids successfully for vehicles, the wholesaler will frequently extend him credit by permitting him to take the vehicles at the conclusion of the auction. The wholesaler effects collection by using a sight draft drawn on the buyer accompanied by the title certificates for the vehicles. After drawing the draft, an illustration of which appears as Document 4-4, the wholesaler attaches the certificates and "deposits" the draft with its bank for collection. The depositary bank, which may or may not give the wholesaler available credit, forwards the draft and certificates through the bank collection system to the buyer's bank. The buyer's bank then notifies the buyer that the draft and certificates have arrived. The buyer goes to his bank, examines the certificates, and honors the draft by putting the bank in funds. At that point, the bank delivers the certificates to the buyer.

In a typical time-draft transaction, an importer of garments will grant 90-day credit terms to his domestic buyer. The terms of the sales contract require the buyer to create **trade acceptances,** which the seller can use to finance his own purchase from the foreign supplier.

Under the contract, the importer will cause the goods to be shipped to the buyer and will obtain evidence of that shipment, probably a nonnegotiable truck bill of lading. The importer will then draw a draft on the buyer in the amount of the purchase price payable 90 days after date, being the date of the bill of lading. The importer will then "deposit" the draft at his bank, which will forward it through the collection chain to the buyer's bank. The buyer's bank will notify the buyer that the draft is available for acceptance. The buyer will then sign the draft on its face. At that point the draft becomes a trade acceptance, which the buyer's bank or some other bank may purchase from the importer. Document 4-6 is an example of a trade acceptance.

The acceptance's attractiveness as an investment will depend in part on the financial reputation of the buyer (the **acceptor**) and also of the importer, who is the drawer and who will indorse the acceptance to any investor. Because the acceptance is a negotiable instrument free from the equities of the underlying contract between the importer and the buyer, it may be an attractive medium of investment in the money market.

The net effect of the arrangement is to give the buyer credit while allowing the importer to be paid. In effect, banks or other financial intermediaries, by purchasing the acceptance, provide the credit. The parties' obligations as drawer, acceptor, and indorser of the acceptance serve as the collateral.

§24.4 PAYABLE-THROUGH DRAFTS

There are occasions when a payor will authorize parties to draw but will want to retain control of payment. In self-administered insurance programs, for example, an insurance company will authorize its insured, an employer providing self-administered health benefits coverage to employees, to draw payable-through drafts on the insurance company. It would be risky for the company to let its many insureds write checks on its account without some control on the part of the company over payment.

The insurance company can achieve that control with the payable-through draft. The employer obtains copies of the employee's medical bills, satisfies itself that there is coverage, and draws a payable-through draft on the insurance company. When the draft arrives at the bank through which it is payable, the bank refers the draft to the insurance company, whose clerks will redetermine that the claim is payable and, if so, authorize the bank to make payment and charge the insurance company's account.

Credit unions and money market funds have also used payable-through drafts in lieu of checks. In the money-market fund transaction, for example, an investor will purchase shares in the fund, which may consist of short-term, highly liquid securities that yield reasonable interest income. When the investor desires to transfer a portion of her investment, she will draw a payable-through draft on the money market fund's account at a commercial bank. The bank will honor the draft if the fund approves it. Document 24-1 is a payable-through draft.

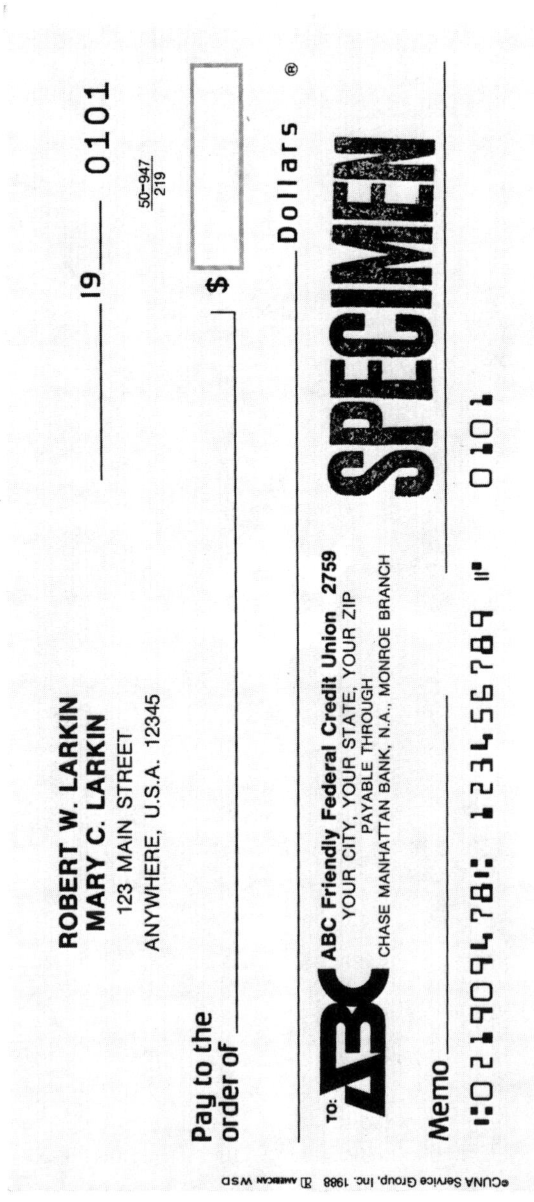

ROBERT W. LARKIN
MARY C. LARKIN
123 MAIN STREET
ANYWHERE, U.S.A. 12345

19___ 0101

50-947/219

Pay to the order of ______ $

______ Dollars ®

TO: ABC Friendly Federal Credit Union 2759
YOUR CITY, YOUR STATE, YOUR ZIP
PAYABLE THROUGH
CHASE MANHATTAN BANK, N.A., MONROE BRANCH

SPECIMEN

Memo ______

⑆021909478⑆ 123456789⑈ 0101

©CUNA Service Group, Inc. 1988

Specimen draft reprinted with permission from CUNA Service Group, Inc. Draft contains collective membership mark that is owned by CUNA and may be used only when authorized by CUNA.

25

Wholesale Electronic Funds Transfer

§25.1 SCOPE

This chapter deals with "wholesale" electronic funds transfer (EFT). By the term *wholesale* in EFT law, we generally mean nonconsumer EFT transactions. This chapter does not deal with debit and credit cards, automated teller machines, and **point of sale terminals,** all of which have important EFT features. Those subjects generally fall under the "consumer" rubric, and Chapter 26 deals with consumer EFT. Electronic transfers initiated by banks, corporations, and other business enterprises are the main concern of this chapter.

This distinction between wholesale and consumer wire transfers parallels the distinction that has evolved in EFT regulation. Generally, the federal government, through the Truth-in-Lending Law and its concomitant, Regulation Z, and the Electronic Fund Transfers Act and its concomitant, Part 205 of Regulation E, deals with *consumer* EFT transactions. On the other hand, under the sponsorship of the American Law Institute and the National Conference of Commissioners on Uniform State Laws, Article 4A of the Uniform Commercial Code is confined in scope to "commercial" or "wholesale" wire transfers.

§25.2 THE PARTICIPANTS

EFT innovations introduce a new lexicon into payments law, and it is worth pausing a bit here to consider the names EFT systems and statutes have given to the parties involved in an electronic payment transaction.

Most wire transfer systems are accessible only to banks. If a nonbank initiates a wire payment or transfer, it must issue a transfer order to a bank participant in the system. This nonbank is the **originator** of the wire transfer "payment order." The bank to which the originator directs the wire transfer order becomes a **sender** when it carries out the originator's order by issuing a new order or transferring the originator's order to a second bank. The first bank, the initial contact in the payments system, is sometimes referred to as the **originator's bank.** The second bank becomes a **receiving bank** upon receipt of the order and, if it passes the order to another bank, becomes a "sender." Ultimately, the order arrives at the bank, the "beneficiary's bank," where the "payee" or **beneficiary** of the transfer order maintains an account. Receipt by that bank of the transfer order prompts the bank to credit the account of the beneficiary and notify

Figure 25-1. Wire Transfer

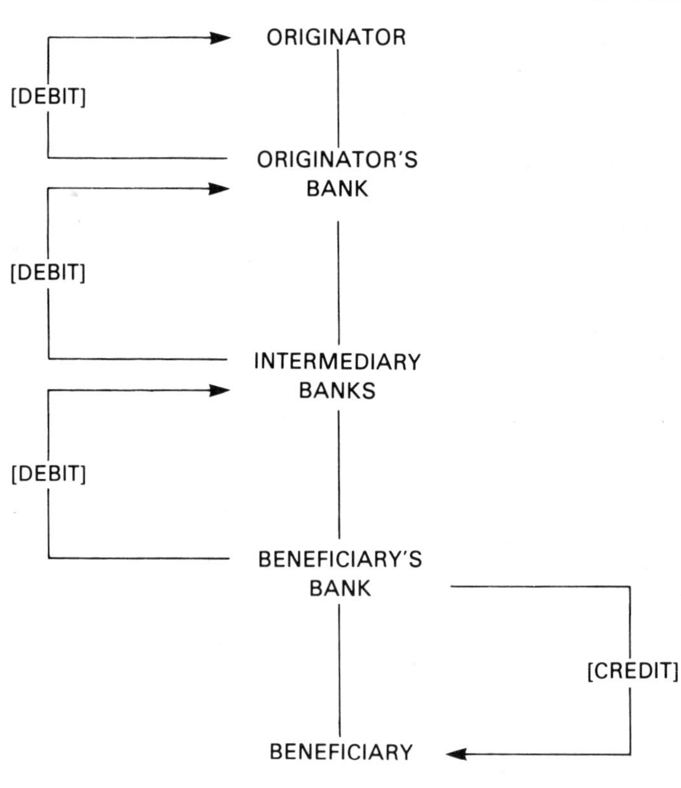

it of the credit. Sometimes, banks initiate transfers and receive transfers for their own accounts. In those cases, there is no nonbank originator or beneficiary. Figure 25-1 illustrates the parties to a wire transfer that involves a nonbank initiator and a nonbank payee.

§25.3 THE "PAPERLESS" SOCIETY

With the advent of the computer, reader-sorter machines, image processors, and other technological advances, some have been predicting the demise of the paper-based payments system and its replacement by electronic funds transfer. The object of these changes would be a system that does not eliminate paper itself from the collection and payments systems but eliminates paper as the medium of payment and replaces it with electronic impulses and computer memory.

Even wire transfers generate paper. Banks that permit consumer customers to deposit and withdraw funds through terminals at home or in shopping centers must provide paper records of those "paperless" transactions. Similarly, banks that wire funds for their large corporate customers provide access to computer-stored information that is available in "hard-copy" form. In these wire transfers, however, there is no piece of paper that serves as the operative instrument. In that important sense, the wire transfer is paperless.

To some extent, we have had wire transfers for a long time. Payments initiated by telephone, **telex,** or telegraph are wire transfers, since there is no piece of paper that embodies the payment order or obligation. For many years bankers accommodated their customers' instructions by telephone. The vacationer who called his banker and asked him to transfer funds from a savings account to a checking account, for example, was effecting a transfer of funds by wire.

For many years, international payments have been effected by telex. A New York importer, for example, could ask its bank to transfer pounds sterling to a British exporter. The New York bank would telex instructions to its London correspondent directing the correspondent to debit the New York bank's pound sterling account and credit the account of the exporter. Since there was no "instrument" in the transaction, though there would have been paper records of the importer's directions to its bank and the New York bank's instructions to its London correspondent (the telex printout), the payment was a true wire transfer.

It was not until the 1960s, however, that the silicon chip and rapid and reliable means of communication made high volume and rapid pace for such transactions practicable. It was the exponential growth of such transfers and the vast variation in systems that developed that gave rise to important distinctions between this payment activity and paper-based systems. Not surprisingly, the law fashioned by the judges of King's Bench in the seventeenth and eighteenth centuries did not always fit these innovations.

§25.4 DISTINGUISHING WIRE AND PAPER PAYMENTS CONCEPTS

Under a paperless system, a debtor uses electronic messages instead of paper to effect payment. An automobile manufacturer in Detroit, for example, can "wire" funds to its suppliers and achieve quick and relatively inexpensive payment. Under such a payments scheme, the manufacturer's computer operator instructs the manufacturer's bank to credit, through an interbank wire system such as Fedwire, the accounts of its suppliers at various banks throughout the country. The arrangement is quicker than payment by check. Transfers occur instantaneously, by the end of the day, or at the beginning of the next day, depending on the interbank settlement arrangements of the wire system. The system will usually be less expensive than a paper system, since the manufacturer avoids check preparation costs and can use stored computer information to generate and record payment for more than one purpose. It is true that the manufacturer may lose **float** by virtue of having reduced the check-collection system's delays, but the manufacturer can time its wire transfer in such a way that payment occurs no sooner than it would under the check-collection system. In short, in this setting, substitution of wire transfers for paper payment makes economic and commercial sense.

In other settings, however, that substitution does not make sense. In the paper-based system, paper, i.e., checks, drafts, notes, and other items, functions not simply as a record of payment or a record of an underlying obligation but becomes an obligation in and of itself. The King's courts long resisted this peculiar merchant innovation. In particular, the judges of King's Bench feared an avalanche of litigation if someone other than the original obligee (the seller of goods, for example) could sue on the obligation (promissory note or acceptance) that the buyer gave the seller. After considerable effort, the English courts of the seventeenth century accepted the idea that a piece of paper can embody an obligation and that that obligation can be independent of the underlying commercial transaction. American courts have accepted the notion from the start.

These ideas are central to the paper-based system, which treats the paper as an obligation of the signatories to it and which gives the holder of the paper, provided he takes in the ordinary course, rights quite apart from the equities of the transaction out of which the paper arises.

This appreciation for the differences between negotiable paper and nonnegotiable wire transfers explains the survival of paper as a means of payment. In fact, the number of paper payments by check and the volume of payments by wire have enjoyed lusty growth in the last two decades, and while the use of drafts and notes has declined, there is evidence that their use continues and that, in the case of notes, is growing again. Some of paper's resilience is, no doubt, a function of its relatively low cost in comparison to wire transactions, but some of it is a function of commercial parties' desire for an obligation that is abstract from the underlying transaction.

Forfaiting, a recent export innovation, involves loans against receivables. In order to make those receivables more attractive in the financial markets, the exporters' lenders have asked the exporter to obtain a negotiable promissory note from the exporter's customer. That note is more marketable than the buyer's naked obligation to pay. The note is negotiable, the obligation to pay arising out of the underlying transaction is not. By using the note, the parties have abstracted the payment obligation from the underlying transaction and rendered the obligation valuable to investors who know nothing about the transaction and do not want to invest in the obligation if it is subject to defenses arising out of the underlying contract. This abstraction feature is also present in the trade-acceptance example discussed in Section 24.2.

The abstraction of the payment obligation, a unique and critical feature of commercial law, enhances the value of the obligation and benefits all parties. Credit becomes more readily available at lower cost. The obligor, of course, loses its contract defenses, but it can protect itself in the contract by providing for security against contract breach (e.g., an escrow arrangement, bond, or letter of credit) or can require an inspection certificate from an independent party. In the alternative, it can save transaction costs and take the risk.

Some commercial parties used the negotiable features of promissory notes unfairly against consumers. In response, there arose a concerted effort by legislators, judges, and many law teachers to limit the use of such instruments. Generally, however, those limitations have confined themselves to the consumer setting. It is fashionable, nonetheless, among law teachers to view the abstraction principle with disdain. Indeed, there is something of a campaign among law school faculties these days against the whole notion of negotiability. Academic literature sometimes argues against this commercial evil. In the consumer context, those arguments are well taken; in the commercial context, they are not.

In recent years, the federal government began paying farmers for not planting crops under a commodity certificate arrangement. Under this system, a farmer in a rural Iowa county, for example, could agree with representatives of the Department of Agriculture not to plant acreage on which he customarily cultivated corn. The government's payment for that agreement consisted of a piece of paper, a commodity certificate, that was denominated in dollars and was redeemable at a specified date.

It makes sense, however, that some holders of certificates would want to convert them into cash early. A certificate issued in May 1989 and redeemable in January 1990 will not pay a June feed bill, a September college tuition statement, or airline expenses for that October trip to Disneyland. The federal government knew, therefore, that the certificates would be more attractive to the farmers they wanted to attract to the program if the certificates were readily transferable. Not surprisingly, the certificates that the government fashioned were negotiable, though not fully. Under the terms of the certificates and the regulations governing them, transfer is effected by restrictive indorsement, and the Commodity Credit Corporation honors them when a holder with a certificate with a proper chain of indorsements presents the certificate. Significantly, the form of certificate adopted by the government provides in blanks on the reverse side for as many as 14 transfers. Document 25-1 is a commodity certificate.

Negotiable paper has its raison d'être. Parties will resort to it when it suits their commercial purpose. Wire transfers have their raison d'être as well, and commercial parties will resort to wire transfers when they suit the transaction.

One might argue that the two ideas, (1) that a piece of paper can embody an obligation and (2) that the obligation exists independently of the transaction out of which the paper arises, are the key elements of "commercial" law that have provided certainty for that field and differentiated it from the ill-defined and litigation-ridden swamp of "contract" law.

A paperless system loses the commercial attributes. Some may see that loss as a threat to the very features of the payments system that render it uniquely fitted for commerce. Others see those features as anachronisms that the system can discard. Arguably, both of those views are erroneous. The first ignores the advantages electronic funds transfers provide to commerce, and the latter ignores the continuing need for a system that provides quick movement of paper.

There are a number of systems fashioned to provide for paperless payments. The balance of this chapter discusses some of them. Readers should bear in mind that this area of commercial activity, perhaps more than any other, is subject to rapid change. Many of these systems are in their infancy. Participants are revising them frequently, creating new systems that compete with them, and discarding some of them altogether.

§25.5 FEDWIRE

Since 1970 when it was first introduced as an electronic payments system and 1982 when it achieved its present form, the Federal Reserve System has operated a wire transfer system. Under the arrangement, more than 8,000 depositary institutions transfer payments by wire among the Federal Reserve Banks and their branches. In addition to the private depositary institution participants, the system serves the federal government, the Federal Reserve Banks themselves, the Federal Reserve Board, and the Treasury.

Under the system, which is now serving more than 100,000 private customers of depositary institutions, a debtor-payor (originator) instructs its bank to transmit funds. The bank, in turn, advises its Federal Reserve Bank or branch to wire the funds to the account of a payee-beneficiary. Daily Fedwire transactions exceed 165,000, and annual transfers aggregate more than $100 trillion. Fedwire transfers are generally large-dollar transfers. The average Fedwire transaction is $2 million, while the average check is only about $600.

Assuming that the originator and the payee-beneficiary maintain accounts at depositary institutions, that is, banks that maintain accounts with Federal Reserve Banks, the transaction is relatively simple. The originator, whose terminal is often connected by telephone to the office of its bank, the depositary institution, signals the bank to transfer funds to the payee-beneficiary's designated account at the receiving depositary institution, the beneficiary's bank.

The message in the Fedwire system actuates the payment, that is, Fedwire is not simply a message system, as **SWIFT,** which is discussed in section 25.7 below, is: Fedwire is a payments system as well. When the receiving Federal Reserve Bank receives the message, it effects payment by debiting and crediting accounts according to its instructions. If both the originator's bank and the payee-beneficiary's bank maintain deposits at the Federal Reserve Bank, the Federal Reserve Bank debits the account of the originator's bank and credits the account of the payee-beneficiary's bank. Figure 25-1 above illustrates the payment.

Only a depositary institution, that is, a financial institution that maintains an account with a Federal Reserve Bank may send funds via Fedwire. If either or both the payor and payee do not maintain deposits at depositary institutions, there must be an additional layer of participants. Assuming that both maintain their accounts at nondepositary institutions, money-market funds, for example, the payor's fund must forward the signal to a depositary institution, and the payee's fund must receive the transfer message from a depositary institution. In both cases, the funds must maintain accounts at the transmitting and receiving depositary institutions or must have other arrangements for reimbursement. Again, if the depositary institutions maintain accounts at the same Federal Reserve Bank, the Federal Reserve Bank debits that of the sending depositary bank and credits that of the receiving depositary bank. The depositary banks must also make corresponding debits and credits to the accounts of their customers, the funds with which the payor and the payee maintain accounts. When the depositary institutions maintain accounts at different Federal Reserve Banks there must be an additional step in the process, that whereby the Federal Reserve Banks settle between themselves.

§25.6 CHIPS AND SIMILAR INTERNATIONAL SYSTEMS

The New York Clearinghouse Association, an organization of money-center banks located in New York City, operates the Clearinghouse Interbank Payments System (CHIPS). The system facilitates international dollar-denominated payments. There are two kinds of CHIPS participants, those that have access to the CHIPS system and those that have access and are settling participants. The former may initiate transfers through the system but must settle through one of the latter.

Assume a French investor agrees to purchase securities from a German seller for a price denominated in dollars. The investor may want to effect payment by transferring funds between accounts at the parties' U.S. banks. If the investor maintains an account at one CHIPS settling participant, First Bank, and the German seller maintains an account at another CHIPS settling participant, Second Bank, the investor will notify First Bank, probably through SWIFT, to make the transfer. First Bank will enter the transaction into the CHIPS computer by designating the account at Second Bank to be credited and the amount of the transaction. Under the rules fashioned by CHIPS participants, the CHIPS computer stores the information until First Bank sends a second signal verifying the stored information. At that point, the transaction occurs under CHIPS rules, and the CHIPS computer will make the corresponding debit and credit entries. Second Bank will notify its customer, the German seller of the credit.

Although CHIPS rules consider the transaction to be final and **unwindable** at the time First Bank verifies its original message, settlement between First and Second Bank does not occur until the end of the day. When the CHIPS day ends, currently at 4:30 P.M. New York time, the CHIPS computer advises CHIPS settling participants of their net positions with respect to all other CHIPS settling participants. At that point, the CHIPS participants must effect settlement among themselves through the New York Federal Reserve Bank. Nonsettling participants must arrange to settle separately with their settling participant correspondents. Figure 25-2 assumes that only settling participants are involved and illustrates the payment in the French investor's purchase of securities from the German seller.

Nonparticipants of CHIPS may use the system but cannot access it without going through a CHIPS participant. If the French investor in the

Figure 25-2. CHIPS Transfer

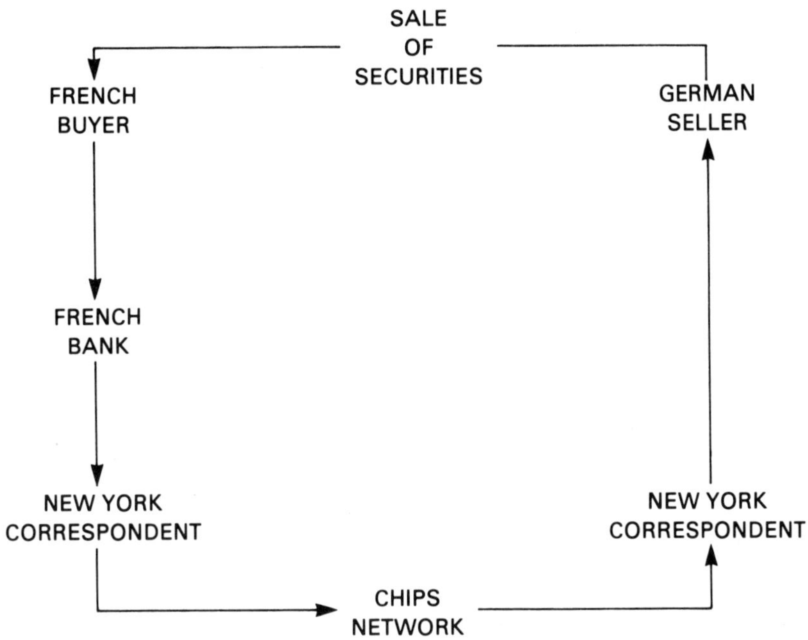

foregoing example did not maintain an account with a CHIPS participant bank, he would have to instruct the bank at which he did maintain an account to arrange for the transaction through a CHIPS participant. The CHIPS participant will be responsible for the transaction under CHIPS rules and will debit an account that the nonparticipant bank maintains at the CHIPS participant bank or otherwise arrange for reimbursement from the investor or his bank. Similarly, if the payee, the German seller, does not maintain an account with a CHIPS participant institution, payment to the seller of the securities requires an additional layer of parties, with the CHIPS receiving bank transferring the funds to the nonparticipant bank where the seller maintains its account. The CHIPS system does not concern itself with transfers outside the system, which are normally made by debiting and crediting correspondent accounts.

The CHIPS system replaces the rather slow process of using **bank drafts,** i.e., checks drawn by one bank on an account it maintains at another bank. Under that system, the French investor would "purchase" a bank draft from a French bank that maintains a U.S. dollar account at a bank, probably in New York. The investor would then send the draft to the German seller, who would deposit it in another bank, probably in New York, where the German seller or his bank maintained its U.S. dollar account. That mode of effecting international payments survives, but it is slower and costlier than using the CHIPS system. Chapter 27 discusses bank drafts and international collections in more detail.

Also surviving is the system of correspondent accounts. Under this arrangement, banks that serve international activity maintain a network of correspondent relationships whereby a domestic correspondent maintains a **nostro account** (in, for example, French francs) at its foreign correspondent and holds a U.S. dollar **vostro account** covering the correspondent's deposit with the domestic bank. Correspondent relationships provide quick and efficient payment. A French bank may telex its U.S. correspondent and instruct it to transfer dollars to the German bank's dollar account with its U.S. correspondent. The practice of maintaining correspondent balances, however, is generally more costly and slower than using the CHIPS network.

CHIPS currently clears as many as 40,000 transfers each day among 140 bank participants. Those daily transfers total about $660 million on an average day. They occur on the day they are initiated, are remarkably free from error, and do not entail the transportation risks that inhere in the mailing of bank drafts. On the first day of the week following a three-day weekend, CHIPS may handle transfers totalling more than $1.25 trillion.

CHIPS began operation in 1970. In 1981, its participants substantially revised its operations. In the same year, the Federal Reserve Bank of Chicago began operating the Clearinghouse Electronic Settlement System (CHESS), which utilized **BankWire** — a private competitor of the Federal Reserve System's Fedwire. When BankWire suspended operations in 1986, CHESS suspended operations also.

FXnet is a London-based limited partnership that provides foreign **exchange** settlements to participating banks. Under the FXnet wire system, two banks can net out their respective positions arising out of foreign exchange transactions. The settlement procedure avoids certain risks and reduces the number of settlements per day between the two banks to one.

English banks have developed their own wire transfer system, Clearing House Automated Payments System (CHAPS), Australian banks their system, Bank Interchange and Transfer System (BITS), and banks of other countries comparable wire-transfer systems.

In short, there are a number of existing electronic systems for transferring funds between and among banks on behalf of their customers. By all indications, the industry is still somewhat in a state of disequilibrium as it evolves into an efficient transfer network.

§25.7 SWIFT

In 1973, more than 200 banks in a number of countries established the **Society for Worldwide Interbank Financial Telecommunications** (SWIFT), a not-for-profit cooperative established under Belgian law. Currently, SWIFT, with more than 1,500 banks now participating in its ownership, is a message, not a payments, system; that is, it facilitates interbank transfer of information but presupposes a separate system for effecting the payments that a given message may indicate. In the CHIPS transaction described in the preceding section, the French investor instructed his New York CHIPS participant by SWIFT, and the New York bank effected the payment through CHIPS.

SWIFT participants transmit messages quickly and inexpensively by using signals that computers encode and decode. An English sender of a message to a New York bank must contact a SWIFT participant, usually a bank, that maintains a SWIFT terminal on its premises. The participant enters the encoded message via telephone lines dedicated to SWIFT usage. The message passes to one of the SWIFT **switching centers.** At the present time, under Phase I of SWIFT, the switching center confirms the message and then transmits it to the receiving bank, which, in this example, is a CHIPS participant.

Under Phase II, SWIFT will replace its switching centers, which store and forward messages and are the hubs of a hub-and-spoke system, with two system control centers that are able to handle the entire SWIFT traffic. Originally, SWIFT was designed to handle 300,000 messages a day, but gradual upgrading of the system permits it to handle up to 1.4 million transactions daily. In an average day, there are slightly more than 1.2 million messages transferred on SWIFT. Under the present SWIFT system, there are five switching centers, all of which are operating close to capacity. The new phase of SWIFT will admit of expanded capacity and additional message-carrying features by adding computers to the two centers. SWIFT managers claim that the new phase, SWIFT-2, will be capable of handling an unlimited number of daily messages and of additional facilities. Among the new operations SWIFT envisions are use of SWIFT as a data base, electronic data interchange, and the handling of recurring payments in a fashion similar to those made through automated clearinghouses.

UNITED STATES DEPARTMENT OF AGRICULTURE

Commodity Credit Corporation

COMMODITY CERTIFICATE

A. Issue Date (Mo., Day, Yr.)	B. St. & Co. Code & C/D	C. Commodity	D. Cash Redemption Start Date
E. Program Code	F. Expiration Date	AMOUNT ⇨ *VOID IF AMOUNT EXCEEDS $50,000.00*	G.

H. This certificate is issued to:

1. This certificate is null and void unless all information in blocks A through H has been completed and the certificate has been signed and countersigned by authorized representatives of the Commodity Credit Corporation (CCC).
2. The Regulations (7 C.F.R. Part 770) "Commodity Certificates, In-Kind Payments, and Other Forms of Payment" (the "Regulations") are incorporated in and made a part hereof by reference. CCC will not honor any certificate made, transferred, or submitted in violation of such Regulations or in violation of the terms and conditions of this certificate.
3. This certificate may be transferred to any person. Any transfer must be in the full amount of the certificate and can be effected only by restrictive endorsement on the back of the certificate, showing the name of the transferee and the date of transfer, and must be signed by the transferor. The person who submits the certificate to CCC for redemption must endorse the certificate to CCC.
4. This certificate shall not be subject to any State law or regulation, including but not limited to State statutory and regulatory provisions with respect to commercial paper, security interests, and negotiable instruments. This certificate shall not be encumbered by any lien or other claim, except that of an agency of the United States Government.
5. This certificate may be used at any time on or before the expiration date (block F) to receive a quantity of certain commodities in CCC inventory which had been pledged as collateral for a CCC price support loan made to the holder. To the extent permitted by the Regulations and in accordance with instructions issued by CCC, any holder may exchange this certificate for commodities owned by CCC. CCC will determine the value of the commodities for which this certificate may be exchanged. In certain instances the Regulations may prohibit the exchange of this certificate for commodities prior to the date contained in block D. In certain instances, as established by the Regulations, CCC may also exchange this certificate for cash. CCC may discount or refuse to accept this certificate if it is submitted after the expiration date (block F).
6. If the term "Generic" appears in block C, this certificate may be exchanged for any CCC-owned commodity made available under the program by CCC. If a specific commodity is designated in block C, this certificate may be exchanged only for such CCC-owned commodity, unless otherwise provided for by CCC.
7. CCC will not be responsible for any loss sustained by any holder resulting from this certificate being lost, stolen, forged or altered.
8. CCC will not honor a joint endorsement of this certificate.

COMMODITY CREDIT CORPORATION · A FEDERAL CORPORATE AGENCY · BY ACT OF CONGRESS · 1948

Signed: **SPECIMEN** Countersigned:

(Authorized Representative of CCC) *(Authorized Representative of CCC)*

CCC-6 (07-10-87) Serial No. 40000071

VOID IF ALTERED OR MODIFIED - DO NOT REPRINT

CCC-6-1 (07-10-87) COMMODITY CERTIFICATE PAYMENT STATEMENT

IDENTIFYING NO.	FARM NO.	LOAN/CONTROL NO.	SERIAL NO.

Document 25-1. *(continued)*

ENDORSEMENTS

THE TRANSFEROR/ENDORSER MUST COMPLETE THE RELEVANT INFORMATION ("TO", "BY", "DATE") FOR EACH TRANSFER. FAILURE TO COMPLETE THE INFORMATION RENDERS THE CERTIFICATE VOID.

TO ______ DATE ______ BY ______	TO ______ DATE ______ BY ______
TO ______ DATE ______ BY ______	TO ______ DATE ______ BY ______
TO ______ DATE ______ BY ______	TO ______ DATE ______ BY ______
TO ______ DATE ______ BY ______	TO ______ DATE ______ BY ______
TO ______ DATE ______ BY ______	TO ______ DATE ______ BY ______
TO ______ DATE ______ BY ______	TO ______ DATE ______ BY ______
TO ______ DATE ______ BY ______	TO ______ DATE ______ BY ______

SPECIMEN

REMOVE THIS STUB BEFORE SIGNING.
DO NOT ENTER ANY SIGNATURES IN THIS AREA

26

Retail Electronic Funds Transfer

§26.1 SCOPE

This chapter deals with those features of electronic funds transfer that involve the bank customer and, importantly, the consumer. By *consumer,* we mean here the customer that uses the bank's system for personal, family, or household purposes. Many of the rules for these transactions will affect business enterprises. Commercial parties use point of sale terminals and automated teller machines, and the largest corporation will maintain a checking account with a bank that uses the automated clearinghouse and check truncation. Yet, in these areas, unlike the **wholesale wire transfer** area, the consumer is a major concern of the law, and the rules are fashioned largely with the consumer in mind. The distinction is an important one, and while there is considerable overlap, differentiating the two kinds of transfers along lines that reflect their importance to the two kinds of parties involved (consumers on the one hand and commercial parties on the other) is working.

§26.2 AUTOMATED TELLER MACHINES (ATMs)

By using a plastic access card and a **personal identification number** (PIN), bank customers may conduct some of their banking without having to deal with long lines in front of the teller window or with early bank closing hours. The ATM, which may be located in a vestibule outside the bank, in a shopping center, or elsewhere, normally permits the customer to make deposits of any kind and to make limited cash withdrawals. By sharing terminals, a consortium of financial institutions can make ATM banking available to their customers in a wide geographic area at a large number of terminals.

The PIN is a computer-generated number given to the customer to be used with the card and memorized or stored in a place away from the card. The mathematical probabilities of a thief's guessing a person's PIN are too low for him to use a stolen card without knowing the number.

ATMs are not without their detractors. Many bank customers avoid them as impersonal and sometimes as unsafe. Enduring the long lines in a cozy bank lobby is often preferable to waiting outdoors on a blustery Minnesota mid-winter day. Criminals are more inclined to essay their fraudulent practices or their thuggery against the young and the elderly at desolate ATM locations than inside a bank, and while they are rare under the watchful eye of bank security personnel, muggings are not uncommon at some ATM sites. Inevitably, many consumers will keep their PIN on pieces of paper in their wallets, where a pick-pocket or thief finds it and the access card.

The evidence suggests that there is a measure of customer fraud and of bank fraud in connection with ATMs. Some customers claim that their transaction statements reflect withdrawals they never made or fail to reflect deposits they did make. Bankers, on the other hand, claim that no one has access to the customer's PIN, without which it is not possible to activate the account and that security measures (usually, two-employee verification of cash-deposit envelopes) make bank fraud unlikely. While industry observers report that some banks are lax in enforcing security measures, other data support the position that some customers make withdrawals and either forget about them or falsely claim that they did not make them. In 1986, fraud losses suffered by banks from ATMs amounted to $40 million. The industry estimates that 10 percent of those losses were from customer fraud and the balance from bank employee fraud.

More sophisticated ATMs may resolve some of the problems. The cost of a camera to record withdrawals and deposits, of a thumbprint recognition apparatus, or of a retina scanner to deter thieves are expensive modifications, however, to a system that has not lived up to early predictions of significant cost savings. Of late, some banks have begun charging customers that use ATMs a fee, this for a service that the banks encouraged their customers to use in the hope that such use would reduce personnel costs and save the bank money.

The industry has estimated that at the present time there are at least 65,000 ATMs in operation that handle roughly 50.2 billion transactions a year, 76 percent of which are cash withdrawals. Financial institutions estimate that they have issued approximately 135 million ATM cards, which are a kind of debit card.

When the ATM is dedicated to a single bank's ranks of customers, it is on line to the bank's computer. Transactions at the terminal are recorded immediately to the customer's account, though deposits are held a sufficient time for verification. When a single terminal serves a number of banks and when one bank's terminals are available to customers of other banks, the communication of deposit and withdrawal data becomes more complicated. First Bank must charge to Second Bank's account cash withdrawals made at First Bank's terminal by a Second Bank customer. Periodically, Second Bank must thereafter charge its customer's account. Deposits at a multibank ATM of necessity require longer availability time than deposits at a terminal dedicated to one bank's customers.

While the terms of the relationship between a card issuer and its customer are to some extent governed by law, most of the rules and regulations are spelled out in the bank/customer agreement, of which Document 26-1 is an illustration.

§26.3 DEBIT CARDS, SMART CARDS, AND THE POINT OF SALE (POS) TERMINAL

While many think of credit cards, which are discussed in Chapter 31, as plastic money, they are, in fact, plastic credit, since the credit-card sale is a credit transaction. Debit cards, on the other hand, are the equivalent of money, or, at least they could be, if the lawmakers would leave the debit-card transaction alone.

The debit card looks much like a credit card. In fact, many credit cards may serve as debit cards. It is the function of the two cards that differs not so much as their appearance or attributes.

Recently "smart" cards have made their debut in consumer wire-transfer transactions. The **smart card** replaces the credit card's magnetic stripe with a silicon chip. While smart cards are relatively more expensive to manufacture than credit cards, the smart card can contain significant amounts of data. That data, moreover, may be accessed and altered by terminals at a merchant's establishment. The smart card, then, does not require the on-line capabilities of the system designed for the cards presently in use. For the most part in the United States, because of the industry's investment in technology that serves present cards, use of smart cards has not proceeded as quickly as some had hoped. Nevertheless, in many transactions, especially the POS transaction, the smart card can achieve efficiencies.

The most common use of debit cards is with ATM machines, where cardholders obtain access to their bank accounts by inserting the card into the machine and entering their PIN. The debit card can also activate a point of sale (POS) terminal. In a few regions of the country, banks have installed these terminals at retail establishments, such as automotive service stations, convenience stores, or super markets. POS growth has been somewhat slow. Presently, there are about 84,000 POS terminals and about 180 million annual transactions.

The POS terminal permits the customer to pay the retailer by inserting the debit card into the terminal, activating the terminal with a PIN, and then entering the amount of the purchase price. If the card is a traditional debit card with a magnetic stripe, the terminal may be on line with the bank's central computer, which receives the information, debits the customer's account, and credits that of the merchant. If the terminal is not on line, the bank must gather the information periodically and make the corresponding debit and credit entries. Under some systems, the bank or other data processor captures the information periodically (usually daily) by telephone line or electronic transmission. Thus, there is under these systems some delay in effecting the transfers and in updating the cardholder's and the merchant's balances. In these cases, the debit card takes on some of the attributes of a credit card and loses some of its advantages as a separate product.

The absence of on-line capabilities also creates problems for credit authorization and verification. Some systems, however, transmit that information daily, usually at off-peak hours. These off-line or "short-term, on-line" systems reduce credit risk but do not eliminate it. During any given day, a merchant will not have up-to-date information on overdrawn accounts or reports of lost or stolen cards that arose during that day. These systems have the advantage, however, of reducing cost. They involve considerably less computer time and less merchant time spent on verification and authorization requests. At the present, systems offering the off-line, smart card POS are marketing their product with low-dollar retailers such as fast-food merchants. The systems, however, are still pretty much in their infancy.

With a smart card and its embedded silicon chip, the on-line capability of the POS is not necessary. Smart cards can be used with equipment that is off-line but that has the capacity to alter the information on the card. For example, a consumer with a smart card can go to the bank and have the card encoded for a given amount of credit. Armed with the card, the consumer can proceed to make purchases. At each merchant establishment, the POS terminal reads the smart card to determine that there is sufficient credit available and deducts the amount of the immediate purchase. When the consumer has exhausted the card's credit, she must return to the bank or an ATM machine to replenish the smart-card credit by withdrawing funds from an account or otherwise purchasing the additional credit.

A merchant using such smart-card equipment must deliver data from its machines to the bank periodically so that the bank can credit its account.

§26.4 CHECK TRUNCATION

In the best of all possible payments worlds, the account information of all payors and all payees would be recorded in a single computer to which all parties would have access. When a payor wanted to transfer credit to a payee, the payor would simply signal the computer to make the corresponding entries.

That world does not now and may never exist. To some extent, all wire transfer systems are partial efforts at achieving the most efficient system. Those efforts include the notion of hybrid paper/wire transfer systems that fall into the general category of "check truncation."

The simplest check truncation system involves the payor bank's interruption of the normal transport of the check. Under the check-collection system, a buyer's check normally travels from the buyer to the seller, who deposits it in the banking system. The check-collection system ultimately delivers the check to the buyer's bank, and the bank pays it and returns the check to the buyer with his monthly statement. In these simplest check-truncation system, the bank does not include the check with the buyer's statement but includes details of the transaction in the statement and destroys the paper. The system saves on mailing and handling costs.

Most banks that have introduced this simple check-truncation system adapt their preprinted checks to the system by providing a carbonless copy arrangement whereby the customer can keep the copy, if he chooses to do so. The carbon copy may not be sufficient evidence of payment for a court or for the Internal Revenue Service, but the payor bank photocopies the check before destroying it and makes the copy available to the customer for a fee. Presumably, bank customers do not need copies of their checks, the information recorded by the customer in the check register and the information in the periodic bank statement being sufficient.

In a somewhat more radical check-truncation program, credit unions have used a combination of the payable-through draft and check truncation. Because credit unions did not have their own system for collecting cash items, when they began offering the **share draft** to their customers, they needed entry to the commercial banking system's check-collection machinery. They achieved that entry via payable-through drafts.

The credit union share draft is a demand item payable through a commercial bank or other financial institution with sophisticated collection facilities. Under the arrangement, the credit union maintains an account with a large financial entity, often a money-center bank. When a credit union member draws a share draft, the draft is on the credit union account at the money-center bank and is payable through the money-center bank. The MICR routing symbols on the share draft permit the payee to route the draft through the commercial bank check-collection system. When the draft arrives at the money center bank, the bank pays it and debits the credit union's account. The bank does not route the share draft to the credit union but supplies the debit information to the credit union by wire and truncates the share draft, that is, photocopies and destroys it.

Presently, there are pilot projects involving even more radical check truncation. Under one of them, checks are truncated at the clearinghouse, under another at the Federal Reserve Bank or regional check-processing center. Image processing is an innovation that increases the possibility of check truncation. An image-processing system captures the check's image in a fashion that permits the storage and retrieval of the image electronically. The system has two clear advantages over the traditional microfilming method of storing images. First, image processing permits high-speed and high-volume transmission of the images. Second, the system permits users to manipulate the stored information. For example, if a depositary bank has full image-processing capabilities, it can program its computer to transmit images of checks according to routing direction on the checks. It can also cull out checks in excess of a threshold amount and forward them while only forwarding data from, but not the image of, the smaller checks. Thus, payor banks could see images of large-dollar checks and verify their signatures but avoid the cost and time of such verification for small-dollar items.

The ultimate effect of the full image-processing capabilities will be to do away with a significant amount of data entry, reader-sorter equipment at depositary and payor banks, and transportation of paper.

Check truncation yields considerable savings, and the earlier the system can replace the paper with an electronic impulse, the greater those savings will be. To date, the costs of implementing radical check truncation have exceeded the benefits, but the system is beginning to overcome the technological obstacles. Of the estimated 50 billion checks collected in the United States each year only 4 or 5 billion are truncated, and few of them are truncated at the bank of first deposit.

§26.5 THE AUTOMATED CLEARINGHOUSE (ACH)

In a sense, the automated clearinghouse (ACH) is misnamed. That name conjures up images of automation substituting for the manual processes currently conducted at the clearinghouse. Section 23.3 discusses the clearinghouse. In fact, there are efforts to render the clearinghouse process amenable to electronic procedures under which members of the clearinghouse would hold or truncate checks at the **depositary bank** and forward them electronically to the drawee or clear them through a central computer to which each clearinghouse member is connected. Those efforts are not included in the phrase "automated clearinghouse."

Essentially, the ACH of today is not so much a facility for clearing checks among local banks as it is a mechanism for handling recurring debits and credits that do not involve checks at all. The similarity between the clearinghouse and the ACH lies in the fact that the ACH substitutes computerized information for the cash letters that member institutions exchange at the clearinghouse.

At present, there are 30 ACHs in the United States, which are connected by an interregional network linking 16,000 depositary institutions. Often the ACH conducts its transactions through a Federal Reserve Bank. However, one of the largest ACHs, the New York Automated Clearinghouse, is a private clearinghouse, and the Hawaii and Arizona automated clearinghouses are private. Recently, Visa's automated clearinghouse in California has begun handling ACH transactions for commercial banks.

The National Association of Automated Clearing Houses (NACHA) establishes rules for the local ACH associations, which are members of NACHA. The local association enters into a contract with the Federal Reserve Bank or other processor, and, in the case of a Federal Reserve Bank, the processor issues a circular to further regulate the ACH. Debits and credits through the nation's ACHs exceed 900 million annually, a little less than half of which are federal payments such as social security, veteran's benefits, and federal employee salary payments. According to recent estimates only about 10 to 12 percent of all insurance premium payments and 6 to 8 percent of all payroll payments are made through the ACH. There is considerable room, then, for growth in this efficient payments system.

In a typical ACH transaction, a payor will initiate the transaction by instructing its bank, a member of the ACH, to forward the computerized information to the ACH, which will act on the information in the fashion described above. If the sending customer's bank is not a member of the clearinghouse, that bank must forward the information to a bank that is a member. Banks usually settle among themselves through the Federal Reserve Banks.

When an employer, for example, offers to make direct deposit of payroll, it will probably use an ACH. The employer prepares the payroll information to include the names and checking account numbers of the employees and transfers that information by telephone wire or by delivering a computer tape to the ACH member, which then forwards it, often in the same form (tape or transmitted computer signal) to the ACH. At the present time, there are efforts on the part of the ACH industry to require all communication with the ACH to be electronic, thereby eliminating computer tapes or paper from the system. The ACH, through its own computer, debits the account of the employer at one ACH member institution, notifies member institutions of the transfers to their depositors (the employees), and credits the account of the member institutions for the aggregate amount transferred to all accounts at that institution. Each member institution, in turn, must credit the account of the designated employee-payee. The depositary institution will send its depositor customer a notice of the deposit and, usually, payroll information similar to that which would otherwise be included on the stub of the payroll check this wire-transfer arrangement replaces. Generally, ACH payments are made in next-day funds, that is, the funds are transferred to the payee on the banking day after the ACH receives the transfer order.

The ACH facility is quick and less expensive to both employer and employee than issuing and collecting a check for each employee and obviates postal delays and the loss of checks, which inevitably occur. The ACH is also far safer than the check collection system, since the ACH avoids the check fraud that has plagued the check-collection process. Figure 26-1 illustrates ACH transfer of payroll when employees maintain their accounts at banks that are all members of one ACH.

Recurring debits also lend themselves to collection through the ACH. Insurance company premiums, mortgage payments, and utility payments can be effected efficiently through the ACH in much the same way that the ACH serves payroll payments. In the insurance premium case, for example, the insurance company first obtains the insureds' debit authorizations for the recurring payments. Next, the company periodically instructs its bank to send the computerized information to the ACH, which then acts to collect the funds. The member institution will credit the account of the insurance company. The ACH will credit the account of the member bank and will debit the accounts of member banks whose depositors have **preauthorized debits**. When the ACH notifies the member banks of the debits, the member banks will debit the accounts of the various preauthorizing depositors.

The efficiency of the arrangement is enhanced by the fact that the same computer input serves to notify the ACH and the member institutions, since the ACH computers and member institution computers read the information supplied by the insurance company's member bank. There is no need to keypunch the information into the system more than once. Usually, the original data is entered on the insurance company's terminal and is transmitted by telephone line to the member bank or delivered to the member bank by tape.

Figure 26-1. ACH Payroll

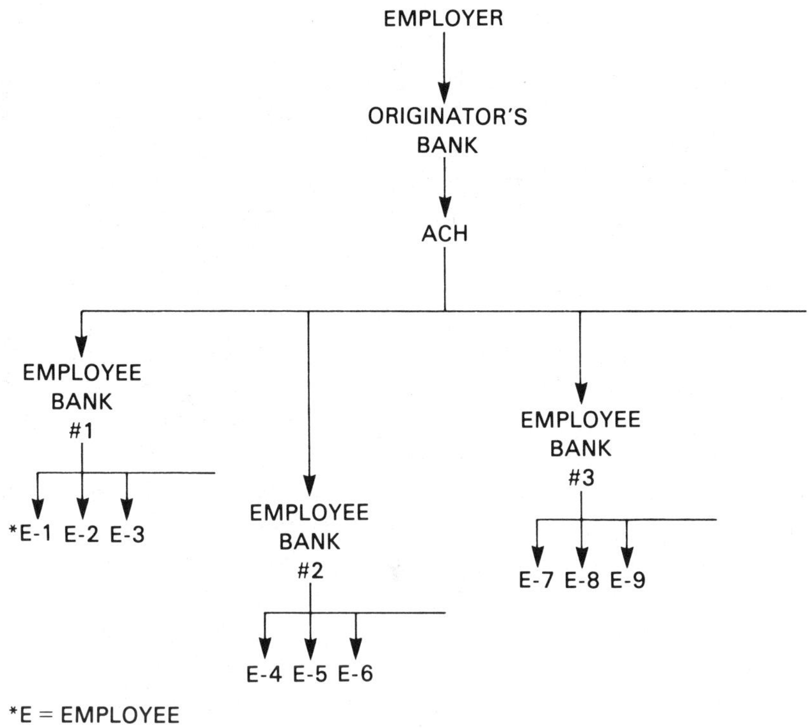

When bankers and commercial parties invented the ACH, they did not anticipate its use as a vehicle for **funds consolidation,** but, in fact, use of the ACH system for that purpose has accelerated. Funds consolidation is the process of bringing a firm's cash to a single point or several points quickly, so that the firm's financial officers can use it. Delay in funds consolidation is expensive, since it forces the firm to borrow or causes it lost investment opportunities. An enterprise with its financial offices in Chicago and retail outlets throughout the country, for example, must bring under the control of the Chicago office cash items received at the retail locations. The ACH lends itself readily to that process.

Periodically, perhaps daily, the Chicago office prepares computerized information instructing the Chicago ACH to debit the bank accounts of the retail outlets. Each afternoon, the retail financial managers signal the Chicago office the amount that will be available for the next morning's debit. The Chicago office then prepares the tape or other computer input, and the following morning, the ACH collects the funds by debiting the accounts of the various banks.

Note that funds consolidation is not a consumer wire transfer, yet it uses the ACH, which was originally designed for and thought of as a retail wire-transfer network. Because the funds consolidation operation traditionally involves sums greater than those involved in retail wire transfers, the chances of excessive daylight overdrafts might be a problem without rules limiting such overdrafts. Even with considerable use of the ACH system for funds consolidation, at the end of 1988, the average ACH transfer was only about $4,000, substantially less than the wholesale wire transfer average over Fedwire and CHIPS, which approximates $2 million.

Some credit-card or debit-card systems are using the ACH to collect charges from their customers. Under these arrangements, the system collects transactional data and, at the end of a day, forwards it to the ACH for collection from the various customers' accounts.

In 1983, the National Automated Clearing House Association (NACHA), the national umbrella organization for all automated clearinghouse associations, developed a system to permit corporations to use the ACH to submit invoices and price information through the ACH. Under this Electronic Data Interchange (EDI) system, merchants that do business with each other on a regular basis may provide each other with up-to-date information on prices, **discounts,** and other credit terms and may substitute electronic communication for such paper transfers as submission of purchase orders, order acknowledgments, and invoices. By combining this feature of the ACH with its debit facility, parties can accelerate the formation of the contract of sale and the invoicing and collection of trade debt.

§26.6 ELECTRONIC CLEARING

At the present time, at least one Federal Reserve Bank (Minneapolis) is experimenting with electronic clearing — the process of presenting items to the drawee electronically in the first instance.

There are two parts to the program. Under the first, participant payor banks in a designated region agree to accept electronic impulses from the Federal Reserve Bank and to make the determination whether to pay or dishonor before the paper arrives. When checks drawn on such an institution arrive at the Federal Reserve Bank, that bank's reader-sorter equipment reads the MICR line on the item and transmits the information to the payor bank. While the payor determines whether to pay or dishonor the item, the Federal Reserve Bank holds the paper under a schedule that permits it to return dishonored items to the bank of first deposit without ever presenting them to the payor. If the payor dishonors, the Federal Reserve Bank returns the item to the bank of first deposit. If the time for dishonor expires, the Federal Reserve Bank forwards the check to the payor for return to its customer with the periodic checking account statement.

Under the second phase of the program, when both the bank of first deposit and the payor bank are participants, the reader-sorter equipment of the depositary bank reads the MICR line of the item. That bank holds the check and forwards the information by "electronic cash letter" to the Federal Reserve Bank. The Federal Reserve Bank then forwards the information to payor participants, who have already agreed to act on it without receiving the paper.

Neither feature of the program involves truncation, since the paper ultimately follows the electronic impulse to the payor. In the case of returns, however, the programs save time — a full day in some cases. Because the Federal Reserve Bank in the first phase of the program and the depositary bank in the second treat the paper on a hold-and-forward basis, paper that is ultimately dishonored travels less than under traditional check-clearing systems.

§26.7 HOME BANKING AND TELEPHONE BILL PAYING

Some banks have marketed a home banking system that uses a combination of telephone lines, cables, home computers, and terminals of various kinds. Under these arrangements, a consumer or a small business can obtain access to its account by telephone or cable. Under most of the programs, the customer can transfer funds among his accounts, pay some bills, stop payments, and obtain account balance information.

Home banking programs suffer from their inability to permit customers to make deposits and withdrawals, and there has been more customer resistance to the innovation than some banks and computer technology experts originally anticipated. The number of banks offering home banking programs has hovered around 50 and showed little inclination to grow until recently, when major banks in the midwest joined a national home-banking organization's system, and a superregional bank in New England began marketing the home-banking facility. Estimates number at 80,000 the households and small businesses that currently subscribe to home banking. In the last year, a bank with one of the larger programs, having 25,000 customers, discontinued the program. Some banks are now combining home-banking programs with brokerage services, data bases (e.g., news and current entertainment schedules), and the purchase of tickets for public events.

Telephone bill paying predates home banking and achieved a higher level of acceptance. Telephone bill paying programs vary, but generally they permit a customer of a bank or of a thrift to use the telephone to order the depository institution to pay creditors. Some systems permit the customer to use a touch-tone or rotary dial telephone to indicate the creditor, the amount of the payment, and the account to be charged. Other systems rely on voice transmission. In a sophisticated system, the institution may permit payments to creditors through the automated clearinghouse. Other systems confine payments to creditors in a smaller geographic area who are depositors at a limited number of institutions. Telephone bill paying systems have lost some of their allure in recent years. Large banks were never much interested in offering them, but savings and loans and some brokerage firms offering money-market accounts still market telephone bill paying systems. Usually, the bank ATM card agreement, which itself is part of the bank-depositor agreement governs the home banking and telephone banking relationships.

Both home-banking programs and telephone bill paying programs permit institutions to market other bank products. When a customer accesses a bank's computer to pay bills by telephone or by a personal computer, the bank program can offer advertising and loan and deposit account information. Some programs permit the customer to compute payment schedules for various loan amounts and various maturities. These programs, which are menu-driven, that is, which provide directions to the customer user, sometimes allow customers to apply for loans, reorder checks, verify that deposits have cleared or that checks have been paid, and indicate the location of the nearest ATM. Banks provide security for these programs by limiting customer access to the facility through use of the customer's bank card number and PIN.

MANUFACTURERS BANK

MNC 6836 (11-88)

ManuWay Agreement and Disclosure Statement

By applying for a ManuWay Banking Card (hereinafter called "Card") the ManuWay Cardholder (hereinafter called "Cardholder") does hereby agree to the following terms and conditions:

1. **AVAILABLE TRANSACTIONS.**
Cardholder may use the Card to:
(a) make deposits to and cash withdrawals from Cardholder's Checking, ManuFund or Statement Savings account;
(b) obtain cash advances from Cardholder's credit card account or revolving credit account;
(c) transfer funds from Cardholder's Checking or ManuFund to Statement Savings account, from Statement Savings to Checking or ManuFund, and from credit card or revolving credit account to Checking or ManuFund;
(d) pay bills, including but not limited to instalment loans, revolving credit accounts, mortgage loans and utility payments;
(e) obtain cash and purchase goods or services, including goods or services obtained by placing mail or telephone orders from certain businesses which have agreed to accept the Card (hereinafter called "point-of-sale transactions").
Some of these services may not be available at all terminals.
Access to Statement Savings accounts is limited to those Cardholders who have adopted Bank's combined statement format.

2. **CARDHOLDER'S LIABILITY FOR LOSS OR THEFT.**
Bank shall issue Cardholder a personal identification number without which the Card cannot be used except at staffed, on-premise electronic funds transfer terminals, in which case other identification will be required.
If Cardholder believes the Card has been lost or stolen, Cardholder must tell Bank AT ONCE and can lose no more than **$50.00** if Bank is contacted within two **(2)** business days. If Cardholder does NOT contact Bank within two **(2)** business days and Bank can prove that it could have prevented the loss if Cardholder had contacted it, Cardholder could lose as much as **$500.00**. Also, if Cardholder's monthly statement shows transfers Cardholder did not make and Cardholder does not contact Bank within sixty **(60)** days after the statement was mailed, Cardholder may not get back any money lost after sixty **(60)** days if Bank can prove that it could have prevented the loss if it had been notified in time (these specified time periods shall only be extended under extenuating circumstances).
Telephoning is the best way of keeping possible losses down.
Notice in writing shall be effective and considered given at the time Cardholder deposits the notice in the mail or delivers the notice for transmission by any other means to Bank.
Bank's business days are Monday through Friday; Bank holidays are not included.
The above provisions are NOT applicable to any cash advances or to overdrafts covered by a line of credit that do not result from an electronic funds transfer.

3. **OPTION TO LIMIT CASH WITHDRAWALS.**
Cardholder has the option to limit the total amount of cash which can be withdrawn via the Card from his/her account in a single day. This option includes, but is not limited to, a single daily access per card and Cardholder shall have the option to limit access to one or more specified accounts. Certain terminals may also have limitations regarding the total amount of cash which can be withdrawn in a single day.

4. **DOCUMENTATION OF TRANSFERS.**
Unless the Card is being used in connection with a check guaranty, a check authorization, to obtain information regarding an account balance or to obtain a cash advance from Cardholder's credit card or revolving credit accounts, or a combination of any of the above, the following provisions shall apply:
(a) Each Card transaction shall be accompanied by a receipt at the time of the transaction. If for any reason a receipt is not obtained, Cardholder may request Bank to issue a subsequent receipt. (Some point-of-sale transactions which do not involve an electronic terminal will not be accompanied by a terminal receipt.)
(b) For any month in which a Card transaction occurs or, at least, quarterly, a statement shall be provided that contains a sufficient description to enable Cardholder to identify any transaction made and to enable Cardholder to relate it to the furnished receipt. (Bank may render monthly statements to Cardholder in lieu of a combined statement.) A receipt and/or statement shall be admissible evidence of an account transaction.

5. **BANK'S LIABILITY FOR FAILURE TO MAKE TRANSFERS.**
If Bank does not properly complete a transfer to or from Cardholder's account on time or in the correct amount according to its agreement with Cardholder, Bank will be liable for Cardholder's losses or damages. However, Bank will not be liable in the following circumstances:
(a) if, through no fault of Bank, Cardholder's account does not contain enough money to make a transfer;
(b) if the transfer would go over the credit limit on Cardholder's overdraft line;
(c) if the automated teller machine where Cardholder is making the transfer does not have enough cash;
(d) if the automated teller machine or the terminal system was not working properly and Cardholder knew about the breakdown when Cardholder started the transfer;
(e) if circumstances beyond Bank's control, such as fire or flood, prevent the transfer, despite reasonable precautions it has taken;
(f) there may be other exceptions.

Printed with the permission of Manufacturers National Bank of Detroit.

6. **ERROR RESOLUTION PROCEDURES.**
If Cardholder thinks his/her statement or receipt is wrong or if Cardholder needs more information about a transfer listed on his/her statement or receipt, Cardholder must call or write Bank no later than sixty **(60)** days after Bank sent Cardholder the FIRST statement on which the problem or error appeared.

Oral complaints or questions must be confirmed in writing within ten **(10)** business days and must include:
(a) Cardholder's name and account number;
(b) the dollar amount of the suspected error;
(c) a description of the error or the transfer in question and an explanation, made as clearly as possible, as to why Cardholder believes an error occurred or why Cardholder needs more information.

An error shall be limited to:
(1) an unauthorized transfer;
(2) an incorrect transfer to or from Cardholder's account;
(3) the omission from a periodic statement of a transfer to or from Cardholder's account that should have been included;
(4) a computational or bookkeeping error made by Bank relating to a transfer;
(5) Cardholder's receipt of an incorrect amount of money from terminal.

Following notification, Bank will inform Cardholder of the results of its investigation within ten **(10)** business days [twenty **(20)** business days in cases of point-of-sale transactions] and will correct any error promptly. (If an oral notification is not confirmed in writing within ten **(10)** business days, Bank may not recredit the accounts.) If Bank needs more time, however, it may take up to forty-five **(45)** days [ninety **(90)** days in cases of point-of-sale transactions] to investigate a complaint or question, but will provisionally recredit Cardholder's account within ten **(10)** business days [twenty **(20)** business days in cases of point-of-sale transactions] for the amount believed to be in error, so that Cardholder will have the use of the money during the time it takes Bank to complete its investigation.

Cardholder's account will not be provisionally recredited when used in connection with the purchase or sale of securities.

7. **FEES.**
Bank reserves the right, without prior notice, to charge a fee for each Card which it issues or reissues under the following circumstances:
(a) if Bank is requested to issue replacements for Card(s) lost, destroyed or misplaced by Cardholder;
(b) if any Card is not used between its date of issuance and date of expiration and Bank is requested by Cardholder to reissue such Card for additional periods.

Bank also reserves the right to assess other charges it may deem necessary in the future. In the event Bank determines that it shall require a fee, such fee will not become effective until thirty **(30)** days after Bank mails notification to Cardholder. Cardholder, however, may terminate this agreement within that thirty **(30)** day period without charge.

8. **OVERDRAFTS.**
Cardholder shall not use the Card to obtain money from an account in excess of the balance then on deposit and Cardholder shall not obtain a cash advance in excess of Cardholder's credit card or revolving credit account limits.

Cardholder agrees to pay upon demand the amount of any overdrafts or any excess over the authorized limits to Cardholder's credit card and revolving credit accounts.

9. **NEW BANKING TRANSACTIONS.**
From time to time Bank may make available to Cardholder other banking transactions that may be accomplished with the use of the Card, and Cardholder agrees that by using the Card for these additional transactions, Cardholder will be bound by this agreement to the same extent as on the transactions now available.

10. **GOVERNING RULES AND REGULATIONS.**
All transactions hereunder shall be subject to the laws of the State of Michigan, the United States, the rules and regulations of the Federal Reserve System and Bank's rules and regulations for the respective accounts.

11. **DISCLOSURES TO THIRD PARTIES.**
Bank will not disclose any information to third parties which shall pertain to Cardholder's accounts, except when necessary to complete transfers, in order to verify the existence and condition of accounts for a third party, such as a credit bureau or merchant, in order to comply, when required, with government agency or court orders, or in accordance with Cardholder's written instructions.

12. **PRONOUNS.**
The pronouns and relative words used herein shall be, where appropriate, construed singular or plural, and if there is more than one Cardholder, each agrees to the terms hereof on a joint and several basis.

13. **AMENDMENTS.**
This agreement may be amended by Bank by sending written notice to Cardholder at Cardholder's last known address or by including a written notice with Cardholder's periodic statement. Any change, however, will not become effective less than twenty-one **(21)** days from the date of such notice, in the absence of extenuating circumstances.

14. **TERMINATION.**
The Card, at all times, shall remain the property of Bank, and Bank may at any time without notice withdraw or revoke its use and may terminate this agreement. Upon demand, Cardholder shall return the Card to Bank.

This agreement may be terminated by Cardholder by delivering the Card to Bank. A termination by either Bank or Cardholder shall not affect prior transactions or existing obligations.

15. **VIOLATIONS BY BANK.**
If Bank violates any of the preceeding provisions, Cardholder may notify the following:

Comptroller of the Currency
Consumers Affairs Division
Washington, DC 20219

16. **NOTICES TO BANK.**
All notices to Bank, required under this agreement, must be given to:

Manufacturers Bank, Electronic Banking Department
P.O. Box 55-001A
Detroit, Michigan 48255-0001
Detroit area: (313) 222-9764
Out-state: 1-800-572-6620

MNC 6836 (11-88)

MANUFACTURERS BANK

ManuWay 24-Hour Banking Application

LAST NAME (PLEASE PRINT)	FIRST NAME	INITIAL	SOCIAL SECURITY NO.
1			
LAST NAME 2	FIRST NAME	INITIAL	SOCIAL SECURITY NO.
LAST NAME 3	FIRST NAME	INITIAL	SOCIAL SECURITY NO.
ADDRESS			HOME TELEPHONE
CITY/STATE		ZIP CODE	BUSINESS TELEPHONE

CHECKING OR MANUFUND NO.	PLEASE ISSUE ☐ 1 CARD ☐ 2 CARDS ☐ 3 CARDS
STATEMENT SAVINGS NO.	MASTERCARD OR VISA OR CASH LINE*

YOU HAVE THE RIGHT TO LIMIT THE DOLLAR AMOUNT AND NUMBER OF DAILY ACCESSES ON YOUR CARD.

DAILY MAXIMUM AMOUNT ALLOWED (NOT TO EXCEED $200.00)	DAILY ACCESSES ALLOWED

* Direct Cash Line access available only at Manufacturers National Bank of Detroit. Access to Cash Line through overdraft protection is available at Manufacturers National Corporation banks offering this service.

THE UNDERSIGNED HEREBY CERTIFIES THAT THE INFORMATION IN THE FOREGOING STATEMENT IS HEREON COMPLETE AND IS SUBMITTED FOR THE PURPOSE OF OBTAINING A DEBIT CARD(S). THE UNDERSIGNED ACKNOWLEDGES RECEIPT OF THE CARDHOLDER AGREEMENT AND DISCLOSURE STATEMENT AND AGREES TO ALL OF THE TERMS AND CONDITIONS THEREOF.

SPECIMEN

SIGNATURE

SIGNATURE DATE
(IF JOINT ACCOUNT, SECOND SIGNATURE REQUIRED)

BANKING USE ONLY

MANAGEMENT APPROVAL	BANK	OFFICE	TELEPHONE	CREDIT CARD/LINE APPROVAL

V $	E $

☐☐☐-☐☐☐☐☐☐☐
MANUWAY CARD NUMBER

COMMENTS

27

Collection of International Payments

§27.1 THE NEED

International trade, investment, and travel are the commercial and private activities that drive international payments. When a French tourist in Morocco uses a Visa card, a U.S. investor acquires eurobonds, or a Dutch refinery buys Nigerian crude oil, the transaction usually cannot proceed to conclusion without the international transfer of **bank credits.**

There are a number of obstacles to these international transfers. Sometimes, for example, the transfers confront exchange problems. If an Afghan merchant wants to buy trucks, he will find that most of the world's sellers of motor vehicles will not accept payment in afghanis, the Afghan currency. Sellers usually will accept only "hard" currencies, that is, currencies that are exchanged freely in international trade and investment.

Other international transactions confront the problem of exchange control laws and regulations. A Venezuelan buyer, for example, may have an adequate supply of funds to his credit at a Caracas bank to purchase the steam-generating facility an American seller wants to sell him, but the buyer may not be able to obtain the necessary government permission to transfer dollars from the Venezuelan central bank or may not be able to obtain the dollars in time to satisfy the American seller.

International traders and investors have devised a number of responses to these problems. **Countertrade,** a form of international barter, and joint ventures are two commonly utilized responses. Both of them, however, as well as the other arrangements adopted in order to overcome the problems of exchange controls and "soft" currencies are less efficient than the quick transfer of bank credits that this chapter describes. Countertrade is probably the least efficient. It leaves the seller with goods that it usually must resell before it has cash or bank credit to use in its business. Only infrequently will a seller who takes goods in countertrade be in a position to use those goods himself. In theory, a seller of computer parts to a Soviet buyer might be able to take Soviet mining vehicles in countertrade and be able to use them in its business, but more often it will have to resell the mining vehicles and often in markets with which it may not be familiar.

Similarly, sales into countries with stiff exchange control laws or regulations are often encumbered by the need to obtain the importing country's approval of the transaction. In such cases, the seller may have to obtain a government functionary's stamp and countersignature on shipping documents or invoices before the buyer's bank will honor a draft drawn under a letter of credit. Obtaining such approval is time-consuming and in some countries creates opportunities for government officials to insist on graft — a practice that is common enough in some regions to be a trade requirement.

The lesson is plain enough: Efficient movement of goods must abide free transfer of international payments. Those who restrict those payments in order to protect domestic industry, to placate political critics, or for whatever other reason are restricting international trade and investment and are reaping the heavy economic burdens of that policy — a lessening of competition with the higher prices, product deficiencies, and other "taxes" that protected industries inevitably exact.

§27.2 THE INTERNATIONAL BANK DRAFT

The international bank draft utilizes a domestic bank's deposits denominated in foreign currencies and held in foreign banks.

A Miami purchaser of automotive parts may agree to pay a Milan seller in lire. The buyer will ask its Miami bank to draw a draft on its correspondent bank in Milan for the purchase price of the parts. The Miami bank will "sell" the draft to its customer, the buyer, who will forward it to the seller by mail. The seller can then deposit the draft at its own bank for collection from the Miami bank's correspondent. Figure 27-1 illustrates the transaction, and Document 27-1 is an example of an international bank draft.

Figure 27-1. International Bank Draft

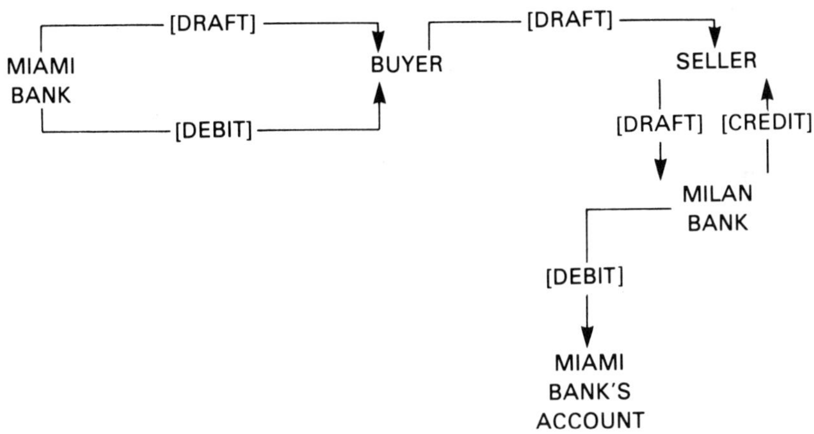

§27.3 PAYMENT BY CORRESPONDENT

The international bank draft is slow and poses a security problem to the extent that the draft might be lost in the mails. Banks that maintain accounts with foreign correspondents can reduce some of the delay and most of the security risk by removing the draft from the transaction. The draft is a negotiable order to pay, and there may be situations in which the buyer wants to use a negotiable order to pay.

Most sellers will not be interested in negotiable drafts, however, and the parties can save the time and the risks of the draft by having the Miami bank wire its Milan correspondent to disburse the funds to the seller. This arrangement is a wire transfer and may be effected by cable, telex, or SWIFT. (For general discussion of wire transfers, see Chapter 25.)

§27.4 PAYMENT BY WIRE

It is inefficient for banks to maintain too many correspondent accounts, so banks engaging in international activity have consolidated their foreign currency accounts in a relatively few banks. They then effect international payments by transferring funds among those few banks. Certain cities such as New York, London, and Hong Kong in countries with hard currencies have emerged as centers for international banking. Large foreign banks with international departments will nearly always maintain a dollar denominated account with one of the New York money-center banks. When the customer of one of those foreign banks wants to transfer dollars to a seller, his bank will initiate payment through the money-center bank network.

When, for example, a Dutch buyer of crude oil on the spot market agrees to pay U.S. dollars to a seller in Dubai, the buyer and seller can agree to use CHIPS, the New York money-center banks' network for international payments. Under the arrangement, the buyer will ask its Dutch bank, First National Bank of Rotterdam, to transfer dollars to the Seller's dollar-denominated account in a New York bank, Second Bank of New York. The Dutch Bank will debit the buyer's account and instruct its New York correspondent to make the payment. The New York correspondent will debit the Dutch Bank's account and will credit Second Bank of New York's account. Second Bank will then credit the Seller's account.

If the Seller does not maintain an account in New York, as it well might not, it becomes necessary to introduce another bank into the transaction. If the seller maintains an account at Third Bank of Dubai, First Bank of Rotterdam's New York correspondent will transfer the funds to the account of Third Bank of Dubai's New York correspondent. Figure 25-2 illustrates a CHIPS transaction.

The volume of these dollar-denominated payments is considerable. On the average day the New York Clearinghouse system for clearing these international transfers handles 60,000 orders, and on a busy day may transfer more than $1 trillion. In order to effect those transfers quickly and without error, the New York Clearinghouse has established CHIPS, a computer system that manages to clear the transfers by wire. Under CHIPS, banks make intraday transfers and net them out at the end of the day. They then settle through the Federal Reserve Bank of New York. For further discussion of CHIPS, see Section 25.6.

§27.5 PAYMENT BY LETTER OF CREDIT

Buyers and sellers under international sales agreements frequently pay by letter of credit. Under an international letter of credit, the seller must present its draft and certain other documents specified in the credit to the nominated bank, that is, the bank designated in the credit as the party that will pay the draft. Sometimes, the issuer of the credit will be the payor bank, but often the credit nominates another bank to make the payment. Frequently, moreover, the seller will want to have a bank local to it confirm the credit, that is, undertake to pay the credit just as the issuer does.

In the oil transaction described in the preceding section, for example, the Buyer's bank, the First National Bank of Rotterdam, will cause a letter of credit to issue in favor of the Dubai seller. The Rotterdam bank might nominate a Dubai bank to confirm the credit and pay the Dubai seller.

At other times, the buyer and the seller will agree to payment in a currency that the issuer does not have on hand. In that case, the issuer will nominate a correspondent that does have the currency in question.

Thus, if the Dubai seller wants to be paid in U.S. dollars, the Rotterdam bank might nominate a New York bank as the payor under the credit and might ask the New York bank to confirm the credit. In this example, the Dubai seller will probably maintain an account in another New York bank.

If the Dubai seller presents its documents in time and if the documents comply with the terms of the letter of credit, the confirming bank or other nominated bank will pay. The paying bank must then seek reimbursement from the issuer of the credit. Usually, the credit recites the arrangement for reimbursement.

When a Dutch buyer agrees, for example, to pay a Dubai seller in dollars, First Bank, the Rotterdam letter-of-credit issuer, might direct the Dubai buyer to draw on Bank of Miami and then instruct Bank of Miami to obtain reimbursement from the Rotterdam bank's New York correspondent where the Rotterdam bank maintains a dollar-denominated account. Figures 5-1 and 5-2 in Part I illustrate the letter-of-credit transaction. Chapter 5 discusses the letter of credit sale in more detail.

§27.6 COLLECTING THE SELLER'S DRAFT

Often, international sellers will vary the letter-of-credit transaction described in the foregoing section. Letters of credit entail bank charges that buyers and sellers may want to avoid. The parties may, nonetheless, still want bank assistance in collecting the seller's draft on the buyer. The seller, for example, may be willing to ship the goods without a letter of credit from the buyer's bank, but the seller may not want to surrender possession of the goods without payment or without the buyer's acceptance of a time draft.

In those cases, the seller will prepare its documents and introduce them into the bank collection system with instructions on the steps the banks should take in collecting the draft. Chapter 4 discusses the documentary draft transaction in greater detail.

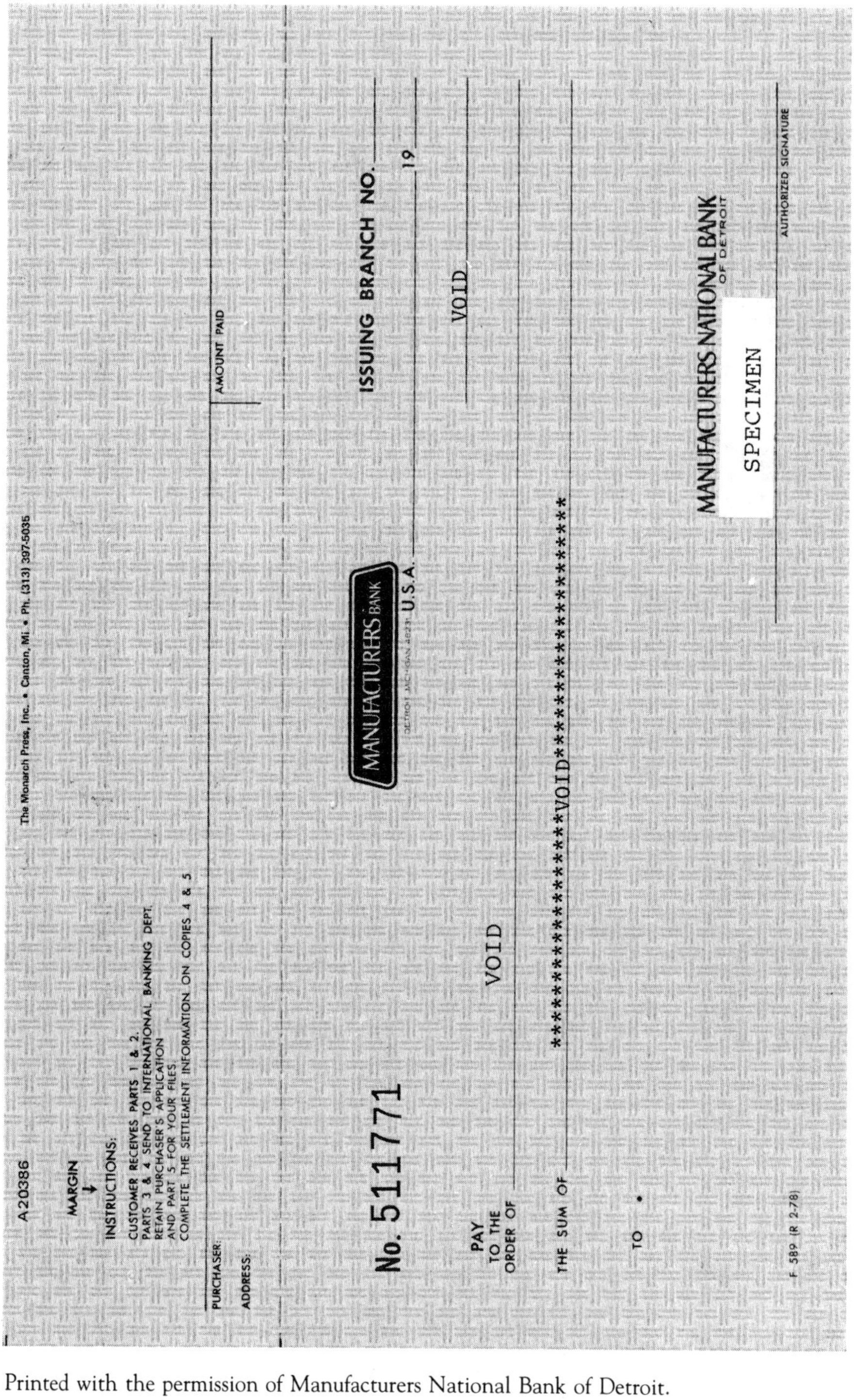
A20386

MARGIN

INSTRUCTIONS:
CUSTOMER RECEIVES PARTS 1 & 2.
PARTS 3 & 4 SEND TO INTERNATIONAL BANKING DEPT.
RETAIN PURCHASER'S APPLICATION
AND PART 5 FOR YOUR FILES.
COMPLETE THE SETTLEMENT INFORMATION ON COPIES 4 & 5

The Monarch Press, Inc. • Canton, Mi. • Ph. (313) 397-5035

PURCHASER:

ADDRESS:

AMOUNT PAID

No. 5111771

MANUFACTURERS BANK

DETROIT, MICHIGAN 48231 U.S.A.

ISSUING BRANCH NO.

19

PAY TO THE ORDER OF VOID VOID

THE SUM OF *******************VOID**********************

TO

MANUFACTURERS NATIONAL BANK OF DETROIT

SPECIMEN

AUTHORIZED SIGNATURE

F 589 (R 2-78)

Printed with the permission of Manufacturers National Bank of Detroit.

28 Giro Accounts

§28.1 PULL ORDERS AND PUSH ORDERS

Drafts and checks, with which most lawyers in the Anglo-American system of law are familiar, are pull orders. They operate to pull funds from an account maintained by the drawer — the person who gives the order. The drawer of a check, for example, mails it to the payee, who deposits it in the collection system in order to pull the funds into his account. Similarly, the seller using a draft draws the draft payable to himself or his agent and deposits the draft in order to pull the funds into his account.

Continental countries generally have not used the check as commonly as the United States and Great Britain. In Continental Europe, the **giro** is more common, and the giro is a **push order**. It operates to push funds from the account of the drawer to the account of the payee.

In a giro system, a buyer or other debtor draws an order, the giro, on his own account and delivers or mails it either to the bank where he maintains that account or another bank that acts as a forwarding agent for his bank. The order specifies the amount to be transferred and the bank account number of the payee. The debtor's bank then debits the account of the buyer and credits the account of the payee's bank and forwards the giro to that bank, so that it can credit the payee's account.

Under the system, when a plumber sells services to a buyer, the plumber's invoice will specify her giro account number. The buyer will draw a giro credit directing a commercial bank or the postal bank to forward the funds to the plumber's account. Under some giro systems, a copy of

Figure 28-1. Giro

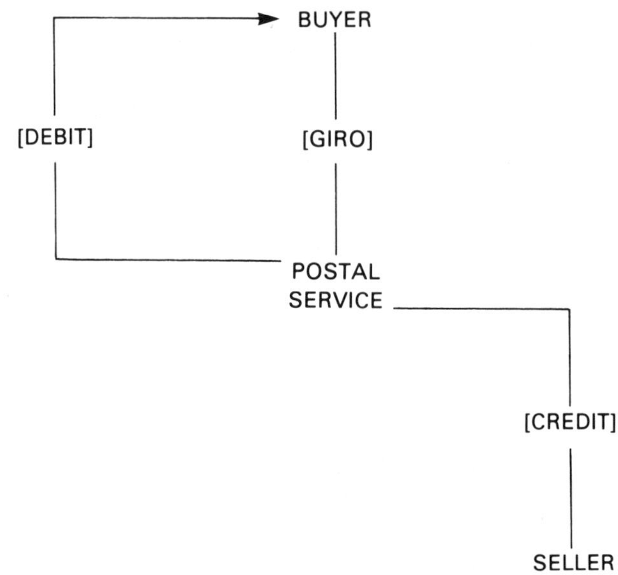

the buyer's order accompanies the fund transfer, but under others, the plumber does not see the giro credit but receives a periodic statement on which the transfer is noted. Figure 28-1 illustrates the giro payment in this simple transaction.

Note that in the giro system, the funds move more quickly than in the check system. Checks are debit instruments, and depositary institutions delay the availability of funds for a period to allow for their collection. There is always the possibility in the check-collection system that the check will arrive at the drawee bank when there are insufficient funds available to pay the check or after the drawer has issued a stop payment order. Although more than 95 percent of all checks clear in the United States, depositary institutions do not know which checks will clear and which checks will not. Depositary institutions also do not know when a check clears. Even though the payor bank decides to pay a check, the depositary bank does not receive notice of the payment. Silence, the absence of notice of dishonor, is the signal that a check is paid.

In the giro system, however, the giro credit moves in the same direction as the funds, as it pushes the funds into the account of the payee. The payee's institution does not have to wait for the giro to clear. When the giro arrives, the funds, in effect, arrive with it.

§28.2 POSTAL GIRO ACCOUNTS

In many countries, the postal service or another nationalized agency operates a giro system. Every person in the country who wishes to participate may establish an account. The postal service's central computer tracks all accounts and makes payments simple and inexpensive. When the plumber in the foregoing example submits her invoice, in place of a bank giro number, she will designate her postal giro number. The homeowner will then prepare a giro payable to the plumber. The homeowner delivers the giro to the postal service that then debits the homeowner's account and credits the plumber's account.

§28.3 BANK GIRO ACCOUNTS

In a bank giro system, the customer who desires to transfer funds is the payor. His bank is the transferring bank, and the bank of the payee is the recipient bank.

When banks operate giro systems along side that of the postal service, they and the postal service arrange for intersystem payments. Banks, because they are independent entities and do not share a single central computer that tracks all accounts and payments, must arrange in the bank giro system to settle periodically among themselves. Similarly, in a market economy, there will be more than one bank, and interbank giro payments require a collection apparatus similar to that employed in a check collection system. Document 28-1 is a bank giro.

§28.4 ELECTRONIC GIRO SYSTEMS

Because the giro system involves push orders, some commentators consider a preauthorized debit system as an electronic giro. Under these systems, debtors preauthorize the payment of insurance premiums, utility bills, mortgage payments, and similar recurring charges. Section 28.5 discusses the automated clearinghouse, an electronic giro system. In a sense, point of sale terminals give rise to electronic giros since they involve the pushing of funds from the account of the buyer who activates the terminal and directs his financial institution to debit his account and credit the account of his creditor. Section 28.3 discusses the point of sale terminal. Similarly, telephone bill paying programs and some features of home banking are a form of electronic giro.

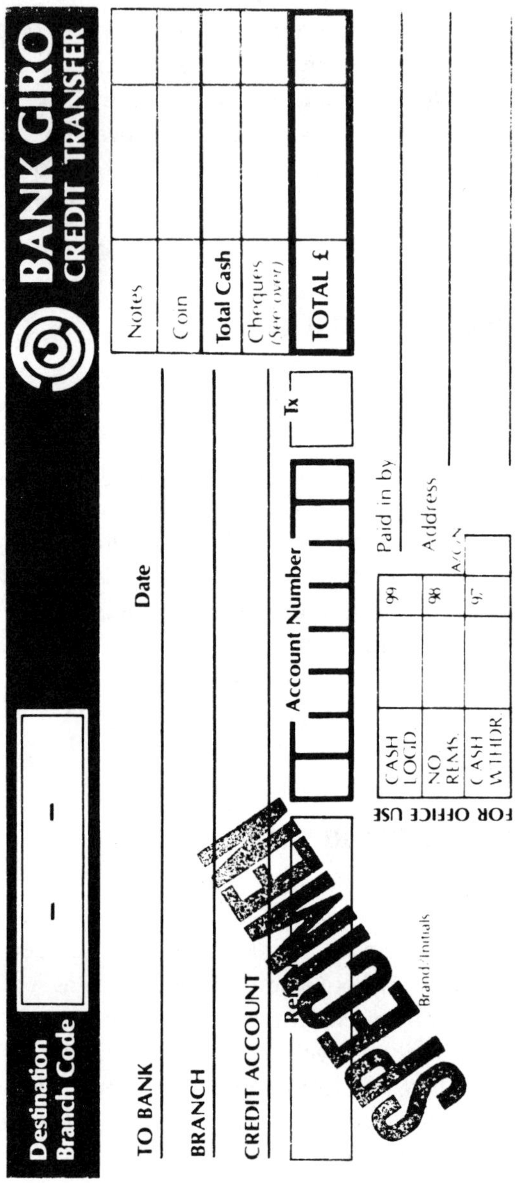

BANK GIRO
CREDIT TRANSFER

Destination Branch Code

TO BANK

BRANCH

CREDIT ACCOUNT

Ref

Account Number

Tx

Date

Notes	
Coin	
Total Cash	
Cheques (See over)	
TOTAL £	

Paid in by

Address

FOR OFFICE USE

CASH LOGD		99
NO REMS		98
CASH W'THDR		97

A/C/N

Branch Initials

SPECIMEN

29 Credit Cards

§29.1 INTRODUCTION

This chapter deals primarily with bank credit cards but includes discussion of **travel and entertainment cards** and single-seller charge cards. Bank credit cards have grown enormously in volume and importance in the retail sector of the economy, replacing many single-seller cards and displacing somewhat the significance of travel and entertainment cards, which predated bank credit cards.

Although the bank card system is efficient once it begins operating, the start-up costs are considerable. Such systems involve several contracts, association bylaws, and an elaborate collection network. Recent figures indicate that annually, there are almost 3 billion bank charge card transactions with an annual volume of about $218 billion, yet there are only two major bank-card systems in the United States.

§29.2 BANK CREDIT-CARD SYSTEMS

While a few banks continue to offer their own credit cards, there are only two national bank credit-card systems: Visa and MasterCard. Both systems operate a national network of bank members or affiliates and an independent payments system. At the present time, however, the two systems are engaging in some cross-processing, whereby merchants authorized to accept cards for one system may accept the other system's cards and use the same processing arrangements for both.

By the late 1980s, there were about 134 million bank cards issued by the two national systems. The outstanding, unpaid credit balances on these cards, that is, the amount of consumer debt generated by them and subject to interest charges, exceeded $50 billion.

There are five basic features of a successful national bank credit-card system. First, it must have a national network of banks that issue cards; second, it must solicit a significant number of merchants to participate in the program by accepting the card from customers; third, it needs to provide a verification service to the merchants; fourth, there must be a network of processors to take the charge slips from the merchants; and fifth, it must provide a quick, inexpensive and reliable interchange system for collecting the charges from the issuer and transmitting them to the merchants' banks.

In the national system, then, banks play two critical roles. The **issuing bank** is the bank that issues a card to its customer and enters into a revolving credit arrangement with the customer. The **merchant bank** or "acquiring bank" is the bank that enters into a contract with a retailer and engages to purchase credit-card **sales slips** from the retailer and to collect them through the system.

Both banks are members of the system and are bound by its bylaws. The bylaws oblige the issuer to honor sales slips when they are "presented" through the system for payment. The bylaws also govern the collection of the sums due under the slips and the rules for charging back disputed amounts and generally displace the common law rules that evolved in the check-collection system.

Sometimes banks play a third role in the system by handling the data processing function, though increasingly banks are referring that business to nonbank data processors.

§29.3 THE CARDHOLDER AND HIS BANK

When the issuing bank issues a card to a customer, the customer enters into a credit-card agreement. Under the agreement, the issuer obligates itself to provide the customer with a revolving line of credit up to a designated amount. The cardholder, in turn, agrees to pay for charges incurred and to pay interest on outstanding balances, which result if the cardholder elects the credit option and defers full payment of the periodic balance.

§29.4 THE MERCHANT AND HIS BANK

Merchants who want to avail themselves of the ability to make credit-card sales must gain entry to the system through a merchant bank. The agreement between the merchant and the merchant bank, a member of the bank-card system, governs matters relating to the bank's purchase or discount of the merchant's paper. In this case, the paper is the credit-card sales slip. Periodically, often at the end of a business day, the merchant will deliver the sales slips to the merchant bank in a batch with an aggregate total. The bank will then grant the merchant either immediate or delayed credit for that total, less a percentage. The percentage, which may range from 1 to 7 percent, is the discount. It is not altogether clear conceptually whether the bank is buying the merchant's sales slips or granting a loan against them, though the parties think of the transaction as a sale of the slips. They acknowledge, however, that the sale is with recourse, that is, that the merchant must repurchase any slip that is not honored. The transaction, in that particular then, resembles a loan that must be repaid if the third party (the cardholder) does not pay it.

Thus it is not clear whether the discount the merchant pays the merchant bank is a charge for the bank's services or, in the case of immediately available credit, the payment of interest for the merchant's use of the funds until the issuing banks pay the cardholders' obligations as evidenced by the slips.

After it has solicited its stable of merchants, the merchant bank's functions are essentially confined to data processing. Some merchant banks have assigned these functions to their data-processing subsidiaries or have contracted the services out to a nonbank data processor.

§29.5 PAYMENT

The broad credit-card transaction involves all four of the parties described in the preceding sections as well as one or more intermediaries.

In a typical sale, the cardholder makes a credit-card purchase of goods from a retailer. The retailer prepares the credit-card slip, sometimes called a **sales draft,** by imprinting it with the credit-card information, filling in the amount of the purchase and a description of the merchandise, and obtaining the cardholder's signature. The clerk is also supposed to compare the signature on the reverse side of the card with that on the sales slip, though, in practice, many clerks fail to perform that operation.

If the amount of the sale exceeds the **floor release limit,** before completing the sale, usually before the cardholder signs the slip, the retailer will run an inquiry through the card system. The purpose of the inquiry is to determine that the card is still valid, i.e., that it has not been reported lost by the cardholder or cancelled by the issuer, and that the cardholder has not exceeded his credit limit. That information is available to the merchant through telephone or on-line computer access where the information is stored or through operators who check for the information. In both cases, the merchant receives an authorization number which he records on the sales slip as evidence that he has received authorization from the system.

Significantly, the process of obtaining authorization permits the card system to capture sales information. When the merchant provides that information to the system, the system's computer reduces the amount of credit available to the cardholder.

By virtue of an agreement between MasterCard and Visa, merchants can engage in cross-processing. Merchants that have an agreement with a merchant bank that is a member of one of the associations has access to information from both associations and, therefore, can honor both cards. The bank-card systems are now beginning to make cross-processing agreements with nonbank systems and especially with travel and entertainment card systems.

Recently, national card associations have provided incentives for merchant banks to encourage merchant use of their terminals for more than verification and authorization purposes. As merchants graduate from telephone verification to computer connected terminals, it becomes possible for the merchant to capture significant information concerning the purchase itself at the time the merchant is verifying the cardholder's credit availability and authority. To the extent that the terminal captures that information and relays it to the merchant bank's terminal, the merchant bank and the national card association will avoid the need to generate that information from the sales slips — a paper process that is labor intensive.

Until the day when all merchants can cheaply deliver that information to the issuing bank, however, the retailer must periodically "deposit" his sales slips with its own bank, the merchant bank. The bank then gives the retailer immediate or delayed credit for the total amount, less the agreed upon discount, of the slips in the batch.

The merchant bank then begins the collection of the slips by forwarding them to a clearing agent that may be a bank subsidiary, a captive of a regional association of banks, or an independent data processing entity. Banks that use a given clearing agent can maintain clearing accounts, and the clearing agent may handle charges against those banks directly by debiting their accounts and crediting the account of the merchant bank. If the member banks do not maintain clearing accounts, they must settle among themselves periodically. Figure 29-1 illustrates the clearing of a sales

Figure 29-1. Credit-Card Collection

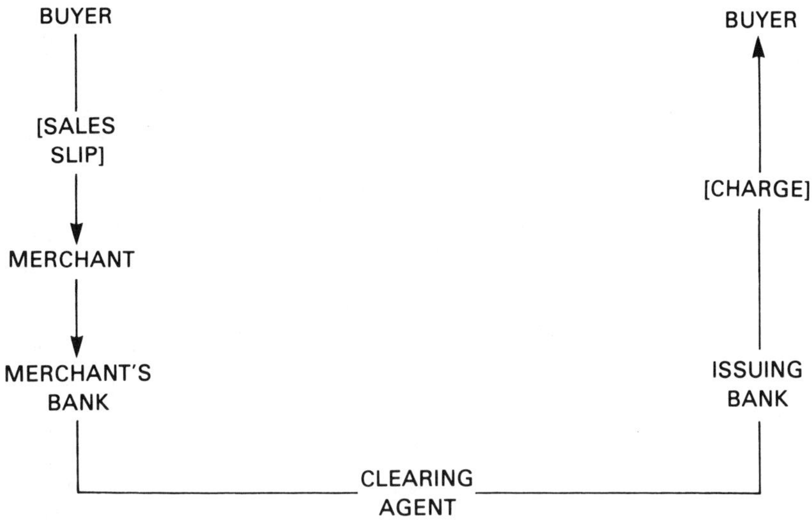

slip when the merchant bank and the issuing bank use the same clearing agent.

Often, the issuing bank and the merchant bank are in different parts of the country and do not use the same regional clearing agent. In that event, the clearing agent must access the bank-card's interchange system. That access is electronic. The clearing agent "truncates" the slips, that is, it subjects them to image processing or photocopies them. Having translated the information on the sales slips into computer usable codes, the processor destroys them after a period of time. The agent then forwards that information by wire to the bank-card system's switching center. The center is the central clearinghouse for the entire bank-card system and makes corresponding debit and credit entries from and to the settlement accounts of the banks in their roles as merchant bank and issuing bank. Figure 29-2 illustrates the transaction when the issuing bank and the merchant bank are in different regions.

Correspondent bank relationships may play a role here, as they do in most collection systems. A merchant bank or an issuing bank may not be a participant directly but may gain access to the system through a correspondent. In that case, there may be an additional layer or two of participants, as the sales slips and the electronic charges pass through the correspondents.

The bylaws of the system and federal and state law provide for charge backs in certain instances. In the event of a charge back, the issuer must give notice to the switch, and the switch must relay the information to the merchant bank. The agreement between the merchant bank and the merchant generally provides that the merchant is responsible for all charge backs.

Figure 29-2. National Credit-Card Collection System

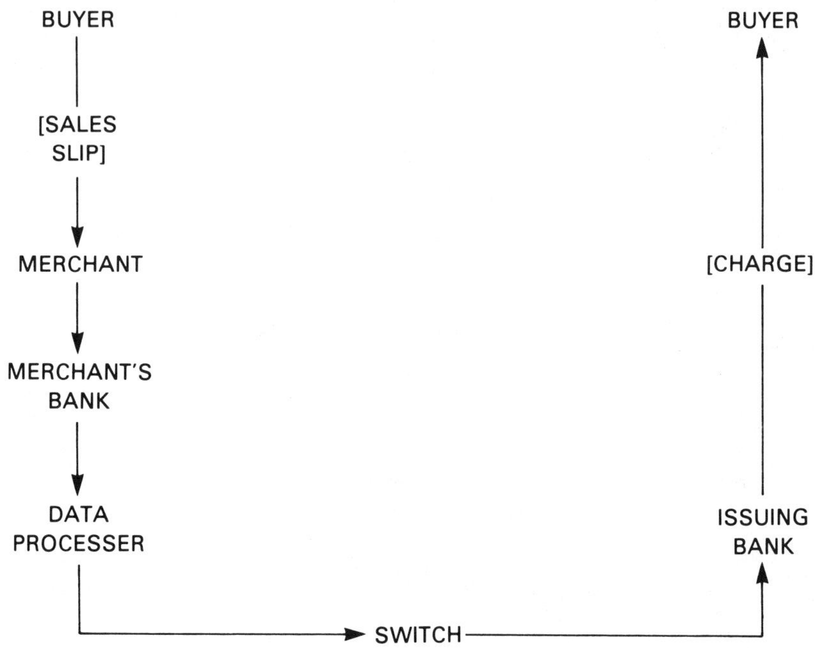

§29.6 TWO-PARTY CHARGE CARDS

Long before the advent of the bank credit card, many sellers, oil companies and department stores, for example, maintained their own charge accounts, and these sellers often gave their customers charge cards. Those cards and traditional telephone charge cards, which are similar, differ from the bank credit card in that they do not involve sophisticated national collection systems. Essentially, they are two-party cards, while bank cards are multi-party.

When a customer uses a department store's charge card, the arrangement calls for the store to grant credit to the customer. Although the store may well finance its accounts with a bank or finance company, the customer generally makes his payments directly to the store and does not deal with any financial institution. Until recently, it was unusual that the card issued by one entity could be used at any other entity. Document 2-3 is a typical department store charge account agreement.

Oil company credit cards are more complex than the customary two-party card, since they frequently involve a service station operator that is independent of the oil company and may include operators of competing brand outlets. In these cases, there is an additional party in the transaction, but the service station operator does not take his charge slips to his bank. He forwards them to the oil company, which acts as the clearinghouse.

A Marathon dealer, for example, forwards his sales slips periodically

Figure 29-3. Oil Company Credit-Card Collections

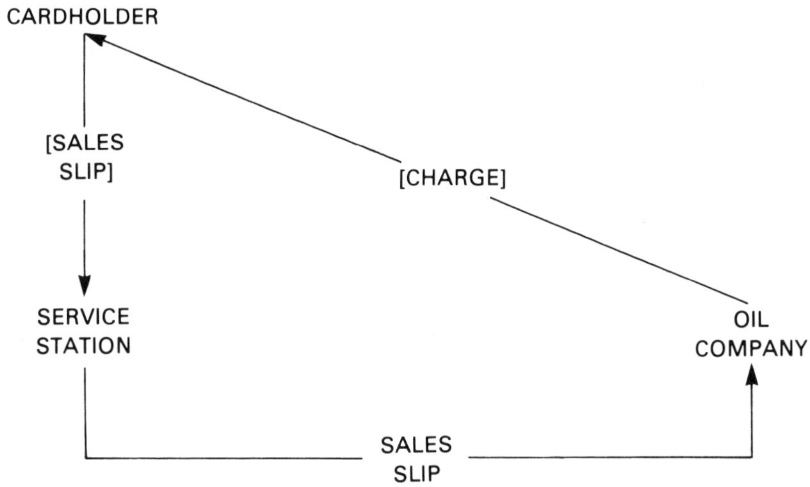

to the oil company's credit-card headquarters. In oil company credit-card operations, traditionally, the service station merchant uses a small hand-operated, mechanical device to imprint the cardholder's account number, the dealer's number, and the amount of the sale on the sales slip in machine-readable form. When the oil company receives the slips, its machines read them and provide batch verification for the company, that is, the machines verify the totals that the dealer submitted to the company with his slips. The company then credits the dealer's account in the amount of the slips or sends him a check.

The company then proceeds to collect the charges from the cardholders by billing them. Because the information has been captured by machines, the company can generate a cardholder's monthly statement from the computer that stored the sales slip information.

Many oil company credit cards are used at service stations other than those of the card issuer. If, for example, the Marathon card is available at an Exxon service station, there must be an arrangement for the Exxon dealer to collect his charges. The oil companies effect that collection by crediting the accounts of their own dealers for charges made on other oil company cards. The oil companies then settle among themselves, treating each other, in effect, as they do a dealer that has generated a significant number of sales slips.

Figure 29-3 illustrates the collection of an oil company credit-card charge. Figure 29-4 illustrates the transaction when a Marathon cardholder uses the Marathon card at an Exxon service station.

Recently, some large national retailers have begun marketing a charge card, such as the Sears Discover card, that the customer can use with other retailers, and AT&T has converted its charge cards into credit cards. Under present marketing arrangements, a Discover card holder, for example, can

Figure 29-4. Oil Company Credit-Card Collections (with Two Companies)

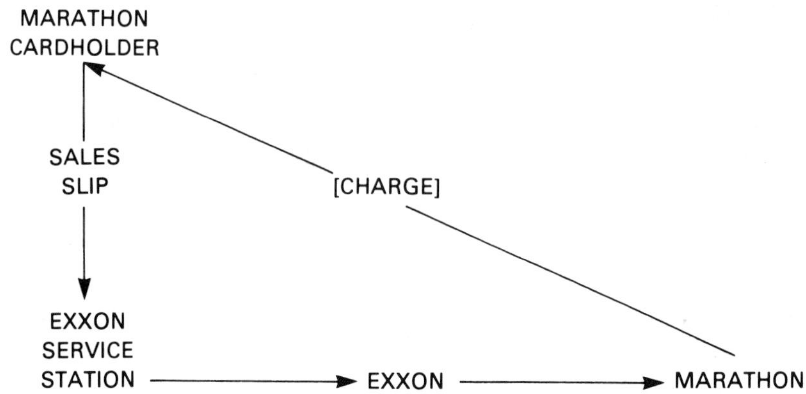

charge purchases at a travel agent unconnected with Sears. The Discover card clearly competes directly with bank cards. Charges under these cards find their way into the bank-card collection system when a credit-card bank issues the card and retailers enter into contracts with banks to collect the charge slips. At first, the national bank-card associations objected to the practice, which they saw as an attempt by retailers sponsoring competing cards to avail themselves of the costly collection system fashioned by the associations for their own cards. To date, those objections notwithstanding, commercial banks are using the national bank-card system to collect charges generated by cards issued by national retailers, and the indications are that the national bank-card associations are accommodating themselves to the fact that nonbank credit cards are a permanent part of the payments system.

§29.7 TRAVEL AND ENTERTAINMENT CARDS

As early as 1950, Diners Club began to market a travel and entertainment (T&E) card. It has since been joined by a number of competing cards. While growth of the T&E cards has slowed and been displaced somewhat by bank credit cards, the T&E industry still handles considerable business. There are approximately 20 million T&E cardholders charging in excess of $60 billion per year for services.

T&E cards allow holders to charge meals, hotel accommodations, and the like and to pay for them periodically, usually monthly. Usually, T&E cards have no credit limit. T&E cardholders tend to use the card, therefore, for higher-priced items such as airline travel and hotel accommodations, and the airline and hotel industries have been more inclined to pay the T&E card company discounts that are generally higher than those charged by banks that take sales slips from merchants accepting bank cards. Retailers, whose sales are relatively small in dollar terms, however, have been reluctant to accept the T&E card with its higher discount. T&E cards also differ from bank credit cards in that usually the cardholder must pay his account in full upon receipt of his periodic statement. There is no credit term beyond the delay between the time of the purchase and the time the T&E company submits its statement. Finally, T&E cards differ from bank credit cards in that the periodic statement from the T&E company usually includes the signed receipts, while bank credit-card issuers truncate the receipts early in the collection process and provide only a printout of purchase made during the billing period.

Recently the lines between bank credit cards and T&E cards have blurred somewhat. At least one T&E card issuer, the subsidiary of a money-center bank, will now extend credit and charge interest on an unpaid principal balance, much as bank credit card issuers do. Bank credit card issuers, furthermore, have been aggressively marketing "gold" cards, which have sufficiently high credit limits that they are useful for travel and entertainment charging, and one bank card issuer is developing procedures for easy override of the credit limit for travel and entertainment purchases.

PART III
GLOSSARY

Accept — the **drawee's** act of executing a **time draft,** usually on its face, as a method of undertaking to pay the **draft** according to its **tenor** at the time it becomes due.

Acceptance — a **time draft** that has been **accepted** by the **drawee.** (*See* **banker's acceptance** and **trade acceptance.**)

Acceptor — a **drawee** that has **accepted** a **time draft.**

ACH (*See* **Automated clearinghouse.**)

Acquirer — in the **bank** credit card industry, the **merchant bank,** that is, the bank that acquires the merchant seller's **sales slips** and processes them or forwards them to a data processor for collection through the bank credit card association.

Affinity card — credit card issued under a marketing strategy that takes advantage of the cardholder's loyalty to an organization by including on the card itself the mark or logo of an organization (e.g., social fraternity, bar association, professional baseball club, or March of Dimes) that receives a fee of a few cents for itself or a designated charity upon each use of the card. [Marine Midland Bank of New York offers a New York Knicks Mastercard. Citibank offers a National Football League Visa card under a program that permits the cardholder to pick his favorite team's logo. Affinity cardholders sometimes obtain discounts on items associated with the designated organization.]

Automated clearinghouse — **wire transfer** facility permitting (1) **payors** to transfer funds to multiple payees and (2) payees to draw funds from multiple payors. [Parties utilize the automated clearinghouse in connection with recurring payments or collections such as social security payments or insurance premium collections.]

Bank — usually a commercial bank, as opposed to a **thrift, credit union,** or other financial institution, but now frequently in the payments context any financial institution that accepts deposits and permits the transfer of them.

Bank credit — **bank** deposits, usually **demand deposits** (checking accounts) that are transferred in the payments system.

Bank draft — **draft** drawn by a **bank** on an account it maintains at another bank, frequently, a bank in another country.

Banker's acceptance — **draft** drawn on and **accepted** by a **bank,** frequently in connection with a commercial letter of credit transaction.

BankWire — a private **wire transfer** network that competed with **Fedwire** and that is no longer in operation.

Beneficiary — in **electronic funds transfer,** the party to whose account the funds are to be transferred, usually, the creditor of the party that originates the funds transfer.

Bill of exchange — in the U.S., an anachronistic term for **draft;** in Great Britain and other Commonwealth countries, a synonym for *draft.*

Board of Governors of the Federal Reserve System — independent agency of the federal government consisting of a seven-member board that governs the **Federal Reserve System,** serves as the principal regulator of state **banks** that are members of the system and of bank holding companies, and acts as the nation's central bank.

Cashier's check — **check** drawn on a **bank** by itself. [A cashier's check bears the **drawee's** signature as **drawer.** It is, in the act of **utterance,** both a **draft** or check and an **acceptance,** since at the time of issuance, it bears the drawee's signature.]

Cash item — a demand instrument for the payment of money drawn on a **bank** as it proceeds through the payments system, e.g., a **check.** (*See* **collection item.**)

Cash letter — document accompanying a batch of **checks** and containing a dollar total of the checks.

Certified check — a **check** that the **drawee bank** has certified. [The certified check differs from the **cashier's check** in that a depositor of the bank draws the former, while the bank itself draws the latter.]

Check — a negotiable **draft** drawn on a **bank** and payable on demand.

CHIPS — Clearing House Interbank Payment System, a creature of an association of New York **banks,** the New York Clearinghouse Association, designed for settlement of international, dollar-denominated payments.

Clear — payment of an **item** or **wire transfer.**

Clearinghouse — traditionally, a meeting place at which members of an association of **banks** exchanged **items** drawn on each other; now, often, an association of such banks.

Collecting bank — **bank** in the collection chain other than the **payor.**

Collection item — **item** that is deposited in the **bank** collection system for collection but that does not require payment by a bank without some authorization and one, therefore, for which the bank of first deposit usually does not give credit until final payment. [**Documentary drafts** drawn on a buyer are often deposited in the banking system. Such **drafts** would be collection items, since they are not payable by any bank but are to be honored by a buyer. Similarly, payable-through drafts are collection items, since they are not payable by the payable-through bank, which must first obtain the authority of the **drawee.**]

Correspondents — **banks** that maintain a continuing relationship. [Often, such banks maintain corresponding balances in accounts with each other, but sometimes, a smaller bank (country bank) will maintain a correspondent relationship with a larger bank (city bank) in order to avail itself of the larger bank's facilities, such as its access to **CHIPS** or an **automated clearinghouse.** In such a case, the smaller bank will maintain an account with the larger bank, but the larger bank will not maintain any account with the smaller bank. In international banking relationships, both correspondents usually maintain exchange accounts with the other.] (*See* **nostro account** and **vostro account.**)

Countertrade — the practice of selling goods not for cash but in return for goods (barter) or for cash but on the condition that the seller will purchase output or other goods at a later time.

Credit cap — limit on **overdrafts** a participant in a transfer system may incur at any given time in the system, among all systems, or against another participant.

Credit item — an **item** sent by an **originator** for debit to the originator's account and, therefore, as a credit to the account of another. (*Compare* **debit item.**)

Credit sale — sales transaction that does not entail immediate payment. [Open account sales, deliveries against postdated **checks,** and sales against **time drafts** are credit sales.]

Credit union — financial institution that accepts deposits from and makes loans, usually for personal, family, or household purposes, to a closed group, e.g., employees of a school district or members of a parish.

Debit cap (*See* **credit cap.**)

Debit card — plastic card, usually with magnetic stripe, that activates computer terminal or similar equipment to effect payment.

Debit item — an **item** sent by an **originator** for credit to the originator's account and, therefore, as a debit to someone else's account. (*Compare* **credit item.**)

Delayed disbursement — the ethically questionable practice of delaying payment of a debt by drawing a **check** or other **item** on a **payor** located in an area distant from the payee. [Cash managers desire to hold funds as long as they can. Some of them follow the practice of using delays in the payments system to effect longer holds than would otherwise arise. A securities broker, for example, with offices in Detroit and New York might pay its New York customers with checks drawn on a Detroit **bank** and its Detroit customers with checks drawn on a New York bank. Because it takes longer for the Detroit payee to collect a check drawn on a New York bank than it would for him to collect a check drawn on a Detroit bank, the **drawer** has managed to keep his funds for an extra day or perhaps longer. The practice also tends to burden the check-collection system since it requires the system to move two checks through the **Federal Reserve System,** which may involve two **Federal Reserve Banks,** while clearing local items might be effected through the local **clearinghouse.**]

Demand deposit — deposit subject to withdrawal on demand, as opposed to a **time deposit,** which is subject to withdrawal only with notice.

Demand draft — negotiable order payable at sight, as opposed to an order payable at a fixed date or after a period of time.

Depositary bank — the first **bank** in the collection chain.

Depositary institution — in the **Federal Reserve System,** a financial institution that maintains a deposit with a **Federal Reserve Bank** and, therefore, that may avail itself of **Fedwire,** the Federal Reserve check-collection system, and other Federal Reserve System services.

Deregulation — the legislative and regulatory process of removing legal inhibitions on the activity in which financial institutions may engage in order to permit them to compete with nonregulated industries that had invaded their traditional markets. [In the 1970s, when the trend began for the securities, insurance, and retail industries to compete with **banks** and **thrifts** for deposits and other traditional banking services, regulators and legislators responded by removing restrictions on bank activity such as the rate of interest that could be paid on deposits and the types of assets that an institution could hold.]

Discount — a function performed traditionally by commercial **banks** that consists of taking paper, e.g., chattel paper or promissory notes, for a discounted price, that is, for a price below par or face value.

Documentary draft — a **draft** accompanied by a document of title such as a bill of lading or a warehouse receipt.

Draft — a negotiable instrument, being an order on a **drawee** to pay (1) bearer or (2) the order of a designated payee.

Drawee — the person designated as the **payor** on a **draft** or **check,** the person who receives the order to pay.

Drawer — the person who draws a **draft** or **check,** the party who gives the order to pay.

EFT (*See* **Electronic Funds Transfer.**)

Electronic Funds Transfer — transfer of **bank** or other credit by telephone, telex, or similar telecommunications, as opposed to transfer by a paper instrument for the payment of money such as a **check** or **draft.**

Eurocheck — a form of **check** that is guaranteed by a **bank** and that is in use in western European countries.

Exchange — converting the currency of one state into the currency of another state.

FDIC (*See* **Federal Deposit Insurance Corporation.**)

Federal Deposit Insurance Corporation — insurer of **bank** and **thrift** deposits through two insurance funds (Bank Insurance Fund and Savings Association Insurance Fund) and regulator of state banks that are not members of the **Federal Reserve System.**

Federal Home Loan Bank Board — former federal agency that regulated **thrifts** and served as their lender of last resort, superseded by the **FDIC,** which now insures thrifts, and the **Office of Thrift Supervision,** which supervises them.

Federal Reserve Bank — a privately owned, federally chartered **bank,** one of twelve that comprise the **Federal Reserve System.**

Federal Reserve Board (*See* **Board of Governors of the Federal Reserve System.**)

Federal Reserve District — one of the twelve districts into which the **Federal Reserve System** is divided. [There are twelve **Federal Reserve Banks,** each serving a district. In addition, there are 25 Federal Reserve Branches, 11 nonbranch offices, and 46 regional check processing centers.]

Federal reserve float — float that results when a **Federal Reserve Bank** makes funds available to a **depositary institution** before the **bank** debits the account of the **payor** bank. [The Federal Reserve Banks make funds available to depositary institutions that submit **checks** to the Federal Reserve Banks for collection according to a funds availability schedule. Since the maximum delay in funds availability under the Federal Reserve Banks' schedule is two banking days, frequently those funds are available to the depositary banks before the Federal Reserve Bank has presented and collected the check from the payor bank. For example, the Federal Reserve Bank of Chicago might make funds available to Second National Bank on Tuesday for a check transferred to the Federal Reserve Bank on Monday. At the same time, the Federal Reserve Bank might not be able to charge the account of the drawee-payor bank (Third National) until Wednesday. For one day, then, Second National and Third National are using the same funds. Hence, the **Federal Reserve System's** efforts to accelerate the collection of **items** has the effect of creating float. In recent years, the Federal Reserve has taken steps to reduce the amount of federal reserve float with considerable success. While federal reserve float averaged $6.7 billion per day in 1979, by 1982 reforms had reduced that figure to $1.8 billion. Under the Monetary Control Act of 1980, the Federal Reserve has reduced that float even further and now prices float, so that any bank that receives the benefit of federal reserve float must pay for it.]

Federal Reserve System — system of 12 **Federal Reserve Banks,** their 25 branches, and 46 regional check processing centers that, among other activity, operates a nationwide check-collection system and **Fedwire.**

Fedwire — a **Federal Reserve System** program for **electronic funds transfer**.

FHLBB (*See* **Federal Home Loan Bank Board.**)

Float — funds in the collection system that, because of collection inefficiencies, belong to one party but are available for use by another party, such as (1) collected deposits that, by virtue of delayed funds availability schedules, are not available to the depositor, (2) funds against which payment orders have been issued but that have yet to be paid, and (3) uncollected funds available for use. ["Holdover" float occurs when computer breakdowns or heavy volumes of **checks** cause processing delays. Bad weather, accidents, and vehicle breakdowns yield "transportation" float. "Disbursement" float occurs when a payor in one area writes a check on a **drawee** in a distant, and often remote, area.]

Floor release limit — in credit-card transactions, the threshold, above which the sales person must obtain authorization from the credit-card system before proceeding with the credit sale.

Funds availability — in a system of **pull orders,** such as **checks** and **drafts, depositary institutions** do not know when an **item** clears and must establish schedules for making deposits available to the depositor or permitting withdrawals on a credit basis. Pursuant to federal legislation, the **Federal Reserve Board** has promulgated schedules for the availability of deposits.

Funds consolidation — the practice of bringing widely scattered funds to a central point or points in order to enable the consolidator to utilize them efficiently.

Giro — a **push order,** common in European countries, for the transfer of funds. [Giro accounts are frequently offered by a country's postal service and often by commercial and savings **banks.**]

Image processing — scanning of documents optically to produce digital images that can be stored on disks or in computer memory and manipulated electronically. [Image processing is a recent and largely untested innovation that may have application in the **check** and the credit-card collection systems. The process has two advantages: (1) it eliminates paper from the collection apparatus; and (2) it facilitates the capture of information from paper, where information is difficult to access and manipulate, and its transfer to computer memory or optical disks, where it is easy to access and manipulate.]

Issuing bank — in credit-card systems, the **bank** that issues the credit or **debit card** to and enters into a revolving-credit contract with the customer.

Item — an instrument for the payment of money. [**Checks, drafts,** and promissory notes are items.]

Lock box — a facility offered by financial institutions for **funds consolidation** whereby a party's customers mail their **checks** to a lock box, i.e., a **bank** or other financial institution local to the customer in order to accelerate the collection of the check. [A mail-order business in Massachusetts, for example, does not want its California customers to mail checks drawn on California banks to the mail-order house in Massachusetts. Since most California buyers would draw checks on California banks, checks received at the mail-order house would have to be collected by depositing them in a Massachusetts bank, which would forward them through the banking chain to California for collection. The mail-order house prefers to have its California customers' checks collected at a bank in California. That bank acts as the lock box and collects the checks for the mail-order house by indorsing them and sending them to the payor banks. When the payor banks honor the checks, the lock-box bank forwards the proceeds to Massachusetts. The lock-box system accelerates the collection and thus saves the seller interest charges.]

Magnetic ink character recognition — (often abbreviated "MICR") said of symbols on **items,** usually **checks** and the like, which pass through the **bank** collection system and are read by reader-sorter machines. [Checks bear preprinted MICR symbols designating the **Federal Reserve District** and the identity of the **payor** bank and the **drawer's** account number. When a payee deposits a check, the **depositary bank's** data-entry clerks print MICR symbols on the check indicating the amount of the check, so that thereafter reader-sorter machines can "read" the amount as well as the preprinted information.]

Merchant bank — (1) in credit-card systems, the **bank** that solicits merchants to accept credit cards and agrees to acquire the **sales slips** generated by the merchant's sales; (2) in Europe and now somewhat in the U.S., a financial institution that engages in investment banking and business counselling, especially with regard to exports and imports.

MICR (*See* **Magnetic Ink Character Recognition.**)

Negotiable order of withdrawal — demand **item** offered by savings **banks** and savings and loan institutions. [Prior to the deregulation of financial institutions, **thrifts** could not offer demand accounts. In the early 1970s, however, some states began authorizing thrifts to accept deposits that would be available by negotiable order of withdrawal. Rather quickly, the practice gained widespread approval, and the thrift industry gradually accepted negotiable order of withdrawal deposits and began facing the problem of fashioning a national collection system for its demand-account items.]

Net — balance after computing all additions and subtractions. [In clearing, it makes no sense for institutions to shuffle payments back and forth all day. It is more efficient to settle only once a day. The **clearinghouse,** for example, usually settles once, late in the afternoon. The amount of that settlement is computed by adding all of the transfers to a party and subtracting all of the transfers from that party to arrive at the net settlement figure, which may be positive or negative.]

Netting — in **electronic funds transfer,** the practice of holding transfers for a period of time, computing net positions at the end of the period, and transferring funds in the net amount. [It is expensive to transfer funds, even over **wire transfer** systems. To the extent that two participants can avoid multiple transfers, they can reduce their transfer costs. Also, multiple transfers can create short-lived **overdrafts,** which are usually reduced by the end of the period but which increase system risks, may violate **debit caps,** and may result in penalties. Two participants in a wire transfer network may be able to avoid some of these problems by holding transfers, say, for a few hours. If, for example, First Bank will be transferring $4 billion to Second Bank during the first hour of a transaction day and Second Bank will be transferring $3 billion to First Bank during the second hour of that day, it may make sense for the two **banks** to hold mutual transfers until the end of the second hour, so that the only transfer expense incurred is for one $1 billion dollar transfer instead of several transfers aggregating $7 billion. The practice, which is not always possible, given the demands of the banks' customers, reduces the number and amounts of the transfers and reduces First Bank's overdraft from a high point of $4 billion to $1 billion.]

Noncash item — an **item** that is not payable by a **bank** in the **check** collection system without some authorization from its customer. [**Documentary drafts** and payable-through **drafts** are noncash items.]

Nostro account — in international banking, the foreign currency account of a domestic **bank** in a foreign country. [In order to facilitate payments to its customers' creditors, a New York bank might want to maintain a pound sterling account. Prior to 1988, domestic banks could not offer their customers accounts in foreign currencies, and most customers would prefer not to maintain such accounts in any event. The New York bank will open an account with its London correspondent. The New York bank will refer to that pound-sterling account as a nostro account. At the same time, the New York bank will offer dollar-denominated accounts to its foreign correspondents and will refer to those accounts as **vostro accounts.**]

NOW (*See* **negotiable order of withdrawal.**)

Office of Thrift Supervision — primary federal regulator of **thrifts.**

Official check — said of a **certified, cashier's, teller's** or other **check** drawn by a **bank** on itself or on another bank.

On-arrival draft — **draft** to be presented to the **drawee** upon the arrival of the goods covered by the accompanying bill of lading or other document of title. [Usually, a **documentary draft** arises in a transaction calling for payment against documents, in which case, the drawee does not have the opportunity to examine the goods before honoring the draft. Parties, however, are free to alter that feature of the transaction by utilizing the on-arrival draft, which allows the presenting bank to hold the draft and accompanying document of title until the goods arrive. At that point, the drawee-buyer will have an opportunity to examine the goods before it must honor the draft.]

Originator — in **electronic funds transfer,** the customer of a **bank,** a participant in a **wire transfer** system, that asks the bank to send a transfer order.

Originator's bank — in **electronic funds transfer,** the first **bank** in a **wire transfer** system to transmit a fund transfer order.

Overdraft — said of an account balance that shows a deficit or of an **item** or transfer that results in a deficit account balance.

Payor — the party designated by an instrument or a **wire transfer** as the party that will pay the order. (*See* **drawee.**)

Personal identification number — computer-generated number given to a credit or debit cardholder for use in computer terminals or other equipment as a method of identifying the user as the person authorized to use the card.

PIN (*See* **personal identification number.**)

Point of sale terminal — computer terminal into which a cardholder can insert a **debit card** for the purpose of transferring funds.

POS Terminal (*See* **point of sale terminal.**)

Preauthorized debit — in **automated clearinghouse** transactions, the authorization of a party for the clearinghouse to make periodic debits to his account. [Frequently, payees such as insurance companies and utilities that collect periodic payments from their customers utilize an automated **clearinghouse** to collect those payments. The **payor's** authorization of the payments is a preauthorized debit.]

Presentation — the physical act of submitting an **item** to a payor. [Presentation can be for payment or acceptance. In the **documentary draft** transaction, for example, if the seller draws a **time draft,** the presenting **bank** will present the **draft** for acceptance. After acceptance, the bank will present for payment. If the draft in such a transaction is a **demand draft,** there will be only one presentation, that for payment.]

Presenting bank — the **bank** in the bank-collection chain that transmits an **item** to the **drawee** or other **payor.**

Pull orders — **drafts** or **checks** that, by their nature, "pull" funds from the drawer's account. (*Compare* **push orders.**)

Purchase — any voluntary transfer. [A transfer by gift is a purchase. A transfer by operation of law, such as the attachment of a judgment lien, is not a purchase.]

Push order — wire order or **item**, such as a **giro,** which the sending party or **drawer** delivers to the institution issuing his account with instructions to transfer the funds to a designated beneficiary or account, hence, the order or item pushes the funds. (*Compare* **pull order.**)

RCPC (*See* **regional check processing center.**)

Receiving bank — in **electronic funds transfer,** the **bank** that receives a transfer order. [If a bank receives a computerized instruction from its customer, the bank is a receiving bank. When it transmits the order to a second bank, that bank becomes a receiving bank, the first bank having also become the **originator's bank.** The last receiving bank is the beneficiary's bank.]

Regional check processing center — center that receives **checks** for collection through the **Federal Reserve System** for collecting checks. [Sometimes, **depositary banks** short circuit the normal collection chain. They bypass the **Federal Reserve Banks** and direct items to regional check processing centers that serve a region that may include all or parts of more than one of the twelve **Federal Reserve Districts.**]

Remitter — the party that supplies the funds represented by an instrument, e.g., the party that provides the funds to a **bank** that issues a **cashier's check.**

Remitting bank — any **bank** transferring funds through the check-collection system. [**Checks** pass from the **depositary bank** to the **drawee-payor** bank. Theoretically, the funds pass in the opposite direction, from the payor to the depositary institution. In fact, of course, the funds move by virtue of credits that each bank gives to the bank prior in the collection chain.]

Sales draft — in credit-card transactions, the piece of paper that bears the imprint of the cardholder's card, a description of the merchandise, the sales price, and the cardholder's signature.

Sales slip (*See* **sales draft.**)

Same day presentment fee — in direct presentment situations, the charge levied by the **drawee-payor bank** against the depositary bank that is making the direct presentment.

Sender — in **electronic funds transfer,** the party that originates an order or transfers an order that it has received.

Share draft — negotiable order for the payment of money drawn by a customer of a **credit union.** [Prior to deregulation, credit unions could not accept **demand deposits,** that is, they could not accept checking accounts. As deregulation commenced and the **thrift** industry began using **negotiable orders of withdrawal,** credit unions commenced using the share draft. Share drafts are usually payable through a **bank** or other financial institution.]

Sight draft — a **draft** payable upon presentation, that is, within a specified short time after presentation. (*Compare* **time draft.**)

Smart card — plastic card resembling a credit or **debit card** with an embedded silicon chip that stores information that can be read and altered by a merchant's or a financial institution's terminals. [The plastic credit card familiar to most U.S. consumers bears a magnetic stripe that contains relatively little information and that requires on-line terminals or human intervention for access to such data as the cardholder's credit line. Smart cards can be operated at terminals without on-line capabilities and can not only read data such as the cardholder's credit limits but can reduce the limit by the amount of a given purchase.]

Society for Worldwide Interbank Financial Telecommunication — Belgian cooperative owned by **banks** and dedicated to the international transfer of information between banks under a system that accepts coded information at terminals, transfers the information to a **switching center,** and relays the information to another bank's terminal where it is decoded.

SWIFT (*See* **Society for Worldwide Interbank Financial Telecommunication.**)

Switch (*See* **switching center.**)

Switching center — a computerized component of a message system serving to accept signals from a terminal, store them, and retransmit them to a second terminal.

T&E Card (*See* **travel and entertainment card.**)

Telex — a system of (1) transmitting messages by electronic impulse over telephone wires and by satellite and (2) recording the message in printed form at a terminal dedicated to telex use.

Teller check — a **cashier's check** or other **check** drawn by a **bank** on itself or another financial institution.

Tenor — the terms of an instrument, i.e., date, amount, etc.

Thrift — usually, a savings and loan association or a savings **bank,** as opposed to a commercial bank.

Time deposit — debt of a financial institution that is payable to the depositor not on demand but at a given period of time after demand or at a specified date.

Time draft — **draft** payable not on demand but a given time after sight or date or on a given date. [Time drafts arise in connection with credit sales and may be payable a certain number of days (e.g., 90) after sight, after the date of the draft, or after the date on a bill of lading. Time drafts are honored twice: first, by acceptance, and second, by payment.]

Trade acceptance — a **time draft** that has been accepted by a merchant or trader as opposed to a time draft accepted by a **bank.** (*Compare* **banker's acceptance.**)

Transaction account — an account against which the depositor may make withdrawals by **check, negotiable order of withdrawal, share draft,** or the like.

Transit item — an **item** for collection that is not an on-us item or one to be cleared through the **clearinghouse,** that is, an item to be cleared through the **Federal Reserve System.**

Transmitting bank — in **wire transfers,** a **bank** that transmits funds through a wire transfer system.

Travel and entertainment card — credit card that usually is (1) marketed by a nonbank entity, (2) requires payment in full at the end of a billing cycle, and (3) has no credit limits.

Truncation — any variant of a paper-collection system that provides for the interruption of the transfer of the paper and the substitution for it of an electronic signal or other form of **wire transfer.** Truncation in the check-collection system may occur at the **drawee bank,** the **depositary bank,** or the **clearinghouse.**

Unwind — in **electronic funds transfer,** the process of undoing a transfer that is partially or wholly complete.

Usance draft — synonym for **time draft.**

Utter — in negotiable-instruments law, the process of issuing a negotiable instrument. [A **drawer** utters a **draft** or **check;** a maker utters a promissory note.]

Value dating — issuing an **item** with instructions that value not be given immediately but at a later date.

Vostro account — in international banking, an account held by a domestic **bank** and owned by a foreign bank. (*Compare* **nostro account.**)

Wholesale wire transfer — **electronic funds transfer** that is initiated by a nonconsumer. [By virtue of the facts (1) that the initial legislation in the field of **wire transfers** differentiated consumer transfers from nonconsumer transfers and (2) that some wire transfer systems entail transfer costs that are not economical for frequent low-dollar, consumer use, the electronic funds transfer industry, regulators, and some legislation have differentiated consumer from nonconsumer or wholesale wire transfers.]

Wire transfer — transfer of funds effected not by paper but by telephonic, telegraphic, computer, or other telecommunication.

PART III
TABLE OF DOCUMENTS

PART III
BIBLIOGRAPHY

Baker, D. & R. Brandel, The Law of Electronic Fund Transfer Systems (2d ed. 1988 & Supps.).

Bailey, H., Brady on Bank Checks (6th ed. 1987).

Board of Governors of the Federal Reserve System, The Federal Reserve System — Purposes and Functions (7th ed. 1984).

Bunn, Bank Collections under the Uniform Commercial Code, 1964 Wis. L. Rev. 278.

Chorafas, D., Electronic Funds Transfer (1988).

Clark, B., The Law of Bank Deposits, Collections and Credit Cards (rev. ed. 1981 & Supps.).

Effros, A Bankers Primer on the Law of Electronic Funds Transfers, 104 Banking L.J. 510 (1988).

Ellinger, E., Modern Banking Law (1987).

Federal Reserve Bank of New York, ACHs (Fedpoints 31 1988).

———, C.H.I.P.S. (Fedpoints 36 1986).

———, Fedwire (Fedpoints 43 1988).

———, Float (Fedpoints 8 1988).

———, Regional Check Centers (Fedpoints 3 1985).

Felsenfeld, C., Legal Aspects of Electronic Funds Transfers (1988).

General Accounting Office, Electronic Funds Transfer — Information on Three Critical Banking Systems, [1989 Transfer Binder] Fed. Banking L. Rep. (CCH) ¶87,580 (Feb. 1989).

———, Check Collections — Competitive Fairness Is an Elusive Goal (1989).

Geva, The E.F.T. Debit Card, 15 Can. Bus. L. 406 (1989).

———, Fedwire Transfer of Funds, 104 Banking L.J. 412 (1987).

———, Daylight Overdrafts and Settlement Failure — Credit Risk Controls in U.S. Wire Systems, Banking L. Bull. 3 (Oct. 1987).

———, The Concept of Payment Mechanism, 24 Osgoode Hall L.J. 1 (1986).

International Chamber of Commerce, Uniform Rules for Collections (ICC Pub. No. 322) (1978).

Jordan, Ending the Floating Check Game: The Policy Arguments for Delayed Availability Reform, 36 Hastings L.J. 515 (1985).

Murdoch, L., Float in the Check Stream (Federal Reserve Bank of Philadelphia).
Nickles, S. et al., Materials for Understanding Payment Systems (1987).
Symons, E. & J. White, Banking Law (2d ed. 1984).
UNCITRAL, Legal Guide on Electronic Funds Transfers (1987).

PART IV

TRANSPORT AND STORAGE

30 Introduction to Bailments

§30.1 INTRODUCTION

There is among law teachers and probably not a few lawyers the notion that **bailments** are a rather quaint subject. The older bailment cases and some old treatises deal with bailment disputes that are somewhat uncommercial. There are cases between restaurant patrons who leave a valuable package in a coat pocket and find it missing when they retrieve the coat from the clothes tree or who lose a hat from the hat rack. Others involve claims by a railroad passenger against the railroad when the parties cannot find baggage checked at the depot. These cases arise in bucolic settings during the last century or the first part of this one. They reflect the pastoral era of the nation's history — the era of the railroad and the time when people actually wore hats, as those faded photographs of your grandfather and his friends as boys testify.

In the commercial arena, as opposed to the classroom, however, bailments are anything but quaint. They are an indispensable part of commerce in goods, comprise a vigorous and growing industry, yield enormous efficiencies, and are the subject of rapid and revolutionary technological innovation. The annual volume of international trade in goods is in the trillions of dollars, and most of it involves bailments. Domestic buyers and sellers transport commodities and manufactured goods largely by truck and rail operated by independent carriers. Energy companies transport oil, natural gas, and their derivatives via a network of pipelines that involve a curious blend of storage and transport of those fungible commodities. In short, the quaint old subject of bailments has become a modern giant in commercial practice.

§30.2 SCOPE

Part IV deals with some of the merchant and banking practices that relate to that modern giant. Bailments are so essential to commercial practices, however, that carving out a discrete niche for them in this study is a difficult exercise. The fact is that good portions of Part I on Sales and Part II on Secured Lending deal with bailments, for bailments play a crucial role in the marketing and financing of goods. Part III on Payments Systems deals with the collection of drafts that are often accompanied by documents of title, paper that **bailees** issue.

This Part rehearses some of those marketing and financing features of bailments but excludes others. Specifically, this Part will not deal with the documentary draft transaction, which Chapter 4 discusses, the documentary letter of credit transaction, which Chapter 5 discusses, and leasing, which Chapter 9 discusses. The documentary draft and letter of credit transactions arise out of bailments and the **bill of lading** that evidences them, and the lease is itself a bailment.

31

The Documents of Title

§31.1 KINDS OF DOCUMENTS OF TITLE

A **document of title** is a piece of paper that a trade or industry treats as evidence of the bailment of goods. That treatment may take different forms. One industry, for example, might treat possession of the document as the equivalent of possession of the goods. Another trade might treat a document as only evidence that the party holding the document is entitled to delivery of the goods from the bailee who issued the document. Other industries might use documents only as presumptive evidence that goods have been shipped.

Documents of title are bound to arise whenever commerce advances beyond the subsistence stage. As producers, manufacturers, and traders generate quantities of goods or produce greater than what they can carry with them, they find the need to deposit their goods with third parties. Eventually, the owner's mother gets tired of having all of those carpets in the kitchen and tells her trader offspring to get that stuff out of the house.

Reluctantly, unless he can find a willing friend or another relative with a big house, the trader turns to a commercial bailee, that is, someone who stores the goods for a charge. In this arms-length bailment, the trader, who is a **bailor,** worries that the bailee may not redeliver the rugs to the trader when he is ready to sell them. Knowing that commercial bailees are not half so reliable as mothers, the cautious trader insists at the time of the bailment that the bailee provide him with a receipt. The receipt, which we now call a **warehouse receipt,** is a document of title. Document 31-1 is a nonnegotiable warehouse receipt.

Traders that transport merchandise themselves do not need to worry about documents of title. Sometimes, however, the trader decides to stay in Kerman and let his nephew in Damascus sell the carpets to French nobles who want to keep their bare aristocratic feet off the castle's damp stone floors. The Kerman trader, therefore, will entrust the carpets to a friend, perhaps another relative, who will take them on the next caravan to Damascus. Although entrustment to a relative was often safe and perhaps the only safe means of marketing goods through third parties until the advent of modern communications at the end of the nineteenth century, eventually the trader found it efficient to entrust to a stranger who had some extra room on his dromedary and who enjoyed a good reputation. That reputation rested on reliability in (1) safekeeping goods from bandits while the goods were in transit and (2) delivering the goods at the caravan's destination. The cautious trader insisted, however, that the stranger (the carrier) issue a receipt for the carpets. After all, the bandits might not get the carpets or the camel but might get the stranger, and who is to say which carpets were the stranger's and which the Kerman merchant's? This receipt is a bill of lading. Document 31-2 is a nonnegotiable truck bill of lading. Document 31-3 is a negotiable truck bill of lading.

In the late middle ages, as commerce grew in importance and volume and gradually replaced agriculture and land ownership as the source of wealth, merchants became frequent travelers. A London merchant might spend as much time in Bristol buying goods as they arrived from Ireland or the American colonies as he did in London arranging for credit from his banker or for sales to his customers. Sooner or later, the merchant would find himself in Bristol when his goods were in London or in London when his goods were in Bristol at a time when he wanted the goods delivered to someone. The goods might be in the hands of a partner, probably a brother, son, or other relative, or they might be in the hands of that stranger bailee.

In all events, the merchant, finding himself in the wrong city, sooner or later would simply issue an order to his bailee to deliver or ship the cotton or the cambric handkerchiefs to a third party, a buyer. The merchant could send the order directly to the bailee or could entrust the order to the buyer. Because merchants knew that the bailee would honor the order, which they came to call a **delivery order,** the buyer was often willing to pay the merchant against surrender of the order. American merchants seem to have forgotten the delivery order, though it does appear from time to time in U.S. commerce. Document 31-4 is a delivery order.

There are other kinds of documents of title. Dock warrants or receipts are, as their names suggest, evidence of delivery to a bailee who holds merchandise until it is loaded on a ship. Carriers that accept goods before they are loaded issue **received-for-shipment bills of lading** and **on board bills of lading** for goods that are on board at the time of issue.

No glossary of document-of-title nomenclature will be complete for long. Merchants are out in that busy commercial world inventing new documents and discarding others. The delivery order has largely disappeared from the American merchant's consciousness, but the bean industry invented "drafts" for the delivery of beans. No doubt, at this moment, a group of merchants is inventing new uses for old documents and new names for old ones.

It is worth mentioning here that the *certificate* of title, which is a creature of modern legislation and which is a piece of paper that is issued by a state official indicating the identity of the owner of goods, such as a motor vehicle, yacht, or aircraft, is not a *document* of title. Certificates of title differ from documents of title in two ways. First, they are not inventions of merchants. They do not serve a private, commercial function. They result from the state's exercise of the police power and serve a public function — identifying the owner of goods for purposes of reducing theft and facilitating licensing and registration. Second, they do not involve any bailment. A document of title, by definition, is issued by a bailee indicating receipt of the goods or is addressed to the bailee directing their delivery.

In the used-car industry, some merchants have used certificates of title in the collection of drafts. When a used car dealer, for example, attends an auction and purchases some vehicles, the auctioneer usually permits him to take the vehicles at the end of the auction. The auctioneer or his principal, collects the sum due by drawing a draft on the buyer and sending the draft through the bank collection system, with instructions to the presenting bank to notify the buyer that the draft has arrived and that the bank will deliver the titles to the buyer upon honor of the draft. The transaction has many of the hallmarks of the documentary draft transaction, but the certificates of title do not function here as the bill of lading functions in that transaction. Chapter 4 discusses the documentary draft transaction.

The function of the certificate of title is to permit the buyer to reregister the vehicle and to obtain a new certificate in the name of his subbuyer. While there has been some confusion over the function of the certificate of title, the courts have generally recognized that the certificate does not stand for the goods, as a negotiable document of title does, and that the delivery of the certificate to the buyer in these cases is a matter of facilitating issuance of the new certificate not as a substitute for delivery of the vehicle. Usually, state authorities will not issue a new certificate without surrender of the old one.

§31.2 THE "CONTRACT" FUNCTION OF THE DOCUMENT OF TITLE

The document of title serves three discrete functions. First, it is similar in nature to a contract, which allocates responsibilities and liabilities between bailor and bailee. A warehouse receipt, for example, usually sets out the terms of the warehouse's obligation to store the goods, the charges for that storage, limits on any liability for loss of the goods, and the warehouse's duty to redeliver the goods upon the owner's request and payment of charges. The bill of lading designates the duty of the carrier to transport the goods to a designated destination and specifies, in one form or another, the party to whom the goods are to be delivered at that destination and the party that the carrier is to notify that the goods have arrived.

Bills of lading almost always include disclaimers of liability, so that, for example, a carrier is not liable if the bailor (the **shipper**) does not fill the cartons with the goods it declares are in them. Usually, carriers do not give a warranty as to the content of packages. Carriers transport merchandise not knowing much about the constellation of merchandise and produce they carry — they are not industry inspectors. Other parties, who have industry expertise, perform that function for a fee, and if the buyer wants an inspection certificate, usually it will have to pay for it separately. Formerly, bills of lading usually incorporated charges under a schedule of charges, called a **tariff,** that the carrier filed publicly. With the advent of deregulation in the transport industry, tariffs have become less important.

§31.3 THE MARKETING FUNCTION OF THE DOCUMENT OF TITLE

Warehouse receipts, bills of lading, and delivery orders play an important role in the marketing of goods and commodities. As Chapter 4 explains, the negotiable bill of lading makes the documentary draft transaction work. Because the buyer of goods from a distant seller that the buyer does not trust can rely on the bill as evidence that the goods have been shipped and on accompanying papers as evidence that the goods conform, and because he can rely on the carrier to deliver the goods to the holder of the document, the buyer may safely pay for the goods before they arrive and before he has seen them. The bill reduces risks. Reducing risks reduces costs, to the benefit of all.

The warehouse receipt has in some industries, especially those that involve storage of agricultural or other fungible commodities, also served as a substitute for the goods themselves. Formerly, cotton growers marketed their cotton by storing it with the gin that processed the cotton. The gin would issue a warehouse receipt for each bale of cotton with a sample from the bale stapled to the receipt. The producer or broker that owned the cotton could then take the receipt to market and sell it, often for cash. The buyer would be able to examine a sample of the cotton before paying for it and would be able to take delivery from the gin after paying for it.

Grain producers and brokers use warehouse receipts issued by elevators to market grain. At harvest time, shortages of rolling stock make it expensive and otherwise inconvenient to transport grain commodities to grain consumers (feed lots, chemical companies, distilleries, etc.). The consumers usually do not have sufficient warehouse space to store all of the grain they are going to need until the next harvest and could not take delivery even if there were sufficient carrier capacity to get it to them. On the grand scale, then, it is best that agricultural commodities are stored and shipped periodically rather than all at once. Thus, farmers often store their grain in a local elevator located alongside a railroad spur.

In the meantime, the owner of the grain, if he feels the price is right and if he needs cash, will want to sell it. Finding a broker, grain merchant, or speculator who wants the grain, the owner can effect the sale by "negotiating" the receipt to the buyer. The seller, a farmer in Iowa with a suntanned visage (from the brow down), and the buyer, a Mercedes owner in Chicago, can consummate the transaction through brokers and can leave the grain at the rail siding on the prairie until the buyer or the grain company or the Soviet trading company the buyer resells the grain to wants to take delivery some months later.

Delivery orders are also an effective device for marketing products, though there is evidence that American, as opposed to British, merchants have forgotten about it. The delivery order may be issued by anyone, but usually the buyer or the seller will issue it. The delivery order is similar to a check. Unlike a check, which is an order to pay money drawn on a financial institution, a delivery order is payable in a commodity and is drawn on a bailee of goods.

A dealer in agricultural commodities, for example, may have title to 50,000 bushels of potatoes stored in a warehouse in Pocatello, Idaho. If the broker is selling to a soup cannery in Sacramento, he may want to be in a position to sell some of the potatoes promptly. The cannery may be willing to buy but only if it has some assurances that it will receive the potatoes and that the potatoes do indeed exist. If the cannery and the broker strike a deal, either one of them may draw a delivery order on the warehouse. That draw creates the document of title, but the cannery is still concerned that there may not be any potatoes or that the warehouse will not deliver them. The cannery will not be certain that it has avoided those risks until the warehouse "accepts" the delivery order. Upon acceptance, the delivery order is the equivalent of a warehouse receipt. Of course, if the dealer and the cannery have been dealing with each other over a long period of time, the cannery may be willing to pay the dealer against his issuance to the cannery of an unaccepted delivery order.

The warehouse will normally check with the dealer when it receives the delivery order if it is drawn by the cannery. The parties may not use the delivery order as a substitute for delivery of the goods but merely as a method of causing the warehouse to ship the goods to the cannery, in which case, of course, the warehouse will want a delivery order from the dealer or assurances the delivery is authorized.

Note that in the delivery order transaction, there may be several documents of title involved. First, the warehouse will probably issue a nonnegotiable warehouse receipt to the dealer, Because the parties anticipate the use of delivery orders, the receipt must be nonnegotiable in this case. The warehouse will not deliver potatoes covered by a negotiable receipt unless the holder surrenders the receipt, so negotiable receipts do not work in this transaction. (For discussion of the negotiable document of title and the ways it differs from the nonnegotiable document, see Section 31.6.) The second document of title is the delivery order, which may or may not be accepted by the warehouse. There will probably be a third document of title, a truck or a railroad bill of lading that a carrier will issue when the warehouse ships the potatoes to the buyer.

§31.4 THE FINANCING FUNCTION OF THE DOCUMENT OF TITLE

The third role of documents of title arises when the owner of stored goods or commodities wants to use them as collateral for a loan. That need for financing is usually short term, sometimes for a matter of days, but may, in the case of distilled spirits that are aging, last for years. In all cases, the owner is using the value of the goods to support its note, that is, to make it more marketable with the lender, so that the lender is more likely to take it (i.e., to make the loan) and more likely to take it at an attractive rate.

Importers and other brokers frequently buy shipments of goods whose value far exceeds the capital of the importer itself. The net worth of the borrower in this transaction, the importer, does not justify the amount of the loan it needs to finance its purchase of the shipment. A broker importing a supertanker of North Sea crude will need millions of dollars to pay its seller and may not be able to resell the oil until it arrives in, say, Bayonne. Someone will have to finance the transaction while the commodity is on the North Atlantic and, maybe, for a period of time while the oil is stored at a tank farm in Bayonne. Because the price of commodities fluctuates daily, there are some risks involved in financing this transaction, but generally the importer will be able to use the value of the oil so that a lender will advance it a significant portion, if not all, of the purchase price.

Remember, the importer knows the U.S. petroleum markets and probably has arranged to purchase the oil from a foreign seller at a price below the U.S. market price. If the foreign seller's price is $100 million, chances are that the value of the oil in the U.S. is above that amount. It would not be impossible, then, for a financial institution or other investor to lend virtually the entire purchase price to the broker, as long as the lender took back as collateral for repayment of the loan a security interest in the oil.

Because a negotiable bill of lading issued by the carrier stands for the oil and because the law generally provides that the supertanker must deliver the oil only to the person who holds the bill of lading, lenders are willing to make the loan in return for possession of the bill with the understanding that if the importer does not repay the loan, the lender will take delivery of the oil, sell it, and use the proceeds to satisfy the loan balance.

Thus, the parties may anticipate that the importer will not repay the loan until it resells the oil, and the parties may know that the resale will not occur until a period of time after it arrives. In that event, the parties arrange for the substitution of one document of title for another.

When the tanker docks in Bayonne, the lender, through its agent or, if it trusts the importer, through the importer itself, will deliver the bill of lading to the tanker and order delivery to a tank storage facility, which issues a new document of title, a warehouse receipt covering the oil. By taking possession of that receipt, the lender uses it to protect its interest in the oil. If the importer defaults after the oil is stored in the tanks, the lender surrenders the receipt to the tank farm against delivery of the oil, which the lender then sells, using the proceeds to satisfy the loan balance.

§31.5 BONDS AND REGULATORS: PROTECTING THE PUBLIC

This discussion should conjure up in the reader's mind all sorts of analogies between bailees and banks. Warehouse receipts and bills of lading are to bailments what certificates of deposit are to banking. Bailments resemble deposits. Delivery orders are analogous to checks and drafts; accepted delivery orders to certified checks. Documents of title are "commodity" paper, paper that stands for an obligation to deliver a commodity; checks, notes, and drafts are financial paper, paper that stands for an obligation to pay money.

In both of these systems, the reliability of the paper depends in part on the financial strength of the issuer. Certified checks lose their attractiveness if the bank that certifies is insolvent. Warehouse receipts lose their value if the market has doubts about the integrity of the warehouse. It would not advance commerce if any dishonest warehouse operator could issue a warehouse receipt for phantom goods and sell them to a gullible market. The states and the federal government have enacted legislation regulating bailees and providing for unannounced audits similar to those conducted by state and federal bank examiners.

Not all audits are successful, however. In the past, bailors have issued receipts for commodities they did not receive, and from time to time we read in the newspapers of insolvent grain elevators that have sold grain that they were supposed to be holding and of vegetable oil tank farms that fooled auditors by filling tanks with water and a film of oil. Insurance can, of course, protect against some of these losses, and some states have established insurance funds to protect bailors and others who sustain losses as a consequence of a bailee's overissuance of documents of title.

The bailment system is like the banking system. It works only as long as commodity paper is sound. To some extent the market assures that soundness. By accepting paper issued by bailees of good repute and rejecting paper issued by those without it, the market fosters good bailment practices. The market has not proved a sufficient policeman by itself, however. To a degree the state must regulate bailees as it regulates financial institutions.

§31.6 REIFICATION

The law merchant long ago accepted the idea that a piece of paper can embody an obligation. A negotiable draft, for example, was not merely a contract, not simply evidence of the underlying obligation, it was the obligation itself, and transfer of it constituted transfer of the obligation. This is the merchant idea of reification, and it was and to some extent still is indispensable to some branches of commerce.

For documents of title, reification is the notion that the document stands for the goods. In fact, when a negotiable document of title issues, the goods cease to exist and become "mere simulacra" — a mere shadow. As long as the negotiable document remains outstanding, anyone desiring to deal with the goods must deal with the document.

Note that this reification notion serves the marketing and financing functions of the document but is not necessary for the contract function. Commercial parties that are not interested in using the document for financing or marketing purposes may decide that they do not want to bother with a document that stands for the goods.

There are serious problems with documents that stand for the goods. First, the bailee will not deliver goods subject to such a document without its surrender. If bailees delivered goods without obtaining and cancelling the document, no one could rely on the document, and it would lose its reification character. In many transactions, surrender of the document becomes problematic. If a Los Angeles seller of goods transports them to his Boston buyer by a carrier that issues a document that stands for the goods, the seller will have to get the document to Boston in order for the buyer to take delivery when the goods arrive. Getting the document to Boston may not be easy, quick, or inexpensive. If the goods travel by air, for example, they may well arrive before the document. Sometimes, documents are lost or stolen. Buyers of goods can arrange to indemnify a carrier against loss incurred by the carrier's delivery of goods without surrender of the document. A bank indemnification agreement can be used by a buyer who wants to take delivery of goods from a carrier without surrendering all copies of a bill of lading that is issued in multiple originals. Indemnification bonds and the like are expensive, however, and procuring them takes time.

In order to avoid the transaction costs that lost or delayed documents entail, merchants decided that it would be advantageous to create a document of title that did not stand for the goods. This document is evidence of a shipment or of a storage contract. It often is sufficient to satisfy a buyer that goods have been shipped or stored and sometimes is satisfactory evidence for lenders. Above all, it is evidence of the bailment, and governs the contractual relationship between the bailor and the bailee. Merchants called this modified document of title "nonnegotiable" in order to distinguish it from the document that embodies the goods. In the transport industry, parties take some pains to distinguish negotiable and nonnegotiable bills of lading. The negotiable bill is an "order" bill, the nonnegotiable bill a "straight" bill.

Document 31-1. Nonnegotiable Warehouse Receipt

AMERICAN WAREHOUSE COMPANY
STREET ADDRESS • CITY & AMERICA 00000
TELEPHONE: (312) – 123-4567

ORIGINAL
NON-NEGOTIABLE WAREHOUSE RECEIPT

DOCUMENT NUMBER
DATE
CUSTOMER NUMBER
CUSTOMER ORDER NO.
WAREHOUSE NO.

AMERICAN WAREHOUSE COMPANY claims a lien for all lawful charges for storage and preservation of the goods; also for all lawful claims for money advanced, interest, insurance, transportation, labor, weighing, coopering and other charges and expenses in relation to such goods, and for the balance on any other accounts that may be due. The property covered by this receipt has NOT been insured by this Company for the benefit of the depositor against fire or any other casualty.

RECEIVED FROM

THIS IS TO CERTIFY THAT WE HAVE RECEIVED the goods listed hereon in apparent good order, except as noted herein (contents, condition and quality unknown), SUBJECT TO ALL TERMS AND CONDITIONS INCLUDING LIMITATION OF LIABILITY HEREIN AND ON THE REVERSE HEREOF. Such property to be delivered to THE DEPOSITOR upon the payment of all storage, handling and other charges. Advances have been made and liability incurred on these goods as follows:

FOR ACCOUNT OF

DELIVERING CARRIER	CARRIER NUMBER	PREPAID/COLLECT	SHIPPERS NUMBER

QUANTITY	SAID TO BE OR CONTAIN (CUSTOMER ITEM NO., WAREHOUSE ITEM NO., LOT NUMBER, DESCRIPTION, ETC.)	WEIGHT	RATE CODE	STORAGE RATE / HANDLING RATE	DAMAGE & EXCEPTIONS
	TOTALS				

NO DELIVERY WILL BE MADE ON THIS RECEIPT EXCEPT ON WRITTEN ORDER.

SPECIMEN

AMERICAN WAREHOUSE COMPANY
BY
AUTHORIZED SIGNATURE

FORM 2 3/70

Reprinted with the permission of American Warehousemen's Association.

Document 31-1. (*continued*)

The property described on this receipt is stored and handled in accordance with the terms and conditions of the Contract and Rate Quotation approved by the American Warehousemen's Association. These Contract and Rate Quotation terms and conditions are repeated below for the convenience of the storer and others having an interest in the property.

STANDARD CONTRACT TERMS AND CONDITIONS FOR MERCHANDISE WAREHOUSEMEN

(APPROVED AND PROMULGATED BY THE AMERICAN WAREHOUSEMEN'S ASSOCIATION, OCTOBER 1968)

ACCEPTANCE — Sec. 1

(a) This contract and rate quotation including accessorial charges endorsed on or attached hereto must be accepted within 30 days from the proposal date by signature of depositor on the reverse side of the contract. In the absence of written acceptance, the act of tendering goods described herein for storage or other services by warehouseman within 30 days from the proposal date shall constitute such acceptance by depositor.

(b) In the event that goods tendered for storage or other services do not conform to the description contained herein, or conforming goods are tendered after 30 days from the proposal date without prior written acceptance by depositor as provided in paragraph (a) of this section, warehouseman may refuse to accept such goods. If warehouseman accepts such goods, depositor agrees to rates and charges as may be assigned and invoiced by warehouseman and to all terms of this contract.

(c) This contract may be cancelled by either party upon 30 days written notice and is cancelled if no storage or other services are performed under this contract for a period of 180 days.

SHIPPING — Sec. 2

Depositor agrees not to ship goods to warehouseman as the named consignee. If, in violation of this agreement, goods are shipped to warehouseman as named consignee, depositor agrees to notify carrier in writing prior to such shipment, with copy of such notice to the warehouseman, that warehouseman named as consignee is a warehouseman and has no beneficial title or interest in such property and depositor further agrees to indemnify and hold harmless warehouseman from any and all claims for unpaid transportation charges, including undercharges, demurrage, detention or charges of any nature, in connection with goods so shipped. Depositor further agrees that, if it fails to notify carrier as required by the next preceding sentence, warehouseman shall have the right to refuse such goods and shall not be liable or responsible for any loss, injury or damage of any nature to, or related to, such goods. Depositor agrees that all promises contained in this section will be binding on depositor's heirs, successors and assigns.

TENDER FOR STORAGE — Sec. 3

All goods for storage shall be delivered at the warehouse properly marked and packaged for handling. The depositor shall furnish at or prior to such delivery, a manifest showing marks, brands, or sizes to be kept and accounted for separately, and the class of storage and other services desired.

STORAGE PERIOD AND CHARGES — Sec. 4

(a) All charges for storage are per package or other agreed unit per month.

(b) Storage charges become applicable upon the date that warehouseman accepts care, custody and control of the goods, regardless of unloading date or date of issue of warehouse receipt.

(c) Except as provided in paragraph (d) of this section, a full month's storage charge will apply on all goods received between the first and the 15th, inclusive, of a calendar month, one-half month's storage charge will apply on all goods received between the 16th and last day, inclusive, of a calendar month, and a full month's storage charge will apply to all goods in storage on the first day of the next and succeeding calendar months. All storage charges are due and payable on the first day of storage for the initial month and thereafter on the first day of the calendar month.

(d) When mutually agreed by the warehouseman and the depositor, a storage month shall extend from a date in one calendar month to, but not including, the same date of the next and all succeeding months. All storage charges are due and payable on the first day of the storage month.

TRANSFER, TERMINATION OF STORAGE, REMOVAL OF GOODS — Sec. 5

(a) Instructions to transfer goods on the books of the warehouseman are not effective until delivered to and accepted by warehouseman, and all charges up to the time transfer is made are chargeable to the depositor of record. If a transfer involves rehandling the goods, such will be subject to a charge. When goods in storage are transferred from one party to another through issuance of a new warehouse receipt, a new storage date is established on the date of transfer.

(b) The warehouseman reserves the right to move, at his expense, 14 days after notice is sent by certified or registered mail to the depositor of record or to the last known holder of the negotiable warehouse receipt, any goods in storage from the warehouse in which they may be stored to any other of his warehouses; but if such depositor or holder takes delivery of his goods in lieu of transfer, no storage charge shall be made for the current storage month. The warehouseman may, without notice, move goods within the warehouse in which they are stored.

(c) The warehouseman may, upon written notice to the depositor of record and any other person known by the warehouseman to claim an interest in the goods, require the removal of any goods by the end of the next succeeding storage month. Such notice shall be given to the last known place of business or abode of the person to be notified. If goods are not removed before the end of the next succeeding storage month, the warehouseman may sell them in accordance with applicable law.

(d) If warehouseman in good faith believes that the goods are about to deteriorate or decline in value to less than the amount of warehouseman's lien before the end of the next succeeding storage month, the warehouseman may specify in the notification any reasonable shorter time for removal of the goods and in case the goods are not removed, may sell them at public sale held one week after a single advertisement or posting as provided by law.

(e) If as a result of a quality or condition of the goods of which the warehouseman had no notice at the time of deposit the goods are a hazard to other property or to the warehouse or to persons, the warehouseman may sell the goods at public or private sale without advertisement on reasonable notification to all persons known to claim an interest in the goods. If the warehouseman after a reasonable effort is unable to sell the goods he may dispose of them in any lawful manner and shall incur no liability by reason of such disposition. Pending such disposition, sale or return of the goods, the warehouseman may remove the goods from the warehouse and shall incur no liability by reason of such removal.

HANDLING — Sec. 6

(a) The handling charge covers the ordinary labor involved in receiving goods at warehouse door, placing goods in storage, and returning goods to warehouse door. Handling charges are due and payable on receipt of goods.

(b) Unless otherwise agreed, labor for unloading and loading goods will be subect to a charge. Additional expenses incurred by the warehouseman in receiving and handling damaged goods, and additional expense in unloading from or loading into cars or other vehicles not at warehouse door will be charged to the depositor.

(c) Labor and materials used in loading rail cars or other vehicles are chargeable to the depositor.

(d) When goods are ordered out in quantities less than in which received, the warehouseman may make an additional charge for each order or each item of an order.

(e) The warehouseman shall not be liable for demurrage, delays in unloading inbound cars, or delays in obtaining and loading cars for outbound shipment unless warehouseman has failed to exercise reasonable care.

DELIVERY REQUIREMENTS — Sec. 7

(a) No goods shall be delivered or transferred except upon receipt by the warehouseman of complete instructions properly signed by the depositor. However, when no negotiable receipt is outstanding, goods may be delivered upon instructions by telephone in accordance with a prior written authorization, but the warehouseman shall not be responsible for loss or error occasioned thereby.

(b) When a negotiable receipt has been issued no goods covered by that receipt shall be delivered, or transferred on the books of the warehouseman, unless the receipt, properly indorsed, is surrendered for cancellation, or for indorsement of partial delivery thereon. If a negotiable receipt is lost or destroyed, delivery of goods may be made only upon order of a court of competent jurisdiction and the posting of security approved by the court as provided by law.

(c) When goods are ordered out a reasonable time shall be given the warehouseman to carry out instructions, and if he is unable because of acts of God, war, public enemies, seizure under legal process, strikes, lockouts, riots and civil commotions, or any reason beyond the warehouseman's control, or because of loss or destruction of goods for which warehouseman is not liable, or because of any other excuse provided by law, the warehouseman shall not be liable for failure to carry out such instructions and goods remaining in storage will continue to be subject to regular storage charges.

EXTRA SERVICES (SPECIAL SERVICES) — Sec. 8

(a) Warehouse labor required for services other than ordinary handling and storage will be charged to the depositor.

(b) Special services requested by depositor including but not limited to compiling of special stock statements; reporting marked weights, serial numbers or other data from packages; physical check of goods, and handling transit billing will be subject to a charge.

(c) Dunnage, bracing, packing materials or other special supplies, may be provided for the depositor at a charge in addition to the warehouseman's cost.

(d) By prior arrangement, goods may be received or delivered during other than usual business hours, subect to a charge.

(e) Communication expense including postage, teletype, telegram, or telephone, will be charged to the depositor if such concern more than normal inventory reporting or if, at the request of the depositor, communications are made by other than regular United States Mail.

BONDED STORAGE — Sec. 9

(a) A charge in addition to regular rates will be made for merchandise in bond.

(b) Where a warehouse receipt covers goods in U. S. Customs bond, such receipt shall be void upon the termination of the storage period fixed by law.

MINIMUM CHARGES — Sec. 10

(a) A minimum handling charge per lot and a minimum storage charge per lot per month will be made. When a warehouse receipt covers more than one lot or when a lot is in assortment, a minimum charge per mark, brand, or variety will be made.

(b) A minimum monthly charge to one account for storage and/or handling will be made. This charge will apply also to each account when one customer has several accounts, each requiring separate records and billing.

LIABILITY AND LIMITATION OF DAMAGES — Sec. 11

(A) THE WAREHOUSEMAN SHALL NOT BE LIABLE FOR ANY LOSS OR INJURY TO GOODS STORED HOWEVER CAUSED UNLESS SUCH LOSS OR INJURY RESULTED FROM THE FAILURE BY THE WAREHOUSEMAN TO EXERCISE SUCH CARE IN REGARD TO THEM AS A REASONABLY CAREFUL MAN WOULD EXERCISE UNDER LIKE CIRCUMSTANCES AND WAREHOUSEMAN IS NOT LIABLE FOR DAMAGES WHICH COULD NOT HAVE BEEN AVOIDED BY THE EXERCISE OF SUCH CARE.

(B) GOODS ARE NOT INSURED BY WAREHOUSEMAN AGAINST LOSS OR INJURY HOWEVER CAUSED.

(C) THE DEPOSITOR DECLARES THAT DAMAGES ARE LIMITED TO ______________________, PROVIDED, HOWEVER, THAT SUCH LIABILITY MAY AT THE TIME OF ACCEPTANCE OF THIS CONTRACT AS PROVIDED IN SECTION 1 BE INCREASED ON PART OR ALL OF THE GOODS HEREUNDER IN WHICH EVENT A MONTHLY CHARGE OF ______________________ WILL BE MADE IN ADDITION TO THE REGULAR MONTHLY STORAGE CHARGE.

NOTICE OF CLAIM AND FILING OF SUIT — Sec. 12

(a) Claims by the depositor and all other persons must be presented in writing to the warehouseman within a reasonable time, and in no event longer than either 60 days after delivery of the goods by the warehouseman or 60 days after depositor of record or the last known holder of a negotiable warehouse receipt is notified by the warehouseman that loss or injury to part or all of the goods has occurred, whichever time is shorter.

(b) No action may be maintained by the depositor or others against the warehouseman for loss or injury to the goods stored unless timely written claim has been given as provided in paragraph (a) of this section and unless such action is commenced either within nine months after date of delivery by warehouseman or within nine months after depositor of record or the last known holder of a negotiable warehouse receipt is notified that loss or injury to part or all of the goods has occurred, whichever time is shorter.

(c) When goods have not been delivered, notice may be given of known loss or injury to the goods by mailing of a registered or certified letter to the depositor of record or to the last known holder of a negotiable warehouse receipt. Time limitations for presentation of claim in writing and maintaining of action after notice begin on the date of mailing of such notice by warehouseman.

OP-097 9/87

SHIPPER PLEASE NOTE ▶ **FREIGHT CHARGES ARE PREPAID ON THIS BILL OF LADING UNLESS MARKED COLLECT**

STRAIGHT BILL OF LADING—ORIGINAL—NOT NEGOTIABLE

☐ **ROADWAY EXPRESS, INC. (RDWY)**

ROADWAY® **GENERAL OFFICES: AKRON, OHIO (DUNS 00-699-8397)**

America's Quality Service Carrier

Thank You For Using Roadway

SPECIMEN

SHIPPER NO. ____________ DATE ____________

CARRIER NO.

FROM SHIPPER:			**TO CONSIGNEE:**		
STREET			**STREET**		
ORIGIN: CITY	**STATE**	**ZIP CODE**	**DESTINATION: CITY**	**STATE**	**ZIP CODE**
ROUTE		**VEHICLE NO.**	**P.O. NO.**		**DEPT. NO.**

NO. SHIPPING UNITS	KIND OF PACKAGING	HM	DESCRIPTION OF ARTICLES, SPECIAL MARKS, AND EXCEPTIONS	NMFC ITEM NO.	CLASS	WEIGHT (LBS) (SUBJECT TO CORR.)	RATE	CHARGES (CARRIER USE ONLY)

REMIT COD TO: (NAME AND ADDRESS IF DIFFERENT FROM SHIPPER)

COD FEE PREPAID ☐ COLLECT ☐ **COD AMT $**

TOTAL CHARGES $

NOTE—When the rate is dependent on value, shippers are required to state specifically in writing the agreed or declared value of the property.

The agreed or declared value of the property is hereby specifically stated by the shipper to be not exceeding:

$ ____________ per ____________

Subject to Section 7 of conditions, if this shipment is to be delivered to the consignee without recourse on the consignor, the consignor shall sign the following statement:

The carrier shall not make delivery of this shipment without payment of freight and all other lawful charges.

____

(SIGNATURE OF CONSIGNOR)

FREIGHT CHARGES ARE PREPAID UNLESS MARKED COLLECT.

CHECK BOX IF CHARGES ARE **COLLECT**. ☐

RECEIVED, subject to the classifications and lawfully filed tariffs in effect on the date of the issue of this Bill of Lading, the property described above and in apparent good order, except as noted (contents and condition of contents of packages unknown), marked, consigned, and destined, as indicated above which said carrier (the word carrier being understood throughout this contract as meaning any person or corporation in possession of the property under the contract) agrees to carry to its usual place of delivery of said destination, if on its route, otherwise to deliver to another carrier on the route to said destination. It is mutually agreed as to each carrier of all or any of said property over all or any portion of said route to destination and as to each party at any time interested in all or any of said property, that every service to be performed hereunder shall be subject to all the conditions not prohibited by law, whether printed or written, herein contained, including the conditions on the back hereof, which are hereby agreed to by the shipper and accepted for himself and his assigns.

This is to certify that the above named materials are properly classified, described, packaged, marked and labeled and are in proper condition for transportation, according to the applicable regulations of the Department of Transportation.

SHIPPER	CARRIER **ROADWAY EXPRESS, INC. (RDWY)**		
PER	PER	DATE	PIECES

1 **MARK "X" IN "HM" COLUMN FOR HAZARDOUS MATERIALS** SINGLE SHIPMENT PICKUP ☐

Reprinted with the permission of Roadway Express, Inc.

CONTRACT TERMS AND CONDITIONS

Sec. 1.(a) The Carrier or the party in possession of any of the property described in this bill of lading shall be liable as at common law for any loss thereof or damage thereto, except as hereinafter provided.

Sec. 1.(b) 1. No carrier or party in possession of all or any portion of the property described in this bill of lading shall be liable for any loss of or damage to the said property or for any delay caused by an Act of God, the public enemy, the authority of law, or the act or default of the shipper or owner. Further, no carrier or party in possession of all or any portion of the said property shall be liable for any natural shrinkage of the property. 2. The carrier shall be liable solely as a warehouseman for loss, damage or delay resulting from fire occurring after the expiration of free time (if any) allowed by the tariffs lawfully on file (such free time to be computed as provided in said tariffs) where such loss, damage or delay occurs: (a) after notice of the arrival of the property at the destination (or, if the property is intended for export, after notice of the arrival of said property at the port of export) has been duly sent or given, and (b) after placement of the property for delivery at destination or tender of delivery of the property to the party entitled to receive it has been made. 3. Except in the case of negligence of the carrier or the party in possession, the carrier or party in possession shall not be liable for country damage to cotton, or for loss, damage or delay which results: (a) when the property is stopped and held in transit upon request of the shipper, owner or party entitled to make such request or (b) from a defect or vice in the property, or (c) from riots or strikes. The burden to prove freedom from such negligence is on the carrier or the party in possession. 4. Except in the case of negligence of the carrier no carrier or party in possession of all or any of the property described in this bill of lading shall be liable for delay caused by highway obstruction, by faulty or impassable highway, or by lack of capacity of any highway, bridge or ferry. The burden to prove freedom from such negligence is on the carrier or party in possession.

Sec. 1(c) In case of quarantine, the property may be discharged at the owner's risk and expense into a quarantine depot or elsewhere as required by quarantine regulations or authorities, or for the carrier's dispatch, the property may be discharged at the owner's risk and expense at the nearest available point in the carrier's judgement. The carrier's responsibility shall cease when the property is so discharged, or the property may be returned by the carrier at the owner's expense to the shipping point, earning freight both ways. All quarantine expenses of whatever nature or kind which are incurred with respect to the property shall be borne by the owners of the property or shall become a lien on the property. The carrier shall not be liable for loss or damage caused by fumigation, disinfection or other acts required or done by quarantine regulations or authorities even though the same may have been done by the carrier's officers, agents, or employees. In addition, the carrier shall not be liable for detention, loss, or damage of any kind occasioned by the quarantine or the enforcement of the quarantine. No carrier shall be liable except in the case of negligence, for any mistake or inaccuracy in any information furnished by the carrier, its agents or officers, as to quarantine laws or regulations. The shipper shall indemnify the carrier for any expense incurred or damages the carriers may be required to pay as a result of introducing the property covered by contract into any place against the quarantine laws or regulations in effect at such place.

Sec. 2.(a) 1. No carrier is bound to transport said property by any particular schedule, train, vehicle or vessel, or in time for any particular market, or in any manner other than with reasonable dispatch. Every carrier shall have the right, in case of physical necessity, to forward said property by any carrier or route between the point of shipment and the point of destination. 2. In all cases not prohibited by law, where a lower value than the actual value of the said property has been stated in writing by the shipper or has been agreed upon in writing as the released value of the property as determined by the classification or tariffs upon which the rate is based, such lower value plus freight charges if paid shall be the maximum recoverable amount for loss or damage, whether or not such loss or damage occurs from negligence.

Sec. 2.(b) As a condition precedent to recovery, claims must be filed in writing with: 1. the receiving or delivering carrier; or 2. the carrier issuing this bill of lading; or 3. the carrier whose line the loss, damage, injury or delay occurred; or 4. the carrier in possession of the property when the loss, damage, injury or delay occurred.

Such claims must be filed within nine months after the delivery of the property (or, in the case of export traffic, within nine months after delivery of the port of export), except that claims for failure to make delivery must be filed within nine months after a reasonable time for delivery has elapsed.

Suits for loss, damage, injury or delay shall be instituted against any carrier no later than two years and one day from the day when written notice is given by the carrier to the claimant that the carrier has disallowed the claim or any part or parts of the claim specified in the notice. Where claims are not filed or suits are not instituted thereon in accordance with the foregoing provisions, no carrier shall be liable, and such claims will not be paid.

Sec. 2.(c) Any carrier or party liable for loss of or damage to any of said property shall have the full benefit of any insurance that may have been effected, upon or on account of said property, so far as this shall not avoid the policies or contracts of insurance. PROVIDED, that the carrier receiving the benefit of such insurance will reimburse the claimant for the premium paid on the insurance policy or contract.

Sec. 3. All property shall be subject to necessary cooperage and baling at owner's cost, except where such service is required as the result of carrier's negligence. Each carrier over whose route cotton or cotton linters is to be transported under this bill of lading shall have the privilege, at its own cost and risk, of compressing the cotton or cotton linters for greater convenience in handling or forwarding, and shall not be held responsible for deviation or unavoidable delays in procuring such compression.

Grain in bulk consigned to a point where there is a railroad, public or licensed elevator, may (unless otherwise expressly noted in this bill of lading and then only if the grain in bulk is not promptly unloaded) be there delivered, and placed with other grain of the same kind and grade without respect to ownership and prompt notice thereof shall be given to the consignor. If the grain in bulk is so delivered, it shall be subject to a lien for elevator charges in addition to all other applicable charges.

Sec. 4(a) In the event that: 1. Said property is not removed by the party entitled to receive it within the free time (if any) allowed by the tariffs, lawfully on file (such free time is to be computed as provided in the said tariffs and notice of the arrival of the property at the destination (or at the port of export, if intended for export) has been duly sent or given, and placement of the property for delivery at destination has been made, or 2. Property is not received at the time tender of delivery of the property to the party entitled to receive it has been made.

Such property may be kept in vessel, vehicle, car, depot, warehouse, or place of business of the carrier, subject to the tariff charge for storage and to the carrier's responsibility solely as warehouseman. Alternatively, at the option of the carrier, such property may be removed to and stored in a public or licensed warehouse at the point of delivery or at another available point, or if no such warehouse is available at the point of delivery or at another available point, then the property may be removed to and stored in another available storage facility, at the owner's cost and held there without liability on the part of the carrier and subject to a lien for all freight and other lawful charges, including a reasonable charge for storage. In the event consignee cannot be found at the address given for delivery then notice of the placing of such goods in warehouse shall be mailed to the address given on the bill of lading for delivery and to any other address given on the bill of lading for notification, showing the warehouse in which the property has been placed subject to the provisions of this paragraph.

Sec. 4.(b) Where non-perishable property transported to the destination stated in this bill of lading is refused by consignee or the party entitled to receive it upon tender of delivery, or said consignee or party entitled to receive the property fails to receive or claim it within 15 days after notice of arrival shall have been duly sent or given, the carrier may sell the property at public auction to the highest bidder, at such place as may be designated by the carrier. PROVIDED, that the carrier shall have first mailed, sent, or given to the consignor notice that the property has been refused or remains unclaimed, as the case may be, and that it will be subject to sale under the terms of the bill of lading if disposition is not arranged for, and that after 30 days have elapsed from the time said notice to the consignor was mailed, sent or given, the carrier shall also have published a notice containing a description of the property, the name of the party to whom consigned (or if shipped order notify, the name of the party to be notified) and the time and place of sale, once a week for two consecutive weeks, in a newspaper of general circulation at the place of sale or nearest place where such newspaper is published.

Sec. 4.(c) Where perishable property transported to the destination stated in this bill of lading is refused by consignee or party entitled to receive it, or said consignee or party entitled to receive the property fails to receive it promptly, the carrier may, in its discretion, to prevent deterioration or further deterioration, sell the property to the best advantage at private or public sale: PROVIDED, that if there is sufficient time to notify the consignor or owner of the refusal of the property or the failure to receive it and to request for disposition of the property, such notification shall be given, in such manner as the exercise of due diligence requires, before the property is sold.

Sec. 4.(d) Where the procedure provided for in Sections 4(b) and 4(c) of this bill of lading is not possible, it is agreed that nothing in these paragraphs shall be construed to abridge the right of the carrier at its option to sell the property under such circumstances and in such manner as may be authorized by law.

Sec. 4.(e) The proceeds of any sale made under this section shall be applied by the carrier: to the payment of freight, demurrage, storage, and any other lawful charges; to the expense of notice, advertisement, sale, and other necessary expense and to the expense of caring for and maintaining the property, if proper care of the property requires special expense. Should there be a balance remaining after all charges and expenses are paid, such balance shall be paid to the owner of the property sold hereunder.

Sec. 4.(f) Property destined to or taken from a station, wharf, landing or other place at which there is no regularly appointed freight agent, shall be entirely at risk of owner after being unloaded from cars, vehicles or vessels or until loaded into cars, vehicles or vessels. Further, except in case of carrier's negligence, when property is received from or delivered to such stations, wharfs, landings, or other places, the property shall be at the owner's risk until the cars are attached to and after they are detached from locomotive or train, or until loaded into and after unloaded from vessels, or if property is transported in motor vehicle trailers or semi-trailers, until such trailers or semi-trailers are attached to and after they are detached from power units. Where a carrier is directed to unload or deliver property transported by motor vehicle at a particular location where consignee or consignor's agent is not regularly located, the risk after unloading or delivery, shall be that of the owner.

Sec. 5. No carrier hereunder will carry or be liable in any way for any documents, coin money, or for any articles of extraordinary value not specifically rated in the published classification or tariffs unless a special agreement to do so and a stipulated value of the articles are endorsed on the bill of lading.

Sec. 6. Every party, whether principal or agent, who ships explosives or dangerous goods, without previous full written disclosure to the carrier of their nature, shall be liable for and indemnify the carrier against all loss or damage caused by such goods. Such goods may be warehoused at owner's risk and expense or destroyed without compensation.

Sec. 7. The owner or consignee shall pay the freight and average, if any, and all other lawful charges accruing on said property according to lawfully filed tariffs of the carrier; but, except in those instances where it may lawfully be authorized to do so, no carrier shall deliver or relinquish possession at destination of the property covered by this bill of lading until all lawfully filed tariff rates and charges thereon have been paid. The consignor shall be liable for the freight and all other lawful charges, except that if the consignor stipulates, by signature, in the space provided for that purpose on the face of this bill of lading that the carrier shall not make delivery without requiring payment of such charges and the carrier, contrary to such stipulation shall make delivery without requiring such payment, the consignor (except as hereinafter provided) shall not be liable for such charges, PROVIDED, that, a consignee shall not be liable for transportation charges (beyond those billed against him at the time of delivery for which he is otherwise liable) which may be found to be due after the property has been delivered to him subject to all of the following conditions (a) The shipper or consignor has instructed the carrier to deliver the property to a consignee other than the shipper or consignor. (b) The consignee is an agent only and has no beneficial title in the property and (c) Prior to delivery the consignee has notified the delivering carrier in writing that he is only an agent and has no beneficial title in the property and (d) In cases where the shipment has been reconsigned or diverted to a point other than that specified in the bill of lading the consignee has also notified the delivering carrier in writing of the name and address of the beneficial owner of said property. Where the consignee is not liable for certain transportation charges in accordance with this provision and the preceding conditions, the shipper or consignor, or, in the case of a shipment so reconsigned or diverted in condition (d), the beneficial owner shall be liable for such additional charges. PROVIDED FURTHER, that where the shipment is designated 'prepaid' the shipper or consignor shall remain liable for undercharges which result from an erroneous determination of the transportation charges assessed.

If the consignee has given to the carrier erroneous information as to who the beneficial owner is, such consignee shall himself be liable for such additional charges. Nothing herein shall limit the right of the carrier to require at time of shipment the prepayment or guarantee of the charges. If upon inspection it is ascertained that the articles shipped are not those described in this bill of lading, the freight charges must be paid upon the articles actually shipped.

Sec. 8. If this bill of lading is issued on the order of the shipper, or his agent, in exchange or in substitution for another bill of lading, the shipper's signature on the prior bill of lading or in connection with the prior bill of lading as to the statement of value or otherwise, or as to the election of common law or bill of lading liability shall be considered a part of this bill of lading as fully as if the same were written on or made in connection with this bill of lading.

Sec. 9.(a) If all or any part of said property is carried by water over any part of said route, such water carriage shall be performed subject to all the terms and provisions of, and all the exemptions from liability contained in the Act approved by the United States Congress on February 13, 1893 and entitled 'An act relating to the navigation of vessels, etc.' and in other United States Statutes according carriers by water the protection of limited liability. Such water carriage shall also be performed subject to the conditions contained in the bill of lading which are not inconsistent with the said Act of Congress and United States Statutes or with this section.

Sec. 9.(b) no such carrier by water shall be liable for any loss or damage resulting from any fire happening to or on board the vessel, or from explosion, bursting of boilers or breakage of shafts, unless caused by the design or neglect of such carrier.

Sec. 9.(c) If the owner shall have exercised due diligence in making the vessel in all respects seaworthy and properly manned, equipped and supplied, no such carrier shall be liable for any loss or damage resulting from the perils of the lakes, seas, or in other waters or from latent defects in the hull, machinery, or appurtenances whether existing prior to, at the time of, or after sailing or from collision, stranding, or other accidents of navigation, or from prolongation of the voyage. And, when for any reason it is necessary, any vessel carrying any or all of the property described in this bill of lading shall be at liberty to call at any port or ports, in or out of the customary route, to tow and be towed, to transfer, trans-ship, or lighter, to load and discharge goods at any time, to assist vessels in distress, to deviate for the purpose of saving life or property, and for docking and repairs. Except in the case of negligence, such carrier shall not be responsible for any loss or damage to property if it is necessary or is usual to carry the property upon deck.

Sec. 9.(d) General Average shall be payable according to the York-Antwerp Rules of 1924, Sections 1 to 15, inclusive, and Sections 17 to 22, inclusive, and as to matters not covered in the said rules, according to the laws and usages of the Port of New York. If the owners shall have exercised due diligence to make the vessel in all respects seaworthy and properly manned, equipped and supplied, it is hereby agreed that in case of danger, damage or disaster resulting from faults or errors in navigation, from the management of the vessel, or from any latent or other defects in the vessel, the machinery or appurtenances (provided the latent or other defects were not discoverable by the exercise of due diligence); or from unseaworthiness, whether existing at the time of shipment or at the beginning of the voyage (provided the unseaworthiness was not discoverable by the exercise of due diligent) the shippers, consignees and/or owners of the cargo shall nevertheless pay salvage and any special charges incurred in respect of the cargo, and shall contribute with the shipowners in general average to the payment of any sacrifices, losses, or expenses of a general average nature that may be made or incurred for the common benefit or to relieve the adventure from any common peril.

Sec. 9.(e) If the property is being carried under a tariff which provides that any carrier or carriers party thereto shall be liable for loss from perils of the sea, then as to such carrier or carriers the provisions of this section shall be modified in accordance with the tariff provisions and the tariff provisions shall be regarded as incorporated into the conditions of this bill of lading.

Sec. 9.(f) The term 'water carriage' in this section shall not be construed as including lighterage in or across rivers, harbors or lakes, when performed by or on behalf of carriers other than water carriers.

Sec. 10. Any alteration, addition or erasure in this bill of lading which is made without the special notation hereon of the agent of the carrier issuing this bill of lading, shall be without effect, and this bill of lading shall be enforceable according to its original tenor.

Document 31-3. Truck Bill of Lading (Negotiable)

SHIPPER PLEASE NOTE **FREIGHT CHARGES ARE PREPAID ON THIS BILL OF LADING UNLESS MARKED COLLECT**

OP-098 5/87

ORDER NOTIFY BILL OF LADING—ORIGINAL—DOMESTIC

ROADWAY EXPRESS, INC. (RDWY)

GENERAL OFFICES: AKRON, OHIO (DUNS 00-699-8397)

SHIPPER NO. ______ DATE ______

CARRIER NO.

SPECIMEN

FROM SHIPPER:	CONSIGNED TO ORDER OF:
STREET	STREET
ORIGIN: CITY / STATE / ZIP CODE	DESTINATION: CITY / STATE / ZIP CODE
ROUTE	NOTIFY / PHONE
VEHICLE NO.	ADDRESS / CITY
	P.O. NO. / DEPT. NO.

NO. SHIPPING UNITS	KIND OF PACKAGING	* HM	DESCRIPTION OF ARTICLES, SPECIAL MARKS AND EXCEPTIONS	NMFC ITEM NO.	CLASS	WEIGHT (LBS) (SUBJECT TO CORR.)	RATE	CHARGES (CARRIER USE ONLY)
			ORDER NOTIFY					

NOTE—When the rate is dependent on value, shippers are required to state specifically in writing the agreed or declared value of the property.

The agreed or declared value of the property is hereby specifically stated by the shipper to be not exceeding:

$ ______ per ______

Subject to Section 7 of conditions, if this shipment is to be delivered to the consignee without recourse on the consignor, the consignor shall sign the following statement:

The carrier shall not make delivery of this shipment without payment of freight and all other lawful charges.

______ (SIGNATURE OF CONSIGNOR)

TOTAL CHARGES $

FREIGHT CHARGES ARE PREPAID UNLESS MARKED COLLECT.

CHECK BOX IF CHARGES ARE **COLLECT**. ☐

RECEIVED, subject to the classifications and lawfully filed tariffs in effect on the date of the issue of this Bill of Lading, the property described above and in apparent good order, except as noted (contents and condition of contents of packages unknown), marked, consigned, and destined, as indicated above which said carrier (the word carrier being understood throughout this contract as meaning any person or corporation in possession of the property under the contract) agrees to carry to its usual place of delivery of said destination, if on its route, otherwise to deliver to another carrier on the route to said destination. It is mutually agreed as to each carrier of all or any of said property over all or any portion of said route to destination and as to each party at any time interested in all or any of said property, that every service to be performed hereunder shall be subject to all the conditions not prohibited by law, whether printed or written, herein contained, including the conditions on the back hereof, which are hereby agreed to by the shipper and accepted for himself and his assigns.

This is to certify that the above named materials are properly classified, described, packaged, marked and labeled and are in proper condition for transportation, according to the applicable regulations of the Department of Transportation.

SHIPPER	CARRIER **ROADWAY EXPRESS, INC. (RDWY)**		
PER	PER	DATE	PIECES

1

MARK "X" IN "HM" COLUMN FOR HAZARDOUS MATERIALS

The surrender of the Original ORDER NOTIFY Bill of Lading properly endorsed shall be required before the delivery of the property. Inspection of property covered by the Bill of Lading will not be permitted unless provided by law or unless permission is endorsed on the Original Bill of Lading or given in writing by the shipper.

SINGLE SHIPMENT PICKUP ☐

Reprinted with the permission of Roadway Express, Inc.

Document 31-3. (*continued*)

ENDORSEMENTS

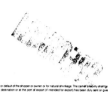

CONTRACT TERMS AND CONDITIONS

Sec. 1. (a) The carrier or party in possession of any of the property herein described shall be liable as at common law for any loss thereof or damage thereto, except as hereinafter provided.

(b) No carrier or party in possession of all or any of the property herein described shall be liable for any loss thereof or damage thereto or delay caused by the Act of God, the public enemy, the authority of law, or the act or default of the shipper or owner, or for natural shrinkage. The carrier's liability shall be that of warehouseman, only, for loss, damage, or delay by fire occurring after the expiration of the free time (if any) allowed by tariffs lawfully on file (such free time to be computed as therein provided) after notice of the arrival of the property at destination or at the port of export (if intended for export) has been duly sent or given, and after placement of the property for delivery at destination, or tender of delivery of the property to the party entitled to receive it, has been made. Except in case of negligence of the carrier or party in possession (and the burden to prove freedom from such negligence shall be on the carrier or party in possession), the carrier or party in possession shall not be liable for loss, damage, or delay occurring while the property is stopped and held in transit upon the request of the shipper, owner, or party entitled to make such request, or resulting from a defect or vice in the property, or for country damage to cotton, or from riots or strikes. Except in case of carrier's negligence, no carrier or party in possession of all or any of the property herein described shall be liable for delay caused by highway obstruction, faulty or impassable highway, or lack of capacity of any highway, bridge or ferry, and the burden to prove freedom from such negligence shall be on the carrier or party in possession.

(c) In case of quarantine the property may be discharged at risk and expense of owners into quarantine depot or elsewhere, as required by quarantine regulations or authorities, or for the carrier's dispatch at nearest available point in carrier's judgement, and in any such case carrier's responsibility shall cease when property is so discharged, or property may be returned by carrier at owner's expense to shipping point, earning freight both ways. Quarantine expenses of whatever nature or kind upon or in respect to property shall be borne by the owners of the property or be in lien thereon. The carrier shall not be liable for loss or damage occasioned by fumigation or disinfection or other acts required or done by quarantine regulations or authorities even though the same may have been done by carrier's officers, agents, or employees, nor for detention, loss, or damage of any kind occasioned by quarantine or the enforcement thereof. No carrier shall be liable, except in the case of negligence, for any mistake or inaccuracy in any information furnished by the carrier, its agents, or officers, as to quarantine laws or regulations. The shipper shall hold the carriers harmless from any expense they may incur, or damages they may be required to pay, by reason of the introduction of the property covered by this contract into any place against the quarantine laws or regulations in effect at such place.

Sec. 2. (a) No carrier is bound to transport said property by any particular schedule, train, vehicle or vessel, or in time for any particular market or otherwise than with reasonable dispatch. Every carrier shall have the right in case of physical necessity to forward said property by any carrier or route between the point of shipment and the point of destination. In all cases not prohibited by law, where a lower value than actual value has been represented in writing by the shipper or has been agreed upon in writing as the released value of the property as determined by the classification or tariffs upon which the rate is based, such lower value plus freight charges if paid shall be the maximum amount to be recovered, whether or not such loss or damage occurs from negligence.

(b) As a condition precedent to recovery, claims must be filed in writing with the receiving or delivering carrier, or carrier issuing this bill of lading, or carrier on whose line the loss, damage, injury or delay occurred, or carrier in possession of the property when the loss, damage, injury or delay occurred, within nine months after delivery of the property (or, in the case of export traffic, within nine months after delivery at port of export) or, in case of failure to make delivery, then within nine months after a reasonable time for delivery has elapsed; and suits shall be instituted against any carrier only within two years and one day from the day when notice in writing is given by the carrier to the claimant that the carrier has disallowed the claim or any part or parts thereof specified in the notice. Where claims are not filed or suits are not instituted thereon in accordance with the foregoing provisions, no carrier hereunder shall be liable, and such claims will not be paid.

(c) Any carrier or party liable on account of loss of or damage to any of said property shall have the full benefit of any insurance that may have been effected, upon or on account of said property, so far as this shall not avoid the policies or contracts of insurance: PROVIDED, That the carrier reimburse the claimant for the premium paid thereon.

Sec. 3. Except where such service is required as the result of carrier's negligence, all property shall be subject to necessary cooperage and baling at owner's cost. Each carrier over whose route cotton or cotton linters is to be transported hereunder shall have the privilege, at its own cost and risk, of compressing the same for greater convenience in handling or forwarding, and shall not be held responsible for deviation or unavoidable delays in procuring such compression. Grain in bulk consigned to a point where there is a railroad, public or licensed elevator, may (unless otherwise expressly noted herein, and then if it is not promptly unloaded) be there delivered, and placed with other grain of the same kind and grade without respect to ownership (and prompt notice thereof shall be given to the consignor), and if so delivered shall be subject to a lien for elevator charges in addition to all other charges hereunder.

Sec. 4. (a) Property not removed by the party entitled to receive it within the free time (if any) allowed by tariffs, lawfully on file (such free time to be computed as therein provided), after notice of the arrival of the property at destination or at the port of export (if intended for export) has been duly sent or given, and after placement of the property for delivery at destination has been made, or property not received, at time tender of delivery of the property to the party entitled to receive it has been made, may be kept in vessel, vehicle, car, depot, warehouse or place of business of the carrier, subject to the tariff charge for storage and to carrier's responsibility as warehouseman, only, or at the option of the carrier, may be removed to and stored in a public or licensed warehouse at the point of delivery or at other available point, or if no such warehouse is available at point of delivery or at other available point, then in other available storage facility, at the cost of the owner and there held without liability on the part of the carrier, and subject to a lien for all freight and other lawful charges, including a reasonable charge for storage. In the event consignee cannot be found at address given for delivery, then in that event, notice of the placing of such goods in warehouse shall be mailed to the address given for delivery and mailed to any other address given on the bill of lading for notification, showing the warehouse in which such property has been placed, subject to the provisions of this paragraph.

(b) Where nonperishable property which has been transported to destination hereunder is refused by consignee or the party entitled to receive it under tender of delivery, or said consignee or party entitled to receive it fails to receive or claim it within 15 days after notice of arrival shall have been duly sent or given, the carrier may sell the same at public auction to the highest bidder, at such place as may be designated by the carrier:

PROVIDED, That the carrier shall have first mailed, sent, or given to the consignor notice that the property has been refused or remains unclaimed, as the case may be, and that it will be subject to sale under the terms of the bill of lading if disposition be not arranged for, and shall have published notice containing a description of the property, the name of the party to whom consigned, or, if shipped order notify, the name of the party to be notified, and the time and place of sale, once a week for two successive weeks, in a newspaper of general circulation at the place of sale or nearest place where such newspaper is published: PROVIDED, That 30 days shall have elapsed before publication of notice of sale after said notice that the property was refused or remains unclaimed was mailed, sent, or given.

(c) Where perishable property which has been transported hereunder to destination is refused by consignee or party entitled to receive it, or said consignee or party entitled to receive it shall fail to receive it promptly, the carrier may, in its discretion, to prevent deterioration or further deterioration, sell the same to the best advantage at private or public sale: PROVIDED, that if time serves for notification to the consignor or owner the refusal of the property or the failure to receive it and request for disposition of the property, such notification shall be given, in such manner as the exercise of due diligence requires, before the property is sold.

(d) Where the procedure provided for in the two paragraphs last preceding is not possible, it is agreed that nothing contained in said paragraphs shall be construed to abridge the right of the carrier at its option to sell the property under such circumstances and in such manner as may be authorized by law.

(e) The proceeds of any sale made under this section shall be applied by the carrier to the payment of freight, demurrage, storage, and any other lawful charges and the expense of notice, advertisement, sale, and other necessary expense and of caring for the maintaining the property, if proper care of same requires special expense, and should there be a balance it shall be paid to the owner of the property sold hereunder.

(f) Property destined to or taken from a station, wharf, landing or other place at which there is no regularly appointed freight agent, shall be entirely at risk of owner after unloaded from cars, vehicles or vessels or until loaded into cars, vehicles or vessels, and, except in case of carrier's negligence, when received from or delivered to such stations, wharfs, landings, or other places, shall be at owner's risk until the cars are attached to and after they are detached from locomotive or train or until loaded into and after unloaded from vessels, or if property is transported in motor vehicle trailers or semi-trailers, until such trailers or semi-trailers are attached to and after they are detached form power units. Where a carrier is directed to unload or deliver property transported by motor vehicle at a particular location where consignee or consignee's agent is not regularly located, the risk after unloading, or delivery, shall be that of the owner.

Sec. 5. No carrier hereunder will carry or be liable in any way for any documents, specie, or for any articles of extraordinary value not specifically rated in the published classification or tariffs unless a special agreement to do so and a stipulated value of the articles are endorsed hereon.

Sec. 6. Every party, whether principal or agent, shipping explosives or dangerous goods, without previous full written disclosure to the carrier of their nature, shall be liable for and indemnify the carrier against all loss or damage caused by such goods, and such goods may be warehoused at owner's risk and expense or destroyed without compensation.

Sec. 7. The owner or consignee shall pay the freight and average, if any, and all other lawful charges accruing on said property according to lawfully filed tariffs of the carrier, but, except in those instances where it may lawfully be authorized to do so, no carrier shall deliver or relinquish possession at destination of the property covered by this bill of lading until all lawfully filed tariff rates and charges thereon have been paid. The consignor shall be liable for the freight and all other lawful charges, except that if the consignor stipulates, by signature, in the space provided for that purpose on the face of this bill of lading that the carrier shall not make delivery without requiring payment of such charges and the carrier contrary to such stipulation shall make delivery without requiring such payment, the consignor (except as hereinafter provided) shall not be liable for such charges. PROVIDED, that, a consignee shall not be liable for transportation charges (beyond those billed against him at the time of delivery for which he is otherwise liable) which may be found to be due after the property has been delivered to him subject to all of the following conditions:

(a) The shipper or consignor has instructed the carrier to deliver the property to a consignee other than the shipper or consignor.

(b) The consignee is an agent only and has no beneficial title in the property and

(c) Prior to delivery the consignee has notified the delivering carrier in writing that he is only an agent and has no beneficial title in the property and

(d) In cases where the shipment has been reconsigned or diverted to a point other than that specified in the bill of lading the consignee has also notified the delivering carrier in writing of the name and address of the beneficial owner of said property.

Where the consignee is not liable for certain transportation charges in accordance with this provision and the preceding conditions, the shipper or consignor, or, in the case of a shipment so reconsigned or diverted as specified in condition (d), the beneficial owner shall be liable for such additional charges.

PROVIDED FURTHER, that where the shipment is designated "prepaid," the shipper or consignor shall remain liable for undercharges which result from an erroneous determination of the transportation charge assessed.

If the consignee has given to the carrier erroneous information as to who the beneficial owner is, such consignee shall himself be liable for such additional charges. Nothing herein shall limit the right of the carrier to require at time of shipment the prepayment or guarantee of the charges. If upon inspection it is ascertained that the articles shipped are not those described in this bill of lading, the freight charges must be paid upon the articles actually shipped.

Sec. 8. If this bill of lading is issued on the order of the shipper, or his agent, in exchange or in substitution for another bill of lading, the shipper's signature to the prior bill of lading as to the statement of value or otherwise, or election of common law or bill of lading liability, in or in connection with such prior bill of lading, shall be considered a part of this bill of lading as fully as if the same were written or made in or in connection with this bill of lading.

Sec. 9. (a) If all or any part of said property is carried by water over any part of said route, such water carriage shall be performed subject to all the terms and provisions of, and all the exemptions from liability contained in, the Act of the Congress of the United States, approved on February 13, 1893, and entitled "An act relating to the navigation of vessels, etc.," and of other statutes of the United States according carriers by water the protection of limited liability, and to the conditions contained in this bill of lading not inconsistent therewith or with this section.

(b) No such carrier by water shall be liable for any loss or damage resulting from any fire happening to or on board the vessel, or from explosion, bursting of boilers or breakage of shafts, unless caused by the design or neglect of such carrier.

(c) If the owner shall have exercised due diligence in making the vessel in all respects seaworthy and properly manned, equipped and supplied, no such carrier shall be liable for any loss or damage resulting from the perils of the lakes, seas, or in other waters, or from latent defects in hull, machinery, or appurtenances whether existing prior to, at the time of, or after sailing, or from collision, stranding, or other accidents of navigation, or from prolongation of the voyage. And, when for any reason it is necessary, any vessel carrying any or all of the property herein described shall be at liberty to call at any port or ports, in or out of the customary route, to tow and be towed, to transfer, trans-ship, or lighter, to load and discharge goods at any time, to assist vessels in distress, to deviate for the purpose of saving life or property, and for docking and repairs. Except in case of negligence such carrier shall not be responsible for any loss or damage to property if it be necessary or is usual to carry the same upon deck.

(d) General Average shall be payable according to the York-Antwerp Rules of 1974, Sections 1 to 15, inclusive, and Sections 17 to 22, inclusive, and as to matters not covered thereby according to the laws and usages of the Port of New York. If the owners shall have exercised due diligence to make the vessel in all respects seaworthy and properly manned, equipped and supplied, it is hereby agreed that in case of danger, damage or disaster resulting from faults or errors in navigation, or in the management of the vessel, or from any latent or other defects in the vessel, her machinery or appurtenances, or from unseaworthiness, whether existing at the time of shipment or at the beginning of the voyage (provided the latent or other defects or the unseaworthiness was not discoverable by the exercise of due diligence), the shippers, consignees and/or owners of the cargo shall nevertheless pay salvage and any special charges incurred in respect of the cargo, and shall contribute with the shipowner in general average to the payment of any sacrifices, losses or expenses of a general average nature that may be made or incurred for the common benefit or to relieve the adventure from any common peril.

(e) If the property is being carried under a tariff which provides that any carrier or carriers party thereto shall be liable for loss from perils of the sea, then as to such carrier or carriers the provisions of this section shall be modified in accordance with the tariff provisions, which shall be regarded as incorporated into the conditions of this bill of lading.

(f) The term "water carriage" in this section shall not be construed as including lighterage in or across rivers, harbors, or lakes, when performed by or on behalf of carriers other than water.

Sec. 10. Any alteration, addition, or erasure in this bill of lading which shall be made without the special notation hereon of the agent of the carrier issuing this bill of lading, shall be without effect, and this bill of lading shall be enforceable according to its original tenor.

ENTRY NO

DATE	OUR REF NO

IMPORTING CARRIER	LOCATION	FROM PORT OF ORIGIN AIRPORT

B L OR AWB NO	ARRIVAL DATE	FREE TIME EXP	LOCAL DELIVERY OR TRANSFER BY (DELIVERY ORDER ISSUED TO)

THIS DOCUMENT, ALTHOUGH A CARBON COPY IS AN ORIGINAL DELIVERY ORDER AND THE ONLY ORIGINAL DELIVERY ORDER PRODUCED TO COVER RELEASE OF THIS MERCHANDISE. IT IS VALID WHEN IT CONTAINS AN ORIGINAL SIGNATURE.

DELIVERY CLERK: PLEASE DELIVER TO

MARKS & NOS.	DESCRIPTION & WT.
	SPECIMEN

CUSTOMS PERMIT ☐ ATTACHED	LODGED WITH ☐ U.S. CUSTOMS	PKG NOS HELD BY U S CUSTOMS—TO FOLLOW	GO #

ORIGINAL DELIVERY ORDER

PER

Form 15-515 Printed and Sold by UNZCO 190 Baldwin Ave., Jersey City, NJ 07306 • (800) 631-3098 • (201) 795-5400

DELIVERY CLERK: ALL DEMURRAGE FOR ACCOUNT OF DRAWEE OF THIS ORDER

ORIGINAL

32

Using the Warehouse Receipt

§32.1 STORING DOMESTIC GOODS

John and Mary Sirois face retirement with a measure of optimism. They have worked hard most of their lives, raised two children, paid off a mortgage, and have purchased a mobile home that will permit them to see the country they never had time or spare money to see. They sell the house and set off for two years of travel to the Grand Canyon, Alaska, and the Great Lakes. When they finish their travels, they will buy a condominium in Florida and move into it. Over the next year or two, they will store their household goods in a warehouse. Their contract of storage is set out in the warehouse receipt the warehouse company issues them, of which Document 31-1 is an illustration.

Note that this receipt is important to the relationship between the Sirois couple and the warehouse, but it will probably not be of concern to third parties. No one anticipates that John and Mary will use this receipt as collateral for a loan or that they will sell their furnishings by selling the receipt. If they lose the receipt, the warehouse will still deliver the goods to them when they return from their travels, provided, of course, that they pay the storage charges. This receipt is nonnegotiable, and the warehouse may not even require its surrender upon redelivery of the furnishings. The warehouse may require John or Mary to sign a receipt acknowledging that redelivery, however. Figure 32-1 illustrates this simple and common bailment.

Figure 32-1. Consumer Bailment

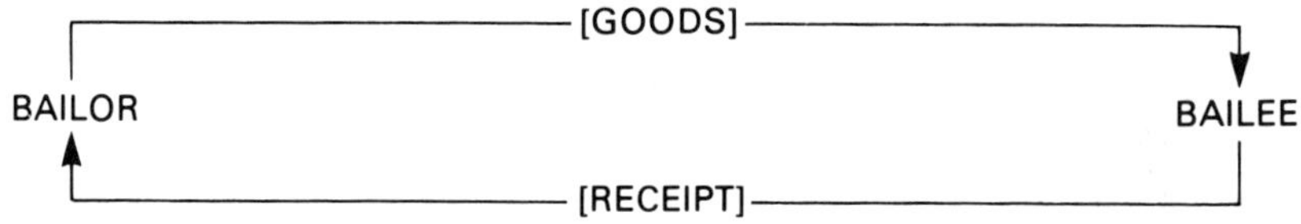

§32.2 STORING AGRICULTURAL PRODUCTS

It would be nice if each month farmers produced commodities in quantities that approximated the market's needs for the next month. Food brokers and processors could then adopt just-in-time inventory controls and save lots of money for themselves and their customers. Unfortunately, farm production does not work that way. Each fall, farmers harvest billions of bushels of grain and legumes, for example, and the industry must accommodate itself to storage of those commodities until they are consumed over the entire year.

Grain elevators, maintained across the nation's grain belt, store the commodities until grain companies, processors, and chemical producers need them. Farmers traditionally deliver the grain to the elevator by their own trucks. The elevators, located along a railroad siding, load the grain onto rolling stock for shipment when the time comes.

In the interim, the grain owners, the farmers themselves or the elevator, which may purchase some grain for its own account, may want to sell the grain or borrow against it.

The federal government, an important source of agricultural credit, lends to farmers and takes a security interest in their grain. The Agricultural Stabilization and Conservation Service (ASCS) makes price-support loans and secures them by taking possession of negotiable warehouse receipts covering stored grain. In the event the farmer does not choose to pay off the loan and sell the grain himself, the ASCS sells the grain or the receipts. Note that by virtue of its possession of the negotiable receipt, the ASCS knows that it has virtual possession of the grain. These receipts, being negotiable, stand for the grain.

If the farmer holds the receipts, he can use them to sell the grain himself, by indorsing the receipts and selling them through a broker. The broker relies on the receipt and takes delivery of the grain later or resells the grain by transferring (negotiating) the receipt to a buyer. During these transactions, the grain, having been dried and stored in a clean elevator, remains out on the prairie free from insects, rodents, mold, and other deleterious effects. It all works rather well. Document 32-1 is an example of a negotiable warehouse receipt, and Figure 32-2 illustrates a transaction with multiple buyers.

Figure 32-2. Marketing Grain

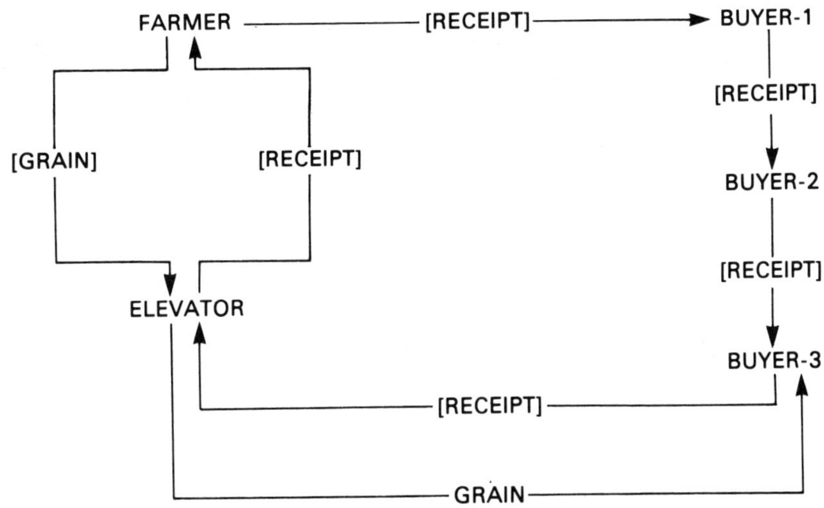

§32.3 THE TERMINAL WAREHOUSE

Some middlemen (brokers, dealers, jobbers, and the like) will purchase goods or commodities that are in transit. These buyers do not usually have warehouse capacity of their own and must turn the goods around, that is, find a buyer for them, quickly. Sometimes, they do not find a buyer who can take delivery when the goods arrive at their destination, and in that case it is necessary for the middleman to store the goods until it does find a buyer. **Terminal warehouses,** often located along rail lines in metropolitan areas, provide a way for the middleman to take delivery of the goods from the carrier and store them during that period. Often, though not always, the terminal warehouse will issue a receipt for the goods. Sometimes the bailor and the warehouse will enter into a warehouse agreement. Document 32-2 is an illustration of such a contract.

§32.4 THE FIELD WAREHOUSE

While the terminal warehouse, being located at the railroad terminal, requires the owner of goods to get them to the warehouse, the **field warehouse** industry takes the warehouse to the goods; hence its name. This warehouse is in the field. Field warehousing occurs when an owner of goods desires to finance them with a seller or an institutional lender of some kind. The creditor, in these transactions, is uneasy about leaving the goods in the borrower's control. Generally, commercial law protects buyers of goods from merchants. Those buyers usually take from the merchant free and clear of any security interest, even when that interest is perfected. Lenders are aware of that rule, and sometimes they are unwilling to make a loan unless they can deprive the borrower of the power to sell the goods. The field warehouse is an efficient and rather ingenious device for effecting that deprivation.

In the field warehouse, the owner of the goods usually has them stored at its own facility. A distiller, for example, may have thousands of barrels of aging whiskey stored in its own warehouse. The distiller does not want to sell the whiskey until it has aged sufficiently and may need to use it as collateral for a bank loan. By turning its own warehouses into a field warehouse, it can effectively deprive itself of possession of that collateral and satisfy the bank's concerns that the distiller not be able to sell the whiskey to a buyer who would have greater rights in it than the bank. Seller-creditors can use the field warehouse to similar effect.

A sawmill that sells millions of board feet of lumber to a lumber company on credit may not want the buyer to be in a position to resell the lumber to sub-buyers without the mill's permission. In this case, the lumber company turns its sheds and open storage areas into a field warehouse, depriving the lumber company of the ability to sell the lumber.

In these illustrations, the owner of the collateral, the distiller or the lumber company, enters into a lease of its own premises with the field warehouse company. The field warehouse company then takes possession of the premises, the warehouse of aging whiskey or the sheds of lumber, and locks them up. The warehouse company usually then issues a nonnegotiable warehouse receipt in favor of the creditor, the bank in the first illustration, the sawmill in the second.

At this point, the creditor is in possession of the collateral through an agent, the field warehouse. When the owner wants to sell some of the collateral, it must seek the creditor's permission. If, for example, some of the whiskey has aged sufficiently and is ready for bottling, the distiller asks the bank to release a certain number of barrels from the warehouse. The bank usually issues a delivery order to the field warehouse authorizing the delivery. Since the whiskey is covered by a nonnegotiable receipt, it is not necessary for the bank to surrender any documents to the warehouse. A distiller in Kentucky, therefore, may do business with a bank in New York, and the bank can issue its delivery orders over the phone or by other teletransmission. The creditor, of course, does not authorize the deliveries if the borrower is in arrears on its loan or is otherwise in default on its loan agreement. The arrangement gives the creditor a measure of protection that a nonpossessory security interest does not give it.

There is a danger in the field warehouse transaction that the field warehouse employee will deliver goods when he is not supposed to. Often, the field warehouse employs as its man on the spot an inventory control officer of the borrower. In the sawmill example, the field warehouse may take the yard manager off the lumber company's payroll and put him on the warehouse company's payroll. The parties guard against the yard manager's malfeasance by bonding him. In the event the manager delivers lumber without having a delivery order or other authorization from the creditor, the unpaid sawmill, the bonding company will make good the sawmill's losses.

There is also danger in the field warehouse arrangement that the borrower will circumvent the field warehouse's security measures. Grain elevator operators have been known to "hot wire" locked-up augurs and empty a grain elevator while the field warehouse managers are miles away. Similarly, sawmill operators can cut through chain link fences and disarm burglar alarms in order to remove collateral from the field warehouse and sell it. Such activity, of course, is unlawful, but business people desperate for cash to save their businesses have done worse.

Note also that there is a considerable measure of activity in the field warehouse transaction. First, there is paperwork: the lease, the change in the yard manager's employment, the warehouse receipt, and delivery orders. All of this documentation results in costs that are, in the last analysis, borne by the borrower. It is in the best interests of the borrower to find a lender or a seller that will extend credit without any field warehouse. The borrower, whose credit is good enough and reputation strong enough that its creditors are willing to trust it, is going to save field warehousing costs. On the other hand, the costs of the field warehouse may not be too great for the new entrant or the troubled business to pay when no one will extend it credit otherwise. Figure 14-6 in Part II illustrates the field warehouse transaction.

Unfortunately, recent liberalization of liability rules has rendered field warehouses common targets for banks and finance companies that lend and then find that the borrower has thwarted the field warehouse's security measures, taken the goods, and sold them. At this writing the number of active field warehouse companies has diminished, and the amount of field warehousing has fallen to a level that may not sustain the industry. The idea is a good one, however, and it is probably only a matter of time and a matter of forging more realistic liability rules, until borrowers and lenders find a need once again for the field warehouse.

VAN DE HOGEN MATERIAL HANDLING INC.
2590 Dougall Avenue
Windsor, Ontario N8X 1T7

RECEIPT NO.
N

________________ 19 ______

THIS IS TO CERTIFY that we have received in Storage Warehouse, ____________________

for the Account of ____________________ EX. ____________________

NUMBER	PACKAGES	OR CONTAIN	MARKS

SPECIMEN

Storage ____________ per ____________ per month from ____________ 19 ________

Handling ____________ per ____________ in and out inclusive

UNDER THE FOLLOWING CONDITIONS: — The above described property subject to all terms and conditions contained herein and on the reverse hereof, such property to be delivered to ____________________ order, upon the payment of all charges, and the surrender of this Warehouse Receipt properly endorsed.

NEGOTIABLE

VAN DE HOGEN MATERIAL HANDLING INC.
claims a lien for all lawful charges for storage and preservation of the goods, also for all lawful claims for money advanced, interest, insurance, transportation, labour, weighing, coopering, and other charges and expenses in relation to such goods.
VAN DE HOGEN MATERIAL

BY ____________________

SPECIMEN

Herald Press Ltd. 31691

Reprinted with the permission of Van de Hogen Material Handling, Inc.

Document 32-1. *(continued)*

The goods mentioned below are hereby released from this receipt for delivery from warehouse. Any unreleased balance of the goods is subject to a lien for unpaid charges and advances on the released portion.

DELIVERIES

DATE	QUANTITY RELEASED		SIGNATURE	QUANTITY DUE ON RECEIPT

LIABILITY—(a) The warehouseman is liable for damage for loss of or injury to the goods caused by its failure to exercise such care and diligence in regard to the goods as a careful and vigilant owner of similar goods would exercise in the custody of them in similar circumstances, but unless otherwise agreed in writing, it is not liable for damages which could not have been avoided by the exercise of such care. The warehouseman shall not be liable for loss damage, delay or demurrage caused by acts of God, civil or military authority, insurrection, riot, strikes, picketing, any other labour trouble, disturbance or interference of whatever cause or nature, whether primary, secondary or tertiary etc., or enemies of the government, or by odors, sprinkler leakage, flood, wind, storm, fire, moths corruption or depredation by rats, mice, insects, parasites or other vermin, or by any other cause beyond the control of the warehouseman or by any cause not originated in the warehouse. No liability is, or will be attributed to or assumed by the warehouseman for loss of weight, for breakage, or for insufficient cooperage, boxing, crating, car bracing, bagging or packing or for wear and tear. The warehouseman shall not be held responsible for loss of goods by leakage or through failure to detect same or for concealed damage. All storage and handling charges must be paid on goods lost or damaged.

(b) The Warehouseman shall not be responsible for any seizure of goods by any court, agency, agent or officer of the federal, state or local government.

LIMITATION OF LIABILITY - THE LIABILITY OF THE WAREHOUSEMAN AS TO EACH ARTICLE ITEM OR UNIT STORED IS LIMITED TO THE ACTUAL VALUE OF SUCH ARTICLE, ITEM OR UNIT.

CLAIMS AND SUITES - (a) The warehouseman shall not be liable for any loss or damage unless the claim therefore has been presented in writing within a reasonable time, and, in any event, not later than thirty (30) days from the date of shipment from the warehouse or, within thirty (30) days from the date the storer requested delivery in the event that shipment is not made. Such notice of claim shall be presented to the warehouseman in person, or by certified mail.

(b) No action at law or in equity shall be brought in connection with any loss or damage prior to the expiration of sixty (60) days after presentation of claim therefor, nor shall such action be brought at all unless brought within one year from the expiration of the sixty day period last mentioned.

WAREHOUSING AGREEMENT

THIS AGREEMENT, Made and entered into this ________ day of ________________, 19____, by and between ____
(Company, City, State)
hereinafter referred to as "DEPOSITOR," and ____
hereinafter referred to as "WAREHOUSEMAN."

WITNESSETH

WHEREAS, DEPOSITOR is desirous of obtaining and utilizing certain warehouse facilities and services in the ____ area; and

WHEREAS, WAREHOUSEMAN has certain warehousing facilities and services of the type and kind desired by DEPOSITOR located at ____; and

WHEREAS, WAREHOUSEMAN desires to make said facilities and services commercially available to DEPOSITOR subject to the terms and conditions herein specified;

NOW, THEREFORE, for and in consideration of the mutual agreements, covenants and promises herein contained, it is hereby mutually agreed, covenanted and promised as follows:

ARTICLE I. TERM OF AGREEMENT

The term of this Agreement shall commence on the date of its execution by the parties thereto and shall continue thereafter in full force and effect for a period of ____________ and shall thereafter automatically renew on a month-to-month basis subject only to either party's right to terminate at any time by serving not less than thirty (30) days prior written notice to that effect upon the other party, said notice to be effective upon receipt. This Agreement shall be deemed cancelled if DEPOSITOR does not store goods with WAREHOUSEMAN for any period exceeding one hundred and eighty (180) days.

ARTICLE II. ACCEPTANCE OF GOODS, RATES AND CHARGES

During the term of this Agreement, and any extensions or renewals thereof, WAREHOUSEMAN agrees to provide for DEPOSITOR certain warehousing facilities and services described in this Agreement and the attached Schedules "A" and "B" which are made a part hereof, and to accept and keep in a neat and orderly condition such goods described in Schedule "A" as from time to time may be tendered by DEPOSITOR. WAREHOUSEMAN further agrees to furnish sufficient personnel, equipment, and other accessories necessary to perform efficiently and with safety the services herein described. Rates and charges for public warehousing services are set forth in Schedule "A" and for extra services and conditions in Schedule "B". For any services not specified in Schedule "A" or Schedule "B", DEPOSITOR shall pay to WAREHOUSEMAN such consideration and compensation as may mutually be agreed upon. Consideration for WAREHOUSEMAN'S performance of this Agreement shall be paid to WAREHOUSEMAN by DEPOSITOR within ____________ days after receipt by DEPOSITOR of WAREHOUSEMAN'S statement.

ARTICLE III. SHIPPING

DEPOSITOR agrees not to ship goods to WAREHOUSEMAN as the named consignee. If, in violation of this Agreement, goods are shipped to WAREHOUSEMAN as named consignee, DEPOSITOR agrees to notify carrier in writing prior to such shipment, with a copy of such notice to WAREHOUSEMAN, that WAREHOUSEMAN named as consignee is a warehouseman under law and has no beneficial title or interest in such property. DEPOSITOR further agrees to indemnify and hold harmless WAREHOUSEMAN from any and all claims for unpaid transportation charges, including undercharges, demurrage, detention, or charges of any nature, in connection with goods so shipped.

ARTICLE IV. TENDER FOR STORAGE

All goods tendered for storage shall be delivered at the warehouse in a segregated manner, properly marked and packaged for handling. DEPOSITOR shall furnish or cause to be furnished at or prior to such delivery, a manifest showing the goods to be kept and accounted for separately, and the class or type of storage and other services desired.

5

ARTICLE V. STORAGE PERIOD AND CHARGES

(A) Storage charges become applicable upon the date that WAREHOUSEMAN accepts care, custody and control of the goods, regardless of unloading date or date of issue of warehouse receipt.

(B) Unless otherwise stated in Schedule "A" hereof, storage rates and charges shall be computed and are due and payable as follows:

1. Goods received on or after the first (1st) day of the month up to and including the fifteenth (15th) day of the month shall be assessed the full monthly storage charge;
2. Goods received after the fifteenth (15th) day of the month up to and including the last day of the month shall be assessed one-half (½) of the full monthly storage charge; and
3. A full month's storage charge will apply to all goods in storage on the first day of the next and succeeding calendar months. All storage charges are due and payable on the first day of storage for the initial month and thereafter on the first day of the calendar month.

ARTICLE VI. TRANSFER, TERMINATION OF STORAGE, REMOVAL OF GOODS

(A) Instructions to transfer goods on the books of WAREHOUSEMAN shall not be effective until said instructions are delivered to and accepted by WAREHOUSEMAN, and all charges up to the time transfer is made shall be chargeable to DEPOSITOR. If a transfer involves the rehandling of goods, it will be subject to rates and charges shown in the attached Schedule "A" or Schedule "B" or as otherwise mutually agreed upon. When goods in storage are transferred from one party to another through issuance of a new warehouse receipt, a new storage date is established on the date of such transfer.

(B) WAREHOUSEMAN may, without notice, move goods within the warehouse in which they are stored; but shall not, except as provided in VI (C), move goods to another location without prior consent of DEPOSITOR.

(C) If, as a result of a quality or condition of the goods of which WAREHOUSEMAN had no notice at the time of deposit, the goods are a hazard to other property or to the warehouse or to persons, WAREHOUSEMAN shall immediately notify DEPOSITOR and DEPOSITOR shall thereupon claim its interest in the said goods and remove them from the warehouse. Pending such disposition, the WAREHOUSEMAN may remove the goods from the warehouse and shall incur no liability by reason of such removal.

ARTICLE VII. HANDLING

(A) Handling rates and charges as shown in the attached Schedules shall, unless otherwise agreed, cover the ordinary labor involved in receiving goods at warehouse door or dock, placing goods in storage, and returning goods to warehouse door or dock. Additional expenses incurred by the warehouseman in loading or unloading cars or vehicles shall be at rates shown in attached Schedules or as otherwise mutually agreed upon.

(B) WAREHOUSEMAN shall not be liable for demurrage, detention or delays in unloading inbound cars or vehicles, or detention or delays in obtaining and loading cars or vehicles for outbound shipment unless WAREHOUSEMAN has failed to exercise reasonable care and judgment as determined by industry practice.

(C) If detention occurs for which WAREHOUSEMAN is liable under Paragraph (B) of this Article, payment of such detention shall be made by DEPOSITOR to the carrier and WAREHOUSEMAN shall reimburse DEPOSITOR for such payment. WAREHOUSEMAN shall keep records concerning the detention of vehicles to assist DEPOSITOR in processing any objection to carrier's imposition of detention charges.

(D) DEPOSITOR shall be responsible for payment of all demurrage charges resulting from receipt by WAREHOUSEMAN of more than ________________ carloads of DEPOSITOR'S goods received in any regular working day.

ARTICLE VIII. DELIVERY REQUIREMENTS

(A) No goods shall be delivered or transferred except upon receipt by WAREHOUSEMAN of complete instructions properly signed by DEPOSITOR. However, when no negotiable receipt is outstanding, goods may be delivered or transferred upon instructions received by telephone, TWX, Dataphone or other agreed upon method of communication, but WAREHOUSEMAN shall not be responsible for loss or error occasioned thereby except as caused by WAREHOUSEMAN'S negligence.

6

(B) When goods are ordered out, a reasonable time shall be given WAREHOUSEMAN to carry out instructions, and if he is unable to because of acts of God, war, public enemies, seizure under legal process, strikes, lockout, riots and civil commotions, or any other reason beyond WAREHOUSEMAN'S reasonable control, or because of loss or destruction of goods for which WAREHOUSEMAN is not liable, or because of any other excuse provided by law, WAREHOUSEMAN shall not be liable for failure to carry out such instructions provided, however, that goods remaining in storage will continue to be subject to regular storage charges as provided for herein.

ARTICLE IX. EXTRA AND SPECIAL SERVICES

(A) Warehouse labor required for services other than ordinary handling and storage must be authorized by DEPOSITOR in advance. Rates and charges will be provided for herein or as mutually agreed by the parties hereto.

(B) Special services requested by DEPOSITOR will be subject to such charges as are provided herein or as mutually agreed upon in advance.

(C) Dunnage, bracing, packing materials or other special supplies used in cars or vehicles are chargeable to DEPOSITOR and may be provided at a mutually agreed upon charge in addition to WAREHOUSEMAN'S cost.

(D) By prior arrangement, goods may be received or delivered during other than usual business hours, subject to a reasonable charge.

(E) Communication expense including postage, teletype, telegram or telephone will be charged to DEPOSITOR if such expense is the result of more than normal inventory reporting or if, at the request of DEPOSITOR, communications are made by other than regular First Class United States Mail.

ARTICLE X. BONDED STORAGE

(A) A charge in addition to regular rates will be made for merchandise in bond.

(B) Where a warehouse receipt covers goods in U.S. Customs bond, such receipt shall be void upon the termination of the storage period fixed by law.

ARTICLE XI. INBOUND SHIPMENTS

(A) WAREHOUSEMAN shall immediately notify DEPOSITOR of any known discrepancy on inbound shipments and shall protect DEPOSITOR'S interest by placing an appropriate notation on the delivering carrier's shipping document.

(B) WAREHOUSEMAN may refuse to accept any goods that, because of infestation, contamination or damage, might cause infestation, contamination or damage to WAREHOUSEMAN'S premises or to other goods in the custody of WAREHOUSEMAN and shall immediately notify DEPOSITOR of such refusal and shall have no liability for any demurrage, detention, transportation or other charges by virtue of such refusal.

(C) All notices required under paragraphs A or B of this Article shall be directed to the attention of ______

____

____.

ARTICLE XII. LIABILITY AND LIMITATION OF DAMAGES

(A) WAREHOUSEMAN shall be liable for loss of or injury to all goods while under his care, custody and control when caused by his failure to exercise such care in regard to them as a reasonably careful man would exercise under like circumstances. He shall not be liable for damages which could not have been avoided by the exercise of such care.

(B) In consideration of the rates herein, DEPOSITOR declares that said damages will be limited to ______

____

ARTICLE XIII. LEGAL LIABILITY INSURANCE

WAREHOUSEMAN shall maintain at its sole expense and at all times during the life of this Agreement a policy or policies of legal liability insurance covering any loss, destruction or damage for which WAREHOUSEMAN has assumed responsibility under the terms of Article XII. WAREHOUSEMAN further agrees to provide satisfactory evidence of such insurance upon request by DEPOSITOR.

ARTICLE XIV. NOTICE OF LOSS AND DAMAGE, CLAIM AND FILING OF SUIT

(A) WAREHOUSEMAN agrees to notify DEPOSITOR promptly of any loss or damage, howsoever caused, to goods stored or handled under the terms of this Agreement. All such notices shall be directed to the attention of ______________________________

____

____

(B) Claims by DEPOSITOR must be presented in writing to WAREHOUSEMAN not longer than either sixty (60) days after delivery of the goods by WAREHOUSEMAN or sixty (60) days after DEPOSITOR is notified by WAREHOUSEMAN that loss or injury to part or all of the goods has occurred, whichever time is shorter.

(C) No action may be maintained by DEPOSITOR against WAREHOUSEMAN for loss or injury to the goods stored unless timely written claim has been given as provided in paragraph (B) of this Article and unless such action is commenced either within nine (9) months after the date of delivery by WAREHOUSEMAN or within nine (9) months after DEPOSITOR is notified that loss or injury to part or all of the goods has occurred, whichever time is shorter.

(D) When goods have not been delivered, notice may be given of known loss or injury to the goods by the mailing of a registered or certified letter to DEPOSITOR. All such notices shall be directed to the attention of ______________________________

____

Time limitations for presentation of claim in writing and maintaining of action after notice begin on the date of receipt of such notice by DEPOSITOR.

ARTICLE XV. RECORDS

DEPOSITOR reserves the right upon reasonable request to enter WAREHOUSEMAN'S premises during normal working hours to examine and count all or any of the goods stored under the terms of this Agreement. WAREHOUSEMAN shall at all reasonable times permit DEPOSITOR to examine its books, records and accounts for the purpose of reconciling quantities and determining with WAREHOUSEMAN whether certain amounts are payable within the meaning of the Agreement.

ARTICLE XVI. INDEPENDENT CONTRACTOR

It is hereby agreed and understood that WAREHOUSEMAN is entering into this Agreement as an independent contractor and that all of WAREHOUSEMAN'S personnel engaged in work to be done under the terms of this Agreement are to be considered as employees of WAREHOUSEMAN and under no circumstances shall they be construed or considered to be employees of DEPOSITOR.

ARTICLE XVII. COMPLIANCE WITH LAWS, ORDINANCES, RULES AND REGULATIONS

(A) WAREHOUSEMAN shall comply with all laws, ordinances, rules and regulations of Federal, State, municipal and other governmental authorities and the like in connection with the safeguarding, receiving, storing and handling of goods.

(B) DEPOSITOR shall be responsible for advising WAREHOUSEMAN of all laws, ordinances, rules and regulations of Federal, State, municipal and other governmental authorities and the like relating specifically to the safeguarding, receiving, storing and handling of DEPOSITOR'S products.

ARTICLE XVIII. NOTIFICATION OF PRODUCT CHARACTERISTICS

DEPOSITOR shall notify WAREHOUSEMAN of the characteristics of any of DEPOSITOR'S products that may in any way be likely to cause damage to WAREHOUSEMAN'S premises or to other products that may be stored by WAREHOUSEMAN.

ARTICLE XIX. ASSIGNMENT

This Warehousing Agreement shall inure to the benefit of and be binding upon the successors and assigns of the parties hereto, provided neither party to this Agreement shall assign or sublet its interest or obligations herein, including but not limited to the assignment of any monies due and payable, without the prior written consent of the other party.

8

Document 32-2. (*continued*)

ARTICLE XX. APPLICABLE STATUTES

The parties understand and agree that the provisions of Article 7 of the Uniform Commercial Code as enacted by the State law governing this Warehousing Agreement shall apply to this Warehousing Agreement. (In the State of Louisiana the provisions of the Uniform Warehouse Receipts Act shall apply.)

ARTICLE XXI. ADDITIONAL TERMS AND CONDITIONS

(Nothing entered hereon shall be construed to extend WAREHOUSEMAN'S liability beyond the standard of care specified in Article XII (A) above.)

ARTICLE XXII.

This Agreement constitutes the entire understanding between DEPOSITOR and WAREHOUSEMAN, and no working arrangements, instructions, or operating manuals intended to facilitate the effective carrying out of this Agreement shall in any way affect the liabilities of either party as set forth herein.

IN WITNESS WHEREOF, the parties hereto have duly executed this Agreement in duplicate the day and year first above written.

WAREHOUSEMAN

By:______________________________

____

DEPOSITOR

By:______________________________

9

Document 32-2. (*continued*)

SCHEDULE A

STORAGE AND HANDLING RATES AND CHARGES

Attached to and made a part of Agreement dated the ______________________ day of ______________________, 19 ____ . by and between ______________________

______________________ and ______________________

DEPOSITOR

SPECIMEN

____

WAREHOUSEMAN

10

Document 32-2. (*continued*)

SCHEDULE B

ACCESSORIAL RATES AND CHARGES

Attached to and made a part of Agreement dated the ______________ day of ____________, 19______,

by and between ____ and

DEPOSITOR

SPECIMEN

____

WAREHOUSEMAN

11

33 Using the Delivery Order

§33.1 IN GENERAL

Delivery orders are curious in a number of ways. They can arise out of nonbailment situations, may be issued by strangers to a bailment, are transformed at times by acceptance into warehouse receipts, and sometimes are used when the original bailee has not issued a document of title.

Delivery orders can occur in any transaction involving the storage of goods, whether as a bailment with a third-party bailee or as an on-premises storage arrangement. In a sense, whenever a sales officer of a company issues directions to the plant or warehouse for the delivery of product to a customer, that officer has issued a delivery order.

Delivery orders are somewhat unique in that anybody may issue one. A stranger to the bailment may issue the delivery order, and sometimes the bailee will obey it. Most of the time, the bailor or its agent issues the delivery order. In any case, whether the bailee will honor the delivery order is far more important than the identity of the issuer, though at times the unaccepted delivery order may be valuable to a holder. Generally, a party that issues a delivery order stands behind it if the bailee dishonors.

Delivery orders may be negotiable or nonnegotiable. The delivery order that begins as nonnegotiable becomes, on acceptance, a nonnegotiable warehouse receipt; while the delivery order issued in negotiable form becomes, on acceptance, a negotiable warehouse receipt.

§33.2 BILL-AND-HOLD SALES

In some industries, the textile industry being an example, manufacturers tool up for a product once a year and make a short production run. Customers that expect to use such a product during that year must place early orders and then hope that they find sufficient business to satisfy their projections. Because manufacturers in these industries are financially strong relative to their customers, they are in a position to dictate these early-order arrangements. The system is optimal, however, since it keeps the down time of the producer's plant to a minimum. The program has much the same inefficient effect, however, that the seasonal harvest has on the agricultural commodity industry. It leaves a large surplus of goods at the beginning of the selling season, a surplus that must be stored.

Manufacturers relieve some of the burden the situation imposes on their customers by selling the product on a bill-and-hold basis. Under this marketing arrangement, the producer enters into a contract with each of its customers at the time the customer orders the merchandise and before the producer manufactures it. After production, the producer holds the product at its mill and bills the customer. The customer, not having much or any warehouse space of its own, leaves the product at the mill until it needs it.

This situation lends itself to the delivery order. If the customer decides that it needs 25 percent of its order in April, it issues a delivery order to the mill directing delivery during that month to the customer's facility or to the plant of the customer's sub-buyer. Sometimes, the customer sells the goods to a third party before the third party wants to take delivery. In that case, the third party or the customer may issue a delivery order to the mill. Note that the mill may not know whether to honor the delivery order without some inquiry. Usually, however, a telephone call to the customer is sufficient to determine whether the customer has in fact authorized the delivery order.

Third-party buyers from the customer who issue a delivery order themselves to the mill or who take a delivery order from the customer are not in a position to know whether the mill will honor the order. It may be that the customer has yet to pay for the product or that it has already taken delivery of all that it ordered. In those cases, the mill dishonors the delivery order. Thus, the third-party that issues a delivery order or takes one from the customer must inquire of the mill whether it will honor. The mill may signal its willingness to honor by accepting the delivery order. That acceptance, of course, renders the delivery order a warehouse receipt.

These features of the delivery order give it considerable flexibility. If the customer's buyer wants to be assured of receiving product stored in Georgia, for example, the buyer can hasten payment and delivery by using

Figure 33-1. Bill-and-Hold Transaction

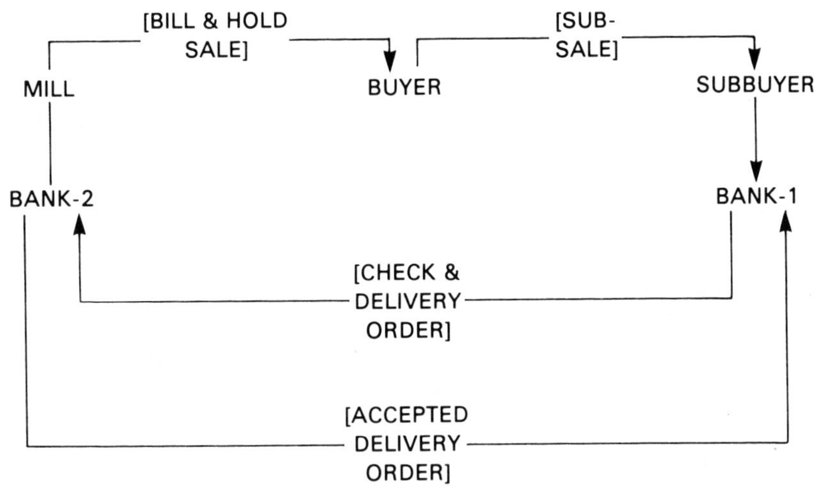

a check and a delivery order. By sending the check to the seller through the bank collection system, the buyer can instruct the presenting bank in Georgia not to give the check to the seller until the seller has the delivery order accepted by the bailee. Once the buyer obtains the accepted delivery order, the Georgia bank releases the check and returns the accepted delivery order to the buyer, who presents it to the bailee when he wants to take delivery.

Alternatively, the parties may use the bank-collection system to pay funds to the mill for the customer's account. In that case, the sub-buyer will send the check to the mill through the system with instructions to the bank to deliver the check upon the mill's acceptance of the delivery order. Document 31-4 is an illustration of a delivery order that might be used in such circumstances. Figure 33-1 illustrates the bill-and-hold transaction.

§33.3 PIPELINE SALES

Large volumes of natural gas and natural gas derivatives move from production facilities in western Canada and the southwestern U.S. to all parts of the country. The pipeline companies that control the flow of these products are common carriers that issue bills of lading to their customers. Refiners that sell the product are located at the pipeline source. They maintain underground storage facilities that they constantly replenish from their refineries. In addition to these sellers, there are bailees that maintain storage facilities at some point along the line. The final party in the pipeline transaction is the wholesaler that buys from the refiner.

Thus, a refiner in Tulsa, Oklahoma, stores gas with a bailee in Conway, Kansas. The refiner sells product to the wholesaler and ships it through the pipeline from the refinery to the underground storage facility. Later, when the wholesaler orders delivery, the refiner ships from the underground storage facility to the buyer's own storage facilities, probably above-ground tanks. Note that the sale may occur at any point before delivery: (1) before shipment to the underground facility, (2) after storage in the facility, or (3) while moving through the pipeline.

Pipelines are expensive operations, and it would be far from efficient for them to lie idle for any appreciable period of time. One pipeline can handle several products at different times but can handle only one product at a time. A pipeline company in Tulsa wants to keep product moving through its pipe without interruption and contracts with various parties to keep the line fully active, sometimes transporting natural gas and at another propane or some other natural gas derivative. The product seller, of course, cannot keep product moving without customers who place orders.

There is, then, a commonality of interests at work here. Pipeline companies want product to be moving through the line constantly. Sellers want to sell product through the line. Buyers want to get product through the line at low prices.

These three players in the gas industry have worked out an efficient arrangement. First, the refinery seller undertakes to supply as much product as the market will need. The local gas wholesalers agree in advance to acquire product, but they may not want to take delivery immediately. The pipeline will transport the product to Conway for storage and will store some product for the wholesaler in the pipeline itself.

Unfortunately, local wholesalers may not know how much product they will need during a given marketing period, and they sometimes buy too much or too little. In fact, sometimes, they speculate by purchasing more than they know they will need. There arises, then, a need for pipeline customers, the wholesalers, to be able to buy and sell product that is in the pipeline or in storage.

Third-party information systems have facilitated that buying and selling by maintaining a computer-accessed market through which wholesalers can indicate their willingness to buy or sell product at quoted prices. In the event two wholesalers strike an agreement over the computerized market, by telephone, or otherwise, the selling wholesaler transfers its product rights in product in the pipeline or in storage at Conway to the buying wholesaler with documents the industry has developed for these purposes. The wholesalers effect delivery of product in storage or in the pipeline by delivery order. Figure 33-2 illustrates the use of pipeline transfer orders.

§33.4 OCEAN SHIPMENTS

From time to time shippers of **bulk cargo,** such as ore, petrochemicals, or grain, want to sell it to traders while the goods are in transit. Parties

Figure 33-2. Pipeline Transfer Orders

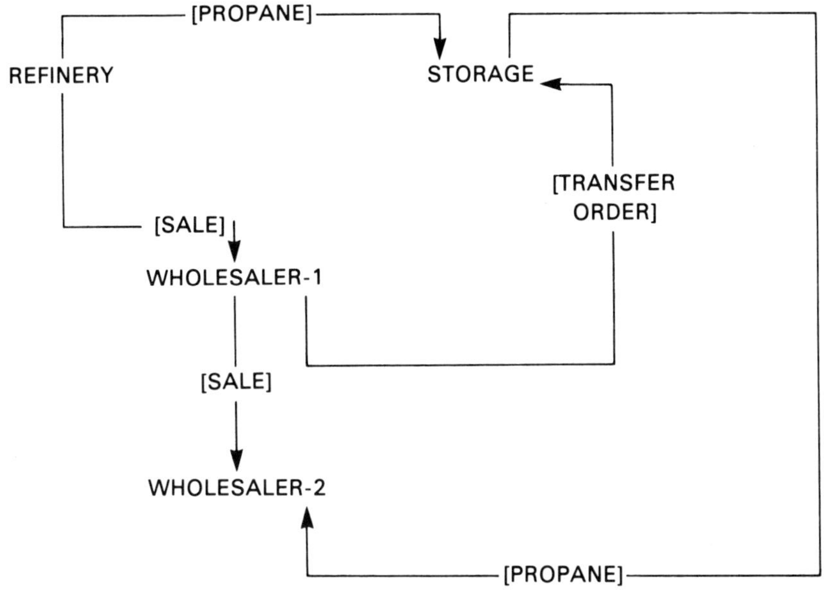

sometimes use negotiable bills of lading for that purpose. At other times they use delivery orders. If the carrier is transporting the cargo under a nonnegotiable bill, the shipper sells portions of the cargo to buyers and issues delivery orders to the carrier instructing delivery at the port of destination.

Assume, for instance, that an importer of bauxite from Georgetown, Guyana, has directed its Guyanese seller to ship the cargo on a **bulker** under a nonnegotiable bill of lading. The importer arranges to sell portions of the shipment in the metals market by issuing delivery orders to the carrier directing delivery of portions of the cargo to the various buyers.

If the cargo is in transit under a negotiable bill, the importer might issue delivery orders to the holder of it. Thus, for example, if the bauxite cargo is subject to a negotiable bill of lading that has been indorsed to a New York lender as collateral for an advance used to pay the bauxite seller in Georgetown, the importer may sell portions of the cargo and issue delivery orders to the lender for each portion sold.

In these cases, the buyers must realize that the delivery orders do not bind the carrier or lender until they are accepted and that the carrier and lender might, before acceptance, dishonor with impunity. In the normal course of affairs, however, buyers utilizing these arrangements either trust the importer or take steps to ensure that the bailee will honor or has honored before they part with value.

34

Domestic Transport

§34.1 BY BARGE, RAIL, OR TRUCK

Much domestic transport, especially local deliveries, occurs in vehicles owned by the shipper itself. When a retailer delivers merchandise to a customer, it uses its own fleet of trucks that pick up the merchandise at the retailer's warehouse and cart it off to the customer's home or office. Wholesalers also frequently maintain their own delivery equipment. Beer distributors, home heating oil suppliers, and some oil refineries, for example, load their trucks and make deliveries at each retail establishment or home that orders product. The same is true for many manufacturers and processors and for farm producers that traditionally haul produce to the grain elevator, the market, or the barge or rail terminal.

In addition, many buyers use their own vehicles to transport merchandise or commodities. It is often more efficient to send one's own truck to the lumberyard to take delivery of plywood than to wait for the lumberyard to make delivery.

Some shippers contract with cartage or **drayage companies** to haul merchandise or commodities, often in **containers** or **trailers** that belong to the shipper. A computer parts manufacturer, for example, might load its own trailers or a railroad company's containers at the manufacturer's plant. When the trailers or containers are ready for transport to a rail terminal, the shipper calls a **cartage company** and arranges for that company to transport the trailer or container to the terminal. If trailers are involved, the cartage company sends a tractor to the shipper's plant, connects it to the trailer, hauls the trailer to the terminal, and delivers the trailer to the railroad. The railroad then loads the trailer, by means of a crane, onto a railroad car. If the shipper is loading containers, the cartage company sends a **chassis** to the shipper's plant, where the shipper places the container onto the chassis for transport to the terminal. There, the railroad offloads it from the chassis onto a railroad car. Under these arrangements, the cartage company does not issue any document of title.

In short, a good bit of the business of transporting goods proceeds without the need to bring a document issuer into the transaction. As a consequence, some of this transport occurs without any bill of lading or equivalent. When a seller delivers from its own truck, the sales department forwards a shipping order to the dispatcher, who supervises the loading of the goods and gives directions to the employee driver for their delivery. By the same token, the purchasing officer of the buyer that takes delivery at the seller's loading dock sends his truck or his cartage company's truck to the seller's premises usually with a copy of the shipping order or of the purchase order or invoice, such latter documents frequently being generated by carbonless copies to the original sales order or from computerized systems that capture the information from one form, manipulate it somewhat, and reproduce it on another.

In a significant number of transactions, however, it becomes necessary for the parties to engage the services of an independent carrier. In fact, many of the short haul transportation arrangements described above are preliminary to the long haul out of which the bill of lading arises. In a long haul, the shipping department must decide which arrangements are superior for getting the merchandise to the buyer. In the United States, with its vast network of rail, truck, air, and barge facilities, a shipping manager has a number of options. In most cases, he contacts independent haulers who send a truck to his loading dock, though at times the shipper must transport the merchandise by its own vehicle or cartage company to a barge, air, rail, or truck terminal. Upon delivery of the merchandise to the independent carrier, the shipper receives a bill of lading. In the vast majority of domestic transport bailments, that bill of lading is nonnegotiable in form. Document 34-1 is an example of a nonnegotiable rail bill.

There may be occasions, however, when the seller and buyer arrange for a domestic sale involving payment against documents. In that transaction, a negotiable bill of lading is necessary. Chapter 4 discusses the documentary draft transaction.

§34.2 BY AIR

Air transport is more expensive than ground transport, but it is, of course, generally much quicker. The manufacturer whose production line is closed for want of a replacement part, the hospital that has an emergency need for supplies, and, above all, the lawyer who must get that contract to the client by 8:00 A.M. on Monday morning avail themselves of air transport to the point that it has become a thriving and profitable business.

Air transport of goods or documents does not lend itself to the documentary sale for a number of reasons. First, the goods that parties ship by air often arise out of isolated transactions in which special arrangements are necessary. If the goods are of high value, as they sometimes are in air shipments, the seller may have a representative at the destination to take delivery from the carrier and hold the goods against payment. Often, of course, the shipment is on open account, and there is no need to obtain a negotiable document. Finally, since the air shipment often arrives at the destination as quickly or more quickly than the air **waybill,** delivery against surrender of a negotiable document is not practical. In air shipments, therefore, the parties use nonnegotiable waybills. Document 34-2 is an air waybill.

Some air carriers specialize in emergency shipments and utilize their own aircraft, which make unscheduled departures on an as-needed basis. Other air freight carriers pick up and deliver merchandise through a hub-and-spoke system. Under this arrangement, an air carrier designates certain airports as hubs for a national or international distribution system. Scheduled flights from the hubs move freight to cities along the spokes. If cities are located on spokes from different hubs, the carrier will move the freight along a spoke to the hub of the first city, then to another hub, and from there along a spoke to the second city.

§34.3 FREIGHT CONSOLIDATION

There is a measure of inefficiency in the shipment of small items of merchandise that the industry has overcome by consolidating freight shipments.

When a patient in Nome, Alaska, needs a kidney from a donor in Los Angeles, there is little concern about saving a relatively few dollars by consolidating shipments. In all probability this transportation arrangement will entail sending a flight directly to Nome to pick up the patient for transport to Los Angeles.

Transporting six cartons of tulip bulbs from Holland, Michigan, to Austin, Texas, however, does not command that kind of extravagance. Thus, the tulip seller delivers the freight to a **forwarder** who arranges to transport it by rail, truck, or air after consolidating this small shipment with other small shipments. By consolidating the freight, the forwarder or **consolidator** can take advantage of rates that favor large shipments in trailers or containers, for example, that can be handled by automation.

Freight forwarders that receive merchandise issue a bill of lading specifically designed for them as nonvehicle-owning common carriers (NVOCC).

§34.4 MULTICARRIER AND MULTIMODAL TRANSPORT

Transhipment is the process of taking freight from one carrier and giving it to a second. For a Los Angeles seller to ship merchandise from California to Detroit by rail, it must arrange to have the goods shipped by more than one carrier, there being no railroad that travels from Los Angeles to Detroit. It makes little sense for each railroad that handles the merchandise to issue a separate bill of lading, though in fact, there is something illogical about the Burlington Northern Railroad's issuing a bill of lading to transport goods across the country when it cannot itself carry the goods to the destination. In theory, the Burlington, when it takes delivery of the goods, acts as a carrier and a freight forwarder, for it carries the goods part of the way to the destination and arranges for the carriage of the goods for the balance of the way.

Thus, for example, the Burlington may carry goods from Los Angeles to Chicago and there deliver them to the Grand Trunk Western for transport to Detroit, but the entire transaction will proceed under the bill issued by the Burlington. The document the industry developed for this transhipment of goods is the **through bill of lading.** Document 34-1 is an example of a through bill.

Sometimes, the transhipment of the goods will involve their offloading from one mode of carrier to another. A shipper of coal from Pittsburgh, Pennsylvania, to a steel mill in Bartonville, Illinois, for example, may arrange for a railroad to transport the coal from the deep mine in western Pennsylvania to a barge terminal on the Ohio River. From there, a barge will transport the coal down the Ohio and up the Mississippi to the Illinois River to a terminal in Peoria. From the Peoria terminal, trucks will take the coal to the steel mill in Bartonville.

Although a coal company may have sufficient transportation management to arrange for each of these shipments, some shippers on **multimodal** journeys will ask a forwarder to arrange for the transhipment in each case.

Uniform Domestic Straight Bill of Lading, adopted by Carriers in Official, Southern, Western and Illinois Classification Territories, March 15, 1922, as amended August 1, 1930 and June 15, 1941

UNIFORM STRAIGHT BILL OF LADING
ORIGINAL—NOT NEGOTIABLE.

Shipper's No. ....

Company — Agent's No. ....

RECEIVED, subject to the classifications and tariffs in effect on the date of the issue of this Bill of Lading.

At .... 19...... **From** ....

the property described below, in apparent good order, except as noted (contents and condition of contents of packages unknown), marked, consigned, and destined as indicated below, which said company (the word company being understood throughout this contract as meaning any person or corporation in possession of the property under the contract) agrees to carry to its usual place of delivery at said destination, if on its own road or its own water line, otherwise to deliver to another carrier on the route to said destination. It is mutually agreed, as to each carrier of all or any of said property over all or any portion of said route to destination, and as to each party at any time interested in all or any of said property, that every service to be performed hereunder shall be subject to all the conditions not prohibited by law, whether printed or written, herein contained, including the conditions on back hereof, which are hereby agreed to by the shipper and accepted for himself and his assigns.

(Mail or street address of consignee—For purposes of notification only)

Consigned to ....

Destination .... State of .... County of ....

Route ....

Delivering Carrier .... Car Initial .... Car No. ....

NO. PACKAGES	DESCRIPTION OF ARTICLES, SPECIAL MARKS AND EXCEPTIONS	* WEIGHT (Subject to Correction)	CLASS or RATE	CHECK COLUMN
	SPECIMEN			

Subject to Section 7 of conditions, if this shipment is to be delivered to the consignee without recourse on the consignor, the consignor shall sign the following statement:
The carrier shall not make delivery of this shipment without payment of freight and all other lawful charges.

Signature of Consignor.

If charges are to be prepaid, write or stamp here, "To be Prepaid."

Received $ .... to apply in prepayment of the charges on the property described hereon.

Agent or Cashier.

Per ....
(The signature here acknowledges only the amount prepaid.)

Charges Advanced:

* If the shipment moves between two ports by a carrier by water, the law requires that the bill of lading shall state whether it is "carrier's or shipper's weight."
Note.—Where the rate is dependent on value, shippers are required to state specifically in writing the agreed or declared value of the property.
The agreed or declared value of the property is hereby specifically stated by the shipper to be not exceeding $.................... per ....

.... Shipper, Per .... AGENT .... PER .... ①

Permanent postoffice address of shipper ....

The Fibre Boxes used for this shipment conform to the specifications set forth in the box maker's certificate thereon and all other requirements of Rule 41 of the Consolidated Freight Classification.

TOPS FORM 3040 LITHO IN U. S. A.

Document 34-1. (*continued*)

CONTRACT TERMS AND CONDITIONS

Sec. 1. (a) The carrier or party in possession of any of the property herein described shall be liable as at common law for any loss thereof or damage thereto, except as hereinafter provided.

(b) No carrier or party in possession of all or any of the property herein described shall be liable for any loss thereof or damage thereto or delay caused by the act of God, the public enemy, the authority of law, or the act or default of the shipper or owner, or for natural shrinkage. The carrier's liability shall be that of warehouseman, only, for loss, damage, or delay caused by fire occurring after the expiration of the free time allowed by tariffs lawfully on file (such free time to be computed as therein provided) after notice of the arrival of the property at destination or at the port of export (if intended for export) has been duly sent or given, and after placement of the property for delivery at destination, or tender of delivery of the property to the party entitled to receive it, has been made. Except in case of negligence of the carrier or party in possession (and the burden to prove freedom from such negligence shall be on the carrier or party in possession), the carrier or party in possession shall not be liable for loss, damage, or delay occurring while the property is stopped and held in transit upon the request of the shipper, owner, or party, entitled to make such request, or resulting from a defect or vice in the property, or for country damage to cotton, or from riots or strikes.

(c) In case of quarantine the property may be discharged at risk and expense of owners into quarantine depot or elsewhere, as required by quarantine regulations or authorities, or for the carrier's dispatch at nearest available point in carrier's judgment, and in any such case carrier's responsibility shall cease when property is so discharged, or property may be returned by carrier at owner's expense to shipping point, earning freight both ways. Quarantine expenses of whatever nature or kind upon or in respect to property shall be borne by the owners of the property or be a lien thereon. The carrier shall not be liable for loss or damage occasioned by fumigation or disinfection or other acts required or done by quarantine regulations or authorities even though the same may have been done by carrier's officers, agents, or employees, nor for detention, loss, or damage of any kind occasioned by quarantine or the enforcement thereof. No carrier shall be liable, except in case of negligence, for any mistake or inaccuracy in any information furnished by the carrier, its agents, or officers, as to quarantine laws or regulations. The shipper shall hold the carriers harmless from any expense they may incur, or damages they may be required to pay, by reason of the introduction of the property covered by this contract into any place against the quarantine laws or regulations in effect at such place.

Sec. 2. (a) No carrier is bound to transport said property by any particular train or vessel, or in time for any particular market or otherwise than with reasonable dispatch. Every carrier shall have the right in case of physical necessity to forward said property by any carrier or route between the point of shipment and the point of destination. In all cases not prohibited by law, where a lower value than actual value has been represented in writing by the shipper or has been agreed upon in writing as the released value of the property as determined by the classification or tariffs upon which the rate is based, such lower value plus freight charges if paid shall be the maximum amount to be recovered, whether or not such loss or damage occurs from negligence.

(b) As a condition precedent to recovery, claims must be filed in writing with the receiving or delivering carrier, or carrier issuing this bill of lading, or carrier on whose line the loss, damage, injury or delay occurred, within nine months after delivery of the property (or, in case of export traffic, within nine months after delivery at port of export) or, in case of failure to make delivery, then within nine months after a reasonable time for delivery has elapsed; and suits shall be instituted against any carrier only within two years and one day from the day when notice in writing is given by the carrier to the claimant that the carrier has disallowed the claim or any part or parts thereof specified in the notice. Where claims are not filed or suits are not instituted thereon in accordance with the foregoing provisions, no carrier hereunder shall be liable, and such claims will not be paid.

(c) Any carrier or party liable on account of loss of or damage to any of said property shall have the full benefit of any insurance that may have been effected upon or on account of said property, so far as this shall not avoid the policies or contracts of insurance: **Provided,** That the carrier reimburse the claimant for the premium paid thereon.

Sec. 3. Except where such service is required as the result of carrier's negligence, all property shall be subject to necessary cooperage and baling at owner's cost. Each carrier over whose route cotton or cotton linters is to be transported hereunder shall have the privilege, at its own cost and risk, of compressing the same for greater convenience in handling or forwarding, and shall not be held responsible for deviation or unavoidable delays in procuring such compression. Grain in bulk consigned to a point where there is a railroad, public or licensed elevator, may (unless otherwise expressly noted herein, and then if it is not promptly unloaded) be there delivered and placed with other grain of the same kind and grade without respect to ownership (and prompt notice thereof shall be given to the consignor), and if so delivered shall be subject to a lien for elevator charges in addition to all other charges hereunder.

Sec. 4. (a) Property not removed by the party entitled to receive it within the free time allowed by tariffs, lawfully on file (such free time to be computed as therein provided), after notice of the arrival of the property at destination or at the port of export (if intended for export) has been duly sent or given, and after placement of the property for delivery at destination has been made, may be kept in vessel, car, depot, warehouse or place of delivery of the carrier, subject to the tariff charge for storage and to carrier's responsibility as warehouseman, only, or at the option of the carrier, may be removed to and stored in a public or licensed warehouse at the place of delivery or other available place, at the cost of the owner, and there held without liability on the part of the carrier, and subject to a lien for all freight and other lawful charges, including a reasonable charge for storage.

(b) Where nonperishable property which has been transported to destination hereunder is refused by consignee or the party entitled to receive it, or said consignee or party entitled to receive it fails to receive it within 15 days after notice of arrival shall have been duly sent or given, the carrier may sell the same at public auction to the highest bidder, at such place as may be designated by the carrier: **Provided,** That the carrier shall have first mailed, sent, or given to the consignor notice that the property has been refused or remains unclaimed, as the case may be, and that it will be subject to sale under the terms of the bill of lading if disposition be not arranged for, and shall have published notice containing a description of the property, the name of the party to whom consigned, or, if shipped order notify, the name of the party to be notified, and the time and place of sale, once a week for two successive weeks, in a newspaper of general circulation at the place of sale or nearest place where such newspaper is published: **Provided,** That 30 days shall have elapsed before publication of notice of sale after said notice that the property was refused or remains unclaimed was mailed, sent, or given.

(c) Where perishable property which has been transported hereunder to destination is refused by consignee or party entitled to receive it, or said consignee or party entitled to receive it shall fail to receive it promptly, the carrier may, in its discretion, to prevent deterioration or further deterioration, sell the same to the best advantage at private or public sale: **Provided,** That if time serves for notification to the consignor or owner of the refusal of the property or the failure to receive it and request for disposition of the property, such notification shall be given, in such manner as the exercise of due diligence requires, before the property is sold.

(d) Where the procedure provided for in the two paragraphs last preceding is not possible, it is agreed that nothing contained in said paragraphs shall be construed to abridge the right of the carrier at its option to sell the property under such circumstances and in such manner as may be authorized by law.

(e) The proceeds of any sale made under this section shall be applied by the carrier to the payment of freight, demurrage, storage, and any other lawful charges and the expense of notice, advertisement, sale, and other necessary expense and of caring for and maintaining the property, if proper care of the same requires special expense, and should there be a balance it shall be paid to the owner of the property sold hereunder.

(f) Property destined to or taken from a station, wharf, or landing at which there is no regularly appointed freight agent shall be entirely at risk of owner after unloaded from cars or vessels or until loaded into cars or vessels, and, except in case of carrier's negligence, when received from or delivered to such stations, wharves, or landings shall be at owner's risk until the cars are attached to and after they are detached from locomotive or train or until loaded into and after unloaded from vessels.

Sec. 5. No carrier hereunder will carry or be liable in any way for any documents, specie, or for any articles of extraordinary value not specifically rated in the published classifications or tariffs unless a special agreement to do so and a stipulated value of the articles are indorsed hereon.

Sec. 6. Every party, whether principal or agent, shipping explosives or dangerous goods, without previous full written disclosure to the carrier of their nature, shall be liable for and indemnify the carrier against all loss or damage caused by such goods, and such goods may be warehoused at owner's risk and expense or destroyed without compensation.

Sec. 7. The owner or consignee shall pay the freight and average, if any, and all other lawful charges accruing on said property; but, except in those instances where it may lawfully be authorized to do so, no carrier by railroad shall deliver or relinquish possession at destination of the property covered by this bill of lading until all tariff rates and charges thereon have been paid. The consignor shall be liable for the freight and all other lawful charges, except that if the consignor stipulates, by signature, in the space provided for that purpose on the face of this bill of lading that the carrier shall not make delivery without requiring payment of such charges and the carrier, contrary to such stipulation, shall make delivery without requiring such payment, the consignor (except as hereinafter provided) shall not be liable for such charges. **Provided, that,** where the carrier has been instructed by the shipper or consignor to deliver said property to a consignee other than the shipper or consignor, such consignee shall not be legally liable for transportation charges in respect of the transportation of said property (beyond those billed against him at the time of delivery for which he is otherwise liable) which may be found to be due after the property has been delivered to him, if the consignee (a) is an agent only and has no beneficial title in said property, and (b) prior to delivery of said property has notified the delivering carrier in writing of the fact of such agency and absence of beneficial title, and, in the case of a shipment reconsigned or diverted to a point other than that specified in the original bill of lading, has also notified the delivering carrier in writing of the name and address of the beneficial owner of said property; and, in such cases the shipper or consignor, or, in the case of a shipment so reconsigned or diverted, the beneficial owner, shall be liable for such additional charges. If the consignee has given to the carrier erroneous information as to who the beneficial owner is, such consignee shall himself be liable for such additional charges. Nothing herein shall limit the right of the carrier to require at time of shipment the prepayment or guarantee of the charges. If upon inspection it is ascertained that the articles shipped are not those described in this bill of lading, the freight charges must be paid upon the articles actually shipped.

Sec. 8. If this bill of lading is issued on the order of the shipper, or his agent, in exchange or in substitution for another bill of lading, the shipper's signature to the prior bill of lading as to the statement of value or otherwise, or election of common law or bill of lading liability, in or in connection with such prior bill of lading, shall be considered a part of this bill of lading as fully as if the same were written or made in or in connection with this bill of lading.

Sec. 9. (a) If all or any part of said property is carried by water over any part of said route, such water carriage shall be performed subject to all the terms and provisions of, and all the exemptions from liability contained in, the Act of the Congress of the United States approved on February 13, 1893, and entitled "An act relating to the navigation of vessels, etc.," and of other statutes of the United States according carriers by water the protection of limited liability, and to the conditions contained in this bill of lading not inconsistent therewith or with this section.

(b) No such carrier by water shall be liable for any loss or damage resulting from any fire happening to or on board the vessel, or from explosion, bursting of boilers or breakage of shafts, unless caused by the design or neglect of such carrier.

(c) If the owner shall have exercised due diligence in making the vessel in all respects seaworthy and properly manned, equipped, and supplied, no such carrier shall be liable for any loss or damage resulting from the perils of the lakes, seas, or other waters, or from latent defects in hull, machinery, or appurtenances whether existing prior to, at the time of, or after sailing, or from collision, stranding, or other accidents of navigation, or from prolongation of the voyage. And, when for any reason it is necessary, any vessel carrying any or all of the property herein described shall be at liberty to call at any port or ports, in or out of the customary route, to tow and be towed, to transfer, trans-ship, or lighter, to load and discharge goods at any time, to assist vessels in distress, to deviate for the purpose of saving life or property, and for docking and repairs. Except in case of negligence such carrier shall not be responsible for any loss or damage to property if it be necessary or is usual to carry the same upon deck.

(d) General Average shall be payable according to the York-Antwerp Rules of 1924, Sections 1 to 15, inclusive, and Sections 17 to 22, inclusive, and as to matters not covered thereby according to the laws and usages of the Port of New York. If the owners shall have exercised due diligence to make the vessel in all respects seaworthy and properly manned, equipped and supplied, it is hereby agreed that in case of danger, damage or disaster resulting from faults or errors in navigation, or in the management of the vessel, or from any latent or other defects in the vessel, her machinery or appurtenances, or from unseaworthiness, whether existing at the time of shipment or at the beginning of the voyage (provided the latent or other defects or the unseaworthiness was not discoverable by the exercise of due diligence), the shippers, consignees and/or owners of the cargo shall nevertheless pay salvage and any special charges incurred in respect of the cargo, and shall contribute with the shipowner in general average to the payment of any sacrifices, losses or expenses of a general average nature that may be made or incurred for the common benefit or to relieve the adventure from any common peril.

(e) If the property is being carried under a tariff which provides that any carrier or carriers party thereto shall be liable for loss from perils of the sea, then as to such carrier or carriers the provisions of this section shall be modified in accordance with the tariff provisions, which shall be regarded as incorporated into the conditions of this bill of lading.

(f) The term "water carriage" in this section shall not be construed as including lighterage in or across rivers, harbors, or lakes, when performed by or on behalf of rail carriers.

Sec. 10. Any alteration, addition, or erasure in this bill of lading which shall be made without the special notation hereon of the agent of the carrier issuing this bill of lading, shall be without effect, and this bill of lading shall be enforceable according to its original tenor.

Document 34-2. Air Waybill

012— 2114 5073 **DOMESTIC AIR WAYBILL** 012—2114 5073

Shipper's Name and Address	Shipper's Account Number	ISSUED BY NOT NEGOTIABLE AIR WAYBILL (AIR CONSIGNMENT NOTE) NORTHWEST CARGO Northwest Airlines, Inc. ST. PAUL, MINNESOTA U.S.A. 55111
		Copies 1, 2 and 3 of this Air Waybill are originals and have the same validity
Consignee's Name and Address	Consignee's Account Number	It is agreed that the goods described herein are accepted in apparent good order and condition (except as noted) for carriage SUBJECT TO THE CONDITIONS OF CONTRACT ON THE REVERSE HEREOF. THE SHIPPER'S ATTENTION IS DRAWN TO THE NOTICE CONCERNING CARRIERS'LIMITATION OF LIABILITY. Shipper may increase such limitation of liability by declaring a higher value for carriage and paying a supplemental charge if required.
Issuing Carrier's Agent Name and City		ALSO NOTIFY NAME AND ADDRESS *(OPTIONAL ACCOUNTING INFORMATION)*
Agent's IATA Code	Account No.	ACCOUNTING INFORMATION
Airport of Departure (Addr. of first Carrier) and requested Routing		

to	By first Carrier (Routing and Destination)	to	by	to	by	Currency	CHGS Code	WT/Val PPD	WT/Val COLL	Other PPD	Other COLL	Declared Value for Carriage	Declared Value for Customs

Airport of Destination	Flight/Date	For Carrier Use Only	Flight/Date	Amount of Insurance	INSURANCE-If shipper requests insurance in accordance with conditions on reverse hereof, indicate amount to be insured in figures in box marked amount of insurance.

Handling Information

No. of Pieces RCP	Gross Weight	kg / lb	Rate Class / Commodity Item No.	Chargeable Weight	Rate / Charge	Total	Nature and Quantity of Goods (Incl. Dimensions or Volume)

Prepaid	Weight Charge	Collect	P UP ZONE	PICKUP CHARGES	ORIGIN ADVANCE CHARGES	DESCRIPTION OF ORIGIN ADVANCE	ITEMS PREPAID
A.				B.	K.		
	Valuation Charge		DEL ZONE	DELIVERY CHARGES	DEST. ADVANCE CHARGES	DESCRIPTION OF DEST. ADVANCE	ITEMS COLLECT
D.				C.	L.		
	Tax			OTHER CHARGES AND DESCRIPTION			
I.			F.				

Total Other Charges Due Agent

Total Other Charges, Due Carrier

Shipper certifies that the particulars on the face hereof are correct and that insofar as any part of the consignment contains dangerous goods (hazardous materials) such part is properly described by name and is in proper condition for carriage by air according to the applicable governmental regulations and, for international shipments, the current International Air Transport Association's Dangerous Goods Regulations.

Signature of Shipper Above and Initial Applicable Box Below.

COD ➡ CURRENCY

☐ THIS SHIPMENT **DOES NOT** CONTAIN DANGEROUS GOODS REGULATED IN AIR TRANSPORT.

☐ THIS SHIPMENT **DOES** CONTAIN DANGEROUS GOODS REGULATED IN AIR TRANSPORT.

Total Prepaid | Total Collect

EXECUTED ON

SPECIMEN

Currency Conversion Rates | Total Collect in Dest. Currency

(Date) (TIME) at (Place) SIGNATURE OF ISSUING CARRIER OR ITS AGENT

For Carrier's Use only at Destination | Charges at Destination | Total Collect Charges

012— 2114 5073

ORIGINAL 3 (FOR SHIPPER)

AC-17 FORM NO. 5-1037 11/89

Reprinted with the permission of Northwest Airlines, Inc.

CONDITIONS OF CONTRACT OF CARRIAGE

1. Unless the Shipper's Option as set forth below is exercised by Shipper as provided in tendering the shipment described herein for carriage. Shipper agrees to these Conditions of Contract, which no agent or employee of the parties may alter, and that this Airbill is non-negotiable and has been prepared by Shipper or on Shipper's behalf by Carrier.
2. As used herein, the term "Carrier" includes Northwest Airlines, Inc., and persons, firms and corporations performing pickup, delivery or other ground services for Northwest Airlines, Inc., in connection with the shipment. These Conditions of Contract apply at all times when the shipment is being handled by or for Carrier and shall inure to the benefit of and be binding upon Carrier, Shipper, Consignee, and other carriers by whom transportation described in this airbill is undertaken.
3. In tendering the shipment for carriage, Shipper warrants that the shipment is packaged adequately to protect the enclosed goods and to ensure safe transportation with ordinary care and handling, and that each package is appropriately labeled and is in good order (except as noted) for carriage as specified.
4. The contents of shipments must be indicated by accurate and specific descriptions on the airbill.
5. Carrier's routing applies unless Shipper inserts on the Airbill specific routing. To expedite movement, shipment may be diverted to motor or other carrier as per tariff rule unless shipper gives other instructions hereon.
6. Delivery will be made by the delivering carrier to Consignee at a point where delivery service is available at applicable charges unless instructions to deliver at city terminal or airport terminal are specified by Shipper on the Airbill under "Instructions to Carrier".
7. Carrier shall not be liable for loss, damage, delay, or other result caused by any circumstance beyond the control of Carrier, including, but not limited to Acts of God, perils of the air, public enemies, public authorities acting with actual or apparent authority in the premises, authority of law, quarantine, riots, strikes, civil commotions, hazards or dangers incident to a state of war, act or default of the Shipper or Consignee, the nature of the shipment or any defect or characteristic or inherent vice thereof, violation by the Shipper or Consignee of any of these Conditions of Contract; compliance with delivery instructions from the Shipper or Consignee, or non-compliance with special instructions from Shipper or Consignee not authorized by the terms of this Contract of Carriage.
8. The carrier shall not be liable for shortage of articles loaded and sealed in containers by the Shipper provided the seal is unbroken.
9. In consideration of the rates charged, Shipper agrees that the liability of Carrier is limited to the greater of $50 or 50¢ per pound based on the weight of the shipment unless a higher value is declared in writing on the Airbill and applicable valuation charges paid. If assembly or distribution service is provided, the limit of liability shall be based on the weight of the individual part.
10. Carrier shall not be liable for special or consequential damages unless at time of receipt of shipment, Carrier is given notice in writing, on the Airbill of the circumstances which could result in such damages; and in no event shall Carrier's liability for such damages exceed the declared value of the shipment.
11. All claims, including claims for overcharges, must be made in writing to Carrier or the originating or delivering carrier within a period of nine months and nine days after the date of acceptance of the shipment by the originating carrier.
12. Damage and/or loss discovered by the Consignee after delivery must be reported in writing to the delivering carrier at destination within 15 days after delivery. While awaiting inspection by the delivering carrier, Consignee must hold the shipping container and its contents in the same condition they were in when damage was discovered insofar as it is possible to do so.
13. No claim with respect to a shipment will be entertained until all transportation charges have been paid, except that a claim for a missing shipment or part thereof will be entertained even though transportation charges thereon are unpaid.
14. Carrier shall not be liable in any action brought to enforce a claim unless such action is brought within one year after the date written notice is given to the claimant that Carrier has disallowed the claim in whole or in part.
15. Shipments from or to a point outside the United States shall not be governed by the rules referred to on this airbill, but by (1) tariffs on file with the U.S. Governments and (2) by the Convention for the Unification of Certain Rules relating to International Carriage by air, signed at Warsaw, October 12, 1929, as amended.
16. Carrier and shipper hereby incorporate by reference in this contract carriers published rules and regulations.
17. This Contract of Carriage shall be interpreted and applied in accordance with the laws of the State of Minnesota.

SHIPPER'S OPTION

Carrier's published rates are reduced rates based upon acceptance by Shipper of the Conditions of the Contract of Carriage hereinabove set forth. Shipper, at his option, may elect not to accept such conditions, and in lieu thereof to have Carrier transport the property with Carrier's liability limited only as provided by common law and by the laws of the United States and the several States insofar as they apply. To elect such option, Shipper must state in writing on the face of this Airbill in the box entitled "Handling Information" (a) the actual value of the shipment, and (b) that Shipper elects Carrier's liability limited only as provided by law. Such actual value of the shipment shall include the amount of any special or consequential damages for which Carrier could be held legally liable. If such option is elected by Shipper, Carrier's applicable rate will be Carrier's published tariff rate plus an additional charge of $1.50 for each $100 of actual value of the shipment.

NOTICE - Northwest Airlines, Inc., Carries Cargo Liability Insurance with limits of four million dollars to protect itself against claims for which it is legally liable.

35 International Shipping

§35.1 INTRODUCTION WITH A FEW DISTINCTIONS

This chapter deals essentially with imports and exports. Import transactions tend to mirror export transactions, since one country's export transaction is another country's import transaction. Domestic lawyers tend to see only one side of each, however. Because international trade, especially that among the western industrialized countries, enjoys a considerable measure of uniformity, what is said here about U.S. exports tends to be true about British or Brazilian exports, though there are certainly many differences. The differences, however, tend to confine themselves to legal rules rather than industry practices.

Exporters utilize many marketing methods. To the extent that they sell products overseas through subsidiaries or related corporations, their shipping arrangements are rather simple. They may ship on their own freighters or tankers or arrange for shipment on a third-party carrier in much the same fashion that an exporter ships goods it is selling on open account to an unrelated buyer. This chapter assumes that the exporter is selling to a third party, for that is the setting in which the complicated and interesting questions arise.

In all of these exporting transactions, the shipment stems from an underlying sales contract and is governed, in large part, by that contract. In addition, there is a considerable body of law that governs international shipping. There are international conventions governing sea and air transport, and there are shipping associations that set rates and adopt standardized forms for bills of lading and other **transport documents**.

Often, the character of the goods shipped will determine shipping arrangements. Since the early 1950s containerization has altered the transport industry's practices significantly. Today, many manufactured goods are shipped in containers that may be filled at the seller's plant and not unloaded until they arrive at the buyer's plant. The container makes transhipment easy, since cranes or other mechanized facilities can load and unload containers with little risk of cargo damage, spillage, contamination, and pilferage. Some containers are on wheels and roll on and off a ship, barge, or railroad car. Others sit on trailers for over-the-road transport and off-loading onto barges, railroad flatcars, or ocean-going vessels.

Still other containers are collapsible, so that they may be returned empty to the shipper. Some ocean-going vessels are designed solely for containers. Companies that own such vessels often own the containers. The ship owners send the containers to the shipper's or the buyer's plant or to a freight forwarder for loading (sometimes called "stuffing") or unloading. Containers may be refrigerated to carry easily spoiled agricultural commodities that otherwise could not be transported long distances.

Containers also streamline the paperwork for exports. Formerly, goods from an inland point might have to be loaded first on a truck or railroad boxcar for transport to the port of exit in the seller's country, then onto an ocean-going vessel for transport to the port of entry in the buyer's region, and then to a truck or railcar for transport to the inland destination. For each leg of the journey, there might be a separate document of title. Containers make it easy for a single document to be issued by a forwarder for the entire voyage.

Some transport activity does not lend itself to containerization. Many agricultural commodities (such as grain and soybean oil), petrochemicals, and similarly bulky commodities are still shipped in bulk either on "bulkers" or tankers. Frequently, these commodities must be off loaded and on loaded at every transhipment point. Thus, grain moving down the Missouri and Mississippi Rivers from Omaha to New Orleans for transport to Vladivostok would have to be loaded on a barge in Omaha and would be unloaded in New Orleans onto the ocean-going vessel. This kind of **breakbulk cargo** is much more susceptible to contamination and loss than manufactured goods shipped portal to portal in sealed containers.

There are a couple of distinctions to keep in mind in reviewing the activity of the transport industries described in this chapter. The first relates to ship-owning companies. Such companies generally fall into one of two categories: lines and **tramps.** Lines are members of a shipping **conference,** such as the Baltic and International Maritime Council (BIMCO). They own **liners,** which are ships that follow published schedules over established routes and charge agreed upon rates. Tramps are ships that wander from port to port in search of business and whose itinerary is determined by the destinations of the cargoes they take on. Often, tramps are subjects of **charter parties.**

Any industry that achieves a degree of sophistication and complexity gives rise to the expert. The ocean transport industry involves more than just shippers, people who want to ship merchandise, and shipping companies, the people that carry the merchandise. There are important middlemen in the industry. The first is the freight forwarder, the second is the **loading broker,** and the third is the **customs broker.**

Generally, freight forwarders are agents of the shipper. They arrange for the shipment by finding a carrier and, frequently, they consolidate the shipment with other shipments in order to take advantage of containerization or other economies of scale. Loading brokers are generally agents of the ship owner. Their function is to find cargo for the ship and to issue the documents in connection with the shipment. Sometimes, freight forwarders, who are supposed to be the agent of the shipper, are also loading brokers, that is, agent of the ship owner. If that arrangement troubles you, you are not alone, but it does not trouble the shipping industry and appears to be working rather well, as arrangements that startle the lawyers so often do. Loading brokers may also act as ship brokers that arrange for charter parties. Customs brokers will take charge of import shipments and see them through customs.

§35.2 SHIPPING TERMS

There has been a measure of standardization in ocean shipping by virtue of the efforts of various organizations, the most successful of which is currently the International Chamber of Commerce (ICC), which has published Incoterms. Generally, Incoterms sets out a lexicon that covers arrangements for delivery of goods, including delivery at the seller's works, multimodal transport of goods portal to portal, and arrangements for single-mode transport of goods from one port to another. The most common export arrangements for shipping goods come under CIF, C&F, or FOB headings, all of which are described in detail in Incoterms.

"CIF" stands for "cost, insurance, freight," with "cost" being the price of the goods, "insurance" being the cost of marine insurance, and "freight" being the charges levied by the carrier for transporting the goods. "C&F" stands for "cost and freight," terms calling for the same arrangement as

CIF without the insurance. A buyer that has its own coverage under a blanket policy would not ask its seller to ship CIF but C&F. "FOB" stands for "free on board" and means that a party must arrange to have the goods loaded on board a named vessel. In each of these cases, additional information is necessary.

A New York importer may order specialty steel from an Italian producer "CIF Cleveland." In that event, the producer must arrange for transport of the steel from its plant to an Italian port, thence by ocean vessel to Cleveland. In the alternative, the producer may be able to arrange for transport on its own trucks to an Italian port with loading on a vessel there that can carry the steel directly to Cleveland. In a sale "FOB Genoa," the producer would have to arrange for loading of the steel on board a ship at the Italian port, but the buyer must arrange for the shipment and must advise the producer of the ship and the schedule.

Under the 1990 version of Incoterms, there are 13 incoterms, and the ICC publication spells out their meaning and the duties of the seller and buyer under each.

The international shipping industry and shippers have fashioned other terms for their contracts. "Pier to House," "House to House," and "Pier to Pier" are examples of phrases that parties use in international shipping by container. While these are not incoterms, they have meanings that the industry assigns to them, with a lesser measure of certainty than in the case of the incoterms.

Despite these efforts at standardization, sometimes shipping terminology has the disconcerting tendency to have one meaning in one region and a different meaning in another. The Uniform Commercial Code, for example, does not always follow international usage. The shipping industry, furthermore, is dynamic; practices and terminology change from time to time. The incoterms have themselves undergone revision and undoubtedly will undergo revision again.

§35.3 THE OCEAN BILL OF LADING

In classic ocean transport, the shipper (the seller or exporter of goods) prepares the goods for transport by packaging them and delivering them to the carrier. The ship owner's agent that receives the goods may be the "mate," (i.e., the captain of the ship or his subordinate) or a loading broker. Upon delivery of the goods, the seller delivers a bill of lading it has prepared on the ship owner's bill-of-lading form. The ship owner's agent examines the goods to determine, to the extent that he can, whether the goods conform to the description in the bill. He then issues a **dock receipt** for the goods. Document 35-1 is a dock receipt.

At this point, the goods are not on board, and there is still considerable risk involved in their loading. They or their packages may be damaged or lost in loading, and, importantly, marine insurance coverage does not apply until the goods pass the ship's rail. Once the goods are loaded on board, the mate compares his receipt with the bill of lading the seller prepared. If everything appears to be in order, the mate then signs the bill of lading. If things are not in order, the mate signs a claused bill, that is, a bill that contains a clause advising, for example, that the goods were damaged upon loading or receipt or that the packages are damaged or dirty. This clausing of the bill is significant because under most letters of credit, banks do not accept claused bills.

Quite often, the ship owner issues a "received for shipment" bill of lading when the seller delivers the goods at the dock. That bill of lading is generally unacceptable to banks and overseas buyers because of the loading and insurance risks mentioned above. Once the goods are loaded on board, however, the ship's agent stamps the received-for-shipment bill with an **on board stamp** and dates and signs the stamp, thereby rendering the bill of lading an on board bill acceptable to buyers and banks.

The description of the goods in a bill of lading is often not reliable. Carriers are not inspectors; they do not open cartons or sealed containers to examine merchandise, and they are not expert enough to determine whether breakbulk cargoes such as grain or tankerload cargoes such as turpentine passes in the trade. Bills of lading, therefore, usually contain disclaimers such as **"said to contain"** or **"shipper's load and count"** (SLC). These disclaimers are not always accorded full effect by the courts, especially U.S. courts, but if they comply strictly with governing law, they are generally effective.

From the standpoint of efficiency, disclaimers make sense. Many sellers and buyers do not want to pay for third-party examination of the goods. They are satisfied with a bill of lading containing such disclaimers. Even banks, which take the bills of lading for value and may look to the goods in the event a buyer fails to reimburse the bank, are generally willing to accept bills with disclaimers. The buyer or bank that wants an examination should pay for it by arranging for an independent inspector's certification that the goods conform to industry standards or to the terms of the contract. Thus, the industry practice is optimal. Those who want inspection must pay for it; those who do not want it do not have to pay for it.

In some industries, especially those involving goods sold on spot markets or goods whose value fluctuates rapidly, traders who ship want to be able to sell or borrow against the cargo while it is in transit. In the oil industry, for example, while North Sea crude is being transported from Britain to Latin America, traders buy, sell, and borrow against the oil at breakneck speed. In fact, during the ten days or so that a tanker of oil traverses the North Atlantic, its cargo may be the subject of hundreds of transactions. Other commodities, such as grain, metals, and some raw materials, may change hands several times. In all of these cases, moreover, even when there is no sale of the cargo during transit, parties need to finance the goods.

In these transfers of cargoes to buyers or financers, the negotiable bill of lading may play a crucial role. By virtue of the fact that the carrier delivers the goods only to the holder of the bill, the bill stands for the cargo, and buyers and banks are willing to give value for it. Document 37-3 is a form that may be used as a negotiable ocean bill of lading.

Traditionally, in order to guard against the loss of the bill, carriers issued ocean bills of lading in a set. Such bills were issued in multiple originals. The carrier would honor any one of the originals. That original having been honored, the outstanding bills became worthless. Bills issued in a set were separated and forwarded to the appropriate party (usually a buyer or a bank) by separate cover, so that if one was lost, at least one would arrive, permitting the buyer to take delivery of the goods. This practice of issuing bills in a set, though not so critical as it once was, survives in many transactions.

It also survives in bank forms, particularly drafts used in the documentary-draft transaction. Such draft forms may contain a clause reciting "**First of exchange** (Second of same tenor and date being unpaid)." That language appeared on the first of the two drafts and indicates that the drafts were issued in duplicate and that one being honored, the other would stand void. The second copy of the draft would recite "**Second of exchange** (First of same tenor and date being unpaid)."

Sometimes, a bill is issued in single copy and becomes lost or arrives after the goods do. In that event, the carrier does not deliver the goods unless the bank or buyer seeking delivery agrees to indemnify the carrier against loss in the event the bill turns up in the hands of a third-party holder. When a bank's customer seeks such a guaranty, the bank will insist, of course, on indemnity from the customer so that the bank can recoup its loss in the event it is called upon to honor its guaranty.

§35.4 CHARTERS

Often, especially in full-capacity shipments, the shipper charters the vessel for a period of time or a voyage. Charters are governed by a contract called a "charter party." Charters may be by demise, in which case the shipper has to hire its own crew for the ship, but most of the time, the charter party leaves the operation of the ship in the owner's control, and the shipper merely delivers the goods for transport.

Charter parties are for a period of time (a time charter party) or for a voyage. In the former, the shipper bears the cost of delays caused, for example, by crowding at a port or unavailability of stevedores or docking facilities. These losses ("demurrage") are borne by the shipper in a time charter party. In a voyage charter party, however, the shipping company undertakes to transport the shipper's goods from one port to another, and the cost of demurrage falls on the shipping company.

When a shipper ships under a charter party, the charter party controls the shipping company's duties to transport and deliver the goods. Bills of lading are sometimes issued by the shipping company, but they customarily recite, and should recite, that they are subject to the charter party. Because third-party buyers and banks do not have the charter party, they are unaware of any terms in the charter party that may be burdensome or contrary to the usual arrangements for the carriage of goods under a bill of lading issued in the form established by a liner conference or a carriers' association. For that reason, charter-party bills of lading, even when they are denominated negotiable, are generally not acceptable to banks and buyers.

§35.5 FORWARDERS

Exporting goods often involves considerable expertise. The occasional exporter or the small operation that ships in less than container loads **(LCL)** often wants to assign the responsibility of obtaining the necessary **export licenses,** letters of credit, inspection certificates, transport documents, and the like to a freight forwarder that offers such services. Freight forwarders know liner schedules and charges and may even be loading brokers for one or more ocean carriers. In addition, some large forwarders own their own containers and maintain container freight stations remote from the docks to which they ultimately deliver the container.

Probably the most significant commercial function of the freight forwarder is its consolidation of shipments. Frequently, LCL sellers want the advantage of container rates and the advantages of container shipment — freedom from risks of loss, spoilage, pilferage, and the like. By engaging a freight forwarder, a number of LCL shippers can deliver their cargoes to the forwarder who consolidates them into full container load (FCL) shipments and delivers the containers to an ocean carrier for transport.

Often, of course, since some freight forwarders are located at places remote from the docks of ocean-going vessels, freight forwarders offer multimodal transportation arrangements to their customers. A shipper in Grand Rapids may ask a freight forwarder in that inland city to arrange for truck, rail, and steamship transport of goods to Buenos Aires. On other occasions the freight forwarders facilities are alongside the docks. A San Francisco exporter delivers its merchandise across the Bay in Oakland where a forwarder holds it until it can ship FCL on a **container ship** that travels between Oakland and Yokohama.

In the multimodal situation, the forwarder issues a document of title to the shipper at the time the shipper delivers the goods to the forwarder. That document will probably be a **combined transport document** that anticipates shipment by various modes of transportation from the time of delivery to the forwarder until delivery to destination. The freight forwarder is not, in fact, a carrier, and the notion that a noncarrier may issue a bill of lading is a curious one. In such transactions, the forwarder styles itself "NVOCC." "NVOCC" means "nonvehicle-owning common carrier," and the banking and transportation industries have pretty much accepted bills of lading issued by such forwarders in that form. Such combined transport bills of lading are not **marine bills,** since they may cover carriage of goods by rail or over the road and perforce are not on board bills. Thus any contract or letter of credit calling for an on board bill or an ocean bill would not be satisfied by the forwarder's bill.

In a typical transaction involving a shipper and a freight forwarder, the shipper prepares the forwarder's bill of lading and delivers the goods to the forwarder, who examines the goods in a manner sufficient only for the purposes of satisfying the bill's disclaimer language (e.g., shipper's load and count) and ascertaining that containers are sealed and that there is no apparent damage to the goods or their packages. The forwarder issues its bill and then arranges with vehicle-owning carriers for the transport of the goods pursuant to its obligations toward the shipper.

In another typical arrangement, the freight forwarder receives an LCL shipment from the shipper, consolidates it with other merchandise into a full container load, prepares the export documents, and delivers the container to the carrier, who issues the bill of lading.

§35.6 MARITIME INSURANCE

When the owner of goods holds them for sale, they are usually covered under the owner's property-damage insurance coverage. When goods leave the premises of the owner, however, that coverage may terminate, and when the goods pass into the hands of a bailee, the cost of extending that coverage to them can become prohibitive. Goods on ocean-going vessels, moreover, may no longer be the property of the seller but that of the buyer or, in effect, that of the bank that is financing the transaction. It becomes efficient, then, that after the goods move out of the bounds of the seller's facility and before they move into the bounds of the buyer's, the insurance coverage be related to the goods themselves rather than to the identity of the person who has an interest in them.

Goods in transport may be the subject of sales and financing, and their value is clearly enhanced if potential buyers and lenders do not have to inquire of the seller or borrower as to insurance during transport.

Long ago the transport and insurance industries responded to this problem with marine insurance policies that are transferable. Under such coverage, the shipper may indorse the policy to a buyer or lender, who then becomes the insured.

Sometimes the shipper cannot obtain a copy of the policy from its insurance broker in time to forward it to the bank or buyer. In that case the parties need to obtain evidence that the policy has, indeed, been contracted for and will issue in due course. **Binders** or insurance **covernotes** are issued by insurance brokers as evidence of that coverage. Some shippers, those doing a significant amount of exporting, may have an **open cargo policy** — a form of blanket coverage that, unlike the marine insurance policy, covers more than one shipment. In the event of that kind of open cargo coverage, the shipper is not in a position to make a policy available to the buyer or bank and uses instead a certificate of insurance.

Of these documents, the policy itself discloses the most information about the coverage — its effective date, the perils insured against, limits, etc. The certificate contains somewhat less information, and the binder or covernote even less. Buyers and lenders are more inclined, then, to accept policies and certificates than they are covernotes or binders.

Note that the transfer of maritime insurance fulfills its anticipated role in these settings only if the transfer is free of equities. If the insurance company could deny coverage to a transferee, for example, by virtue of the company's right of setoff against the transferor, the maritime insurance apparatus would not work. For that reason, maritime insurance policies, which travel with the goods, are akin to negotiable instruments. In fact, maritime insurance is some of the oldest insurance that we have, and the negotiability feature of it is similar to the negotiability features of the document of title and the bill of exchange (draft) that also come to us out of maritime commerce.

There is a great deal of learning in and a considerable lexicon for maritime insurance. Some terms arise with sufficient frequency that they are worth mentioning here, especially because they arise in connection with the letters of credit and payments that the exports generate.

Average is the maritime insurance concept of partial damage, as opposed to total loss of the goods. **General average** is the concept that in the event of extraordinary danger to the ship's cargo, the master may deliberately sacrifice some cargo to save the rest. In that event, cargo that is saved must participate in the loss, which contributed to its being saved. **Particular average** is a partial loss caused, for example, by seawater leaking into the hold and not caused by such deliberate decision by the master of the ship to sacrifice cargo.

Some insurance coverage is described as **FPA,** that is, free of particular average. That coverage would not protect the insured from partial losses caused by accident. A marine policy covering particular average is **WA** or **WPA,** that is, with average or with particular average.

Often, marine policies contain a deductible expressed as a specified **franchise.** WPA subject to a 10 percent franchise would require the insurer to protect against partial losses exceeding 10 percent of the amount of the loss.

The term **all risks** modifying coverage in a marine policy does not mean that the policy covers all risks. Losses caused by a malfunction of refrigeration equipment or by virtue of the inherent nature of the goods (e.g., bananas that rot because of delays) and similar losses are not included in all risks coverage.

The insurance industry has fashioned so-called cargo clauses, which were originally devised by the Institute of London **Underwriters.**

§35.7 EXPORT DOCUMENTS

Exports are the subject of considerable regulation by the federal government. In order to advance certain political agendas and to restrict the transfer of technology that might be harmful to the national defense, the government requires the licensing of all exports. Most exports, however, fall under the general license procedure. Only those commodities that are listed on the Export Administration's Commodity Control List and that are destined for countries to which exports are restricted fall within the more burdensome validated license procedure. While the government provides administrative personnel to assist exporters in determining whether they must obtain a validated license and what they must do to obtain it, the process is bureaucratic and subject to delay, paperwork, and all of the other headaches that such procedures inevitably entail.

Exporters that ship goods of a value in excess of $500 or that are subject to a validated license must file a **shipper's export declaration** (SED). General licenses are issued automatically, without application, but validated licenses must be applied for. The process of obtaining a validated license may be accelerated by a procedure whereby the importer or importing country verifies that the goods will not be reexported to a restricted country or that the goods will not be used for military or other restricted purposes.

§35.8 MARITIME FRAUD

With international trade's great distances, time changes, language and currency differences, and communications difficulties, the rogue finds opportunities to ply his trade. Sellers guard against that fraud with documentation and the letter of credit. Those procedures are sensitive, however, to maritime fraud, of which there is a considerable amount.

Maritime fraud can arise in a number of ways. In the most egregious case, a fraudulent ship owner of a rusty tub issues bills of lading for nonexistent merchandise and scuttles the ship at sea. False bills of lading can sometimes give rise to insurance fraud, when the ship owner or its agent issues bills of lading for nonexistent or worthless cargo, which it sells or, in the previous case, for which it obtains maritime insurance.

When third world countries ordered more goods than their ports could handle, some shipping companies, in order to avoid demurrage, offloaded merchandise at the wrong port or even sold cargoes to third parties.

Sellers, buyers, and banks are victims of these acts of fraud and take a number of steps to avoid them. The first and most important step is to avoid commerce with rogues. Shippers are well-advised to investigate the creditworthiness of shipping companies or to engage experienced freight forwarders to represent them. Buyers and banks who are taking documents of title from questionable carriers can insist on independent cargo surveys to determine the seaworthiness of the vessels or independent loading certificates to determine that cargo has, indeed, been loaded on board.

§35.9 IMPORTS

Often, the U.S. party to an international sale is not an exporter but an importer. In these cases, the foreign seller usually arranges for the transport of the goods, though the buyer's foreign agent or employee may perform that task.

Those arrangements do not include the all-important task of seeing the goods through customs. That task usually falls to the importer, and generally customs brokers, who are often freight forwarders, perform those functions for the inexperienced or infrequent importer. Getting goods into the country can be an expensive, slow, and exasperating task. The multitude of goods and commodities that pass in international trade make it difficult for government customs inspectors to classify goods and impose customs duties, though efforts at international uniformity in the classification of goods and commodities are proving helpful.

It is a tribute to the ingenuity of all concerned that the system works as well as it does. Graft in U.S. customs activity is remarkably uncommon. It might even be fair to say that delays are rather uncommon, though they do occur, as do disputes that must be resolved with litigation, lawyers, and all the expense that goes with that activity.

Under customs statutes and regulations, only the owner of goods or their purchaser or a customs broker may enter goods into the country.

There may be difficulty in determining the identity of a party and its relationship to the goods. Anyone holding a duly indorsed negotiable bill of lading will satisfy the Customs Service that he is entitled to enter the goods. In the absence of such a bill of lading, a carrier may certify the identity of the person with authority to enter the goods.

When merchandise arrives at a port in the United States several things might happen. First, the merchandise might be entered for consumption, that is, the goods might be entered by a party that is going to use or consume it in the country. Second, the goods might "arrive" at a port but not be entered there. If goods arrive in New York but are going to be transported to Chicago for "entry," New York is only the port of arrival: Chicago is the port of entry, that is, the port where the goods will be classified under the Harmonized Tariff Schedule and where the duty will be paid. Third, merchandise might be brought into the country to be warehoused for a period of up to five years during which the goods are stored in a bonded warehouse until the importer brings them into the country for consumption or re-exports them. Fourth, goods might be brought into a U.S. foreign trade zone or subzone. Under U.S. law, goods that are going to be subjected to a manufacturing process and reexported are not subject to duty if the manufacturing facility is in a foreign trade zone or qualifies as a foreign trade subzone.

Once the Customs Service is satisfied that the duty on goods will be paid, it will release the goods, subject to later determination of the duty — a process that sometimes takes time, especially if the importer and the Service disagree on the classification of the goods. The Service requires a commercial or **pro forma invoice** and an entry summary form, so that it can compute duties and collect statistical information concerning imports. Document 35-2 is a pro forma invoice. In addition, the importer must file an entry **manifest**.

In all events, the Customs Service will not permit entry of goods without payment of the duty unless the importer posts a bond. If the importer is using a customs broker, the broker's blanket bond may stand for the obligation to pay the duty. After the Service determines the appropriate classification of the imported goods, of course, the duty must be paid. Failing that payment, the Service resorts to the bond. If the importer does not arrange for release of the merchandise pending resolution of any dispute with the Service, the merchandise remains in a bonded warehouse.

DOCK RECEIPT

2. EXPORTER (*Principal or seller-licensee and address including ZIP Code*)

ZIP CODE

5. DOCUMENT NUMBER

5a. B/L OR AWB NUMBER

6. EXPORT REFERENCES

3. CONSIGNED TO

7. FORWARDING AGENT (*Name and address — references*)

8. POINT (STATE) OF ORIGIN OR FTZ NUMBER

4. NOTIFY PARTY/INTERMEDIATE CONSIGNEE (*Name and address*)

9. DOMESTIC ROUTING/EXPORT INSTRUCTIONS

12. PRE-CARRIAGE BY

13. PLACE OF RECEIPT BY PRE-CARRIER

14. EXPORTING CARRIER

15. PORT OF LOADING/EXPORT

10. LOADING PIER/TERMINAL

16. FOREIGN PORT OF UNLOADING (*Vessel and air only*)

17. PLACE OF DELIVERY BY ON-CARRIER

11. TYPE OF MOVE

11a. CONTAINERIZED (*Vessel only*) ☐ Yes ☐ No

MARKS AND NUMBERS (18)	NUMBER OF PACKAGES (19)	DESCRIPTION OF COMMODITIES in Schedule B detail (20)	GROSS WEIGHT (*Pounds*) (21)	MEASUREMENT (22)	D OR F (23)

DELIVERED BY:

LIGHTER
TRUCK ____________

ARRIVED— DATE ________ TIME ________

UNLOADED— DATE ________ TIME ________

CHECKED BY ____________

PLACED IN SHIP / ON DOCK LOCATION ____________

RECEIVED THE ABOVE DESCRIBED GOODS OR PACKAGES SUBJECT TO ALL THE TERMS OF THE UNDERSIGNED'S REGULAR FORM OF DOCK RECEIPT AND BILL OF LADING WHICH SHALL CONSTITUTE THE CONTRACT UNDER WHICH THE GOODS ARE RECEIVED, COPIES OF WHICH ARE AVAILABLE FROM THE CARRIER ON REQUEST AND MAY BE INSPECTED AT ANY OF ITS OFFICES.

FOR THE MASTER

BY ____________
RECEIVING CLERK

DATE ____________

SPECIMEN

ONLY CLEAN DOCK RECEIPT ACCEPTED.

PROFORMA INVOICE

SHIPPER

SOLD TO

SHIP TO

PRO FORMA INVOICE NO. | DATE ISSUED

TERMS AND CONDITIONS OF SALE

MODE OF TRANSPORT | CARRIER

AIR/OCEAN PORT OF EMBARKATION | LOADING PIER

AIR/OCEAN PORT OF UNLOADING | CONTAINERIZED ☐ Yes ☐ No

MARKS:

GROSS WEIGHT:

QUANTITY	U/M	DESCRIPTION OF MERCHANDISE	UNIT PRICE	AMOUNT
		SPECIMEN		
			FREIGHT	
			EXPORT PACKING	
			INSURANCE	
			MISC	
			TOTAL	

WE HEREBY CERTIFY This Invoice Is True and Correct and that the merchandise described is origin of the United States of America.

Authorized Signature | Title

Form 10-080 Printed and Sold by UNZ&CO 190 Baldwin Ave., Jersey City, NJ 07306 • (800) 631-3098 • (201) 795-5400

Reprinted with the permission of Unz & Co., 190 Baldwin Ave., Jersey City, NJ 07306 USA.

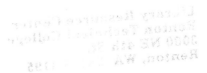

PART IV
GLOSSARY

All risks — in maritime insurance, coverage that includes losses caused by fortuity but not all losses. [For example, damage caused by hooks or malfunctioning of refrigeration equipment or by delays are not covered by an all risks policy. The all risks coverage has been displaced by the Institute Cargo Clause A.]

Average — in maritime insurance, a partial, as opposed to total, loss. (*See* **general average, particular average.**)

Bailee — the party to whom personal property is delivered under a **bailment.**

Bailment — arrangement between a **bailor** and a **bailee** for the transport, storage, or use of personal property. [In a bailment, the bailee has the right to hold the goods but does not acquire the "property," i.e., the title. There are many examples of bailment in commerce and private activity. Agisters, who graze cattle for the owner, are bailees. Lessees of equipment are bailees. A neighbor who borrows a pair of hedge clippers is a bailee. This Part deals primarily with commercial bailees: those who store or transport goods for compensation.]

Bailor — in a **bailment,** the party who causes goods to be put in the possession of a **bailee.**

Bill of lading — a **document of title** issued by a **bailee** who agrees to transport or arrange for the transport of the bailed goods.

Binder — in maritime insurance, the broker or agent's brief summary of the insurance coverage and certification that the insurance policy will issue in due course.

Breakbulk cargo — **bulk cargo** that is subject to separate **bills of lading.**

Bulk cargo — cargo that is not shipped in **containers**. [It is often not efficient to ship cargo in containers, the cost of loading and unloading the ship's hold or tanks being less than the cost of shipping in individual containers. Ores, crude oil, agricultural commodities, and many other fungibles are shipped in bulk.]

Bulker — a ship that carries bulk rather than **container** cargo.

Cartage company — a trucking company, often one that makes short hauls of goods, say, from a shipper's dock to a rail siding or dock. [Often cartage companies send their tractors to pick up **trailers** or send tractors with **chassis** to pick up **containers**.]

Cellular container ship — ocean-going vessel that is designed to carry large **containers**.

Charterer — the party that rents a ship to carry goods or passengers under a contract called a **charter party** with the owner.

Charter party — the contract between the owner of a ship and the party that undertakes to use it for a voyage or a period of time.

Chassis — a device on which a **container** may be placed for hauling by a truck tractor.

Combined transport document — a **document of title** covering the transport of goods by more than one mode of transportation, e.g., by truck and rail or by barge and ship.

Combined transport operator — a **bailee** that transports or arranges for the transport of merchandise on more than one mode of transport. [A combined transport operator may be a carrier that uses trucks and rail, for example, or may be a **freight forwarder** that arranges for such transport.]

Commercial invoice — document, prepared by the seller of goods, submitted to the buyer requesting payment. [The commercial invoice usually includes a number of important terms of the sales agreement: the description and quantity of the goods and the payment and delivery provisions. The commercial invoice is of interest to third parties such as customs officials and bankers who are financing the transaction. The seller must take care that the commercial invoice conforms to customs and banker usages. U.S. customs officials, for example, expect the commercial invoice to include all handling and shipping charges, the currency in which payment is to be made, and drawbacks or rebates that may come due, the country of origin, and other matters. Banks that issue letters of credit will not pay drafts accompanying commercial invoices that do not describe the goods as the letter of credit describes them. The commercial invoice, then, is an important document whose preparation requires considerable care and expertise.]

Conference — association of ship owners or **liners** that publishes schedules and sets charges.

Consignee — the party designated on a **bill of lading** as the party to whom the carrier should deliver the goods. [The term "consignee" is somewhat anomalous in negotiable **bills of lading,** since the party to whom the goods are to be delivered under a negotiable bill is the holder of it. Nevertheless, modern bill-of-lading forms use the term in both negotiable and nonnegotiable bills.]

Consignment note — a nonnegotiable receipt for goods with the terms for their transport. (*See* **waybill.**)

Consolidator (*See* **freight forwarder.**)

Container — box, usually of corrugated steel, or tank into which merchandise is "stuffed" for shipment.

Container ship — ship designed for **container** rather than **bulk** cargo.

Covernote — in maritime insurance an agent or broker's certification that insurance coverage has been purchased and that the policy of insurance will issue. (*See* **binder.**)

Customs broker — party that offers importers the service of getting goods through customs. [A custom broker's services include preparing the documentation, seeing to the offloading of goods into bonded warehouses, and, sometimes, paying charges for the importer. Customs brokers may have blanket type bonds under which goods may be released by the customs service before the duty is computed. Many customs brokers are also **freight forwarders.**]

Customs invoice — special invoice prepared in order to satisfy the customs service of the importing country. [Some countries specify the terms to be included in the commercial invoice and accept that invoice for customs purposes. Other countries have, at times, required a special customs invoice on their own forms, and still other countries require the commercial invoice to be "consularized," that is, examined by consular official of the importing country in the exporting country. The consular official then stamps and signs the invoice, thereby consularizing it. In all of these cases, the government officials use the invoice information to determine import duties, to enforce import restrictions, and to generate statistical information.]

Data freight receipt (*See* **waybill.**)

Delivery order — a **document of title** issued by any party, sometimes a stranger to the **bailment**, requesting the delivery of goods, usually that are the subject of a bailment. [Delivery orders arise in any number of transactions. Their independent value as documents of title depends on the parties that sign them. When they are accepted by a **bailee,** they become the equivalent of a **warehouse receipt**.]

Destination control statement — statement appearing on an invoice, **bill of lading**, or **shipper's export declaration** providing notice of the foreign destinations to which a shipment may be transported and used as a method of government control of exports.

Disponent owner — in a sub-**charter party**, the party granting the right to use the vessel to the **charterer**. [It is not uncommon for a ship to be the subject of more than one charter. The owner may charter the vessel to *X*, who in turn, subcharters it to *Y*. In the subcharter, *X* is the disponent owner.]

Dock receipt — receipt evidencing delivery of goods to an agent of the shipping company. [The shipping company's agent may take delivery of the goods prior to the issuance of the **bill of lading**. In that case, the dock receipt serves as a document covering the **bailment.**]

Document of title — commodity paper, that is, paper that (1) stands, in the event the document is negotiable, for the goods themselves while they are in the possession of a **bailee** and (2) evidences the **bailment** arrangement between the **bailor** and the bailee. [Documents of title may be negotiable or nonnegotiable. In the former event, they stand for the goods; in the latter, they merely evidence the bailment and the terms of it.]

Door-to-door — shipment term indicating that the goods will be shipped in **containers** stuffed at the seller's facility and delivered unopened at the buyer's facility.

Drayage company (*See* **cartage company.**)

Equivalents — standard length measurements for **containers**, e.g., 20 ft., 40 ft.

Export license — (*See* **general export license, validated export license.**)

FCL — full **container** load.

FIATA — acronym for the French name of international **freight forwarders** association: Fédération Internationale des Associations de Transitaires et Assimilés.

Field warehouse — company that operates a warehouse or warehouses at the premises of another party, usually, a debtor whose creditor desires to deprive the debtor of possession of its inventory, which is stored in the field warehouse.

First of exchange — recital on a draft used in international trade indicating that the draft is the first of two or more, the draft having been issued in multiple copies. [In the international documentary draft transaction, because of the risk that documents might be lost in the mails, it was common in the past and survives to some extent today for sellers to assemble two or more sets of documents in order to send them to the buyer by mail and by ship. If the documents arrived by mail, the buyer or bank to which they were directed would use them, and the duplicate set would be void. If the documents did not arrive by mail, the buyer or bank, as the case might be, would go to the steamship that carried the goods and ask the captain to deliver the duplicate set of documents that the **shipper** has entrusted to him and that he had carried in the ship's safe. Drafts drawn under the practice contained a recital indicating the draft as the first or the second in the set. Thus, "first of exchange" indicated that the draft was the first copy. **"Second of exchange"** indicated that it was the second. Customarily, following these recitals there was further language indicating the number of drafts drawn and the consequences of honor of one of them. After "first of exchange," the draft would recite "second of same tenor and date being unpaid." Thus if the duplicate draft had been paid, the drawee knew not to honor the first.]

Forwarder (*See* **freight forwarder.**)

FPA — in maritime insurance, "free of **particular average**," that is, coverage that does not extend to particular average losses. (*Compare* **WPA, general average.**)

Franchise — in maritime insurance, a kind of deductible, expressed in a percentage or in dollar terms.

Freight forwarder — agent of the **shipper** who arranges for the transport of the shipper's goods. [Often, the forwarder is a **consolidator,** that is, he accepts **LCL** shipments from his clients and consolidates them into **FCL** shipments. Forwarders are also sometimes **customs brokers** and often are **loading brokers.**]

General average — partial loss allocated among surviving cargoes as a consequence of the ship captain's decision to sacrifice cargo in order to save ship or cargo from extraordinary peril.

General export license — U.S. export license covering all exports except those covered by a **validated export license.**

Gross weight — weight of cargo including contents and packaging or **container.**

House bill of lading — said of a **bill of lading** issued by a **freight forwarder.**

IATA — acronym for International Air Transport Association.

Insurance binder (*See* **binder.**)

Insurance certificate — document certifying that there is coverage, usually under an **open cargo policy**, of a designated shipment.

LCL — less than **container** load.

Lighter — a small vessel or barge used to transport merchandise from ship to ship or from ship to dock and back in port.

Liner — ship that travels established routes under **conference** schedules and rates.

Loading broker — agent of the ship owner whose duty it is to obtain cargo for the ship. [In addition, the loading broker may perform some of the ship owner's functions in connection with the issuance of the **bill of lading**, the affixation of the **on board stamp,** and the like.]

Manifest — ship's record of cargo the ship is carrying.

Marks — (as in "marks and numbers") markings on goods or packages identifying the goods and their destination. (*See also* **numbers.**)

Marine bill of lading — **bill of lading** issued by an ocean-going carrier, as opposed to a **house bill of lading** or bill of lading issued by a **freight forwarder**.

Multimodal — said of transport of goods by more than one mode, i.e., by rail and steamship. (*Compare* **unimodal.**)

Net weight — weight of contents only, i.e., exclusive of weight of packages or **containers**.

Numbers — designation on a series of packages, when a shipment consists of more than one package.

NVOCC bill of lading — a **bill of lading** issued by a nonvessel-owning common carrier, a **freight forwarder**. (*See also* **transport document.**)

On board bill of lading — **bill of lading** indicating that the goods have been loaded on board. [For risk of loss, title passage, insurance, and other purposes, it may be critical for parties to know that the goods have been loaded on board the ship. **Received-for-shipment bills of lading** are issued by carriers or by **freight forwarders** and do not indicate that the goods are loaded on board unless the received-for-shipment bill contains an **on board stamp**, signed and dated by the ship's agent.]

On board stamp — notation superimposed on **received-for-shipment bill of lading**, signed and dated by the ship's master or agent, and indicating that the cargo has passed the ship's rail.

Open cargo policy — marine insurance policy in the nature of a blanket policy, that is, one policy that covers many shipments.

Order bill of lading — a negotiable **bill of lading.**

Packing list — detailed description of the contents of packages that contain the cargo.

Particular average — in maritime insurance, an accidental, partial loss and specifically not a **general average** loss.

Pro forma invoice — an invoice, incomplete in one or more respects, sometimes used as a seller's quotation or offer to sell. [The pro forma invoice suggests that the buyer and seller have yet to conclude all of the terms of their sales contract, but the document permits the buyer to approach customs authorities or other officials and present documentation that will permit him to obtain preliminary approval of his imports and preliminary calculation of duties and other charges. When the **commercial invoice** issues, if its terms differ materially from the pro forma invoice, the preliminary approval and calculations will be revoked, and the whole purpose of the pro forma invoice will be frustrated. The pro forma invoice, therefore, is usually a draft of the commercial invoice with the words "pro forma" superimposed. In the event the transaction proceeds as the parties plan, the terms of the commercial invoice may be identical to those of the pro forma invoice.]

Received-for-shipment bill of lading — **bill of lading** issued by a carrier or **freight forwarder** indicating that the **bailee** has received the cargo but not indicating that the goods are loaded on board. (*Compare* **on board bill of lading.**)

Roll-on roll-off — said of **containers** that are on wheels and can roll on and off **chassis**, railcars, or other carrier equipment.

Said to contain — a carrier's disclaimer, often found in **bills of lading**, indicating that the carrier has not verified the description of the goods on the bill. (*See also* **shipper's load and count.**)

Second of exchange (*See* **first of exchange.**)

SED — **shipper's export declaration.**

Shipper — the **bailor**, the party that delivers the goods to a carrier or **freight forwarder** for shipment.

Shipper's export declaration — document required by the U.S. Department of Commerce for all export shipments of a value in excess of $500. [The shipper's export declaration permits the Commerce Department to enforce export control regulations and statutes and provides data for the Department's statistical reporting role.]

Shipper's load and count — (sometimes "shipper's load, weight, and count") a disclaimer, often found in **bills of lading,** indicating that the carrier is not vouching for the description of the goods in the bill of lading. [Disclaimers in **documents of title,** especially bills of lading, are common and reasonable attempts to avoid claims that the goods, which are often in sealed **containers** or packages, do not conform to the description in the document. In most transportation arrangements, for instance, the **shipper** fills out the bill of lading for the carrier's agent to execute. It is not efficient for the carrier to inspect all shipments. Most buyers, banks, and other parties that take the bill of lading are content to rely on the honesty of the shipper. The disclaimers, of which **SLC** is but one, are an effort to alert the amateur buyer or taker of the document that the carrier does not stand behind the description. If a buyer wants verification of the packages' contents, he must arrange for an independent inspector or require a document that does not contain the disclaimer. Some courts have been reluctant to enforce these disclaimers, and there is statutory and case law applicable to them in domestic and international shipments.]

SLC — shipper's load and count.

SRCC — in maritime insurance, "strikes, riots, and civil commotions," perils that may be included or excluded from the underwriter's insurance obligation.

Stale bill of lading — generally, a **bill of lading** that is outstanding more than 21 days after issue. [In the banking industry and among parties that take bills of lading as a method of purchasing goods, there is concern that the bill not cover merchandise that has already been unloaded. Sometimes, carriers will deliver goods without surrender of the bill. If the bill is lost, for example, the **consignee** may obtain a guaranty to indemnify the carrier against the possibility that the bill is in the hands of a holder who has rights in the goods. In order to balance the interests of all innocent parties (i.e., true owners, carriers, and indemnitors), the industry has fashioned the rule that any bill of lading that is more than 21 days old is suspect. Persons who take such a bill are warned, therefore, that something may be amiss and that they may not qualify as holders who take by due negotiation, in which event, they will not take a superior interest in the goods covered by the bill.]

Stevedore company — a company that loads and unloads ships.

Straight bill of lading — a nonnegotiable **bill of lading.**

Tariff — a schedule of shipment charges. [Prior to the deregulation of the domestic transportation industry, virtually all shipments by truck and rail were made under tariffs that were published with a federal, state, or quasi-official agency. Those tariffs prevented what some saw as abuse by carriers, in particular the long haul-short haul differentials that have riled **shippers** since the great railroad era of the last century. Deregulation of the domestic transport industry permits carriers to negotiate freight rates, and more and more shipments are now handled by private contractual arrangements.]

Terminal warehouse — warehouse located at a rail, truck, or ship terminal, as opposed to a **field warehouse**, which is located "in the field."

Through bill of lading — a **bill of lading** that is issued by the initial carrier and that covers transport by that carrier and one or more subsequent carriers. [Under the through bill, the initial carrier acts as the agent of the **shipper** for the purpose of engaging other carriers to complete the transport of the goods. Thus if a Detroit shipper desires to ship merchandise from Detroit to Los Angeles, it may deliver the goods to the Grand Trunk Railroad in Detroit. The GT will transport the goods to the end of its line and deliver them to a Burlington Northern train, which will haul them to California. In the through-bill situation, the Grand Trunk collects the entire freight charge from the shipper and the Burlington draws on the Grand Trunk and collects its share of the charge through a clearinghouse maintained by the railroads.]

TPND — in maritime insurance, "theft, pilferage, and nondelivery," perils that may or may not be covered by the maritime insurance policy.

Trailer — a **container** that is on wheels and may be hitched to a truck tractor.

Transport document — the equivalent of a **bill of lading** issued by a noncarrier. [It offends the logic of some in the banking and transport industry that noncarriers, such as **freight forwarders,** may issue a bill of lading — a document indicating that the issuer will carry the goods. In some areas, therefore, noncarrier issuers do not issue bills of lading but "transport documents." In the United States, freight forwarders issue an **NVOCC bill of lading.**]

Tramps — ships that travel from port to port in search of cargo and do not follow a published route and schedule. (*Compare* **liner.**)

Transhipment — (sometimes transshipment) the act of off loading goods from one vessel, which completes part of a voyage, and on loading them to a second vessel for another leg of the voyage. [Transhipment may be **unimodal** or **multimodal** and may involve more than two legs to a single voyage.]

Underwriter — in maritime insurance, the insurance carrier.

Unimodal — said of a shipment that will occur on one type of carrier only, e.g., by truck only and not by truck and rail or rail and ship. (*Compare* **multimodal.**)

Validated export license — government grant of authority to a specified exporter to export specified goods. [Validated licenses must be applied for and are used when the goods are national-security sensitive or are destined for a country that is, often for political reasons, the subject of U.S. export restrictions.]

WA — in maritime insurance, "with average," i.e., said of insurance coverage that extends to **average**.

Warehouse receipt — a **document of title** issued by a **bailee** and covering the storage of goods or commodities.

Waybill — nonnegotiable document indicating the terms of a shipment. [In the air transport industry, the air waybill is the only document that the carrier issues. In the rail industry, the waybill is usually a carbon copy of the nonnegotiable **bill of lading** that the carrier issues. The waybill is attached to the railroad car, so that railroad personnel will know where to direct the shipment.]

Weight note — document, executed by the seller of merchandise or by a third party, certifying the weight of the shipment.

WPA — in maritime insurance, "with particular average," i.e., said of coverage that extends to **particular average**. (*Compare* **FPA**.)

Part IV
TABLE OF DOCUMENTS

PART IV
BIBLIOGRAPHY

American Bankers Association, Letters of Credit (2d ed. 1983).

Francis, D., The Countertrade Handbook (1987).

Guadagnoli, L., A Practical Guide to Export Financing and Risk Management (1989).

Guild, I. & R. Harris, Forfaiting (1986).

Henson, R., Documents of Title Under the Uniform Commercial Code (1983).

Hervey, Countertrade — Counterproductive?, Economic Perspectives (1989).

International Chamber of Commerce, Guide to Documentary Credit Operations (ICC Pub. No. 415) (1985).

———, Incoterms (ICC Pub. No. 350) (1980).

———, Guide to Incoterms (ICC Pub. No. 354) (1980).

———, The Development of International Container Transport (ICC Pub. No. 314) (1977).

———, Uniform Customs and Practice for Documentary Credits (ICC Pub. No. 400) (1983).

———, The Problem of Clean Bills of Lading (ICC Pub. No. 283) (1963).

Letters of Credit Report (Executive Enterprise Publications Co., Inc., 22 West 21st St., New York, NY 10010-6904 (212) 645-7880).

Letter of Credit Update (Government Information Services, 1611 North Kent Street #508, Arlington, VA 22209 (703) 528-1000).

Todd, P., Contracts for the Carriage of Goods by Sea (1988).

Schmitthoff, C., Export Trade (8th ed. 1986).

Sullivan, E., The Marine Encyclopaedic Dictionary (2d ed. 1988).

Watson, A., Finance of International Trade (2d ed. 1981).

U.S. Department of Commerce, A Basic Guide to Exporting (1986).

U.S. Department of the Treasury, U.S. Customs Service, Importing into the United States (1989).

Index

All references are to section numbers.

Index

DATE DUE
